American Pomology: Apples

by Doct. John A. Warder

with an introduction by Roger Chambers

Self Reliance Books

Introduction

I am pleased to present yet another title on Gardening.

The work is in the Public Domain and is re-printed here in accordance with Federal Laws.

As with all reprinted books of this age that are intended to perfectly reproduce the original edition, considerable pains and effort had to be undertaken to correct fading and sometimes outright damage to existing proofs of this title. At times, this task is quite monumental, requiring an almost total "rebuilding" of some pages from digital proofs of multiple copies. Despite this, imperfections still sometimes exist in the final proof and may detract from the visual appearance of the text.

I hope you enjoy reading this book as much as I enjoyed making it available to readers again.

Roger Chambers

1858

8

PREFACE.

All patriots may realize a sense of pride, when they
consider the capabilities of the glorious country in which
we are favored to live; and while fostering no sectional
feelings, nor pleading any local interests, yet, as Americans
and as men, we may be allowed to love our own homes,
our own neighborhoods, our States and regions; and we
may be permitted to think them the brightest and best
portions of the great Republic to which we all belong.
Therefore the writer asks to be excused for expressing a
preference for his own favored *Northwest*, and while claim-
ing all praise for this noble expanse, he wishes still to be
acknowledged as most devotedly an AMERICAN CITIZEN,
who feels the deepest interest in the prosperity of the
whole country.

His fellow-laborers in the extensive field of Horticulture, who are scattered over the great Northwest, having
called upon him for a work on fruits which should be
adapted to their wants, the author has for several years
devoted himself to the task of collecting materials from
which he is preparing a work upon AMERICAN POMOLOGY,
of which this is to be the first volume.

The title has been adopted as the most appropriate, because the book is intended to be truly American in its
character, and, though it may be especially adapted to the
wants of the Western States, great pains have been taken

to make it a useful companion to the orchardists of all portions of our country.

When examining this volume, his friends are asked to look gently upon the many faults they may find, and they are requested also to observe the peculiarities by which this fruit book is characterized. Much to his regret, the author found that it was considered necessary to the completeness of the volume, that the general subject of fruit-growing should be treated in detail, and, therefore, introductory chapters were prepared; whereas, he had set out simply to describe the fruits of our country. To this necessity, as it was considered by his friends, the author yielded reluctantly, because he felt that this labor had already been thoroughly done by his predecessors, whose volumes were to be seen in the houses of all intelligent fruit-growers. From them he did not wish to borrow other men's ideas and language, and therefore undertook to write the whole anew, without any reference to printed books. But, of course, it is impossible to be original in treating such familiar and hackneyed topics as those which are discussed at every meeting of horticulturists all over the country, and which form the subject of the familiar discourse of the green-house and nursery, the potting-shed and the grafting-room, the garden and the orchard.

After the introductory chapters upon the general or leading topics connected with fruit-culture and orcharding, the reader will find that especial attention has been paid to the classification of the fruits under consideration in this volume. Classification is the great need of our pomology, and, indeed, it is almost a new idea to many American readers. The author has fully realized the difficulties attendant upon the undertaking, but its importance, and its growing necessity, were considered sufficient to warrant the attempted innovation. It is hoped that American students of pomology will appreciate the efforts which have been made in their behalf. The formulæ which have been adopted may not prove to be the best, but it is believed that they will render great assistance to those who desire to identify fruits; and that, at least, they may lead to a more perfect classification in the future.

On the contrary, with these simple formulæ, under which the fruits are arranged, the student has only to decide as to which of the sub-divisions his specimen must be referred, and then seek among a limited number for the description that shall correspond to his fruit, and the identification is made out.

In the systematic descriptions of fruits, the alphabetical succession of the names is used in each sub-division. An earnest endeavor has been made to be minute in the details without becoming prolix. A regular order is adopted for considering the several parts, and some new or unusual characters are brought into requisition to aid in the identification. Some of these characters appear to have been strangely overlooked by previous pomologists, though they are believed to be permanent and of considerable value in the diagnosis.

In deciding upon the selection of the names of fruits, the generally received rules of our Pomological Societies have been departed from in a few instances, where good reasons were thought to justify differing from the authorities. Thus, when a given name has been generally adopted over a large extent of country, though different from that used by a previous writer, it has been selected as the title of the fruit in this work.

To avoid incumbering the pages, authorities for the nomenclature have not been cited, except in a few instances, nor have numerous synonyms been introduced. Such only as are in common use have been given, and those of foreign origin have been dropped.

The attention of the reader is particularly directed to the catalogue of fruits near the close of the volume, which also answers as the index to those which are described in detail. This portion of the work has cost an immense amount of labor and time, and, though making little display, will, it is hoped, prove very useful to the orchardist. In it the names of fruits are presented in their alphabetical order, followed by information as to the average size, the origin of the variety, its classification, from which are deduced its shape, flavor and modes of coloring; next is noted its season, and then its quality. This last character is, of course, but the result of private judgment, and the estimate may differ widely from that of others; the quality, too, it should be remembered, is here intended to be the result of a consideration of many properties besides that of mere flavor.

This catalogue will furnish a great deal of information respecting the fruits it embraces. Unfortunately, it is not so full nor so complete as it should be, but it is offered as the result of many years' observations, and is submitted for what it is worth.

ACKNOWLEDGMENTS.—It is but an act of common justice for an author to acknowledge his indebtedness to those who have aided him in his labors, especially where, from the nature of the investigations, so much material has to be drawn from extrinsic sources. Upon the present occasion, instead of an extended parade of references to the productions of other writers, which might be looked upon as rather pedantic, it is preferred to make a general acknowledgment of the important assistance derived from many pomological authors of our own country and of Europe. Quotations are credited on the pages where they occur.

But the writer is also under great obligations to a host of co-laborers for the assistance they have kindly rendered him in the collecting, and in the examination and identification of fruits. Such friends he has happily found wherever he has turned in the pursuit of these investigations, and there are others whom it has never been his good fortune to meet face to face. To name them all would be impossible. The contemplation of their favors sadly recalls memories of the departed, but it also revives pleasant associations of the bright spirits that are still usefully engaged in the numerous pomological and horticultural associations of our country, which have become important agencies in the diffusion of valuable information in this branch of study.

To all of his kind friends the author returns his sincere thanks.

With a feeling of hesitation in coming before the public, but satisfied that he has made a contribution to the fund of human knowledge, this volume is presented to the Horticulturists of our country, for whom it was prepared by their friend and fellow-laborer,

Aston, January 1, 1867.   JNO. A. WARDER.

INTRODUCTION.

——◦◦◦——

IMPORTANCE OF ORCHARD PRODUCTS — GOVERNMENT STATISTICS — GREAT VALUE OF ORCHARD AND GARDEN PRODUCTS — DELIGHTS OF FRUIT CULTURE — TEMPERATE REGIONS THE PROPER FIELD FOR FRUIT CULTURE, AS FOR MENTAL DEVELOPMENT — PLANTS OF CULTURE, PLANTS OF NATURE — NOMADIC CONDITION UNFAVORABLE FOR TERRA-CULTURE — NECESSITIES OF AN INCREASING POPULATION A SPUR — HIGH CIVILIZATION DEMANDS HIGH CULTURE — HORTICULTURE A FINE ART, THE POETRY OF THE FARMER'S LIFE — MORAL INFLUENCES OF FRUIT-CULTURE — SINGULAR LEGISLATION RESPECTING PROPERTY IN FRUIT — INFLUENCE UPON HEALTH — APPLES IN BREAD-MAKING; AS FOOD FOR STOCK — SOURCES AND ROUTES OF INTRODUCTION — AGENCY OF NURSERYMEN — INDIAN ORCHARDS — FRENCH SETTLERS — JOHNNY APPLE-SEED — VARIETIES OF FRUITS, LIKE MAN, FOLLOW PARALLELS OF LATITUDE — LOCAL VARIETIES OF MERIT TO BE CHERISHED — OHIO PURCHASE — SILAS WHARTON — THE PUTNAM LIST.

FEW persons have any idea of the great value and importance of the products of our orchards and fruit-gardens. These are generally considered the small things of agriculture, and are overlooked by all but the statist, whose business it is to deal with these minutiæ, to hunt them up, to collocate them, and when he combines these various details and produces the sum total, we are all astonished at the result.

Our government wisely provides for the gathering of statistics at intervals of ten years, and some of the States also take an account of stock and production at intermediate periods, some of them, like Ohio, have a permanent statician who reports annually to the Governor of the State.

Our Boards of Trade publish the amounts of the leading articles that arrive at and depart from the principal cities, and thus they furnish us much additional information of value. Besides this, the county assessors are sometimes directed to collect statistics upon certain points of interest, and now that we all contribute toward the extinction of the national debt, the United States Assessors in the several districts are put in possession of data, which should be very correct, in regard to certain productions that are specified by act of Congress as liable to taxation. By these several means we may have an opportunity of learning from time to time what are the productions of the country, and their aggregate amounts are surprising to most of us. When they relate to our special interests, they are often very encouraging. This is particularly the case with those persons who have yielded to the popular prejudice that cotton was the main agricultural production of the United States; to such it will be satisfactory to learn that the crop of corn, as reported in the last census, is of nearly equal value, at the usual market prices of each article. Fruit-growers will be encouraged to find that the value of orchard products, according to the same returns, was nearly twenty millions, that of Ohio being nearly one million; of New York, nearly three and three-quarters millions; that the wine crop of the United States, an interest that is still in its infancy, amounted to nearly three and one-quarter millions; and that the valuation of market-garden products sums up to more than sixteen millions of dollars' worth. It is to be regretted that for our present purpose, the data are not sufficiently distinct to enable us to ascertain the relative value of the productions of our orchards of apples, pears, peaches, quinces, and the amount and value of the small fruits, as they are termed, since these are variously grouped in the returns of the census takers, and cannot now be separated. Of their great value, however, we may draw our conclusions from separate records that have been kept and reported by individuals, who assert the products of vineyards in some cases to have been as high as three thousand dollars per acre; of strawberries, at one thousand dollars; of pears, at one hundred dollars per tree, which would be four thousand dollars per acre; of apples, at twenty-five bushels per tree, or one thousand bushels per acre, which, at fifty cents per bushel, would produce five hundred dollars.

But, leaving this matter of dollars and cents, who will portray for us the delights incident to fruit-culture? They are of a quiet nature, though solid and enduring. They carry us back to the early days of the history of our race, when "the Lord God planted a garden eastward in Eden ...... and out of the ground made the Lord God to grow every tree that is pleasant to the sight, and good for food ...... and the Lord God took the man and put him into the garden of Eden, to dress it and to keep it." We are left to infer that this dressing and keeping of the garden was but a light and pleasant occupation, unattended with toil and trouble, and that in their natural condition the trees and plants, unaided by culture, yielded food for man. Those were paradisean times, the days of early innocence, when man, created in the image of his Maker, was still obedient to the divine commands; but, after the great transgression, everything was altered, the very ground was cursed, "thorns and thistles shall it bring forth to thee, and thou shalt eat of the herb of the field. In the sweat of thy face shalt thou eat bread."——From that day to the present hour it has been the lot of man to struggle with difficulties in the cultivation of the soil, and he has been driven to the necessity of constant watchfulness and care to preserve and to improve the various fruits of the earth upon which he subsists. In the tropics, it is true, there are many vegetable productions which are adapted for human food, even in a state of nature, and there we find less necessity for the effort of ingenuity and the application of thought and labor to produce a subsistence. Amid these productive *plants of nature*, the natives of such regions lead an idle life, and seldom rise above a low scale of advancement; but in the temperate regions of the globe, where the unceasing effort of the inhabitants is required to procure their daily food, we find the greatest development of human energies and ingenuity—there man thinks, and works; there, indeed, he is forced to improve the natural productions of the earth—and there we shall find him progressing. As with everything else, so it is with fruits, some of which were naturally indifferent or even inedible, until subjected to the meliorating influences of high culture, of selection, and of improvement. Here we find our *plants of culture*, which so well repay the labor and skill bestowed upon them.

In the early periods of the history of our race, while men were nomadic and wandered from place to place, little attention was paid to any department of agricultural improvement, and still less care was bestowed upon horticulture. Indeed, it can scarcely be supposed that, under such conditions, either branch of the art could have existed, any more than they are now found among the wandering hordes of Tartars on the steppes of Asia. So soon, however, as men began to take possession of the soil by a more permanent tenure, agriculture and horticulture also, attracted their chief attention, and were soon developed into arts of life. With advancing civilization, this has been successively more and more the case; the producing art being obliged to keep pace with the increased number of consumers, greater ingenuity was required and was applied to the production of food for the teeming millions of human beings that covered the earth, and, as we find, in China, at the present time, the greatest pains were taken to make the earth yield her increase.

High civilization demands high culture of the soil, and agriculture becomes an honored pursuit, with every department of art and science coming to its assistance. At the same time, and impelled by the same necessities, supported and aided by the same co-adjutors, horticulture also advances in a similar ratio, and, from its very nature, assumes the rank of a fine art, being less essential than pure agriculture, and in some of its branches being rather an ornamental than simply a useful art. It is not admitted, however, that any department of horticulture is to be considered useless, and many of its applications are eminently practical, and result in the production of vast quantities of human food of the most valuable kind. This pursuit always marks the advancement of a community. —As our western pioneers progress in their improvements from the primitive log cabins to the more elegant and substantial dwelling houses, we ever find the garden and the orchard, the vine-arbor and the berry-patch taking their places beside the other evidences of progress. These constitute to them the poetry of common life, of the farmer's life.

The culture of fruits, and gardens also, contributes in no small degree to the improvement of a people by the excellent moral influence it exercises upon them. Everything that makes home attractive must contribute to this desirable end. Beyond the sacred confines of the happy hearthstone, with its dear familiar circle, there can be no more pleasant associations than those of the garden, where, in our tender years, we have aided loved parents, from them taking the first lessons in plant-culture, gathering the luscious fruits of their planting or of our own; nor of the rustic arbor, in whose refreshing shade we have reclined to rest and meditate amid its sheltering canopy of verdure, and where we have gathered the purple berries of the noble vine at a later period of the rolling year; nor of the orchard, with its bounteous supplies of golden and ruddy apples, blushing peaches, and melting pears. With such attractions about our homes, with such ties to be sundered, it is wonderful, and scarcely credible, that youth should ever be induced to wander from them, and to stray into paths of evil. Such happy influences must have a good moral effect upon the young. If it be argued that such luxuries will tend to degrade our morals by making us effeminate and sybaritic, or that such enjoyments may become causes of envy and consequent crime on the part of those who are less highly favored, it may be safely asserted that there is no better cure for fruit-stealing, than to give presents of fruit, and especially of fruit-trees, to your neighbors, particularly to the boys—encourage each to plant and to cherish his own tree, and he will soon learn the meaning of *meum* and *tuum*, and will appreciate the beauties of the moral code, which he will be all the more likely to respect in every other particular.

Some of the legislation of our country is a very curious relic of barbarism. According to common law, that which is attached to the soil, may be removed without a breach of propriety, by one who is not an owner of the fee simple; thus, such removal of a vegetable product does not constitute theft or larceny, but simply amounts to a trespass: whereas the taking of fruit from the ground beneath the tree, even though it be defective or decaying, is considered a theft. An unwelcome intruder, or an unbidden guest, may enter our orchard, garden, or vineyard, and help himself at his pleasure to any of our fruits, which we have been most carefully watching and nursing for months upon trees, for the fruitage of which we may have been laboring and waiting for years, and, forsooth, our only recourse is to sue him at the law, and our only satisfaction, after all the attendant annoyance and expense, is a paltry fine for *trespass* upon our freehold, which, of course, is not commensurate with our estimate of the value of the articles taken: fruits often possess, in the eyes of the devoted orchardist, a real value much beyond their market price.

Were I asked to describe the location of the fabled fountain of Hygeia, I should decide that it was certainly situated in an orchard; it must have come bubbling from earth that sustained the roots of tree and vine; it must have been shaded by the umbrageous branches of the wide-spreading apple and pear, and it was doubtless approached by alleys that were lined by peach trees laden with their downy fruit, and over-arched by vines bearing rich clusters of the luscious grape, and they were garnished at their sides by the crimson strawberry. Such at least would have been an appropriate setting for so valued a jewel as the fountain of health, and it is certain that the pursuit of fruit-growing is itself conducive to the possession of that priceless blessing. The physical as well as the moral qualities of our nature are wonderfully promoted by these cares. The vigorous exercise they afford us in the open air, the pleasant excitement, the expectation of the results of the first fruits of our plants, tending, training and cultivating them the while, are all so many elements conducive to the highest enjoyment of full health.

The very character of the food furnished by our orchards should be taken into the account, in making up our estimate of their contributions to the health of a community. From them we procure aliment of the most refined character, and it has been urged that the elements of which they are composed are perfected or refined to the highest degree of organization that is possible to occur in vegetable tissues. Such pabulum is not only gratefully refreshing, but it is satisfying—without being gross, it is nutritious. The antiscorbutic effects of ripe fruits, especially those that are acid, are proverbial, and every fever patient has appreciated the relief derived from those that are acidulous. Then as a preventive of the febrile affections peculiar to a miasmatic region, the free use of acid fruits, or even of good sound vinegar made from grapes or apples, is an established fact in medical practice—of which, by the by, prevention is always the better part.

Apples were esteemed an important and valuable article of food in the days of the Romans, for all school boys have read in the ore rotundo of his own flowing measures, what Virgil has said, so much better than his tame translator :

" New cheese and chestnuts are our country fare,
With mellow apples for your welcome cheer."

But in more modern times, beside their wonted use as dessert fruit, or evening feast, or cooked in various modes, a French economist " has invented and practiced with great success a method of making bread with common apples, which is said to be very far superior to potato-bread. After having boiled one-third part of peeled apples, he bruised them while quite warm into two-thirds parts of flour, including the proper quantity of yeast, and kneaded the whole without water, the juice of the fruit being quite sufficient ; he put the mass into a vessel in which he allowed it to rise for about twelve hours. By this process he obtained a very excellent bread, full of eyes, and extremely light and palatable." *

Nor is this class of food desirable for man alone. Fruits of all kinds, but particularly what may be called

---

* Companion for the Orchard.—Phillips.

the large fruits, such as are grown in our orchards, may be profitably cultivated for feeding our domestic animals. Sweet apples have been especially recommended for fattening swine, and when fed to cows they increase the flow of milk, or produce fat according to the condition of these animals. Think of the luxury of eating apple-fed pork! Why, even the strict Rabbi might overcome his prejudices against such swine flesh! And then dream of enjoying the luxury of fresh rich milk, yellow cream, and golden butter, from your winter dairy, instead of the sky-blue fluid, and the pallid, or anotto-tinted, but insipid butter, resulting from the meager supplies of nutriment contained in dry hay and fibrous, woody cornstalks. Now this is not unreasonable nor ridiculous. Orchards have been planted with a succession of sweet apples that will sustain swine in a state of most perfect health, growing and fattening simultaneously from June to November; and the later varieties may be cheaply preserved for feeding stock of all kinds during the winter, when they will be best prepared by steaming, and may be fed with the greatest advantage. Our farmers do not appreciate the benefits of having green food for their animals during the winter season. Being blessed with that royal grain, the Indian corn, they do not realize the importance of the provision of roots which is so great a feature in British husbandry; but they have yet to learn, and they will learn, that for us, and under our conditions of labor and climate, they can do still better, and produce still greater results with a combination of *hay* or *straw*, *corn meal* and *apples*, all properly prepared by means of steam or hot water. Besides, such orchards may be advantageously planted in many places where the soil is not adapted to the production of grain.—The reader is referred to the chapter on select lists in another part of this volume, in which an attempt will be made to present the reader with the opinions of the best pomologists of various parts of the country.

It were an interesting and not unprofitable study to trace the various sources and routes by which fruits have been introduced into different parts of our extended country. In some cases we should find that we were indebted for these luxuries to the efforts of very humble individuals, while in other regions the high character of the orchards is owing to the forethought, knowledge, enterprise, and liberality of some prominent citizen of the infant community, who has freely spent his means and bestowed his cares in providing for others as well as for his own necessities or pleasures. But it is to the intelligent nurserymen of our country that we are especially indebted for the universal diffusion of fruits, and for the selection of the best varieties in each different section. While acting separately, these men were laboring under great disadvantages, and frequently cultivated certain varieties under a diversity of names, as they had received them from various sources. This was a difficulty incident to their isolation, but the organization of Pomological Societies in various parts of the country, has enabled them in a great measure to unravel the confusion of an extended synonymy, and also by comparison and consultation with the most intelligent fruit-growers, they have been prepared to advise the planter as to the best and most profitable varieties to be set out in different soils and situations.

Most of our first orchards were planted with imported

trees. The colonists brought plants and seeds. Even now, in many parts of the country, we hear many good fruits designated as English, to indicate that they are considered superior to the native; and we are still importing choice varieties from Europe and other quarters of the globe.

The roving tribes of Indians who inhabited this country when discovered and settled by the whites, had no orchards—they lived by the chase, and only gathered such fruits as were native to the soil. Among the earliest attempts to civilize them, however, those that exerted the greatest influence, were efforts to make them an agricultural people, and of these the planting of fruit-trees was one of the most successful. In many parts of the country we find relics of these old Indian orchards still remaining, and it is probable that from the apple seeds sent by the general government for distribution among the Cherokees in Georgia, we are now reaping some of the most valuable fruits of this species. The early French settlers were famous tree-planters, and we find their traces across the continent, from the St. Lawrence to the Gulf of Mexico. These consist in noble pear and apple trees, grown from seeds planted by them, at their early and scattered posts or settlements. These were made far in advance of the pioneers, who have, at a later period, formed the van of civilization, that soon spread into a solid phalanx in its march throughout the great interior valley of the continent.

On the borders of civilization we sometimes meet with a singular being, more savage than polished, and yet useful in his way. Such an one in the early settlement of the northwestern territory was Johnny Apple-seed—a simple-hearted being, who loved to roam through the forests in advance of his fellows, consorting, now with the red man, now with the white, a sort of connecting link—by his white brethren he was, no doubt, considered rather a vagabond, for we do not learn that he had the industry to open farms in the wilderness, the energy to be a great hunter, nor the knowledge and devotion to have made him a useful missionary among the red men. But Johnny had his use in the world. It was his universal custom, when among the whites, to save the seeds of all the best apples he met with. These he carefully preserved and carried with him, and when far away from his white friends, he would select an open spot of ground, prepare the soil, and plant these seeds, upon the principle of the old Spanish custom, that he owed so much to posterity, so that some day, the future traveler or inhabitant of those fertile valleys, might enjoy the fruits of his early efforts. Such was Johnny Apple-seed—did he not erect for himself monuments more worthy, if not more enduring, than piles of marble or statues of brass?

In tracing the progress of fruits through different portions of our country, we should very naturally expect to find the law that governs the movements of men, applying with equal force to the fruits they carry with them. The former have been observed to migrate very nearly on parallels of latitude, so have, in a great degree, the latter; and whenever we find a departure from this order, we may expect to discover a change, and sometimes a deterioration in the characters of the fruits thus removed to a new locality. It is true, much of this alteration, whether improvement or otherwise, may be owing to the difference of soil.   Western New York received her early fruits from Connecticut, and Massachusetts ; Michigan, Northern Illinois, and later, Wisconsin and Iowa received theirs in a great degree from New York.   Ohio and Indiana received their fruits mainly from New Jersy, and Pennsylvania, and we may yet trace this in the prevalence of certain leading varieties that are scarcely known, and very little grown on different parallels.   The early settlement at the mouth of the Muskingum river, was made by New England-men, and into the " Ohio-purchase," they introduced the leading varieties of the apples of Massachusetts.   Among these, the Boston or Roxbury Russet was a prominent favorite, but it was so changed in its appearance as scarcely to be recognized by its old admirers, and it was christened with a new name, the Putnam Russet, under the impression that it was a different variety.   Most of the original Putnam varieties have disappeared from the orchards.   Kentucky received her fruits in great measure from Virginia ; Tennessee from the same source and from North Carolina, and these younger States sent them forward on the great western march with their hardy sons to southern Indiana, southern Illinois, to Missouri, and to Arkansas, in all which regions we find evident traces in the orchards, of the origin of the people who planted them.

Of course, we shall find many deflections from the precise parellel of latitude, some inclining to the south, and many turning to the northward.   To the latter we of the West are looking with the greatest interest, since we so often find that the northern fruits do not maintain their high characters in their southern or southwestern migrations, and all winter kinds are apt to become autumnal in their period of ripening, which makes them less valuable; and because, among those from a southern origin, we have discovered many of high merit as to beauty, flavor, and productiveness—and, especially where they are able to mature sufficiently, they prove to be long keepers, thus supplying a want which was not filled by fruits of a northern origin. There may be limits beyond which we cannot transport some sorts to advantage in either direction, but this too will depend very much upon the adaptability of our soils to particular varieties.

In every region where fruit has been cultivated we find local varieties grown from seed, many of these are of sufficient merit to warrant their propagation, and it behooves us to be constantly on the look out for them; for though our lists are already sufficiently large to puzzle the young orchardist in making his selections, we may well reduce the number by weeding out more of the indifferent fruit, at the same time that we are introducing those of a superior character. It has been estimated that there may be as many as one in ten of our seedling orchard trees that would be ranked as "good," but not one in a hundred that could be styled "best."* Certain individuals have devoted themselves to the troublesome though thankless office of collecting these scattered varieties of decided merit, and from their collections our pomological societies will, from time to time, select and recommend the best for more extended cultivation. Such devoted men as H. N. Gillett, Lewis Jones, Reuben Ragan, A. H. Ernst, who have been industriously engaged in this good work for a quarter of a century, are entitled to the highest com-

* Elliott—Western Fruits.

mendation; but there are many others who have contributed their full share of benefits by their labors in the same field, to whom also we owe a debt of gratitude. Two of the chief foci in the Ohio valley from which valuable fruits have been distributed most largely, were the settlement at the mouth of the Muskingum, with its Putnam list given below; and a later, but very important introduction of choice fruits, brought into the Miami country by Silas Wharton, a nurseryman from Pennsylvania, who settled among a large body of the religious Society of Friends, in Warren Co., Ohio. The impress of this importation is very manifest in all the country, within a radius of one hundred miles, and some of his fruits are found doing well in the northwestern part of the State of Ohio, in northern Indiana, and in an extended region westward.

There are, no doubt, many other local foci, whence good fruits have radiated to bless regions more or less extensive, and in every neighborhood we find the name of some early pomologist attached to the good fruits that he had introduced, thus adding another synonym to the numerous list of those belonging to so many of our good varieties.

A. W. Putnam commenced an apple nursery in 1794, a few years after the first white settlement at Marietta, Ohio, the first grafts were set in the spring of 1796; they were obtained from Connecticut by Israel Putnam, and were the first set in the State, and grafted by W. Rufus Putnam. Most of the early orchards of the region were planted from this nursery. These grafts were taken from the orchard of Israel Putnam (of wolf-killing memory) in Pomfret, Connecticut. In the Ohio Cultivator for August 1st, 1846, may be found the following authentic list of the varieties propagated : —

"1. Putnam Russet, (Roxbury).
2. Seek-no-further, ('Westfield.)
3. Early Chandler.
4. Gilliflower.
5. Pound Royal, (Lowell).
6. Natural, (a seedling).
7. Rhode Island Greening.
8. Yellow Greening.
9. Golden Pippin.
10. Long Island Pippin.
11. Tallman Sweeting.
12. Striped Sweeting.
13. Honey Greening.
14. Kent Pippin.
15. Cooper.
16. Striped Gilliflower.
17. Black, do.
18. Prolific Beauty.
19. Queening, (Summer Queen?)
20. English Pearmain.
21. Green Pippin.
22. Spitzenberg, (Esopus ?)

Many of these have disappeared from the orchards and from the nurserymen's catalogues."

2

CHAPTER II.

HISTORY OF THE APPLE.

———◦◦◦———

In attempting to trace out the history of any plant that has long been subjected to the dominion of man, we are beset with difficulties growing out of the uncertainty of language, and arising also from the absence of precise terms of science in the descriptions or allusions which we meet

26

respecting them. As he who would investigate the history of our great national grain crop, the noble Indian maize, which, in our language, claims the generic term corn, will at once meet with terms apt to mislead him in the English translation of the Bible, and in the writings of Europeans, who use the word corn in a generic sense, as applying to all the edible grains, and especially to wheat—so in this investigation we may easily be misled by meeting the word apple in the Bible and in the translations of Latin and Greek authors, and we may be permitted to question whether the original words translated apple may not have been applied to quite different fruits, or perhaps we may ask whether our word may not originally have had a more general sense, meaning as it does, according to its derivation, any round body.

The etymology of the word apple is referred by the lexicographers to *abhall*, Celtic; *avall*, Welch; *afall* or *avall*, Armoric; *aval* or *avel*, Cornish; and these are all traceable to the Celtic word *ball*, meaning simply a round body.

Worcester traces the origin of apple directly to the German *apfel*, which he derives from *æpl*, *apel*, or *appel*.

Webster cites the Saxon *appl* or *appel;* Dutch, *appel;* German, *apfel;* Danish, *æble;* Swedish, *aple;* Welsh, *aval;* Irish, *abhal* or *ubhal;* Armoric, *aval;* Russian, *yabloko.*

Its meaning being fruit in general, with a round form. Thus the Persian word *ubhul* means Juniper berries, and in Welsh the word used means other fruits, and needs a qualifying term to specify the variety or kind.

Hogg, in his British Pomology, quoting Owen, says, the ancient Glastonbury was called by the Britons *Ynys avallac* or *avallon*, meaning an apple orchard, and from this came the Roman word *avallonia*, from this he infers that the apple was known to the Britons before the advent of the Romans. We are told, that in 973, King Edgar, when fatigued with the labors of the chase, laid himself down under a wild apple tree, so that it becomes a question whether this plant was not a native of England as of other parts of Europe, where in many places it is found growing wild and apparently indigenous. Thornton informs us in his history of Turkey, that apples are common in Wallachia, and he cites among the varieties one, the *domniasca*, "which is perhaps the finest in Europe, both for its size, color, and flavor." It were hard to say what variety this is, and whether it be known to us.

The introduction of this word apple in the Bible is attributable to the translators, and some commentators suggest that they have used it in its general sense, and that in the following passages where it occurs, it refers to the citron, orange, or some other subtropical fruit.

"Stay me with flagons, comfort me with apples." — Songs of Solomon ii, 5.

"As the apple-tree (citron) among the trees of the wood, * * * I sat me down under his shadow with great delight, and his fruit was sweet to my taste."—Sol. ii, 2.

* * * "I raised thee up under the apple-tree."—Solomon viii, 5.

"A word fitly spoken, is like apples of gold in pictures of silver."—Prov. xxv, 11.

The botanical position of the cultivated apple may be stated as follows : — Order, *Rosaceæ ;* sub-order, *Pomeæ ;* or the apple family and genus, *Pyrus.* The species under our consideration is the *Pyrus Malus,* or apple. It has been introduced into this country from Europe, and is now found in a half-wild state, springing up in old fields, hedge-rows, and roadsides ; but, even in such situations, by their eatable fruit and broad foliage, and by the absence of spiny or thorny twigs, the trees generally give evidence of a civilized origin. It is not that the plant has changed any of its true specific characters, but that it has been affected by the meliorating influences of culture, which it has not been able entirely to shake off in its neglected condition. Sometimes, indeed, trees are found in these neglected and out-of-the-way situations, which produce fruits of superior quality—and the sorts have been gladly introduced into our nurseries and orchards.

Very early in the history of horticulture the apple attracted attention by its improvability, showing that it belonged to the class of culture-plants. Indeed it is a very remarkable fact in the study of botany, and the pivot upon which the science and art of horticulture turns, that while there are plants which show no tendency to change from their normal type, even when brought under the highest culture, and subjected to every treatment which human ingenuity can suggest, there are others which are prone to variations or sports, even in their natural condition, but more so when they are carefully nursed by the prudent farmer or gardener. These may be called respectively the plants of nature and the plants of culture. Some of the former furnish human food, and are otherwise useful to

man; but the latter class embraces by far the larger number of food-plants, and we are indebted to this pliancy,
aided by human skill, for our varieties of fruits, our escu-
lent vegetables, and the floral ornaments of our gardens.

The native country of the apple, though not definitively
settled, is generally conceded to be Europe, particularly
its southern portions, and perhaps Western Asia: that is,
the plant known and designated by botanists as *Pyrus
Malus,* for there are other and distinct species in America
and Asia which have no claims to having been the source
of our favorite orchard fruits. Our own native crab is
the *Pyrus coronaria,* which, though showing some slight
tendency to variation, has never departed from the
strongly marked normal type. The *P. baccata,* or Siberian crab, is so distinctly marked as to be admitted as a
species. It has wonderfully improved under culture, and
has produced some quite distinct varieties; it has even
been hybridized by Mr. Knight, with the cultivated sorts
of the common Wilding or Crab of Europe, the *P. Malus.*
Pallas, who found it wild near Lake Baikal and in Daouria,
says, it grows only 3 or 4 feet high, with a trunk of as
many inches diameter, and yields pear-shaped berries as
large as peas.

The *P. rivularis,* according to Nuttall, is common in
the maritime portions of Oregon, in alluvial forests. The
tree attains a height of 15 to 25 feet. It resembles the
Siberian Crab, to which it has a close affinity. The fruit
grows in clusters, is purple, scarcely the size of a cherry,
and of an agreeable flavor; sweetish and sub-acid when
ripe, not at all acid and acerb as the *P. coronaria.**

* North American Sylva, Nuttall II, p. 25.

Among the early writers upon the subject of pomology, we find some very crude notions, particularly in regard to the wonderful powers of the grafter, for this art of improving the Wilding by inserting buds or scions of better sorts, and thus multiplying trees of good kinds, was a very ancient invention. Pliny, the naturalist, certainly deserves our praise for his wonderful and comprehensive industry in all branches of natural history. In regard to grafting, which seems to have been well understood in his day, he says, that he had seen near Thuliæ a tree bearing all manner of fruits, nuts and berries, figs and grapes, pears and pomegranates ; no kind of apple or other fruit that was not to be found on this tree. It is quaintly noted, however, that "this tree did not live long,"—is it to be wondered that such should have been the case ? Now some persons may object to the testimony of this remarkable man, and feel disposed to discredit the statement of what appears so incredible to those who are at all acquainted with the well-known necessity for a congenial stock into which the graft should be inserted. But a more extended knowledge of the subject, would explain what Pliny has recorded as a marvel of the art. The same thing has been done in our own times, it is a trick, and one which would very soon be detected now-a-days by the merest tyro in horticulture, though it may have escaped the scrutiny of Pliny, whose business it was to note and record the results of his observations, rather than to examine the modus of the experiment. By the French, the method is called Charlatan grafting, and is done by taking a stock of suitable size, hollowing it out, and introducing through its cavity several stocks of different kinds, upon each of which may be produced a different sort of fruit, as reported by Pliny. The needed affinity of the scion and stock, and the possible range that may be successfully taken in this mode of propagation, with the whole consideration of the influence of the stock upon the graft, will be more fully discussed in another chapter.

Though it be claimed and even admitted that the wild apple or crab was originally a native of Britain, and though it be well known that many varieties have originated from seed in that country, still it appears from their own historians that the people introduced valuable varieties from abroad. Thus we find in Fuller's account, that in the 16th year of the reign of Henry VIII, Pippins were introduced into England by Lord Maschal, who planted them at Plumstead, in Sussex.

, After this, the celebrated Golden Pippin was originated at Perham Park, in Sussex, and this variety has attained a high meed of praise in that country and in Europe, though it has never been considered so fine in this country as some of our own seedlings. Evelyn says, in 1685, at Lord Clarendon's seat, at Swallowfield, Berks, there is an orchard of one thousand golden and other cider Pippins.* The Ribston Pippin, which every Englishman will tell you is the best apple in the world, was a native of Ribston Park, Yorkshire. Hargrave says: "This place is remarkable for the produce of a delicious apple, called the Ribston Park Pippin. The original tree was raised from a Pippin brought from France.† This apple is well-known in this country, but not a favorite.

---

* Diary

† History of Knaresborough, p. 216.—Companion of the Orchard, p. 34.

At a later period, 1597, John Gerard issued in an extensive folio his History of Plants, in which he mentions seven kinds of Pippins. The following is given as a sample of the pomology of that day: —

"The fruit of apples do differ in greatnesse, forme, colour, and taste, some covered with red skin, others yellow or greene, varying infinitely according to soil and climate; some very greate, some very little, and many of middle sort; some are sweet of taste, or something soure, most be of middle taste between sweet and soure; the which to distinguish, I think it impossible, notwithstanding I heare of one who intendeth to write a peculiar volume of apples and the use of them." He further says: "The tame and grafted apple trees are planted and set in gardens and orchards made for that purpose; they delight to growe in good fertile grounds. Kent doth abounde with apples of most sortes; but I have seen pastures and hedge-rows about the grounds of a worshipful gentleman dwelling two miles from Hereford, so many trees of all sortes, that the seruantes drinke for the moste parte no other drinke but that which is made of apples. * * * Like as there be divers manured apples, so is there sundry wilde apples or crabs, not husbanded, that is, not grafted." He also speaks of the Paradise, which is probably the same we now use as a dwarfing stock.

Dr. Gerard fully appreciated the value of fruits, and thus vehemently urges his countrymen to plant orchards: "Gentlemen, that have land and living, put forward, * * * * * graft, set, plant, and nourish up trees in every corner of your grounds; the labor is small, the cost is nothing, the commoditie is great, yourselves shall have plentie,

2*

the poor shall have somewhat in time of want to relieve
their necessitie, and God shall reward your good minde
and diligence." The same author gives us a peculiar use
of the apple which may be interesting to some who never
before associated *pomatum* with the products of the orchard. He recommends apples as a cosmetic. " There is
made an ointment with the pulp of apples, and swine's
grease and rose water, which is used to beautify the face
and to take away the roughness of the skin; it is called
in shops *pomatum*, of the apples whereof it is made." *
When speaking of the importance of grafting to increase
the number of trees of any good variety, Virgil advises to

" Graft the tender shoot,
Thy children's children shall enjoy the fruit."

So high an estimate did Pliny have of this fruit, that he
asserted that "there are apples that have ennobled the
countries from whence they came, and many apples have
immortalized their first founders and inventors. Our best
apples will immortalize their first grafters forever; such
as took their names from Manlius, Cestius, Matius, and
Claudius."—Of the Quince apple, he says, that came of a
quince being grafted upon the apple stock, which "smell
like the quince, and were called *Appiana*, after Appius,
who was the first that practiced this mode of grafting.
Some are so red that they resemble blood, which is caused
by their being grafted upon the mulberry stock. Of all
the apples, the one which took its name from Petisius,
was the most excellent for eating, both on account of its

---

* Our lexicographers give it a similar origin, but refer it to the shape in which
it was put up. Others derive it from *poma*, Spanish, a box of perfume.

sweetness and its agreeable flavor." Pliny mentions twenty-nine kinds of apples cultivated in Italy, about the commencement of the Chistian Era.*

Alas! for human vanity and apple glory! Where are now these boasted sorts, upon whose merits the immortality of their inventors and first grafters was to depend? They have disappeared from our lists to give place to new favorites, to some of which, perhaps, we are disposed to award an equally high meed of praise, that will again be ignored in a few fleeting years, when higher skill and more scientific applications of knowledge shall have produced superior fruit to any of those we now prize so highly; and this is a consummation to which we may all look forward with pleasure.

In this country the large majority of our favorite fruits, of whatever species or kind, seem to have originated by accident, that is, they have been discovered in seedling orchards, or even in hedge-rows. These have no doubt, however, been produced by accidental crosses of good kinds, and this may occur through the intervention of insects in any orchard of good fruit, where there may chance to be some varieties that have the tendency to progress. The discoveries of Linnæus, and his doctrine of the sexual characters of plants, created quite a revolution in botany, and no doubt attracted the attention of Lord Bacon, who was a close observer of nature, for he ventured to guess that there might be such a thing as crossing the breeds of plants, when he says: —" The compounding or mixture of kinds in plants is not found out,

* Phillips' Companion, p. 82.

which, nevertheless, if it be possible, is more at command than that of living creatures; wherefore it were one of the most noteable experiments touching plants to find it out, for so you may have great variety of new fruits and flowers yet unknown. Grafting does it not, that mendeth the fruit or doubleth the flowers, etc., but hath not the power to make a new kind, for the scion ever overruleth the stock." In which last observation he shows more knowledge and a deeper insight into the hidden mysteries of plant-life than many a man in our day, whose special business it is to watch, nurse, and care for these humble forms of existence.

Bradley, about a century later, in 1718, is believed to have been the first author who speaks of the accomplishment of cross-breeding, which he describes as having been effected by bringing together the branches of different trees when in blossom. But the gardeners of Holland and the Netherlands were the first to put it into practice.*

The following extract is given to explain the manner in which Mr. Knight conducted his celebrated experiments on fruits, which rewarded him with some varieties that were highly esteemed : — "Many varieties of the apple were collected which had been proved to afford, in mixtures with each other, the finest cider. A tree of each was then obtained by grafting upon a Paradise stock, and these trees were trained to a south wall, or if grafted on Siberian crab, to a west wall, till they afforded blossoms, and the soil in which they were planted was made of the most rich and favorable kind. Each blos-

* Phillips' Companion, p. 41.

som of this species of fruit contains about twenty chives or males (stamens,) and generally five pointals or females (pistils,) which spring from the center of the cup or cavity of the blossom. The males stand in a circle just within the bases of the petals, and are formed of slender threads, each of which terminates in an anther. It is necessary in these experiments that both the fruit and seed should attain as large a size and as much perfection as possible, and therefore a few blossoms only were suffered to remain on each tree. As soon as the blossoms were nearly full-grown, every male in each was carefully extracted, proper care being taken not to injure the pointals; and the blossoms, thus prepared, were closed again, and suffered to remain till they opened spontaneously. The blossoms of the tree which it was proposed to make the male parent of the future variety, were accelerated by being brought into contact with the wall, or retarded by being detached from it, so that they were made to unfold at the required period; and a portion of their pollen, when ready to fall from the mature anthers, was during three or four successive mornings deposited upon the pointals of the blossoms, which consequently afforded seeds. It is necessary in this experiment that one variety of apple only should bear unmutilated blossoms; for, where other varieties are in flower at the same time, the pollen of these will often be conveyed by bees to the prepared blossoms, and the result of the experiment will in consequence be uncertain and unsatisfactory." * * *

In his Pomona Herefordiensis, he says: — " It is necessary to contrive that the two trees from which you intend to raise the new kind, shall blossom at the same time;

therefore, if one is an earlier sort than the other, it must be retarded by shading or brought into a cooler situation, and the latest forwarded by a warm wall or a sunny position, so as to procure the desired result."

We must distinguish between hybrids proper and crosses, as it were between races or between what may have been erroneously designated species, for there has been a great deal of looseness in the manner of using these terms by some writers. A true *hybrid* * is produced only when the pollen of one species has been used to fertilize the ovules of another, and as a general rule these can only be produced between plants which are very nearly allied, as between species of the same genus. Even such as these, however, cannot always be hybridized, for we have never found a mule or hybrid between the apple and pear, the currant and gooseberry, nor between the raspberry and blackberry, though each of these, respectively, appear to be very nearly related, and they are all of the order *Rosaceæ*.

In hybrids there appears to be a mixture of the elements of each, and the characters of the mule or cross will depend upon one or the other, which it will more nearly resemble. True hybrids are mules or infertile, and cannot be continued by seed, but must be propagated by cuttings, or layers, or grafting. If not absolutely sterile at first, they become so in the course of the second or third generation. This is proved by several of our flowering plants that have been wonderfully varied by ingenious crossing of different species. But it has been found

---

* Balfour's Manual.

that the hybrid may be fertilized by pollen taken from one of its parents, and that then the offspring assumes the characters of that parent.*

Natural hybrids do not often occur, though in diœcious plants, this seems to have been the case with willows that present such an intricate puzzle to botanists in their classification, so that it has become almost impossible to say what are the limits and bounds of some of the species. Hybrids are, however, very frequently produced by art, and particularly among our flowering plants, under the hands of ingenious gardeners. Herbert thinks, from his observations, " that the flowers and organs of reproduction partake of the characters of the female parent, while the foliage and habit, or the organs of vegetation, resemble the male."

Simply crossing different members of the same species, like the crossing of races in animal life, is not always easily accomplished; but we here find much less difficulty, and we do not produce a mule progeny. In these experiments the same precautions must be taken to avoid the interference of natural agents in the transportation of pollen from flower to flower; but this process is now so familiar to horticulturists, that it scarcely needs a mention. In our efforts with the strawberry, some very curious results have occurred, and we have learned that some of the recognized species appear under this severe test to be well founded, as the results have been infertile. Where the perfection of the fruit depends upon the development of the seed, this is a very important matter to the fruit-grower; but fortunately this is not always the case, for

* Balfour's Manual.

certain fruits swell and ripen perfectly, though containing not a single well developed seed. It would be an interesting study to trace out those plants which do furnish a well developed fleshy substance or sarcocarp, without the true seeds. Such may be found occasionally in the native persimmon, in certain grapes, and in many apples; but in the strawberry, blackberry, and raspberry, the berry which constitutes our desirable fruit, never swells unless the germs have been impregnated and the seeds perfect. In the stone-fruits the stone or pit is always developed, but the enclosed seed is often imperfect from want of impregnation or other cause—and yet the fleshy covering will sometimes swell and ripen.

One of the most successful experimenters in this country is Doctor J. P. Kirtland, near Cleveland, Ohio, whose efforts at crossing certain favorite cherries, were crowned with the most happy results, and all are familiar with the fruits that have been derived from his crosses. The details of his applying the pollen of one flower to the pistils of another are familiar to all intelligent readers, and have been so often set forth, that they need not be repeated in this case—great care is necessary to secure the desired object, and to guard against interference from causes that would endanger or impair the value of the results.

Van Mons' theory was based upon certain assumptions and observations, some of which are well founded, others are not so firmly established. He claimed correctly that all our best fruits were artificial products, because the essential elements for the preservation of the species in their natural condition, are vigor of the plant and perfect seeds for the perpetuation of the race. It has been the object of culture to diminish the extreme vigor of the tree so as to produce early fruitage, and at the same time to enlarge and to refine the pulpy portion of the fruit. He claimed, as a principle, that our plants of culture had always a tendency to run back toward the original or wild type, when they were grown from seeds. This tendency is admitted to exist in many cases, but it is also claimed, that when a break is once made from the normal type, the tendency to improve may be established. Van Mons asserted that the seeds from old trees would be still more apt to run back toward the original type, and that "the older the tree, the nearer will the seedlings raised from it approach the wild state," though he says they will not quite reach it. But the seeds from a young tree, having itself the tendency to melioration, are more likely to produce improved sorts.

He thinks there is a limit to perfection, and that, when this is reached, the next generation will more probably produce bad fruit than those grown from an inferior sort, which is on the upward road of progression. He claims that the seeds of the oldest varieties of good fruit yield inferior kinds, whereas those taken from new varieties of bad fruit, and reproduced for several generations, will certainly give satisfactory results in good fruit.

He began with seeds from a young seedling tree, not grafted upon another stock; he cared nothing for the quality of the fruit, but preferred that the variety was showing a tendency to improvement or *variation*. These were sowed, and from the plants produced, he selected such as appeared to him to have evidence of improvement, (it is supposed by their less wild appearance), and transplanted them to stations where they could develop themselves. When they fruited, even if indifferent, if they continued to give evidence of variation, the first seeds were saved and planted and treated in the same way. These came earlier into fruit than the first, and showed a greater promise. Successive generations were thus produced to the fourth and fifth, each came into bearing earlier than its predecessor, and produced a greater number of good varieties, and he says that in the fifth generation they were nearly all of great excellence. He found pears required the longest time, five generations; while the apple was perfected in four, and stone fruits in three.

Starting upon the theory that we must subdue the vigor of the wilding to produce the best fruits, he cut off the tap roots when transplanting and shortened the leaders, and crowded the plants in the orchard or fruiting grounds, so as to stand but a few feet apart. He urged the "regenerating in a direct line of descent as rapidly as possible an improving variety, taking care that there be no interval between the generations. To sow, re-sow, to sow again, to sow perpetually, in short to do nothing but sow, is the practice to be pursued, and which cannot be departed from; and, in short, this is the whole secret of the art I have employed." (*Arbres Fruitiers.*)

Who else would have the needed patience and perseverance to pursue such a course? Very few, indeed—especially if they were not very fully convinced of the correctness of the premises upon which this theory is founded. Mr. Downing thinks that the great numbers of fine varieties of apples that have been produced in this country, go to sustain the Van Mons doctrine, because, as he assumes, the first apples that were produced from seeds brought over by the early emigrants, yielded inferior fruit, which had run back toward the wild state, and the people were forced to begin again with them, and that they most naturally pursued this very plan, taking seeds from the improving varieties for the next generations and so on. This may have been so, but it is mere assumption —we have no proof, and, on the contrary, our choice varieties have so generally been conceded to have been chance seedlings, that there appears little evidence to support it—on the contrary, some very fine varieties have been produced by selecting the seeds of good sorts promiscuously, and without regarding the age of the trees from which the fruit was taken. Mr. Downing himself, after telling us that we have much encouragement to experiment upon this plan of perfecting fruits, by taking seeds from such as are not quite ripe, gathered from a seedling of promising quality, from a healthy young tree (quite young,) on its own root, not grafted, and that we " must avoid 1st, the seeds of old trees; 2d, those of grafted trees ; 3d, that we must have the best grounds for good results "—still admits what we all know, that " in this country, new varieties of rare excellence are sometimes obtained at once by planting the seeds of old grafted varieties; thus the Lawrence Favorite and the Columbia Plums were raised from seeds of the Green Gage, one of the oldest European varieties."

Let us now look at an absolute experiment conducted avowedly upon the Van Mons plan in our own country, upon the fertile soil of the State of Illinois, and see to what results it led : --

The following facts have been elicited from correspond-
ence with II. P. Brayshaw, of Du Quoin, Illinois. The
experiments were instituted by his father many years ago,
to test the truth of the Van Mons' theory of the improvement of fruits by using only the first seeds.

Thirty-five years ago, in 1827, his father procured twenty-five seedling trees from a nursery, which may be supposed to have been an average lot, grown from promiscuous seed. These were planted, and when they came into
bearing, six of them furnished fruit that might be called
"*good*," and of these, "four were considered *fine*." One
of the six is still in cultivation, and known as the *Illinois
Greening*. Of the remainder of the trees, some of the
fruits were fair, and the rest were worthless, and have
disappeared.

Second Generation. — The first fruits of these trees
were selected, and the seeds were sown. Of the resulting
crop, some furnished fruit that was "good," but they do
not appear to have merited much attention.

Third Generation.—From first seeds of the above, one
hundred trees were produced, some of which were good
fruit, and some "even fine," while some were very poor,
"four or five only merited attention." So that we see a
retrogression from the random seedlings, furnishing twenty-five per cent. of good fruit, to only four or five per cent.
in the third generation, that were worthy of note.

Fourth Generation.—A crop of the first seed was again
sown, producing a fourth generation; of these many were
"good culinary fruits," none, or very few being of the
"poorest class of seedlings," none of them, however, were
fine enough "for the dessert."

Fifth Generation. — This crop of seedlings was destroyed by the cut-worms, so that only one tree now remains, but has not yet fruited. But Mr. Brayshaw appears to feel hopeful of the results, and promises to continue the experiment.

Crops have also been sown from some of these trees, but a smaller proportion of the seedlings thus produced were good fruits, than when the first seeds were used— this Mr. Brayshaw considers confirmatory evidence of the theory, though he appears to feel confidence in the varieties already in use, most of which had almost an accidental origin.

He thinks the result would have been more successful had the blossoms been protected from impregnation by other trees, and recommends that those to be experimented with should be planted at a distance from orchards, so as to avoid this cross-breeding, and to allow of what is called breeding in-and-in. If this were done, he feels confident that " the seedlings would more nearly resemble the parent, and to a certain extent would manifest the tendency to improvement, and that from the earliest ripened fruits, some earlier varieties would be produced, from those latest ripening, later varieties, from those that were inferior and insipid, poor sorts would spring, and that from the very best and most perfect fruits we might expect one in one thousand, or one-tenth of one per cent., to be better than the parent. This diminishes the chance for improvement to a beatifully fine point upon which to hang our hopes of the result of many generations of seedlings occupying more than a lifetime of experiments.

Mr. Brayshaw, citing some of the generally adopted

axioms of breeders of animals, assumes that *crosses*, as of distinct races, will not be so likely to produce good results, as a system of breeding in-and-in, persistently carried out. This plan he recommends, and alludes to the quince and mulberry as suitable species to operate upon, because in them there are fewer varieties, and therefore less liability to cross-breeding, and a better opportunity for breeding in-and-in. He also reminds us of the happy results which follow the careful selection of the best specimens in garden flowers and vegetables, combined with the rejection of all inferior plants, when we desire to improve the character of our garden products, and he adopts the views of certain physiologists, which, however, are questioned by other authorities, to the effect that violent or decided crosses are always followed by depreciation and deterioration of the offspring.

The whole communication referring to these experiments, which are almost the only ones, so far as I know, which have been conducted in this country to any extent, to verify or controvert the Van Mons' theory, is very interesting, but it is easy to perceive that the experimenter, though apparently very fair, and entirely honest, has been fully imbued with the truth and correctness of the proposition of Van Mons, that the first ripened seed of a natural plant was more likely to produce an improved variety, and that this tendency to improvement would ever increase, and be most prominent in the first ripened seeds of successive generations grown from it.

The theory of Van Mons I shall not attempt in this place to controvert, but will simply say that nothing which has yet come under my observation has had a tendency to make me a convert to the avowed views of that great Belgian Pomologist, while, on the contrary, the rumors of his opponents, that he was really attempting to produce crosses from some of the best fruits, as our gardeners have most successfully done in numerous instances, in the beautiful flowers and delicious vegetables of modern horticulture, have always impressed me with a color of probability, and if he were not actually and intentionally impregnating the blossoms with pollen of the better varieties, natural causes, such as the moving currents of air, and the ever active insects, whose special function in many instances appears to be the conveyance of pollen, would necessarily cause an admixture, which, in a promiscuous and crowded collection, like the "school of Van Mons," would at least have an equal chance of producing an improvement in some of the resulting seeds.

The whole subject of variation in species, the existence of varieties, and also of those partial *sports*, which may perhaps be considered as still more temporary variations from the originals, than those which come through the seeds, is one of deep interest, well worthy of our study, but concerning which we must confess ourselves as yet quite ignorant, and our best botanists do not agree even as to the *specific* distinctions that have been set up as characters of some of our familiar plants, for the most eminent differ with regard to the species of some of our common trees and plants.

RUNNING OUT OF VARIETIES.

It has been a very generally received opinion among intelligent fruit-growers, that any given variety of fruit can

have but a limited period of existence, be that longer or
shorter.   Reasoning from the analogies of animal life this
would appear very probable, for it is well known that individuals of different species all have a definite period of
life, some quite brief, others quite extended, beyond which
they do not survive.   But with our modern views of vegetation, though we know that all perennial plants do eventually die and molder away to the dust from whence they
were created, and that many trees of our own planting
come to an untimely end, while we yet survive to observe
their decay, still, we can see no reason why a tree or parts
of a tree taken from it, and placed under circumstances
favorable to its growth from time to time, may not be sem-
piternal.   Harvey has placed this matter in a correct
light, by showing that the true life and history of a tree
is in the buds, which are annual, while the tree itself is
the connecting link between them and the ground.   Any
portion of such a compound existence, grafted upon another stock, or planted immediately in the ground itself
and established upon its own roots, will produce a new
tree like the first, being furnished with supplies of nourishment it may grow indefinitely while retaining all the
qualities of the parent stock—if that be healthy and vigorous so will this—indeed new life and vigor often seem to
be imparted by a congenial thrifty stock, and a fertile soil,
so that there does not appear to be any reason why the
variety should ever run out and disappear.

The distinguished Thomas Andrew Knight, President
of the London Horticultural Society, was one of the leading advocates of the theory that varieties would necessarily run out and disappear as it were by exhaustion.

In his Pomona Herefordiensis, he tells us that "those apples, which have been long in cultivation, are on the decay. The Redstreak and Golden Pippin can no longer be propagated with advantage. The fruit, like the parent tree, is affected by the debilitated old age of the variety." And in his treatise on the culture of the apple and pear, he says: "The Moil and its successful rival, the Redstreak, with the Must and Golden Pippin, are in the last stage of decay, and the Stire and Foxwhelp are hastening rapidly after them." In noticing the decay of apple trees, Pliny probably refers to particular trees, rather than the whole of any variety, when he says that "apples become old sooner than any other tree, and the fruit becomes smaller and is subject to be cankered and worm-eaten, even while on the trees."—Lib. XVI, Chap. 27.

Speechly combated the views of Mr. Knight, and says: "It is much to be regretted that this apparently visionary notion of the extinction of certain kinds of apples should have been promulgated by authors of respectability, since the mistake will, for a time at least, be productive of several ill consequences."

Some of the old English varieties that were supposed to be worn out or exhausted, appear to have taken a new lease of life in this country, but we have not yet had a long enough experience to decide this question. Many of the earlier native favorites of the orchard have, for some reason, disappeared from cultivation —whether they have run out, were originally deficient in vigor, or have merely been superseded by more acceptable varieties, does not appear.

Mr. Phillips, in his Companion, states "that in 1819, he
3

observed a great quantity of the Golden Pippin in Covent Garden Market, which were in perfect condition, and was induced to make inquiries respecting the health of the variety, which resulted in satisfactory replies from all quarters, that the trees were recovering from disease, which he thought had been induced by a succession of unpropitious seasons. He cites Mr. Ronald's opinion, that there was then no fear of losing this variety; and Mr. Lee, who thought that the apparent decay of some trees was owing to unfavorable seasons. Mr. Harrison informed him that this variety was very successfully grown on the mountains of the island of Madeira, at an elevation of 3000 feet, and produced abundantly. Also that the variety was quite satisfactory in many parts of England, and concludes that the Golden Pippin only requires the most genial situation, to render it as prolific as formerly."

It is quite probable, as Phillips suggests, that Mr. Knight had watched the trees during unfavorable seasons which prevailed at that period, and as he found the disease increase, he referred it to the old age of the variety, and based his theory to that effect upon partial data.

Mr. Knight's views, though they have taken a strong hold upon the popular mind, have not been confirmed by physiologists. For though the seed would appear to be the proper source whence to derive our new plants, and certainly our new varieties of fruits, many plants have, for an indefinite period, been propagated by layers, shoots or scions, buds, tubers, etc., and that the variety has thus been extended much beyond the period of the life of the parent or original seedling. Strawberries are propagated and multiplied by the runners, potatoes by tubers, the

Tiger Lily by bulblets, some onions by proliferous bulbs, sugar cane by planting pieces of the stalk, many grapes by horizontal stems, and many plants by cuttings, for a very great length of time. The grape vine has been continued in this way from the days of the Romans. A slip taken from a willow in Mr. Knight's garden pronounced by him to be dying from old age, was planted in the Edinburgh Botanic Garden many years ago, and is now a vigorous tree, though the original stock has long since gone to decay.*

---

* Balfour's Manual, p. 284.

CHAPTER III.

PROPAGATION.—SECTION I.

———◦◇◦———

ALL GROWTH IS DEPENDANT UPON THE DEVELOPMENT OF CELLS—THE
SEED AND THE BUD; THEIR RESEMBLANCE—THE INDIVIDUALI-
TY OF BUDS—THE BASIS OF ALL PROPAGATION—BUDS ARE DEVEL-
OPED INTO TWIGS; HAVE POWER OF EMITTING ROOTS—IMPORTANCE
OF THE STUDY OF CELL-GROWTH——BY CUTTINGS: PREPARATION
AND SELECTION—HEEL-CUTTINGS—SOFT WOOD—HARD WOOD—
SEASONS FOR EACH—FALL PLANTING—THE CALLUS, OR DEVELOP-
MENT OF CELL-GROWTH—BOTTOM HEAT; WHY BENEFICIAL—WHY
SPRING CUTTINGS FAIL—STIMULUS OF LIGHT UPON THE BUDS,
CAUSES THEM TO EXPAND, AND THE LEAVES EVAPORATE TOO FREE-
LY—ROOT CUTTINGS; DIFFERENT FRUITS THUS PROPAGATED——
BY SUCKERS: OBJECTIONS TO ANSWERED—SUCKER ORCHARDS;
BEAR EARLY—SUCKER TREES APT TO SUCKER AGAIN——BY LAY-
ERS: A NATURAL METHOD—HOW PERFORMED—THE RASPBERRY
AND THE GRAPE—ILLUSTRATIONS OF NATURAL AND ARTIFICIAL
METHODS—QUINCE STOCKS—ADJUVANTS TO LAYERING, NOTCHING,
ETC——BY SEEDS: HOW IT DIFFERS FROM THE OTHERS—APPLE
SEEDLINGS—THEIR TREATMENT, SEPARATING, AND PREPARING THE
SEED—APPARATUS—SPROUTING—SOWING—CULTIVATION—SEED-
LINGS—TREATMENT—SORTING—PACKING.

All propagation of plants must depend upon the development of seeds or of buds, and all will arise from the
growth and extension of cells. The seed and the bud are
much more nearly related than a casual observer would at

first sight suppose. The early phylologists thought they discovered that in the seed was enwrapped the image of the future tree—a dissection of the seed would appear to demonstrate this. It is composed of separate parts which are capable of being developed into the root, stem, and appendages, but they have yet to be so developed; the several parts that we find in the seed are merely the representative parts. But the seed has the future of the tree within itself, it has certain qualities of the future tree impressed upon it in its primary organization, within the capsule of the fruit of the parent plant, so that in a higher sense the image of the future tree does exist within the seed. Within the bud, still more plainly and more distinctly visible, is the future tree manifest, and we may produce a tree from a bud as certainly as we do from a seed. Subjected to circumstances favorable for growth, the bud, as well as the seed, will emit roots, will form its stem, branches and appendages, and will become a tree; differing from the product of the seed only in this, that in the latter the resulting organism constitutes a new individual which may vary somewhat from its parent, in the former it is only a new development of a part of a previously existing organization. The similarity existing between the two is exceedingly close, and is a matter of great importance in horticultural operations. Dr. Lindley, in the Gardener's Chronicle, says very truly, that "every bud of a tree is an individual vegetable, and a tree, therefore, is a family or swarm of individual plants, like the polype with its young growing out of its sides, or like the branching cells of the coral insect." Similar opinions, more or less modified, have been expressed by subsequent physiologists, and are familiar to men of science in every country and, we may add, are also universally accepted as true by all who claim a right to express an opinion upon the subject.—Men of science recognize the individuality of buds. —Nobody doubts the individuality of buds.—In a gardening aspect, the individuality of buds is the cardinal point upon which some of our most important operations turn; such, for example, as all modes of propagation whatever, except by seed. If this be not fully understood, there is no possible explanation of the reasons why certain results are sure to follow the attachment of a bud, or the insertion of a graft, or the planting of a cutting, or the bending of a layer, or the approach of a scion, or the setting of an eye—our six great forms of artificial multiplication." In his Elements of Botany, the same writer says: " An embryo is a young plant produced by the agency of the sexes, and developed within a seed—a leaf bud is a young plant, produced without the agency of the sexes, enclosed within the rudimentary leaves called scales, and developed on a stem." " An embryo propagates the *species*, leaf-buds propagate the *individual*." He shows each to be " a young plant developing itself upwards, downwards and horizontally, into stem, root, and medullary system."

Dr. Schleiden thus beautifully expresses his views of their individuality: " Now the bud essentially is nothing more than a repetition of the plant on which it is formed. The foundation of a new plant consists equally of a stem and leaves, and the sole distinction is that the stem becomes intimately blended at its base with the mother plant in its growth, and has no free radical extremity like that exhibited by a plant developed from a seed. However, this

distinction is not so great as at the first glance it appears.
Every plant of high organization possesses the power of
shooting out adventitious roots from its stem, under the
favoring influences of moisture; and very frequently, even
plants that have been raised from seed, are forced to content themselves with such adventitious roots, since it is
the nature of many plants, for instance the grasses, never to
develop their proper root, although the radicle is actually
present. We are, it is true, accustomed to look upon the
matter as though the buds must always be developed into
twigs and branches, on and in connection with the plant
itself; and thus in common life, we regard them as parts
of a plant, and not as independent individuals, which they
are in fact, although they, like children who remain in
their paternal home, retain the closest connection with the
plant on which they were produced. That they are at
least capable of becoming independent plants, is shown
by an experiment frequently successful when the necessary care is taken, namely the breaking off and sowing of
the buds of our forest trees. The well-known garden
operations of grafting and budding are also examples of
this, and layering only differs from the sowing of the
buds, in that the buds on the layers are allowed to acquire
a certain degree of maturity before they are separated from
the parent plant. All here depends upon the facility with
which these bud plants root as it is called, that is develop
adventitious roots, when they are brought in contact with
moist earth. * * * Nature herself very often makes
use of this method to multiply certain plants in incalculable
numbers. In a few cases, the process resembles the artificial sowing of buds, as when the plant spontaneously

throws off the perfect buds at a certain period; an instance of this is afforded by some of our garden Lilies, which throw off the little bulb-like buds which appear in the axils of the lower leaves. The more common mode of proceeding is as follows: Those buds which have been formed near the surface of the soil, grow up into shoots provided with leaves; but the shoots are long, slender and delicate, the leaves too are stunted into little scales; in their axils, however, they develop strong buds, which either in the same or in the following year take root, and the slender shoot connecting them with the parent plant, dying and decaying, they become free independent plants. In this manner the strawberry soon covers a neglected garden." *

Upon the development of a cell in any living tissue, and its power of reproducing other cells, and upon its function of communicating by endosmosis and exosmosis with other like cells, depend all our success in propagating vegetables, whether from seeds or buds, and parts containing these. We must study the circumstances that favor the development of cells, if we would be successful in propagating plants. Each bud being considered an individual, and capable, under favorable circumstances, of taking on a separate existence, we can multiply any individual variety indefinitely, and be sure of having the same qualities of foliage and fruit that we admire in the original, and that we may desire to propagate. This applies equally to a group of buds, as in cuttings, grafts and layers, etc.; but, more wonderful still, there are cells capable of developing buds where none existed before, and

* The Plant, a Biography. M. J. Schleiden, p. 68.

even in tissues or parts of a plant where we do not usually find buds—hence we have a mode of propagation of many woody plants, by root cuttings, and by leaves, and even parts of leaves.

PROPAGATION BY CUTTINGS.—Many fruits are multiplied by this means. Healthy shoots of the previous year's growth are usually selected and taken when the parent is in a dormant state, or still better, when it is approaching this condition. Sometimes a small portion of the previous year's growth is left with the cutting, making a sort of *heel;* when this is not to be had, or not preferred, the slip is to be prepared for planting by cutting it smoothly just below a bud, as this seems to be the most favorable point in many plants for the emission of roots. Some plants will throw out radicles at any point indifferently along the internodes or merithalls. The preference for heel-cuttings depends upon the fact, that near the base of the annual shoot there are always a great number of buds, many of which, however, being imperfectly developed, are inconspicuous, but though dormant, they seem to favor the emission of rootlets. Cuttings may be made to grow if taken at any period of their development, but when green and soft, they require particular conditions of heat and moisture in the soil, and atmosphere, that are only under the control of the professional gardener. They are usually taken in the dormant state, because they are then susceptible of being made to grow under the ordinary conditions of out-door gardening. If cut early in the season, on the approach of autumn, after the wood-growth has been perfected, they may be planted at once with good prospect of success, or they may be put into the

3*

soil, out of doors, in the cellar, or in a cold frame or pit, and a very important step in the progress of their growth will commence at once. The leafless sticks are not dead, and whenever the temperature will admit of the quiet interchange of fluids among their cells, this curious function will go on, and will be accompanied by the development or generation of new cells that soon cover the cut surfaces, constituting what the gardeners call the *callus*. This is the first step toward growth, and it most readily occurs when the earth is warmer than the air; hence the value of fall planting, whether of trees or of cuttings, if done before the earth has been chilled, and hence also, the importance of bottom heat in artificial propagation. If on the contrary the air be warm and the ground cold, the buds are often stimulated to burst forth, before the rootlets can have started. The expanding foliage which so delights the tyro in propagation, offers an extended surface for evaporation, the contained juices of the cutting itself are soon exhausted, no adequate supply is furnished, and the hopeful plant soon withers, or damps off, and dies.* The cutting, like the seed, must have "first the root, then the blade." The length of time that is allowed for cuttings to prepare for rooting, if they are designed for spring planting, should be as great as possible, and the circumstances under which they are kept should be such as to favor the development of the cells, so that roots may form freely with the breaking of the buds, if not before.

Root-cuttings should be made in the spring, just before the usual period of the bursting of the buds in the plant to be propagated. The tendency to develop buds appears

---

* Because it had no root, it withered away. Mat. 13, 6.

to be then most active. Gentle bottom heat, though not
essential, is still very desirable, and will conduce to the
success of the operation. Some plants are best propagated by this means, and those too, which never naturally produce suckers, may often be successfully grown by
sections of the roots. All plants do not equally admit
of propagation by division as cuttings, some woody
tissues refusing to emit roots under almost any circumstances.

Nobody thinks of propagating the stone fruits, such as
the cherry, plum, peach, or apricot, by attempting to plant
cuttings, and yet some of these will emit roots very freely, as we may often observe when the shoots or trimmings
are used as supports for plants in the green-house. The
plum tree is exceedingly apt to form new roots when
planted too deeply, and upon this fact depends the success
or failure of the finer varieties when worked upon certain
varieties of the wild stock. If the young trees are earthed
up in the nursery, and set rather deeply in the orchard,
they will soon establish a good set of roots of their own,
emitted above the junction of the scion and stock, which
is very preferable to the imperfect union and consequent
enlargement that often results from using uncongenial
stocks. The raspberry and blackberry do not grow so
well from cuttings of the wood, which is always biennial
in this genus, as they do from root-cuttings.

In some parts of the country, peaches are mainly produced, or the favorite varieties are multiplied, by planting
the sprouts that come from the base of the trunk of the
trees; these have little or no roots when taken off with
the mattock, but they soon establish themselves and make

good trees, bearing fruit like their parents, in soils and climate that are well adapted to this fruit.

Refined and scientific horticulture has been extensively applied to the multiplication of the grape, which is now produced in immense numbers, from single eyes, or buds. Formerly our vineyards were formed by planting long cuttings at once in the field in the stations to be occupied by the vines, or by setting them first in a nursery, whence they were transplanted to the vineyard, when one or two years old. Only the most refractory kinds, which would not grow readily in the field, or such as were yet rare, were propagated from cuttings, by using the single eye and artificial bottom heat. Now, however, the appliances of our propagators are called upon for the production of grape-vines by the million, and they find it advisable to multiply all the varieties in this manner. The propagation of the grape by using single eyes affords the most beautiful illustration of the subject of the individuality of buds, and though denounced by some as an unnatural, steam-forcing process, it is really an evidence of the advance of horticulture, since every step is supported by a philosophical reason, and the whole process, to be successful, is dependent upon the application to practice of well established scientific truths.

It has already been stated that the first effect of cell-growth upon a cutting, is the production of a callus. This callus may form upon any cut surface, or even where the bark has been abraded. It is the first effort of nature to repair an injury by the reproduction of new parts; it is most generally found at the base of the cutting, but under favorable circumstances, it will be seen also at the up-

per end of the shoot if this has been placed in contact
with the earth. Cuttings will sometimes be set up-side
down, when we find the callus upon the smaller end, and
roots will be emitted from that portion whence we should
have expected to see the branches issue. Upon this fact,
and to multiply the chances of living, has been based the
French method, as it is called, or that of inserting both
ends of the cuttings. The common mode, (fig. 1), is to

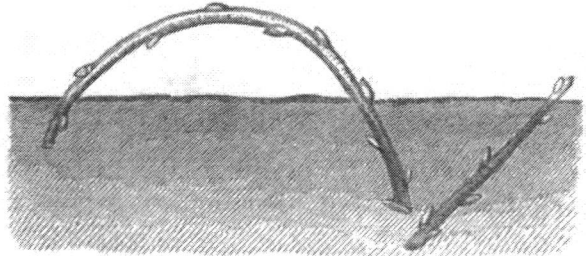

Fig. 1.—FRENCH AND COMMON MODES OF SETTING CUTTINGS.

set the cuttings in a slanting direction in the ground, so
placed that the upper eye or bud only shall reach the surface. Formerly there was a preference for long cuttings,
and these were often made eighteen inches or more in
length. The practice with most of our cultivators has
been modified in this particular, and they have reduced
the length of the slips to six and eight inches, so as to
have in grape wood about three or four eyes. Some have
gone still further, and use but two, even for out-door
planting of the grape, and some have been very successful when using but a single joint. The Germans have advocated longer cuttings, upon the theory that there was a
retroaction in the pith of the internodes and in all the
buds of the cutting, upon the lower point, enabling it to
push roots more strongly from a long than from a short

cutting. This theory has for its support the fact, that there is in such a cutting a larger amount of organizable matter to be developed into the new parts to be produced, and certainly, if neglected, short cuttings will be very apt to suffer from drought, but in practice, it is found that the short cutting plants have better roots, which are near the surface, and even those plants, grown from single eyes, are better furnished than long cuttings produced upon the old plan, which placed the roots deep in the soil.

Fig. 2.—ONE-EYE CUTTINGS OF THE GRAPE.

There are various methods of preparing the single-eye cuttings, some of which are represented in fig. 2.

Among our cultivated fruits there is but a limited number that need to be propagated by cuttings, though, where it becomes necessary, many of them may be grown in this manner, to which procedure there are no serious objections, though there are some of a theoretical nature.   The currant and the gooseberry are increased almost exclusively from cuttings, they strike root very readily, and are multiplied to any extent; their seeds are sown only to produce new varieties. The grape is propagated very extensively by cuttings; the slips are often planted in the field and in the stations where the vines are wanted for the vineyard; but some varieties are so unsatisfactory in their results, that other more elaborate and scientific means must be taken for their propagation. Among the larger fruits, those constituting our trees, we do not depend upon cuttings, except in the quince, which is not only grown for its fruit, but is also largely produced as a stock for the dwarfed pear, and is extensively propagated from cuttings. The Paradise apple, a dwarf stock, is multiplied in the same way. Pears and apples may be grown from cuttings, but this plan is not pursued with them to any extent. Those that are root-grafted, or budded very low, especially the pear on quince stocks, will often produce roots if favorably situated, but there is a great difference in varieties, some rarely produce a root, while others are very prone to do it; from observations of this fact, a new phase of dwarf-pear culture has been inaugurated.

SUCKERS.—One of the simplest methods of multiplying varieties consists of increasing and encouraging the suckers thrown up by the roots; these are separated and set out for trees. We have been told by some physiologists that there was an absolute difference in structure between the root and the stem, that they could not be substituted the one for the other; and yet the oft quoted marvel of the tree which was planted upside down, and which produced flowers and leaves from its roots, while its branches emitted fibres, and became true roots, is familiar to every one.

Here, as in other cases, our teachers have led us into error by attempting to trace analogy with animal anatomy and physiology, and by directing our attention to the circulation of plants, as though they, like the higher animals, possessed true arterial and venous currents of circulating fluids. The cell circulation is quite a different affair, and can be conducted in either direction, as every gardener knows who has ever layered a plant, or set a cutting upside down. So with the roots—they are but downward extensions of the stem; under ordinary circumstances they have no need for buds, but these may be, and often are developed, when the necessity for their presence arises. Buds do exist on roots, especially upon those that are horizontal and near the surface, and from them freely spring suckers, which are as much parts of the parent tree as its branches, and may be planted with entire certainty of obtaining the same fruit, just as the twigs when used as cuttings, or scions, when grafted, will produce similar results.

Whole orchards are planted, in some sections of the country, with the suckers from old trees; apples, pears, plums, and even peaches, as well as raspberries and blackberries, are multiplied in this primitive way. There are some varieties of apples that have been so propagated for half a century, and extended for hundreds of miles in this way by the pioneer emigrants, without ever having been grafted, until their merits have at length accidentally become known to the Pomological Societies and nurserymen, when the propagation of them by grafting soon supercedes the more primitive method. Sucker trees are objected to upon the grounds that they are not healthy and

thrifty, that they do not have good roots. Inherent disease of the parent tree will of course be transmitted with
its other peculiarities, but I cannot imagine that this would
be any more likely to occur in a sucker than in a layer, or
cutting, or graft. As to the roots, they may be more developed upon one side than another in the young tree, and
this state of things may continue in the adult; we often
observe the same condition in the stumps of the monarchs
of our forests, which were never suspected in the day of
their glory and pride of having such a fault. But such a
condition of roots is not essential to the sucker, which
may be made to have as fine a system of lateral roots, and
as evenly and regularly distributed as those of a seedling
tree. Another objection to this mode of propagation has
much truth and some force; that is, that suckers are very
apt to produce suckers again. This is particularly
the case with the Morello cherry, which is a favorite
stock, upon which to work many of the choice varieties. As an offset to this it may be urged, that the
small fibrous roots, which are supposed to conduce to
early fruitfulness, abound in trees propagated by this
means, and this may be the reason why the fruit trees
that have been thus multiplied, are very generally remarkable for their precocious fruiting. Some of the
apples that have been long increased in this manner, bear
so early, and so bountifully, as to prevent them from ever
forming very large trees; they often have a stunted appearance, and not infrequently present a peculiar inequal-
ity upon the bark, portions being swollen or enlarged
like warts—from which, in some cases, it is easy to force
out shoots or sprouts; they are indeed true gemmules like

those of the old olive trees, and like them might be used for the propagation of the variety; a similar condition, no doubt, exists in the roots, whence the tendency to sucker. The common Morello cherry; the Damson; the Chickasas, and other varieties of plum; the blackberry, and many raspberries, are multiplied almost exclusively in a similar manner.

LAYERS are portions of the branches of a plant that have been induced to throw out roots, and which can thus set up an independent existence if removed from the parent tree. This mode of propagation is a very natural one, and was probably an accidental discovery. In its traits, it is the reverse of the mode we have just been considering. Here the branch emits roots, instead of the root emitting branches, as in the case of the sucker. Layering is frequently resorted to as a mode of propagation, it is very simple, easily performed, and, with some species, very certain in its results. Some plants will root readily if merely placed in contact with the ground, or very slightly covered with soil; others require some artificial interference, such as ringing, or twisting, or slitting. The raspberry, known as the *Rubus occidentalis*, or Black-cap, belongs to the first class, and it even places itself in contact with the soil by recurving its branches so as to bring the tips to the earth, where they strike root, and make new plants. The grape comes under the second category, needing only a little assistance, and it is multiplied to a considerable extent in this manner. In the spring, the vines are laid out in a little shallow trench, and pegged down closely; as the buds burst, they throw up shoots which are trained vertically by tying them to sticks, and as soon as these shoots have acquired a certain degree of maturity and firmness, the mellow earth is drawn up to them and they emit a beautiful system of roots, and by the fall they form very fine plants, (fig. 3). The layered

Fig. 3.—PROPAGATING THE GRAPE BY LAYERING.

branch is then taken up and the several plants are separated, when it will be found that the best roots are chiefly from the lower joints of the new wood, rather than from the old canes that were laid down in the spring.

Fig. 4.—LAYERING THE QUINCE.

Quinces are considerably increased by a sort of layering, as the twigs emit roots very freely; they are often bent down, slightly twisted, or not, as the case may be, and covered with mellow soil, when they readily emit roots, become firmly established, and may be set out by themselves, (fig. 4). There is, however, another method of layering, much practiced in the multiplication of the quince; that called propagation by stools. The plants are set in open rows, four feet wide, and three or four feet apart in the rows; they should be so planted as to stand below the general surface, that is in trenches. When cut off at the ground in the spring, they throw up a great number of shoots, and the earth is gradually worked up to these to encourage their rooting, (see

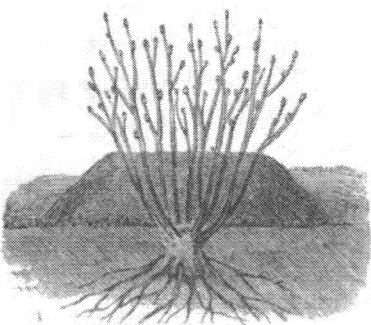

Fig. 5.—STOOL LAYERING THE QUINCE.

figure 5), which is often sufficient for removal the first season; if, on inspection, the roots are not found to be sufficiently large or abundant, the earthing is continued until the autumn of the next year, when they are removed, the stools trimmed of their lower roots, and reset in new trenches. The plants, thus raised from stools, are cut back severely, and are then ready to set out in nursery rows for budding. With the quince, cultivated in this manner, nothing is required but to accumulate the mellow earth about the shoots; but in many plants it is necessary to notch the wood by splitting, or cutting it for an inch or two, (as in fig. 6), making a tongue that separates from the lower portion of the shoot, and from which the roots are emitted. This slit should be commenced just below a bud, and the knife is drawn upward, cutting halfway through the wood. If commenced at one side instead of at the depending portion, the tongue is more sure to be separated from the stock, to which it might otherwise reunite. To insure rooting, some persons insert a little stick or chip between the separated portions, to prevent a re-union of the parts. The shoot, after being notched, is fastened down, and fine soil or compost is brought about it to encourage the development of roots. Few of the hard wooded fruit trees have been extensively prop-

Fig. 6.—MANNER OF CUTTING AND PEGGING DOWN A LAYER.

agated by means of layers; they might be so produced, but it has not been found profitable nor necessary.

A very common opinion prevails that layering exhausts the mother plant, or vine, which is used in this mode of propagating. If properly conducted, there is no reason why this should be; but if the whole top of any plant is bent down and made to take root, and to form independent roots, there can be little or no return from the branches to the original stock to strengthen it. A certain amount of healthy growing wood should always be left in its natural position, and no danger to the plant need be apprehended.

The wood growth of the strawberry, when allowed to

take its natural bent, is directed into the stolons or runners, which form natural layers. Their production de-
tracts from the central wood-growth of the plant, and
exhausts its strength to such a degree, that it often dies,
whereas, by a constant removal of the runners, as fast as
they appear, we practice a sort of summer pruning or
pinching, which results in the production of a large branching stool, with many points or centers for the production
of foliage and flowers, and thus insure the greatest abundance of fruit. The strawberry, like one species of the
raspberry, and many other of our native plants, offers illustrations of natural layering.

SEEDS.—The most common as well as the most natural
mode of multiplying the individual plants of most of our
fruit trees, is by sowing the seed; from this source we
procure stocks upon which are worked, by budding or
grafting, the several varieties we may desire to propagate.
As an illustration of this process, I propose to speak of
apple seedlings.

The almost universal means of increasing the number
of apple trees, is by sowing the seed. This is generally
selected and separated from the fresh pomace left on the
press in cider-making. The old and slow process of hand-
washing has given way, in this age of labor-saving machinery, to more economical methods. The most approved
apparatus is constructed upon the principle of separating
the seeds from the pulp by means of their greater specific
gravity; it is, indeed, much like a gold washer, being a
series of boxes or troughs through which a current of water is made to flow; this carries the lighter portions away
from the seeds, the contents of the boxes being agitated

from time to time. At the close of the process, the clean seed is found in the bottoms of the boxes, whence it is removed and carefully dried, by putting it in an airy place, and stirring it frequently to prevent mildew and fermentation. Well prepared seed is plump and bright, and should feel cold to the hand. When the pips are broken, they should be white and clear within ; but the best test of their quality, is to sprout a portion, and count the plants produced by a given number of seeds.

Sowing.—The seeds may be put into the ground, either in the fall, or spring. The soil having been well prepared, and deeply pulverized, is thrown up in beds a few feet wide, and the seed sown in close drills across ; or without the beds, it may be sown in broad drills, by hand, or with a machine, the rows at such a distance as to allow of culture by horse-power. It is desirable, in either case, to get an early start and a good stand ; the weeds must be kept under from the very first, and not allowed to have the mastery for a single day. Thorough culture during the season, upon a deeply tilled soil, of such a character as to retain moisture, will be found highly advantageous in the production of this crop, and will insure immunity from leaf-blight and other adversities. Some recommend sprouting the seed a little before planting. If it have been kept during the winter mixed with its bulk of sand, which is a good plan, the whole may be subjected to a gentle heat as in a hot-bed, for a few days, just before planting. During this time the mass must be stirred and turned every day, to prevent fermentation and to secure an even start. Whenever the germ makes its appearance at the points of the seeds, which is called *pipping*, the

sowing must begin, and should be done as quickly as pos·
sible; the covering is to be slight, and the earth should
be friable and not disposed to bake. The depth at which
the apple seed is to be covered will depend upon the present and prospective state of the weather, lighter if moist,
heavier if dry, for a continued drouth might be fatal to
sprouted seed, if it were planted too near the surface; but
when the weather is not dry, it is advised that the
shallower the seed is sown, the better. The objection has
been made to sprouting, that if the process have advanced
too far, the seedlings will be apt to have a crook at or
near the collar, instead of the straight fusiform appearance they should possess when presented to the grafter.

These seedlings furnish the stocks upon which to work
the finer varieties of the apple. They are taken up in the
autumn with their long clean roots, which are often longer
than their tops, the leaves are stripped off, and they are
assorted; the larger are packed away in earth or saw-dust
in the grafting department, or heeled-in out of doors, and
covered in such a way as to be accessible at any time they
may be needed during the winter. The smaller stocks
are heeled-in for spring planting in nursery rows for budding, or they may be left in the original rows for another
year's growth as seedlings. If the plants have been well
grown and not too thick, so that the majority are of sufficient size, it will be better to take them all up at once and
assort them as just indicated, otherwise the largest only
may be drawn separately when the ground is soft with
autumnal rains, leaving the smaller seedlings for another
year's growth. In assorting and selling the stocks, nurserymen make about three classes. The very largest, as

thick as a lead-pencil, are called extra, or two-year old, and command a higher price. The next size, called 1st class stocks, are large enough for co-aptation to the average scions, and long enough to make two cuts each for grafting; and those that fall below this requisition are considered second class, and are either thrown aside or set out for budding, and for stock or collar-grafting in the rows.

4

PROPAGATION.—SECTION II.—GRAFTING.

GRAFTING is but a modification of propagation by cuttings. The scion is a cutting of the variety we wish to propagate, which, instead of being committed to the ground to emit its own roots, is placed in contact with tissues of a nature similar to its own, through which it is to form a connection with the roots and the soil. The success of the operation depends upon the formative cell in this instance also, as in the cutting; new cells are formed upon the cut surface, and the intercommunication takes place through them. Hence we have anatomical limits to grafting; there are physiological bounds beyond which we cannot pass, in our combinations of scion and stock. Our success is in the direct ratio of the affinity that exists between them ; thus apple grows best on apple, and even among these we find the *closest union* and the best results, where there is a similiarity between the style of growth, and probably in the character of the cells.

We say, as a general rule, that stone fruits must be grafted upon stone fruits, those bearing seeds, upon seed fruit; but there are limits even here which confine us upon one hand, and give us more latitude upon the other. Thus the cherry may be worked upon the wild cherry (*Prunus Virginiana,*) but it forms a very poor union ; the pear will grow upon the thorn, which has a very different seed, but the union is very imperfect and the tree is short-lived; the apple would appear to be much nearer of kin, since it belongs to the same genus, but though the pear will grow vigorously upon this stock, it is no more permanent than upon the thorn : either of them will answer when grafted low, or in the root, to start the cutting, as the scion may then be considered, and to sustain it until it shall have supplied itself with roots. In top-grafting the pear upon a tree of either species, it is found essential to success, and it conduces to the greater durability of the tree, for some branches of the original stock to be left intact to secure the circulation of the trunk, as the union of the dissimilar cells is so imperfect that it does not furnish sufficient vent for the sap. In the case of the cherry we find that the varieties appear to have a greater affinity for those of their own race; thus the Dukes and Morellos do well when grafted upon the Morello stocks, whereas the Hearts and Biggarreau sorts do not make a good union upon these stocks, but prefer the Mazzard, which has a freer growth more like their own.   Most varieties will do well upon the Mahaleb stock, which is used as a means of dwarfing this fruit, though not a dwarf.   Upon the wild cherry, which belongs to quite a different section of the genus, the cultivated varieties will grow, but they form a very imperfect union.

The peach may be worked upon the plum stock, and is claimed to be somewhat dwarfed by it, and to produce superior fruit.   This stock is more congenial to the apricot, which is frequently propagated upon it. Both plums and apricots may be worked upon the peach stock, and they will grow very vigorously, as they will upon the wild plum, but they soon over-grow, and are very apt to break off.   When either of these species is used as a stock for the plum or apricot, they should be considered merely as a nursing mother, like the apple or thorn to the pear, which may be wanted to help the cutting until it shall be prepared to stand alone, and feed itself from its own roots.   In other words, they should be grafted, *not budded*, into these uncongenial stocks, and the operation should be performed in the collar or below it, in the root, so that the growing scion may be earthed up, and encouraged to furnish itself with a good system of roots of its own.   The success will then depend upon the ability of the scion to emit roots freely.

We must never forget that in grafting, we are confined to very narrow limits.   Our scion must be of a similar nature with the stock, each must have cells of a similar character, capable of transmitting their nutritious fluids from one to the other. We must recollect likewise, that the parts must be so co-apted that the cells of wood growth shall be brought into as close connection as possible, in both scion and stock; these cells are found in the layer, called the cambium, which is between the wood and the bark. The crude sap from below will often pass from cell to cell, when the elaborated sap of the cells in the scion is wholly unfitted for the formation of wood cells in the stock below it; of course the union in such a case must be very imperfect, and the product of such a grafting will be subject to accident, and will be short-lived, though the result in fruit, while the union continues, may be very precocious, abundant, and of superior flavor.

Natural grafting may often be observed by the student of nature when wandering among his favorites of the sylvan shades. There can be no doubt that the first hint was thus communicated to the early gardeners. In nature we always find the grafting to be inarching, or grafting by approach; two limbs or even two trees approximating closely, have abraded one another, and have afterward united their tissues most firmly together. This is generally a union of two trees of the same variety or species; but such is not always the case; sometimes trees of very dissimilar natures unite in this manner, but when we examine them we find only a dove-tailing, only a mechanical union, but no vital action subsists between them. The ancients give us some fancy sketches of the unions by grafting of very dissimilar trees, and some moderns who have no higher claim to poetry than their romancing, tell

us that we may graft the peach upon the Willow and But-
tonwood, and form other equally impossible unions.

The different methods of performing the operation of
grafting vary with the character and size, and
condition of the stocks to be worked; thus we
have splice grafting, whip, cleft, saddle, and side
grafting with modifications, and also grafting
by approach, which is generally called inarching
—though sometimes also practiced where we
desire to renew the roots of a tree that are unhealthy, or to restore those
that have been removed by
accident or by the erosion
of some rodent animals.

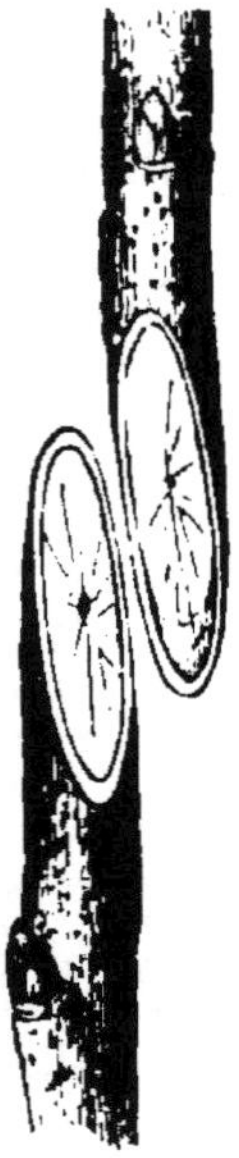

SPLICE GRAFTING is the
simplest process, and is applicable only where the size of
the stock and of the scion correspond pretty nearly; the
two are cut with a sloping curve, each
of which being made at the same angle,
will coincide with the other when they
are applied together, as represented
in the engraving, fig. 7.

Fig. 7.

WHIP GRAFTING is a modification of

Fig. 8.—WHIP GRAFT-
ING.

the above. Each portion is cut in a sloping manner as in the splice grafting, but
each is also split with a thin-bladed knife, as represented
in fig. 8. The object in this is to give a firmer union
to the two portions, and also to present a more extended
surface for the effusion of the new cell tissue that is to

form the bond of union in cementing them together. In both these methods, but especially in the first, the parts must be held together in co-aptation by some kind of bandage; this is generally composed of grafting wax, spread upon cloth or paper, or even, as now extensively practiced, upon fine thread. Cotton yarn No. 3 is drawn through melted grafting wax, and as it cools, it is wound

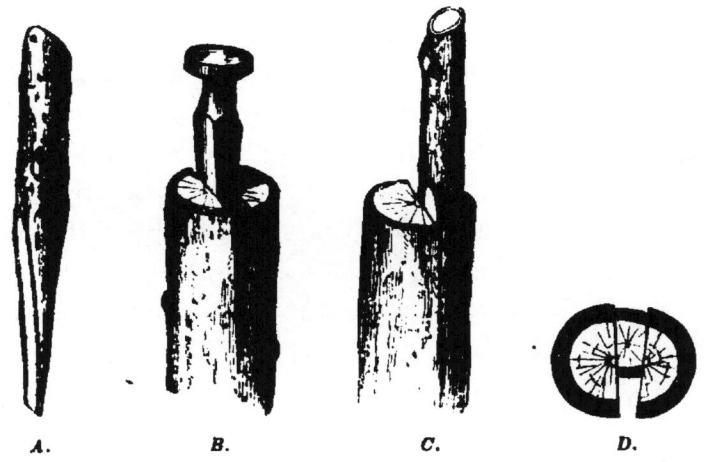

A.   B.   C.   D.

Fig. 9.—DIFFERENT STEPS IN CLEFT GRAFTING. *A*, SCION PREPARED FOR SETTING. *B*, THE CLEFT OPENED BY A WEDGE. *C*, THE SCION INSERTED. *D*, SECTION OF STOCK AND SCION TO SHOW THE CO-APTATION OF THE PARTS OF THE TWO.

upon a reel at the other side of the room, whence it is drawn as wanted by the grafter or tyer. Tying or wrapping is always a good precaution, and when the splice or cleft graft is not very close, it becomes necessary; but thousands of grafts will unite equally well where the parts are covered with earth, without any such appliance.

CLEFT GRAFTING is generally done when the stock is larger than the scion, and also where the operation is performed at a point above the ground. The stock is split downward, after having been cut off at the point where the grafting is to be done. The knife should be sharp, and the bark should be cut through first, to avoid its being torn, and so that the sides of the cleft shall be smooth. A wedge is inserted to keep the cleft open for the inser-

Fig. 10.—CLEFT GRAFTING WITH BOTH SCIONS IN- CLINED INWARD.

tion of the scion, which is cut on each side like a fine wedge; but the two planes not being parallel, the bark will be left on one side to the very point of the wedge, while on the other it will be removed a part of the way, making a feather edge, *A*, fig. 9. The object of this is to have the pressure of the cleft greatest upon the outer side, where the union is to be effected. It is well to have a bud on the strip of bark left between the two cuts used in forming the graft, this should be near the top of the cleft. One or two grafts may be inserted into a cleft, or more clefts may be made, in large stocks, or in re-grafting the large limbs of an old tree, but usually one is sufficient to leave growing; and in the young tree, only one should ever be allowed to remain. When the scion is nicely set into the cleft, so that the inner bark of the stock and graft shall coincide, or rather cross a very little, (see fig. 10,) the wedge, whether of hard wood, or of iron, should be gently withdrawn, and then the elasticity of the stock will hold the scion firmly to its place; this pressure should not be too severe. In this kind of grafting, if the pressure be sufficiently firm, and if the operation have been performed below the sur-

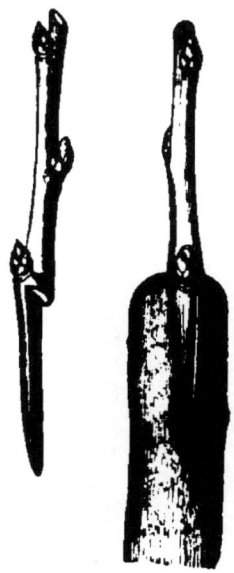

face of the ground, it may not be necessary to make any other application than to press the moist earth about the parts, and cover all but the top of the graft with soil, and place a stick to indicate the plant and protect it from injury. If, on the contrary, the pressure of the cleft be not sufficient to hold the scion firmly, as in small stocks, the graft must be tied. For this a piece of bass matting, or cotton twine, may be used; and if the operation has been performed above ground, the whole must be covered with grafting wax, applied, either hot with a brush, or cold, after having been worked with the hands, or by wrapping with strips of muslin or paper previously spread with the wax. In old times grafting clay was used, and applied with the hands as a lump around the junction; but this disagreeable and clumsy appliance has given way to more elegant and convenient arrangements.

Fig. 11.—SIDE GRAFT-ING.

Fig. 12.—SIDE GRAFTING—THE STOCK NOT CUT BACK.

SIDE GRAFTING is performed in two ways. In one it is a modification of cleft grafting in which there is no cleft,

4*

but the bark is started from the wood, and the scion, cut as shown in figure 11, is pressed down between the wood and bark. This can only be done late in the spring, after the sap has begun to flow in the stock, so that the bark will run; it is indeed more like budding than grafting. The other modification is done without cutting off the stock. The knife is applied to the side of a stock of medium size, and a cut is made downward and extending to

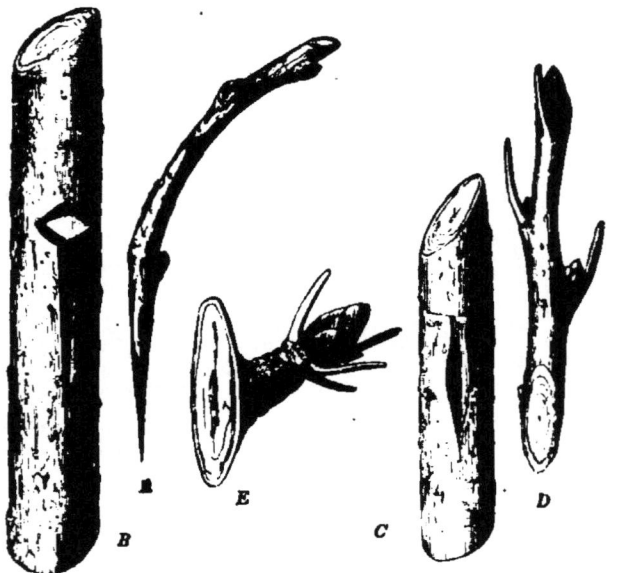

Fig. 13. — TWO FORMS OF SIDE GRAFTING. — A, B, THE SCION AND STOCK FOR THE RICHARD SIDE GRAFT. C, STOCK FOR THE GIRARDIN SIDE GRAFT. D, SCION, AND E, FRUIT BUD FOR THE SAME.

one-third the diameter, fig. 12; the scion is cut as for cleft grafting, and inserted so as to have the parts well co-apted, and then secured as usual. This plan is useful where there is danger of too free a flow of sap from the roots. Two other kinds of side graft are shown in fig. 13 The left-hand figures show the Richard side graft, in which an arched branch, *A*, is used. This is inserted under the bark of the stock, *B ;* above the graft an incision is made in the stock down to the wood, to arrest the flow of sap. After the insertion, the wound is covered with grafting wax. The Girardin side graft is illustrated at the three right-hand figures. A fruit bud, *E*, or a graft with a terminal fruit bud, *D*, is inserted under the bark of the

stock, *C*, in August, or whenever suitable buds can be obtained and the bark will run. The wound is tied and covered with wax, as before. The object of this grafting is to secure immediate fruitage. Another kind of side grafting consists in plunging a dirk-shaped knife directly through the tree, inclining the point downward, into this opening the graft is inserted; the object being to establish a limb on a naked portion of the trunk.

SADDLE GRAFTING is used only with stocks of small size; it is per-

Fig. 14.—SADDLE GRAFT-ING.

formed by making a double slope upon the stock, and by opening a corresponding space in the graft, by cutting two slopes in the scion, from below upwards, so that they shall meet in the centre, as seen in fig. 14. Some merely split the scion.

GRAFTING BY APPROACH, or as it is generally termed, *inarching*, is often practiced where there is difficulty in making the scion unite with the stock; it is not often needed in the culture of our orchard fruits, but may be

here described. The stock upon which we wish to graft
the scion, must be planted near the variety or species to
be increased. A small twig of the latter, which can be
brought close to the stock, is selected for the operation;
a slice of bark and wood is then removed from the twig,
and another of equal size from the stock, so managed, that
these cut surfaces can be brought together and secured
in that position until they have united, after which the
twig, that has been used as a scion, is cut from its parent
tree, and the top of the stock is carefully reduced until
the scion has sufficiently developed itself to act as the top
of the ingrafted tree, which may afterward be transplanted
to its proper station.

A modification of this grafting by approach, is, however, sometimes of great service, where we have a valuable
tree that has suffered from disease in the roots, or from injury to them. It consists in planting some thrifty young
stocks, with good roots, about the base of the tree, after
having prepared the ground by thorough digging, and by
the addition of good soil if necessary. These stocks are
then inserted upwards into the healthy portion of the
trunk, by the process of side grafting reversed or inverted, or by the usual method of inarching.

RING GRAFTING OR BARK GRAFTING is not much used,
and in small stocks it is rather a kind of budding, for then
a ring of bark is removed at the proper season of year,
generally about midsummer, and it is replaced by a similar
ring of bark from a shoot of the same size, taken from a
tree of the variety to be propagated; this ring of bark
must be furnished with a healthy bud. This method has
little to recommend it, and can only be applied when both

the stock and the scion are in a growing condition, so that the bark will run freely; care also must be exercised to avoid injuring the eye of the bud, in peeling off the ring. A modification of bark grafting may be applied with great advantage, however, to an old tree, that has met with an injury to a portion of its bark. The injured part, should be pared smoothly to the sound bark and wood.

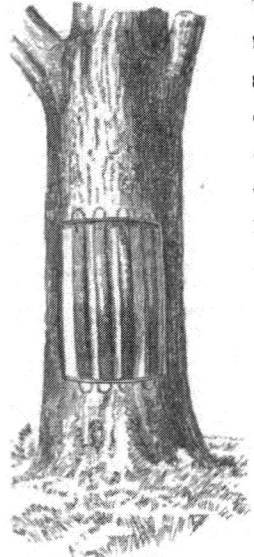

This may be done with a sloping cut, or. the edge may be made abrupt and, square with a chisel and mallet; a piece of fresh wood and bark is then to be cut from a healthy tree and fitted precisely to the fresh wound, and secured in its place with bandages, and grafting clay or wax is then applied, thus making what the surgeons would call a sort of taliacotian operation. Instead of a single piece of wood and bark, a number of young shoots may be used to make the communication complete; these are set close together and secured in the usual manner; see fig. 15.

Fig. 15.—BARK GRAFT-ING, TO REPAIR AN INJURED TREE.

RE-GRAFTING OLD ORCHARDS. — Old orchards of inferior fruit may be entirely re-made and re-formed by grafting the limbs with such varieties as we may desire. A new life is by this process often infused into the trees, which is due to the very severe pruning which the trees then receive; they are consequently soon covered with a vigorous growth of young healthy wood, which replaces the decrepid and often decaying spray that accumulates in an old orchard, and the fruit produced for several

years by the new growth is not only more valuable in
kind, according to the judgment used in the selection of
grafts, but it is more fair, smooth and healthy, and of better size than that which was previously furnished by the
trees.   Certain varieties are brought at once into bearing
when thus top-grafted, which would have been long in developing their fruitful condition if planted as nursery
trees.   Others are always better and finer when so worked,
than on young trees.   Some of the finest specimens of the
Northern Spy apple, exhibited at the fairs, have been produced by grafts inserted into the terminal branches of old
bearing trees.   There is a theory held by some orchardists, that the further the junction of the graft with the
stock is removed from the root, the better will be the
fruit.   This, however, is not well supported, and the circumstance, when observed, is probably dependent upon
other causes.

In renewing an old orchard by grafting its head, it will
not be a good plan to attempt the whole tree at once ; the
pruning would be too severe, and would be followed by a
profusion of succulent shoots breaking out from the large
branches, such as are called water-sprouts.   Those who
have practiced most, prefer at first, to remove about one-
third of the limbs for grafting, and those should be
selected at the top of the tree.   The new growth thus has
an open field for its development, and the lower limbs
will be invigorated, while they tend also to preserve the
equilibrium of the tree in a double sense, physically and
physiologically.   The next year another third of the limbs
may be grafted, and the remainder the year following, as
practiced by Mr. Geo. Olmstead, of Connecticut, who, on

the sixth year from the first grafting, harvested 28½ bushels of choice apples from a single tree that was 75 years old, and which before only produced inferior fruit. J. J. Thomas recommends, "to give a well-shaped head to such newly formed trees, and to prevent the branches from shooting upward in a close body near the centre of the tree; that the old horizontal boughs should be allowed to extend to a distance in each direction, while the upright

Fig. 16.—RENEWAL OF THE TOP OF AN OLD TREE.

ones should be lopped;" see fig. 16. The same writer also advises, "instead of cutting off large branches and grafting them at once, it is better to prune the top in part, which will cause an emission of vigorous shoots. These are then budded, or grafted. · * * * And as the grafts gradually extend by growth, the remainder of the top may, by successive excisions, be entirely removed."

GRAFTING IN THE NURSERY is either done at or near the collar of the stock, or it is performed in-doors upon the roots or sections of roots of young stocks. The latter may be first described, as it constitutes the most extensive means of multiplying fruit trees. It is a sort of machinery, with division of labor, and appliances, that enable the operators to turn out immense numbers. Machinery has indeed been applied to the business; we have grafting apparatus to facilitate the work. The Minkler machine consists of a frame or guage which regulates the angle of the slope, which is cut with a broad chisel that reduces the roots and scions to a condition for putting them to gether; by its use an immense number of grafts can be cut, and another hand binds them together with the waxed thread, without any tie. Mr. Robey's machine consists of a complicated shears to cut the slope and tongue at one operation, preparing the pieces for whip grafting. Mr. S. S. Jackson, of Cincinnati, has also invented an apparatus for this purpose, which proves to be very useful.

ROOT GRAFTING.—The methods of performing the operation vary somewhat, but all agree in the object to be attained: the co-aptation of the scion with a piece of root. Some grafters use only the upper portion of the root, thinking the original collar of the seedling stock the only point at which the most perfect and successful union between the aërial and terrestrial portions of trees should or can be effected — theoretically this may be very well, but the practice constantly pursued, in myriads of cases, abundantly proves that the grafting need not be restricted to this part, and that a perfect union may be effected at any point of the root, and that this may even be inverted. The very common practice has been to take two or more cuts from the root, when it is of sufficient size and length;

and though some of our best propagators restrict themselves to two cuts from each, others, who have experimented carefully, insist that the third section will average as well as the others. A lot of trees, worked especially for a test in this matter, gave the following results.

In 1859 an average lot of roots and scions, about fifty in each lot, were treated as follows, White Pippin and Willow-leaf being used as scions : —

White Pippin—No. 1, being on the first cut of the root, had made a fair growth.

No. 2, being on the second cut, were quite as good or better.

No. 3, being on the third cut, were not quite so good as the others, the ground being partially shaded by a large tree.

Another, of Willow-leaf—No. 1, on the 3d cut of root, very good growth.

No. 2, on very slender roots, nearly as good.

No. 3, only 1 inch of root to 1 inch of scion; not so good growth nor so good a strike, but shaded by a tree.

No. 4, on 2d cut of root, not so good as the third.

No. 5, on average lot, not waxed, as good as any.

No. 6, roots worked upside-down, mostly failed.

D. O. Reeder exhibited some 2-year old apple trees, worked on the root inverted, they were of very good growth.

For root grafting, thrifty stocks are wanted of one or two years' growth, the smoother and straighter the roots, the better. These should be taken up from the seed-bed in the fall, selected, tied in bundles, and stored in the cellar or cave, or buried in the soil where they shall be accessible at any time, and where they will be kept fresh and plump. The roots and scions having been prepared and under shelter, the work of grafting may proceed at any time during the winter. The stocks, if not clean, should be washed, and one hand trims off the side rootlets. The grafter cuts a hundred scions of the appropriate length, which he puts into a shallow box on the table; he takes up a stock, cuts the slope near the collar, and a dextrous hand will at the same time make the sloping cut to receive the first graft and also the tongue, if that style of grafting is to be done, as is usually practised. He then picks up a scion, from a lot which himself or another hand has already prepared with a slope and tongue, and adapts it to the root, the tongue keeping the two together; a portion of the root is then cut off with the graft, and the process is repeated upon the next section. Two or three or more grafts, are thus made from one seedling root; the length of the sections vary from two to four inches, according to the fancy of the operator, or of his employer. Some persons recommend a long scion with a short root, and others prefer to reverse those terms. The whole root graft should not be more than six or seven inches long.

When any given number of scions are fitted to the roots, a boy completes the process of grafting, by applying melted wax with a brush, in which case they are dropped into water to harden the wax, or they are wrapped with waxed strips of muslin or paper, or, better still, they are tied with waxed thread. No. 3 cotton yarn is drawn through a pan of melted wax, and wound upon a reel placed at the other side of the room, so that the wax may harden. This waxed thread is a very convenient tie; the graft being held in the left hand, the thread is wound about it two or three turns; as the wax causes the bandage to adhere to itself where it crosses, no knot is needed, and the thread is broken off with a quick jerk.

In splice grafting, whether performed with any of the machines, or if the slopes of root and scion be cut with the thin grafting knife, the tying must be done by the same hand that selects and places the scion upon the root. This does not admit of the same division of labor, and the fingers, becoming sticky from the wax, cannot be so nimble, and are unfit for cutting. When the lot is tied, they are set into the box, which should be inclined at an angle, and interspersed with earth or saw-dust; for transportation. Saw-dust, just as it comes from the mill, neither wet nor dry, is preferred by some as a packing material, and it has been found very efficacious, excluding and admitting the air just in the right proportions to prevent desiccation, and to promote the union, which very soon takes place between the graft and the root, if the boxes be stored in the cellar. In an ice-house root grafts have been kept in saw-dust more than a year, and then planted and grown successfully. The boxes should be deep enough to receive the whole graft—say from 10 to 12 inches—and then they can be packed upon one another without injuring the scions; these should be distinctly marked with the name and number, so as to be ready for planting out in the spring.

Much discussion has been had upon the merits and demerits, or disadvantages of root grafting, and much theoretical argument has been brought against the practice; but beautiful trees are thus made in immense numbers in the extensive nurseries of our country, and until better arguments can be produced against the practice, nursery-men will continue to graft on sections of root, such va-rieties, as are suitable for this procedure—especially ap-ples, in a large proportion of the varieties cultivated, some pears, some peaches, grapes, and other fruits.

Root grafting is now of almost universal application with the apple. It has many advantages, which may be summed up as follows: Two or more plants may be pro-duced from the root of one stock; these may be made with great rapidity; the work may all be performed in-doors and during the whole winter season, when nothing can be done outside; they are of small bulk, and great numbers may be stowed away in little space, they may be trans-ported to any distance in this condition, and are ready for planting with the opening of spring, when they may be set in the nursery rows at once; or, they may be bedded out in a small space and mulched, to protect them from drouth, and the weeds can easily be kept under. Another advantage of bedding out the root-grafts is, that they may be assorted according to their size the next season, when transplanted into the nursery rows. This very transplant-ing too is a great advantage, for the roots will be much improved by the process.

The theoretical objections to root grafts have yielded to sound philosophy, based on and supported by practical observation. The very many advantages of this more economical and convenient and agreeable process, will necessarily sustain root-grafting in this fast age, when so many millions of trees are needed for the rapidly extend-ing wants of this nation of tree planters. We may, how-ever, consider some of the practical objections which have been brought forward against this plan of multiplying the apple. In our very changeable climate, and particularly in the North-west, upon the prairies, the cold of winter often supervenes with great suddenness, after the young trees have made a prolonged and vigorous growth in the fertile soil, and produces terrible devastation among those that are there exposed, without protection of any kind, to the rude blasts of the storm-king: in a less degree, injury is very frequent with many such late-growing kinds, at the first access of a severe frost; this is manifested in the bursting of the bark near the base of the stem. The same thing is not so often seen in the same varieties, when they have been budded or stock grafted a foot or more from the ground upon hardy seedling stocks, hence judicious propagators have selected the "tender" varieties for this kind of working, and confine their root-grafting to those less liable to the injury. There are other varieties which do not readily and promptly form a strong upright growth, so as to be profitable trees to the nurseryman if root grafted; these are selected for stock working, either on strong seedlings, or upon hardy upright sorts that have been root grafted for the purpose of being thus double-worked. This plan has been pursued to a limited extent only, but its advantages in the production of good trees of the slender growing varieties, begin to be appreciated, and as the demand increases, our intelligent nurserymen will very soon furnish the requisite supply.

Planting.—When the weather is fine, and the soil in good condition, the root-grafts are to be set out with a dibble, by the line; they should be planted rather deeply, one bud projecting above the surface of the ground. The

culture must be thorough, the plants should be kept perfectly clean, but it is questionable whether the growth
should be pushed late in the season; indeed, it is preferable to check the vegetation at mid-summer. For this
purpose it has been recommended to cease cultivating the
soil, or even to sow the ground with a heavy seeding of
oats, so as to check the growth before winter. In good
soils, with good culture, the average hight in the rows
will be two feet, but there is a great difference in the
kinds; some will considerably exceed this hight. Intelligent nurserymen no longer endeavor to have an excessive growth in the first year, and many prefer the bedding
plan above alluded to.

Trimming, Pinching, or Heading.—The growth during the first year is generally a single shoot, sometimes
two. If there be a second, it should be subordinated by
pinching off its extremity, never by trimming it off; indeed, laterals should always be encouraged, and this will be
more and more the case, since the demand for low-headed
trees is increasing, as the laws of physiology are better
understood. A young tree, well furnished with laterals,
is always more stocky, and every way better, though not
so tall as that which has been drawn up to a single stem.
To encourage this condition, some advise the pinching out
the terminal bud in the midst of the growing season,
which will cause the swelling and subsequent breaking of
the lower buds, so as to furnish plenty of laterals. If
done later in the season, especially with strong-growing
varieties, a branching head may be formed higher up, during the first season, making very pretty trees. This is,
however, seldom attempted with root-grafts the first sea-

son, though it is very common for collar-grafted trees, and for buds on strong stocks to make a fine branching growth the first year. The second season the trees should all be headed-in, and the laterals spurred-in early in the spring, or in mild weather during the winter, if the scions are wanted. This method of making stocky plants cannot be too highly commended, nor can the opposite plan, of trimming off all the side branches, and even of stripping the leaves from the lower part of the shoots, during the first summer, be too severely condemned.

Stock Grafting has many advocates, and for some varieties this plan is preferable. The union may be effected at any point from the collar upward. Formerly, the place was selected to suit the convenience of the grafter, and many old orchards show very plainly where they were worked, the stock or the scion having overgrown, and it is very curious that some varieties may be indicated as good feeders of the stock below them, and the contrary. At present, tree planters are more fastidious, and object to these irregularities in the stems of their trees. They will purchase nothing that shows the point of union above ground, hence the more common use of collar grafting, as it has been called, or the insertion of the scion at or near the surface of the ground. Stocks that have been cultivated one or two years in the nursery row, are selected for this purpose; the earth is removed from them, they are cut off and grafted as they stand, and with their fine strong roots undisturbed, the result of one summer's growth is very satisfactory, making beautiful trees fit for the orchard. Older trees, especially those with straight clean stems, are often grafted standard high, so as to produce a fine salable tree at once, or in one season. This is a very good plan with some of the slender and straggling varieties, such as are called poor growers, and which are unprofitable to the nurseryman when propagated in the usual manner. Grafting or budding upon such stocks is also resorted to very often, when it is desirable at once to furnish large, or salable trees of new varieties.

In grafting upon a large stock, or upon the tops of an old tree, the process called cleft grafting is generally used. Here, as in all forms of this process, the object to be attained, is the co-aptation of the inner bark of both stock and scion. The latter is held in its place by the clasping of the former, and is also covered by some material that is pliant, and which will exclude the air and moisture.

The advantages of stock-grafting are the changing of an old tree from bad to good fruit, which is produced in a few years; it is also applicable to large stocks, and produces an immediate result, making salable trees in one year. It is also desirable for some poor-growing varieties, which are slow in making a tree from the ground; but it has its disadvantages also. The nurseryman must wait until his stocks have been grown one or more years in the nursery, his trees will sometimes be larger than he desires, they will be apt to have the mark of the grafting as a blemish upon the stalk sometimes during the life of the tree; and worse than all, he is restricted to a brief period in the spring, when he is obliged to perform the operation out of doors, and often in very unpleasant weather.

As a result of all the discussions upon this subject, it is found that stock-grafting, whether at the collar or at some distance above the ground, is still practiced, and has many warm advocates, as a better means of making the best trees. The only objections are the greater expense of culture of the stocks, and greater labor in grafting; the limited period at which the work can be performed, and the exposure of the workman during its performance, which is often at a stormy season, and always during a busy portion of the year. The trees too, in the orchard, are often somewhat deformed by an irregularity of growth, and have an enlargement either above or below the union, which is unsightly.

The kind of grafting will depend upon the size of the stocks; splice and whip-grafting on the smaller, and cleft-grafting on the larger ones, must be practiced. The waxing may be done by any of the methods indicated, according to the fancy; but it must always be more thoroughly done in aerial, than in underground grafting, whether this be in the collar or upon sections of the root; in the former the whole of the cut surfaces must be covered, to prevent desiccation by the winds, or the inroads of insects, or of wet from rains.

WAX.—Various combinations of the materials used in the preparation of grafting-wax, have been recommended by different operators. The desideratum being to have a material that shall-be sufficiently pliant, and at the same time firm enough to withstand the elevated temperatures to which it may be exposed. A mean is preferred, neither too hard nor too soft, and the proportions of the ingredients are varied according as it is proposed to use it out of doors, or in the house, in cold weather or warm.

7

A favorite recipe, with a practical nurseryman of great experience, is :

Rosin, six parts,   ⎫
Bees-wax, one part, ⎬ melted together.
Tallow, one part,   ⎭

This is to be used warm, when grafting in the house.

For out-door work he used the following :

Rosin, four or five parts.
Bees-wax, one and one-half to two parts.
Linseed oil, one to one and one-half.

This is made into a mass to be applied by hand. A very pleasant and neat mode of using the wax is to pour it when melted, upon thin muslin or strong paper, and spread it thin with a spatula. The tissue is then cut into strips of convenient size. The application to cotton yarn for root-grafting, has already been mentioned.

The French use the preparation given below, sufficiently warm to be liquid, but not so hot as to injure the tissues of the tree, and apply it with a brush :

Black pitch..........................28 parts.
Burgundy pitch.......................28   "
Bees-wax.............................16   "
Grease 14   "
Yellow ochre...... 14   "
                                   _____
Making.......................100 parts.*

Mr. Du Breuil also refers to Leport's liquid mastic in terms of commendation, but speaks of it as a secret composition.

Downing recommends melting together:

Bees-wax.............................8 parts.
Rosin................................3   "
Tallow...............................2   "

---

* Du Breuil, Culture of Fruit Trees; English Translation.

He says, the common wax of the French is

Pitch... ....one-half pound.
Bees wax...................... " "
Cow-dung ....one pound.

To be boiled together, and laid on with a brush, and for using cold or on strips of muslin, equal parts of tallow, bees-wax, and rosin, some preferring a little more tallow.

J. J. Thomas, whose practical knowledge is proverbial, recommends for its cheapness

Linseed oil...........................one pint.
Rosin...... ....six pounds.
Bees-wax.................. ......one pound.

Melted together, to be applied warm with a brush, or to be put on paper or muslin, or worked with wet hands into a mass and drawn out into ribbons.

The season for grafting is quite a prolonged one, if we include the period during which it may be done in the house, and the ability we have of retarding the scions by cold, using ice. It should be done while the grafts are dormant, which is at any time from the fall of the leaf until the swelling of the buds. As the grafts would be likely to suffer from prolonged exposure, out-door grafting is done just before vegetation commences in the spring, but may be prolonged until the stocks are in full leaf, by keeping back the scions, in which case, however, there is more danger to the stock unless a portion of its foliage is allowed to remain to keep up the circulation; under these circumstances, too, side-grafting is sometimes used with the same view.

The stone fruits are worked first; cherries, plums, and peaches, then pears and apples. With regard to grafting grapes, there is a diversity of opinion. Some operators prefer very early in the season, as in February, and others wait until the leaves have appeared upon the vine to be grafted.

SCIONS OR GRAFTS are to be selected from healthy plants of the variety we wish to propagate. They should be the growth of the previous year, of average size, well developed, and with good buds, those having flower buds are rejected. If the shoots be too strong, they are often furnished with poor buds, and are more pithy, and therefore they are more difficult to work and are less likely to grow. Grafts, cut from young bearing orchards, are the best, and being cut from fruiting trees, this enables us to be certain as to correctness of the varieties to be propagated; but they are generally and most rapidly collected from young nursery trees, and as an orchardist or nurseryman should be able to judge of all the varieties he cultivates by the appearance of their growth, foliage, bark, dots, etc., there is little danger in taking the scions from such untested trees.

Time for cutting Scions.—The scions may be cut at any time after the cessation of growth in the autumn, even before the leaves have fallen, until the buds burst in the spring, always avoiding severely cold or frosty weather, because of the injury to the tree that results from cutting at such a time, though the frost may not have injured the scion. The best nurserymen prefer to cut them in the autumn, before they can have been injured by cold. They should be carefully packed in fine earth, sand, or sawdust, and placed in the cellar or cave. The leaves stripped from them, make a very good packing material; moss is often used, where it can be obtained, but the best material is saw-dust. This latter is clean, whereas the sand and soil will dull the knife. If the scions should have become dry and shriveled, they may still be revived by placing them in soil that is moderately moist, not wet— they should not, by any means, be placed in water, but should be so situated that they may slowly imbibe moisture. When they have been plumped, they should be examined by cutting into their tissues; if these be brown, they are useless, but if alive, the fresh cut will look clear and white, and the knife will pass as freely through them as when cutting a fresh twig.

The after-treatment of the grafts consists in removing the sprouts that appear upon the stock below the scion, often in great numbers. These are called robbers, as they take the sap which should go into the scion. It is sometimes well to leave a portion of these as an outlet for excess. When the graft is tardy in its vegetation, and in late grafting, it is always safest to leave some of these shoots to direct the circulation to the part, and thus insure a supply to the newly introduced scion; all should eventually be removed, so as to leave the graft supreme.

It may sometimes be necessary to tie up the young shoot which pushes with vigor, and may fall and break with its own weight before the supporting woody fibre has been deposited; but a much better policy is to pinch in the tip when but a few inches long, and thus encourage the swelling and breaking of the lateral buds, and produce a more sturdy result. This is particularly the case in stock-grafts and in renewing an orchard by top-grafting.

PROPAGATION.—SECTION III.—BUDDING.

———◇———

BUDDING, or inoculating, is the insertion of eyes or buds. This is a favorite method of propagation, which is practiced in the multiplication of a great variety of fruits. The advantages of budding consist in the rapidity and facility with which it is performed, and the certainty of

102

success which attends it. Budding may be done during a long period of the growing season, upon the different kinds of trees we have to propagate. Using but a single eye, it is also economical of the scions, which is a matter of some importance, when we desire to multiply a new and scarce variety.

It has been claimed on behalf of the process of budding, that trees, which have been worked in this method, are more hardy and better able to resist the severity of winter than others of the same varieties, which have been grafted in the root or collar, and also that budded trees come sooner into bearing. Their general hardiness will probably not be at all effected by their manner of propagation; except perhaps, where there may happen to be a marked difference in the habit of the stock, such for instance as maturity early in the season, which would have a tendency to check the late growth of the scion placed upon it—the supplies of sap being diminished, instead of continuing to flow into the graft, as it would do from the roots of the cutting or root-graft of a variety which was inclined to make a late autumnal growth. Practically, however, this does not have much weight, nor can we know, in a lot of seedling stocks, which will be the late feeders, and which will go into an early summer rest.

Certain varieties of our cultivated fruits are found to have a remarkable tendency to make an extended and very thrifty growth, which, continuing late into the autumn, would appear to expose the young trees to a very severe trial upon the access of the first cold weather, and we often find them very seriously injured under such circumstances; the bark is frequently split and ruptured for sev-

eral inches near the ground. The twigs, still covered
with abundant foliage, are so affected by the frost, that
their whole outer surface is shriveled, and the inner bark
and wood are browned; the latter often becomes perma-
nently blackened, and remains as dead matter in the centre
of the tree, for death does not necessarily ensue.   Now intelligent nurserymen have endeavored to avoid losses
from these causes, by budding such varieties upon strong
well-established stocks, though they are aware that these
are not more hardy than some of the cultivated varieties:
a given number of seedling stocks has been found to suffer
as much from the severity of winter, as do a similar amount
of the grafted varieties taken at random.*   That the serious difficulty of bark-bursting occurs near the surface of
the ground, does seem to be an argument of some weight in
favor of budding or stock-grafting at a higher point.   The
earlier fruiting of budded trees than those which have
been root-grafted, does not appear to be a well established
fact, and therefore need not detain us; except to observe
that the stocks, upon which the buds were inserted, might
have been older by some years than the slip of root upon
which the graft was set, so that the fruiting of the former
tree should count two or three or more years further back
than from the period of the budding.   There are so many
causes which might have contributed toward this result
of earlier bearing, that we should not be too hasty in
drawing conclusions in this matter.

   The philosophy of budding is very similar to that of
grafting.   The latter process is performed when the plant-
life is almost dormant, and the co-apted parts are ready to

---

* A. R. Whitney, Franklin Grove Nurseries, Lee Co., Ill.

take the initiative steps of vegetation, and to effect their
union by means of new adventitious cells, before the free
flow of sap in the growing season. Budding, on the contrary, is done in the hight of that season, and toward its
close, when the plants are full of well matured and highly
organized sap, when the cell circulation is most active, and
the union between the parts is much more immediate than
in the graft; were it not so, indeed, the little shield, with
its actively evaporating surface of young bark, must certainly perish from exposure to a hot dry atmosphere. The
cambium, or gelatinous matter, which is discovered between the bark and the wood when they are separated, is
a mass of organizable cells. Mr. Paxton, using the gardener's expression, calls it the " pulp." Budding is most
successfully performed when this matter is abundant, for
then the vitality of the tree is in greatest degree of ex-
altation.

The individuality of the bud was sufficiently argued in
the first section of this chapter, it need not now be again
introduced, except as appropriately to remind us of the
fact where the propagation depends upon this circumstance—the future tree must spring from the single bud
which is inserted. Mr. A. T. Thomson, in his Lectures on
the Elements of Botany, page 396, says:—"The individuality of buds must have been suspected as early as the
discovery of the art of budding, and it is fully proved by
the dissection of plants. * * Budding is founded on
the fact, that the bud, which is a branch in embryo, is a
distinct individual. It is essential that both the bud and
the tree into which it is inserted should not only be analogous in their character, as in grafting with the scion, but

3*

both must be in a state of growth at the time the operation is performed. The union, however, depends much
more upon the bud than upon the stock—the bud may be
considered a centre of vitality—vegetative action commences in the bud, and extends to the stock, connecting
them together."—" The vital energy, however, which commences the process of organization in the bud, is not necessarily confined to the germ, nor distinct from that
which maintains the growth of the entire plant; but it is
so connected with organization, that when this has pro-
ceeded a certain length, the bud may be removed from
the parent and attached to another, where it will become
a branch the same as if it had not been removed."

The season for budding has already been indicated in
general terms, it is usually done in mid-summer and the
early part of autumn, reference being had to the condition
of the plants to be worked; these should be in a thrifty
growing state, the woody fibre should be pretty well advanced, but growth by extension must still be active, or
the needful conditions will not be found. The "pulp"
must be present between the bark and the wood of the
stock, so that the former can be easily separated from the
latter; in the language of the art, the bark must "run;"
this state of things will soon cease in most stocks, after the
formation of terminal buds on the shoots. The success
of spring budding, however, would appear to indicate
that the cambium layer is formed earlier in the season
than is usually supposed; for whenever the young leaves
begin to be developed on the stock, "the bark will run,"
and the buds may be inserted with a good prospect of
success. In this case we are obliged to use dormant buds
that were formed the previous year, and we have to exer-

cise care in the preservation of the scions, to keep them back by the application of cold, until the time of their insertion.

The condition of the bud is also important to the success of the operation. The tree from which we cut the scions should be in a growing state, though this is not so essential as in the case of the stock, as has been seen in spring budding—still, a degree of activity is desirable. The young shoot should have perfected its growth to such an extent as to have deposited its woody fibre, it should not be too succulent; but the essential condition is, that it should have its buds well developed. These, as every one knows, are formed in the axils of the leaves, and, to insure success, they should be plump and well grown. In those fruits which blossom on wood shoots of the previous year's growth, as the peach and apricot, the blossom buds should be avoided; they are easily recognized by their greater size and plumpness. In cutting scions, or bud-sticks, the most vigorous shoots should be avoided, they are too soft and pithy; the close jointed firm shoots, of medium size, are much to be preferred, as they have well developed buds, which appear to have more vitality. Such scions are found at the ends of the lateral branches. These need immediate attention, or they will be lost. The evaporation of their juices through the leaves would soon cause them to wither and wilt, and become useless. These appendages are therefore immediately removed by cutting the petioles from a quarter to half an inch from the scion; a portion of the stem is thus left as a convenient handle when inserting the shield, and this also serves afterward as an index to the condition of the bud. So soon as trimmed of their leaves, the scions are tied up, and enveloped loosely in a damp cloth, or in moss, or fresh grass, to exclude them from the air. If they should become wilted, they must not be put into water, as this injures them; it is better to sprinkle the cloth and tie them up tightly, or they may be restored by burying them in moderately moist earth.

The early gardeners were very particular as to the kind of weather upon which to do their budding. They recommended a cloudy or a showery day, or the evening, in order to avoid the effects of the hot sunshine. This might do in a small garden, where the operator could select his opportunity to bud a few dozen stocks; but even there, wet weather should be avoided, rather than courted. But in the large commercial nurseries, where tens of thousands of buds are to be inserted, there can be no choice of weather; indeed, many nurserymen prefer bright sunshine and the hottest weather, as they find no inconvenience arising to the trees from this source. Some even aver that their success is better under such circumstances, and argue that the " pulp is richer."

Most trees in their mature state make all their growth by extension or elongation very early in the season, by one push, as it were; with the first unfolding of the leaves, comes also the elongation of the twig that bears them. In most adult trees in a state of nature, there is no further growth in this way, but the internal changes of the sap continue to be effected among the cells during the whole period of their remaining in leaf, during which there is a continual flow of crude sap absorbed by the roots, and taken up into the organism of the tree to aid in the perfection of all the various parts, and in the preparation of the proper juice and the several products peculiar to the tree, as well as its wood and fruits. When all this is transpiring within its economy, the tree is said to be in its full flow of sap; at this stage the young tree is in the best condition for budding, but it continues also, if well cultivated, to grow by extension for a greater or shorter portion of the season, and this is essential to the success of the operation as already stated. After the perfecting of the crop of fruit, the main work of the tree seems to have been done for the year, and we often observe, particularly with the summer fruits, that the trees appear to go to rest after this period, and begin to cast their foliage. Now, to a certain extent, this is true of the young trees. The varieties that ripen their fruit early, make their growth in the nursery in the earlier portion of the summer, they stop growing, and their terminal bud is formed and is conspicuous at the top of the shoots. Very soon the supply of sap appears to be diminished, there is no longer so much activity in the circulation, the bark cleaves to the wood, it will no longer run, and the season of budding for those stocks has reached its terminus; hence the nurseryman must be upon the look-out for the condition of his trees. Fortunately, those species which have the shortest season, are also the first to be ready, the first to mature their buds, and they must be budded first. We may commence with the cherry, though the Mahaleb stock, when it is used, continues in condition longer than other varieties, and may be worked late. The plum and pear stocks also complete their growth at an early period in the season; the apple continues longer in good condition, and may be worked quite late. Grapes, if worked in this way, should be attended to about mid-season, while they are still growing; but quinces and peaches may be kept in a growing state much later than most other stocks, and can be budded last of all.

How to do it.—The stocks being in a suitable condition as above described, they should be trimmed of their lateral shoots for a few inches from the ground. This may be done immediately in advance of the budder, or it may have been done a few days before the budding. The stock may be one year old, or two years; after this period they do not work so well. The usual method is to make a **T** incision through the bark of the stock, as low down as

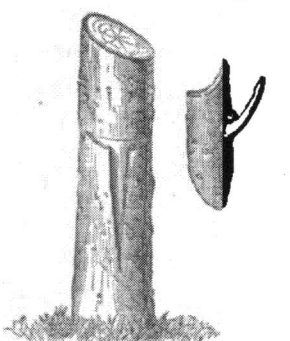 

possible, but in a smooth piece of the stem; some prefer to insert the shield just below the natural site of a bud. The knife should be thin and sharp, and if the stock be in good condition, it will pass through the bark with very little resistance; but if

Fig. 17.—BUDDING, WITH THE WOOD RE-MOVED. *b*, THE INSIDE OF THE SHIELD SHOWING THE BASE OF THE BUD.

the stock be too dry, the experienced budder will detect it by the different feeling communicated through his knife, by the increased resistance to be overcome in making the cut. The custom has been to raise the bark by inserting the haft of the budding knife gently, so as to start the corners of the incision, preparatory to inserting the bud; but our best budders depend upon the shield separating the bark as it is introduced. The bud is cut from the scion by the same knife, which is entered half an inch above the bud, and drawn downward about one-third the diameter of the scion, and brought out an equal distance below the bud; this makes the shield, or bud. The authorities direct that the wood should be removed from the shield before it is inserted; this is a nice operation,

requiring some dexterity to avoid injuring the base of the bud, which constitutes its connection with the medulla or pith within the stick. The base of the bud is represented by *b*, figure 17. Various appliances have been invented to aid in this separation, some use a piece of quill, others a kind of gouge; but if the bark run freely on the scion, there will be little difficulty in separating the wood from the shield with the fingers alone. All this may be avoided by adopting what is called the American method of bud-

Fig. 18. — AMERICAN BUD-DING. *b*, THE BUD WITH THE WOOD REMAINING.

ding, which consists in leaving the wood in the shield, (fig. 18, *b*) that should be cut thinner, and is then inserted beneath the bark without any difficulty, and may be made to fit closely enough for all practical purposes. Like everything else American, this is a time-saving and labor-saving plan, and therefore readily adopted by the practical nurseryman, who will insert two thousand in a day.

A division of labor is had generally, so far as the

tying is concerned; for this is done by a boy who follows immediately after the budder, and some of these
require two smart boys. S. S. Jackson has carried this
principle of division of labor still further, and, as appears,
with advantage; one hand cuts the shields for another who
inserts them.   He never uses the haft of his knife to raise
the bark, but, after having made the longitudinal cut
through the bark, he places the knife in position to make

Fig. 19.—MR. JACKSON'S METHOD OF MAKING THE INCISION.

the transverse incision, and as he cuts the bark, the edge
of the blade being inclined downward, the shield is placed
on the stock close above the knife, which is then still
further inclined toward the stock, resting upon the shield
as a fulcrum; thus started, the bark will readily yield to
the shield, which is then pressed down home into its place.

J. W. Tenbrook, of Indiana, has invented a little instrument with which he makes the longitudinal and transverse
incisions, and raises the bark, all at one operation, and in-

serts the bud with the other hand.   On these plans, two persons may work together, one cutting, the other inserting the buds; these may change work occasionally for rest.   In all cases it is best to have other hands to tie-in the buds, two or three boys will generally find full occupation behind a smart budder.   It will be apparent that the above processes can only be performed when the stock is in the most perfect condition of growth, so that the bark can be pressed away before the bud; a good workman will not desire to bud under any other circumstances.

In budding, it is found that the upper end of the shield is the last to adhere to the stock; it needs to be closely applied and pressed by the bandage, and if too long, so as to project above the tranverse incision, it should be cut off.

Another expedient for facilitating the operation of budding is made use of by some of the nurserymen who grow peach trees extensively.   It consists in preparing the stick of buds, as shown in the engraving, figure 20.   A cut is made, with a sharp knife, through the bark, around each bud, as in the figure. The budder then removes the buds as they are wanted, with a slight side-

Fig. 20.–STICK OF BUDS. wise pull, and has the shield in the right condition to insert, without the trouble of removing the wood. When working in this manner, the stick of buds must not be allowed to dry, and the work must be done at a time when the bark parts with the greatest ease.

Among the modifications of the process of budding, that, called ring-budding, fig. 21, may be mentioned, rather as a curiosity however, though preferred by some, especially for the grape, which is said to be very easily budded, though we seldom see the operation practiced.

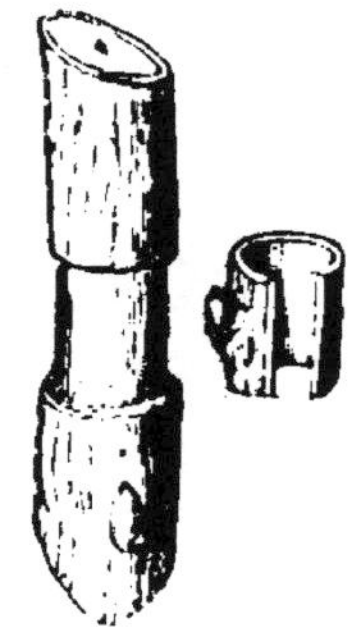

Fig. 21.—RING BUD-DING.

Those who are anxious to commence budding early in the season, prepare the scions they expect to use, by pinching the ends and cutting off a portion of the leaves; the effect of this check to the wood growth is to hasten the ripening or development of the buds, which rapidly swell, preparatory to breaking, in their attempt to reproduce the foliage that had been removed.

TYING should be done as soon as convenient after the buds have been inserted; though under very favorable circumstances the bud may adhere and do well without any bandaging, no one thinks of leaving the work without carefully tying in the buds, and most budders lay a great deal of stress upon the necessity for covering the whole shield and cut with a continuous bandaging, that shall exclude the light, and air, and moisture. The material most used is bass matting, brought from Russia, as a covering to the packages of sheet iron for which that country is famous. This is the inner bark of the *Tilia Europea*, but our own Bass-wood, *T. Americana*, furnishes an excellent bass, and is procured by our nurserymen directly from the trees, by stripping the bark in June, and after it has lain a few days in water, the inner portion separates easily, is dried, and put away for future use. Those who have not provided the bass, are content to apply woolen yarn to tie in the buds; its elasticity adapts it well to the purpose. The ingenious budder, without bass, often finds a substitute for it, and a very good tie, in the soft husks of corn ears, the inner husks are torn into strips and used a little damp, when they are pliant and

 easily tied, answering a very good purpose. Many nurserymen, who have tried the corn-husk, prefer it to all other material, because it saves them the trouble of removing the bandages, as it decays rapidly, and yielding to the growth of the stock, it falls off before it cuts the bark, which a firmer bandage is apt to do.

S. S. Jackson, whose improvements in budding have already been mentioned, also adopts another in tying. He holds that it is not at all necessary to hide the bud with the tie, the only requisite being to retain the parts in contact.

Fig. 22.—MR. JACKSON'S MANNER OF TYING THE BUD.

tact. He uses No. 3 cotton yarn, cut in lengths of a few inches, more or less, according to the size of the stocks; a couple of strands are pulled out from the cut bundles; the first turn around the stock secures the end of the string by its own pressure, one turn more is taken below the bud and one or two above it, when the free end is passed into a cleft made through the bark above the point where the bud is inserted. This is found to secure the string sufficiently, and is easily loosened when necessary to relieve the tension caused by the continued growth, (fig. 22).

All ties should be loosened in the course of a couple of weeks, if the stocks be growing freely; otherwise they will injure the tree by strangulation. Sometimes it will be necessary to replace the bandage to prevent the effects of desiccation upon the bud, this is particularly the case with the cherry, and other fruits, that are budded early; but the tie is often left on the stock all winter, as a sort of protection to the bud. When loosening the ties, the buds are inspected and their condition ascertained; if they have failed, they may be replaced, if the stocks continue in a suitable condition. It is very easy to tell the success of the budding; the portion of the petiole left upon the shield is a very good index; if the bud has withered, this will also be brown and will adhere firmly to the shield; but, on the contrary, the bud and its shield having formed a union with the stock, the leaf-stalk remains plump, but changes color. Like a leaf-stem in the autumn, it assumes the tint of ripeness, and it will separate with a touch, and soon falls off.

The common method of removing the ties is to cut them with a single stroke of a sharp knife, when the bandage is left to fall off. Mr. Knight recommended two distinct ligatures, and left the one above the bud for a longer time uncut. When the buds have not been very fully developed, and when the stocks are very thrifty, it sometimes happens that the excessive growth about the incisions made for the insertion of the bud, completely cover up this little germ of a future tree, which is then said to be "drowned." Judicious pinching and shortening of the stock will prevent this effect, but care is needed not to pursue such treatment too far.

The stocks are generally headed back to within an inch or more of the bud, just as vegetation starts the next spring; but early set buds may be headed back so soon as they have taken, and will often make a nice growth the same season. This, however, is not generally preferred, and a late start in the growing weather of our autumns is particularly to be avoided, as the young shoot will not become matured before winter, and may be lost.

The advantages of propagating by budding may be summed up in the following remarks, which are presented even at the risk of some repetition.

This favorite method of multiplying varieties has some advantages over grafting, and is by many preferred on account of the facility with which it can be performed, and because it affords a means of increasing sorts in the nursery that have not been grafted, and of filling up gaps in the rows where grafts have missed; and it has been reported, that budded trees of certain varieties were more hardy than those which had been root-grafted. The objections, if such they can be called, are, that the period of performing the operation is limited, and that the young shoots from the buds generally have a curve that makes a crook or blemish in the tree when it goes from the nursery—neither of these objections constitute any real difficulty; on the contrary, the advantages quite over-balance them: as already suggested, it is a good plan for double-working certain varieties. The season for budding is at the period when the longitudinal growth of the stock is nearly completed, and when the wood-forming process is most active, so that the bark will part most freely from the wood—in other words, while the stock is still quite active in its circulation, but has, in a measure, made its growth. The scions used must have so far completed their growth for the season as to have filled their buds handsomely, but yet be so young as to allow the wood to part freely from the bark of the shields when they are cut. Those who desire to bud early, may accelerate the development of the buds by nipping off the points of the shoots to be used, this, in a few days, causes the buds to swell. The season of budding will thus depend upon the high culture of the nursery, and upon the condition of the trees from which the scions of buds are to be cut. Budding should never be done unless the stock is in perfectly good condition, if otherwise, it is labor lost. The old writers recommended damp, cloudy, or even showery weather; but under our bright summer skies our large establishments would never be able to dispose of their work, were they to wait for such suitable weather. Fortunately it is not found necessary to select such a season, but the greatest success attends the budding that is done in fine bright and even hot weather. The scions should be kept wrapped in a damp cloth, excluded from the rapid evaporation to which they would be subjected if exposed—this is better than to keep them in water, which exhausts them by dilution of the sap they contain. The scions should have their leaves removed, so soon as they are cut from the tree; this is done with a knife or the thumb nail, leaving a short piece of the leaf-stalk for convenience when inserting the buds.

Spring budding is sometimes desirable, either to fill up gaps in the nursery-rows, or to secure varieties, the scions of which may have been received too late for grafting, or when it is desirable to multiply them as much as possible, by making every bud grow. When the operation is to be performed in the spring, the scions must be kept back, by placing them in the ice-house until the stocks are in full leaf, when the bark will peel readily, and the buds may be inserted with a pretty fair prospect of success; of course, the American method must be used in this case, as the wood and bark of the dormant scion will not separate.

The stocks should be cut down as early in the spring as the buds begin to swell, with a sharp knife, applied just above the bud, and on the same side; the whole upper portion of the stock must be removed by a clean cut; this is better than to leave a stump of three or four inches, as is often recommended, as a support to which to tie up the buds in their tender growth. All shoots from the stock should be rubbed out while young; this may need repeating a second time.

If the stocks were strong, the buds will make handsome sturdy trees the first season; the branched form may be assisted by pinching the points when a few inches high, as recommended with the grafts. Two year old stocks should make pretty trees, at one year old from the bud.

PROPAGATION.—SECT. IV.—THE NURSERY.

———◦◦◦———

THE NURSERY.—Be not alarmed, brother nurseryman,
think not that all the arcana of your craft are to be exposed to the public; one small chapter cannot injure you,

120

even were it wise and proper to retain knowledge exclusively in the hands of the guild ; on the other hand, ye need not be afraid that one who owes you so much would turn tell-tale, and expose all your weaknesses to the gaze of the multitude. From my friends in the craft, the many intelligent men and keen observers, who have ever been foremost in the ranks of our country's pomologists, no censure is apprehended for attempting to dash off a few brief directions for the amateur, or even the nurseryman, who is just beginning to pursue as a business the pleasant occupation of growing trees. Any censure from others, if such there be, who would feel afraid to trust their knowledge to the world, and who might think in this enlightened age that such a thing as secrets of the trade could be long retained in their own hands,—any censure, from such a source, would fall harmless—it is not dreaded. Indeed, though not of the trade, it would be easy to expose the ignorance that is sure to be found among those who might claim to be the exclusive conservators of knowledge, such however is not the object in view, it is rather to extend useful knowledge, to popularize it and to bring it with'n the reach of those who may need it, that this chapter is undertaken ; and the labor is the more willingly entered upon, in the firm conviction that the more the knowledge of plants and the love for them is diffused among the masses of our population, the greater will be the success of those who are engaged as professional nurserymen and gardeners, who need not fear the competition of amateurs, but should rather encourage it, upon the score of such persons being and continuing to be their best customers—if not from any higher and more noble

6

sentiments of affiliation with men of congenial tastes and pursuits.

SITE AND SOIL FOR THE NURSERY.—A somewhat elevated position should be selected for the ground that is to be appropriated for the production of trees; the surface water should be able to escape rapidly, instead of standing in the paths, and furrows, and trenches. The fresh air should be able to blow freely over the young trees, swaying them about, trying their fibres, and at the same time giving them new strength and vigor: not that they should be too much exposed to the rude blasts, as they might be upon the vast savannas of the West, where a protecting belt of deciduous and evergreen trees, to a moderate extent, will be found of service, and conducive to the healthy development of young trees in the nursery. But even the naked prairie, exposed for miles in every direction, would offer a better location for the nursery, than a few acres cleared out among the heavy timber. Here the little trees, if crowded together, must be drawn up to meet the light, and will be poorly furnished with lateral branches, and unprepared to meet the rude battle with the elements that awaits them in their future orchard homes, which, indeed, too often become rather their graves, into which they are thrust, buried, not planted, and whence they rise no more, but after a fruitless struggle, dwindle and die.

A somewhat elevated situation is also valuable, on account of its greater probable immunity from frost, than a lower level; and this is often a matter of great importance in the successful cultivation of fruit trees.

The soil should be a good strong sandy loam, one that

contains the needful elements for the growth of trees, and at the same time has a composition that will freely permit the passage of water through it, and be easily worked by the cultivator. Heavy soils, abounding in clay, are strong; but they are more retentive of water, they require more labor to keep them in a friable condition, and they are sometimes objectionable on account of the character of the roots produced in them. These are less abundantly furnished with fibres, as a general rule, when the tree has been grown in a stiff clay, than when it has been produced in a lighter and more porous soil. Mucky soils are too light, and should not be used for permanent nurseries, though valuable for seedlings, cuttings, and newly transplanted forest evergreens for a short period; unless the muck be underlaid by clay, and that it is near enough to the surface to be reached in the preparation of the soil, and to become mixed with its staple in cultivating it. Trees, for the orchard, should never be grown upon a mucky or peaty soil.

The different character of the roots formed by trees growing in particular soils, should not be overlooked by the propagator, since much of his reputation as a nurseryman, and the success attendant upon the labors of his customers, will depend upon the healthy development of these important organs, which have been called the mouths of plants. As elsewhere observed, peaty and mucky soils do not produce roots of a character well adapted to transplanting into upland soil. Very stiff clays furnish trees with long straggling roots that have feeble and scattered fibres; such roots do not present themselves in a good condition, nor are they easily separated from the soil, the tenacity of which often injures the slender fibrous portions, which it is desirable to preserve in transplanting. Sandy soils and sandy loams produce the very best roots, most evenly distributed, and also most easily preserved and removed when the trees are dug from the earth.

Much may be done by the intelligent cultivator, in any kind of land, to make good roots by proper treatment of his soil and trees. A thorough preparation of the ground, and disintegration of the soil, will conduce to this result; and thorough culture will maintain the good condition thus produced. Frequent transplanting will encourage the production of new roots from the cut ends of those that were ruptured in digging, and these will be within reach at the next removal. When taking up young trees, or when setting out seedlings in the nursery rows, the tap roots, and indeed all long straggling roots, should be cut back, with a view to producing the same result. When trees have remained for three or four years in the nursery rows, the fibres will have extended so far in search of food and moisture, that in digging them, the best portions of the roots will be left in the ground, and the young trees will suffer upon being transplanted in this mutilated condition. Such should be root pruned the season previous to their removal. This process is performed by removing the earth on either side of the row, until the roots are exposed, when they are cut off at from ten inches to a foot, from the tree, and the earth replaced upon them, the object being the formation of new fibres that shall be within the reach of the spade when they come to be dug for the orchard. Another plan for root pruning is, to use a very sharp spade, which is set down and pressed deeply into the ground, a few inches from the tree, so as to cut all roots that pass that limit. This, though a ruder method, is followed by good results.

DIGGING THE TREES, is a process that should be conducted upon very different principles from those exercised in grubbing a thicket. The nurseryman wishes to clear his block, but the purchaser hopes to save his trees, and to have them live, he wants a good share of their roots with them. No one need expect, however, to have anything like a large proportion of the roots of a tree removed from the ground; that is out of the question, unless they have been grown in walled stations, confining the roots, like those of green-house plants in their flower-pots. In open culture, they will have spread through the soil in every direction, and cannot be preserved and removed. Repeated root pruning will be of the greatest service in furnishing a great many fine roots within reach ; but at the best, a great deal of damage is necessarily inflicted upon the roots by digging, and the older and larger the tree, the greater will be the injury, and the smaller the proportion of roots to the branches.

In digging trees, it is important to remove the soil very carefully on each side of the row to expose the roots, always holding the spade in such a position that its side and edge shall be in the direction of a radius, from the stem of the tree as a centre. Never stand facing the tree to be dug, but keep it next the elbow, at one side. On finding a root, withdraw the spade, and try again; and, having ascertained its direction, endeavor to loosen the outer extremities first. Proceed all around in this manner, and by gently swaying the trunk, the points of resistance will be indicated; these should be loosened and freed until all appear to be free, when, by grasping the collar as low down as possible, the tree is to be lifted gently and freed from the soil; no force should be used beyond that which is absolutely necessary, to lift the plant from its bed.

In the great commercial nurseries, all this care cannot be exercised; everything must be done in the large way, and labor-saving appliances, the valuable results of

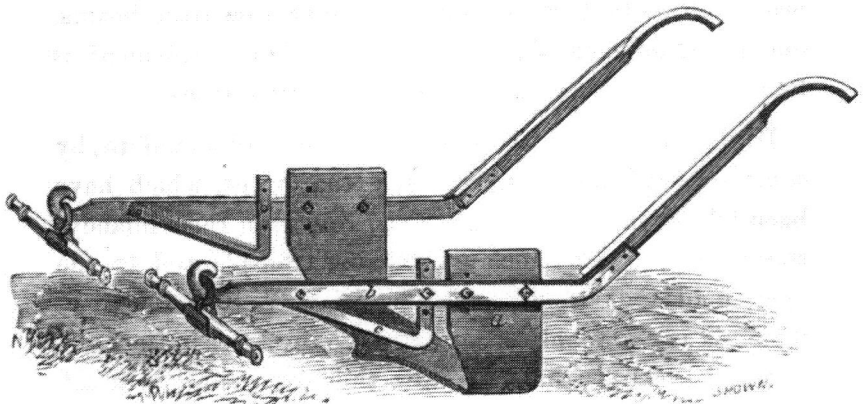

Fig. 23.—HARKNESS' TREE DIGGER.

human thought, but still not thinking nor observing intelligences, must be used. One of this class is the tree-digger, which, in the prairie soils, is used with very good success. It consists of a very large deep plow, without any mold-board, but with a wide sharp steel share, which is turned up at the edges, so as to cut the lateral roots at some distance from the trees. It is drawn on each side of the row, by four horses, hitched *ad tandem*. The trees may then easily be lifted from the loose prairie soil. The accompanying engraving shows the tree digger of Mr. E. Harkness, which is much used in the nurseries of Illinois and other Western States. The figure is sufficiently clear, without much explanation. The broad steel blade runs under the rows and is drawn by four horses, two working one before the other, or *tandem*, each side of the row. Some of our Western nurserymen find great advantage from the use of this digger in their free soils, and also for root pruning trees that are to remain in the rows.

In the sandy loams of New Jersey, a similar tool is used for digging peach trees, which is drawn by a span of heavy horses that are attached to the two separate beams, one being on each side of the trees. This implement is found to be entirely satisfactory in its operations.

High manuring in the nursery has been objected to by some orchard planters, who say that trees, which have been forced into a too luxuriant growth in their infancy, receive so severe a shock upon being transplanted to the open field, that they never recover. With the neglect which is so commonly accorded to young trees in the orchard, it is really wonderful how they ever survive at all, whether they had been stimulated in their culture or not. The large majority of purchasers at the nursery always select those trees which are most vigorous, notwithstanding the prejudice against stimulating the trees, and then with mutilated roots, they probably omit cutting back the limbs sufficiently, and when their neglected orchard fails, they complain of the forced trees. The change from the good cultivation of the nursery to the careless culture and even neglect of the farm, is certainly hard for the poor things to bear. Late growth, encouraged by high manuring, is injurious. There is a much more serious fault of the nursery than stimulating with manure and high cultivation, and that is the too common error of crowding the trees; but even this has its origin partly with the pur-chaser, who too often wishes to have his trees drawn up as high as possible; instead of demanding low heads he asks for high ones, and will sometimes offer a premium for trees that have grown in one season, the second from the root graft, eight or ten feet in a single shoot, so that he may at once calculate upon forming the head where he wants it, out of the reach of his horse; a calculation, how-ever, which he will not realize.

THE PREPARATION OF THE SOIL for a nursery should be as deep and as thorough as possible, for some things it is best even to trench the ground; but generally, the thorough plowing, with a deep-tiller, or a trench-plow, will be sufficient, and if followed by the subsoil lifter, so much the better. One of the most intelligent horticultur-ists, and most successful nurserymen in the country, finds that he can produce a better result in depth and fineness of tilth, by using the Double Michigan plow, than he can with the spade. A piece of clover-sod thus plowed in the fall, and subsoiled at the same time, will be in fine order for nursery purposes, after a thorough cross-plowing and harrowing in the following spring. If the land has been under-drained, so much the better. There is little good land that would not be much improved for nursery pur-poses by tile draining.

If manure is to be applied, it may be spread upon the clover-sod before plowing, or it may be thrown upon the plowed ground at once or at any time during the winter, to be worked into the soil by the spring plowing; if com-posted, it may be spread just before the spring stirring.

LAYING OUT. — In laying out the nursery, some taste

may be exercised by the planter; the sections and blocks should be distinct, and alleys should be located at convenient distances, so that all parts may be easily accessible with the wagon. The rows should be laid out straight, and they ought to be far enough apart—four feet might be a good average for nursery trees; cuttings and seedlings may, of course, be nearer. The trees should not be set too closely in the rows, one foot apart is plenty close enough for most kinds, and that is little enough room for the development of good lateral branches, or for those which have to remain three or four years before transplanting. For peaches, for dwarf pears, and indeed for any of the varieties that are to be taken from the nursery as maiden trees, a less space may be allowed—say eight inches apart. Apple stocks for budding, or for collar grafting, may be set ten inches apart, and they will have room to make very good plants, even should they remain until two years old.

Most nurserymen set out their apple grafts in the rows where they are to be grown to full size, and cultivate them from two to three years; while this saves the trouble of transplanting, the trees will not be as well assorted for size, nor will they have the benefit of the transplanting, (which will enhance their value much more than it costs, in the improved character of their roots), as have those that have been treated on the bedding plan, practiced by some nurserymen. This consists in setting the root grafts closely together, in a bed of very well prepared ground; they are covered at once with a good mulching of sawdust, which keeps the ground moist, and insures the growth of almost all the plants, while for the first season they occupy very little space, and are readily kept clean, as the mulching prevents the growth of weeds. In the fall, or in the following spring, they are taken up, assorted for size, and re-planted in the nursery-rows where they are to stand. This transplanting improves the character of their roots, which are more fibrous and shorter than in those trees which have stood three or four years without being disturbed. Purchasers, now-a-days, begin to look at the roots of their trees, as well as the tops; and it may become necessary for the nurserymen to gratify this fancy for low-headed, stocky trees, that have abundant fibres to insure their growth, and their early fruitfulness.

CULTURE of the nursery should be thorough; the soil should be frequently stirred, and kept mellow and loose, to insure cleanliness and thriftiness, and to make handsome trees. The mellow soil upon the surface, is, by some persons, considered equal to a good mulching, and indeed it answers the indications of one. Cultivation, to kill the weeds as fast as they appear, will admit both air and moisture; a share of both of these is retained by the mellow earth, which, thus treated, is indeed a very good mulch. The cultivation may be done with the small turning plow, with the double shovel, or with any of the many approved cultivators in use everywhere throughout the country. The surface should be kept as level and even as possible. In some soils the roller, made short enough to pass between the rows, is highly esteemed, and is considered a most valuable implement in the nursery. As a general rule, cultivation should not be continued too late in the season, but should be suspended about mid-summer, so as to prevent a late growth and to encourage the plants to finish their summer's work in time to ripen their wood thoroughly before the advent of winter. This is particularly necessary where the climate is severe, especially on new lands, where the trees are very vigorous. Upon the approach of winter, it is a good practice to plow a light furrow against the trees on each side; this protects the collar from cold, prevents heaving by the frost, and gives a good surface drainage to excess of water.

For deeply loosening the ground between the rows, the one-horse subsoil lifting plow is a very valuable instrument; this can be used in very narrow spaces. This plow prepares the ground admirably for the pronged hoe, and it may be used between rows of cuttings and seedlings.

THE PRONGED HOE.—One of the most valuable implements in the nursery to clean out the weeds from between the trees, and also to work among cuttings, and other plants, that are set too closely for the use of the horse, is

Fig. 24.—THE PRONGED HOE.

the pronged hoe; it makes the best shallow culture, prevents the soil from becoming hard, and it is the best destroyer of small weeds that can be used. The flat hoe is never sharp enough to cut all of the weeds effectually, it produces little tilth, and the result of its use is too often a disappointment, but half killing the weeds, in some places, and dragging them out by the roots in others, and often leaving the ground hard and in miserable condition.

PLANTING CUTTINGS.—Some of the small fruits, as cur-

rants, gooseberries, as well as the quince, are propagated,
to a great extent, by cuttings. The ground for growing
them, should be very ·well prepared by trenching or ·
trench-plowing; the difference in the growth between cuttings set on well or on poorly prepared ground is astonishing, and the advantage in favor of trenched land is
sufficient to pay for the extra expense bestowed upon the
preparation. The soil should be rather sandy, decidedly
loose and mellow, and rather moist than dry.

In setting the cuttings, the rows may be quite close, as
horse labor is seldom employed among them; but they are
tended by hand, or the ground is mulched. They may
also be set quite thickly in the row, as they are to remain
but a short time in the cutting bed, from which they are
transplanted at one year old, though sometimes alternate
rows may be left over another season. When the trench is
opened for them, the cuttings are set, three or four inches
apart, next the line, so that only the top bud shall reach
the surface; a little mellow soil is thrown upon them, and
they are tramped firmly at the base, when the remainder
of the earth is thrown in and the next trench is opened
for another row. If they be planted in the autumn, it is
well to cover them with a mulch, and for this leaves from
the forest are an excellent material. Some propagators
insist very strongly upon the necessity for removing all
the buds from the lower portion of the cutting, particularly in the currant and gooseberry, so as to prevent suck-
ering and to grow the bush as a miniature tree, with a
single stem. This is not desirable when the bushes are
liable to have the stems destroyed by the currant borer.
Indeed, the nature of the currant appears to require a re-

newal of the wood by these shoots, which come to replace the old exhausted branches.

The grape is grown in immense quantities from cuttings, which are either planted in a nursery, or set at once in the vineyard. In the former they are planted closely in rows, that are about twenty inches apart. Sometimes the ground is trenched, and the cuttings set at the same operation. When the first trench is opened in a rich mellow loam, which may be sod or clover lea, the edge of the dug soil is dressed to the line with the spade, then the cuttings are placed so as to have one eye at or above the surface, and soil is thrown in and tramped closely to the base of the cuttings. Then the next trench is made with the spade, digging the ground as you proceed.

Grape cuttings are generally made eighteen or twenty inches long; and those which have a heel of old wood are preferred, and command a higher price. The earlier these are taken from the vines, after the fall of the leaves, the better success will attend the plantation; provided they are not too long exposed to the air. Fall planting is very desirable, but if not then planted, the cuttings should be put into the ground and covered as soon as convenient, and they will be better prepared for spring planting. A deep trench is opened, into which the bundles are set in a vertical position, and loose earth filled in about them and slightly covered over them; they will then be ready for planting by the spring. The length of the cuttings has latterly been much reduced, with advantage; some of the most successful planters make them from six to eight inches long: these are much more easily dug than the longer slips, and are better provided with roots.

TRIMMING should be practiced in the nursery with a definite object in view, and not at random; much less with any expectation of increasing the hight of the trees by trimming them up. The object in pruning nursery trees should be to develop them in every part, to produce a stout stocky sturdy little tree, one that may be turned out upon the bleak prairie, and be able to withstand the blasts. To produce this result, the leaves should never be stripped from the shoots to make them extend their growth, for the sake of making more leaves; the nurseryman should know the value of leaves, as constituting the great evaporating surface that plays a most important part in causing the ascent of the crude sap, and also in its elaboration after it has been taken up into the organization of the plant. Leaves should be carefully preserved, and in the trimming, which is necessary, this should be borne in mind. To make vigorous, stocky trees, the side branches should be encouraged rather than pruned off. The tops may sometimes need to be pinched, to force out the laterals, and to encourage their growth; if two shoots start together as rivals, one of them should be topped or cut back, or twisted and broken, but not cut off at its origin, unless there be plenty of lateral branches or twigs to furnish the tree. When these become too long, they may be spurred-in, either in the fall and winter when cutting grafts, or in the summer, during the growing season. Whenever it becomes necessary to trim off any of these laterals, it is best to do it at mid-summer, as the healing of the wounds made at this period is very rapid. Heading off the nursery trees is done to force them to branch out uniformly the second year, to form their heads at the right place; this is to be done toward spring, and is applicable especially to those varieties that are prone to make a single shoot the first year without branching, and which have not been pinched-in or headed during the previous summer to force out side branches. Cherries, plums, and pears, and some apples, are very apt to make this kind of growth. It should have been premised that all nursery trees ought to be grown to one main stem, or leader, from which all the branches arise, and to which they should all be made to contribute their quota of woody fibre. It has been asserted that the wood of a tree, instead of being a cone, as its stem appears to be and is, it should be a column of nearly equal size from the bottom to the top; that is, the mass of all the branches taken together, should equal the diameter of the trunk at any point below. A well-grown stocky nursery tree, with its abundance of lateral branches approximates this idea; but the main stem of such an one is very perceptibly a cone, rapidly diminishing in diameter from the collar upwards.

AGE OF TREES FOR PLANTING.—This depends so much upon the views of planters, that the nurseryman cannot always control the period at which he shall clear a block of trees. Peaches should always be removed at one year from the bud. Plums and dwarf pears will be ready to go off at two years from the bud or graft; so with apples and cherries. But many persons, purchasers and sellers, prefer larger trees, and they recommend that the trees should remain one, two, or even three years longer in the nursery. Others, a new school of planters, prefer to set out the maiden tree, in most of the species above named, except some very feebly growing varieties, that will scarcely have attained sufficient size to risk in the orchard. The nurseryman should beware of keeping his trees too long on his hands; they may become unprofitable stock, and are sure to require much more labor in the digging and handling. The purchaser is his own master, and his tastes and wishes must be consulted; if he wants large trees, by all means, let him be indulged; he will have to pay in proportion, he will have more wood for his money, more weight to carry, or more transportation to pay for, more labor in planting, and vastly increased risk of the life of his trees; but, let him be indulged with his five year old trees, while his neighbor, for a smaller sum invested, with less freight, less wood, less labor, and infinitely less risk, will plant his maiden trees, and five years hence will market more fruit.

The risk of transplanting large or old trees from the nursery, may be greatly diminished, and their value will be vastly enhanced, by judicious root pruning in the nursery-row. This may be done by digging, on either side, on alternate years, and cutting off the straggling roots, and particularly those that run deeply; this will be followed by the production of a multitude of fibrous roots that put the tree into a good condition for transplanting. In the great nurseries of the West, there is a peculiar plow, which is used for root pruning the nursery rows.

THE HOME NURSERY has been recommended by Mr. Field in his *Pear Culture*, as a means of enabling the orchardist to amuse himself, and to grow his trees in such style as he may prefer. He advises to select trees " of two or three years' growth, and prepare a piece of ground for the home nursery. For this a rich, deep, dry soil should be spaded and thoroughly pulverized to the depth of two feet, (trenched). In it plant the trees in rows four feet distant, and three feet apart in the rows. Two hundred trees would thus occupy a space fifty feet square. The roots having been carefully examined, and, as before mentioned, the laterals pruned to six or eight inches, are spread out horizontally, and gently covered with earth. It will be seen that the labor of pinching, pruning, and cultivating, will be much less on so small a spot, than when the cultivator is obliged to travel over three or four acres upon which they are ultimately to be planted.

"If at the end of two years it is still desirable to allow them to remain, a sharp spade should be thrust down around them, at a distance of fifteen or eighteen inches, in order to cut the long straggling roots, and thus induce the formation of fibres nearer home. This will fit them for transplanting at an advanced stage of growth. In this case, if at the end of two or three years, they are removed at the proper season, and with care, they will suffer scarcely any check. By pursuing this plan, they receive better care, grow faster, and are not liable to damage; and as only the good trees will, in this case, be set in the fruit grounds, none of those unseemly breaks in the rows, caused by the injury or death of a tree, need occur. Where, however, older trees, at least once transplanted, cannot be obtained, and it is desirable to set out the orchard at once, stout two-year old trees are decidedly preferable. Such trees have not stood sufficiently long to send their roots beyond a limit whence they can be removed; and with careful digging, removal and planting, the purchaser need not fear a loss of more than two per cent."

THE NURSERY ORCHARD, as practiced by A. R. Whitney, of Lee Co., Ill., now one of the largest orchardists of the country, is well worthy of imitation by all those nurserymen, who desire also to become fruit-growers. In laying off the blocks of nursery stock, the varieties that are wanted for the orchard, should be planted in such a manner, that they shall be in every fourth row, so that the orchard trees will stand in rows sixteen to twenty feet apart, according as the nursery-rows are four or five feet wide. In cultivating and trimming these rows in the nursery, a plant is selected, every twelve or sixteen feet, which is to remain as the orchard tree when the block shall be cleared. A good tree is selected, and special care in the pruning is bestowed upon it to secure the desired form, and low branches; if necessary, the tree on either side of it is removed, to give it room. By the time the block is cleared, these orchard trees are often in bearing, and while his customers are struggling to save their trees, and nursing them after their transplanting, the nurseryman will have become an orchardist, and is enjoying his fruits. The nursery will have become an orchard — one rather closely planted to be sure—but the trees can be dwarfed by root pruning with the plow, they shelter one another from the prairie blasts, and when too thick, alternate trees may be removed to the wood-pile, and thus cheer the owner on a winter's day.

WINTER-KILLING is a serious evil in the nursery, as by it whole rows and blocks of certain varieties are sometimes destroyed, or very seriously injured. It has been observed to be most marked in its effects upon those sorts of trees that make the most vigorous and sappy growth, and those which continue to grow late in the season. Such varieties have very naturally acquired the epithet of *tender*, especially as orchard trees of the same kinds, even in a bearing state, have been similarly affected; in some sections of the country, these kinds have been thrown out of cultivation. The bark looks shriveled and withered, the twigs seem dry when cut, and resist the knife; when thawed by the fire, or on the return of spring weather, the bark seems loose, and the inner bark, instead of being greenish-white, becomes brown, and the whole tree looks as though it was dead. In old trees, large portions of the bark start from the stem and large limbs, and hang loosely for awhile and then fall off. The buds alone retain their vitality, and upon the return of spring they sometimes succeed in establishing the necessary connection with the soil, and restore the circulation of the sap; the results are the deposit of the usual annular layer of woody matter, which encases the dead portions within, that become like a *sequestrum* of dead bone in an animal. The best treatment for the trees that have been winter-killed, is to cut them back very severely, in the hope of producing a vigorous wood-growth the next season, to repair the injury.

A partial winter-killing often affects small nursery trees, especially on low and wet, undrained soils; the plants recover, but for years they have a black point in the heart which embraces all of the wood-growth that was affected—all their wood at the period of the disaster. This is enclosed and surrounded by clear, healthy wood; but such trees are not desirable, they are so fragile, as to be easily broken.

The best preventive for winter-killing in the nursery, is

to encourage early ripening of the wood, and to drain the land, is one of the best means of producing this effect; another is the cessation of culture at mid-summer, and the sowing of oats very thick at the last cultivation, has been practiced, and, it is thought, with excellent effects. The rank growth absorbs the superfluous moisture, robbing the trees, and afterwards forms a good protective mulch during the winter. The objections to it are, that it encourages the mice, which, by girdling the trees, effectually winter-kills them.

Many nursery and orchard trees often present a black discoloration of the bark, which is quite unsightly, and excites alarm for the health of the tree. This is often caused by trimming at unfavorable periods; in the spring pruning of bearing trees, the large stumps sometimes bleed, but in the nursery trees it arises from cutting them, and especially in the barbarous trimming up, during severely cold weather, when they are frozen.

INJURIOUS ANIMALS AND INSECTS. — The nurseryman sometimes suffers from the depredations of some of the smaller animals, which cause him great annoyance. The mole, though highly recommended by the naturalists as a harmless beast, who is an aid to horticulture by his insectivorous habits, is nevertheless injurious in his *ways;* for he often makes his run in the seed bed, or along a row of root grafts, and raising them from their stations break their tender rootlets, when the sun and air soon destroy them. Mice, of different kinds, are still more destructive, particularly in the winter, when they will often girdle young trees near the collar, and do much mischief. They also devour many seeds after they have been committed to the ground, particularly those sown in the autumn. For both of these animals, the best preventive is to catch them, which may be done with traps. They may also be poisoned. The young trees may be protected from the mice by keeping them clear of rubbish, that would shelter these animals, and when snow falls, it should be trodden down closely about the trees. Owls and cats will do their share in the destruction also, but they will also take the friendly little birds.

Rabbits are also very apt to bite off young shoots, and to bark trees of larger growth in the nursery, as well as those that have been set out in the orchard. Various methods have been suggested to prevent their injuries. Wrapping the stems with strips of rags or with ropes of hay, was formerly the method practiced by those who wished to save their young trees; the process is tedious and troublesome. A few pieces of corn-stalk have been placed by the stem of the tree and tied to it; this, too, is a troublesome procedure, though, like the others, it is efficacious. A still better plan in this class of preventives, is a half sheet of common brown wrapping paper, made to encircle the stem, like an inverted funnel; this need be fastened only at the top, by a little thin grafting wax applied with a brush at the instant, or the paper may be tied with some common white cotton string. This envelope keeps off the rabbits, and lasts through the winter; the string will decay before the growing season returns, so there is no danger of strangulation. All the other wrappings must be removed, or they will injure the trees and afford harbor for insects. It will be observed that all applications of this class, are adapted only to trees that have a clean bole without branches, but are not suited for those which are made to branch at or near the ground. Besides, in countries where snow abounds, these little marauders are elevated above the wrappings, and have fair play at the unprotected parts of the tree—on this account another class of preventives has been adopted.

These consist in applications that are obnoxious to rabbits, which, being nice feeders, are easily disgusted. White-wash, and white-wash made with tobacco water, soap, whale-oil soap, grease, blood, and especially the dead rabbit itself, freshly killed, have all been used with happy results, in that they have driven these animals to seek their food elsewhere. A very good application, and one that may be used upon a low-branched tree as well as to the smooth clear stem of one that is higher, is blood. This is put on with a swab; a few corn husks tied to a stick, answers very well. Dipping this into the vessel of blood, the swab is struck gently against the stem or the branches, as the case may be, and the fluid is spattered over it. A very little will answer to keep the rabbits away, and the effect will continue all winter, notwithstanding the rains.

Certain insects also prove injurious in the nursery, among these the most numerous are the *aphides*, which are found upon the roots of some fruit trees, especially the apple. Others of this disagreeable insect appear upon the foliage, among these one of the most disgusting is the one which causes the black curl, on young cherry trees. The pear tree slug, (*Selandria cerasi*), destroys the foliage of many young trees in the nursery; caterpillars also do their share of mischief. A serious trouble in old nur-

sery grounds, especially where manure is used, is the grub
of the May beetles, of which there are several species.
These grubs are whitish, nearly as thick as the little
finger, with a brownish head. They cut off the young
nursery trees at three or four inches below the surface.
We have seen two-year old stocks cut in this manner, and
the work of destruction was so complete, that the proprie-
tor of the nursery was a long time in attributing it to
such an apparently inadequate cause as this sluggish,
soft-bodied grub. All of these, with other insects injurious
to fruit, will be considered in their appropriate place.

CHAPTER IV.

DWARFING.

DWARFING consists in so controlling the growth of plants as to reduce the natural size of any of our fruit trees, and bring them within comparatively narrow bounds. The objects of dwarfing are to enable us to plant a large number of specimen trees, or of varieties upon a small piece of ground, or to have small trees beside the alleys of our gardens. Such plants are also well adapted for growing in pots, or in the borders of an orchard-house. It is claimed for dwarfed trees, that they are more prolific than those which are worked on free stocks, which are often erroneously called standards, and it is also asserted that these dwarfed trees will bear sooner and produce finer and larger fruit.

The terms used may as well be explained at once. When we speak of dwarfing stocks, we mean such as are so uncongenial as to check the wood-growth; and thus, while producing smaller trees, they have a tendency to early fruitfulness if properly managed. But this condition may be superinduced by other means than these. Hence in speaking of dwarf pear trees, it does not follow that they have been worked on the quince or other uncongenial stock. A dwarf tree, of whatever kind, is simply one that has been caused to assume diminutive proportions. Dwarfing stocks are contrasted with free stocks, or those which would have attained the full size of the species, and which, when grafted, produce large trees. These are often mis-called standards, when contrasted with those that have been worked on the quince, or other dwarfing stock. Whereas, the trees propagated on free stocks, may also be dwarfed, by means that will be presently detailed; and the term standard refers really to the mode in which the training of the specimens has been performed. Those which are trimmed up as orchard trees are usually treated as standards, and are said to be trimmed to standard hight. Those branching at a lower point are called

7

half standards. Those which are branched so low as to conceal the stem of the tree, and in which the limbs are so well managed that the lower ones are always the longest, and those above them gradually contracted to the point at the top, are called pyramids, or more properly conical trees. Whether dwarfed or not, trees may be trained in a variety of forms, such as the columnar, sometimes called the *quenouille ;* the vase or goblet form may be given them, or the parasol shape, and they may be made to assume the form of a fan or other mode of extension laterally, when trained upon a wall or espalier frame, as may be seen in the illustrations given by Du Breuil; but it is seldom that our gardeners are willing to bestow the care and attention necessary to produce these results.

The vertical and oblique *cordons* represented and recommended by Du Breuil are very attractive, and admirable methods of training and dwarfing fruit trees, and of crowding a great many into a small space. His method of making an edging to the fruit-border with dwarf apples, inarched together so as to form a connected tree for its whole length, is a capital illustration of the control we may exercise upon vegetation.

Standards and pyramids are often trained as weeping trees, for the sake of gratifying the fancy of the cultivator, and with a view of bringing on that early productiveness which results from the check of the upward current of sap that is incident to such a mode of treatment. This is really a kind of dwarfing so far as it goes, and if commenced early in the life of the tree, it may become very effective, especially when combined with other means of reducing the growth. These are formed by arching the branches, tying their tips to a ring of wire or hoop secured near the ground, or simply by fastening weights to them sufficient to keep them in the desired position, and by tying the upper limbs to the lower ones. As is well known, the sap flows most readily toward the shoots that occupy a vertical line; it will be seen that its ascent will be seriously retarded in those that are bent, and their vigor will be diminished, and fruit-bearing will be promoted. This process must not be continued too perseveringly, lest the tree become exhausted by over-production.

Du Breuil recommends laying bare the principal roots of the tree in the spring of the year, so as to expose them for the most of their length, and leaving them in this condition during the summer. This exposure of roots to the sun and air diminishes the vigor of the tree, and hence it tends to the production of fruit. He also recommends the removal of a part of the roots in the spring, and replacing the earth; considering this a more energetic operation than the preceding, he advises caution, lest we injure the tree. This is simply root-pruning, a plan that has been pretty thoroughly tested in this country, where, perhaps, its beneficial effects are more needed than in any other, and where we shall even find it advantageous to have recourse to mechanical means for its performance in large orchards by horse-power, as will be set forth in another place.

A very successful method of obtaining the desired effect of dwarfing, which is early and abundant fruiting, consists in transplanting the trees in the autumn; this should be done very carefully, so as to preserve the roots from mutilation as much as possible. The effect of this will be to check the wood-growth the ensuing summer, and fruit-buds will be formed, for it is well known that these two opposite conditions of plant life are complementary the one to the other, and while we always desire to see them both proceeding together in a healthy tree, the wood-growth must have been moderated before we can expect to receive any fruit.

The French and English excel us in training upon walls and espaliers, and we may willingly yield them the palm; since, in this country, it is rarely necessary to incur so great expense for the production of good fruits, and as a means of dwarfing our trees, it is more expensive and requires more skill, care, and watchfulness, than other methods of producing this effect. Espalier training, however, affords the most beautiful opportunity for the illustration of many of the important principles of vegetable physiology, but it should never be undertaken by any one who is not familiar with these, and at the same time willing to exercise great patience and perseverance in their application to the subjects under his control. No blind pursuance of the abstract rules of the art can enable the mere routine gardener to become a successful grower of espalier trees. The modes of training are various, to suit the whims and necessities of the artist. Trees are fastened directly to the walls, or to trellises of wood or of iron, that are placed at a little distance from the masonry, or they may be entirely independent of any such structures, and exposed to the air and light freely on both sides. The trellises may be either vertical, or inclined. The limbs may be made to issue nearly opposite to one another, and be trained horizontally in two directions, with successive stages to the top of the wall or trellis, or they may be trained in a fan shape, with various modifications of what M. Du Breuil calls the *palmette* form. And a simple modification of this method of dwarfing may be made with some varieties of fruit, by training a single stem horizontally within a foot of the ground, as a border or edging between the path-ways and the cultivated ground.

The favorite method of training in France, at the present day, appears to be that called the *cordon*. This may be either the vertical or inclined. In this kind of espalier, the trees are dwarfed by crowding them closely together, and by successive pinching and other mutilation, such as bending and even breaking the shoots, which results in early productiveness. The trees are planted sixteen inches apart, and are trained to single stems, and so treated as to be furnished with the requisite number of fruit-spurs on their whole extent. This is quite a new application of principles, and one which is rudely imitated by Mr. Field's pear hedges, which, however, bear but little resemblance to the elegant cordons of Du Breuil beyond that of dwarf-ing by crowding and pinching. We are told that among the many advantages of this method, are the diminished time required to cover a wall or trellis with fruit, and the greater facility of replacing a dead or defective tree, which, in the usual espalier methods, is a very serious matter, requiring several years for its restoration and the production of a crop.

We are so blessed, in most parts of this country, with soil and climate that are well adapted to the production of fruit in the open field, upon sturdy orchard trees, that there is less necessity for introducing these elegant methods of pursuing the fine art of horticulture; and yet there are reasons in the uncertain climate of our winters, why these plans of training and dwarfing should be pursued by those who have the talent and the means for doing it. Until within a few years, there were not many dwarfed pear or apple trees in this country, and they were confined chiefly to French gardens and to the establishments of the wealthy. But since their more general introduction, immense numbers have been propagated and planted, and extensive orchards, particularly of dwarfed pears, have been set out with a view to profit. Some of these have been eminently successful, others are failures; the results will very much depend upon the amount of care which may be bestowed upon them.

The French have long practiced the dwarfing of certain varieties of fruits, and have been very successful in their results; but that wonderful people, the Chinese, excel all others in this branch of horticulture, for which they display a remarkable talent.

DWARFING BY UNCONGENIAL STOCKS. — The usual mode, which is literally a partial starvation of the tree by limiting the supplies of crude sap, consists in the use of uncongenial and dwarf-growing stocks, upon which the desired varieties are budded or grafted. These are, for the dwarfed pear, either Quinces, Thorns, the Mountain Ash, or the Amelanchiers; for the apple, the Paradise and the Doucin varieties of apple stocks; for the peach and plum, the Chickasas, or other dwarf plum stock may be used. The free-growing cherries are worked on the Mahaleb or the Morello varieties; but it must be confessed, that some of these do not produce a perfect dwarf without other treatment.

To produce a dwarf by grafting on an uncongenial stock, this should be so uncongenial as to form an imperfect union, which checks the downward circulation; the sap that has been elaborated by the organs of the scion is thus kept above the junction of the two woods, and, being so checked, the result is the early formation of fruit-buds, and a premature fruitage of the trees results in a direct proportion to the incompleteness of the union of scion and stock. This is often so very imperfect as to be very easily ruptured, the grafts are often broken out by a very small force being applied to them, sometimes even the weight of the fruit is sufficient to effect a separation, and an examination of the rupture will show how very slight or imperfect the union between the parts has been; in other cases, however, it is difficult to trace the fibres of wood-growth that belong respectively to the stock and to the scion, even when these have been so different as pear and quince, or plum and peach.

It is also considered desirable that the roots of the stock should be small and fibrous, and not long, naked, and straggling; the former will furnish the crude sap in more limited amounts, and are less-likely to produce an excessively rampant or luxurious growth in the scion.

Many persons have been disappointed in the Mahaleb cherry, which has been reputed to be a dwarfing stock. It is found, that without the application of other means, the so-called dwarfed cherries grow as freely, at least in their early years, as those worked on the free stock, known as the Mazzard cherry. They will never make such large trees, however, and those who would enjoy dwarf cherry trees, should combine the different methods of producing the result.

By Pinching.—There are other means of producing the desired effects of dwarfing and early fruiting, which should be mentioned. These consist in systematic efforts to curtail the development of the wood-growth, by judicious pinching, of the tips or points of the branches, and to prevent the rambling of the roots by root-pruning. These it is designed now to examine. Pinching is practiced in the green-house with the happiest effects, and it results in the production of the most perfect form of the plants, and most abundant display of flowers. The constant check which is thus given to the wood system, causes the sap to seek new outlets, and instead of the one limb into which it had been flowing, and causing it to be developed; its flow is now directed to the other buds along its course, which presently burst out into lateral growths, none of which are so strong as the first, and these are induced to change the character of the buds so as to result in the production of flowers and fruit.

This system applied to fruit-trees has been most thoroughly carried out by the French, and is admirably described and illustrated by Du Breuil, in a work called *Scientific Culture of Fruit Trees*, and reproduced in our own language by Wm. Wardle, an English gardener and orchardist of high reputation.

It is not to be expected that in this country, where fruits are so easily produced, we shall soon reach such a point of horticultural practice as to lead us to the adoption of the European system of walls and espalier training, but we shall do well to watch the application of the very important principles involved in their practice, since these may be applied to our orchards with manifest advantage. In reference to the form and management of trained trees, it is established as an axiom that their permanency is dependent upon an equal diffusion of the sap being kept up throughout the whole extent of their branches. This occurs naturally in all trees, because they develope themselves in the forms natural to them, but in our gardens and orchards we make our trees assume unnatural forms. The sap flows to the highest parts by a law which is well known, though not so well understood; as a consequence, the lower branches do not receive their needed supplies, and being smothered by those above them, they eventually die and decay, leaving a naked stem supporting a top, or the common form of the natural tree. To maintain the shape we desire—be this the pyramid, the vase, or the espalier of whatever kind—certain operations must be performed from time to time, as the conditions of the tree may indicate.

Among these, Du Breuil advises to prune the strong branches short and allow the weaker ones to grow long, and thus to restore the balance: This may be done at the spring pruning, and also at any time during the growing season, when it may be necessary to check excessive growth at any one point: and upon this principle depends some of the most important practice of the summer pruning of our vineyards. The sap flows towards the leaves, and by removing them from one part, and leaving a preponderance upon another, we change the direction of its

7*

flow. As the strongest flow is toward those parts that are in a vertical direction, we may also check this tendency, or encourage it, by altering the position of the branch, as is done in the vineyard by tying up the canes we wish to have developed, and depressing the laterals with their fruit; so in a tree, we may depress the shoots which are too strong, and elevate those that are weak, to produce the desired effect. We may also greatly diminish the flow of sap to a strong branch by removing early all its useless buds; this is a sort of premature pinching to be sure, but when we consider the powerful influence exerted by these organs as centers of vitality, we can realize their attractive force in drawing the sap towards them. After the production of the full number of shoots upon the weaker branch, if the foliage continue to predominate upon the stronger shoot, it may be partially removed by early pinching, or cutting through the petioles, not by tearing them off; and as late as possible, remove the surplus and useless shoots from the weaker branches, which were at first needed to encourage the flow of sap in that direction.

The true pinching of the young laterals, or new shoots, should also be done as early as possible to keep them in check on the strong branches, while the same operation may be delayed on the weaker, from which we should remove only those that will be supernumeraries. M. Du Breuil also recommends the stimulation of the weaker limbs, by bathing all the green portions with a solution of sulphate of iron, made by dissolving twenty-four grains in a pint of water. This should be applied in the evening, when it is absorbed by the leaves, and acts as a powerful stimulant.

It is a well established principle, that the chief growth by extension will be made by the terminal bud, and this should either be removed by cutting back, or left upon the limb, according as we desire to grow our wood; if extension of the shoot be our leading object, all the lateral buds must be subordinated. So also, it is well known, that all circumstances, which retard the circulation, are followed by a diminution of the wood-growth, and by the development of flower-buds.

The culture of the strawberry affords one of the best illustrations of the benefits and effects of pinching. The runners of this plant may be viewed in the light of wood-growth, or the increase of the plant by extension; even though these slender threads are not permanent, and they only serve to convey a bud to a distance from the parent plant, and place it under favorable circumstances for the formation of a natural layer. They are but annual productions, and hence there is no considerable deposit of woody matter, as in the limbs of trees, but they are thrown out from the parent plant just like woody branches, and are so much substance withdrawn from it, which, if retained or thrown back upon the plant, would have resulted in an enlargement of the main stem of the strawberry plant, and in the development of buds upon the crown, which become stored with the proper juices that result in the production of more abundant blossom buds. The result, however, is so admirable an illustration of this important element in the management of permanent and woody fruit-trees, that we may well look at an herbaceous plant, be it even so humble an individual as the prostrate earth-berry, as our ancestors called the delicious *Fragaria.*

DWARFING THE APPLE

Apples are generally dwarfed by working them upon the French Paradise stock, which is a very diminutive tree or bush, seldom rising more than a few feet high. This is the true stock for those who wish to indulge in the luxury of dwarf apple trees. Such are very appropriate for the small garden, or for the specimen grounds of a nursery establishment, and they sometimes make beautiful objects in the lawn or among the shrubbery, but they are wholly unsuited for orchard planting, as many a poor deluded purchaser has found out to his sorrow, a few years after having been beguiled by the smooth-spoken tree peddlers, who have sold many thousands through the country to farmers to plant as orchard trees.

There is a more vigorous stock which has been used for the same purpose, but it possesses much less dwarfing power. It is called the Doucin, or English dwarfing stock. This, however, exerts so little of the dwarfing influence, that at the end of eight or ten years the trees are generally about as large as those worked upon free stocks; but it happens unfortunately that early fruitage, the great object of dwarfing, is not attained by their use, for they will not have produced any more fruit than the common trees similarly treated.

BY ROOT PRUNING.—Among the many valuable hints which horticulturists have received, with the beautiful flowering and other plants, from our antipodes in the "Flowery Land," none has been of greater value than the practice of root-pruning. In this art of dwarfing even the large forest trees by mutilations of the roots and by other means, this curious people excel all others, as has frequently been stated. In Europe, and in this country also, root-pruning has been extensively practiced with the effect of partially dwarfing the trees, but more especially with the object of inducing prematurely the fruitfulness we so much desire, and which is a natural result of the diminished supplies of crude sap furnished by the contracted roots of a tree that has been treated in this manner. The balance between the wood-growth by extension, and that which results in fruitful spurs is sooner established, and the sap is directed to the formation and support of the fruit.

We should not commence the application of this severe treatment until our trees have been allowed to establish themselves firmly in their stations, unless we desire at the same time to produce decided dwarfs by means of root-pruning. In this case the treatment may be commenced in the nursery itself; the stocks should be transplanted once or oftener before being worked, and the young trees should be moved annually, which will so shorten the roots as to make them a mass of fibres, occupying the whole soil close about their main divisions, and the subsequent removals can then be easily effected, with but a slight check to the tree, which becomes furnished with fruit spurs at a very early period of its existence, instead of its requiring years to reach its natural period of fruitfulness, as is the case with some varieties, particularly of the pear.

As generally practiced, however, root-pruning is postponed until the trees have made a free and vigorous growth, and have become well established in their stations. Then if the growth be too vigorous, and there do not appear any indications of the formation of fruit spurs, as is often the case in the fertile soils of the West, our impatient orchardists complain of the barrenness of their trees, and seek a remedy in root-pruning. This is generally performed with a sharp spade, with which a trench is dug in a circle around the tree. The excavation should be deep enough to reach all of the lateral roots; these are generally within a foot of the surface. The ditch need not be much wider than the spade, and the soil can be thrown back at once, but all the roots should be severed, if we desire to produce the effect of checking the wood-growth. The diameter of this circle will depend upon the size and vigor of the tree to be operated upon. As a general rule, it may be made in the proportion of one foot to each inch of the tree's diameter. The work may be done at any time after the spring growth has begun to harden, or during the autumn and winter, and until the buds are about to break in the spring. The operation is wonderfully conducive to the end we have in view, and we often see a vigorously growing but barren subject, transformed in a single season into a fruitful tree, covered with blossom-bearing spurs that are full of promise of delicious fruits. In some varieties, however, these fruit spurs require more than a single season for their perfection.

Now it may be objected that this labor will be expensive, and so it is, as all hard work with the spade must be; but what of that, when we consider the happy results that ensue in golden harvests. But it has been suggested that this labor may be performed by farm machinery, using a strong plow, or rather a sharp cutter attached to a plow beam, and drawn by a powerful team at the requisite distance on either side of the rows of trees, and in directions crossing each other at right angles. This, of course, like all mere mechanical applications, must be uniform, whether the necessities of the trees be equal or not; whereas, by hand-labor, we may vary the distance at which the roots are to be cut, according to the vigor and size of the trees demanding the treatment.

This topic will be again referred to in the chapter on Pruning, where also it will be necessary to recur to the subject of Training, which was incidentally alluded to in connection with Dwarfing.

CHAPTER V.

DISEASES.

—◦◦◦—

DIFFICULTIES IN THE OUTSET — WHAT CONSTITUTES DISEASED ACTION — NO ANALOGY TO ANIMAL SICKNESSES — CONGENITAL DEFECTS — DEBILITY — DEFICIENT STRENGTH OF FIBRES — DEFECTIVE FOLIAGE — IMPERFECT AND REDUNDANT BLOSSOMS — THE CIVILIZED AND CULTIVATED PLANT MAY BE ABNORMAL ALTOGETHER — UNSATISFACTORY ACCOUNTS OF DISEASES IN PLANTS — LANKESTER'S CLASSIFICATION CONSIDERED — EFFECTS OF THE EXCESS OR PAUCITY OF MOISTURE, HEAT, AND LIGHT — MODE OF ACTION OF FROST — INJURY RATHER REFERRIBLE TO THE CONDITION OF THE CIRCULATION THAN TO THE DEGREE OF COLD IN MANY HARDY PLANTS — INFLUENCE OF THE SOIL — LIGHT THE GREAT STIMULUS, ITS WITHDRAWAL SUSPENDS HEALTHY ACTION — ITS SUDDEN RESTORATION CAUSES DEATH BY SUN SCALD — INJURY BY SUNSHINE IN WINTER — POISONOUS GASES — MIASMATA — POISONS IN THE SOIL — PARASITIC PLANTS, EPIPHITES, FUNGI, PEAR BLIGHT — VARIOUS THEORIES — WHAT WE KNOW, AND WHAT WE DON'T KNOW — TREATMENT — ROOT PRUNING SUGGESTED — SATISFACTORY RESULTS — MILDEW BLIGHT IN PEACH AND APPLE — TWIG BLIGHT IN APPLE AND QUINCE — THE APPLE BLIGHT — BITTER ROT — CRACKED FRUIT — SCAB — MILDEWS — KIRTLAND'S VIEWS AND SUGGESTED REMEDY — WOUNDS AND INSECTS — NEEDING THE AID OF SURGERY RATHER THAN MEDICINE — DESTRUCTION OF FOLIAGE BY INSECTS IMPAIRS THE HEALTHY CONDITION OF THE PLANT — RESUME — SELECT HEALTHY TREES OF HEALTHY VARIETIES — EMPIRICAL CHARACTER OF TREATMENT USUALLY RECOMMENDED FOR DISEASED TREES — THE BLACK KNOT — THE ROT AND MILDEW OF THE GRAPE.

In opening a discussion upon the nosology of vegetation, it may be expected that one who had spent many years of his life in the investigation of the diseases of the human family, and at the same time was something of a student of comparative anatomy and physiology, tracing analogies between the animal and vegetable kingdoms, should be familiar also with the diseases of plants. Such an anticipation, it is feared, will not, in the present instance, be realized. Indeed, the writer feels very much at a loss how to proceed in discussing this branch of the subject, and hardly knows what departures from undoubted health and vigor should be considered worthy of the title of disease. Nor is it easy to trace the causes of the conditions that are generally viewed in the light of maladies. We find the manifestations both in the tree or plant, and in its several parts, and also in the products which chiefly interest us; the fruits themselves, are often deteriorated by what is called diseased action of different kinds. The analogy to diseases of animals is certainly not very distinct. We do not find anything like fevers, or gout, or rheumatism, in plants, but we may consider some of their conditions somewhat in the light of dropsies, and plethora or hypertrophy on the one hand, and of anæmia or atrophy upon the other; we may consider canker and the death of some parts of a plant analogous to gangrene, and mortification in the animal subject. Then again we find congenital defects in individuals among plants, just as we do among animals. Some are always less vigorous than others, and thus certain varieties seem possessed of a degree of inherent disease that perpetually prevents them from displaying the requisite strength and vigor which we so much desire in our plantations. Certain varieties that, from the size and excellence of their fruits, have attracted the attention of pomologists, are so deficient in health and vigor as to be

considered diseased, and are therefore very properly condemned as unworthy a place in our orchards and gardens;
others appear simply deficient in the production of some
one part, as is illustrated by the inferior strength of the
woody fibres of some trees, which break easily under the
weight of their own fruit, and thus destroy the symmetry
of the tree and diminish its productiveness. Others have
defective foliage, which is attended by the imperfect performance of the functions of growth, both in the fruit and
in the sustaining woody fibres; others again produce defective blossoms with either a redundancy or deficiency of
the parts that are necessary for the production of the
seeds needed for the perpetuation of the species. When
the parts are deficient, the flowers are called barren or infertile. A redundancy or multiplication of parts is seen in
double flowers of our gardens, where they are much prized
for their beauty, though considered monstrosities by the
botanist, and perhaps properly referred to diseased action
by the nosologist. .

It is evident, that very often the conditions of a plant
and its products, which we most highly prize, and towards
which all our efforts in its culture are directed, are really
departures from the natural and healthful status; in other
words, what we covet, is really a state of diseased and
abnormal action. With the other secondary objects of
occupying and ornamenting the barren wastes of the earth
with plants, and thus supplying food to hosts of insects,
and to the higher animals, nature also has primarily in
view, the production of perfect seeds for the perpetuation
of their species, by the plants that are profusely scattered
over the globe. Man, on the contrary, often rejects the

true seeds as worthless when compared to their juicy
fleshy envelopes that constitute his favorite fruits, or the
enlarged and succulent roots, tubers, stalks, and leaves,
that characterize his garden vegetables and field crops;
while in the grains proper he seeks sustenance in the true
seeds, which become the object of his greatest care and
ingenuity to enlarge, to increase, and to develope, particularly in regard to their nutritive qualities.

Most writers upon the diseases of plants have given us
very indistinct notions upon the subject, and have done
very little to enlighten their readers; while they have
written voluminously upon the unhealthy and unsatisfactory condition of certain vegetables, and have given us
most extensive accounts of the treatment by which they
propose to remedy the evils complained of, we gather little of the information needed to enable us to understand
the true state of the case, or of the causes of the disease,
if it is to be considered such. The reader need not expect
that he will be more enlightened by this chapter than he
has been by the essays to which reference is here made,
but he will be led to a consideration of some of the causes
of those departures from health and vigor which are considered diseased action, and in this way he may possibly
be put upon the track which will lead him to the avoid-
ance of disastrous results. More than this will not be attempted.

Perhaps the most satisfactory account of diseases of
plants is that given by Lankester, in which he divides
them according to their causes, as follows:

1st—Those produced by changes in the external conditions of life, such as redundancy or deficiency of the in-

gredients of soil, of light, of heat, air, and moisture.

2d—Those produced by poisonous agencies, as by injurious gases, miasmata in the air, or by poisons in the soil.

3d—Those arising from the growth of parasitic plants, such as the various Fungi, Dodder, Mistletoe, etc.

4th—Such as are caused by mechanical injuries or wounds, and by the attacks of insects.

These may be considered separately: 1st—It may be assumed, and has been already well established by botanists, that every plant has its own peculiar constitution, adapting it to certain atmospheric conditions, and that for its healthful and successful culture, these must be understood and adhered to, within comparatively narrow limits. Tropical plants, as is well known, cannot be cultivated beyond their natural limits, except under circumstances where their natural conditions are nearly imitated by the gardener; and even in our stoves and hot-houses, these plants do not compare in vigor with their fellows that luxuriate in the hot and steaming atmosphere of the tropics, under the stronger light of such a clime as is natural to them. On the contrary, the plants of northern latitudes will not grow and produce seeds where temperature is too elevated. Those from a humid atmosphere suffer in an arid clime, and those which thrive in dry sandy regions suffer equally when introduced into a humid atmosphere.

Thus we find, that where there is too much moisture for some of our cultivated plants, they are inclined to be too succulent, and this very excess may produce a dropsical condition that is really a state of disease. Thus we suffer in a loss of fruit, which will fall badly before its period of maturity, and that which remains its full time is found to be thin and watery, deficient in the high spicy aromatic flavor which is so highly appreciated by the connoisseur of these choice products. When, on the other hand, the arid character of the soil and climate prevail to an extent that is uncongenial to any particular fruit, we shall find that its growth is arrested, and that its highest qualities are not adequately developed: this is frequently observed in an unusually dry season — and in California, where irrigation is required to enable the orchardist to produce some of the succulent fruits, the most remarkable size and beauty have been attained, but we are told that it was often at the expense of the desired flavor that the same varieties acquire, under circumstances more advantageous to the development of their superior qualities.

So in many of our fruits, the successful results depend upon the hygrometric condition of the atmosphere, and Liebig suggests that a very prolific source of diseased action in plants, arises from the suppressed evaporation and transpiration consequent upon such atmospheric conditions.

Too much moisture prevailing at the time of the blossoming of our fruits, especially moisture precipitated in the form of rain during this period, is sometimes disastrous to our crops, both of cereals and of orchard fruits. Continuous showers prevent the development of the pollengrains, and their transfer to the stigmas of the blossoms, so that the fruit does not set well. Fortunately this does not often occur in our glorious climate, which is so highly favored by an abundance of light and sunshine, which are the great and essential stimuli of the higher orders of plants. The loss of our fruit crops in some parts of the Ohio Valley in the years 1862, 1865, and 1866, was fairly attributed to this cause.

We must not overlook the unhealthy influences produced by an excess of moisture in the earth. Many plants that naturally delight in a dry porous soil, become weak, unfruitful, or even seriously diseased when they are planted in low wet grounds, or upon such as are underlaid by a very tenacious sub-soil, while an opposite condition is equally unfavorably to those that are naturally more aquatic in their tastes and habits. In the former case we learn to avoid such soils and situations, unless we are able to change their character in this respect by thorough under-draining, which will completely remove the evil, and the remedy becomes merely a question of expense.

A certain amount of temperature may be assumed as requisite to every plant, or rather it may be affirmed that some plants cannot exist and thrive except within a certain range, and it has been asserted that each class of plants requires a mean temperature for the year that shall not vary many degrees: the range of this variation has perhaps never been satisfactorily ascertained. But it is well known, that both heat and frost act injuriously upon vegetation. Mr. Lindley tells us that "the extreme limits of temperature which vegetables are capable of bearing, without destruction of their vitality, have not been determined with precision." When the temperature is maintained at a higher point than is natural, the plant is excited to undue activity of growth; but this is attended with an enfeebled condition, often seen in badly managed green-houses. Mr. Knight found that certain plants were rendered abortive by the production of male flowers only, when exposed to too great heat, and by an opposite treatment, when subjected to a low temperature for a long time, others produced only female flowers. In some plants a high degree of heat, with moisture, results in the production of leaves only, and Humboldt found that wheat was grown about Xalapa, Mexico, as a fodder plant, because it produced an abundance of grass, but did not form ears nor grain.

A diminished temperature, on the contrary, removes the stimulus of growth, and leads to the suspension of all vital action in proportion to its reduction. At the freezing point it is probable that all such action ceases, though in this regard there is great difference among plants; the mosses and lichens w ll flourish, and the Chickweed will vegetate and blossom at a temperature very little above freezing. The access of frost, after vegetation has somewhat advanced, often proves very disastrous, and we not unfrequently lose our crops of fruit by such an occurrence during the period of blossoming, or even afterward.

Some plants in a dormant condition, will endure uninjured a great depression of temperature, while others will be destroyed by the slightest approach of frost. According to De Candolle, this may depend upon the greater or less amount of water they contain, upon the greater or less viscidity of their fluids, or the rapidity with which these fluids circulate. Those with larger cells he thinks most easily injured by frost, and those which contain a great deal of air are able to resist it best. The freezing point will vary according to the quality of the sap, for we know that different vegetable juices congeal at different

temperatures. The manner in which cold acts upon plants
depends upon their physical structure. Lindley says,
freezing is attended with the following effects: — The
fluids contained within the cells of tissue are congealed
and expanded—this produces a laceration of the cell-walls,
and impairs excitability by the unnatural extension to
which the cells are subjected; the air is expelled from the
air-vessels and introduced into parts naturally intended to
contain only fluid; the green coloring matter and other
secretions are decomposed, and the vital fluid or latex is
destroyed, and the action of its vessels is paralyzed. The
interior of the tubes, in which fluid is conveyed, is ob-
structed by a thickening of their sides. So we have as a
result, both mechanical, chemical, and vital changes.[*]

Our hardy fruit trees are woody perennials that hybernate during the winter. Yet we find that even these suffer upon some occasions from a great depression of temperature; it has been asserted that a certain degree of
cold would inevitably destroy the blossom buds at least,
and we often find that the bark is burst off from the wood,
and in some instances the wood itself is so injured as to
suffer from a kind of decomposition, and to become affected with a change generally known as the dry rot, losing
its elasticity and hardness, and acquiring a whitish color,
which is supposed may arise from the introduction of the
mycelia of fungous growths. Now it is believed that
these injuries do not arise so directly from the degree of
cold to which the tree has been exposed, as to the condition of its circulation at the time of the exposure. If the

---

[*] Trans. Horticultural Society, London, Vol. II. p. 308; and Am. Journal of
Science and Arts, March, 1840.

sap have been excited by mild or warm weather, as is so apt to be the case in our changeable climate, the sudden depression of temperature will produce disastrous effects, even when the cold has not been very severe. This is manifested by the bursting of the bark in young trees in the early part of winter, while they are yet holding their leaves, and of course having a circulation somewhat active. Hence the importance, now very well understood by our nurserymen, of checking the growth of young trees in time to have their terminal buds thoroughly ripened before the approach of frost. This, to a certain extent, is subject to our control; but we cannot foresee the character of the seasons upon which the safety of our orchard trees will, in a great measure, depend, and they are less easily managed. When the autumn is dry, and continued late into winter, as sometimes happens, we see a perfect ripening of the wood, with a great development of blossom buds, and then we may confidently calculate upon the safety of our fruits, provided they be not exposed to a warm period at mid-winter, that shall excite some activity in their circulation, which would suffer terribly from any sudden and great depression of temperature such as frequently occurs, carrying the mercury from summer heat to a point below zero, in a few hours. Such a change has amounted to 68 degrees in nine hours.*

The influence exerted by the soil upon the healthiness or unhealthiness of our trees has already been alluded to incidentally, but it is an important subject of inquiry whether this may arise from a redundancy or a paucity of some particular ingredients necessary to sustain the plants

---

* Trans. Cincinnati Horticultural Society, 1805.

we desire to cultivate.   Liebig has pointed out how chemistry may be brought to our assistance in solving such a question.   As all the inorganic elements found in a tree and its fruits, must have been derived from the soil in which it grew, he suggested that the ashes of the plant would show us exactly what it needed, and then an examination of the soils would inform us whether they contained all the necessary elements, and in the right proportion. Hence arose the doctrine and the practice of applying special manures, which has been so fashionable in our day. Though there be many doubters as to the efficacy of such investigations and practices, most sensible and enlightened agriculturists admit the truths which Liebig has propounded.

Light is the great stimulus of vegetation, an essential element to its existence: its withdrawal is followed by an arrest of some of the most important functions of vitality, and yet we find that there is a great difference among different species, as to their requirements of this element, and also that various parts and several products of vegetation require very different degrees of light for their perfection.   It is also found that a sudden exposure of parts from which it had been withheld, is often attended with disastrous consequences.   Its withdrawal does not so immediately destroy the plant, being attended with the etiolation of the parts that are usually colored, but a sudden re-exposure to the sun's rays will now destroy the plant. So the removal of a portion of the foliage from a tree, or the exposure of the bare stem of one that had been previously sheltered, is often attended with severe effects, known as sun-scald—for which there is no remedy, but very easy modes of prevention. The best of these is to provide against the evil by reserving the lower branches to shade the stem. There are other excellent reasons for this practice, which will be brought forward in the chapter on Pruning.

Frequently, however, the nurseryman, or perhaps the injudicious efforts of the planter himself, may have removed all the side branches of the young tree, and as these cannot be replaced, we may substitute for them a shelter from the scorching sun to which the newly planted tree is exposed. This may be done by tacking two narrow boards together at their edges, like a gutter spout, and setting them upright on the south side of the tree to shade it. A wisp of straw, tied loosely to the stem, will answer a very good purpose; but both of these appliances are objectionable, because they furnish a shelter for insects, and thus they fall short of the natural shading of the stem by the foliage of its own branches.

It is not only the scorching suns of summer that damage our young trees that are thus exposed by injudicious trimming. Even the bright rays of a mid-winter sun, falling upon the frozen stem, will often effect the most serious damage, and should be guarded against with equal care; but here the natural protection will answer, for the shade of the naked spray of the laterals is found all-sufficient in the well-trained tree.

2d—To resume the consideration of Lankester's causes of disease, it must be admitted that some diseased conditions may be produced by poisonous gases, but the usual result will be the death of plants confined in such an atmosphere. The natural power of diffusion of all gases among one another in the open air, prevents the danger that would ensue in a confined situation. The accidental production of sulphurous and other poisonous gas, or the escape of smoke from the flues, or from the tobacco-pan in the green-house, sometimes produces the most disastrous effects upon the plants subjected to their action. So, in crowded cities, it often happens that the effects of coal smoke and other gases, generated in the furnaces and manufactories, are very injurious to vegetation. The coal soot falls in flakes like lamp-black, which covers the surface and obstructs the transpiration of the stomata, and thus seriously affects the health of plants in such situations.

The action of *miasmata*, suggested by Lankester, is as obscure in the effects produced upon plants as in those upon animals. The presence of these atmospheric conditions cannot be detected by any of our tests, nor can their effects be prevented by any means in our power; we know little or nothing about their characters, yet we cannot deny their existence: finally, they serve as a very convenient explanation, though a very unsatisfactory one, for the incursions of maladies that are of an obscure or unknown character. Whether of a miasmatic nature or not, no one can deny the existence of certain atmospheric conditions, which appear to produce disastrous effects upon some of our vegetable productions whether these be inherent to the air itself, or are only conveyed by it from one place to another. The inexplicable potato disease may owe its origin and diffusion to such a cause, and the grape malady, which appears to be dependent upon atmospheric causes, may at least be carried from one vine to another upon this medium, in the form of the minute spores or seeds of the fungi that are believed to be the cause of the trouble.*

Poisons in the soil are frequently very deleterious to vegetation, and we often find extensive injuries to our plants produced by this class of agents. When these are of a chemical nature, as is usually the case, they may be satisfactorily treated by applications that will neutralize their effects. In cities the escape of the illuminating gas, that is carried in subterranean pipes, has often so poisoned the soil as to destroy the shade trees by the side of the streets.

An excess of certain saline and alkaline ingredients often produces barrenness in the soil, by a sort of poisoning, even with those articles that in smaller quantities are used as manures with the happiest effects.

3d—The influence exerted upon vegetation by the growth of parasitic plants, cannot be observed without forcing us to the conclusion that they are prejudicial to the health of the plants they infest—since they either cover and smother the foliage by twining upon it, as is the case with the Dodder; or fasten themselves upon a limb, appropriating the sap that was intended for its support, and thus starve it, as does the Mistletoe; or attaching themselves to the bark, they interfere with its functions, as is done by the lichens and mosses; or, following the descending scale, in the size of these parasites, but meeting in them foes of much greater importance, we find the minute but innumerable fungi attacking the wood, the bark, the foliage, and the fruits, of our gardens and orchards, and committing incalculable damage—thus entailing serious

---

* Cincinnati Hort. Soc. Report.

disease. A very important question has arisen, however, as to whether the inroads of fungi were the cause or the consequence only of disease. A question which it will be necessary to leave to wiser heads, only observing that these epiphytes do appear, under certain atmospheric conditions, to invade some plants that had previously seemed to be in perfect health. That they are transported upon the air, in the form of very minute sporules, is unquestioned, and that their growth is dependent upon certain atmospheric conditions, is equally admitted, but whether they induce disease, or are only able to take possession of a plant that is not in a perfectly healthy condition, does not yet appear so clear. The very eminent Mr. Solly is of the opinion, that in the potato at least, the existence of parasitic fungi is a secondary result of previous disease. So it may be with our fruits, and there is considerable testimony to favor such a belief in many cases, where we find, with the appearance of these fungi, other causes of unhealthiness.

The leaves of the apple trees in some seasons become coated with a black efflorescence, that gives the tree a very sombre appearance, and seems to affect its health. I am not aware that any one has yet made any microscopical investigations of this condition of the foliage, which looks as though it were dusted with coal-smoke. It has been supposed, however, to be the result of a fungous growth.

Pear Blight.—This is a subject upon which so much has been said and written, that any one may well shrink from its discussion. The condition in which the invasion of the malady finds the tree has been pretty thoroughly ascertained, and the sad state in which it is left after the attack, is too well known to need any learned description. It is well called *the blight*, for nothing short of scorching by fire can more effectually destroy the life of the tree and blight our hopes of its usefulness. The varied theories and suggestions that have been advanced in attempted explanation of this state of things are altogether unsatisfactorn, so that it may be said we know nothing about the disease, nor whether it be occasioned by frozen sap, by fungous invasion, or by insect attacks, all of which have been set forward as causes of the difficulty. None of these explanations have been clearly proved, and they seem rather guesses than established facts in the history of the disease, which breaks out in the midst of the season of growth, and attacks those trees that are in the midst of the most vigorous production of succulent shoots; but it is not confined to the young wood; on the contrary, it appears first in the hard bark of limbs, that are two or more years old. This turns brown, becomes desiccated, and thus the circulation is arrested, and the foliage as well as the bark is affected. The outer extremities of the leaves wilt, die, and turn suddenly brown and then black, and often remain adhering by their petioles for months—sad testimonials of the destruction caused by the blight. The disease appears to extend in some instances, but it is not proved that there is any poisonous matter generated by a blighted limb that could have entered the circulation, and then have been transmitted to other parts of the tree. The apparent extension of the disease is rather believed to have been the successive development of the trouble from different foci, which had successively invaded so much of the bark as to have more or less completely arrested the flow of the sap. In some limbs of small size, a patch of dead tis sue of moderate dimensions would entirely arrest healthy action early in the season, and destroy the portion of the branch beyond it; in other branches of greater size, quite a large patch of the dead bark might exist for a long time without entirely surrounding them, and arresting the circulation, which would thus be kept up until a later period, when at length this occurred, the symptoms of blight would appear.

The treatment of this malady is quite unsatisfactory, and gives us no clue to the cause of the trouble. Various plans have been suggested, the most satisfactory is the removal of the affected limbs—not that it cures the disease, but because it takes from us the sad mementos of our loss. We have been advised to pare away the diseased portion of old bark with a spoke-shave, or some similar instrument; but it is apprehended that few persons would ever find this patch of dead bark until they have the fatal evidence of the blighted foliage, and no possible good can result from its removal at that time.

This trouble is connected, in many instances, with an excessively vigorous growth of shoots; indeed, some of those varieties which are most thrifty, suffer the most, while those which make firm and moderately short shoots, seldom blight. Hence it has been inferred by some, that if we can check this excessive vigor, and reduce the wood growth to a moderate amount, not exceeding ten or twelve inches, annual extension, we shall be able to prevent the occurrence of blight. This object is easily attained by root-pruning the trees severely in the spring of the year. So far, we can only say that trees so treated, have not blighted; but it does not follow that they would have suffered if let alone.

Another form of blight may often be seen in the peach and in the apple; it consists in a loss of vitality of small twigs and their foliage in several parts of the tree, especially in the inner portions that are not freely exposed to the air and light. In the peach, this disease is accompanied with the decay of the fruit upon these twigs, which rots and becomes moldy. This trouble is usually attributed to mildew, and it is probably owing to some form of fungus invasion.

Quite a different affection of the twigs is that known as the "blight" in apples and quinces. This attacks only the young shoots of the current season's growth, which suddenly wither and become brown at mid-summer. The same condition occurs also in the shoots of the Italian mulberry. The cause of this malady is not very apparent; by some persons it is attributed to the punctures of minute insects, but they have escaped the scrutiny of other observers, who attribute this blight to atmospheric causes.

The true apple blight is a malady of very serious character, that invades many orchards in the Western States. In its nature, and in the mode of its invasion, it very much resembles the dreaded fire-blight of the pear, with which most orchardists have unfortunately become already but too familiar. Like it too, all the guesses which Solons have offered for the explanation of its cause, appear equally unsatisfactory.

A whole branch or limb of the tree becomes simultaneously affected; sometimes one quarter or even one half of the top is destroyed by the disease, and the removal of

8*

the dead portions is not followed by the reproduction of healthy branches. Certain varieties are more subject to this blight than others, and they seem to poison the grafts that are inserted into them, to produce a new top to the tree with a more healthy variety.

BITTER ROT.—Our excellent and observing friend, H. N. Gillett, of Lawrence Co., Ohio, furnishes the following description of this disease to the Ohio Cultivator:

"The disease generally presents itself on the skin of the apple in very minute brown spots, from one to a dozen or more in number, generally after the fruit is pretty well grown. These gradually spread and penetrate the flesh of the apple, producing a black rot, almost as bitter as aloes, but this taste is confined to the discolored portion. The fruit ceases growing, and falls prematurely. The rot occasionally begins at the center, and extends outward, so that the fruit appears perfectly sound for some time," on which account he advises against too early gathering of the fruit.

The late Dr. Barker, of McConnellsville, Ohio, who was one of our most observing pomologists, referring to this disease as peculiar to certain varieties, concludes in an article in the paper above quoted, vide Vol. VI, p. 283, that this malady is different from what is called Bitter Rot in other places, and which affects other varieties with a discoloration of the flesh and a bitter taste. He thinks this malady is different from that described by Mr. Gillett, and that it, the true Bitter Rot, is caused by a fungous growth, the spores of which are carried on the air from tree to tree, like a similar fungus producing mold in the cherry, plum, and peach. He also traces a resemblance of this disease to the vaccination in the human subject, except that the scab does not separate and fall off. Hence he suggested the name of *pock*, instead of *Bitter Rot.* High culture, manure, lime, trimming, and pasturing hogs in the orchard, have all been recommended as remedies.

CRACKED FRUIT—MILDEW.—Certain fruits become partially covered with what appears to be a fungous growth, which occupies the skin in such a manner as to prevent the development of the succulent tissues beneath it. This may result in a deformity consequent upon the irregular growth, and the fruit is called scabby, or it may strike deeper into the tissues, which become dry and corky and crack open, being thus utterly worthless. Some varieties, which formerly produced the most beautiful fruits, have been so severely affected by this malady as to yield absolutely nothing in certain localities, and are only rendered profitable by top grafting with other sorts that are not affected with the cracking. That this is not caused by the wearing out of the variety, as has been suggested, it may be added that the same fruit ripens perfectly and is quite fair in other regions of the country. The trouble, however, is extending, and it is hardly safe to plant largely of those varieties that have proved subject to the malady. No explanation has been satisfactory as to the cause, nor has any treatment been successful.

Dr. Kirtland addressed the Ohio Pomological Society upon this subject, and an abstract of his remarks is here given:—

"The disease known as the blight or the fire-blight, is at this day proving the most serious obstacle to the successful cultivation of the pear, in many sections of the country. Early in the present century it prevailed extensively in New England, coincidently with the spotted fever, and other disorders of a low grade of action, which at that period swept epidemically over that region of the country. It was a popular opinion that all these diseases, both of the human family and vegetable kingdom, arose from one cause; — an opinion not, however, tolerated by medical men and men of science in that day.

"Various theories have been advanced to account for the origin of this blight. Insects, frozen sap, electricity, excessive evaporation, and exhaustion of the soil, have, at different times, been assigned as the cause. Investigation of each fails to meet and explain the phenomena attendant on the rise, progress, and results of that disease. It is time they all should be abandoned, and that researches for a cause be extended in some other direction.

"As a starting point in this undertaking, I will suggest another hypothesis, which may perhaps explain the pathology of the blight, and call into use an effectual remedy or preventive. *Pathology*, Dr. Webster defines to be 'the doctrine of the causes and nature of diseases.'

"1. The Pear-tree blight is produced by the poisonous impression of the seeds (*sporules*) of a microscopic fungus.

"2. Several combinations of iron, especially the sulphate (*copperas*), will, to some extent, counteract that impression.

"It will be understood that these two propositions are merely hypothetical. If sustained by analogies, subsequent observations, and experience, they will be accepted as truths; if not thus sustained, they will of course be rejected.

"The extensive prevalence of the cholera, over large portions of the globe, commencing in the year 1818, led medical men to seek for its cause. Dr. Cowdell, of London, in 1848, published 'A Disquisition on Pestilential Cholera, being an attempt to explain its phenomena, nature, cause, prevention and treatment, by reference to an extrinsic fungous origin.'

"In 1849, Prof. J. K. Mitchell, of Philadelphia, issued a more elaborate work, 'On the Cryptogamous Origin of Malarious and Epidemic Fevers.' It abounds in numerous facts and correct reasoning, and should be consulted by every investigator of disease, animal and vegetable.

"These publications attracted the attention of the medical profession, both in America and Europe, so long as that epidemic continued its ravages, and the theories they advanced gained extensive credence during that time. They were, however, lost sight of when that epidemic subsided. Recently they have been substantiated as plain matters of fact, so far as malarious diseases are concerned, by the labors and investigations of Prof. J. H. Salisbury, of Cleveland.

"It is well established, then, that a number of diseases of the animal system are produced by fungi. 'Under this name botanists comprehend not only the various races of mushrooms, toadstools, and similar productions, but a large number of microscopic plants, forming the appearances called mouldiness, mildew, smut, rust, brand, dry rot, etc.' They are universally diffused in nature. It is difficult to conceive of a place where they do not exist. They are among the most numerous of all plants, in regard to genera and species, and with very few exceptions are deleterious in their impressions on the animal system. Even the palatable mushroom is always poisonous to some persons, and may become so to all under certain circumstances. It is equally evident that fungi frequently occasion diseases in the vegetable kingdom. The smut of wheat and maize, the rust of wheat, ergot of rye and grass-seeds, and specks, cracks, and discoloration of the skin of the apple and pear are of this nature.

"The microscopical examinations of Prof. Salisbury and others have detected the presence of certain species, infesting extensively pear trees about the period of attack by the blight. They have made similar discoveries that lead to the conclusion that the curl of the peach leaf, the potato disease, and the blight of pear trees, all have their origin from the cause assigned in my second proposition.

"Under this head still another disease of our fruit should be noticed. I have watched carefully the sudden and premature decay of our plum crop, at the period of its ripening, for the last fifteen years. From hints afforded by the work of Prof. Mitchell, and several microscopic observations of my own, I was induced to publish an article in 'The Florist,' of Philadelphia, in the year 1855, in which I imputed the origin of the disease to the Torula or some analagous species of parasitic fungi. The disease still prevails among us, and it is sure to destroy all the plums which escape puncture by the curculio. It is, however, generally overlooked by pomologists, and its effects are charged to the depredations of that insect. Similar disease occasionally impairs our peach and apple crops, to a less extent. Whenever it occurs on either of these varieties of fruit, the spurs and young wood blight or canker, and cease to be fruitful for several years

"If these discoveries and analogies establish, with any degree of certainty, the hypothesis of the cryptogamous origin of the pear tree blight, we have made important progress in laying down true indications for its cure or prevention. Among the means suggested for effecting that end, certain combinations of iron have already been named. The authority for such practice is founded on the following facts:

"1. It is a popular belief that iron exerts a favorable influence over the health of fruit trees. Hence arises the practice of driving nails into the body of such trees, and loading their limbs with scraps of iron. Both the belief and the practice may be visionary, yet in such instances of popular belief, investigation usually discovers them to be founded on some shadow of truth.

"2. An intelligent and observing gentleman of Cleveland informs me that he prevents the curl of the peach leaf by depositing in the earth, about the bodies of the trees, fragments of rusty stove pipe and worthless pieces of iron.

"3. Twenty-four years since I called the attention of the public to the isolated fact, without reference to any theory, that a large pear tree in Columbiana county, Ohio, with its body surrounded with many wagon loads of boulders, scoria, scales of iron and accumulations from a blacksmith shop, retained its health, vigor, and fruitfulness, while all other pear trees in that region of country had either died, or were suffering from blight. *Vide* New England Farmer, December 3, 1840, page 153. At this late day this tree still continues healthy.

"4. I recollect reading in that reliable journal, Hovey's Magazine of Horticulture, some years since, a statement that the finest prize pears seen in the Parisian market, were produced by investing the growing fruits with folds of cotton or linen cloth, and daily, or oftener, moistening them with a solution of sulphate of iron. This treatment was said to result in developing the size, beauty, and quality of the fruits to a high degree, and especially to free them from parasitic blotches.

"5. Four years since, Mrs. Weller Dean, of Rockport, Ohio, informed me that blight might not only be prevented in healthy pear trees, but might be successfully arrested, in many trees, after it had made considerable progress, by means of repeatedly washing the bodies of the trees with a saturated solution of sulphate of iron (copperas), at a time when the sap is in active circulation.

"This was a confidential communication, with the condition annexed that I should thoroughly test the plan, and if it should prove successful, I was to publish it; and furthermore, if any merit or more substantial reward should be deemed due to any one by the public, she was to be the recipient.

"This plan has yet been only imperfectly tried. Age and infirmities will probably prevent its completion by me. I will therefore report that I have tested it on a number of my partially blighted pear trees, while a greater numbers has been left to die unmedicated. Of the former, not one has yet perished, while of the latter very few survive. It has appeared, in every instance, to arrest the progress of the disease, and to impart a healthy condition to the bark wherever applied. The apparent results may have been coincidences and not the effect of the remedy. There is much false experience in horticulture and agriculture, as well as in medicine.

"These views suggest the expediency of extensively applying a solution of the sulphate of iron by means of a green-house syringe or garden engine to the tops and foliage of trees, laboring under any of the diseases suspected of a cryptogamous origin. It also becomes a query whether the same agent may not be successfully employed at some period to counteract the potato disease, either by watering with it the growing plant, or washing the tubers in it in autumn, after they are dug. No injury has ever arisen to pear trees by a free use of a *saturated* solution of copperas.

"In conclusion, I would observe that the discovery of the cryptogamous origin of the many disorders of the human system is effecting important changes in their treatment. May we not hope that an extension of these discoveries to the vegetable kingdom, may result as favorably in shaping the practice in diseases of fruits and fruit trees?"

4th—Wounds, and the attacks of insects, may be considered more in the light of mechanical injuries by a loss of substance, hence they belong rather to the department of surgery, and can scarcely be considered as disease. The breaking of a branch, or the removal of a portion of the bark, may inflict a serious injury, but it is one which, under ordinary circumstances, will be recovered from, without any impairment of the health of the tree—unless where the wound is so large that the new growth will not soon cover it over, in which case exposure to the moisture of the atmosphere may result in decay of the woody tissues, or, if the sap exudes, at certain seasons, it may produce canker and fungous growths. In some varieties of our cultivated fruits, wounds of this character are often attended by an effusion of gummy matter; this is particularly the case with those that are known as stone-fruits, and in these the excision of a large limb is seldom followed by a deposit of woody matter in the way of healing over the wound, which is always desirable; hence in such cases particularly, it is well to cover the exposed surface with something to exclude atmospheric moisture, whether this be paint, varnish of shellac, or common grafting wax.

Insects, by eating the foliage extensively, very materially injure the healthy condition of a tree — even the minute aphides that suck the sap from the leaves and tender bark, will seriously impair the health of our plants; but the borers that mine under the bark, extensively consuming the vital cambium, and even burrow into the solid wood, reducing it to a honeycomb, cannot fail to affect the healthy condition of the tree materially, and often cause its premature death. Some knowledge of the habits of these little creatures is considered of so great importance, that the subject will be brought before the reader's notice more at length in another part of this volume.

There is no doubt, however, that many unhealthy conditions of our trees, that might be traced to other causes, but which are not manifestly dependent upon a want of care on the part of the orchardist, nor upon a deficiency in the constitution of the soil, are often attributable to the inroads of these minute foes, which, in some cases at least, are made the scape-goats upon which is laid the blame that should be applied to our own neglect, or want of forethought and care.

After having reviewed the whole subject, it may be safe for us to conclude that what is called disease in our cultivated vegetables of whatever kind, is a departure from full health and productiveness of sound fruits. And further that this may arise from a lack of the necessary ingredients in the soil, from a want of proper conditions as to its quality and constitution, particularly with regard to the important elements of moisture, heat, and light; and especially, that this condition of unhealthiness and unproductiveness, when not an inherent failing of the variety, may in many instances be attributable to want of proper care on our part, and to our allowing the trees to injure themselves by overbearing, while we neglect to keep up the proper supply of nourishment.

In making selections of trees for planting, it is important that all weak or unhealthy varieties should be avoided. Secure healthy and vigorous stocks, that appear to be possessed of a sound constitution, even though the fruit should not be quite so fine and beautiful as that produced by some of the sickly and less vigorous varieties. There is more difference apparent, in this respect, among pears than among apples; but of the latter there are varieties that should be avoided on account of their deficient vigor. There are others that might be considered as coming under the ban, because the trees are not long-lived; and yet some of these appear to be perfectly healthy in every other respect, and seem literally to wear themselves out by excessive bearing, producing annual crops of large and

handsome fruit, until, utterly exhausted, they reach a pro
mature end.

Some varieties, that for many years yielded very fine
crops of the most beautiful fruit, and of the highest character for flavor, have afterward ceased to furnish any perfect specimens — the whole crop being covered and deformed with the black scab or fungus, that prevents their
development, or else ruined by the disagreeable bitter-rot
which entirely spoils them for any use. Various remedies
have been suggested for these maladies, all of which are
more or less unsatisfactory, because from our ignorance of
the causes of the troubles; these applications are wholly
empirical.

The Black-knot, which has become very common in
some parts of the country, is well discussed by Benjamin
D. Walsh, in the Practical Entomologist, for March, 1866,
page 48.

This essay is the more valuable because of the absence
of the empiricism just complained of: —

" It is a black, puffy, irregular swelling on the twigs and
smaller limbs of plum and cherry trees, and, in one instance that came under my personal observation of peach
trees, making its first appearance in the latitude of New
York early in June, and attaining its full growth by the
end of July. Usually a tree, that is attacked in this manner, is affected worse and worse every year, until it is
finally killed; and wherever one tree of a group is affected, the malady usually spreads to them all in process of
time. In 1865 whole cherry orchards were destroyed in
Western New York by this disease, and I have myself seen
many groups of wild plum trees in Illinois that were gradu-

ally perishing by it; but in Southern Ohio, as I am told, the Black-knot is never met with. In the Eastern States it has been observed from time immemorial, and various contradictory opinions have been broached as to its real nature and origin.

"In 1865 I watched the Black-knot carefully through all its stages, from its earliest commencement to its complete maturity, experimenting at the same time on numerous specimens collected week after week, so as to ascertain what insects bred in it. The practical conclusion I have arrived at, is simply this:—*If the diseased twigs are all cut off and destroyed early in July in the latitude of New York, or a little earlier or later according to the latitude, taking care to cut a few inches below the affected part, the Black-knot can be checked and probably entirely eradicated; but if this operation is delayed till August, it will be of no benefit whatever.* Hence we can easily account for a circumstance which has puzzled many men wonderfully, viz.: That cutting off and burning the diseased twigs is pronounced by some to be a sovereign remedy, and by others to be a delusive humbug. Those that do this early enough, find it effectual; those that delay it till too late, find it of no use.

"This perhaps will be sufficient for some few impatient souls, who take everything upon trust that they see in print, and care nothing about the *rationale* of a mode of treatment, so long as it be practically available. But for the benefit of that large class of intelligent agriculturists, who have been deluded by too many quack prescriptions to place much faith in any man's *ipse dixit*, and who in any case like to understand the principle of a remedy before they apply it, I subjoin a full account of all that is at present known on this subject, and of the different theories respecting it entertained by different writers.

"Three radically different theories have been broached as to the nature and origin of Black-knot: 1st, that it is a mere disease of the tree, like the cancer or the gout in the human race, which is the view maintained by Dr. Fitch, the State Entomologist of New York; 2d, that it is what naturalists term a "gall," produced by some unknown insect depositing its eggs in the twig —just as the well-known "oak-apples" are produced by a Gall-fly, (*Cynips*), depositing its egg in the bud of the oak — which is the opinion that I myself formerly held and maintained, before I had fully examined into the subject; (*Proceedings Ent. Soc., Phil.*, III, p.p. 613–618;) and 3d, that it is what botanists term an epiphytous fungus, growing on the tree as a mushroom or toad-stool grows on the ground, which is the opinion of the botanist Schweinitz, and which has recently been re-asserted by Mr. Glover, the Entomologist of the Bureau of Agriculture at Washington, (*Ag'l Rep.*, 1863, p. 572.) This last is the opinion which, upon full inquiry, I have now adopted.

"Before discussing these theories, the facts arrived at by myself in the summer of 1865, must first be briefly noticed. It should be premised that the old, dry Black-knot remains on the tree for many years, and that the place to look for the new Black-knot is on such trees as have been already attacked and are loaded with old Black-knot, without being as yet completely killed by it.

"1st. By the middle of June the new Black-knot is pretty well developed, and may then be readily distinguished from the old by its dull, opaque, brown-black color, while the old is coal-black and more or less glossy. When cut into, it is found to be fleshy inside, like an apple, but not juicy, and of a pale greenish-yellow color, with fibres radiating from the axis of the twig, while the old Black-knot is internally hard and woody, and of a reddish-brown or rust-red color. The brown-black color of the external surface is retained till the last week in July, when the surface of the new Black-knot becomes gradually covered all over with little, coal-black, hemispherical plates, appearing when viewed through a pocket glass, about the size of the head of a pin, each of these is a distinct fungus, named long ago by Schweinitz '*Sphæria morbosa.*' Even on the old Black-knot this fungus may be readily seen, at any time of the year, covering its entire surface. So far I have added little to the information already published on this subject, except by the specification of dates. But in addition to these facts, I discovered that about the last of July or the first week in August, there grows from each fungus on the surface of the Black-knot a little cylindrical filament about one-eighth of an inch long, which no doubt bears the seed or "spores," as they are technically termed, of the fungus, and that these filaments very shortly afterwards fall off and disappear, leaving behind them the hemispherical plates, which alone had been hitherto noticed by the botanists. In another Epiphytous fungus, which grows commonly and abundantly in Illinois on the Red Cedar, but which differs from the Black-knot in being attached to the twig by a very short stalk or peduncle, and in being roundish and externally of a reddish-brown color instead of elongate and black, there is a precisely similar phenomenon; except that the plates and filaments are very much larger, and that each filament, when it falls off, leaves a ragged scar behind it. In a single specimen of Black-knot noticed August 6th, I discovered that the filaments not only covered the entire surface of the Black-knot itself, except where a few of them had already fallen off, but that they were thinly studded over the twig for an inch or two above and below the swollen black part; thus proving that the fungus sometimes extends rather further than on a cursory view it would appear to do. Towards the middle of August, the new Black-knot, having perfected its seed, gradually dries up and becomes internally of a reddish-brown color. In other words, like so many other annual plants, it dies shortly after it has perfected its seed, just as a stalk of wheat or of corn dies shortly after the grain is ripe.

"2d. During the months of June and July I collected from time to time very numerous specimens of Black-knot, some of which I cut into to see what larvæ they contained, and some I preserved to see what perfect insects could be bred from them. Besides seven specimens of the common "Curculio," which many persons had previously bred from Black-knot, I bred for the first time therefrom no less than five distinct species of insects, none of which can be considered as gall-makers, but not a single true gall-maker; and I can confirm Dr. Fitch's assertion, that some specimens are wholly free from larvæ of any kind when cut into.

"We will now take up in order the three different theories respecting the nature and origin of Black-knot, which, as already stated, have been maintained by different writers.

"1st. *That Black-knot is a mere disease like the cancer.*—Dr. Fitch, who maintains this opinion, allows that the black granules found on the Black-knot are a true fungus, 'that the surface of these excrescences, when mature, is always covered with this plant,' and that 'this plant never grows, or at least has never been found, in any other situation.' (*Address N. Y. State Ag'l Soc.*, 1860, p. 21.) * * *

"2d. *That Black-knot is a gall.*—As already stated, there is no true gall-making insect that inhabits the Black-knot, so far as I can discover on the fullest and most extensive investigation that I have been able to give to the subject. The minute holes commonly found in the old dry Black-knot, which are too large either for the 'Curculio' or for the small moths bred by myself from Black-knot, are of a suitable size for either of the two dipterous insects which I have enumerated in a note as bred by myself from Black-knot. Consequently the argument which I based upon the existence of these minute holes (*Proc. Ent. Soc. Phil.* III, p. 614) falls to the ground; and although I found on one occasion the larva of a Gall-gnat embedded in a cell in a Black-knot, yet this was most probably that of the Guest Gall-gnat which I actually bred from Black-knot, as stated in the note, and not of a true gall-making Gall-gnat.

"3d. *That Black-knot is a fungus.*—Just as Dr. Fitch, having proved to his own satisfaction that Black-knot is neither a gall nor a fungus, infers by the method of exhaustion that it must be a disease; so, having proved that

9

it is neither a disease nor a gall, we may infer by the method of exhaustion that it must be a fungus, or rather an assemblage of funguses. In confirmation of this theory may be adduced the very remarkable analogies between the structure of the Black-knot and that of the fungus, described above as occurring on Red Cedar. That this last is really and truly a fungus and not a gall, is shown by the fact, that it is scarcely ever inhabited by insects; for out of hundreds of specimens that I have cut into, both green and dry, not more than two or three contained the larvæ of the moths, but one contained what was probably the larva of an Ichneumon-fly, and all the rest were perfectly solid and unbored. On the other hand, Black-knot is so infested by insects, that it is almost impossible to find a mature specimen that is not all bored up by them. The cause of this remarkable difference may be attributed to. the well-known repugnance of almost all kinds of insects for Red Cedar.

"If, then, Black-knot is a fungus, and if, as I think I have shown, it is an annual plant propagating itself by seed or the so-called 'spores,' and the 'spores' make their appearance about the end of July in latitude 41° 30′, then it must be obvious that if all the Black-knot on a particular tree is cut off and destroyed in the fore-part of July, or a little earlier or later as you go further south or further north, an effectual stop will be put to its further propagation. It is true that the 'spores' are in the form of an impalpable powder, so that they may be carried some considerable distance from other infected trees by the wind; and it may possibly be further true, that certain 'spores' may lie dormant in the bark for over a year, as the seeds of weeds will often lie dormant in the ground. Still, with all these possible drawbacks, I have little doubt that the above remedy will, as a general rule, if applied according to directions, be found effectual."

The foregoing is interesting as giving the conclusions of an entomologist who had investigated the subject, and arrived at the same result that had been reached by a botanist many years before. Schweinitz, in 1832, published the correct history of the Black-knot in the Transactions of the American Philosophical Society. In the *American Agriculturist*, April, 1863, p. 113, Mr. C. F. Austin confirmed Schweinitz's observations, and gave a popular account of the botany of this fungus, with figures. It may be considered as fully established that the knot is of vegetable origin; and whenever insects or larvæ are found in it, it is only because they find a diseased portion of the tree suited to their necessities.

ROT AND MILDEW upon the grape both destroy our crops, and render the vines unhealthy. Would that I were able to give the reader some encouragement as to its cause and prevention, or cure; but some of our oldest and most experienced vine-planters have come to the conclusion, as to treatment, that "the more they find out, the more they don't know." It is now generally conceded that it is caused by a fungus growth. That on the leaves is probably the *Oidium Tuckeri*, and it is generally supposed that the mildew and rot of the berries is owing to the same cause. The microscope clearly indicates its fungoid character. As to the causes, it must be admitted that the weather favors or prevents its access, and that so far it is a proximate cause, but that the spores are the true origin of the trouble. The Cincinnati Horticultural Society, whose members have long had opportunities of studying this malady, have come to the following conclusions, which, it will be seen, are not very satisfactory.

To the Cincinnati Horticultural Society: — We have been appointed by you to discharge a certain function. Having examined the premises and considered the subject, we do now report: That, notwithstanding the discouragements attendant upon the experience of most vine-dressers during the past season, we are determined to persevere in viticulture, for the following among other reasons:

We have our capital invested in a way which *has been* profitable, and we believe *will be* so again.

Our lands are occupied with a growth that has required time and labor to produce, and which we are unwilling to sacrifice.

We do not believe that the diseases to which the vines and fruit have been subjected, are dependent upon long pruning or short pruning, upon deep culture or shallow, nor any of the causes to which it has been attributed, that are under the immediate control of man, but that the cause is CLIMATIC.

We do not believe that the rot and mildew can be warded off by leaving the wood upon the vines, nor that the usual vineyard method called short pruning, will render our vineyards more subject to this disease.

We do believe, however, that we have yet much to learn in regard to the *philosophy of pruning* which it were well for us to study, and that by so doing we may gather some useful hints in relation to this very important part of a vine-grower's duties.

We do believe, as a result of our observations, that some varieties of grapes are more healthy and vigorous than others; and, on the other hand, that some are peculiarly subject to the inroads of these maladies which have so terribly affected the fruit, the foliage, and the green wood of our vines. We do firmly believe, that our societies should avoid recommending the extensive planting of any trees or vines that have not proved themselves general healthy, and free from the maladies in question, for a number of years, after trial in different situations.

We do believe that systematic efforts should be made with different remedial and preventive agents, to avert the disasters that have overtaken our vine-crops of late years, and, with this view, as we have reason to believe that the difficulty depends upon the existence of some epiphytic plant, and as we are informed that sulphur and sulphate of iron exert an obnoxious influence upon the whole class of fungi, we recommend our brother vine-dressers to take courage, and to make vigorous and systematic efforts to ward off the difficulty the coming season, by the regular and persevering applications of these substances to their grape vines.

For your encouragement, we will also refer you to the history of the vineyards of Europe, which have suffered in like manner, and which have at length recuperated their energies and become productive. Why may not the same good fortune await us?

Very respectfully submitted, by

R. BUCHANAN, Chairman.

CHAPTER VI.

THE SITE FOR AN ORCHARD.

A MATTER OF IMPORTANCE, NOT OF MERE CONVENIENCE — LOW VALLEYS LEAST DESIRABLE — BASINS, EVEN IF ELEVATED, SUBJECT TO FROSTS — LOCAL DIFFERENCES OF TEMPERATURE, OFTEN FATAL TO TENDER VEGETATION — THE FROST LINE NOT DEPENDENT UPON MERE ELEVATION, BUT UPON RELATIVE ALTITUDE — MODERATE BLUFFS BESIDE VALLEYS, OR RIDGES IN A PRAIRIE, ARE BETTER THAN HIGH VALLEYS AMONG MOUNTAINS — DRIFT FORMATIONS, PRESENT INEQUALITIES OF SURFACE — FAVORABLE INFLUENCE OF THE WATER OF RIVERS AND LAKES UPON THE CLIMATE — INSULAR POSITIONS AND LACUSTRINE SITUATIONS HAVE A PECULIAR CLIMATE — FOGS — LATENT HEAT BECOMING SENSIBLE — METEOROLOGY WILL FURNISH AID TO THE ORCHARDIST — COLD STORMS — *Aspect* — PROTECTION FROM WINDS, ESPECIALLY A PRAIRIE QUESTION — EFFECTS OF AGITATION IN THE ATMOSPHERE — BELTS AND SCREENS OF TIMBER DESIRABLE — WINTER KILLING OFTEN DEPENDENT UPON THE CONDITIONS OF THE TREE — VARIETIES MOST SUBJECT TO THIS — LISTS — SOILS, PERMEABLE AND TENACIOUS — ADAPTATION OF SORTS TO SOILS — GEOLOGICAL FORMATIONS TO BE OBSERVED IN MAKING SELECTIONS.

SITE.—The selection of a suitable site for an orchard is a matter of no small moment to him who would be a successful grower of fine fruits. Without, at this time, pausing to inquire into the characters of the soil, let us examine more particularly the *aspect* of the field to be ap-

198

propriated to this important crop; for the orchard is a permanent investment, and so much depends upon the site, that we should make some sacrifice of our convenience, rather than commit any error in this particular. In the first place, then, let it be understood that the orchard should be well exposed to the sun and air. The least desirable positions for orchard planting are narrow valleys, particularly limestone valleys in a mountainous country, traversed by a small brook, or where the surface is *spouty* from springs or sudjacent water. Even if such depressions are considerably elevated, but surrounded by higher and abrupt elevations, they will be found obnoxious to late and early frosts in spring and fall, especially the former, which are often disastrous in such situations, after the fruit-buds have expanded in these sheltered nooks. Every one at all conversant with meteorological observations made in a broken country, is aware of the different range of temperature that will be indicated by instruments suspended at different elevations.* When the cooling influence of radiation has lowered the temperature of the surface of the earth and of objects near it, the stratum of air in immediate contact will be chilled, and growing heavier, will flow down into the most depressed situations, and, accumulating there, will cause a difference of several degrees of temperature. This, when near the freezing point, will be of the greatest consequence to tender vegetation, which may be preserved in perfect safety at forty degrees, but will be destroyed at thirty degrees, or even at a higher point, in some cases.

* See Lawrence Young's Experiments, in *Western Horticultural Review*. Vol. I. page 190. In Report of Kentucky State Fruit Committee to American Pomological Congress, for 1850.

The *frost line* becomes a very important subject of inquiry in the selection of an orchard site, and in some countries we find that its position may be definitely settled within a limited range of elevation; not that a certain level can be indicated, above which there will always be an immunity from frost, while all below will suffer, but we may approximate, in certain situations, so nearly as to indicate that certain sites are safe or unsafe.

Nor is it the absolute elevation alone that is to be taken into the account; in any given locality, we may assume that the higher the orchard is situated above the water levels, the safer it will be, and that the lowest depressions are the most unsafe or frosty. It is not always the mere elevation, but rather the relative elevation of the site, that renders it more desirable than another in the same region. There are many orchards that are situated upon a moderate bluff, with a rapid descent of only a few feet or yards, into a swale or valley of moderate extent; these we find to be uninjured, when another at a greater elevation, but in a depressed basin surrounded by higher lands, will be found to have suffered from the influence of frost. In the one case, the cold air could flow off rapidly into the adjoining depression, while in the other, the cold air from adjoining slopes would collect, and accumulate in the situations described.

In the great plateaus of the world, we often find immense tracts of land so nearly of the same level as scarcely to afford sufficient drainage for the surplus water; of course, we should expect to find, in such places, little variation of temperature arising from difference in elevation. But even in such situations, whether we examine the table-lands of our timbered regions, or the extended areas of the prairie country, we shall find that the drift formation which covers these vast tracts, has not been distributed evenly, but that there are successive rolls or swells frequently recurring, which give, in some instances, considerable variations of level. A bold ridge, of fifty feet or more in hight, rises abruptly from the level prairie, stretching along for miles, and affording admirable exposures for orchard sites. Such places are observed to be free from late and early frosts. In other places, there is an abrupt depression of the surface, answering the same purpose — drawing off the cold air. These may be very moderate in their extent, as the prairie sloughs, or they may be small vales, the courses of the minor streams, or of larger extent, the valleys of rivers, or the depressions of lakes. In these latter cases, the modifying influences of considerable bodies of water enter into the frost problem as an element of no mean value.

It may be asked: How do these masses of water affect the frost? Science answers: By their evaporated moisture influencing the atmosphere. This may save us from the blighting influence of frost, by enveloping the frozen vegetation in a wet blanket of fog; enabling it to be thawed in the dark, as it were, by which we avoid the influence of a bright sunshine, that would have destroyed the tissues had they been suddenly exposed to it when frozen. An equally important result is derived from the direct influence of the humidity of the atmosphere, which modifies the temperature remarkably, as in the immediate vicinity of large bodies of water. Insular situations especially, even when low, are known to have a more genial climate in

9 *

consequence of this condition of the atmosphere, which depends upon the large amount of caloric that is present in the latent form, in the vapor, and which becomes sensible heat as fast as the moisture is condensed; as well as by the sensible caloric, the absolute warmth of the water, affecting the temperature of the atmosphere.

We thus see that very opposite situations, in regard to mere elevation, may both be recommended for orchards; but the latter are the exceptions rather than the rule, for we can not always count upon the saving influence of a fog, nor are the modifying effects of a moderate sheet of water always to be depended upon at the time when most needed. Still, we may find a few favored spots, where an insular position, in a lacustrine situation, receives a double influence — acting at both extremities of the season of vegetation, in quite an opposite way, but in both acting favorably. In such places we shall discover that the spring opens late, being retarded by the cold atmosphere flowing over the chilled waters, that may be even icy, when inland places in the same latitude are rejoicing in a mild and genial temperature, tempting the expansion of the flower-buds. Vegetation on an island thus situated is retarded until all danger of frost has passed, and the air has received the full benefit of warmth from the water. Then, again, in the autumn, when we are in danger from the access of an early frost, such as sometimes, north of latitude forty degrees, destroys the whole crop of corn, almost universally, over hundreds of miles, these favored spots have really a warmer atmosphere, from the influence of a great extent of water, that has enjoyed a summer's sunshine, and which warms the air by giving off its heat very steadily, but slowly; and besides, as the surface of the land cools by radiation and condenses the watery vapor, it receives accessions of temperature that had been locked up, or was insensible in the vapor. Hence we find that in these places, though the opening of spring was retarded a month, the approach of winter and autumnal frosts is warded off for two months, making the season really one month longer than in the same latitude inland.

It must be confessed, however, that the subject of meteorology is not fully understood. We have but a glimmering of the light that we hope is to be shed upon the subject when the deductions from millions of observations, long continued and systematically conducted, shall have been wrought out for the benefit of the orchardist and the general agriculturist.

We also have storms accompanied by a low temperature, passing across the country, in which, at times, the greatest intensity of cold is at the southern border. Such a one passed from the west to the east in January, 1852, in which the mercury, near Marietta, O., sank to thirty degrees below zero; at Zanesville, O., on the same river, it was twenty-seven degrees; at Lancaster, O., thirty-two degrees; while at Cleveland, O., it was only fifteen degrees below, and at Aurora, on Cayuga Lake, N. Y., influenced by the unfrozen water, its greatest depression was only four degrees below zero.*

ASPECT.—When considering the orchard site, the best *aspect* of the ground becomes a matter of interesting inquiry. To all vegetation, the morning sun is a welcome visitant after the night's repose; for plants, as well as ani-

* Western Horticultural Review; also, Statistics of Storm, Jan. 1, 1864.

mals, rest from their functions at night, and all nature rejoices in the return of day; hence an eastern or a southeastern exposure is generally preferred, but we find that practically there is little difference in the different parts of an orchard that can be fairly referred to this cause. Some planters prefer a southern slope, thinking that the fullest exposure to the sun is essential; others select a northern aspect, in the hope that they may there avoid a too early excitation of vegetable life, and also that the heats of summer may be thus moderated. In my own opinion, the aspect is a matter of little consequence to the success of an orchard, though my predilections are in favor of an easterly exposure. The danger of a southern aspect in summer, and the advantages of the northern slope, may, in a great degree, be obtained or obviated by judicious planting and pruning, as will be set forth in another place.

A theory has been started by those who are opposed to a northerly slope, that vegetation continues later in the season in such situations, especially with young trees, and that hence they are not in so good a condition to resist the access of very severe weather at the sudden setting in of winter. The hypothesis is not sustained by long-continued observation, although many facts noted in the autumn and winter of 1859 induced persons to embrace the theory; these were particularly the killing of the peach-buds, upon northern slopes, by the December frosts. There is no evidence that there was any want of perfect ripening of the wood in these situations; on the contrary, it is well known that, long before December, the growth of these very trees had been checked, the wood had been well ripened, and the foliage had been cast to the ground.

The warmer exposure of a southern slope may, and often does, favor the premature swelling of the buds and starting of the sap during mild, pleasant, and bright weather in the winter, and vegetation is often seriously injured from this cause.

In many parts of the country, it is much more important to consider the exposure to the prevailing winds of the region, and to select the site and aspect that shall enjoy the benefit of protection. This, I am aware, is a proposition that has had opponents, as well as advocates, in the broad savannas of the West, where, especially, it becomes a question of the greatest importance. There are benefits as well as evils attendant upon the motions of the atmosphere. The swaying of the limbs, when agitated by the breeze, gives them tone and strength, and may assist in the circulation of the sap within their cells; and the constant agitation of the atmosphere, commingling the warmer with the colder portions, will often modify the temperature to such an extent as to give an immunity from the frost in the open prairie, at the same moment that the more tranquil air, within a limited clearing of forest lands, has been cooled down, by radiation, to the frost point. On every account, therefore, the moderate and reasonable exposure to the influences of a mobile atmosphere is rather to be courted than shunned.

The views that have been advanced by the advocates of protection for orchards on the prairies, have been somewhat modified since they were first promulgated. We are now told, by those who have opposed " protection," that narrow timber-belts of evergreens and deciduous trees, should be planted on the windward sides of orchards, to

moderate, not to cut off, the aerial currents; in this all
will agree, and those who have any sympathy for a tree
will surely prefer to have the blasts, that sweep over miles
of open country, somewhat checked and tempered before
reaching either themselves or their orchards.   The testimony as to the effects of cold in sheltered and in exposed
situations, it must be confessed, appears somewhat contradictory; but this is because we have not all the elements
of a complex problem.

WINTER-KILLING.—A most serious evil, both to the nurseryman and orchardist, is the severe injury sometimes
done to the trees by frost.   This is commonly known by
the term "winter-killing," which has, at times, destroyed
millions of trees, and thus blighted the hopes of long-continued labor and large investments of capital.   Some orchardists have been disheartened, and have given up in
despair.   The investigation of the causes of this disaster,
and the conditions under which it occurs, will be of great
value to future planters; and though, perhaps, we have
not yet at command sufficient data for the full explanation
of the phenomenon, it may be well to look into the attendant circumstances that have been observed; and as some
of the most important considerations depend upon the soil
and exposure, they may be well introduced in this place.

I have already alluded to the theory, that the north hill-
sides maintain a later growth than other situations, and
have stated that the facts do not sustain the position.
The warm exposures on southern slopes and sheltered
nooks, are apt to favor the premature starting of the sap
in the mild weather that often occurs during the winter,
in our changeable climate.   On the prairies, and on flat

lands elsewhere, an excess of humidity in the soil will contribute to this disaster; and in such situations we may often observe the most terrible destruction following a great and sudden change of temperature. Exposure to long-continued cold, with severe winds, seems to dry up the juices of the plants, in some instances, and thus effect their destruction. This, in the far North, is believed to be a frequent cause of the evil. The condition of the tree upon the access of severe cold is too important a subject to be lost sight of, and has already been alluded to.

Of any given variety, the more perfectly dormant the plant, and the more complete its condition of hybernation, the greater will be its immunity from this evil. The atmospheric changes and conditions we can not control, and we can modify them only in a very limited degree, by hedges, by timber-belts, and by evergreen screens, the value of which begins to be appreciated. The state of the soil, as to its moisture, is under our control, and by thorough and surface-drainage, we may obviate one very important condition that conduces largely to the injury under consideration — the excess of moisture in and upon the soil.

The more perfect ripening of the wood, is likewise a matter of great moment, and this is also subject to our control, particularly in young trees in the nursery and orchard.

Certain varieties are much more subject to injury from cold than others. Among these are some of the most thrifty and free growing sorts. There appears to be an inherent quality of hardiness in others, that enables them to resist the most trying alternations of temperature.

Why some should be thus hardy, and others tender, we do not know, but it is not their Northern or Southern origin; some having the former are most tender. Sad experience has taught us the fact, and since the dreadful winters of the past decade, in some parts of the West, the first question asked, respecting a new variety of fruit, is that regarding its hardiness. Pomological societies have endeavored to collate the names of the hardy and tender kinds, and have thus, by their united experience, been enabled to present lists of a few of the known hardy apples, for the guidance of planters.

SOILS.—It will be proper, in this place, to say something about the soils best adapted to orcharding. The apple is a gross feeder, but a good-natured one, and, like a good citizen and a cosmopolite, it submits to surrounding circum stances. In our own country, it flourishes alike on the gran ite hills of New England, or the mountain ranges stretching thence to the southwest, in the limestone valleys amid these ridges, on the sandstones and shales that form the southeastern rim of the great valley of the West, upon the vast drift formations that overlie the rocks from the tide-waters of the St. Lawrence to the sources of the Missouri, upon the rich diluvial and alluvial deposits of our river bottoms, and our vast prairies. I have said that the apple flourishes *alike* upon these various soils and under these so different circumstances; perhaps this expression should be somewhat modified; there are varieties that appear peculiarly adapted by their nature for all of these different situations; there are, perhaps. none that will thrive equally well in all.

The orchardists of each section of the country must ascertain for themselves what varieties are best adapted to the peculiarities of their soil and climate; hence, no one region can furnish lists of varieties to be taken as a guide for the planting of others differently situated. Hence, too, the importance of local organizations for pomological study, and the great value of the labors of those who are engaged in the prosecution of these investigations in the American Pomological Society, which will, it is fondly hoped, ultimately give us corrected lists of fruits that are adapted to all the varying circumstances of soil and climate, in each of the great geological regions of our country. This has already been proposed by the excellent general chairman of Fruit Committees, as an important work for the National Society; and so soon as the subject receives a fair consideration, its merits will be appreciated, and a union of the best minds, and the best experience of the pomologists of each district, will be concentrated upon this labor.

Let me not be misapprehended in the statement, just made, with regard to the wide distribution of which the apple appears to be capable. There are soils and situations, in all of the widely-separated regions alluded to, that are wholly unfitted to orchard culture, upon which it were folly to plant an apple-tree; and yet, many of those may be rendered entirely suitable, if subjected to treatment, suggested by science, and executed by human ingenuity and industry; the missing element may be supplied, the compactness of the soil may be overcome by mechanical comminution, and by that effected by aeration; the excessive moisture may be removed by surface and thorough drainage; other disqualifications, such as those of situation and climate, may not be so readily overcome; they have already been alluded to; and even in them we may hope for improvement with the advance of science.

Different soils may be designated as porous and compact. Leaving out of view for the present, their chemical composition, let us look to their mechanical structure. Porous soils are composed of materials that always allow of the escape of superabundant moisture; they are generally underlaid by beds of diluvial gravels, or by rocks of a porous character. Such lands are peculiarly adapted to orchard planting. The compact soil, on the contrary, is made up of the finest materials, among which alumina largely predominates. Such are called clayey soils or clays, and are among the most valuable upon the surface of the earth, not because alumina is a component of vegetation, but because the elements associated with it, are all of them in a state of extreme comminution.

Clays are compact soils, not only by reason of the fineness of their particles, but because the predominating alumina swells and becomes pasty when it is wet, and thus prevents the passage of water through them. On this account, soils that are too compact, especially if they be underlaid by stiff clay subsoils, are not so well adapted to orcharding as those that are more porous. This is especially true of level lands, upon which water accumulates, to the great injury of the fruit-trees planted upon them; but even in hilly situations, with good natural surface drainage, the excess of clay is indicated by a "spouty" condition of the surface. So many varieties succeed in clayey lands, however, and some are so superior in their products when planted upon clays, that we need not be discouraged by this apparent difficulty; it may be overcome by the ingenuity of the skillful farmer. Thorough or under-drainage will remedy all the evils of clay soils, and bring out their superior advantages. This will be more fully explained in another place. Much may be done toward removing the redundant moisture, even in the flat clay lands of the prairies and other extended plateaus, by the simple means of ridging up the lands with the plow. What is familiarly called "back-furrowing" enables the plowman to raise a ridge upon which to plant his trees, and at the same time he opens a furrow for the escape of surface water. While a portion of the redundant moisture is thus removed, another great object of drainage is not attained: I allude to the aeration of the soil.

From what has been said upon a previous page, it might be inferred, that as the apple may be cultivated upon soils of such great diversity as those that occur over the range of territory indicated, as well as upon the western coast of this continent, and in the temperate regions of the Old World, the peculiar soils that are characterized by their underlying rocks would be equally acceptable, whether these were granites, shales, sandstones, or limestones. Such is not the fact, however, and we have found, in this utilitarian age, that geology has much to do with the planting of an orchard. There are varieties that succeed better upon one rock than upon another, and there are those that fail to be remunerative when transplanted to a rock, which to them is obnoxious, though it may be a very paradise to other varieties.

These observations are becoming a matter of great importance to orchardists, and we may hope that the study of this subject will be developed into some certain data, and that the future discussions of our pomological societies will furnish reliable information to orchard planters.

CHAPTER VII.

PREPARATION OF THE SOIL FOR AN·ORCHARD.

DRAINAGE — ITS ADVANTAGES — SURFACE DRAINS — MADE WITH THE PLOW — MAY BE FOLLOWED BY TILES, OR MOLE PLOW — THOROUGH PLOWING — TRENCHING — TRENCH-PLOWING — SUBSOIL PLOWING — MANURING NOT OFTEN NEEDED IN A NEW COUNTRY — CHARACTER OF MANURES — LIME, ALKALIES — CLOVER — HOW CLOVER ACTS — EXHAUSTED FIELDS TO BE IMPROVED BEFORE PLANTING — DIGGING THE HOLES — DONE WITH THE PLOW — STAKES — THEIR FUNCTION AND OBJECTS — NOT TO TIE TO — HOW TO TIE A TREE WHEN NECESSARY — PLANTING — PREPARING THE TREES — TRIMMING, BRANCHES AND ROOTS — PUDDLING — SET TO THE NORTH OF THE STAKES — DEPTH TO PLANT — LEANING TREES TO THE SOUTHWEST — SEASON FOR PLANTING — FALL OR SPRING BANKING UP AFTER FALL PLANTING — MULCHING, ITS OBJECTS — MATERIAL TO BE USED — CLOVER MULCH.

The more thoroughly the preparation of the soil, the greater will be the success of the orchardist. Good results, fair crops amply remunerating all outlay, often follow the most careless or almost accidental orchard planting; but trees that are properly set, in well-prepared land,

213

upon a judiciously selected orchard site, and for a few
years subjected to proper culture, are infinitely more satisfactory in their results, and much more profitable to their
owner.

The importance of drainage can not be too often reiter-
ated, not merely for the sake of leading away the excess
of water that at some seasons prevails in much of our
best lands, but on account of the more thorough admission
of the beneficial air to the soil and the roots; this, of
course, can only be had by thorough under-draining of the
land. Spouty or springy land is not to be selected for an
orchard, and yet we often find spots of this character in
fields that we wish to appropriate to orcharding; these
should certainly be drained.

Mere surface drainage may be cheaply effected by the
plow, and should always be done in level lands, especially
where the subsoil is compact and tenacious. The expense
of thorough drainage is so great, and the success of our
orchards, as commonly planted, even on ill-prepared
ground, is so generally good, that we can not expect the
majority of farmers to use drain tile at present. Still, the
importance of draining can not be doubted: the best results follow its use, and he who would reap the best harvests, and attain the highest success, will underdrain his
land. For the most of us, surface drainage alone, is all
that we can do; this should never be neglected, for no
crop can be successful in land that is subject to an occasional drenching with a surplus of water that stands for
days, filling it to the surface, causing the fermentation and
souring of the organic matter it contains. The fruit tree,
certainly, will not thrive in such a situation, and is as sure

to fall into a decline, or consumption, if condemned to wet feet, as would a delicate girl under similar exposure.

The expense of under-draining is the only objection that can possibly be urged against it; even this is no real objection, for it has been repeatedly proved that the outlay, whatever it be, insures such increase of crops as to pay a good interest upon the investment, except where the natural under-drainage of the soil, by a porous stratum of rock or gravel, already provides a ready discharge of the superabundant water. It is thus only a question of the cash capital to be invested in the business, for most of our orchard sites are of such a character of soil as to be immensely benefited by the process. With many of us, in this country, the capital is not to be had, or can not be spared, to put underground; our means are limited, and we do not drain our farms, as we should.

Surface drainage may be more cheaply effected, and, on land at all flat and retentive of moisture, it should never be neglected. It may be done while preparing the soil for planting — done with the plow. It has already been premised that the orchard site should be elevated; such land is generally somewhat undulating; indeed, the flattest field that should ever be planted, will always present some inequalities of surface. Let these be noted before laying off the lands for the plow; calculate to have the furrows cross these inequalities of surface, and gather tho furrows in narrow lands, lapping them together just where the row of trees is to be placed. This process may be repeated, and thus quite a ridge will be thrown up for the trees, and a corresponding depression will be left in the middle of the space between the rows, which will serve as a gutter to carry off an excess of surface water; thus, a cheap method of superficial drainage may be effected by the mere plowing of the land judiciously; and this will be found of great advantage in level lands with a stiff subsoil. When such fields are selected for the orchard, this plan should always be pursued; nor does it preclude the subsequent use of tile, which is the best draining material, at any period afterward. These gutters being at a distance from the tree rows, can be deepened, and the tile laid, without disturbing the roots; or the mole drain plow may be drawn through these furrows, if the subsoil be of a suitably tenacious character to admit of the use of this implement.

Very satisfactory preparation of the soil is done with the plow and a good team; indeed, except for the limited surface of a small fruit garden, no other and no better implement need be desired. With it we can produce a very thorough disintegration and perfect subversion of the soil; these are the objects we have in view. But here we have a choice of instruments, in which we must be guided by the character of the soil to be dealt with. If this be shallow, or thin, and underlaid by a sterile subsoil that would be unfit for the surface, we must plow more shallow, but there are few sites, in the Western country, where we do not find a sufficient depth of soil to satisfy the most thorough plowman, and beneath it a subsoil that will be benefited by aeration, and which will become good surface soil if subjected to the influences of the atmosphere.

We have few soils that may not be trenched with the plow or spade to any depth that is attainable. And here let me explain what is meant by *trenching :* it is the trans position of two layers of the soil more thoroughly, and to a greater depth, than is done by simply digging or plowing, in which a limited amount, only a thin layer of the soil, is inverted. In trenching with the spade, a narrow strip of land is excavated across one end of the piece to be trenched, eighteen or twenty inches wide, and as deep as the spade can take it out at two diggings. The earth thus removed is thrown aside, to be used at the end of the work. The trench being now open, a similar space is laid off, and the surface soil, to the depth of the spade, is dug and thrown into the bottom of the first trench, after which the subsoil is dug to the same depth, the length of the space, and thrown on top of the surface soil that was put into the bottom of the first trench. A second trench is thus opened, and a third strip being then marked off, the same processes are continued, until the whole piece is trenched, when the pile of earth first excavated is brought into requisition to complete the work, by filling up the last trench. This is common trenching, which reverses the two layers of soil, and stirs the whole to the depth of eighteen or twenty inches. It is an expensive operation, but very desirable in a small fruit-garden—not at all applicable for extensive orchard planting, though often applied to the preparation of extensive vineyards.

Trench plowing is conducted upon the same principle, and is done by using two plows in the same furrow, the first taking off the surface soil and throwing it into the deep furrow of the second plow, which is so constructed as to lift the lower soil and throw it high up over the furrow slice laid by the first, and at the same time, leaving a deep furrow open behind it to receive the next cut of

10

surface soil. The two layers are thus inverted and reversed at the same time, and with a proper plow, the whole soil is finely comminuted and reduced to a perfect seed-bed, suitable for a garden. To perform this work, the Double Michigan plow is the favorite implement. It should be properly constructed, for much depends upon having the plow well made; the mold-boards should be formed upon the best models for their respective offices of reversing the surface soil, and of upheaving and comminuting that which lies below it; and these mold-boards should be made of steel. Such plows are manufactured at several points, but all the Double Michigan patterns are not equally good, and some are quite unsatisfactory.

The Deep Tiller plows will do very good work in certain soils, and may often be used to advantage in the preparation of the orchard grounds, either alone, or to follow another plow when trench plowing is desired, and the trench plow is not at hand. These plows, as made at Moline, Illinois, are much used, and give great satisfaction in that State.

Subsoiling is a very useful addendum to deep plowing; its object is to stir the deep layers of the soil without bringing the earth to the surface. This aerates and loosens the subsoil, and thus effects the combined objects of increasing the fertility of the land, of retaining moisture for the crops, and, to a certain extent, of allowing any excess of moisture to percolate away. Subsoiling is most efficacious when combined with draining, but it is of great use without, unless where permanent water is found near the surface. There is a great improvement in the subsoil plows. Those first made were provided with a share on one side, and this wing, as it was called, was tilted up several inches, thus increasing the draft unnecessarily. We now use a sharp steel share, of diamond shape, cutting on both edges, right and left, and very slightly elevated in the centre, only two inches, or two and a half at the most. If the soil is stirred with this implement, the hard earth at the bottom of the furrow, made by the turning plow, is thoroughly broken up, and it does not fall directly back into its place, but the crumbled portions support one another, and the furrow appears to be filled with loose earth. The result is astonishing, when we consider the flat, diamond-shaped plow sole that has done the work.

The depth to which this implement may be made to disintegrate the soil, depends upon its strength, the power of the team, and the character of the subsoil. I have seen it tear up several inches of the shales and other rocks, and aid in making a good soil of them. I have seen it sink to the beam in the alluvium of our river bottoms, and I have seen it almost refuse to do its office in some of the hard white clay subsoils, when drawn by a heavy team, while in more yielding but tenacious clays I have seen it trembling under the strain of three yoke of good cattle, that were scarcely able to pull it through the adhesive soil.

MANURING.—The importance of the application of manures to the orchard, as a part of the preparation of the soil, will depend entirely upon its strength and condition. Trees are great feeders; they need a reasonably fertile soil, for though their roots run wide and deep, in search of nourishment, if the necessary food be not in the soil, they will certainly fail to thrive as they should. The analysis of the ashes of our fruit trees, which contain the elements they have derived from the soils on which they grew, enables us to ascertain what kinds of plant-food should be present in the soil we are about to use, or what materials we may safely and judiciously add to it as manures. Lime, and the alkalies, are generally safe and useful additions, in connection with clover as a green manure; these may be applied to almost any worn soils with great advantage. Clover is an invaluable assistant. Its long roots pierce deeply into the soil, bringing up from below hidden treasures, which are left in the upper layers, modified by the digestion of the plant, and by new chemical changes and combinations, rendered fit food for succeeding crops. The mere disintegration of the soil produced by the roots of clover, is, in itself, a valuable mechanical preparation, quietly performed, without plow or team. The clover lea may be limed with great advantage; an application of twenty-five to fifty bushels of slacked lime to the acre will improve the growth of clover, and will exert its appropriate influence upon the soil, with very happy results for the succeeding crop of orchard trees. Alkalies may be applied, in the form of wood ashes, either at the preparation of the soil, or at any subsequent period, as may be found most convenient. Stable manure, and composts, will seldom be required in lands that have not been nearly exhausted, and therefore unfit for an orchard. In case it becomes necessary to use such a field, the manuring should be done all over the surface, and a crop of clover should be grown and plowed in before planting the trees; upon no account should fresh stable manure be brought into immediate contact or close proximity with the roots of the young tree. If the necessity for planting on such a piece of land impel immediate action, very thoroughly decomposed composts may be applied, mixed with the soil about the tree, but successive applications of manures will be needed over the entire surface, for the roots are destined to occupy the whole extent of soil between the trees.

The next step in the preparation is the digging of the holes for planting the trees. Some persons lay great stress upon the importance of having these made large and deep, which may be very well in a grass lawn with a few trees, but it is a very expensive matter for the orchard of thousands or even of hundreds. The holes should be prepared as wide as the field, and as deep as the plow can stir it, as already directed; that is the kind of holes that should be dug; if the land have been prepared in this manner, the opening of the holes and planting the orchard, either deep or shallow, becomes a very simple matter.

Having determined the distance at which the trees shall stand from one another, and the order or plan of planting, flag poles are to be set in the line to be occupied by the first row of trees, and a deep furrow is then opened with a large plow, drawn by a pair of steady horses. The poles are moved and set for the next row of trees, and so on, until the whole is laid off, making the furrows as straight as possible. This done, a single horse with a lighter plow is driven across these deep furrows at the proper distance, so that the intersections shall indicate the stations for the trees. Strong stakes, about four or five feet long, are then driven firmly at these intersections, and if the marking-

out has been well done, they will range in six directions
—N. and S.—E. and W.—N.-E. and S.-W.—N.-W. and
S.-E., or to corresponding points of the compass; for it is
not a matter of much consequence in what direction the
rows of trees stand.   The holes are the deep furrows, and
tree stations are the spaces beside the stakes, always main-
taining the same relative position throughout the orchard;
the northern side is to be preferred, on account of the partial shade of the stake.   By adopting this plan, there
need be no trouble, as is often experienced, in sighting the
trees to have them straight, for if the stakes have been
correctly placed, the trees will also be right, and will
range in every direction, when planted.

Before dismissing the subject of stakes, let us understand their object and function: it is not to tie up the
trees, and to force them to attain an erect posture; no,
that is not to be effected by staking, as will be set forth in
another place.   Rather than tie a tree to a stake, it were
better to cut it down to the ground, and grow it over
again.   The real objects of the stakes are, first, to show
the planter where to set a tree; second, to show where
the tree has been planted; third, to indicate to the plowman and to his horse where to exercise care in passing the
infant tree during the first years' culture, for an intelligent
animal will very soon learn what objects it is intended for
him to avoid injuring during his labors in the field; a
fourth function of the stake is to ward off the single-tree
which the careless laborer may allow to strike the tree to
its manifest injury, tearing the bark, and even breaking
the stem.   The passage of the wagon through the field
will also be directed, by these stakes, to the interspaces,

instead of passing over the trees.   Here are reasons
enough for the use of stakes, but tying the trees to them
is not among the number; indeed, it might be called the
abuse of the stakes rather than their use, except in rare
cases.   Even in the windy prairie country, no stakes
should be used, as supports, in a properly regulated orchard.

When necessary to support a tree with stakes, after
an injury or accident, the plan of C. Rosenstiel, Free-

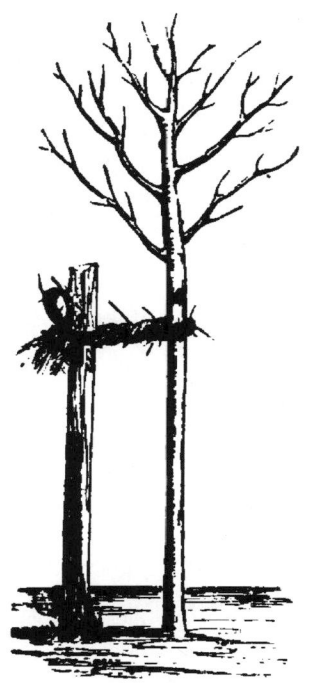

Fig. 25.—MANNER OF STAK-
ING A TREE.

port, Ill., is the best I have seen.
He adopts it as a means of keeping his trees from being inclined
by the wind.   He drives a stake
firmly into the ground, about a
foot to the southwest of his tree;
a band of rye straw is cast about
the tree a few feet from the
ground; the two ends are twisted
and entwined together, forming
a stiff rope from the tree to the
stake, about which it is then cast,
and the ends are secured with a
piece of twine.   By this appliance,
the tree is maintained in an erect
position without chafing; it can
only yield to the wind by wav-
ing to the right or left; the
band, by its tension, prevents it
from leaving the stake, and, by its stiffness, holds it at a
proper distance, and prevents its approach.

PLANTING comes next in order to the marking out, or

hole-digging, for these are synonymous; it should be done
as soon as possible after the plow, on account of the fresh
furrow with its mellow soil.   It is really a simple matter
and upon this method may be executed with great rapidi·
ty.   The trees now receive their necessary trimming,
which consists in a liberal shortening of the branches, a
careful inspection of the roots, and a removal with a sharp
knife of such as may have been bruised or torn, and cut·
ting away any mat of fibres; after this, they should be
puddled, and then carried out to their stations by a boy.
The planter follows; with a bright spade he removes any
excess of soil at the station, scraping away such portions
of earth as he may find in the way of the roots when the
tree is placed by the stake.   If the furrow has not been
recently made, it will be well always to remove a portion
of the surface, so as to have fresh soil next the roots.
The tree being placed near the stake, the roots are care·
fully spread out in their natural direction, and the moist
mellow earth is filled in among them, using the fingers
when necessary, and gently shaking the tree so as to leave
no empty cavities among the fibres.   Pretty firm pressure
should now be made with the foot, especially upon the fine
earth placed above the ends of the roots; this excludes
the air, by bringing the particles of soil in close proximity
to the roots, ready to receive the new fibres that will soon
be emitted from them.   It also secures the tree in its place
better than tying to the stake, for each root acts as a guy
rope.   In this manner the work may progress very rapid·
ly, and, at the same time, may be well done.   Some plant·
ers always pour a liberal supply of water upon the mellow
earth, instead of pressing it with the foot.   This will set·

tle the fine soil about the roots very effectually; fresh earth should always be thrown on after the water, to prevent the surface from being caked and cracked.

The depth at which the tree should be planted is a question of interest. Most authorities and most successful planters endeavor to regulate this, so that, when settled, the original collar of the young tree may be at the surface of the ground; deep planting has few advocates. The position of the tree as to the points of the compass, is now believed to be a matter of very little moment, although there are still those who insist that the north side of the tree in the nursery row should be made to occupy the same position in the orchard. With low-headed trees this can make no difference; no others are recommended; on the contrary, if, unfortunately, none but tall trees with naked stems can be procured, it is advised to cut them back severely at planting time, so as to form a new head where wanted. Those who have not the heart to cut back a fine tree, may attempt and will sometimes succeed in bringing out branches below, by nicking the bark with a large sharp pruning-knife, at several points along the stem, on all sides, but especially to the southwest, where the shelter of the branches is most needed. This, however, requires us to wait at least one season, and that the most trying one to the young tree, during which the naked bark is exposed to the sun and insects; and the winds may add to the difficulty, by inclining the stem from the southwest. All this may be avoided by planting trees with low branches, which are becoming more and more common as their merits are more highly appreciated. Some of the most judicious planters, especially in windy districts, have

10*

adopted the plan of inclining all their trees to the south-west at the time of planting, expecting thus to overcome the difficulty so commonly observed everywhere with tall trees—their leaning to the northeast, and then becoming scorched and injured by the frost and sun, and damaged by the borers.

The season for planting is a question of some importance, and must be settled by the attendant circumstances. Fall planting has many advocates and many advantages, but the fewest practice it. In the far north, with a long, trying winter approaching, it can not be recommended; but, as the spring advances, there is a great press of work; everything is to be done at once, and all is hurry; hence, for the milder latitudes, with our charming autumnal weather, comparative leisure, and the soil in good condition, everything invites us to plant in the autumn, and with those south of latitude forty degrees, the planting season will often continue until mid-winter. If we commence this work before the fall of the leaves, care should be taken to strip these appendages from the trees in the nursery, before digging them. Instead of leaving the soil about the tree at or a little above the general level, it should be heaped up in a little mound, which will shed off the rains, support the stem, and, to some extent, protect the roots from frost. This last suggestion is a matter of much importance, for one of the great advantages of autumnal planting, depends upon the fact that, except in the most severe weather, the tree is not dormant—the hybernation is not complete; in mild weather there is some action in the buds and branches, and considerable activity exists in the roots; new fibres are emitted, and, with the first opening of spring, the young tree is ready for its summer's growth. Such is not the case with trees that have been badly planted in the fall, in a wet, tenacious soil, where their roots have been immersed in mud and water for months, and the swaying top has strained them in every direction. For such a soil, draining is needed; but, even then, the mound will be of material advantage in fall planting.

MULCHING is a process about which much has been said and written, but of which, it is to be feared, very little is known and understood. The very objects of mulching do not appear to be properly appreciated by many persons. Its uses are two-fold: primarily, to keep the surface of the earth moist by preventing evaporation, and to maintain that open, friable condition we always find in the forest, under the natural mulching of the leaves. · Mulching keeps the earth cooler in summer and warmer in winter; the first, by shading from the burning rays of the sun, the second, by protecting from frost; the material itself, and the confined air among it, being bad conductors of heat. Now, what material shall we use for producing these results? Almost anything that will fulfill these indications will answer—either stones, chips, boards, twigs, saw-dust, tan-bark, weeds, straw, either long or cut, coarse manure, hay, freshly-cut grass, or, perhaps the very best for all the purposes of mulching, leaves themselves, except that they are difficult to retain in their place. A combination of leaves and twigs, small branches or weeds, may be made to answer a very good purpose, for winter mulching especially. For summer mulching there is another material which has been found to answer an admirable purpose, though not mentioned in the above list; it is mellow earth—yes, mellow earth admirably fulfills most of the conditions of a good mulching material, but it must be kept mellow by constant stirring. The air is thus admitted, and deposits its moisture whenever the earth is cooler than the atmosphere; the presence of the air among the particles of the soil makes it a worse conductor of heat than when it is compacted together.

Mulching the newly-planted trees is a very valuable application, whether in summer or winter, and should be practiced wherever it is possible, always remembering that we can not well combine with it culture, which, for the summer treatment, is most essential to the successful growth of trees, and in winter we shall present a harbor to the mice if the mulch be placed too near the tree. He who may have been induced, by the recommendations of high authority, to plant an orchard in a stiff blue-grass sod, or who may allow such sod to surround his trees, in the belief that this constitutes a good mulch, will be sadly disappointed; for, though the surface is shaded, the grass will absorb the moisture from the soil at the expense of the young trees. Clover, on the contrary, makes a denser shade, and seeking its supplies more deeply, is less injurious, while its abundant broad foliage attracts ample supplies of dew to irrigate the soil. In this respect it resembles the Indian corn, which is considered the best crop to put among young trees, as it produces shade, attracts the dew, and, more than all, it demands and receives the thorough culture which the trees also require.

CHAPTER VIII.

SELECTION AND PLANTING.

IMPORTANCE OF JUDICIOUS SELECTION — LARGE TREES NOT DESIRABLE — THRIFTY YOUNG TREES PREFERRED — REASONS FOR THE PREFERENCE — ADVANTAGES OF SMALLER TREES — LOW HEADS AND THE PROTECTION BY LATERAL BRANCHES — PERSONAL INSPECTION AND SELECTION RECOMMENDED — DIGGING THE TREES — CAREFULLY AVOID MUTILATION OF THE ROOTS — PUDDLING — TYING AND LABELING — PACKING — AVOID EXPOSURE TO SUN, AND WIND, AND FROST — TREATMENT OF FROZEN TREES IN COLD WEATHER — HEELING-IN — MULCHING — MAKING RECORD — DRIED TREES, HOW RESTORED — SEASON FOR PLANTING — BANKING THE TREES — MULCHING — DISTANCE BETWEEN TREES — DEPENDENT UPON THE HABIT OF THE VARIETY — ASSORTING THE VARIETIES ACCORDING TO SIZE — CLOSE PLANTING — COMBINATION PLANTING — DIFFERENT CROPS — APPLES AND PEACHES, OR CHERRIES — SMALL FRUITS BETWEEN — ORDER OF PLANTATION — QUINCUNX — ASSORTING VARIETIES — CONVENIENCE IN HARVESTING TO HAVE EACH KIND GROUPED TOGETHER.

We now come to the consideration of a matter of great importance to the success of the future orchard — the selection of the plants we are to set therein. No matter how favorable the site, how good the soil, nor how thorough the preparations may have been; all may be spoiled by a bad selection of trees, and subsequent disappointment will be the consequence.

229

Formerly, and in some sections of the country even now, very erroneous notions prevailed upon this subject. Large trees, of several years' growth in the nursery, were preferred by those who were planting orchards: trees, ready to bear fruit, were eagerly inquired for, and preferred; even if they had been crowded together so as to be drawn up to a great hight without any lateral branches, and had formed their heads at the hight of seven or eight feet, so as to be out of the way of browsing by cattle and horses, they were the more admired by the purchasers. Now-a-days there is a great change in the sentiment of tree-planters as to the age, size, and shape of the trees that are to be set out.

Thrifty young trees are preferred to older and larger ones on many accounts. They are more vigorous and will endure the disturbance of digging, transportation, and change of locality from the nursery to the orchard, much better than larger and older trees. They are more easily dug, and will have a larger proportion of roots removed with them than those which have stood longer in the nursery-rows, so as to have pushed their fibres beyond the reach of the spade. Such trees are more stocky, and are furnished with lateral branches, or they should be so furnished, but these would be smothered and removed from older trees in crowded rows, as they are usually found in the nurseries. If these younger trees be not already furnished with laterals and elements for the formation of low heads, by the judicious treatment of the nurserymen who produced them, the orchardist can at least bend them to his will. He may make of them just what he pleases by his own manipulations at the time of planting or afterwards, without feeling that he is sacrificing to his fancy and judgment the growth of two or three years, by freely using the knife and saw, in the removal of the surplus and overgrown top, leaving him only a bare and mutilated stock to set out at the beginning of his orchard.

Another advantage of selecting small trees, especially to those at a distance from the nursery, is, that they are so much more easily transported, and freight bills are a serious item in the expense account of a large orchard plantation—these may be reduced to a minimum by the selection of small instead of large trees. As to forming the heads of our trees, if we cannot get the nurserymen to do this for us, since we are unwilling to remunerate them for the extra labor, and greater space required to form such stocky specimens as we prefer, the difficulty is obviated by planting out young trees upon which we may form the heads where we please.

As already suggested, there is a great revolution going on in the minds of tree-planters as to the proper age for planting. Instead of the inquiry for huge and cumbrous, overgrown trees, that had stood four or five years or more in the nursery, we now find a growing demand for small, stocky trees, of two or three years, or even less. Of many thriftily growing kinds, good yearlings are much better for the orchard than large trees, especially such as have been crowded in the nursery and are devoid of side branches, and whose tall naked stems are exposed to the burning heats and blasting cold of their new homes in the open field, and to the depredations of hosts of insects. Those purchasers, who seek after the tall trees, with bare stems, running up like fishing poles, they who desire to buy their trees by the running yard and to get as great a length as possible for their money, can be accommodated by the nurseryman, who will produce the article to order; but such planters will soon find that their orchards are much less satisfactory than those set with short and stocky trees, and which have been encouraged to branch out so as to form low heads. As set forth in the chapter upon *The Nursery*, such trees can be produced, and they are greatly to be preferred on many accounts, but their production by the nurserymen must depend upon the intelligence of the orchardists producing a demand for trees of such a character, and a willingness on their part to pay the grower a liberal price for the increased labor and expense, (in space at least), requisite for their production. This no one should object to, for there is economy in planting good trees; the successful orchardist will purchase the best; he will not have the refuse or trash that may be offered him at a low figure, for he well knows that it is dear at any price.

Where it is practicable and within reach, it is best for the planter to visit the nursery and make his own selection of the trees, especially if the demand be for a limited number; but he may generally depend upon the judgment and honesty of the nurseryman, if he has given his order distinctly as to the shape of the trees he desires to purchase. In a common nursery, he will often observe at the ends of the rows, and where there may have been a gap or break in the continuous line of any variety, so that the trees are less crowded, some trees that are better furnished with lateral branches, and are consequently more stocky than where the rows are crowded. Here he will be likely to find the specimens that suit his fancy, and he will mark them for removal.

DIGGING.—At the proper season, and for most kinds this is at the fall of the leaf, the trees should be dug from the ground. This operation, as usually and necessarily conducted in large establishments, has to be done expeditiously and with less care than the amateur will be disposed to bestow upon this very important operation; and it sometimes happens that he will offer to pay the nurseryman a bonus for the privilege of digging his own trees with his own hands.

In performing this operation he will be very careful to avoid mutilating the roots with the spade, or by using more force than is absolutely necessary in lifting the loosened tree from its bed after the roots have been pretty thoroughly liberated from the soil. He will follow the directions given under this head in the appropriate section of the chapter on *The Nursery*. The importance of puddling the roots as soon as the trees are dug, cannot be too forcibly impressed upon the planter and nurseryman; its value to the trees is so great as a protection of the tender covering of the roots from exposure to the blighting influences of light, wind, and frost, that the trifling labor and expense involved in the operation, should not receive a moment's consideration.

A puddle hole should be within convenient reach of the nursery-rows where the digging is in progress, and each sort should be taken to it as soon as dug. The excavation should be about a foot deep, or more, for large plants, and as wide as is necessary to receive all the roots of the trees to be puddled. A plentiful supply of water should be at hand to put into the hole, and fine dry loamy soil should be sifted into this, or simply thrown in from the shovel, and thoroughly mixed, so as to bring the fluid to the consistency of thick cream. Into this mud the roots are dipped, until every fibre is endued with a coating of the fine material; the trees then are ready for tying snugly together, and a little dry dirt may be sprinkled or sifted upon the roots while they are still wet, so as to give them a further protection from the elements. They are then securely bound, each kind by itself, and each carefully labeled, if not already done; and as soon as all are grouped together, they are ready for transportation to their new homes. If the distance be short, so that the trees may be carried on the farm-wagon, no packing is used, unless the weather proves very inclement, but it is always safer to guard against both wind and sun, by covering the roots from their influence. For distant transportation, too much care cannot be taken to have the trees well packed to protect the roots from drying and freezing.

In our uncertain climate, it not unfrequently happens that we receive an invoice of trees in the midst of a severe storm of cold, when the ground is frozen hard, and we have reason to suppose that the roots in the cases are frozen. This need not discourage nor alarm us, if the packing be good, for we have only to be patient and allow them time to thaw out thoroughly in the dark, and we shall find our trees all right. The packages should be placed at once in a dark cellar, and allowed to thaw gradually—if no such convenience be at hand, the boxes may be buried in the soil, or covered heavily with straw or hay, materials which are generally abundant in a prairie country, where commodious cellar room is not always at command.

HEELING-IN, as it is called, is a very important operation to be performed so soon as possible after the receipt of the trees It consists in placing the fibrous roots in immediate and close contact with the fresh and mellow soil, at some point convenient to the future planting. A ditch is dug with the spade, or a deep furrow is opened with the plow, in a sheltered, but elevated and dry situation, and in light mellow soil; into this the trees are placed as fast as they are removed from the packages, each kind being separated from the next by a distinct marking stick, and it is well to place the labeled tree first, as taken from bundles when untied. The trees are inclined at an angle, generally leaning towards the south, so as to have the stems shaded by their own branches. They are carefully placed separately and held in this position by one person, while the fine mellow earth is thrown upon the roots by another, who should take great care to see that all the interstices are filled with soil, so as to exclude the air from the fibres. This is especially necessary where the trees are to remain in this situation during the winter, when they will be alternately frozen and thawed. To secure them from injury, the earth should be banked up against them several inches; and it is well also to cover this with a heavy coating of leaves or some other mulching material, if it can be safely used without danger of attracting the field mice, which might ruin the trees. It is well at once to make a record of the trees as they stand, so soon as they are heeled-in, beginning at one end of the ditches or rows, and pursuing a definite order. This record will prove of great value, and very convenient in selecting the different kinds at the time of planting, and will enable us to restore the names in case of accidental loss of labels during the winter. The heeling-in of trees as they are received is recommended, even if everything is ready for immediate planting, unless the number be very small; but if the weather and our convenience permit us to place them at once in their permanent stations, the trees need not be heeled-in with so much care as when they are to remain for a longer period.

It sometimes happens that, from accident, detention by the way, bad packing, or exposure, we receive our trees in bad condition; they are dried, and the bark appears to be shriveled and shrunken—they seem to be dead. Such trees may often be entirely restored by a little care, and will grow as well as any. The best treatment for such is to bury them at once. Opening a sufficiently large trench, a layer of trees is placed flat upon the bottom, fine mellow earth is sifted upon, and among their roots and branches, another layer of trees is spread down and covered in the same way, and so on until they are all secured, when they are left to quietly and slowly absorb the moisture from the soil. In a few days they will be found to be well plumped, and will look as fresh as ever, and should be exhumed, trimmed, and planted, selecting a moist or showery day for the operation.

Season for Planting.—This topic has already been discussed, and the advantages of fall planting have been presented: but it is well to bear in mind that there are reasons for preferring the spring, and for some fruits the latter season is generally preferred.

When planting an orchard in the fall, it has been recommended to raise an embankment of earth about the stem, for the double purpose of protecting the roots from the frost, and also of preventing the action of the wind swaying the tree and straining the roots. A copious mulching is sometimes applied to keep out the frost, or at least to prevent the frequent thawing and freezing of the surface in our variable winters; but whenever loose material is left near the base of a young tree, we must expect damage from the mice, which are attracted and sheltered, and may commit sad devastations upon the bark before spring. The banking and mulching may be combined with advantage, and with less danger from the mice, which only work under cover and are often more injurious upon older trees, surrounded with grass and weeds in neglected orchards, than upon those newly planted and mulched, if a little care has been taken to remove the straw or tramp it down near the stem.

DISTANCE.—The distance between the trees is a matter that should be carefully determined. Their habit should be considered, and their size, when fully developed, must be studied. Some varieties will be more crowded at forty feet apart, than others at fourteen. If possible, the larger and widely spreading sorts should be assorted and planted by themselves, and the more compact, upright and smaller ones should be grouped together. It is difficult to do this, however, for want of the necessary data; we can only make an approximation to the desired result. Thus, the Yellow Bellflower, Summer Queen, Fall Pippin, King of Tompkins County, Talman's Sweet, Golden Sweet, Pennock, Northern Spy, and several others, are of the largest kind of trees, and may be allowed as much as forty feet of space between them, while the upright character and moderate growth of the Lady, Bullock's Pippin, Red June, Benoni, Early Joe, American Summer Pearmain, Summer Rose, Red Astrachan, and others, of similar habit, would enable us to crowd them into half as much space without serious injury—and there are trees of intermediate size and vigor, such as the Winesap, Rambo, Greening, Russet, Early Harvest, Fall Wine, Autumn Strawberry, Hubbardston, Jonathan, and a host of others that, at the same ratio, should have thirty feet spaces between them.

There is also a great diversity of opinion among orchardists as to the proper allowance of space for each tree, and many western planters are advocates of close planting of the apple, which I have seen placed as near as sixteen feet, occupying the whole space in a very few years, and bearing luxuriantly. The advocates of such crowding urge, that they protect one another, and that alternate trees can easily be removed whenever they become too much crowded. In other places, the old rule, of allowing two rods (33 feet), or even forty feet, between the trees, is still followed and considered the best.

A favorite method with some planters of fruits is, to make a combination of different kinds in the same orchard, so as to have the whole surface occupied from the first. In this way, by introducing a temporary crop of another variety which will make speedy returns, and will soon be ready to come away and make room for the permanent plantation, the ground may be rendered productive of remunerative crops from the first. It is a very common plan to combine in this way the apple and the peach—the latter come into bearing rapidly, and are generally ready to be removed by the time the apple trees need the whole space. Alternate rows and alternate trees are usually planted with peaches, and the small growing cherries, such as the Early May, often called the Early Richmond, can be planted in the same way. I have seen a still further combination of fruits made by the introduction of the raspberry, or even of the blackberry, the currant, and the gooseberry, in alternate rows, so that, by setting the apple trees at forty feet, with alternating cherry trees, and the cherry rows in the middle space, or twenty feet each way from the apple and cherry rows, and in the intermediate strips of twenty feet the berries, which were also set between the trees, the whole ground was laid off in rows of fruit separated by strips of ten feet wide. Nothing is then needed for the full occupation of the ground, and to yield a return of fruit the next year, but to plant a single row of strawberries in each of these ten feet spaces; these, if well treated, would make four beds in the spaces between every two of the apple tree rows, or each ten feet, which is nearly half as much as would be planted in the open field; and these would yield a half crop the next year after planting, and as much the next season, when they should be plowed up to give cultivation to the berry bushes that would then also bear a crop of fruit, and continue to do so until the larger trees needed the ground for their support. The peaches or cherries would commence bearing the third or fourth year, and some of the apples would follow quickly afterward, yielding partial crops. By such a combination, as has been represented, the land is made to yield a succession of paying fruit crops from the second year of the foundation of the orchard.

The order of planting is a matter of some consequence, and should be settled upon before commencing the work. The simplest form, and that most usually adopted, is the square; furrows are drawn across the field, at whatever distance the plants may be desired to stand, and crossed by others equally distant and at right angles to the first. These will, by their intersections, indicate the stations to be occupied by the trees. Some planters introduce a tree at the centre point between each four, and this has been called *quincunx*, but erroneously—for the true *quincunx* is constituted by one central tree surrounded by six, and all are equidistant, as illustrated by the diagram, figure

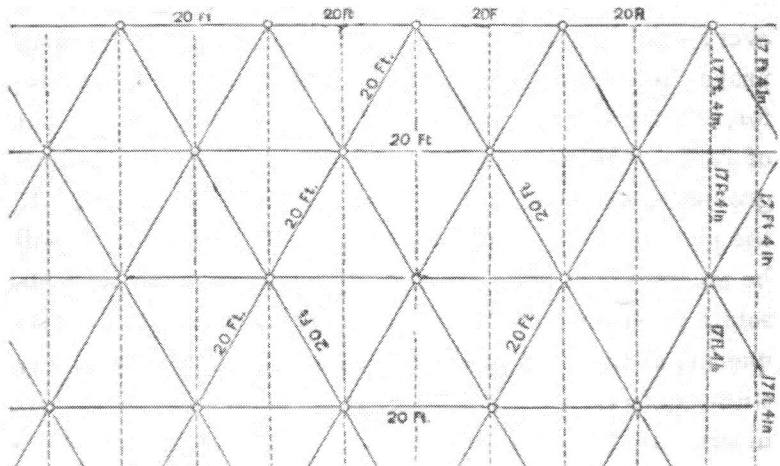

Fig. 26.—DIAGRAM OF PLANTING QUINCUNX.

26. This gives as many trees as possible upon the ground, all equidistant, at twenty feet apart, or at any other, distance. It will be seen, that, in laying off this ground, whether with the plow or simply with stakes to

indicate the stations which the trees are to occupy, we may first strike our furrows or set our sight poles, all in one direction, parallel, and at seventeen feet four inches apart. Crossing these at right angles, we may draw parallel furrows every ten feet, and by setting our stakes at each alternate intersection of these furrows, the proper stations will be found for planting trees in the true *quincunx* order, in which every tree will occupy the corner of an equilateral triangle, and will be equidistant from six surrounding trees. If any one prefers to dig holes with the spade, instead of the more economical method proposed, by using the plow, the stakes may be set in parallel rows, in such a manner, that in every alternate row the first stakes shall be advanced one-half of the desired distance from the base line. It will be desirable in this, as in every other system, to have a measuring-line at hand to prove the work from time to time, and make corrections; for, otherwise, the most careful planter will soon get out of range. When the stakes are set properly, on level ground, they should range correctly in all directions. If the plantation be upon an uneven or hilly surface, it will be found almost impossible to lay off the ground with absolute precision; but this is a matter of very little consequence, as the growth of the trees will soon conceal any slight defects, particularly if they be trained with low heads. In the small fruit garden greater precision is desirable, and should be attempted, but in the commercial orchard, containing hundreds or thousands of trees, such exactitude is scarcely attainable if it were desired. Sometimes the aid of the civil engineer, with his instruments, is called in by the very precise planter.

11

CHAPTER IX.

CULTURE, ETC.

—◦◦◦—

THOROUGH CULTURE SHOULD FOLLOW THOROUGH PREPARATION — HOED CROPS RECOMMENDED — NO WHITE STRAW CROPS, NOR GRASSES ALLOWED — HOW LONG SHALL WE CULTIVATE THE ORCHARD ? — LIMITS — THE SPADE AND FORK, AND MULCHING SUBSTITUTED — HORSE CULTIVATORS NECESSARY IN LARGE ORCHARDS — THESE SHOULD NOT BE DEEP TILLERS, BUT SHALLOW, TO AVOID DISTURBING THE ROOTS — SEEDING WITH CLOVER — MULCHING IMPRACTICABLE ON A LARGE SCALE — CLOVER MULCH — THE MELLOW EARTH AS A MULCH — PASTURING AN ORCHARD — OBJECTIONS — DAMAGE DONE BY HORSES AND MULES — BY CATTLE, BY GOATS — SHEEP — THEIR ADVANTAGES — SWINE AND POULTRY MAY BE ADMITTED — HOW THEY MAY BE USEFUL — DESTRUCTION OF INSECTS — POULTRY AND CURCULIO

In a previous chapter, reference has been made to the necessity of thorough cultivation of the soil among young trees; but the importance of the proper attention to orchard culture is so great, that it deserves separate consideration. The thorough preparation of the soil before committing the roots of our trees to its embraces, which was fully impressed upon the orchardist, might have induced some

242

to think that this was to be sufficient for them; but it ought rather to be inferred that any crop for which these preliminary labors were recommended, should receive continuous attentions of a similar character. It is with the desire that these views should obtain, and to indicate and specify, some of the most suitable modes of procedure, that the following remarks are presented in this place.

If the ground, which has been appropriated to the orchard, be also occupied as farming land, as is usually done for a few years after planting, while the trees are small, it should be exclusively devoted to hoed crops; by which is meant those that require constant cultivation and stirring of the soil. Indian corn is a favorite on account of the thorough culture which is bestowed upon it, but there are some objectors to its use; by such it is considered too rank a grower; it is thought to absorb too much of the moisture of the soil, and too greatly to over-shadow the young trees if they be so small as has been recommended under the head of *Selection and Planting*. To this objection, however, it is urged by others that the partial shade during the latter part of summer is a benefit rather than an injury. If the stalks be left standing upon the ground during the winter, they modify the force of the winds, and may even be of benefit, by the protection they furnish to the stems of the young trees; and when they fall to the ground, with their abundant foliage, these materials constitute a winter mulching of considerable value. Even if the fodder has been cut up, as is usually done by prudent farmers, the shocks scattered through the fields must exercise a considerable protecting influence.

Melons, cucumbers, cabbages, potatoes, turnips, and

other root crops, which require frequent cultivation, are preferred by some orchardists, because of their being lower, and thus they will shade only the surface of the ground, without affecting the trees themselves. Let it ever be remembered, particularly in respect to soils that are of poor or of moderate fertility, that all these crops will remove their full share of plant-food from the land that we have already appropriated to another object, and that the main crop which we desire to draw its sustenance from the earth for a long series of years, may thus be robbed of its proper nourishment. Under such circumstances we must meet the emergency by applications of fertilizing materials. I am aware that it may be urged by the theorists of agriculture, that these crops call upon the soil for different elements, and that, according to the customary views of the objects attained by a rotation, they may even be of advantage to those which are to follow. Others will make the practical observation that the fertilizing materials of common use in modern agriculture, may so readily be applied to compensate for these abstractions from the soil, that this is a matter of little moment, and not worthy of serious consideration. But it should be observed that, while men will often be induced to apply fertilizers to the temporary crop, counting upon an immediate return for their outlay, they seldom feel willing to make any return to the soil in compensation for what they have already removed from it, and rather wait until the necessity for such enrichment becomes painfully apparent in the diminished productiveness of their fields.

Hoed crops, such as those above mentioned, should alone be allowed to occupy the space between the young trees, and on no account should any white straw crops, or grasses be introduced, at least for several years, nor until the orchard shall have become well established. In many species of fruits, it is undoubtedly better to keep up the surface cultivation continuously, at least wherever the characters of the site and soil will permit it; but there are many situations where the abruptness of the declivities appropriated to fruit-growing, and often admirably adapted to such purpose, absolutely forbid continued cultivation. In such places it will be necessary soon to withdraw the plow, and to depend upon loosening the soil about the trees with the spade or fork, and upon the mellowing and meliorating effects of mulching. The expense of all the operations that are performed by human labor renders them inapplicable, except in small orchards and gardens; and in all large plantations we must depend upon the common earth-workers that are drawn by horses. Among these, a preference should be given to such as stir and pulverize the soil near the surface only; shallow culture of the upper layers of earth effects the objects in view better than that which is deeper. The intruding weeds are subdued and a mellow condition of the earth is the result, while the roots are not torn and bruised, but are encouraged to turn their feeding fibres into the stratum of mellow soil above them. When the trees have become well established, or when the nature of the soil and the broken character of the surface of the orchard require it, we may seed down the ground with clover, which is preferred to any of the grasses: the broad foliage will shade the ground, and may remain on the surface as a mulch, or be moderately pastured by suitable stock.

Mulching the young orchard has some advantages over cultivation, but except in the proximity of the salt-marshes of the East, or near the great straw piles on the vast grain fields of the Western prairies, it is almost impossible to procure mulching materials for extensive orchards; so that, unless we consider the clover and other legumes as a living mulch, or grow such crops upon the land itself, to be used in this way, we shall be thrown back upon culture of the surface, which, in the mellow soil thus produced, furnishes a most admirable mulching, that fills all the indications, at least in the season when it is most needed. This is a matter of the greatest importance, especially during the first year after planting, when our trees so imperatively demand the protection of a mulch; and it is found that when the usual applications of straw or similar material cannot be obtained, or are unsuitable for the situation, especial attention to the condition of the upper layer of earth about the trees is of the greatest importance; this should be kept thoroughly loosened and finely disintegrated for the admission of air and moisture.

Mulching, even of an old and apparently exhausted orchard, has been found to exercise a most happy effect upon its health and productiveness. Such a one growing upon a tenacious clay, which had ceased to yield any crops for years, was restored to abundant fruitfulness by covering the ground with a couple of inches of spent bark from an adjoining tannery, and similar effects have been produced by the application of straw, and of the bagasse from sorghum, where those materials could be procured; but these were necessarily limited to a small number of trees, and they can never be adopted in the treatment of large orchards. Fortunately, for us, however, in some kinds the trees themselves provide us shade for the ground, when they are properly trained and closely planted, which will prevent the intrusion of weeds and grasses, and the falling leaves and spray will also yield a mulching of no mean value. Indeed, the trimmings from the orchard, as well as the decaying foliage that annually falls to the ground, belong to the soil, and might be left upon it with great advantage to keep up its fertility by their decay, and even to increase it, as they do in the natural forest, were it not for the slovenly appearance they produce.

Dr. Ward, of New Jersey, has practiced mulching rather extensively, and with excellent results. He uses salt hay from the marshes; after plowing the ground in the spring, he applies the mulching in a heavy layer, which keeps down the weeds, preserves the moisture of the soil, and exerts a very happy influence upon the trees.

From what has preceded, the reader may infer that the orchard is not to be used for a pasture field, and yet this is a very common appropriation of the inclosure that contains our fruit trees—at least after they have attained sufficient size to be considered out of the way of serious injury. Let it not be supposed that the indiscriminate pasturing of an orchard is advocated; on the contrary, it is wholly deprecated, except as will be indicated below. All stock will trample and harden the soil. Low-headed trees will be sadly injured by live stock of all kinds. Horses and mules will often ruin the trees by destroying the bark, and trimming off the twigs, as high as they can reach. Horned cattle will browse the spray, and where within reach they will also break and twist branches of considerable size. Though much smaller, goats are entirely inadmissable, since they not only trim off all the foliage within their reach, but they will also greedily devour the bark from the trees, and thus commit sad havoc among them. Sheep, on the contrary, may often be introduced into an orchard with advantage, as they will eat off a great many weeds, and thus clear the land of such intruders; but they will also spoil low-headed young trees by eating all the leaves within their reach, and they should never be allowed access to the orchard in winter, at least not while there are any trees remaining with smooth bark, as they will often attack such and strip off all that they can get at: sheep are often very desirable in cider orchards when used to crop off the herbage closely, just before the ripening and fall of the fruit.

The only domestic animals which should ever be allowed free range in the orchard, are swine, and the different sorts of poultry. All of these will prove really useful in the destruction of vast numbers of the insects that are particularly injurious to our cultivated fruits, and which are often enormously multiplied in our old orchards. Swine, it is true, will sometimes learn to climb small trees that have very low branches, which they break off in their attempts to help themselves to the fruit—this has been observed particularly in peach and cherry orchards. These animals are of use too as earth-workers, when they have not been mutilated, for with their peculiarly formed snouts they will turn over a large extent of the surface, while in pursuit of the larvæ and pupæ of many of the destructive insects, that in such stages of their existence occupy the soil beneath our fruit trees; in this manner, swine are valuable adjuvants to the practical entomologist. The hog is a most useful scavenger, and also a great economist in the orchard, for, being omnivorous, after feeding upon the luxuriant herbage of the red clover, he takes his dessert from the fallen fruit, which, being defective, would otherwise be wasted: but we must remember that most of these wind-falls are occupied by the larvæ of insects which are thus put out of the way of doing further harm, while contributing variety to the porcine diet. The additions of manure to the soil, which are distributed over the orchard by these animals, are also found to be of service. Trees, which are frequented by swine, are generally healthy, and the bitter-rot is reported to have disappeared from orchards that were badly affected with that malady before the swine were admitted.

The advantages resulting from keeping both swine and poultry, but particularly the latter, confined among plum trees, is a matter of general notoriety; nor need we inquire whether this depends upon the far-reaching instinct of the insect, which warns her against depositing her eggs where the progeny must surely be destroyed, or upon the actual destruction of the larvæ by these animals, to such an extent as to diminish the number of depredators the following season. We must not, however, depend upon these and other valuable aids, to the exclusion of personal efforts, if we desire to secure good crops of the delicious fruits that usually fall a prey to their attacks.

In conclusion, the orchardist cannot be too strongly impressed with the importance of cultivating his young trees in the most thorough manner; nor can he exercise too much care in avoiding injury to the stems and roots, in

11*

practising this constant culture of the soil. In collections of dwarf fruit trees, he will have less difficulty on this score, because he will be restricted to hand-labor; but the spade and fork will be found much more expensive in their use than the plow and cultivator.

PLOWING UP OLD ORCHARDS.—A question frequently arises as to the best course to be pursued with an old neglected orchard, which has become covered with a dense sod of grass, and this often of an inferior character, and full of disagreeable weeds. Orchards that have been widely planted, and which have gaps from the decay of trees, especially when these have been trimmed up with high stems and long naked branches, do not cast sufficient shade upon the ground to prevent the growth of grass and weeds. These intruders occupy the surface soil to the disadvantage of the roots of the fruit trees, and we may wonderfully improve the health of such orchard by plowing the ground, and at the same time severely pruning the branches and cleansing the bark of these old trees. These good results may be continued by shallow culture of the soil, with suitable applications of manure where needed. By giving a dose of lime, or of marl, and ashes, we shall infuse a new life and growth and productiveness that will astonish and delight us, and reward us for our labors and outlay.

It may be urged as an objection to breaking up the sod, that the most careful plowman will unavoidably damage some of the roots that approach the surface, but this is an injury that must be submitted to; and after all it is not such a serious affair, and is overbalanced by the advantages of renewing the productiveness of the exhausted orchard.

CHAPTER X.

PHILOSOPHY OF PRUNING.

———◦◦◦———

PRUNING, NATURE'S — WE PRUNE, FIRST, FOR SHAPE AND COMELINESS; SECOND, FOR FRUIT — PRUNING YOUNG TREES IN THE NURSERY — RULES FOR — SEASON FOR — PRUNING FOR FRUIT IS TO BE DONE CHIEFLY IN SUMMER — THINNING OUT—SHORTENING-IN—ROOT PRUNING — PHILOSOPHY OF — ADVANTAGES OF - CHARACTER OF ROOTS PRODUCED BY IT — IN THE VINE — SEVERE IN WINTER TO PRODUCE WOOD AND DIMINISH BLOSSOMS — ADAPT TO VARIETIES — IN SUMMER TO DIMINISH EXCESSIVE FRUITAGE, AND TO DIRECT SAP INTO NEW CANES — TRIMMING IN GARDENESQUE, REQUIRING A CORRECT EYE AND GOOD TASTE — PRUNING SHOULD BE CONDUCTED UPON TRULY PHILOSOPHICAL PRINCIPLES, OR NOT AT ALL — QUALIFICATIONS REQUIRED IN THOSE WHO PRUNE — THE OPERATION SELDOM WELL PERFORMED — PRUNING OF THE GRAPE, SHORT AND LONG — REASONS FOR AND OBJECTIONS TO EACH — SEASONS FOR PRUNING THE VINE.

Pruning is one of the most important operations that we perform upon plants,—especially woody plants. Pruning, in some sort, has to be performed at all periods of their existence and growth, and upon all plants, from the noble forest tree, or the fruit trees of the orchard, of what-

251

ever kind, to the humble bushes and brambles that yield us
their abundant and most welcome fruits: the trailing vine
that adorns our arbors and covers our trellises with its
rich and tempting clusters of grapes, also needs to be pruned. Many herbaceous plants are also submitted to judicious pruning, and yield in consequence an increased product of fruit. Our ornamental gardeners and plant-grow-
ers practice pruning most admirably upon their house-
plants, and by their successful practice, they produce the
most wonderful effects, which are manifested in the vigor,
thrift, symmetry, and blossoming of their specimens.

And yet, when we come to travel about the country,
and to see the shrubberies, the parks, the orchards, fruit-
gardens, and vineyards, as they are, we shall be struck
with the great amount of ignorance or neglect manifested
by what we everywhere behold! Still more shall we be
surprised, when we hear nurserymen and orchardists, men
who have had opportunities for extended observation, and
those too, who are considered successful cultivators, advo-
cate the idea that trees should not be pruned at all. An
apology may be found for them in the many instances of
bad pruning that may frequently be met with. They may
say that no pruning is better than such mutilation, and
with some varieties of fruit, they may have a show of
reason on their side, as there are many sorts that will
very naturally produce an open head, everywhere provided
with abundant fruit-spurs, which are the great desiderata
of the fruit-grower.

We prune our plants for the most opposite purposes; we
prune to make them assume some desired form, we prune to
produce symmetry, and we prune to tórture them as much

as possible from their natural habit. Again, we prune to make them grow vigorously, and we perform other pruning operations, in order to dwarf and stunt our specimens, and to make them as diminutive as possible. The experienced orchardist will tell you to prune a barren but thrifty tree, in order to make it productive of fruit; and he will also tell you to *prune* one that has expended all its energies in fruit-bearing, and appears likely to exhaust itself to its own destruction. Upon very high authority, supported by universal and annual practice, the vine dresser will tell you to prune your vine in order to make it fruitful; the same authority will advise you to prune in such a manner as to prevent an over-production—and he will insist that you shall prune again during the season of growth, to promote the same objects.

Thus it appears that the ends to be attained by this important operation are exceedingly diverse, and apparently contradictory: nor is it any wonder that the novice should feel bewildered in the midst of directions so opposite, nor even that those who have grown gray in the orchard, should have arrived at the strange conclusions just mentioned, *not to prune at all.* And yet, notwithstanding these apparent contradictions, there is a reason for each of these various modes, as well as for the different seasons that have been recommended for performing the several operations of pruning.

It may be said that in natural trees, whether standing alone in the midst of a prairie, thinly grouped in the "opening," or crowded together in the dense forest, we may behold the most perfect models of beauty and fruitfulness; yet these have never been subjected to the action of the knife, the saw, nor the hatchet. True, and yet they have all been pruned by *nature*. She prunes and trains magnificently, and gives us the finest models for imitation, whether for park scenery, as in the lone tree of the prairie, or in the scattered groups of the island groves that are so often seen in the broad savannas of the West, or in forests of noble shafts, gazed at with admiration, then felled by the ruthless ax, and converted to man's economic uses. She also shows us the pattern in the dense pineries, and other timber tracts of our country. All these have been pruned into their present condition by the hand of nature. In the single specimen, free access of air and light have enabled it to assume its full proportions, developing itself on every side, and giving us the grand and beautiful object we behold. The winds have tossed the branches and some have been broken, the lower ones have quietly and gradually yielded to the smothering influence of those above them, which, in turn, have swept downward toward the ground. In the groves, the scattering trees have for a while enjoyed the same opportunities for development; but at length their branches have met together, and interlocked in friendly embrace. Those that were nearest the ground had already begun to suffer from the denser canopy above them but the great sturdy boughs that had shot upward so as to form a part of the crown, were able to retain their vantage ground, and continue as important members of the trees. In these illustrations, we have seen more of nature's training than of her pruning; but it must be remembered that training is one of the objects, and indeed, a leading element of pruning, and is very properly a matter for our consideration.

In the dense primeval forest we see nature's pruning exhibited upon a grand and perfect scale; tall, straight, and noble trunks rise majestically on every hand; not a twig nor limb breaks the symmetry of the gradually tapering shafts, that are clothed in bark which does not indicate that they had ever been furnished with branches; and yet they have borne branches from their base to their summit, and nature has so neatly removed them that we cannot detect the marks of her pruning-saw. How this has been effected, may be seen in any dense thicket of young forest growth. It is simply a smothering of the lower branches by those next above them, which has destroyed their vitality, and their decay has soon followed; while a new growth of branches at a higher point, in turn, performs the same office of destruction upon those next below them. As there is no outlet for the wood-growth but in an upward direction, upwards they must needs go, and as there is no light nor air for lateral branches under such a canopy of shade, death and decay ensue, and down they perforce must come.

If it be asked why we prune at all, it may be answered in general terms that in the orchard, our objects in performing this operation, are two-fold.

1st—We prune for shape and comeliness, and for the removal of dead and dying branches, in aid of nature, but working in sympathy with her.

2d—We prune for the sake of inducing fruitfulness.

Let us consider some of the principles that are to guide us in these operations.

The first object, that of producing the desired shape of the future tree, is chiefly done upon the young subject, even in the nursery-row. The judicious pruner, being well aware of the upward tendency of young growth, and that this is increased by the crowded condition of the trees in the nursery square, seeks to overcome the evil by proper pruning. If the growth be altogether upward, with no side branches the first season, the stem will be slender, often so much so as to bend over with its own weight. The wise nurseryman carefully avoids disturbing the leaves or lateral branches, well knowing their importance in forming the woody trunk. At the proper season he trims his trees down, instead of trimming them up—this he does by heading them back to the hight at which he desires them to form their branches—at the same time, he shortens in the laterals; his object in both instances being to check the upward tendency of growth by removing the strong terminal buds, which would naturally have formed the new shoots the coming season. The result of this treatment is to call into action several buds at the upper part of the stock. These are to form the arms of the tree, and hence a very important part of the pruning and training of the plant is thus performed at once by this simple operation of heading-back the young nursery tree. But further attention is needed, as these arms develop themselves during the next season of growth; they should not be too numerous, nor too much crowded together; they should not be too nearly matched in strength, and one should be kept as a leader, stronger than the rest. Never allow two shoots to remain contending for the mastery; one of them should be subordinated by cutting, breaking, or twisting, as soon as it is observed; for how beautifully developed, a tree grown in this way, may appear when well balanced, there is always danger of its splitting down when heavily laden with fruit. This very common error of our orchards used to be quaintly illustrated by a dear old friend on the prairies of Illinois, who cited the advice of a Scotch jockey to whom he had applied for counsel in the purchase of a piece of horse-flesh. "Ne'er buy a horse whose twa fore-legs cum oot frae ae hole," said he, and Mr. W. Stewart applied the same principle to his young fruit trees, by never allowing them to have two equal leaders, branching from one point. It is also important to have the lateral branches regularly distributed on different sides.

The precise point or elevation point at which this heading-back should be done, will depend very much upon the object of the cultivator, and whether he desires to produce a high or a low head, a standard, half standard, or a dwarf, or conical tree—such as are often called pyramids. He will study the wants and fancies of his customers in this matter, but we of the West, have learned the importance for us, at least, of *trimming our trees down*, and not trimming them up, as is often done by those who anticipate plowing and planting crops under the shade of their orchards. The proper point for forming the branches to make the head, will very much depend, however, upon the habit of the variety; whether it be drooping, spreading, or upright. The former will require the branches to be started at a higher point. The proper season for performing this kind of pruning is in the early spring, or after the severe frosts of winter have passed; and with some kinds of orchard trees, it may be done at the time of transplanting them, when they need a severe pruning.

The second object of pruning being done with a view

to the production of fruitfulness in the tree, is to be practised chiefly in the summer.   At the same time, or during
the growing season, much may be done to advantage, both
in thinning-out and shortening-in such parts of the tree,
as may need these plans of treatment.   Various methods
are pursued to produce fruitfulness, all of them depending
upon the fact that this condition arises from the natural
habit of a tree to make its wood-growth freely for a series
of years.   After it has built up a complicated structure
of limbs and branches, with some consequent obstruction
to the flow of sap, depending upon the hardening of the
woody tissues, and the tortuous course of its circulation,
it then appears to have reached its maturity, or its fruit-
bearing condition.   It then ceases to make such free
wood-growth, and prepares a set of buds, which develop
flowers and fruit.

Now this period of growth and unfruitfulness may continue for a longer or shorter time in different varieties of
fruits; and the shortening of this, is the great object of
summer pruning, and of other methods of producing
fruitfulness that may be classed under this second head of
the objects of pruning.

To appreciate their importance and the mode in which
the effect is produced, we must ever bear in mind the two
great acts of vegetable life, that of wood-growth or
growth by extension, and the wonderful morphological
change of this growth into flowers and fruit.   These are,
in some sense, antagonistic.   The first is essential to the
production of timber, to the building up of the tree, and
should be encouraged to do its work undisturbed, up to a
certain point, that we may have a substantial frame-work

by which our fruits can be supported. The latter, however, is the ultimate desideratum with fruit-growers, and in our impatience to reap a quick reward, we often resort to measures that tend to curtail the usefulness, size, and beauty, as well as the permanence of our trees. This is an illustration of the axiom, that whatever threatens the vitality of a plant, tends to make it fruitful; it calls into activity the instinctive effort to perpetuate the species by the production of seed, that may be separated from the parent, and establish a separate and independent existence, to take the place of that, the life of which is threatened.

Summer pruning and pinching interferes with the growth by extension, and threatens the very life of the tree; the entire removal of all new shoots and their foliage, and the removal of the successive attempts by the tree at their reproduction, will cause its death in a little while. Their partial abstraction, as practiced in summer pruning and pinching, being an attack of the same kind, results in the formation of fruit-buds. The operations of budding and grafting upon an uncongenial stock, interrupting the circulation by ringing, by ligatures, by hacking, twisting, and bending downward, all tend to check the growth by extension, and are attended by similar results, since they are antagonistic to the mere production of wood. Shortening-in the branches of some species, which form their fruit-buds upon the shoots of the current year, has the effect to give them a fuller development, if performed during the summer, but if deferred until the following spring, it will have the directly opposite result, and will cause the production of woody shoots at the expense of the fruit.

The season for pruning has been made the subject of much discussion, and different periods have been very confidently advised by different authorities, from which it may safely be inferred that all are somewhat right, or may be supported by good reasons. This refers of course to pruning in its general sense, of trimming, and applies to the removal of limbs of greater or less size. We always desire to avoid the removal of large limbs, and should endeavor to provide against the necessity of such removal, by trimming our orchards sufficiently when they are young, and while the branches are small; but when such removal becomes absolutely necessary, it should be performed late in the autumn, when vegetation is at rest, because it is found that such large wounds, which cannot be soon healed over by the new growth, will at this season dry in, and resist the action of the elements better than if the section had been made when the wood was full of sap in active circulation.

Early spring is a favorite period for pruning, chiefly because it is comparatively a period of leisure; the weather is less inclement than in winter, and the absence of foliage affords us an opportunity to see our work and to anticipate its effects upon the tree. So soon as the buds begin to swell and the foliage to expand, pruning should be arrested, unless in small trees, because the sap is in active motion, and the material called *cambium* is not yet developed, hence the wounds will bleed, and are not so readily healed over; besides, the bark at this season is very readily separated from the wood, and bad wounds are thus frequently produced by the pruner, which may seriously damage the tree. Then follows a period when pruning had better be suspended until the time that the trees have completed their growth by extension, and formed the terminal bud at the ends of their shoots. The date cannot be given, but it is sufficiently indicated by this mark in nature's calendar; the formation and full development of the terminal bud, and by the copious deposits of woody matter throughout the tree. The annual layer of fibres is then being produced, and the tissues are in the formative stage; the tree now possesses within its own organism the best of all plasters to cure and cover the wounds made by the saw and knife, now the tree possesses the true *vis medicatrix naturæ* in the highest degree.

A few intelligent nurserymen have learned this very important lesson, and have applied it in the preparation of their trees, for the exposure incident to their removal from the nursery to the orchard. A very few practice it systematically; I knew one, (alas, for the lamented Beeler, of Indiana), who acted upon the suggestion made to him by observations and experiments in vegetable physiology. He left the side branches, though subordinated by shortening when necessary, in order to give stocky stems to his trees, and then removed them with the knife during the summer before they were to be sold and planted, instead of waiting until they were dug and sent to the packing house in the fall or spring. The result was, that while his stems were stout and stocky, they were also smooth, the wounds neatly healed over with new bark, instead of being open from the fresh cuts and liable to crack or bleed, as they would have done had this pruning been deferred until after digging, either in the fall or spring. This may be considered a small matter, but it is an illustration of the principle involved in selecting the period for pruning.

For the removal of small limbs from young trees, hardly any time can come amiss — better to do it out of season than to neglect it, and it is a good rule to have a sharp pruning knife always at hand when passing through our young orchards. There is but one time when pruning is absolutely interdicted, and that is when the wood is frozen. When so circumstanced, it should never be cut nor disturbed in any manner — not even to gratify your best friend, by helping him to a few grafts from your proved tree of some coveted variety. Let him wait for a thaw, or go away without the grafts, rather than commit such an outrage upon your tree: as to approach it with a knife when frozen.

While considering the question of the proper season for pruning, there is one axiom of great importance which should be firmly impressed upon the mind of the orchardist. Much will depend upon which of the two leading objects, above indicated, he may have in view — vigor of growth and symmetry of form, or simply fruitfulness, as the result of his labors in pruning his trees. Pruning at one season will induce the former result, at a different period of the year the same work will conduce to the latter; hence the postulate *Prune in winter for wood; in summer for fruit.*

CHAPTER XI.

THINNING.

———◦◦◦———

Every person who has looked at a bearing fruit tree in the winter season, must have been struck with wonder at the great profusion of fruit-buds with which it was clothed; they are crowded along the slender spray of some varieties as thickly as a necklace of beads, or still more abundantly, like clusters of pearls, they are crowded to-

263

gether upon the little fruit-spurs. We are inclined to cavil at this profusion of nature, and to ask why this waste of vegetative effort. But we may rest assured that it is only another evidence of the unerring wisdom of Him who doeth all things well.

All blossoming and fruiting is but a changed condition of those buds that would otherwise have produced leaves and wood-growth. Every tree, sooner or later, reaches a point which we call its period of maturity, when some of its buds are thus modified. The same elemental parts are still present; but those that were arranged for the production of an elongated shoot, with leaves set around it in some definite manner, and destined for the formation of woody growth, are now so constituted as to have a growth of very short extension, and furnished with modified leaves, so changed, that we scarcely recognize them thus crowded together upon this shortened and modified axis. We here take our first lesson in the very interesting study of morphology, or the science of the changes of form to which the parts of a plant are subjected, in the production of flowers and fruit, from what were otherwise the source of shoots and leaves. This will be found one of the most interesting branches of the study of botany, as it leads us to the investigation of one of the most beautiful displays of Divine power, and, like all such studies, gives us more and more elevated views of the exalted wisdom and benevolence of an All-wise Creator, who has produced nothing in vain, and who, while creating worlds and systems of the greatest magnificence, has condescended to prepare the most tiny flower, and its previous bud, in the most perfect manner. ·

The study of morphology which gives us such an insight into the mechanism of the plant, and which leads us into such mazes of wonder and admiration, cannot now detain us further than to be named and referred to as the explanation of the formation of what we call fruit or blossom buds. The reader is referred to the full explanations of this subject by the famous philosopher and poet, Goethe; or, if more conveniently accessible, to his English translators, or to the appropriate chapters in any of the modern text books of botany.

When the plant is young, its chief object is to grow; it must acquire size and development, to enable it to produce and bear up the enormous crop it is destined one day to yield. Hence in the early years of a tree there is none, or very little of this transformation of the buds, which are all of the pointed character, and when excited into growth, they all produce shoots and leaves only, which result in the formation of an increase of the woody fabric, that we call the tree. This period of adolescence is longer or shorter in different species and varieties—in some it may extend through many years. Thus, the American Aloe is called the Century Plant, from the common belief that it must survive a hundred summers before this stage of maturity and blossoming is reached; whereas this plant only needs a period of thirty years or less to produce its blossoms, when it is favorably situated as to soil and climate.

There is, it is probable, a definite period at which each kind of plant will have these changes occur in the buds, when they will begin to flower and to produce fruit. This period may be accelerated or retarded, to some extent, by human means; for we have observed, that whatever pro-

12

duces excessive vigor, is attended with the formation of leaf buds; whereas, all those conditions and circumstances that check the vigorous growth by extension, provided they do not too greatly impair the vitality of the plant, will conduce to the formation of flower-buds.

Some of these conditions consist in starving the tree, or by planting it in a sterile soil, that has deficient moistuie; by severely crowding the roots, or by cutting them, as in root pruning; in grafting a portion of the young plant upon an old or an uncongenial stock, or one that is naturally dwarfish; in ringing the bark; in frequent transplanting, or in continued summer pinching; in short, almost any circumstances which appear to threaten the life of the tree, seem to excite within it an effort for the preservation and perpetuation of the species, by changing the bud plants, attached to the parent, into seed plants, that may and will be separated from it to reach the soil eventually, and there to establish an independent existence.

As the tree advances in growth, and approaches toward its natural period of maturity, it is supposed that there is an accumulation of nutritive matter within it, and at the same time the roots will have exhausted the soil, to some extent, of the elements that contributed to the production of wood-growth, and the result is the formation of flower-buds. Now it becomes a nice matter to preserve the proper balance between these two systems of growth, the wood producing and the fruit forming. Two opposite systems of production have become established in the tree, the one infertile, the other producing the desired fruits; the one preserving the health and vigor of the tree, the other tending to preserve the species at the same time that it satisfies our demands for fruit, but also meanwhile tending to the destruction of the tree, for all old trees are apt to overbear. Young trees, on the contrary, in which the vigor of wood-growth remains in full activity, very often produce fruit-buds and blossoms, but do not perfect their fruit, which either fails to set, from some imperfection of the organs of reproduction, or falls prematurely, in consequence of the wood system absorbing the nutriment, or failing to prepare the proper juices for their support. Trees, in these different conditions, require an entirely opposite treatment. The younger need summer pruning and pinching, to check their too great vigor, and to develop the laterals or spurs with their blossom buds; the older need winter pruning, for the double purpose of reducing the amount of fruit, and also to excite renewed vigor in the production of wood growth that shall take the place of that which has been removed. This subject will be more appropriately discussed in another chapter, to which the reader is referred; while we proceed to the legitimate topic of thinning fruit.

Thinning fruit is not practiced as it should be, particularly on the apple; old trees are often too fruitful, so much so as not only to deteriorate the fruit, but to injure the tree itself. This is so much the case with certain varieties, as to constitute a serious objection to planting them; other sorts so exhaust themselves by over-production in one season, as to be barren, or nearly so, the next year, during which period of rest they are able to recuperate their energies and to provide a new set of flower-buds. These are called biennial bearers, and such are quite numerous in our orchards. Those kinds that are prone to overbear every year, are often objectionable on account of the diminished size and inferior character of their fruits, which result from this cause, particularly when the trees have become old. The great desideratum, especially with those who object to the trouble of thinning the fruit, is to find a variety that will produce an even or well distributed, continuous, and moderate yield—an annual bearer, that does not exhaust itself by the production of one enormous crop so as to require it to rest and recuperate. Such varieties are to be found in our collections, and should be highly prized.

But to return to our topic, the bold method of reducing the crop by winter pruning, has already been alluded to, and is highly recommended for such old trees as have ceased producing thrifty shoots of wood-growth at their tips, and have taken on an excessive tendency to fruitage. There are other methods of producing this desired effect, diminishing the amount of fruit when excessive, and thereby greatly enlarging the size, and improving the flavor of that which is left behind: some of these will now be mentioned.

DISBUDDING.—One of these consists in the removal of alternate buds, or even a greater proportion than one half; this may be performed either in the end of winter or in early spring, or even after the buds have pushed, still later in the season. This work may be done with the fingers, a knife, or by using the shears, when the buds are terminal, as in old bearing apples and pears, or on some cherries. This plan has been practiced with very good success upon the Duchesse pear, by T. W. Field, who accidentally had his attention directed to the feasibility of making this variety very productive. He had observed that certain trees, which were rubbed so by the cart-wheels as to be stripped of a portion of their buds in the winter season, instead of being injured thereby, were more productive than those which retained all of their abundant spurs and blossoms, and which, nevertheless, often bore sparsely. Improving upon this hint, he has since planted some such varieties in close rows or hedges, which he trims annually with the shears to keep them within bounds, and at the same time to diminish the amount of blossoms. Disbudding is systematically pursued in the European fruit-gardens, and we have elaborate directions for the season and mode of performing the operation, which is extensively practiced, particularly on the trees that are grown as espaliers, and those kept in orchard houses. If neglected, the trees become exhausted by over-production; and the failure of production by the fruit-spurs which results, causes vacant spaces upon the tree, which are afterward, with difficulty, restored to a profitable condition.

Another method, and the one usually pursued by those who practice thinning, is, to go over their trees after blossoming, while the fruit is still small, and systematically remove such a proportion as they may deem sufficient to relieve them of the surplus; and while so doing, they select for removal all the inferior specimens. This is found to pay very well in the increased size, appearance, and flavor of those that remain, and is practiced by all good horticulturists.

It is found in some varieties that the thinning may be done when the fruit has attained to one-half its usual size, so that it may be marketed, and yet those which are left, will swell out to their full proportions after this removal, and will realize, when harvested, more money, and will even be of greater weight than if the whole crop had been left upon the tree until its natural period of maturity. The reason is obvious, and depends upon the greater size and fuller development of the fruit, which remains after thinning.

SUMMER PRUNING has already been alluded to as one of the methods of producing fruitfulness. When it is here introduced as a means of thinning the fruit, the recommendation may appear somewhat paradoxical—yet it is not so. Neither is this cutting a parallel operation to that in which we seek to check the excessive vigor of young shoots by pinching and heading-in, with a view to directing the sap to the lateral buds so as to cause their development for the formation of fruit-spurs, which will insure a greater production of fruit: whereas this summer pruning removes a portion of the crop to be supported by the tree. This plan is most successfully practiced by judicious orchardists, among whom may be named Dr. Hull, of Alton, Ill., who has thus treated his peaches, nectarines, and plums. This process consists in cutting off the ends of the shoots that are laden with fruit, while these are yet quite small; the superabundance is thus removed in a great degree by the knife, and the excess of foliage is also diminished so as to expose the fruit freely to the sun and air, which insures an increased size and heightened color, particularly to the peaches and nectarines. The remaining fruit is also suitably thinned so that no specimens shall crowd one another. The exact distances between them must be determined by the judgment of the operator;

some have decided that peaches should not be nearer than nine inches; plums and nectarines may be separated by a smaller distance; but it is not easy to lay down a precise rule.

Thinning is not often practiced upon the strawberry crop, which appears able upon suitable soils to produce a great abundance of fine fruit, but it may. be done by the curious, and enormous show specimens, such as are often exhibited at fairs, are produced by special care and high manuring, aided greatly by judicious thinning; not only by cutting back a portion of the crowns, so as to throw the whole force of the plant into one or two trusses, but still further, by removing with the scissors a portion of the blossoms or fruit, so that the few which are left may become enormously distended with the nutriment that had been stored up in the plant for a much greater number. Some may consider this one of the tricks of the trade, and so it is when merely done for the sake of deceiving the public, who are asked to purchase the variety by the sample of fruit, without detailing the arts by which the results were accomplished: but there can be no objection raised against such practices when pursued by the amateur for the sake of producing unusually large fruits of any variety.

The English pursue a similar method with their show gooseberries; by means of thinning and high feeding, with great attention to watering, these fruits are made to assume gigantic proportions that are little dreamed of by cultivators of the smaller varieties, which are chiefly grown in this country.

The grape is very prone to over-production, and the

crop, as well as the vine itself, is often much injured by a want of attention to this particular. So avaricious is man, that few persons will exert the needed firmness and perseverance to remove the excess which the beautiful vine annually affords. The result of this neglect is apparent at the vintage, especially when from any fault of the season, or from the invasion of insects or of mildew, the foliage may have been damaged, as it frequently is, to a considerable extent. Then we find large quantities of the grapes so deficient in color and flavor as to be worthless; in some varieties whole bunches will hang flaccid, withered, and insipid—while perhaps a few, more favorably situated, will have their proper flavor. The grape vine is well called beautiful, and it is capable of sustaining most wonderful amounts of fruit; but on young vines, especially, it is very bad policy to allow of this over-production.

The tendency to fruitage may be met in different ways, a few of which will now be pointed out, and all planters are urged to observe and to practice some of these plans for reducing the exuberance of this kind of fruit. In the first place we practice winter pruning, regardless of its established and well-known effect of producing an increase of wood-growth, for this is what we desire to obtain in the vine, on account of its habit of yielding its fruit on wood of the previous year's growth; by this means we are able to pursue the renewal system, which is so generally preferred, and thus we may keep our vines perpetually clothed with new wood, or canes as they are technically called. By this winter pruning we can reduce the amount of wood that is of a bearing character, to any point which may be deemed desirable, according to the strength and

age of the vine, and thus the crop is thinned by a whole-
sale process of lopping off the superabundance of buds,
that would have produced an excess of fruit. Another
method of thinning is, to rub out a portion of the shoots,
this may be every alternate branch in close jointed varieties of the vine: this is to be done soon after the buds
have burst, and while the branches are yet quite small, so
that the vital forces may be directed to those that remain.
Wherever double shoots appear, the weaker should always
be removed.

Still another method of reducing the superabundance,
remains to be noticed; this consists in thinning the grapes
themselves, the separate berries, which, in some varieties,
are often so crowded upon the bunch, as to prove a serious
injury to one another. In hardy out-door culture this is
seldom practiced, being less necessary than in the large
varieties of foreign grapes that are grown under glass.
These are systematically thinned with the scissors, so that
none shall crowd together; and this process, repeated from
time to time, is found to produce much finer and larger
berries and heavier bunches than when all are left.

A very rude method has sometimes been pursued in
thinning the superabundance of fruit upon apple trees. It
appears so very Gothic that its description may only excite a smile, when it is stated that it consists in threshing
the tree with a long slender pole, by which a portion of
the fruit is cast to the ground. Rude and primitive as
this method may appear, it is surely better than no thinning at all, and is attended with this good result, for which
it deserves some commendation; the threshing removes
portions of the excessive twiggy spray that always abounds

12*

upon such trees as those under consideration, and thus, in a degree, it prevents the recurrence of so heavy a crop the following year. Whenever an old orchard has reached this condition of over-fruitfulness, however, the best method of thinning is to give a severe winter pruning; removing portions of the spray and encouraging the free growth of young wood in various parts of the top, to replace the older portions that were removed.

CHAPTER XII.

RIPENING AND PRESERVING FRUITS.

———◦◦◦———

RIPENING FRUITS.—Having succeeded in bringing our trees into a productive condition, we now come to a period of their history which is possessed of great interest to the orchardist. While he is contemplating the rich returns for his capital and labor expended upon the orchard, however, he will find many circumstances in the functions of his plants that will amply repay him for their careful study. Nor should he consider these only as matters of philosophical interest, for they will often lead him into courses of treatment that will enable him to secure richer returns than he would otherwise attain. A few of these will be presented in the commencement of this chapter, nor need any apology be offered for quoting one of the highest authorities in the language upon this branch of botanical study. Balfour gives the following account of the changes which occur in the vegetable economy during the formation and ripening of fruits, under which term he includes, in botanical language, all seeds, whether the dry pericarps, or the pulpy drupes, and other appendages, which are recognized as fruits proper in pomological language.

" While the fruit enlarges, the sap is drawn towards it, and a great exhaustion of the juices of the plant takes place. In annuals, this exhaustion is such as to destroy the plants; but if they are prevented from bearing fruit, they may be made to live for two or more years. Perennials, by acquiring increased vigor, are able better to bear the demand made upon them during fruiting. If large and highly flavored fruit is desired, it is of importance to allow an accumulation of sap to take place before the plant flowers. When a very young plant is permitted to blossom, it seldom brings fruit to perfection. When a plant produces fruit in very large quantities, gardeners are in the habit of thinning it early, in order that there may be an increased supply of sap for that which remains. In this way, peaches, nectarines, apricots, etc., are rendered larger and better flavored. When the fruiting is checked for one season, there is an accumulation of nutritive matter which has a beneficial effect upon the subsequent crop.

"The pericarp is at first of a green color, and performs the same functions as the other green parts of plants, decomposing carbonic acid under the agency of light and liberating oxygen. Saussure asserts that all fruits, in a green state, are adequate to perform this process of deoxidation. As the pericarp advances to maturity, it either becomes dry or succulent. In the former case it changes into a brown or white color, and has a quantity of ligneous matter deposited in its substance, so as to acquire great hardness, where it is incapable of performing any process of vegetable life; in the latter it becomes fleshy in its texture, and assumes various bright tints. In fleshy fruits, however, there is frequently a deposition of ligneous cells in the endocarp, forming the stone of the fruit; and even in the pulpy matter of the sarcocarp, there are found isolated cells of a similar nature, as in some varieties of pear, where they cause a peculiar grittiness. The contents of the cells near the outside of succulent fruits are thickened by exhalation, and a process of endosmose goes on, by which the thinner contents of the inner cells pass outward, and thus cause swelling of the fruit. As the fruit advances to maturity, however, this exhalation diminishes, the water becoming free and entering into new combinations. In all pulpy fruits, which are not green, there are changes going on by which carbon is separated in combination with oxygen.

* * * "Succulent fruits contain a large quantity of water along with cellulose or lignine, sugar, gummy matter or dextrine, albumen, coloring matter, various organic acids, as citric, malic and tartaric, combined with lime and alkaline substances, beside a pulpy gelatinous matter, which is converted by acids into pectine, whence pectic acid is formed by the action of albumen. Pectine is soluble in water, and exists in the pulp of fruits, as apples, gooseberries, currants, strawberries, etc. Pectic acid is said to consist of C. 14, H. 3, O. 12 + H.O. It absorbs water, and is changed into a jelly-like matter, hence its use in making preserves. Each kind of fruit is flavored with a peculiar aromatic substance. Starch is rarely present in the pericarp of the fruit, although it occurs commonly in the seed. * * *

"During the ripening much of the water disappears, while the cellulose or lignine and the dextrine are converted into sugar. Berard is of opinion that the changes in fruits are caused by the action of the oxygen of the air. Freney found that fruits, covered with varnish, did not ripen. As the process of ripening becomes perfected, the acids combine with alkalies, and thus the acidity of the fruit diminishes, while its sweetness increases. The formation of sugar is by some attributed to the action of organic acids on the vegetable constituents, gum, dextrine, and starch; others think that the cellulose and lignine are similarly changed by the action of acids. The formation of sugar is said to be prevented by watering the tree with alkaline solutions. * * * In seasons, when there is little sun, but a great abundance of moisture, succulent fruits become watery and lose their flavor. The same thing frequently takes place in young trees with abundance of sap, and in cases where a large supply of water has been given artificially." Travelers, who have eaten the magnificent specimens of fruits produced by irrigation, in California, tell us that they are deficient in flavor, and the same thing is sometimes observed as a result of an unusually wet season.

"It is not easy in all cases to determine the exact time when the fruit is ripe. In dry fruits, the period immediately before dehiscence,* is considered as that of maturation; but in pulpy fruits, there is much uncertainty. It is usual to say that edible fruits are ripe when their ingredients are in such a state of combination as to give the most agreeable flavor.. After such are ripe, in the ordinary sense, so as to be capable of being used for food, they undergo further changes by the oxidation of their tissues, even after being separated from the plant. In some cases these changes improve the quality of the fruit, as in the case of the medlar, the austerity of which is thus still further diminished. In the pear, this process renders it soft, but still fit for food, while in the apple it causes a decay which acts injuriously on its qualities. By this process of oxidation, the whole fruit is ultimately reduced to a putrescent mass, which probably acts beneficially in promoting the germination of the seeds when the fruit drops on the ground.

"The periods of time required for ripening the fruit, varies in different plants. Most fruits ripen within a year from the expansion of the flower, some come to maturity within a few days, others require months. Certain plants,

---

* Bursting open of the pods, or of the hulls of nuts.

as some Coniferæ, require more than a year, and in the Metrosideros the fruit remains attached to the branch for several years. The following is a general statement of the usual time required for the maturation of fruits: —

Grasses and Grains............................13 to 15 days.
Raspberry, Strawberry, Cherry.......................2 months.
Bird-cherry, Lime-tree..............................3　"
Roses, White Thorn, Horsechestnut.................4　"
Vine, Pear, Apple, Walnut, Beech, Plum, Nut, Almond.....................................5 to 6　"
Olive, Savin..7　"
Colchicum, Mistletoe.................. ....8 to 9　"
Coniferæ......................................10 to 12　"
Some Coniferæ, certain Oaks, and Metrosideros................... ....above 12　"

"The ripening of fruits may be accelerated by·the application of heat, the placing of dark-colored bricks below it, and by removing a ring of bark, so as to lead to an accumulation of sap. It has been observed that plants, subjected to a high temperature, not unfrequently prove abortive; this seems to result from the over stimulation, causing the production of uni-sexual flowers alone. Trees are sometimes made to produce fruit by checking their roots when too luxuriant, and by preventing the excessive development of branches." [*] Here we have the explanation of the processes of root pruning and of summer pinching, and shortening-in, which have been more extensively introduced upon another page; as well as the plan for inducing fruitfulness in such trees as are tardy from excessive wood-growth, by hacking the bark to interrupt the flow of sap from the buds to the roots; by

---

[*] Balfour's Manual.

this, some of the former are changed to flower-buds.

We may learn to judge of the condition of ripeness of our larger succulent fruits, such as apples and pears, by a little experience. When ready to be picked, they will have attained their maximum size, their color will have changed somewhat from its greenness, and they will assume a sort of translucency that indicates the approach of maturity; but the best practical test for the fruit-gatherer, is the ready separation of the stem from its attachment. In those fruits, which are suspended by a stem of considerable length, and in which this organ belongs to the fruit itself, and is intimately connected with its tissues, we shall find that it will part easily from the branch at that period of ripeness when it is best to separate it. Such fruits are often much improved by a continuation of the process of ripening after they are gathered, but this more properly belongs to another division of the subject. There is another class of fruits which are found to attain their greatest excellence and most perfect ripening upon the tree itself, and these can never be enjoyed elsewhere in so great perfection as in close proximity to the place of their production; because, so soon as they are separated from their connection with the plant, a process of decomposition commences, they begin to decay, and many of them soon become really unwholesome. Most of those that are called stone-fruits are of this character, such as peaches, nectarines, apricots, plums, and cherries—all of which have a very transitory period of excellence. The same is still more remarkably the case with most of the berries, hence all of these classes of fruits are better adapted to a near than to a distant market.

With apples and pears, however, the case is quite different. Some of these, it is true, especially some of the summer varieties, will attain a perfect state of ripeness while yet attached to the tree, and some of them will even remain hanging to the twig, until they reach that condition of over-ripeness in which they lose a portion of their fine juices and become mealy, or incipient decay may set in, so as to make them rotten at the core. Hence, in nearly all varieties, it is found best to pluck the fruit a little prematurely, and we are guided by the natural indication of the falling of a portion of the crop. By this means we can, in a degree, control the final ripening of our fruits; and we have the great advantage of being able to ship them in a firm condition to distant markets, so as to arrive at the end of a long journey in prime order; whereas, if thoroughly ripe, they could only be transported a few miles, and then needing the greatest care in their handling. Our summer varieties always require to be near their ultimate ripeness when gathered, for, if plucked too soon, they will wither, and be worthless. Among these, there are some varieties, particularly of the apple, which continue ripening for a long period. In the limited family orchard this quality is a great desideratum in the summer fruits, but it is quite otherwise in the orchards, which are planted for profit in the market, because of the increased expense of gathering only a few at a time repeatedly, instead of clearing the tree at once. It is also found to be an advantage in shipping, to have a considerable quantity of a kind to send off at one time.

GATHERING.—We now come to the important matter of harvesting our crops of fruits that have been the cause of so much care and anxiety, as well as of pleasure. This will require new considerations as to its disposition and preservation to the best advantage, and will call for a discussion of the best modes of packing, storing, ripening, and transportation to market.

From what has already been said with regard to the process of ripening of fruits in the natural way upon the tree, it will be understood that we must gather some kinds before they have reached their perfect condition of maturity. There is a point at which they have obtained, from their connection with the parent tree, all the elements that are necessary to the development of their highest qualities. They may now be separated, not only with safety, but with decided advantage in many instances, as they are improved by the further process of maturation under different circumstances from those supplied by nature, and when properly treated, they will acquire a much finer condition as to delicacy and flavor than is ever reached by ripening upon the tree exposed to the light and air. This, it will be remembered, is not the case with all fruits; for, as has already been stated, there are those which must remain upon the tree until they acquire their most perfect ripeness, and which begin to depreciate in quality so soon as they are separated from their connection with the fruit-bearing twig. These need to be at once disposed of, and the consideration of the best means of transportation, is a question of more importance than any plans for their temporary preservation. They must be sold or used at once, and should be handled with the greatest care, packed in suitable boxes or baskets in the most judicious manner for a good display of their beauties, for their preservation from bruising and decay, and for sending them forward to their destination with the least possible delay: the details of these several parts of the business will be left for the exercise of the ingenuity of the parties most deeply interested. In the class of fruits which are so constituted as to bear and indeed to require picking, before they have reached the period of perfect ripeness we shall find several particulars that need consideration. First, it will be found that the proper time for gathering them varies considerably. Thus, with early apples and pears, a few days only embrace the best period, during which they may be gathered without becoming wilted if plucked too soon, or decaying if left too late. Even with winter fruits, we find that, to have them in perfection, some varieties require to be gathered much earlier than the time usually assigned for harvesting the general crop. It is somewhat singular also, that this course very considerably extends their time of keeping, and that some of those varieties which would become dry, mealy, and insipid, early in the winter, if gathered too late, will remain sound, firm, plump, and juicy, and retain all their fine flavor through the winter, if they have been taken from the tree at an earlier period of the season. They must be left upon the tree until properly developed, however, and then be carefully kept in a cool apartment.

The usual season for gathering winter fruits is October, before the access of severe frosts, and at a time when the wood-growth for the season has been completed, and the foliage is nearly ready to separate from its attachment to the tree. The fruits will then generally part readily from the twigs, without either breaking them or rupturing the fruit-stem, which should always be preserved, and from the apple especially, it should never be pulled out, as is apt to happen in certain varieties, when proper care is not exercised in picking them. Some of the apples that require to be gathered early, are, the Rambo, Pryor's Red, Hubbardston, Westfield, Rhode Island Greening, several Russets, and all those which evince a tendency to fall prematurely. There are others which may be left to a later period with impunity, some of these will even bear a little freezing without serious damage, but we should always endeavor to anticipate the exposure of our fruits to any great depression of temperature while they remain attached to the trees. An early and severe frost has often proved disastrous to a fine crop of apples, thus left too long upon the trees.

For all fruits it is essential that the weather should be fine at the time they are gathered. They should be perfectly dry when plucked, and they must be handled with the greatest care to avoid bruising in the slightest degree. Each specimen must be taken separately in the hand and turned to one side, when, if it do not part readily from the twig, the thumb and finger must be applied to the stem, to aid the separation at the proper point; each is then to be placed in a gathering basket, which should be shallow, and for delicate sorts should be lined loosely with fresh leaves or with soft moss, or a little wilted grass. From the baskets, the fruit should be transferred to its permanent winter quarters, by a careful and judicious hand, who should select them and reject all that are bruised, specked, or otherwise defective, and place them on the shelves, or pack them in the boxes or barrels into which they are placed for preservation, or transportation to market. In packing, it is best to use no material but the fruit itself, which should be so closely placed that they shall not jostle and bruise one another when moved. Some persons use a bag, slung around the neck, when gathering the fruits from the tree; into this they are placed as fast as they are plucked, and successively transferred to the barrels, or poured in piles upon the ground. With very firm varieties, this may be done without serious damage, but the bruising that necessarily ensues will be very prejudicial to all the more delicate fruits, and will materially depreciate the value of such as are also of a pale color. A want of care in this matter of handling fruit is, no doubt, the chief reason for the popular preference of red apples in our markets, since those, that are well covered with a deep color, do not show the bruises that are so unseemly upon the fair cheek of the lighter colored varieties.

The modes of keeping winter fruits are exceedingly various, and some of them are quite primitive. The desiderata are coolness and dryness, which should not be carried to the extent of freezing, nor of desiccation. The simplest method is to place the fruit in a pile upon a dry piece of ground, to cover it thickly with clean dry straw, and, as the winter approaches, to apply a heavy layer of earth, sufficient to keep out the frost. Sometimes this is kept from the straw by a simple roof of boards, which support the earth from pressing upon the fruit, and leave it in a sort of cave, which can be entered occasionally during the winter. This plan is only recommended for those who have no cellars or other suitable apartments, for many fruits acquire an earthy flavor from this near con tact with the soil. Another primitive plan, and one which is well adapted to the preservation of cider apples, and might be used for the keeping of those needed for stock feeding, is to build a rail-pen, four square, like a field corn-crib, into which the fruit is put upon straw, and a lining of the same material is placed at the sides and upon the top, which may also be sheltered with boards to shed off the rain. In our mild winters, many varieties of fruits can be sufficiently well preserved in this manner for the purposes mentioned. In a proper establishment for cider-making, large bins and rooms are provided within the building, which afford sufficient protection from the frost, so that cider-making may be carried on during the winter; and in well arranged farm-steads, the feeding barns should be provided with suitable compartments for the safe storage of fruits or roots, that are to be fed to the stock during the inclement season, when they are so much needed.

All farm-houses should be provided with good deep and dry cellars, which will prove the best place for the storage of fruits. These may be placed in bins, or, still better, upon shelves, as it is not desirable to have too great a bulk together. When but one, or at most, but two layers of fruit are deposited upon each shelf, and when each of these is placed at a sufficient distance from those above or below it, the whole may be easily inspected from time to time, and defective specimens can be removed without disturbing the rest. These shelves should be made of narrow strips, separated from one another by a space that will admit of thorough ventilation. The whole apartment devoted to fruit, should be kept cool and dark, and free from moisture or dampness.

Many large orchardists prefer to select their fruit from the picking baskets, and pack at once in new barrels, which are made for this special purpose, and are not so tight as those used for flour. In packing these, it is desirable to place the fruit carefully in layers, filling the space completely as the work proceeds, putting each specimen down by hand, and when the vessel is filled to about an inch above the chine, the heads are put on, a follower placed upon them, and the whole brought under the pressure of a lever, which forces the mass together so that there shall be no possibility of motion among the fruit. It is better that the outer layers should be somewhat indented by the barrel heads, than that the whole should be spoiled by the bruising that would follow from loose packing. These barrels are often left under the trees for some time, or they may be placed under an open shed for protection, prior to transportation. It is a common practice, before barreling, to deposit the fruit in piles as it is gathered, giving it only a covering of straw to allow it to throw off a part of its moisture, a process generally termed sweating. Now it cannot be gainsaid that there may be an escape of the fluids by transpiration through the pores of the skin, and we know that there is a loss of weight and even of plumpness, in many varieties, by exposure in a dry atmosphere; but the excessive moisture observed upon the surface of fruits that have been exposed to a low temperature, when they are brought into a warmer apartment, is unquestionably the simple precipitation of atmospheric moisture, and entirely independent of the juices of the fruit itself. The advantages of this method of treatment are, that more time is given for the careful selection of the fruits before placing them in the barrels, and a better opportunity for selection, and the rejection from the packages of all those which are in any way defective. The disadvantages are the increased labor and the greater amount of handling to which the fruits are subjected. The surface of our seed-fruits, (*pepins*), is endued with a peculiar coating of a waxy nature, which is of great value for their preservation, and should not be removed, hence the less fruit is handled, the better it will keep, and it should never be rubbed nor wiped; if too wet, or " sweating," it should be exposed to a dry atmosphere, until the surplus moisture shall have quietly evaporated before it is transferred or handled.

It is often observed of particular varieties that they are more prone to wilt than other kinds: this is particularly the case with Russet apples, and is believed to result from a deficiency of this protecting outer covering or waxy exudation, which appears most plentiful in those that retain their plumpness.

In packing for market, besides the directions already given as to prevent motion, it is very desirable to have the packages, of whatever form, whether boxes or barrels, of a neat appearance and uniform full size. The fruits should be well selected, and of a like average quality throughout, and not fixed up for market with the best only at the ends or sides that are to be first opened, while the inferior fruit is concealed within. *Honesty is the best policy everywhere, and dealers soon learn to discriminate in favor of the brands of honest packers. It is believed that any orchardists, who will take pains in the selection of their fruits, and in the excellence and honest measure

13

of their packages, will soon establish a reputation that will be of great value to them in their future offerings.

FRUIT-ROOMS.—For those who wish to reap the highest rewards and the greatest profits from a near and convenient market, as well as those who desire to preserve their fruits, prolong their enjoyment of them, and to bring them to the highest perfection, the fruit-room or fruit-house becomes indispensable. These should be so constructed as to meet the required conditions of an equable and cool temperature, with darkness, and a sufficient amount of dryness to insure freedom from mold and damp. To avoid the precipitation of atmospheric moisture, the apartment should be tight, and seldom opened, particularly in damp weather. To absorb the exhalations from the fruit itself, and that emitted from the burning candle or the breathing of the visitor, the introduction of certain chemical absorbents has been suggested; among these, freshly burned lime has been recommended and used, but Mr. Du Breuil advises the introduction of dry chloride of calcium, which has so great an affinity for moisture as to absorb it completely from the atmosphere. This is the material used by B. M. Nyce, of Cleveland, Ohio, in his patent fruit preserving establishments; and this mode of preserving a dry atmosphere is a leading, and indeed, the chief feature and element of his success.

In the construction of fruit-houses, the fluctuations of the outer atmospheric temperature must be guarded against by making double walls, and by filling the spaces with non-conducting materials. The floors and the ceiling should be similarly arranged—unless where the cooling is effected by a layer of ice above the fruit-room, when the ceiling should be metallic, so as to enable the caloric to be rapidly abstracted from the space below. The house, patented by Prof. Nyce, is essentially a large refrigerator, with the ice at the top, and provided with absorbents for removing *from* the air the moisture it has received from the fruit. Its construction will be understood from the accompanying diagrams and description. The lettering of similar parts is the same in all three diagrams; the description is that of the inventor.

(*A*) Foundation walls. The ground floor is leveled off, and made solid, and even with the foundation walls.

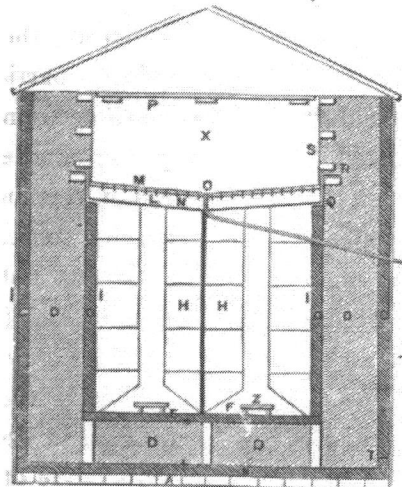

Fig. 27.—NYCE'S FRUIT PRESERVING HOUSE. (CROSS SECTION.)

(*B*) A covering of *tar* and *pitch*, one-half inch thick, put over the ground and foundation walls, to prevent the entrance of moisture. The tar and pitch should be mixed so as to be only moderately hardened by the temperature of the ground. (*D*) The filling between the walls is composed of short dry shavings, chaff, or other poor conductors, 3½ feet thick, on the bottom and sides. (*C*) Joist for plank floor, 3½ feet above the ground. The floor is made level throughout. (*F*) Chloride of calcium, or *dried waste-bittern*, from salt works, spread on every part of the floor of the preserving room, to absorb moisture. (*I I*) Air-tight casings, made of common sheet-iron, No. 26; the edges thickly painted, and nailed to upright studding. The outer casing in some houses is made of brick. The inside of the brick wall is covered with roofing cement, or pitch, or some other air-tight coating. (*K K*) doors 6 or 8 inches thick, filled with chaff or shavings, and fitted tightly to the door-frames, by listing or cloth nailed over thin layers of cotton. (*X*) The ice-chamber. (*L*) Joists to support the ice floor, resting 2 inches on the posts at *Q*. (*N*) Iron bars, 1¼ inches wide, and ¼ inch thick,

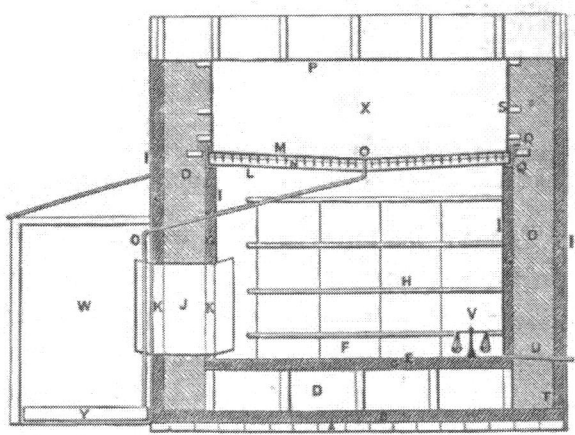

Fig. 28.—NYCE'S FRUIT PRESERVING HOUSE. (LONGITUDINAL SECTION.)

gained ½ inch into the joists, and placed crosswise to them. A bar must always be put directly under the seams and rivets. Three bars are enough to be under a sheet 30 inches wide. (*M*) The galvanized-iron ice floor, No. 18 or 20; the edges joined with rivets not more than 1 inch apart, and very carefully soldered. The ice floor is put on the edges of the iron bars so as to expose every part of its surface, on which ice directly rests, to the air of the room below. (*S*) Sides of ice room made of upright planks. Better have it lined with zinc or galvanized-iron, inside of the plank. Scantling, 2 by 6 inches, are placed on the ice, 4 feet apart, made even with the ice. Wide plank (*P*) are placed loose across the scanting, the edges

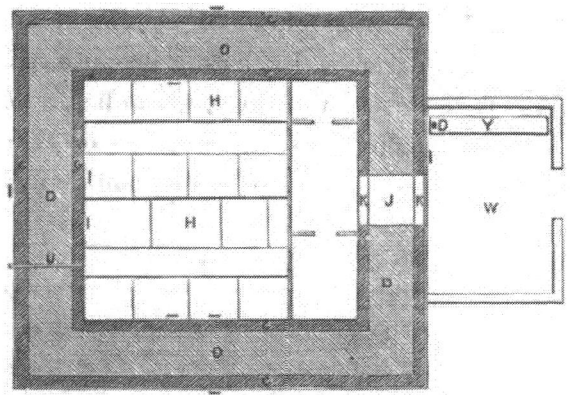

Fig. 29.—NYCE'S FRUIT PRESERVING HOUSE. (GROUND PLAN.)

as close as may be put together, to prevent the filling falling on the ice. Saw-dust, 6 inches thick, is placed on the plank (*P*). Shavings are not compact enough on the top to keep the air from the ice. (*O*) A discharge pipe to conduct the water from the ice. (*W*) An ante-room with an ice-water trough, (*Y*), in which canned fruit is kept, in large stone crocks, for retailing by small measure.

The following estimates are given by the inventor, for a house, with room 15 ft. square, 8 ft. high, 22 ft. square on outside, with capacity for holding 500 bushels. The cost would be about as follows:

Common iron, at 7¼ cts. per lb., cost in the house...........$210 00
Galvanized iron, No. 26, at 20 cts. per lb................... 105 00
Galvanized iron, No. 20, at 18   " 80 00
Whole cost, probably... 800 00

The frame and roof being simple, their cost need not exceed that of similar structures.

CHAPTER XIV.

INSECTS.

——•◦•——

When the preparation of this work was undertaken, the author desired to make it as perfect as possible in all its parts. He very soon discovered, from his own observations in the orchard, that one of the greatest difficulties we all have to contend against in fruit-growing, was the ravages committed upon our fruits and fruit-trees by hosts of noxious insects.

Here then was a new branch of investigation, a new field of study to be entered. He was not an entomologist, nor could he gain any assistance from his friends who were such, because, though they were scientific, and able to assist him in names and descriptions of the insects presented, still they were not *practical entomologists ;* their knowledge of these creatures was purely scientific, and while they could descant learnedly upon the systems set up by the great masters of the science, for the most perfect classification of insects, they could render us practical men but little aid in combatting our insect foes. Great

294

assistance they have rendered, however, in providing names for all these wonderful creatures, in describing their habits and their economy, and in assigning them places in the beautiful classification that has been provided for them.

On turning from men to books, but little more assistance or encouragement was met with; these too would only give the names, the places, and the descriptions, in the most approved language of the science, but they are not attractive nor intelligible to the unlearned. Any person can soon acquire the language of the science, with a little study, but these scientific books do not give us directions how to rid ourselves of the pests.

Among the books that are accessible and that are adapted to the general reader, and to the student of practical entomology, two were found of eminent utility as far as they went. These are the excellent reports to the Massachusetts and the New York Agricultural Societies, by Messrs. Harris and Fitch, which are clothed in popular language, and which treat particularly of the insects injurious to vegetation, and they put us in the way of combating our foes. The former, which has been reprinted and illustrated in beautiful style, is worthy of a place in every farmer's library, and will prove a valuable aid in the study: the latter is printed in connection with the Society's reports. To both of these, the author acknowledges his indebtedness, and from both has he drawn liberally.

Other popular treatises, though attractive, have proved of very little practical value, and the student will find even the reports above referred to imperfect, as they were prepared for a limited region, and do not mention several insects that are common in other parts of the country than the States for which these reports were prepared. It were much to be desired, that every State Society would have similar reports, respecting the insects, peculiar to its state.

Thus the author found himself compelled to investigate this broad field of study for himself—it became necessary to grasp the elements of the classification, and to go into the field and the orchard, to use his eyes, and to observe for himself. This was a labor of time, and required considerable effort; but it brought its own reward in the pleasure attendant upon this delightful study. At the same time there was great satisfaction in the thought that all these facts, gathered from the works of men of science, confirmed by personal observation, and rendered useful and applicable in practice by his fellow laborers in the garden and orchard, would be a valuable contribution to them, and would constitute a useful portion of the *American Pomology* he was then preparing.

Unfortunately for himself, he has discovered that his collections, in this department, covered several hundred pages of manuscript, and that, if printed, they would render his volume too cumbrous. Upon consulting with his publishers, it was concluded best to lay the matter aside, for the present at least, and to prepare anew a brief account of some of the insects most injurious to the orchard, with short suggestions as to the best methods of combating their ravages. This conclusion has been the more readily yielded to, because the public now have a medium of communication with the scientific entomologists, which well supplies the great want we had begun to experience. I refer to a monthly publication, issued by the Entomological Society of Philadelphia, in which the questions, that are constantly occurring to farmers, are answered in the most simple, clear, and satisfactory manner.* Besides this, we find in our best agricultural journals, a page or a column, devoted to the consideration of insects injurious to vegetation.**

For the sake of convenience and system, these notes will be presented in the order of the approved classification of insects. Omitting further introduction or discourse upon the wonderful instincts and habits of insects, and explanation of their metamorphoses and the principles of classification, and confessing my poor qualification for the task, let us proceed at once to the catalogue.

COLEOPTERA.—Beetles.

In this class of insects we find both, friends and foes. The former assist us by their voracious appetites, that can only be satisfied with gourmandizing upon other insects, particularly the juicy bodies of their larvæ. The latter embrace some of our most troublesome pests, especially as they consume vegetable matters, in the perfect as well as in the larval condition, and in both stages are exceedingly voracious. Moreover, they generally commit their depredations under cover, or at night. Some live in the soil and consume the roots of our plants, and others mine their way into the solid wood of the stems of our finest trees; while some only affect the twigs and smaller branch-

* *Practical Entomologist*, 518 South 13th street, Philadelphia, fifty cents a year, in advance.

** Vide *Prairie Farmer, American Agriculturist, Country Gentleman*, etc.

13*

es, and others devour the foliage, flowers, and fruits. A few of the most familiar and troublesome of these will now be introduced; and allusion will also be made to some of those which befriend us by their destruction of other insects.

Saperda bivittata, (*Say.*)—The Apple Tree Borer.— This is a nocturnal insect, which has been found very destructive to our orchards. The female deposits one egg in a place, generally low down on the stem of the tree; this hatches, and enters the tissues of the bark, where it feeds for a time, a footless grub. As it grows, it burrows deeper, and upward, until it reaches the sap wood, upon which it feeds. When half grown, it burrows still deeper, and upwards into the heart of the tree, and then outward through the sap wood to the bark, but retires again toward the centre, as to a place of safety, to undergo its transformation, after packing the hole with shreds of wood and with its castings to make its retreat secure. In the spring, the perfect insect opens its way outward, and emerges to the light of day.

REMEDY. — Observe the bark of young trees very closely during the summer, to discover the castings that are ejected; notice the discolored or depressed portions of bark, and cut into them to find and destroy the worm —if it has penetrated the solid wood, pursue it with a piece of stout but flexible wire.

PREVENTIVES.—Alkaline washes have been highly recommended, as a means of driving away the mother beetle; soft soap may be used, and a portion of soft or hard soap, placed in the forks of the branches, will dissolve with the rains, and wash down on the bark. These applications, to be efficacious, should be made in May or June. In August, the bark should be examined, and when the worms are cut out, the soap suds may be injected with advantage, especially if the larvæ have not been reached. Birds should be encouraged, particularly the Picæ tribe, which destroy many grubs of the wood-boring insects.

Chrysobothris femorata, or the Thick-legged Buprestris, is another kind of apple-tree borer, very common in some parts of the West. The perfect insect may be seen running up and down the stems of our trees, in June and July. It is a blackish beetle, about half an inch long. The hole, bored by the grub, is flat, and not cylindrical like that of the *Saperda.* This beetle attacks the stem higher up than the *Saperda*, but burrows under the bark, and then sinks into the wood much in the same way.

REMEDIES and PREVENTIVES are similar to those above mentioned. Seek for the young worms in their shallow burrows in August, before they have gone deeply into the tree.

Dicerca divaricata, (*Say*), or the Cherry-tree Borer, is similar in its habit of boring in 'the sap wood under the bark, and may be combated in the same way. The perfect insect appears in June and July.

Prenocerus supernotatus, or the American Currant Borer, feeds upon the pith of the stalk. The larva is a small, white grub, which changes into a slender, long-horned beetle; black, edged with chestnut-brown. The wing covers are marked with two small grey dots, anteriorly, and a crescent-shaped one behind the middle.

It is very injurious to the currant bushes in many parts of the country, and constitutes a serious obstacle to growing the plants to a single stem, tree fashion. In the bush form of this plant, the constant reproduction of new shoots compensates for the destruction caused by the borer.

There is another currant borer, an European, which is confined to young shoots; as it is not the larva of a beetle, but of a butterfly, it will be treated in its proper place.

Bostrichus bicaudatus, or the Apple-twig Borer, affects the small twigs, and when numerous, will produce an effect like that called twig-blight, by causing the death of the part and the withering of the leaves, at mid-summer. A small hole will be found near the axil of a leaf; this turns with the twig, and often extends several inches along the pith. The insect is a small, chestnut-brown beetle, 0.25 to 0.35 of an inch long, and is characterized by two projections or horns at the hinder end. Has been found rather common from Michigan to Kansas.

REMEDY.—Kill, when found.

Scolytus pyri, or the Pear-blight Beetle, affects twigs of pear, apple, and other fruits, which wither and die at mid-summer. Small perforations, like pin holes, will be found, and issuing from them small cylindrical beetles of a deep brown or black color.

REMEDY—not known.

Lucanus dama, or Horn-beetle, is a large insect, the larvæ of which are said to feed upon the trunk and roots of old apple and other trees. The perfect insects are of a dark mahogany color, smooth, and polished. Like other Stag-beetles, they fly at night, are not very harmful, and are believed to be several years in reaching the perfect state.

Leptostylus aculiferus, bores under the bark of apple trees. It is a short, thick, brownish-gray beetle, with thorns upon its wing-covers; hence, the scientific name of needle-bearer. Length, 0.35 inch; season, August. The larvæ are small worms, occurring in multitudes under the bark, and making long-winding burrows.

Tomicus mali, or the Apple-bark Beetle, is described by Dr. Fitch as new. He says, it is a small, smooth, black or chestnut-red, cylindrical beetle; the larvæ feed under the bark, and then enter the wood, killing the young tree.

Conotrachelus Nenuphar, (*Herbst*), is the noted and notorious and yet little known Plum Weevil, that is such an abomination to plum planters, and which has proved very injurious to our peaches and is even accused of producing deformities in our pears and apples.

The egg is deposited in the fruit, where it soon hatches and feeds, approaching the stone. This causes the fruit to fall, and when the grub has attained its full size it descends into the ground to perform its transformation. The perfect insect, a small, dark-gray beetle, either crawls up the stem, or flies to the trees. Mr. Walsh reminds us that Dr. Trimble has found these insects hybernating in sheltered places.

REMEDIES.—It is lamentable that we have been able to do so little to prevent the ravages of this insect. The plan of shaking off, and destroying the affected fruits, promises the best results, by diminishing the next crop. It was suggested by David Thomas, of New York, but is most successfully practised by Dr. E. S. Hull, of Illinois, who has invented an inverted umbrella on wheels, which receives the insects, as well as the defective fruits, when it is bumped against the trees. By the use of this, he is enabled to harvest splendid crops of stone-fruits.

Pomphopæa Sayi, (or *Cantharis pyrivora,* of *Fitch*), is called by him the Pear Blister-fly. He describes it as a long blistering beetle, of a green-blue color; found on a pear tree about the first of June, eating the young fruit voraciously.

Euryomia Inda, or the Indian Cetonia, is a beetle about six-tenths of an inch long. The head and thorax dark, copper-brown, thickly covered with short, greenish-yellow hairs; wing-cases light yellowish-brown, changeable, with metallic tints. These are called flower-beetles, because they consume the pollen, and bury themselves in our flowers; but in the autumn, they consume our choicest fruits, especially peaches.

Lachnosterna fusca, (*Frœlich*), is the White Grub, or May Beetle. A heavy brown insect, an inch or more in length, which makes its appearance with the first warm evenings, when the Black Locust begins to open its fragrant blossoms, to which these beetles are attracted. They also attack the foliage of other trees, particularly the cherry, which they entirely strip of leaves and fruit. Though very destructive in the perfect form, these insects are most to be dreaded while in the larval condition, which is supposed to continue for some years. They then work under cover, and can only be traced by the ravages they commit. Every strawberry grower is familiar with the large White Grub that so often destroys his hopes of a crop, by killing the plants when in full growth and fruitage, by cutting off all the fibres.

REMEDY.—The full-grown insects are very busy in the evening, but become stupid and lethargic before morning, clinging to the leaves and twigs, when they may be shaken down, caught on sheets, gathered, and destroyed. If let alone, they will fall to the ground toward day break, and secrete themselves in the grass and soil until night. All that can be killed in this stage of their existence, the better, as this will prevent the deposition of innumerable eggs. The White Grubs must be destroyed one at a time in cultivated grounds; kill them whenever found. Encourage chickens and birds to follow the plow and spade, as they will consume great numbers. Hogs will find and eat them greedily, and may be allowed to root them out even from a meadow, if badly affected; for, though a harsh remedy, it is not so bad as the disease.

Pelidnota punctata, or the Spotted Pelidnota, is a large yellowish insect, with a black dot on each side of the thorax, and three others on the outer side of each wing-cover. It is found in the day time, upon the leaves of the grape vine. Like the rest of the tribe, these insects are voracious, and the grubs may also feed upon the roots of the grape; therefore they had better be destroyed, though as their numbers are seldom large they are not found to be very injurious.

Haltica chalybea, or the Grape Vine Flea-beetle, appears early in the season, and eats holes in the buds and leaves. It is small, 0.16 inch long, oval; shining, deep greenish-blue, or deep green, or purple. This insect spends the winter in the earth about the roots of the vine, and feeds upon them.

Anomala lucicola, or the light-loving Anomala, is found on the grape vine in July. It resembles the May Beetle, but is smaller, being 0.35 inch long.

These are not all the beetles that feed upon the grape vine.

Macrodactylus subspinosa, or the Rose-chafer, is another melolonthian beetle, which is exceedingly destructive to grapes and various other plants in many parts of the country, in May and June. This insect is smaller than the others of its group, but is equally destructive as a leaf-eater, on account of its numbers. On the grape, it cuts off the young bunch of buds and blossoms, and thus seriously diminishes the crop, as well as by destroying the foliage. It is of a buff-yellow, with black feet, about 0.33 inch long. They continue to ravage vegetation about a month, and then retire into the ground, an inch deep, and deposit their eggs, which hatch in about twenty days, and the young grubs feed upon tender roots, attaining their full size, three-quarters of an inch, before winter, when they descend deeper to hybernate.

The Rose-beetle has many natural enemies, among which are the Dragon-flies; but we must depend upon human efforts for their destruction, an almost hopeless task, for their name is legion, but so much the greater necessity for the effort, and as they are sluggish, they may easily be caught and thrown into hot water, or otherwise destroyed.

Tree Pruners are the larvæ of beetles that excavate a burrow in small limbs of trees, so as to make a section almost across their substance; most of them then bore upward into the limb, and await the action of the winds to break off the part and waft them to the ground, where they pass through their change to the perfect insect. They exercise a wonderful instinct in leaving just fibres enough to support the branch until they are ready for their descent, but it often happens that the twig breaks off partially and hangs by a thread, dying, of course; we see the brown leaves on the trees, and this is the first indi-. cation of the presence of the insects. If we examine the fallen spray, we shall be surprised to observe the cause of its falling. In the case of the oak tree, the damage is done by the *Elaphidion villosum*, (Fabricius), a long-horned beetle. The larva remains in these twigs until the next season, hence the importance of gathering and burning all that fall to the ground.

An insect of somewhat similar habits often cuts off stout shoots of the Hickory, making a very neat section of a small limb, leaving only the bark, so that it readily breaks off with the wind; and a similar effect has been observed in strong annual shoots of the pear, toward the end of summer. The fallen piece and the stump are cut as neatly as by the shears, but no perforation is discovered along the axis, in which the larva could be concealed; hence we have but to suffer the trimming thus performed without our will, and look upon it as a sort of natural shortening-in of our trees.

Blister-flies, or Beetles.—There are several species of these insects, each of which appears to have its favorite pasturage. They are exceedingly voracious, but confine themselves chiefly to the destruction of herbaceous vegetation, and are therefore obnoxious to the farmer and gardener, who know them as the potato insects, than to the fruit-grower. Their appetites are not very discriminating,

however, and when they are abundant they may consume
the foliage of our trees.   These Blister-flies belong to the
genus *Lytta*, and are used as a substitute for the Spanish-
fly of Europe, as they are possessed of blistering qualities
in no mean degree.   They are wholly different from the
new potato destroyer of the West, the *Doryphora* 10-*li-
neata*, which is hemispherical, and is a leaf-eater, in the
larval as well as in the perfect state.

REMEDY.—Catch and kill all that can be found in the
garden, or potato field ; scald, dry, and sell to the apoth-
ecary.

Before closing this section, it is but due to our many
insect friends in this order, to introduce a few of them to
the reader.   There are several large families that are really
serviceable to man ; some of these are called Scavengers,
because they consume large quantities of decaying matter that might prove noxious to us, were it allowed to decay upon the surface of the ground.   Among these are
the Dung-beetles, and the Carrion-beetles : others are carnivorous, and some of these are called *Cicindelidæ*, or Tiger-
beetles, from their voracious consumption of other insects, which they devour in great numbers, both in their
larval and in their perfect form.   These day beetles are
large, brightly colored, and very active in their movements, as they run about in the sunny paths and roads,
and cannot fail to attract attention.   Few persons are
aware, however, of the valuable aid they are rendering
to man, nor of the credit that is due to them for the preservation of our crops from the invasion of other insect
foes.   Too often they are either unobserved and overlooked, or even treated with the aversion and cruelty of men

who ignorantly attempt to stamp out all insect life, as though these creatures were intruders upon their pre-emption. The intelligent observer of nature will soon learn to respect each aid, which has been so wisely furnished to assist him in his labors as a cultivator of the soil, and all may admire the Wisdom that has provided at the same time such beautiful and such useful creatures for the work.

Calosoma scrutator, is well named the handsome, for it is one of our most beautiful insects of this class. This, and the red-spotted *C. calidum,* may be seen upon trees, seeking caterpillars, upon which they feed. One of our most intelligent horticulturists has so high an appreciation of these insects, that he will not allow them to be disturbed, and whenever he sees any caterpillars in his orchard, he takes these beetles to the tree, and gives himself no further concern, knowing that the Calosoma will soon destroy every worm.

Coccinelidæ, or Lady-birds, are most valuable aids to the cultivator, who is constantly liable to have his crops destroyed by the various species of Aphides. These little hemispherical beetles are familiar to every one, and known to the children as Lady-birds; but all may not know their value, nor be so well acquainted with the larvæ of these insects, which are the chief agents in the destruction of our troublesome plant-lice. Most persons would be very apt to crush these curious, diminutive, lizard-looking creatures, even at the time they were attacking the Aphides, instead of leaving them to carry on the warfare more effectually without our aid.

These little friends have had a superstitious regard shown

to them in many countries, which indicates that a glimmering idea prevailed respecting their usefulness. The Germans call them the *Marienkaefer*, or Lady-beetles, of the Virgin Mary. The French call them *Vaches de Dieu*, the Lord's cows, and our own children are all familiar with the nursery rhyme about the Lady-birds. These insects find their way to trees or plants that are infested with their proper food, the Aphides.

These beetles hide under the leaves that cluster in sheltered nooks about or between the large roots of forest trees, where they can be found on any mild winter day, and may be carried to the green-house or to the window plants that are infested with plant-lice. They will not only devour these pests, but will soon lay eggs that hatch and produce the larvæ which are so voracious as to clear the plants in a short time. A little attention to the habits of these insects may spare us great losses from the plant-lice.

----♦----

ORTHOPTERA.—GRASSHOPPERS.

The insects of this order have an imperfect transformation. The eggs hatch at once into young insects, that resemble their parents in form and habits, excepting that they do not get their wings till they approach the adult state. The young consume food voraciously, and the perfect insects are not only still more hungry, but, having increased powers of locomotion, they are more widely destructive. These are the true *Locusts*, and though chiefly injurious to the farm and garden, infesting the meadows and corn-fields, the grasshoppers, when winged, often attack the foliage of our young orchard trees toward the end of summer. But when we contemplate the invasion of the great western plague, belonging to this order, which rivals that terrible scourge, the Locust of the eastern continent, in numbers and voracity, we may well dread their increase and appearance in other parts of the country. The grasshoppers that have invaded Kansas and other Western States are, like all the rest of this group of *Orthoptera*, true Locusts.

This order is called *Orthoptera*, from their straight wings; it embraces several groups, cockroaches, crickets, grasshoppers, or locusts, etc., which are all injurious, except the *Mantis*, which is predacious, and therefore useful.

HEMIPTERA.—Bugs and Harvest-flies.

This order contains many insects that are injurious to the nurseryman, to the orchardist, and to the gardener. They are characterized by having a proboscis instead of a mouth with jaws; they can suck, but they cannot bite. The proboscis is often horny, and armed with two pair of bristles, when it becomes a more formidable weapon for attack. Bugs have four wings; they do not pass through the usual metamorphoses of insect life; but are born with legs and feeding apparatus like the perfect insects, except that some have no wings. Bugs are all injurious to man, excepting such as are predacious, which are serviceable by destroying other insects. Many are very small; and yet their countless numbers and wonderful fecundity enable them to do immense damage, as is true of the *Aphides* and *Coccidœ*, the *Tingis*, the *Tettigonia vitis*, called the Thrips by our vine-dressers; and still more so of the Chinch-bug of the Western prairies, which destroys whole crops of our most important cereals.

The colored juice of some bugs is used in the arts. The coccus of the prickly pear, in Central America, is gathered and dried to form the cochineal of the shops.

Hemipterous insects are divided into two groups. True bugs, called *Hemiptera heteroptera*, having the wing-covers opaque at the base, and laid horizontally, and crossing each other obliquely at the end, overlapping; and the Harvest-flies, such as Plant-lice and Bark-lice. These, the *Hemiptera homoptera*, have the wing-covers of one texture throughout, not horizontal, but more or less sloping, and not crossing one another behind. Among these, which all feed upon plants, some very troublesome pests will here be noticed.

COCCIDANS.—Bark-lice.

Aspidiotus conchiformis, or the Apple Bark-louse, is very numerous in many parts of our country, particularly north of latitude 40 degrees. It commits sad devastations in some sections. Individually, it is but a little scale; but these animals are wonderfully prolific and soon cover every twig of the tree, obstructing its transpirations, and abstracting its vital juices; the leaves, and even the fruit are overrun with these miserable scales, but the twigs are their favorite resort. These scales are oblong, shaped like an oyster shell; flat and brown, often crowding upon one another. In the winter and spring, they contain or cover a number of small, round, white eggs, which hatch out in the spring, in May, attach themselves to the bark, and absorb the juices: various remedies have been suggested, and more or less thoroughly tested. The restoration of the thrifty growth of the tree is considered essential to success; and without this, all remedies are looked upon as unavailing. Some orchardists think that thorough drainage and cultivation of the land would alone banish the lice, but this can hardly be hoped. Strong lye, or solutions of potash, or soda, white-wash, and sulphur, have been used, and tobacco boiled in lye, soft-soap and tar mixed with linseed oil, which makes a kind of varnish. Mr. Walsh tells us that applications, to destroy this insect, are better made in May or June, as the eggs are protected by the scale in winter, and it is impermeable to watery solutions. This pest has been imported from Europe. Walsh recommends the use of Lady-birds to check the Bark-lice.*

Lecanium pyri, (*Fitch*), or the Pear Bark-louse, is a hemispherical brown scale, as large as a split pea. They may be found in summer on the under side of the limbs, and are the remains of dead females, which cover the eggs and young brood. This insect would be very injurious, were it to increase in numbers considerably. Let young trees be examined in June, when the scales may easily be found, removed, and destroyed.

Lecanium persici, or the Peach Bark-louse, is described, by Fitch, as similar in size to the above, found on

---

* See Practical Entomologist, Vol. II, p. 32.

smooth bark near a bud; it is blackish, uneven, shining, with a pale margin.

Another pear tree bark-louse was described by the lamented A. O. Moore, of New York, as a white, papery scale, giving a claret-colored juice when scraped. This, in the winter, consists of a defunct mother and her brood of eggs, the breaking of which gives the color. Alkaline washes are recommended to be applied in the spring. Mr. Walsh thinks this insect cannot be the same as that mentioned by Dr. Harris, on p. 222 of his report, under the name of *Coccus cryptogamus*, (*Dalman*), who found it upon the Aspen, and therefore he has named it *Coccus? Harrisii.**

Lecanium vitis, (*Linn.*), or the Vine Bark-louse, is mentioned by Fitch as having been found on grape vines in June. It is hemispherical and brown. A cottony substance was extruded from one end of the scale, and this increased until July, when minute insects crept out and scattered over the bark, upon which they fixed themselves. This insect is not very common, but its first appearance should be closely watched, and its destruction promptly effected.

APHIDES.—PLANT-LICE.

These are the most extraordinary insects, being found upon almost all parts of plants, and there is scarcely a species which does not support one or more kinds peculiar to itself. Then they are so exceedingly prolific! Reau-

---

* See Practical Entomologist, Vol. II, p. 31.

mur proved that one individual, in five generations, may become the progenitor of nearly six thousand millions of descendants. Most of these insects, which we find so abundant upon our trees, are wingless females. Winged insects, both male and female, appear later in the season, and after laying their eggs, they soon perish. Some lay in the fall, others wait till spring. When these eggs hatch, the brood consists wholly of females, which are wingless, and do not lay eggs, but are viviparous and produce from fifteen to twenty young lice in the course of a day. This second generation are also wingless, and at maturity produce their young, and so on to the seventh generation, without the approach of a single male, until the autumn, when a brood of males and females appears, which are both winged at maturity, and then the eggs are laid for the next year's brood, and the parents die.*

The injuries occasioned by plant-lice, are much greater than would at first be expected, from an observation of the small size and extreme weakness of the insects; but these make up by their numbers what they lack in strength individually, and thus become formidable enemies to vegetation. By their punctures and the quantity of sap they draw from the leaves, the functions of these important organs are deranged, or interrupted, the sap is withdrawn or contaminated, and unfitted to supply the wants of vegetation. Plants are differently affected; some wither and cease to grow, their leaves and stems become sickly, and die from exhaustion. Others, not killed, are greatly impeded in their growth; the tender parts, which are attacked, become stunted and curled. The punctures of the

* Harris, p. 205.

14

lice appear to poison some plants, producing warts or swellings, which are sometimes solid, sometimes hollow, containing within them a swarm of lice, descendants of a single individual.* These last are often seen upon the leaves of the Elm, and upon some Poplars, and other trees; but I have not found any upon the foliage of our cultivated fruits, unless it be those on the grape.

Aphis mali, or the Apple Leaf-louse, is a small, green insect without wings, accompanied by a few black and green ones having wings. These are all crowded together upon the green tips of twigs, and under the leaves, sucking the sap. The eggs remain in deep cracks of the bark during the winter, and hatch as soon as the buds expand in the spring. The most successful treatment is to scrape off the loose bark, and to apply to the stems of the trees alkaline or lime washes. Many of our familiar little winter birds consume these eggs. In the spring and summer, alkaline solutions may be used with advantage, syringed or sprinkled upon the affected shoots and foliage.

The smell of these insects is peculiar, which, indeed, is generally characteristic with bugs. Each sort seems to derive a special flavor from the tree or plant upon which it feeds. Most insects of this family secrete copiously a sweetish fluid, called the honey dew, which is ejected from two little horns or nectaries, that project, one on each side of their bodies. This sweet material attracts a great many flies, and other insects, particularly ants, which are the constant attendants of these creatures, and are said to protect them from their enemies in order to obtain their

* Harris' Report, p. 810.

sweet secretion. Some entomologists have called *Aphides* the Ants' cows.

No one, who is acquainted with the *Aphides*, and the various insects which prey upon them, will ever permit a valuable plant to suffer injury from these pests. He will collect some of the *Aphis'* enemies alive, carry them to the affected plant, and set them free to do their work; there they will remain while the food lasts. The *Aphides* have more numerous, more active, and more inveterate enemies than insects of any other group — these are the means by which their wonderful fecundity is kept in check. Among them are the Aphis-lions, which are the larvæ of the Golden-eyed and Lace-wing flies, belonging to the order *Neuroptera*. They are reddish-brown, with a dark stripe down the middle, and a cream-colored one on each side; bodies long, narrow, and wrinkled transversely. Their jaws are long, curved like sickles, projecting forward from their heads horizontally.*

The *Coccinellidæ*, mentioned as useful members of the order *Coleoptera*, on a previous page, are among the most active enemies of the *Aphides*. The eggs are laid in clusters of twenty to forty on the under side of a leaf, to which they are closely glued; they are oval, and light yellow. They hatch into small blackish larvæ, which are active, and which boldly attack an *Aphis* much larger than themselves, leaving only the empty skin. They consume hundreds while in the larval state, about two weeks, when they attach themselves by the tail, and go into the pupa state. One of the largest of these Lady-birds is the

* For further details of these insects, the reader is referred to Fitch's Report, pp. 88 to 98.

Mysia 15–*punctata ;* the larva is a clear white, the middle of the back tinged with red, and two or three black spots on each segment—nearly a hundred species of Ladybirds are found in this country. The perfect insect, as well as the larvæ, feed upon *Aphides,* and instead of being destroyed, they should be cherished and encouraged.

Besides these, there are other inveterate enemies of the plant-lice in the *Syrphidæ,* which are two-winged flies, resembling the common house-fly, but handsomer. They deposit their eggs where *Aphides* exist; the maggot, which hatches from these, seizes upon the first *Aphis* that comes within his reach, and sucks its fluids. A medium-sized worm will consume a hundred lice in an hour. They are always found in a colony of *Aphides.**

Aphis prunifoliæ, or the Plum Leaf-louse, is black, with pale green abdomen. It is found on the under side of the leaves, which become wrinkled and distorted. It is not so abundant as some other species, but its habits are similar. **

Aphis cerasi, (*Fabric.*), or the Cherry Plant-louse, is very common, very numerous, and very black. They appear with the first expansion of the leaves, and continue or are renewed when destroyed, and remain until mid-summer, when they generally disappear. Their numbers are almost incredible, and they give a young cherry tree a wretched appearance. On the under surface of a small leaf, three-fourths of an inch long, Mr. Fitch counted one hundred and ninety lice, on one-side only of the midrib. Their natural enemies come to the rescue to check

* Rept. cit., p. 100.
** Rept. cit. p. 122.

their wonderful increase, and sometimes will utterly rout the *Aphides* in a single week.*

The remedies advised for the apple tree *Aphides*, are equally applicable to those of the cherry, and their natural enemies are the same and equally efficacious; but *Aphides* have internal foes likewise, that may be named here. The Ichneumon-flies are parasitic, their larvæ feed upon the substance of the *Aphides*. The genus *Aphidius* is particularly provided to furnish parasites to these insects, in which they deposit a single egg, selecting a louse of the proper size to sustain their progeny: the egg hatches to a larva, which exhausts the *Aphis* by the time it has attained its growth, when the poor creature fastens itself securely to the leaf, and dies, leaving its carcase a secure resting place for the pupa of the Ichneumon. These parasitic insects, which feed internally upon the *Aphides*, are as effective in their destruction as the Aphis-lions, or any other class of their enemies.**

Aphis persicæ, or the Peach Tree-louse, punctures the leaves of this plant, and Dr. Fitch † thinks, is the common though not the only cause of the curl in the peach tree leaves. Our intelligent orchardists have found these insects occasionally in the curled leaves of the peach, but do not agree with this distinguished entomologist, in considering them a cause of that malady.

Aphis vitis?, or the Vine *Aphis*, is often quite troublesome on vigorous young shoots of the grape vine, both wild and cultivated, particularly the former. These in-

---

* Rept. cit. p. 125.
** Rept. cit. p. 184.
† Trans. N. Y. Ag'l Soc., 1856, p. 359.

sects soon cripple the growth of the shoot. The species is not known to be different from that of Europe. This insect is briefly mentioned by T. Glover, in Patent Office Rept. for 1854, p. 79. Dr. Fitch describes as a grape leaf-louse, the *Pemphigus vitifolia*, which inhabits the gall-like excrescences upon the foliage of some varieties, particularly those with thin leaves.

Aphis ribis, (*Linn.*), is the *Aphis* of the currant. It causes the leaves to present a blistered appearance above; the lice are found on the under side; the wingless are pale yellow, the others have glossy wings, mostly black, with abdomen light green.*

Aphis lanigera, now called *Eriosoma*, or the Woolly *Aphis*, was first described in 1801 as infesting the apple trees in Germany. It has been noticed in England in 1787, and has since acquired the name of American Blight, from the erroneous supposition that it had been imported from this country; but it was known to French gardeners for a long time previous.

The eggs of this insect are microscopic, and are enveloped in a cottony substance. They are deposited in chinks of bark, and crotches of limbs, at or near the surface of the ground. When first hatched, the insects are covered with short down; as they grow, the down increases in length. When fully grown, they are one-tenth of an inch long; the head, antennæ, sucker, and skins, are blackish, the abdomen of a honey-yellow color. Their punctures produce warty excrescences, the limbs become sickly, the leaves turn yellow and drop off, and the whole tree perishes as the insects spread over it. The remedies

---

* Lib. cit. p. 435.

appear futile on badly affected trees. Young trees were treated by painting over the affected parts with a mixture of melted resin and fish oil, in equal parts, applied warm. Sir Joseph Banks removed them with a stiff brush. Spirits of tar, turpentine, oil, and soft soap, have been recommended. After scraping off the rough bark, wash the tree with alkaline solution, apply the same to the main roots after laying them bare of earth.*

Phemphigus pyri, *Eriosoma pyri,* (*Fitch*), or *Pemphigus Americanus?,* (*Walker*),.is the Apple-root Blight. It produces a similar condition in the roots, and was also called the American Blight in England. It is composed of warty excrescences upon the roots, containing in their crevices minute lice, having their bodies covered with a white cottony subtance. Removal of the earth, and the application of soapsuds, has been recommended as a probable remedy for the injuries done by this insect.* *

Psylla Pyri.—Some *Aphides* have the power of leaping, like the leaf-hoppers, but they differ from those insects in having very large transparent upper wings, which cover the sides of the body like a steep roof. The genus embracing these insects, is called *Psylla.* One of the species was observed by Dr. Harris, upon a pear tree. They live by suction, and having gorged themselves, the juice runs down on the bark, producing a blackish color; young trees suffered excessively. As Dr. Phumb, of Salisbury, Conn., had observed them in 1833 on some imported pear trees, of which he lost several hundred in a

---

* Harris' Rept. p. 211.

* * For further particulars respecting these insects, consult Dr. Fitch's Rept., p. 5, and Harris' Rept., p. 241.

few years, Dr. Harris suspected the insect to be the *Psylla pyri*, of Europe. Kollar recommends brushing off the insects, and crushing them under foot; and also advises to destroy the winged females in the spring. This being tedious and uncertain, it is recommended to wash the twigs with a brush, dipped in a mixture of strong soap-suds and flowers of sulphur, before the buds expand, to deter the insects from laying their eggs. A weaker solution, or the whale oil soap, might kill the young insects after they have fastened upon the bark, if applied with a syringe.*

Cicada septendecim, or the Seventeen-year Locust, as it is erroneously called, is no Locust at all, but should be called *Cicada*, because, as already stated, when considering the order *Orthoptera*, the true Locusts, are, what we call Grasshoppers.

This insect is remarkable for the long period of its pupal existence, which is subterranean, and during which it feeds upon the juices of roots. In its perfect state, it does not eat, and is neither able to bite nor to sting. The injury it does to our orchards is effected by its piercer in depositing its eggs, causing twigs to break and fall off. There are several Harvest-flies that belong to this order.

Tree Hoppers, being members of the same order, feed upon the juices of plants, through their suckers, and are thus injurious; but their numbers are not sufficient to render them of much consequence.

Palæothrips mali, (*Fitch*), is the name of an insect described by Dr. Fitch ** as infesting apple trees in the

---

* Vide Harris' Rept., p. 232.
** Rept., p. 403.

month of August, where they were attacking the fruit. They excavated a little hollow near the blossom end of the apple about the size of a pea, which was occupied by small insects. Until the habits of the insect are more thoroughly understood, it will be difficult to advise any remedies.

There is quite a number of insects in this class that affect the grape vine, some of which may become troublesome, and we should watch their habits. The following accounts are condensed from Dr. Fitch's Report:

Raphigaster sarpinus, or the large Green Tree-bug, is grassy-green, edged with yellow, and a black point at every joint of the abdomen; found in September.

Pentatoma ligata, or the Bound Tree-bug, is also grassy-green, but more widely bordered all round, except the head, with pale red, and has a pale red spot on the middle of its back and on the apex of its scutel; antennæ green.

Arma modesta, or the Modest Tree-bug, is tawny yellowish-gray, thickly dotted with brown punctures; the wing-covers are red at the apex of their leathery portion, and have a brown spot at the tip of the hyaline portion; the under side is whitish, with a row of black dots along the middle, and another on each side.

Thelia univittata, (*Harris*), or the Single-striped Tree-hopper, is chestnut-brown, shaped like a beech-nut, with a perpendicular protuberance on the fore part of its back, higher than wide. It is tawny white in front, a white stripe along the back to the tip; length 0.37 inch; July and August.

Ceresa bubalus, or Buffalo Treehopper, is of a light

14*

grass-green, freckled with whitish dots; with a sharp short point on each side, projecting like horns.

Ceresa taurina, is like the preceding, but the space between the horns is concave.

Acutalis dorsalis, is a small, triangular, shining Tree-hopper, with a smooth round back; it is greenish-white, with a large black spot, from the anterior corners of which a line runs off to each eye. Plentiful about the last of July, a few remaining until October.

Erythroneura vitis, (*Harris*), or the Vine-leaf hopper, is pale yellow, with two broad blood-red bands, and a third dusky one on the apex. Swarms of these small insects occur in August, and often bleed the foliage so as to injure it seriously.

Erythroneura tricincta, or the Three-banded Leaf-hopper, is like the preceding species, but the bands are narrower.

Erythroneura vitifex, or the Vine-destroying Leaf-hopper, is yellowish-white; the wing-covers have oblique confluent, blood-red bands, and a short, oblique, black line on the middle of their outer margin. The thorax commonly has three red stripes, the middle one forked anteriorly and confluent, with two red stripes on the crown of the head. When the wing-covers are closed, they look red, with a cream-colored spot, shaped like a heart placed anteriorly, and on the middle, a large diamond-shaped spot, with a small red spot in its centre.

These insects are sometimes seen in such numbers upon the grape vines in September, that, when the leaves are disturbed, they fly out and resemble a shower of snowflakes. The young resemble their parents, but are destitute of wings.

A REMEDY is much needed.

Erythroneura vulnerata, (*Fitch*), or the Wounded Tree-hopper, is tawny yellowish, sometimes tinged with red; the wing-covers have white spots and veins, and on the middle of the outer margin an oblique black streak, between two creamy white spots; the hind one smaller, and an oblique blood-red line at its end; tips smoky-blackish; length 0.12 inch; September.

Otiocerus Coquebertii, is a slim fly of yellowish-white color, with a bright carmine-red stripe along each side of the body and wings, which are widely forked behind. Length 0.42 inch; July until autumn, on the wild grape vine.

There are a great many insects of this order, which are familiar to most country residents on account of their unpleasant smell. These are the true bugs, and belong to the sub-division called *Heteropterous Hemiptera.* The Squash-bug is a familiar illustration of these insects; it is called the *Coreus tristis,* from its sad dull color; they are quite destructive to all plants of the Squash family.

Reduvius trinotatus, is one of this order, which is a valuable aid to the horticulturists, because its sucker is armed with sharp instruments, that enable it to pierce and consume other insects, many of which are destroyed by it. This insect has been introduced into the West for the sake of its valuable services.

ORDER LEPIDOPTERA.

The insects of this order are very numerous, and in their larval or caterpillar state they are often very destructive. In the perfect form of butterflies and moths, they commit little or no depredations, because their jaws have been transformed into a sucking apparatus. They consume, in their perfect state, little else than honey.

The order has been divided into three great sections: Butterflies, *Papiliones*; Hawk-moths, *Sphinges*; and Moths, or *Nocturnes*. Of these, the *Ægeridæ* constitute a very distinct family, resembling bees and wasps rather than butterflies; their caterpillars also differ, being borers, and nearly naked. Butterflies are produced from caterpillars that are not generally very injurious to our crops. Hawk-moths are large insects, and have great power of flight; their caterpillars are large and voracious. It is the moths proper, a very numerous family, which do us the most harm, and which will demand the largest share of our attention. They vary much in size and appearance. Some of the females are destitute of wings.

The *Arctians*, or Woolly Bears, are a very numerous division of the tribe of *Bombyces* or Spinners, so called from the name of the Silk-worm; some of these will be mentioned.

Orgyia leucostigma, or the Vaporer Moth, is a very beautiful caterpillar, frequently seen upon our fruit trees, though not confined to them. They feed separately, and therefore we can best destroy them in the egg. Fortunately, these may easily be found during the winter, for the female, being wingless, never quits her cocoon, but deposits the eggs in a mass upon the outside of it. The whole contrivance is one of the many illustrations of the wonderful instinct of insects. When about to spin, the worm secures two or more leaves, by entwining her silk about their stems, and also around the woody twig upon which they grow; she then attaches them together by bands of silk, and spins her cocoon between them. She thus secures a winter resting place for her eggs, and her progeny, when they hatch the next summer, are upon the tree that furnishes them their appropriate food. These dead leaves will attract our attention during the winter, and should be gathered and burned. Many of the caterpillars are destroyed by a little Ichneumon-fly.

Orgyia antiqua, or the Rusty Vaporer Moth, of Europe, has been introduced into this country, and has been quite destructive to thorn-hedges in Rhode Island. They may become troublesome to our orchards.

Several of these *Arctians*, or Tiger-moths, may be seen about our houses on a summer evening, as they are chiefly nocturnal. One of the most common is

Arctia phalerata, or the Harnessed Moth, so called from the markings on its wings. Another distinctly marked one is *Callimorpha militaris*, now called *C. Lecontei*. Beautiful illustrations of these are given in Dr. Harris' Report.

Spilosoma Virginica, is the beautiful White Moth, or "Miller," that we see in May; it is the imago or perfect insect of a large hairy caterpillar, of a yellowish color, frequently seen in our gardens, and quite destructive to vegetation.

Hyphantria textor, or the Fall Web-worm, is very troublesome upon shrubs and trees during the summer and fall. They are called the Web-worms from their habit of feeding gregariously in large numbers, and spinning a web that envelopes the leaves and the whole branch, as they devour the foliage.

This insect commits sad ravages upon our cultivated trees of various kinds, for it is not a choice feeder, consuming but one species, like many other insects. Their most common pasture is the mulberry, and the related Osage Orange is frequently attacked. The Elder bushes appear very attractive to them, and are often covered with their unsightly webs. Elms suffer very much; our favorite fruit trees are attacked; apples, pears, cherries, quinces, and, occasionally, even the peach trees are eaten by them. Even the repulsive Ailantus, which has often been recommended as a wormless tree, is greedily devoured by these caterpillars, notwithstanding its disagreeable odor.

The eggs, from two to three hundred in number, are deposited on the under side of a leaf, near the end of a twig. These soon hatch, and the larvæ commence feeding on the upper surface, spinning their threads from side to side, and then, attaching two or three leaves together, they soon make a web. They continue feeding and spinning along the twig, as they consume the tender portion of the leaf, leaving the mere skeleton.

The caterpillars are small, of a pale yellow color, with a broad blackish stripe on the back, and another beneath. They are thickly clothed with whitish hair; the head and feet are black. Worms of the same nest vary in size and colors. When about an inch long, they disperse, and spin their cocoons. The moth is milk white, without any

. markings on its wings, and is 1.25 to 1.35 inch in width. (Vide Harris, p. 358).

Though called the Fall Web-worm, these caterpillars appear about Cincinnati in the end of May quite abundantly, and from that time until October, they are more or less frequent; most so in August. In the North, they may be later; I have seen large tracts of forest defoliated on the lake shore, in August, 1865.

REMEDIES.—For the destruction of these pests we must resort to hand-picking, when they are in the caterpillar state. The twig or branch should be taken off, and the worms crushed or burned. It is fortunate for us that they are gregarious and that they spin a web, for we can detect them while they are yet young, and when confined to one or two leaves, so that the whole brood may be destroyed with very little effort. Birds, and some insects, aid us in keeping them in check.

Clisiocampa decipiens, (*Walker*), or *C. Americana*, (*Harris*), is commonly known as the Tent-caterpillar, or Nest-caterpillar. The larvæ are not indiscriminate feeders, but prefer the foliage of certain members of the *Rosaceous* family of plants. Their natural food appears to be the common wild cherry, but they attack the apple so vigously, that they are often called the apple tree worm. Mr. Fitch thinks they do not feed upon the peach; but I have frequently found them upon this tree since 1855. The moth appears to be endowed with wonderful instinct in depositing her eggs; selecting a terminal shoot that has completed its growth, they are placed to the number of 200 or 300 around it in a broad ring or sheath, and covered with a sort of varnish that protects them.

Very early in the spring, when the buds of the apple have just begun to swell, the eggs hatch, and the little worms traverse the twig, spinning a slender thread; when they reach another branch, they halt in the bifurcation, and, moving about, soon create a slight web with the silken threads, and from this they emerge in search of food, spinning a thread along their route, and when they return, they travel about, and thus enlarge their web.

REMEDIES.—These insects may be attacked in the egg or in the larval state. The former are so arranged as to be conspicuous on the naked spray at any time during the winter—whenever seen, they should be broken or cut off, and carried to the fire. In the early spring, we must watch for the little tents in the bifurcations of the limbs, and remove the nests with all the worms; this may be done when they are small, by using the thumb and finger; if larger, it is a disagreeable task, but no orchardist should hesitate when he recollects that six hundred leaves is a day's ration for one colony. They can easily be gathered in their web, thrown upon the ground, and crushed with the foot. Mr. Needham, of Massachusetts, has invented, what he calls, a caterpillar scourge; it is a little cone of wood, clothed with a piece of wool-card. This is attached to a pole: when thrust into the web, the whole nest is gathered by the card-teeth and brought down. An old dry mullein stalk has often been used for the same purpose, and some recommend burning the nest, or shooting it; but I have more faith in thumb and finger work, believing it to be more thorough.

Among the natural enemies of these caterpillars are the Tiger-beetles, which a successful orchardist of Illinois uses systematically for their destruction. He catches a beetle, and puts it upon a tree containing a nest of the Tent-caterpillar, after which he finds the worms soon disappear.

Gastrophaca Americana, (*Harris*).—The Lappet-caterpillars are found on apple trees. The worms are flat, and when at rest on a limb, they often escape observation from their gray color resembling the bark. A fringe of hairs, along their sides, gives them this flat appearance. They feed only at night. Dr. Harris found some in September that measured two and one-half inches in length, and above half an inch in breadth.

SATURNIANS, CERATOCAMPIANS, ZEUZERIANS.

Platysamia (Attacus) cecropia, (*Linn.*), the Cecropia Emperor Moth, is found as a large cylindrical, pale green worm, three or four inches long, and as thick as one's thumb, and having two rows of pale blue, projecting points along each side, and two rows of pale yellow ones upon the back, with four larger, bright orange, or red ones anteriorly, all ending in little black prickles. The moth is large; its wings dark gray; each has a large white, crescent like spot in the centre, margined with red, and a red band crossing both wings. Appears in June; width five to seven inches.

There are others of this family of noble moths whose names have been indicated above, but they are not very destructive to the orchard.

Then come, in Dr. Harris' classification, the *Zeuzerians*, a group of moths which, like *Ægerians* among the Sphinges, pierce the roots and stems of trees. Among these is *Xyleutes* (*Cossus*) *robiniæ*, or the Locust-tree Boring-moth.

The Saturnians are a group of large, naked caterpillars, which are generally short, thick, clumsy, and cylindrical; they are leaf-eaters, and some of them, when young, keep together in families, but separate as they become older, when they spin large· silky cocoons sometimes among leaves, which they secure by silk to the twigs, sometimes attaching them to the stems and limbs, and at others at, or beneath, the surface of the ground. This group contains some of the largest and most beautiful moths, with large woolly bodies, and widely extended, highly colored· and ornamented wings. They lay a great many eggs; some females deposit several hundreds. Still they are seldom so numerous as to commit serious devastations.

"Among these are the *Telea Polyphemus*, *Tropæ aluna*, *Callosamia Promethea*, *Platysamia cecropia*, (formerly known under the genus *Attacus*, which is now restricted to the immense *A. Atlas*, and another species of China), and the *Euchronia Maia*, and *Hyperchiria varia*, (formerly known under the genus *Saturnia*, which is now retained for several European species). The latter species, (*H. varia*), has been generally known among us under the name of *Saturnia Io*, but according to Dr. Packard, (who published 'a Synopsis of the Bombycidæ of the United States,' in the Third Volume of the Proceedings of the Entomological Society of Philadelphia), our species has been confounded by authors with Cramer's species '*Io*,' from South America, and which belongs to a different genus."—[E. T. Cresson, Mss.

These moths may yet become valuable for the production of a kind of silk, as they are enclosed in large cocoons, the fibres of which surpass those of the Silk-worm in strength, and might be employed in the formation of fabrics, similar to those manufactured in India from the Tusseh and Arrindy Silk-worms, the strength and durability of which are proverbial. Mr. Pullein, who experimented with the cocoons of the *Cecropia*, found that twenty threads of this silk, twisted together, would sustain nearly an ounce more in weight than the same number of common silk.—(Vide Harris, pp. 295–303.)

Psychidæ are curious caterpillars, which, being naked, cover themselves during the larva state with a case that protects their bodies, though open at both ends, and which they carry about with them; these cases are made up of fragments of leaves, generally the stems and veins, which they connect together by threads of silk. The Germans call them Sack-bearers. Huebner called them *Canœphorœ*, or Basket-carriers, because the cases, often made of little sticks, resemble a basket. One genus is called *Œceticus*, or House-insect; and the common species, which, in some parts of the country, commits great devastation upon the leaves of trees, is called the Drop-worm, or the Basket-worm, in many places.

We have several genera and species belonging to this sub-family, the most common of which are the *Thyridopteryx ephemeraformis*, and *Œceticus coniferarum*. The best means for the destruction of this pest consist in persevering efforts for their individual destruction; each case should be cut or torn off in the winter, when they show very plainly upon deciduous trees; they may be crushed, but had better be committed to the flames.

The Notodontians are so called from a hump or horn, which rises from the top of the fourth ring of the caterpillar; the tail is always raised when the insect is at rest. One of these is called, from its horn, *Cœlodasys* (*Notodonta*) *unicornis*. Some species consume the foliage of our fruit trees, particularly the apple and quince; one of these, the *Datana ministra*, (the *Eumetopona ministra* of Fitch, or the *Pygœra ministra* of Harris), will be noticed below.

Eudryas grata, and **E. unio.** — The Beautiful Wood-nymph, and the Pearl Wood-nymph.—The worms are very much alike, and resemble the Spotted Forrester. The moths come forth in July; the fore-wings are milk white, bordered behind and on the outer side, from the base to the middle, with rusty brown, edged on the inner side with greenish olive; hind-wings nankeen yellow, with a blackish-brown border. These worms are best removed by hand-picking.

Datana ministra, or the Hand-maid Moth.—The moths are troublesome visitors to the evening student in June; they are brown, hairy, thick-bodied, and measure rather more than an inch across the wings. This creature is destined to give us a great deal of trouble by her progeny, for she deposits her numerous eggs on the under side of the leaf on a twig of quince, apple, and cherry trees, where they hatch into worms, that, during their existence of about four weeks, consume immense quantities of foliage, often stripping the trees bare.

The worms feed gregariously, lying side by side in solid phalanx. They are of a dark brown in their younger state, but become lighter and more clearly marked at each successive moulting, so that they are distinctly striped with black and yellow. The peculiar character of this worm is, that when at rest, the head and tail are carried up in the air, or recurved over the body, which is supported by the six prop legs placed near the middle. When disturbed, these caterpillars often throw their heads from side to side, as though in anger. They are sparingly furnished with hairs, and they spin but little; though when young, the worms will sometimes drop from the leaves when disturbed, and hang suspended by a fine strand of silk. At full size, these creatures are an inch and three-quarters to two inches long, and as thick as a goose quill, so that we can readily imagine the amount of destruction which may be committed by one of these armies or family groups of one to two hundred worms.

TREATMENT.—Constant vigilance is required on the part of the orchardist, and unremitting efforts while the insect is in the larval condition. Fortunately for us, their habits are such as to aid us in a remarkable way. They may be looked for in July, but they become numerous only about the end of August, and in September. Some late broods may be seen on the access of early frosts, but by the end of September, the worms generally perfect their growth, and descend into the earth to undergo their changes for the next season, when the moths will again appear.

When we may be inspecting our orchards, in the summer and autumn, we should observe any defective foliage, as this is often an indication of the inroads of insects.

If our trees have been neglected, we may be alarmed by observing some of the thriftiest shoots and branches quite stripped of their leaves; and, lying along the stems, or crowded together, we shall see these unpleasant worms, unless they be foraging upon an adjoining, or sometimes upon quite a distant branch; for, in changing their pasture, they descend one twig and pass out upon another, which may diverge considerably from the first.

In the early stages of their existence, however, the little worms consume only the upper surface of the leaves, and it is at this period that we may most advantageously attack them. The leaves that have thus had their substance eroded become dry and whitish, and attract our attention. They are generally found upon a single twig or spray, usually a lateral, and it should at once be examined, as we may now easily destroy the whole brood by rolling a single leaf between the thumb and finger.

NOCTUÆ, OR OWLET-MOTHS, CUT-WORMS.

The perfect insects are thick-bodied, and of dull colors; they fly at night. The caterpillars are naked, live in the soil, and feed above ground at night, when they do considerable damage. The common Cut-worm, *Agrotis*, is an illustration. There are several sorts, which have received different names, but the worms all have very similar habits.

The moths are supposed to lay their eggs in July, when they soon hatch and feed during the season; they attain siderable size and hybernate in the soil.

REMEDIES.—Fall and winter plowing has been recommended, as it exposes the worms to the birds, and to the weather, but especially because it destroys the vegetation upon which they might subsist in the early spring. The only safe way, is to watch their traces among our plants, and dig down beside them, find the worm, and destroy it. Though this does not restore the plant already killed, we prevent further damage, and may hope to thus diminish the pest in future years, which is no small matter. A knowledge of their nocturnal habits has induced some gardeners to go among their young plants with a lamp or candle at night, when they may find the caterpillars feeding. A few choice plants may be protected by wrapping their stems with a strip of paper, or a stout leaf, (hickory), at the time of transplanting into infested grounds; this will save them. Tobacco water has been found very effective, applied to the plants, which it does not injure. .

Mamestra arctica, (*Hadena amica*, of Harris, and *H. amputatrix*, of Fitch), is a Cut-worm of a brownish color, about one and a half inch long. It is sometimes quite destructive in the nursery and garden, ascending woody plants, and cutting them off where succulent, in the month of May. It can only be checked by seeking for it, in the soil, near the base of the plants affected.

All these Cut-worms are eaten by birds, among which the crow is a valuable aid to the farmer, and should be cherished for his services instead of being condemned as a bird of ill-omen. Predacious insects also consume numbers of them; one of these is the larva of a beetle, *Harpalus calaginosus*. A large Ichneumon-fly has been found hunting after the worms, and is considered their natural enemy.

GEOMETERS, SPAN-WORMS, CANKER-WORMS.

The measuring worms take their name from their peculiar method of locomotion; having their legs at each end
of their long bodies, they walk by progressive leaps, arching up their backs by bringing their hind-legs forward, and
then thrusting their heads out to their full length. Many
of them drop from the trees, and hang suspended by a
thread of silk, when disturbed, or when seeking the earth
to undergo their transformations. Some of them are naked, or have few hairs; most are smooth, often striped, or
of an uniform color, like the bark of the trees on which
they feed.

The moths are slender-bodied; the wings large; of some
the females have no wings. These are the *Hybernians*,
including the Canker-worm, *Anisopterix vernata*. These
caterpillars are very numerous and destructive; they do
not feed gregariously, and are difficult to combat in that
form. The pupæ are under ground, and, as the female
moths are wingless, and must ascend the trees to deposit
their eggs, we can destroy them in the perfect form by
meeting them on the highway they have to pass. Ingenious devices have been invented for this purpose; among
the most effective of these are vessels of oil, fastened
closely around the bole of the tree. The moths emerge
from the ground in early spring, but many come out during pleasant mild days in the winter, and some even in the
autumn; so the remedies must be applied early to be of
any use.

Harris describes a smaller species as the *Anisopterix
pometaria.*

Hybernia tiliaria, or the Span-worm of the Linden, is

abundant in June, growing to the length of an inch and a half. A belt of tar, applied to the trees, has been found effective in preventing the ascent of the wingless females; this needs renewing daily, until the season of their rising has passed.

Ellopia ribearia, or the Currant-moth, was figured and described by Fitch as the *Abraxas? ribearia,* in New York Reports for 1856. The worm is light yellow, with black dots. It eats the leaves of currants and gooseberries, in June. The moth ascends from the ground in July; it is nankeen-yellow; quite a common insect in some parts of the country. It must have some natural enemies, for, where very abundant one year, it sometimes disappears altogether the next. Hand-picking is the only remedy known, and this is quite a tedious process.

— ◦◦◦ —

TORTRICES, DELTA MOTHS, OR LEAF-ROLLERS.

The Leaf-rollers are a numerous tribe, and some of them are troublesome upon our cultivated trees and vines. They curl up the edge of the leaf upon which they feed, and fasten it with little bands of silk, and thus shelter themselves from the weather and from their enemies. They are naked worms, and generally light colored, and exceedingly active. Some live in the unfolding leaves and flower-buds, fastening them together so they cannot expand, while they devour the tender tissues. Some enter the young fruit, which they cause to ripen and fall prematurely. The moths are generally small, often prettily marked, and fly only in the evening.

15

Loxotænia rosaceana, (*Harris*), is found soon after the buds of the apple begin to expand. They curl up and fasten them together, and do considerable damage.

Penthina oculana, (*Harris*), has similar habits, and preys upon the apple; both must be killed by hand.

Brachytænia melania, or the Many-dotted Apple Leaf-worm, is mentioned by Fitch* as eating holes in the leaves, in June and September. It is rather thick, light green, an inch and a quarter long, with five white lines and numerous white dots; the worms spin their cocoons in a leaf. There are two crops.

Loxotænia cerasivorana, (*Fitch*), or the Cherry Tortrix, is a deep yellow worm, with black head and feet. Found in July, fastening the leaves together and living in families, forming a large nest.**

Desmia maculalis, or the Spotted-winged Sable, or Grape Leaf-folder, is a slender, active green worm, that feeds upon and disfigures the leaves of our grape vines, rolling them with great regularity, and fastening them with strong bands of beautiful white silk. The pupa is formed within the rolled leaf. These worms begin in June, but continue to fold the leaves during the season of growth.

They can be destroyed by hand-picking, but it requires quickness and dexterity, as the worm escapes from either end of the open pipe when disturbed. The warblers are very fond of them, and destroy a great many.

Carpocapsa pomonella, or the Codling-moth, is one of these Tortrices, which gives great trouble. It has been in-

* Rept., p. 241.
** Vide Fitch, in N. Y. Trans. 1856, p. 392.

troduced from Europe, but is steadily increasing as our orchards grow older, until we now have few perfect fruit. The moth appears early in the summer to lay the eggs of the first crop of worms. This insect is figured and described by different authors, among whom Dr. Trimble, of New Jersey, has paid it especial attention in his recent work.

The eggs are dropped singly upon the blossom end of the apple, that affords an entrance to the young worm, which passes to the core, about which it consumes the pulp and the seeds. The worm is whitish, becoming flesh-colored. In warm weather it attains its growth in three or four weeks, and makes its exit by gnawing through the side of the fruit. It instinctively seeks the stem of the tree to secrete itself under the scales of bark, and this affords us an opportunity to destroy it in the pupa state, for it will creep under any shelter that may be put in its way.

The REMEDIES will depend upon the habits of the insect. The moth, being nocturnal, may be destroyed by burning lamps or fires in the orchard during June, when they are first at work; cheap coal-oil may be used for the purpose. The pupæ can be entrapped in large numbers, by putting a piece of old rag in the crotch of the tree, beneath which the worms will crawl to spin their cocoons, when they may easily be destroyed. Dr. Trimble has used a trap, made by twisting a hay rope and fastening it about the trunk of the tree; under the rope immense numbers will be found. This trap should be examined fortnightly, as the moths hatch out during hot weather in a shorter time than later in the season, when some remain over winter in the pupal state.

All wormy fruit should be gathered as soon as it falls

from the trees, and either be boiled, or at once fed to swine. Hogs and sheep, kept in the orchard, will generally consume the fruit as fast as they fall to the ground; and this is the simplest and cheapest method of destroying the worms.

Chætochilus pometellus, (*Harris*), is commonly called the Palmer-worm. It feeds upon the leaves of our orchard and forest trees in June. Sometimes it appears in immense numbers, and, coming after the period for the production of new leaves, great damage is done to the trees; old trees, and limbs of younger ones, are sometimes killed. There have been two celebrated invasions of this insect in the Eastern States, those of 1791 and of 1853.*

GRAPE VINE FEEDERS.

Grape vines are subject to the attacks of many lepidopterous insects. Dr. Harris gives the history of seven American larvæ, mostly of large moths, which feed upon grape leaves.

Pterophorus periscelidactylus, or the Gartered Grape vine Plume, is a pale green worm, half an inch long, which hides itself in a hollow ball of leaves, fastened together with silken threads. It is described at length by Dr. Fitch, in the New York Agricultural Transactions.

Ohis myron, (*Chœrocampa pampinatrix*, of *Harris*), called also the Vine Dresser, is somewhat troublesome in the vineyards, as it eats the leaves, and cuts off the bunches

---

* For interesting details vide Fitch's Rept., p. 221.

of grapes when half grown. This worm is thick, cylindrical, tapering anteriorly, pale green, freckled with pale yellow dots, and, when mature, a pale dusky olive; 2.25 inches long. The pupa is found under leaves on the ground; the moth emerges in June.

Philampelus satellita, and **P. Achemon,** the Satellite and Achemon Sphinges, are large green worms that feed upon the vine. They bury themselves in the ground when going into the pupa state, and remain until the next July. The worms are seen in August and September.

Procris Americana, or the American Forrester, is found feeding upon the grape leaves at mid-summer, (June 22). The worms feed gregariously on the surface of a leaf, some twenty side by side, leaving only a skeleton behind them when small, and consuming the leaf when older. They are small, 0.60 inch long; yellowish. The moth is blue-black, with a bright orange neck.

Alypia 8-maculata, or the Eight-spotted Forrester, is a light blue worm, 1.25 inches in length. They leave the vines in July, and spin a web on the ground; the moth appears in May; it is black, with orange shanks; each of the fore-wings has two large, light yellow spots; the hind-wings have two white ones. Width 1, to 1.50 inch.

ÆGERIANS.

Egeria exitiosa, (*Say*), or *Trochilium exitiosum*, is well known in its larval state as the Peach tree Borer, and is often so destructive as to kill the trees. The habits of the worm as a borer, and its situation at the base of the tree, are somewhat similar to those of the apple tree borer; but while that is the footless grub of a beetle, this is a true caterpillar, the larva of a butterfly or moth, with feet. The females deposit their eggs from June to October, placing them upon the bark at the surface of the ground, sometimes in the forks of the large limbs. The larva enters, and works downward; first consuming the bark, but afterwards eroding the wood also. Gum exudes from the wound, mixed with their castings, and indicates their presence. When ready to enter the pupa form, the worms come to the surface, excavate a hollow in the wood, and prepare a tough leathery follicle or pod, three-fourths of an inch long, in which they repose as pupæ.

This, or an analagous insect, attacks the plum tree, and behaves in a similar manner. The double-flowering Almond of our shrubberies is also attacked by the borer.

The perfect insect looks more like a wasp than a butterfly, for the wings of all this group are partially clear of feathers, and transparent. It varies in size from a half to three-quarters of an inch in length, and from eight-tenths to one and three-tenths of an inch across. The female varies more than the male, and her wings are larger in proportion to the body, which is heavier. The male is of a deep steel-blue color, with sulphur-yellow marks, and glossy luster. The wings are transparent and glossy; the veins margined and fringed steel-blue.

REMEDIES will depend upon the habits of the insect, and must be directed to the pupa and larva, though valuable preventives are applicable to the perfect insect. The worms may be sought out by scraping away the gum and cutting the dead bark until we find them, often along the main roots; the follicles with the pupæ should also be sought. This work can be done in the autumn and spring; if at the former season, the removed earth should be left away from the stem, when coal tar may be applied to destroy any worms left in the tree and to act as a preventive against future attacks, but this substance should be used with great caution. If applied, the earth should be thrown back to the tree. Boiling soap-suds has been used with good effects.

PREVENTIVES are sometimes better than cures, and in this case they have been very successfully used. They all consist in means to keep the moth from depositing her eggs in the part of the tree where, alone, the borers can be harmful. Some raise a little mound of earth about the tree in the spring, and allow it to remain there all summer. The first application of this principle consisted in placing a chimney crock about the base of the young tree when planted; into this coal ashes, cinders, or even gravel was placed, which protected the base of the tree. In the autumn the crock was lifted, and the materials scattered. An open box, made of four bits of board, tacked together, answered the same purpose. A cone of coarse brown paper, tied about the tree with grocers' string, or pasted upon the tree itself, when applied, will answer a very good purpose in keeping off the fly.

A small portion of sulphur thrown about the tree is said to have the desired effect, but the statement has not been confirmed by trial. It has been recommended to plant Tansy with every peach tree, but doubt attaches itself to this suggestion also.

In the *American Agriculturist*, for February, 1865, is a notice of a peach tree protector made of sheet-iron, like a stove-pipe; and in the April number, Mr. Bouthorpe, of Massachusetts, says, he had used a similar apparatus made of zinc, eight inches long, and twice the size of the tree, which was of easy application; the contained space next the tree was to be filled with loose dirt. They were found to be a perfect protection.

Ægeria tipuliformis, (Linn.), or the Currant Borer, has been imported from Europe. The eggs are laid near a bud; when hatched, the worms penetrate the pith of young shoots, killing them.

Ægeria pyri is mentioned by Dr. Harris[*] as having done a good deal of damage to pear trees, by boring under the bark. The perfect insect resembles that of the Currant Borer, and makes its appearance near the end of summer, leaving its chrysalis skin projecting from the hole in the bark, whence it had escaped.

Ægeria polistæformis, or Grape Vine Borer, is mentioned by Mr. Glover in the Patent Office Report for 1854, p. 80. He had received it from North Carolina, where it was very destructive to all vines, except the Scuppernong. This insect has become rather common in the vineyards about Cincinnati, and its depredations, in consequence of the large size of the caterpillar, are very serious. The eggs are laid near the roots of the vine, and the larvæ bore into the bark and wood during the summer, consuming them so completely, that the vine sickens and dies, and often breaks off at the ground, or just below the surface. When fully grown, they measure

---

[*] Rept., p. 256.

from an inch to an inch and three-quarters in length, are thick and whitish, and they form a pod-like chrysalis, similar to that of the Peach Tree Borer, but within or beside the injured roots.

The moths are of a dark brown color, tinged with tawny-orange, and banded with bright yellow on the edge of the second ring of the body; the fore-wings are dusky, and the hind ones transparent.

REMEDIES.—No effectual methods of prevention are known; but it is well to inspect the vines, and when the presence of the insects is suspected, examine the roots, to find and destroy the worms.

NEUROPTERA, HYMENOPTERA, AND DIPTERA.

These several orders will be introduced together for convenience, as they may be disposed of in a briefer mention than some of their predecessors; because they do not contain so many species that are noxious by preying upon our cultivated plants. Some are even of advantage to us by their carnivorous propensities.

Among the **Neuroptera** are several which are aquatic in their larval condition, but when winged, they devour many insects; among these are the Dragon-flies, commonly called Devil's-needles by the children, who dread them, but they are harmless creatures. The Ant-lions were referred to under the head of Aphids, in the consideration of the order *Hemiptera*, as most voracious destroyers of Plant-lice. Reference was also made to the Lace-winged Flies, *Hemerobius*, which, in the larval state, consume

15*

immense numbers of the same pests. A few of these insects are injurious; among them are the White-ants, Wood-lice, and the Wood-ticks, which are annoying, though they do not affect our crops.

Of the **Hymenoptera** there are many which, in a perfect state, consume the juices of our choice fruits, as well as the pollen and honey of flowers. Their services among these last, as aids in fertilizing the germs, is often of great importance to the fruit-grower. But, while acknowledging our gratitude to many for this service, and to the industrious bee for gathering abundant stores of the nectared sweets, we have a serious charge to bring against the family for their depredations. The wasps especially are often troublesome, particularly in the vineyard, and their stings are annoying. Some ants are quite injurious.

The larvæ of some species are destructive as wood borers and as leaf-eaters, and others cause an excrescence or warty growth upon the twigs and leaves where the eggs have been deposited; these are called *Gall-flies*. The great benefits rendered by a very large class of insects in this order, however, may compensate for all the evil done by the others. I refer to the tribe of *Ichneumon-flies* of several genera. Some of these are very small, and deposit their eggs within other insects, where they hatch and destroy them by feeding upon their juices.

Many of the wasps are predaceous, and destroy numerous insects to feed their larvæ. Some of these exercise a wonderful instinct in preparing and securing this food for their.young, which is stored up in safe caskets with the egg, and are ready to serve as food to the young larvæ.

The *Diptera*, or two-winged insects, form an extensive

order, containing many species, and these are composed of very numerous individuals. Flies and mosquitos are exceedingly annoying to man and animals, and many species, in the larval state, consume vegetable matters; but even here they are often of use in consuming decayed vegetation, and like many others of the order may be considered scavengers, consuming, as they do, immense quantities of filth and carrion, that would otherwise continue to taint the air and produce disease.

Some of the most destructive insects of this order are the *Gall-gnats*, among which are the Wheat-fly and the Hessian-fly, which often sadly interfere with the farmer's prospects.

A few insects will now be noticed more in detail.

Selandria cerasi, or *Blennocampa cerasi*, is the common Slug of the cherry and pear trees, and quite a troublesome hymenopterous insect. In some parts of the United States these little creatures are so numerous as to strip the substance from the foliage of pears and cherries.

Our Slug resembles the *Selandria œthiops* of Europe, but is declared to be different. The larvæ are at first white, but the slimy substance that oozes from their bodies covers them with an olive coating. They have twenty very short legs; when fully grown, the largest are about nineteen-twentieths of an inch long. The head is concealed under the fore part of the body, which is largest before, and tapers behind. They attain their growth in twenty days, casting their skins five times, eating them until the last time, after which they remain free from viscidity, and are of a clear yellow color. They leave the tree and enter the ground to the depth of one or three inches, to form their chrysalids. In three days they come up as flies, in July and August, to lay eggs for a second brood, the pupæ of which remain in the ground during the winter.

Another insect of this genus is very destructive to our rose bushes; it is called *Selandria rosœ.*

Selandria vitis, is a species that appears upon our grape vines, and is quite troublesome in some vineyards in July. They feed in companies of a dozen or more.

REMEDIES.—Shaking them off the leaves has been recommended, but does not promise to be effectual. When few, they should be sought for and crushed, to prevent their increase. Though troublesome, this may be effectually done, and their ravages leave traces that will direct us to the leaves which contain them.

When more numerous, the foliage may be syringed with common soapsuds, or with the whale oil soap, two pounds to fifteen gallons of water.

Air-slaked lime has been dusted upon them with good effect; ashes, and even dry dust from the road, will destroy them, by adhering to the slimy surface. These applications are best made when the foliage is wet after a shower, or with the dew. The great difficulty consists in their habit of going under the leaves, and thus being protected.

Mr. Parkman, the noted rose fancier, has found a mixture of soap and petroleum of great service, as it kills the slugs without injuring the buds and foliage. To a gallon of soft soap he adds two-thirds of a pint of petroleum, mixes them thoroughly, and dissolves in half a barrel of water; to be applied with a syringe.

Diptera.—Dr. Fitch describes as a new species *Malo-brus mali*. He found them in a fruit that had been perforated by the Codling-moth. The larvæ are transparent; the flies resemble the Hessian-fly, that destroys the wheat plant.*

Cecidomyla grossulariæ, or Gooseberry Midge, attacks the fruit, giving it the appearance of ripening prematurely. Considerable fruit is lost in this way.**

In closing this chapter, the author feels obliged to express his regrets that no more space could have been appropriated to this important subject. He could only indicate some of the most troublesome insects of our orchards and vineyards, and he hopes that the reader will be induced to pursue the investigation for himself. He knows, by experience, that the study will bring its own reward in the information that is received, and which is absolutely necessary to enable us to combat these troublesome pests successfully.

* See Fitch's Report, p. 176.
* * See Fitch's Report, p. 202.

CHAPTER XV.

CHARACTERS OF FRUITS AND THEIR VALUE.
TERMS USED.

———◦◦◦———

IMPORTANCE OF SEIZING THE STRONG MARKS — EXTERNAL; WEIGHT, SHAPE, SIZE, SURFACE — BASIN AND EYE — CAVITY AND STEM — INTERNAL; FLESH, CORE, AXIS, SEEDS, FLAVOR — THESE CONSIDERED SEPARATELY AND ILLUSTRATED — EXPLANATION OF TERMS USED — SHAPE REFERRED TO RELATIONS OF THE DIAMETERS; AXIAL AND TRANSVERSE — LEADING FORMS DESCRIBED AND ILLUSTRATED — SIZE, A COMPARVTIVE TERM — SKIN CHARACTERS, COLOR; ITS USE IN CLASSIFYING — PERMANENCE OF STRIPES — LINES — DOTS AND SPECKS — FUNGOUS SPOTS — FORMS OF BASIN AND EYE, OF CAVITY AND STEM, ARE VALUABLE; TERMS USED — THE INTERIOR, AXIS, CORE, SEEDS, FLESH — FLAVOR UNCERTAIN — SWEET AND SOUR GOOD CHARACTERS — QUALITY, TERMS EXPRESSIVE OF.

In the description of a fruit, it is very desirable for the writer to catch the strong characters, so that he, who reads, may the more readily identify the specimen he holds in his hand. Among these several characters there is considerable difference as to their permanence and value; some are evanescent, some variable, while others are

350

found to be more reliable and constant. Let us consider some of these in the systematic order by which they will be taken in the descriptions that are to follow.

In describing a fruit, the firmness, weight, and external characters, first claim our attention, then the internal; these are taken up in the following order: externally, its shape, size, surface, color, and dots are examined. In the apple and pear the basin is next observed and its characters noted, with any peculiarities connected with the eye, by which term the triangular space is designated that is embraced by the calyx, as shown in an axial section of the fruit; at the same time the length and breadth and shape of the calyx segments are noted. The other end of the fruit is then explored as to the form and markings of the cavity, and the length, size, and peculiarities of the stem. Having thus disposed of the externals, we are now to investigate the nature of the internal structure; to do this, a section is made vertically through the middle of the fruit from the eye to the stem, which exposes the flesh, the axis with its core and the seeds, and which enables us to investigate some very important characters, such as the length of the axis, its form and that of its carpels, and the manner of their union, whether they form an open core or otherwise.

The number, color, and shape of the seeds are noted. The color of the flesh, its texture and juiciness are examined; the latter qualities are always tested by the teeth, and then the palate gives us an account of the degree of richness, acidity, or sweetness and flavor. The investigator is now prepared to render judgment; having the testimony of his organs of touch, sight, taste and smell, he can pronounce his decision as to quality, and is prepared to specify the particular uses to which the fruit is especially adapted; whether for the table as a dessert, for the kitchen, as in baking and stewing, or for drying, or whether it be valuable for cider-making. A good judge will now be able to decide whether the fruit be especially adapted for the market or for the amateur. The season of ripening should be noted in this place, with any remark as to qualities not already provided for.

FORM is one of our most permanent characters; though subject to modifications, the general shape of the specimens is always characteristic of the variety. Even a novice will soon learn the peculiar outline of a variety of fruit.

Before, commencing the study of these varieties of form, it will be well to explain some of the leading terms introduced. By referring to the illustrations, it will be observed that the outlines are inscribed in circles to which they are compared; these are drawn with dotted lines, and they are bisected with cross lines representing the two diameters referred to in the classification by form: the vertical or axial diameter, *AA*, passing through the axis of the fruit, and the transverse diameter, *BB*, at right angles to the vertical.

The FORM may be *round* or *globular* when it is nearly spherical; the two diameters, the axial and transverse, being nearly equal; fig. 30.

Globose is another term of about the same meaning.

Conic, or *conical*, indicates a decided contraction toward the blossom end, fig. 31; *Ob-conic* implies that the cone is very short or flattened.

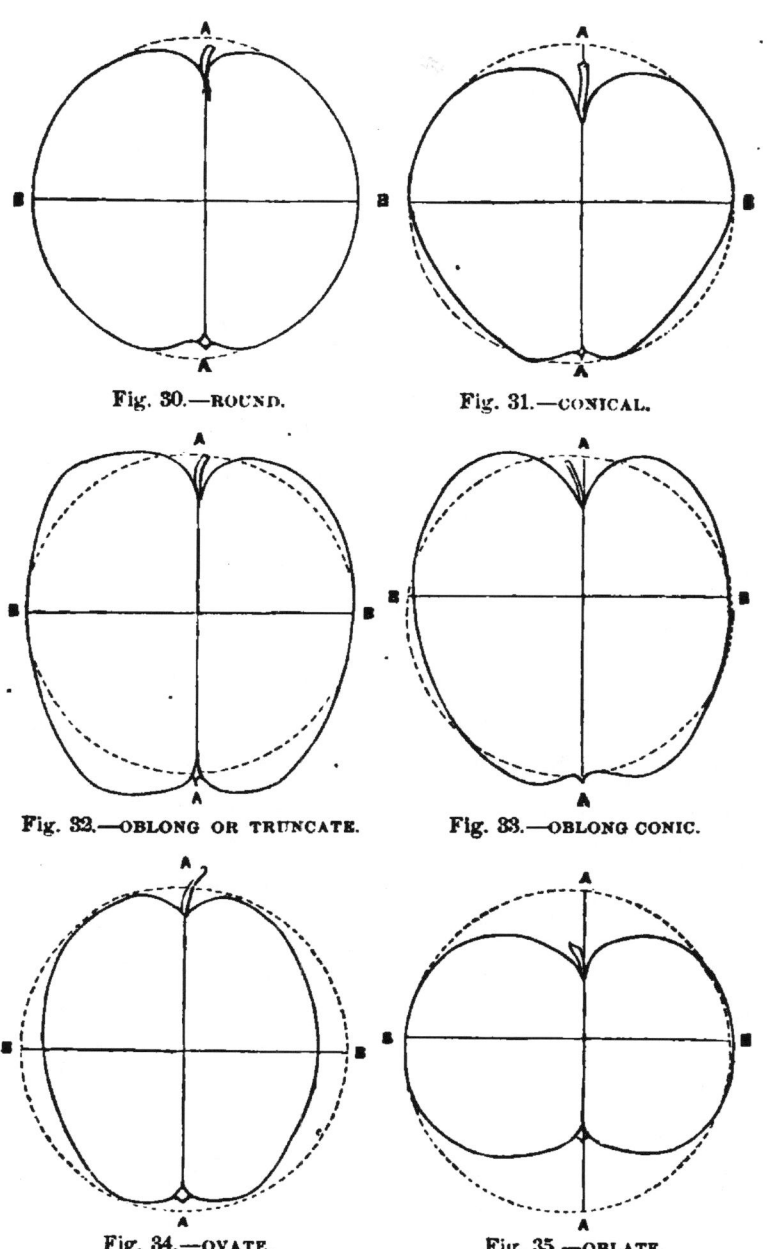

Fig. 30.—ROUND.

Fig. 31.—CONICAL.

Fig. 32.—OBLONG OR TRUNCATE.

Fig. 33.—OBLONG CONIC.

Fig. 34.—OVATE.

Fig. 35.—OBLATE.

Oblong means that the axial diameter is the longer, or that it appears so, for an oblong apple may have equal diameters; fig. 32.

Oblong-conic, that the outline also tapers rapidly toward the eye; fig. 33.

Oblong-ovate, that it is fullest in the middle; and like

Ovate, which means egg-shaped, that it tapers to both ends; fig. 34.

Oblate, or flattened, when the axial diameter is decidedly the shorter; fig. 35.

Obtuse is applied to any of these figures that is not very decided.

Cylindrical and *truncate* are dependent upon one another, thus a globular, or still more remarkably, an oblong fruit, which is abruptly truncated or flattened at the ends, appears cylindrical in its form.

Depressed is an unusually flattened oblate form.

Turbinate or top-shaped, and *pyriform* or pear-shaped, are especially applicable to pears, and seldom to apples.

When these forms are described evenly about a vertical axis, as shown by a section of the fruit made transversely, or across the axis, the specimen may be called *regular* or *uniform,* fig. 36; if otherwise, it is *irregular,* fig. 37, *unequal,* fig. 38, *oblique* or *lop-sided,* fig. 39, in which last cases the axis is inclined to one side. If the development at the surface is irregular, as in the Duchesse d'Angouleme and Bartlett pears, the fruit is termed *uneven.*

When a transverse section of the fruit, made at right angles to the axis, gives the figure of a circle, the fruit is *regular ;* if otherwise, it may be *compressed* or flattened at the sides, fig. 40; *angular, quadrangular,* fig. 41;

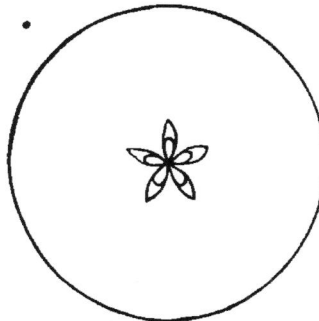

Fig. 36.—REGULAR.

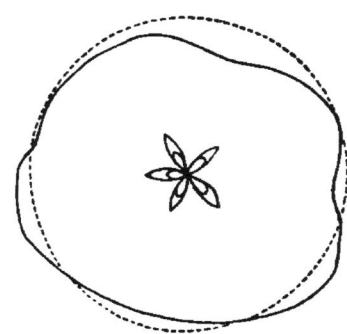

Fig. 37.—IRREGULAR.

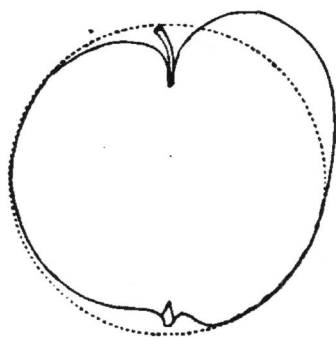

Fig. 38.—UNEQUAL.

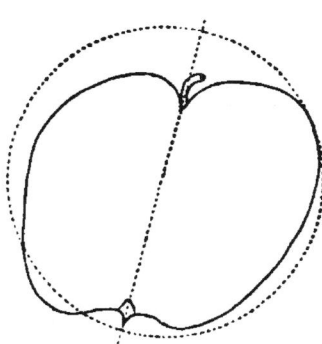

Fig. 39.—LOP-SIDED.

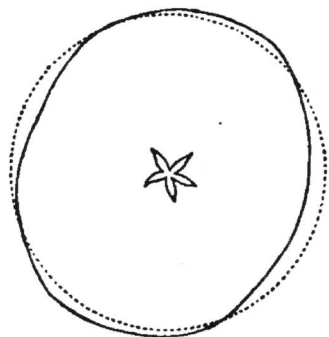

Fig. 40.—COMPRESSED.

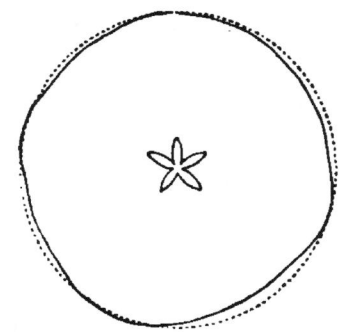

Fig. 41.—QUADRANGULAR.

sulcate or *furrowed*, fig. 42, when marked by sulcations; or *ribbed*, fig. 43, when the intervening ridges are abrupt.

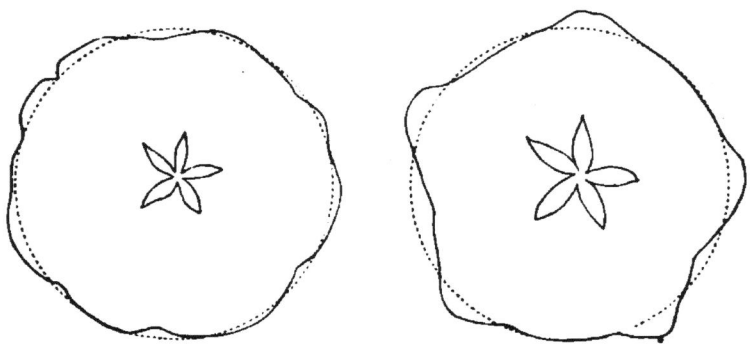

Fig. 42.—SULCATE.   Fig. 43.—RIBBED.

Heart-shaped is a form that applies more especially to the cherry, than any other kind of fruit.

Size is a character of but second rate importance, since it is dependent upon the varying conditions of soil, climate, overbearing, etc. It has its value, however, when it is considered as comparative or relative. The expressions employed in this work to indicate size, are: *very large*, *large*, *medium*, *small*, *very small*, making five grades.

The characters of the Skin and surface are generally very reliable, though the smoothness of the skin as well as the coloring depend upon both soil and climate. We find, however, that a striped apple which has been shaded, though pale, will always betray itself by a splash or stripe, be it ever so small or rare, nor will any exposure so deepen and exaggerate its stripes as to make it a self-colored fruit; and no circumstances will introduce a true stripe upon a self-colored variety. Hence we may consider this kind of marking a reliable character, and apply it as an element of our classification. We sometimes find *lines* on self-colored fruits that are as distinctive as the stripes, but entirely distinct from them.

The skin itself may be either *thick* or *thin, smooth rough*, or *polished*, and it is sometimes *uneven ;* it may be covered with a *bloom*, it may be *russeted* in whole or in part, and this may be thickly or thinly spread over the surface, or only net-veined. A sort of russeting occurs about the stem only in some varieties, and is never seen in others, making a pretty good character, but in the same variety it is often much increased or diminished.

This character, russet on the skin, has been very puzzling to young pomologists in the study of pears, owing to its liability to exaggeration in some varieties, under the influence of certain climatic conditions that have even produced it in varieties in which it had not been previously suspected. Some pears are characterized by this russeting of the skin, either generally spread over the surface or confined to a limited area at either end of the fruit, particularly about the insertion of the stem; others have never shown any disposition to put on this character, but, under certain circumstances some varieties, which should have been smooth and fair, become thickly spread with this russeting, that seems even to thicken the skin and which deteriorates the qualities of the fruit. In some cases this appearance is local, occupying one end of the fruit, or making a band around the middle and contracting it like a cincture, as though its presence prevented the proper growth and development of the sarcocarp or fleshy mass of the fruit.

The colors themselves being as various almost as the hues of the rainbow, will be designated by their appropriate or customary names; the manner of their laying on will require the use of certain definite terms, which should be understood to comprehend the classification, which, in part, depends upon this circumstance. Thus a fruit is called *self-colored* when it is not striped, though it may be *blushed* or *bronzed*, and the coloring may be so broken, without stripes, as to be *mixed* or curdled, *blotched*, marbled, *mottled, clouded, spotted, stained, shaded* or *dappled;* but some of these characters are often found associated with striping also, or they are observed in those kinds of fruit that are always devoid of stripes. Striped fruits are often so deeply colored that the separate stripes do not appear so distinctly, as when there are fewer of them on a lighter ground and they can scarcely be perceived. When the stripes are long and distinct, they are called *streaks;* when short and broken abruptly at their ends, the surface is said to be *splashed.* Certain pears are striped by a paleness or faintness of color, these are called *panache*, and are considered sports of their namesake varieties which they resemble in other respects. A few peaches are distinctly striped; some plums and cherries obscurely so.

Another class of surface or skin characters consists in the DOTS and SPECKS, which appear to be very valuable distinctive markings, on account of their uniformity in different varieties. These may be *large* or *small, numerous* or *scattered, darker* or *lighter* colored, *prominent* or *indented.* In shape they are *round* or *elongated*, and this last is a valuable character because quite rare. Sometimes the dots are characterized by having a green base or areola around them, which is very noticeable, and in some varieties these marks, which are perhaps the stomata of the skin, are surrounded by distinct rings of a gray color, that resemble *ocellations* or eyes. No reliance can be placed upon the delicate coloring that is often to be seen upon the surface of certain light colored fruits, making rose, red, or purplish tints about these dots, as they are accidental only and not distinctive markings.

No one should confound these pores, that are designated as the *dots*, with the superficial and extraneous marks that appear to be the accidental growth of some fungus or lichen, and which are very commonly found upon the surface of many fruits, often giving them a quite pretty appearance that would be seized upon by the fruit painter as a special beauty, unless when so abundant as to produce an unpleasant smutchiness or cloudiness, such as is often found in the product of apple orchards that are situated in low bottom lands, and which peculiarity is attributed to the influence of fogs.

The BASIN or APEX of a fruit consists of that portion most distant from the stem. In the apple and pear it is commonly called the blossom end, and is often more or less depressed; hence the term *basin*. In other fruits it is called the point or *apex*. Both are characterized by peculiarities of form that serve as distinctive marks in the description of fruits, and these are characters of considerable value on account of their permanence. In respect to its form, the basin, according to its depth, is called *deep*, fig. 44; *shallow*, fig. 45; *very shallow*, or *medium*. It is *abrupt*, fig. 44, when the edges are steep; it is *narow* and *pointed*, fig. 46, or *wide ;* it is *regular,* or *wavy, wrinkled, plaited, folded, ribbed* or angular, fig. 46—when these peculiarities exist.

Fig. 44.—DEEP AND ABRUPT.   Fig. 45.—SHALLOW.

Some fruits are *russeted* at this part of their surface only, but this marking is a variable character and is found in

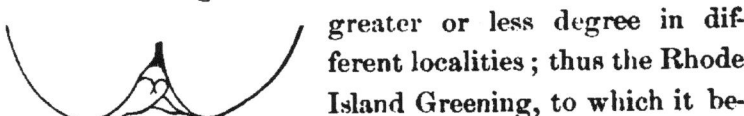

greater or less degree in different localities ; thus the Rhode Island Greening, to which it be-

Fig. 46.—NARROW AND FOLDED longs, is sometimes almost entirely divested of the russeting, and in other localities the surface is thickly spread with it half way to the stem ; the Westfield Seek-no-further, which is slightly marked with this character in the North, often becomes a russet apple in more southern latitudes.

The basin of some fruits is very apt to crack into irregular fissures, and this appears to be peculiar to certain varieties, though it is not esteemed a very reliable mark ; the term *cracked* is used to express this. In some fruits, however, we find a very peculiar cracking that forms a permanent character, upon which great dependence may be placed : all the rim of the basin in these is marked with a slightly cracked appearance that does not rupture the skin, and which resembles the incipient breaking of the surface of a piece of dry leather ; it has, therefore, received the name of *leather-crack.* This is characteristic of a few sorts, and hence a valuable mark.

Within the basin is the EYE, which furnishes characters of great value. This I consider to mean the meeting of

the segments of the calyx, and more particularly in the apple, the triangular space enclosed by these parts, in which the remains of the stamens and pistils are found. Hence the Eye can only be displayed by making a vertical section of the fruit. There are but a limited number of expressions used in its description; thus the eye is said to be *large, small, long* or *short*, and it may be *open* or *closed*. The segments of the calyx may be *converging* or *reflexed, persistent* or *obsolete*, according to their condition in the ripe fruit, and these several characters are quite reliable; but the simple fact that the eye is *open* or *closed*, may depend upon the accidental breaking away of the segments of the calyx, and is of little value as a sign.

The next character to be considered is the attachment of the stem, which, in some fruits, is so depressed as to constitute what is called the CAVITY. In the apple this portion has many variations that are quite characteristic of certain varieties of fruit.

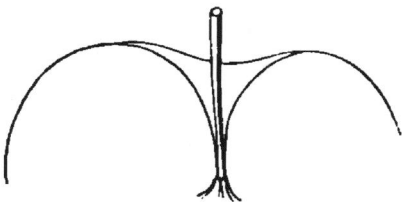

Fig. 47.—DEEP, STEM LONG.

In form the cavity may be either *deep*, fig. 47, or *shallow; regular* or *irregular; wide*, fig. 48; or *narrow*, and *acute*,

Fig. 48.—WIDE, STEM STOUT.   Fig. 49.—WAVY, STEM CLUBBED.

wavy, fig. 49; and *uneven, folded*, and even *lipped*, fig. 50; as when a portion of the flesh protrudes against the

16

stem, as in Pryor's Red, Roman Stem, and other apples, and in some pears. This portion is sometimes defaced by *cracks* that separate the skin; it is occasionally green, and

this is a good and distinguishing character of a limited number of fruits, both apples and pears. The

Fig. 50.—CAVITY LIPPED.   cavity is also *brown* or "*russeted*" in some fruits, and, though this character is quite variable in its depth, amount and extent, we may consider the *brown* or *russeting about the stem* quite reliable in both pears and apples.

The stem has its place of insertion in the region we have just been considering. It is the peduncle of botanists, and in some species it separates from the fruit by a joint—in others it remains attached and separates from the twig; when it is considered a part of the fruit itself, as in the apple and pear. The shape, average length, thickness, and other characters, and especially its mode of attachment to the carpos * in the pear, give us some important characters, but these are always somewhat uncertain and variable; hence they are rather relative than positive traits. In apples, stems may be *long*, fig. 47, *short*, fig. 48, or *medium*, according to their projection beyond or concealment within the cavity, being called *medium* when they simply reach the contour of the outline. They are *slender*, fig. 47; *medium* or *thick, fleshy, knobby* or *clubbed*, fig. 49, according to the amount of their substance and its arrangement. They are *curved* or *straight*, and *direct* and *axial*, or *inclined*, according to their direction

---

* From καρπος, Greek, for fruit.

and relation to the axis of the fruit; and in pears, they often have a peculiarity of the insertion dependent upon their being more or less fleshy; in both plums and pears, this fullness is often arranged in rings surrounding the base of the stem.

Some pomologists have taken great pains to measure the length of the stems, which they report in inches and lines. As above stated, this is an uncertain quantity, and therefore of little value, except when taken in relation to other measurements by way of comparison; hence I have preferred to use the above-mentioned terms only in their relation to the axial diameter in describing the apples, unless where their extension is unusual. The variable length of this organ in some varieties is remarkable, and we often find the smallest fruits having the longest stems.

When we come to examine the interior portions of a fruit, if it be an apple or pear, we make a vertical section through the axis from basin to cavity. This exposes the internal structure and enables us to judge of the color and other characters of the fleshy pericarp, the length of the axis, the size of the core and carpels, and the number and appearance of the seeds. These characters are possessed of value, and are quite reliable; in many fruits the seeds furnish distinctive indications, and this is particularly the case with the stone fruits, many of which are readily identified by the form and markings of the stones or pits, the *endocarps* of botany.

In the apple particularly, we first have our attention drawn to the AXIS, which is sometimes very *short*, so that in some decidedly oblate specimens, with deep basin and cavity, there is scarcely room between them for the core, which is shortened to correspond with the oblate character of the fruit. This is illustrated by many of the outlines given in Class I. It is well also to observe and note whether the axis be inclined. The form of the *core* is not very reliable, but it has characters that are permanent and peculiar to certain varieties. Thus it is always *open* in some, and always *closed* in other sorts of the apple. In the pear it is *gritty* in some varieties, and surrounded with fine grained flesh in others. The core is *large, medium,* or *small,* and these distinctions are permanent. Its outline, embracing the group of carpels, may be *regular* or *irregular, long* or *short, cordate, wide* or *compressed ;* it may reach the eye or otherwise, and it frequently clasps that portion.

The SEEDS are *numerous* or otherwise; they are *long* or *short, acuminate* or *rounded, flat, angular, imperfect,* or *plump, large* or *small ;* they may be *pale,* even *yellow,* or *brown, dark,* and nearly *black ;* and these shades are distinctive, often enabling the pomologist to decide upon the variety when other characters are less marked. The peculiarities of the stones of peaches, plums and cherries, and of the seeds of the grape, had better be described in immediate connection with those species of fruit.

In the FLESH of fruits we find characters that most pomologists, even the amateurs, are generally pleased to have under practical consideration. They are also very reliable, for if the fruits be in good condition, they are always the same in any given variety. In its consistency, this tissue is either *firm* and *compact,* or *spongy ;* it is *fine grained, granular, gritty. fibrous,* or *breaking,* on the one hand, or *tender, buttery* and *melting,* on the other;

the flesh is either *dry* or *juicy*, and tinted with various shades of color. In some we find a satisfying *richness*, while others are *thin* and poor. Some have a fine aroma, while others have an unpleasant flavor or are scentless.

So intimately associated are our organs of taste and smell, that it is difficult to separate and distinguish the impressions we receive through these senses. For our present purpose it will be best to consider all under this head, whether really belonging to one or the other sensation; and the lexicographers themselves admit the commonalty of taste and smell in the word *flavor*. These qualities of a fruit depend upon so many accidents of season, culture, and especially of the condition of ripeness, that they are of comparatively little value in descriptions, except in their broadest expressions of acidity and its opposite, which indeed are sufficiently pronounced to be used in the classification of fruits.

With regard to their FLAVOR, fruits may be said to be *vinous*, *sub-acid*, *acid*, and *very acid*, or *sugary*, *sweet*, *very sweet*, and *honey sweet ;* they may be *flat* and *insipid*, or *highly flavored*, *mild*, or *astringent ;* and as to fragrance, in which they may remind us of many other agreeable odors, they may be said to be *perfumed* and *aromatic*, or otherwise.

In deciding upon the quality of the fruit that has thus been subjected to this series of tests, and to this thorough examination, we shall find that the decision will depend upon the individual tastes, the likes and dislikes of those who are called upon to render judgment, and that, at best, the result must be arbitrary. The terms expressive of this division are *inferior*, *good*, *very good*, and *best*.

CHAPTER XVI.

CLASSIFICATION.

———•◦•———

The need of some classification grows more and more
pressing, as our fruit lists have become more extended,
and they now reach many hundreds. A good and reliable
systematic classification has become absolutely necessary,
and has received a great deal of consideration.

Upon what principle shall this classification be founded?
The common alphabetical arrangement of most text books
may be very convenient for a mere dictionary of fruits,
but is utterly useless to the novice who does not know
the name of his specimen. The arrangement by season

366

and size has its difficulties in the uncertainty and variation of these characters in the different soils and climates
of our extended country, and a sub-division and group-
ing of fruits by their quality of excellence is not only unreliable, but is altogether arbitrary, and subject to the
greatest diversity of opinion arising from the various
tastes of different individuals. We must look to some
marked and reliable characters that are always present,
easily recognized, and permanent or fixed. Among these
shape or figure stands pre-eminent, notwithstanding the
acknowledged fact that some varieties are almost protean.
The shape of the general outline appears to be the best character for the broad divisions of a classification. A sub-
division may again be made, which is to be based upon
the regularity or irregularity of the shape.

The next character, and one of considerable value, is
that dependent upon *flavor* in its broadest characters of
sweet and sour, which, though sometimes giving rise to
a puzzling question, is, in most varieties, sufficiently
marked to constitute the basis of a minor sub-division.
Color, which is notoriously the poorest character and least
esteemed by botanists in their descriptions, on account of
its liability to variation, is, however, of sufficient importance in pomology to take a high rank and to appear very
prominently in fruit nomenclature. Still it should be re-
served for the lowest sub-divisions of a classification.

Among our American writers, who deservedly stand
prominent as pomologists, the most satisfactory attempt
at classification is found in the little work prepared by J.
J. Thomas. No one who has realized the advantages to
be derived from the simple and clear sub-divisions made

by this author, will ever be satisfied with a fruit-book that is not arranged upon the basis of some classification. Thomas, in his excellent work, makes three great divisions of apples according to their period of ripening, as the *Summer*, *Autumn*, and *Winter* fruits, to which some of us would desire to add *Spring*, or long-keepers. Each of these he has divided into two classes—those characterized by their flavor as *sweet* apples, and those possessed of more or less acidity; and each of these classes is subdivided into two sections, according to their color, as striped with red and not striped; so that in this arrangement we have eighteen groups, and, with specimen in hand, this synopsis enables us at once to decide in which of these groups of moderate dimensions we may look for the description we desire; and, if it be contained in the book, it may readily be found. The labor of searching through the whole list is thus obviated.

The Germans have made many attempts at the classification of fruits. Christ, Diel, Dochnal, Manger and Sickler, have been engaged in this work; and Diel's Synopsis, though far from perfect, has been generally adopted. He makes seven classes, with orders under each. Dochnal, a later writer, has modified this by making two sections according to the shape, whether *angular* or *spherical*, and four classes also based upon their form.

Robert Hogg, in his *British Pomology*, which is an excellent account of the apples cultivated in England, has given a modification which answers a good purpose for classification. He makes three great sections, according to season, *Summer*, *Autumn*, and *Winter*. Each of these is divided into two classes, according to shape: 1st,

Round, roundish, or *oblate;* and 2nd, *Oblong, conical, oval,* or *ovate.* These again are grouped according to their colors: A, *pale;* B, *striped;* C, *red;* and D, *russet.*

As a matter of interest I will give Diel's classification.

CLASS I.—RIBBED APPLES.

1. They are furnished with very prominent, but regular ribs around the eye, extending also over the fruit, but which do not render it irregular.

2. Having wide, open, and very irregular cells.

ORDER I.—TRUE CALVILLES.

1. They taper from about the middle of the fruit toward the eye.

2. They are covered with bloom when on the tree.

3. They have, or acquire, by keeping, an unctuous skin.

4. They are not distinctly and purely striped.

5. They have light, spongy, delicate flesh.

6. They have a strawberry or raspberry flavor.

ORDER II.—SCHLOTTER ÆPFEL.

1. The skin does not feel unctuous.

2. They are not covered with bloom.

3. They are either of a flat, conical, cylindrical, or tapering form.

4. They have not a balsamic, but mostly a sweetish or sourish flavor.

5. They have a granulous, loose, and coarse-grained flesh.

ORDER III.—GUELDERLINGE.

1. They are not balsamic, like Order I.; but of an aromatic flavor.

2. They have a fine flesh, almost like that of the Reinettes.

3. They are either of a conical or flat shape.

4. They are most prominently ribbed around the eye.

CLASS II.—ROSENÆPFEL—ROSE APPLES.

1. They are covered with blue bloom when on the tree.

2. They have not unproportionally large, but often only regular cells.

16*

3. They emit a pleasant odor when briskly rubbed.

4. The skin does not feel unctuous.

5. They are handsomely and regularly ribbed around the eye, and often also over the fruit.

6. They have a tender, loose, spongy, and mostly fine grained flesh.

7. They have a fine rose, fennel, or anise flavor.

8. They are mostly of short duration, and are often only summer or autumn apples.

9. They are mostly striped like a turnip.

ORDER I.—FRUIT TAPERING OR OBLONG.

ORDER II.—FRUIT ROUND OR FLAT.

CLASS III.—RAMBOURS.

1. They are all large apples, and comprise the largest sorts.

2. They have mostly, or almost always, two unequal halves—namely, one side lower than the other.

3. They are constantly furnished with ribs around the eye which are broad, rising irregularly, one above the other, and extending over the fruit so as to render it irregular in its shape; they are also compressed, and have one side higher than the other.

4. They are constantly broader than high, and only sometimes elongated.

5. They have all a loose, coarse grained and often very pleasant flesh.

ORDER I.—WITH WIDE CELLS.

ORDER II.—WITH NARROW CELLS.

CLASS IV.—REINETTES.

1. They have a fine grained, delicate, crisp, firm flesh.

2. They are mostly the ideal of a handsomely shaped apple; in them the convexity or bulge of the middle of the apple towards the eye is the same as that towards the stalk, or not much different.

3. They are all gray dotted, or have russety patches, or completely covered with russet.

4. They have rarely an unctuous skin.

5. They have all the rich, aromatic, sugary, and brisk flavor, which is called the Reinette flavor.

6. They decay very readily, and must, of all apples, hang longest on the tree.

7. The really sweet and at the same time aromatic apples belong to the Reinettes, only as regards their shape, their character, and their fine and firm flesh.

8. Apples with fine, firm, crisp flesh, which cannot of themselves form a distinct class; for instance, the Pippins belong to this class.

ORDER I.—SELF-COLORED REINETTES.

1. Having a uniform green ground color, which changes to the most beautiful golden yellow.

2. Having no lively colors or marks of russet on the side next the sun, except those that are very much exposed, and which assume a slight tinge of red.

3. Having no covering of russet, but only slight traces of russety stripes.

ORDER II.—RED REINETTES.

Having all the properties of the self-colored Reinettes, but of a pure red on the side next the sun, without any mixture of russet.

ORDER III.—GRAY REINETTES.

1. The ground color is green, changing to dingy dull yellow.

2. The coating of russet, or the russety patches, spread over the greater part of the fruit, are very conspicuous.

3. The side next the sun is often dull brownish or ochreous red.

ORDER IV.—GOLDEN REINETTES.

1. On the side next the sun they are washed or striped with beautiful crimson.

2. The ground color changes by keeping to a beautiful deep yellow.

3. Over the ground color, and the crimson of the exposed side, are spread light thin patches, or a complete coat of russet.

CLASS V.—STREIFLINGE—STRIPED APPLES.

1. They are all, and almost always, marked with broken stripes of red.

2. These stripes are found either over the whole fruit, or only very indistinctly on the side exposed to the sun.

3. The stripes may be distinct—that is to say, truly striped; or between these stripes on the side next the sun the fruit is dotted, shaded, or washed with red; but on the shaded side the stripes are well defined.

4. The cells are regular.

5. They are of a purely sweet, vinous, or acid flavor.

6. They have not the same flavor as the Rose apples.

7. They do not decay, except when gathered before maturity.

ORDER I.—FLAT STREIFLINGE.

1. They have the bulge at the same distance from the eye as from the stalk, and are broadly flattened.

2. They are constantly half an inch broader than high.

ORDER II.—TAPERING STREIFLINGE.

1. They are broader than high.

2. They diminish from the middle of the apple towards the eye, so that the superior half is conical, or pyramidal, and not at all similar to the inferior half.

ORDER III.—OBLONG OR CYLINDRICAL STREIFLINGE.

1. The hight and breadth are almost equal.

2. They diminish gradually from the base to the apex.

3. Or from the middle of the fruit they gradually diminish toward the base and apex equally.

ORDER IV.—ROUND STREIFLINGE.

1. The convexity of the fruit next the base and the apex is the same.

2. The breadth does not differ from the hight, except only about a quarter of an inch.

3. Laid in the hand, with the eye and stalk sidewise, they have the appearance of a roundish grape.

CLASS VI.—TAPERING APPLES.

1. They have the cells regular.
2. They are not covered with bloom.
3. They are not striped, and are either of a uniform color, or washed with red on the side next the sun.
4. Constantly diminishing to a point towards the eye.
5. They are sweet or vinous, approaching a pure acid.
6. They do not readily decay.

ORDER I.—OBLONG, CYLINDRICAL OR CONICAL.

Characters the same as Order III. of the Streiflinge.

ORDER II.—TAPERING TO A POINT.

Characters the same as Order II. of the Streiflinge.

CLASS VII.—FLAT APPLES.

1. They are constantly broader than high.
2. They are never striped.
3. They are either of a uniform color, or, on the side exposed to the sun, more or less washed or shaded with red.
4. They have regular cells.
5. They are not unctuous when handled.
6. They do not readily decay.
7. Flavor purely sweet, or purely sour.

ORDER I.—PURELY FLAT APPLES.

1. The difference is obvious to the eye.
2. The breadth is constantly half an inch more than the hight.

ORDER II.—ROUND-SHAPED FLAT APPLES.

1. The eye cannot easily detect a distinction between the breadth and hight.
2. The breadth rarely exceeds the hight by a quarter of an inch.
3. The fruit, cut transversely, exhibits almost or quite two equal halves.

DOCHNAHL'S CLASSIFICATION.

SECTION I.—PLEUROIDEA.—ANGULAR OR RIBBED.

Having sharp or flat ribs, which extend over the length of the fruit and are most prominent around the eye, where they are most generally situated.

CLASS I.—MALA CYDONARIA—QUINCE-SHAPED.

ORDER I.—CALVILLES.

1. They have large heart-shaped cells, open towards the axis, or often entirely torn; the cells extend very often from the stalk even to the tube of the calyx.
2. They diminish from about the middle of the fruit, or a little above it, towards the eye.
3. They are regular, and provided generally with fine ribs, which do not disfigure the fruit.
4. On the tree, the fruit is covered with bloom.
5. They are never distinctly striped.
6. Their flesh is soft, loose, fine and light, of a balsamic flavor, similar to that of strawberries or raspberries.
7. The eye is frequently closed.
8. Many of them acquire by keeping an oily or unctuous skin.

GROUP I.—Fruit red, almost entirely covered with red.

GROUP II.—Fruit parti-colored; yellow; very much striped or washed with red.

GROUP III.—Fruit yellow; of a whitish, greenish, or golden yellow.

ORDER II.—PSEUDO-CALVILLES.

1. The cells are almost the same as the true Calvilles—very large and open.
2. The calycinal tube is wide and generally very short.
3. They are slightly narrowed toward the eye, and flattened toward the stalk.
4. Their ribs are very prominent, especially around the eye.
5. They are aromatic, and have not the balsamic flavor of the true Calvilles.

6. Their flesh is fine, opaque, a little succulent, and almost equal to the Reinettes.

GROUPS I., II., III., as above.

CLASS II.—MALA PYRARIA—PEAR-SHAPED.

Their flavor is neither balsamic nor aromatic; they are purely sweet or acid; their flesh is granulous and loose.

ORDER I.—TREMARIA—SEEDS LOOSE.

1. They are almost always large apples, the skin of which is neither unctuous nor covered with bloom.

2. They are also furnished with ribs; but they are not so regular as in the Calvilles.

3. The cells are very large, irregular, widened, and generally open.

4. The calycinal tube is most generally widely conical, and does not extend to the cells.

5. They are of a flattened, conical, cylindrical or pointed shape.

6. Their flesh is loose, more often a little coarse, and of a slightly balsamic flavor.

7. The leaves of these trees are very large, rather deeply dentated, and less downy than those of the Calvilles.

GROUP I. — *Unicolores*— Green, greenish, yellow, or golden yellow, and slightly tinged with red.

GROUP II.—*Bicolores*—Yellow or green, and distinctly striped or washed with red.

ORDER II.—RAMBURES.

1. They are all very large.

2. They have almost always the two halves unequal.

3. They are constantly broader than high, and appear sometimes higher than they are.

4. They are not furnished with ribs, except around the eye; these are often irregular in numbers, and frequently form broad projections on the fruit.

5. They do not decay, but shrivel when they have passed maturity.

6. The flesh is coarsely granulous, rarely aromatic, nevertheless often very agreeable.

GROUP I.—*Capsulis amplis*—Wide cells.

GROUP II.—*Capsulis angustis*—Narrow cells.

SECTION II.—SPHŒROIDÆ—Spherical.

They have sometimes prominences on the fruit and around the eye, but never true ribs.

CLASS III.—MALA MESPILARIA—Medlar-shaped.

Their flavor is sweet, aromatic, similar to that of the Rose, fennel or anise.

ORDER I.—APIANA, or Rose Apples.

Their flesh is soft, loose, marrowy, very fine grain, and of a snow white color.

2. The cells are almost always regular and closed.

3. They are regularly ribbed around the eye, and often also over the fruit, but sometimes not at all ribbed.

4. They have a balsamic flavor, accompanied with a very agreeable odor.

5. They emit a pleasant odor when briskly rubbed.

6. When on the tree they are frequently covered with a blue bloom, and striped like a Tulip.

7. The fruit is mostly small, or middle sized.

8. They are mostly of short duration, and lose their good flavor the same year.

Group I.— *Oblongi*—Oblong fruit.

Group II.—*Sphœrici*—Round or flattened.

ORDER II.—REINETTA—Reinettes.

1. These are apples which generally have the most regular and handsome shape, having the bulge in the middle, at the same distance from the eye as from the stalk.

2. All are dotted, clouded, or entirely covered with russet.

3. They are very rarely inclined to be unctuous, but generally rough when handled.

4. They all decay very readily; (they must therefore be left as long as possible on the tree.)

5. Their flesh is fine grained, crisp, firm, or fine and delicate.

6. They are all charged with only a balsamic, sugary acid, which is called Reinette-flavored.

GROUP I. — *Unicolores.* — 1. Having uniform green ground color, which changes to the most beautiful golden yellow.

2. Having no lively colors or marks of russet on the side next the sun, except those that are very much exposed, and are slightly tinged with red.

3. Having no covering of russet, but only slight traces of russety stripes.

GROUP II.—*Rubri*—Fruit red; having all the properties of the self-colored Reinettes; but on the side next the sun they are of a red color, with a mixture of russet.

GROUP III.—*Ravi*—Russeted.

1. Their ground color is green, changing to dingy, dull yellow.

2. The coatings of russet are very conspicuous.

3. The side next the sun is often dingy, brownish, or ochreous red.

4. They all decay very readily.

GROUP IV.—*Aurei*—Yellow or golden fruit, Golden Reinettes.

1. On the side next the sun they are washed or striped with beautiful crimson.

2. The ground color changes, by keeping, to beautiful deep yellow.

3. Over the crimson there is a light thin trace, or a complete covering of russet.

CLASS IV.—MALA MALARIA—PERFECT OR PURE APPLE-SHAPED.

They are of a perfectly sweet or vinous flavor, approaching to pure acid.

ORDER I.—STRIOLA, OR STRIPED.

1. They are almost always marked with broken stripes of red.

2. These are either over the whole fruit, or only indistinctly on the side exposed to the sun.

3. The stripes may all be distinct—that is, clearly and finely striped; or between these stripes, on the side next the sun, the fruit is dotted, shaded or washed with red; but on the shaded side the stripes are well defined.

4. The cells are regular.

5. The fruit does not decay, except when gathered before maturity, or after the period when it has been properly ripened.

GROUP I.—*Depressa*—Flat.

1. They have the bulge at the same distance from the eye as from the stalk, and are broadly flattened.

2. They are always half an inch broader than high.

GROUP II.—*Acuminati*—Pointed.

1. They are broader than high.

2. They diminish from the middle of the apple toward the eye, so that the superior half is conical, and is not at all similar to the inferior half.

GROUP III.—*Oblongi*—Oblong or cylindrical.

1. The hight and breadth are almost equal.

2. They diminish gradually from the base to the apex.

3. Or, from the middle of the fruit they gradually diminish toward the base and apex equally.

GROUP IV.—*Sphœrici*—Round.

1. The convexity of the fruit next the base and the apex is the same.

2. The breadth does not differ from the hight, except only about a quarter of an inch.

3. When laid on their side they present a spherical shape.

ORDER II.—CONTUBERNALIA—Storing Apples.

1. Having the cells regular.

2. They are not striped, and are either of a uniform color or washed with red on the side next the sun.

3. They do not readily decay.

4. They are not unctuous when handled.

5. They are never covered with bloom.

GROUP I.—*Acuminati*—Tapering, diminishing toward the eye.

GROUP II. — *Depressi* — Flat. These are constantly broader than high.*

After a long and careful consideration and study of this subject, I have prepared the following formula for the

---

* As translated for R. Hogg's British Pomology.

CLASSIFICATION OF APPLES. It consists of four classes that are based upon the general figure of the fruit; with two orders, that are distinguished by a modification of the form, causing the fruit to be regular, or irregular, and angular. The characters upon which the classes are founded are exemplified by a vertical section through the length of the axis of the fruit. Those by which the Orders are distinguished are shown by a transverse section, made at right angles to the axis, or by holding the fruit with the blossom end toward the eye.*

Each of these Orders may contain two *Sections*, characterized by their flavor as sweet and sour; and each of these may again be sub-divided into three *Sub-sections*, that are based upon color.

CLASS I.—OBLATE OR FLAT, having the axis shorter than the transverse diameter.

ORDER I.—REGULAR.

ORDER II.—IRREGULAR.

SECTION 1.—Sweet.

SECTION 2.—Sour.

SUB-SECTION 1.—Pale or blushed, more or less, but self-colored and not striped.

SUB-SECTION 2.—Striped or Splashed.

SUB-SECTION 3.—Russeted.

CLASS II.—CONICAL, tapering decidedly toward the eye, and becoming OVATE when larger in the middle and tapering to each end, the axial diameter being the shorter.

ORDERS I and II.

SECTIONS 1 and 2.

SUB-SECTIONS 1, 2, and 3.

---

* Figures 36 to 46, pp. 355 to 356.

CLASS III.—ROUND, GLOBULAR or nearly so, having the axial and transverse diameters about equal, the former often shorter by less than one-quarter of the latter. The ends are often so flattened as to look truncated, when the fruit appears to be cylindrical or globular-oblate.

ORDERS, SECTIONS, and SUB-SECTIONS, as above.

CLASS IV.—OBLONG, in which the axis is longer than the transverse diameter, or appears so. These may also be truncate or cylindrical.

ORDERS, SECTIONS, and SUB-SECTIONS, as above.

DESCRIPTIONS OF APPLES.

ARRANGED ACCORDING TO THEIR CLASSIFICATION ALPHABETICALLY,
UNDER EACH DIVISION.

CLASS I.—FLAT APPLES.

ORDER I.—REGULAR IN FORM.

SECTION 1.—SWEET.

SUB-SECTION 1.—SELF-COLORED, NOT STRIPED.

Camack Sweet.

This newly introduced sort is said to have originated in North Carolina or Georgia. The trees cultivated in the

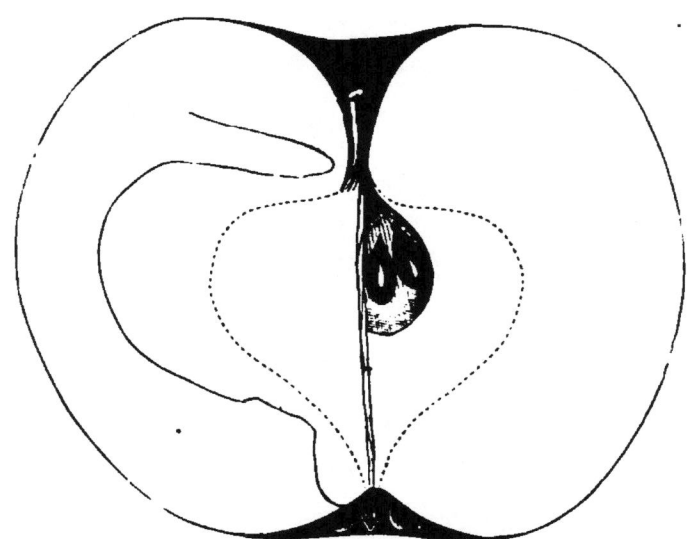

Fig. 51.—CAMACK SWEET.

Northern States are yet too young for us to judge of their characteristics, but they appear to be healthy and vigorous.

381

Fruit medium to large, flat, regular.

Surface smooth, greenish-white, rarely blushed with red.

Basin broad, shallow, and regular or wavy; Eye medium, open.

Cavity deep, acute; Stem rather long; Flesh yellowish, firm, rather tough, but juicy, rich and sweet.

This variety keeps well, lasting until **May**. Not yet sufficiently tested in the North.

Campfield.

NEWARK SWEETING.

Tree vigorous, spreading, productive. This fruit is especially valuable for cider, but it may be used also in the kitchen; being a long keeper and often beautifully

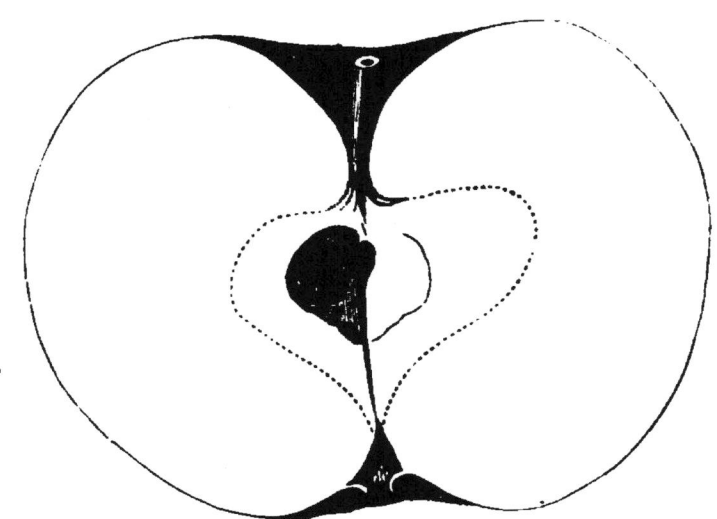

Fig. 52.—CAMPFIELD.

colored at maturity in the spring, it is often exposed on the fruit-stands, where it attracts purchasers by the great beauty of its brilliant colors.

Fruit always fair, but its figure is variable, being sometimes globular or conical. The characteristic form is round-oblate, regular; Size medium.

Surface very smooth, of a dull green, often suffused with a faint blush on the exposed side; but at maturity, bright lemon yellow, shaded with carmine; Dots minute, gray and indented.

Basin shallow, regular; Eye rather large, closed; Segments of medium length.

Cavity regular, with medium width and depth; Stem medium, rather stout.

Core wide, regular, closed, meeting the eye; Seeds numerous, plump; Flesh white, firm, tough; Juice very sweet and rich at maturity, making excellent cider.

Season, December until March.

Dillingham.

This variety was found in an old orchard of D. C. Richmond, near Sandusky, Ohio. Tree productive, and sufficiently vigorous.

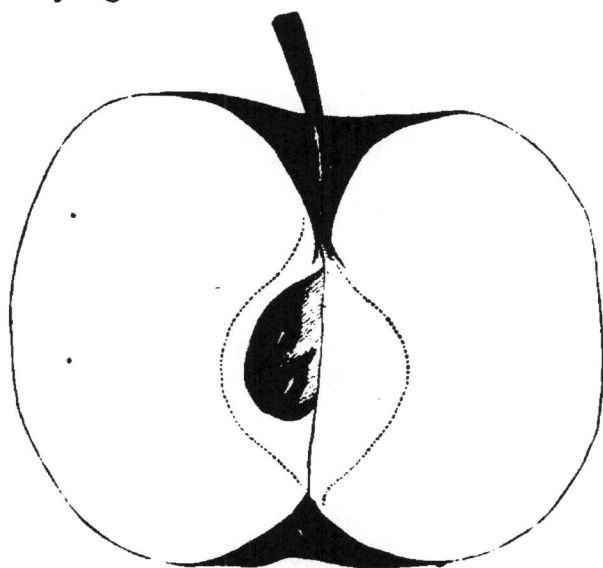

Fig. 53.—DILLINGHAM.

Fruit round-oblate rather than flat, generally regular and of medium size; Surface rough, yellowish-green, and bronzed, or shaded with a purplish tint; Dots numerous russet.

Basin wide, folded; Eye small, closed.

Cavity rather deep, wide, regular, wavy, brown; Stem sometimes long, of medium size, red.

Core small and closed, meeting the eye; Seeds numerous, large, brown.

Flesh yellow; Flavor sweet, juicy; Use, good for baking; Season, November to February. Not highly esteemed nor largely cultivated, though its productiveness and sweetness would render it desirable for stock-feeding.

Eue's Winter Sweet.

From J. S. Downer, Elkton, Kentucky; a southern fruit of some merit.

Fruit medium, flat, regular; Surface roughish, uneven, greenish-yellow, blushed and russeted; Dots numerous, minute, russet veined.

Basin abrupt, regular, leather-cracked; Eye large, open.

Cavity wide, wavy, brown; Stem medium.

Core round, closed, clasping; Seeds numerous, angular, imperfect; Flesh yellow, fine grained; Flavor very sweet, rich; Quality quite good; Use, table; Season, December.

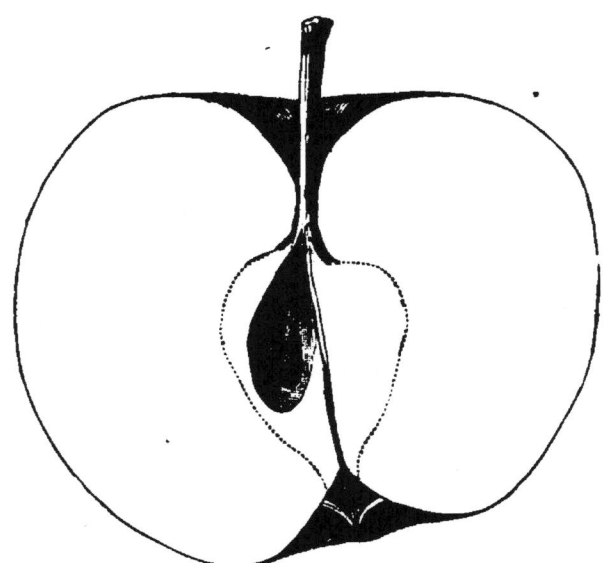

Fig. 54.—GREEN SWEET.

Green Sweet.

HONEY GREENING.

Tree vigorous and productive in most situations where cultivated, but is not much planted in the West.

Fruit rather small, regular, and usually flat, though sometimes conical; Surface smooth, green; Dots whitish, with green bases.

Basin rather shallow and wavy; Eye large, closed.

Cavity wide, regular and brown; Stem long and stout.

Core closed, regular, meeting the eye, containing numerous angular, acuminate brown seeds; Flesh greenish-white, breaking, tender, juicy and fine grained; very sweet, and valued for baking and market; those who do not admire sweet apples would hardly consider it second rate.

Season from December to February, or March.

Haskell's Sweet.

Found in the orchard of Dr. Geo. Haskell, at Rockford, Illinois.

Fruit large, flat, regular; Surface green, bronzy; Dots numerous, large, white.

Basin deep; Eye small, closed.

Cavity deep, acute, wavy; Stem short.

Core closed; Seeds numerous, plump; Flesh yellow, juicy; Flavor sweet, rich; Quality very good; Use, baking; Season August, September.

A practical test at the table of mine host must convince any one that either the apple or the cook, or both, are eminently deserving. This is supposed to be the Massachusetts variety of the same name.

Hay Boys.

I do not know where this summer apple was produced, or christened with its peculiar cognomen; Specimens received from H. N. Gillett, Lawrence Co., Ohio.

Fruit large, oblate, regular or slightly angular; Surface pale yellow; Dots numerous, dark, prominent.

Basin wide, abrupt, wavy; Eye medium, closed.

17

Cavity wide, folded, green; Stem long.

Core very wide, flat, open, clasping the eye; Flesh yellow, fine grained, breaking; Flavor sweet; Quality good, to very good; Use, table and baking; Season, August.

Lancaster Sweet.

Origin unknown, grown in Central Ohio, where it is much admired for baking and apple butter.

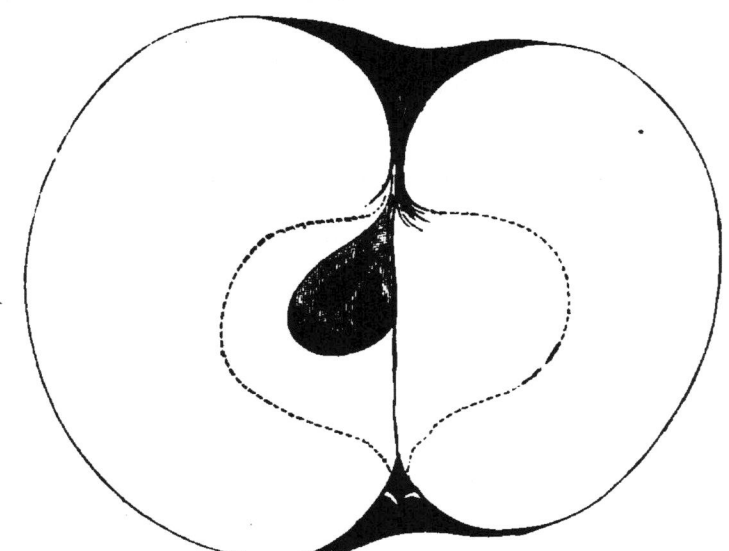

Fig. 55.—LANCASTER SWEET.

Fruit medium, regular, oblate, slightly conical; Surface green; Dots scattered, dark, minute.

Basin medium, regular; Eye small, closed; Segments of calyx long and reflexed.

Cavity wide, wavy; Stem very short and small.

Core medium, regular, closed, meeting the eye; Seeds numerous, dark, plump; Flesh greenish-white, tender, fine grained, juicy, rich; very sweet.

Quality not first rate, except for cooking; Season September and October.

London Sweet.

This vigorous, upright, and productive tree is supposed to have had its origin near Dayton, Ohio, whence it has been largely disseminated, giving entire satisfaction to all of its planters. Foliage abundant, and quite dark colored.

Fruit always fair, regular, flat, and of large size; Surface smooth, pale yellow, with scattered dots that are often colored.

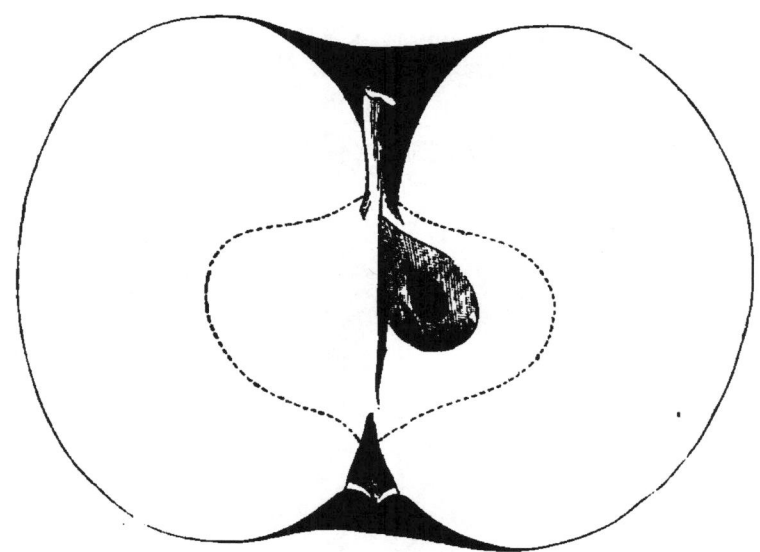

Fig. 56.—LONDON SWEET.

Basin abrupt, regular, often having concentric cracks; Eye small and closed.

Cavity wide, regular; Stem short, rather thick.

Core medium width and closed, clasping the eye; Axis very short; Seeds variable, some being plump and some imperfect; Flesh yellowish-white, breaking, rather dry, but very sweet; Quality good; and considered by some persons the very best baking apple of its season, which is from November to January or later.

Mountain Sweet.

MOUNTAINEER.

From Pennsylvania; exhibited by Joel Wood, before the Ohio Pomological Society.

Fruit large, beautiful, but too delicate for transportation, oblate; Surface smooth, light, yellow; Dots minute.

Basin wide, wavy; Eye small, closed.

Cavity deep, acute, wavy; Stem short, slender.

Core wide, open, dark, clasping the eye; Seeds numerous, pointed; Flesh white, breaking, very tender, fine grained, juicy; Flavor sweet; Quality good to very good; Use, table, baking; Season, December.

A rival of *Broadwell* or *Ladies' Sweeting.*

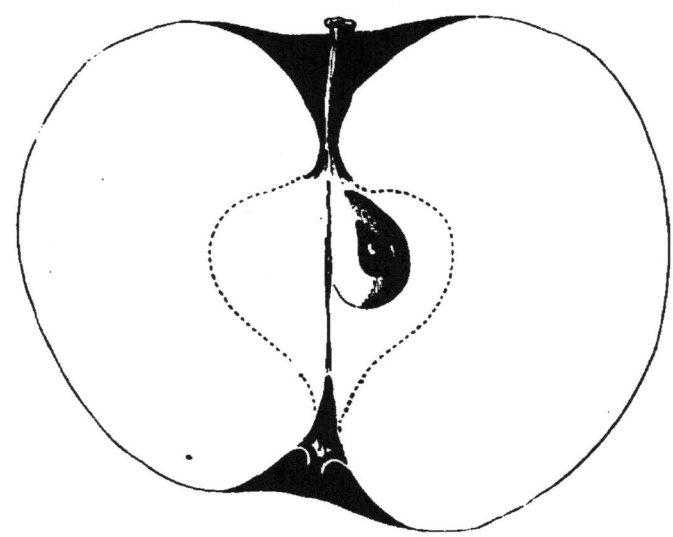

Fig. 57.—MUNSON SWEET.

Munson Sweet.

ORANGE SWEET.

This New England variety is considered quite promising in its new western homes, where, however, it is not yet widely known or tested. Tree vigorous, spreading, and productive when established; said to be a regular bearer.

Fruit medium, flat; Surface smooth, green, becoming yellow; Dots minute.

Basin small, abrupt, often folded or plaited; Eye medium, closed.

Cavity wide, wavy, green; Stem medium or short.

Core small, closed; Seeds plump; Flesh yellowish-white, fine grained, tender, juicy; Flavor very sweet; Quality nearly first rate; Valuable for baking; Season early winter.

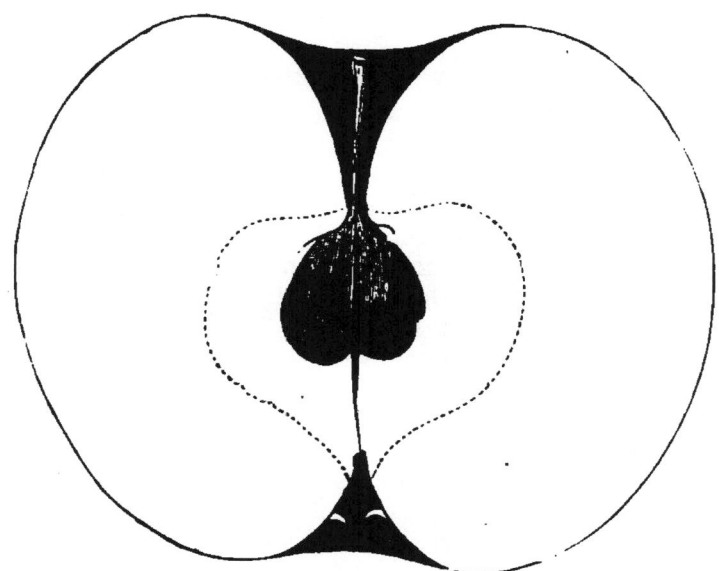

Fig. 58.—SNEPPS'.

Snepps'.

JNO. SNEPPS'.

This fine apple is believed to have originated at Edinburgh, Indiana, and was brought to the notice of the State Society by the orchardist whose name it bears, and by whom it has been distributed. As it appears to be distinct from any known fruit, it is here described. Tree vigorous and sufficiently productive.

Fruit above medium, almost large, flat, generally regular.

Surface nearly smooth, of a dull green, becoming pale yellow, with numerous dark dots, that often give it a gray appearance.

Basin rather shallow, sometimes folded or wavy; Eye large and closed; Segments of the calyx coarse.

Cavity acute, regular, rather deep; Stem medium to short, stout.

Core large but closed; Seeds numerous, pointed, brown; Flesh yellowish, breaking, fine grained, juicy; Flavor very rich, and agreeably sweet when ripe; Use, fine dessert fruit, and good for cooking; Season, December to March.

Superb Sweet.

This variety is worthy of more attention than it has received; native of Massachusetts, where it is a vigorous and productive tree. Its period of maturity makes it less valuable than it would otherwise be.

Fruit above medium, roundish; Surface smooth, of a pale yellow color, often shaded with red.

Basin rather shallow, broad; Calyx large, open.

Cavity regular, deep; Stalk long.

Flesh white, fine grained, tender, juicy; . Flavor rich, sweet.

Cole gives its season as September and October, in Massachusetts.

Trumbull Sweet.

FENTON SWEET.

This is another fine white sweet apple, originating in Ohio, which, notwithstanding its beauty, is less esteemed on account of its season, but its productiveness makes it valuable for stock-feeding. Tree vigorous, spreading, productive, and an early bearer.

Fruit above medium, regular, flat; Surface very smooth, pale yellow, or white, resembling ivory; Dots scattering, minute.

Basin deep, regular; Eye large, rather open.

Cavity deep; Stem short.

Core closed; Seeds numerous, plump; Flesh white, fine

grained, breaking, juicy; Flavor very sweet; Quality very good; Use, baking and stock; Season September and October.

CLASS I.—FLAT APPLES.
ORDER I.—REGULAR.
SECTION 1.—SWEET.
SUB-SECTION 2.—STRIPED.

Baltimore.—[*Of Elliott.*]

FLUSHING SPITZENBERG, OF NORTHWEST.—CABLE'S GILLIFLOWER.—
ROYAL PIPPIN IN ILLINOIS.

The origin of this very satisfactory second rate fruit is unknown, though it is extensively cultivated in western

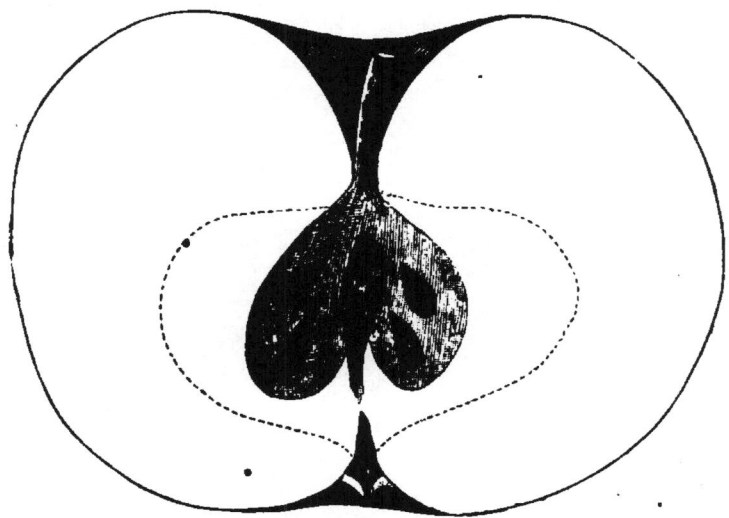

Fig. 59.—BALTIMORE.

orchards, especially in the lake country, for it is scarcely known within the Ohio river fruit region.

Tree thrifty, sufficiently vigorous but with slender growth, very productive, spreading.

Fruit medium, regular, oblate, almost round in some specimens, Surface smooth, red, striped with deep red and often covered with whitish or gray markings that give it a blue appearance like a bloom; Dots scattered, large, yellow or fawn color.

Basin shallow, regular; Eye small, closed.

Cavity wide, regular, brown; Stem short to medium.

Core large, closed; Seeds numerous, plump; Flesh yellow, fine grained, juicy, almost sweet, aromatic, lacking character; Of second quality, but valuable for market; December and January; Not disposed to rot, does not show bruises.

Butter.

FULKERSON'S.

The origin of this fruit has not been definitely traced, and though not very widely diffused, it is a prime favorite with its acquaintances, and the lovers of rich apple-butter.

Fruit small, very regular, oblate; Surface very smooth, and so covered with mixed red as rarely to show the yel-

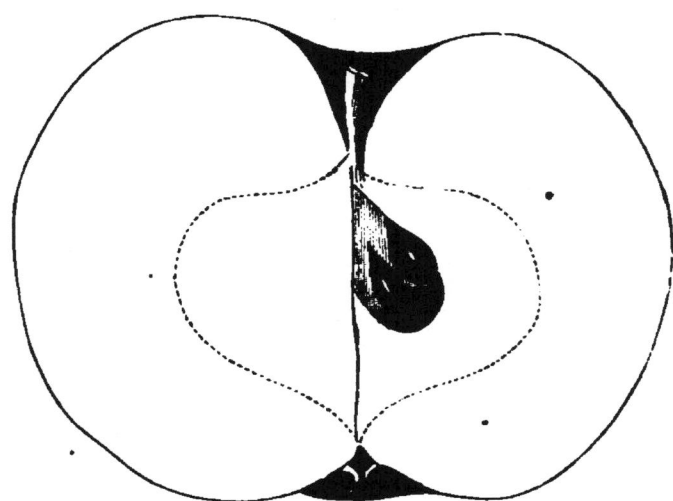

Fig. 60.—BUTTER.

low ground color; upon this are laid darker stripes of deep red; Dots minute and inconspicuous.

Basin medium, regular, or folded; Eye rather large, closed.

Cavity acute, regular, brown; Stem of medium thickness, rather long.

Core wide, large, closed; with large, plump, pointed seeds; Flesh yellow, tender, fine grained, juicy; with a sweet, rich and aromatic flavor. Valuable for stock and for apple-butter; Season, October to January.

Conant's Red.

This variety is cultivated in southern Ohio and adjacent regions, to which it has been distributed by the venerable Pomologist, H. N. Gillett, of Quaker Bottom, to whom the author is under many obligations for valuable information connected with the fruits of that productive region.

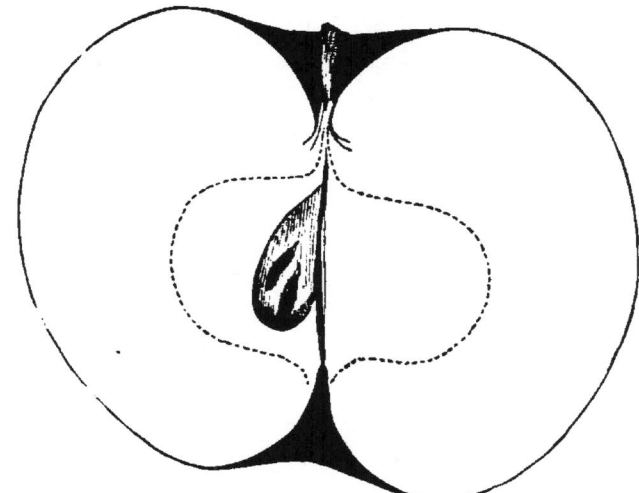

Fig. 61.—CONANT'S RED.

Fruit full medium, regular, oblate, and sometimes nearly round.

In appearance this apple is not very prepossessing, as the surface is rough, the yellow ground is obscured by mixed red, upon which are red stripes and streaks of russet; dots are numerous, minute, indented, yellow or fawn colored.

Basin rather deep, abrupt, regular or wavy; Eye small, closed.

Cavity wide, wavy or regular, green; Stem medium to long, slender.

17*

Core large, regular, closed; Seeds numerous, some are imperfectly developed; Flesh yellow, fine grained, juicy; flavor sub-acid to sweet, very aromatic, agreeable, fitting it admirably for a dessert fruit, as which it is nearly first rate. Season from September to December.

Connett Sweet.

The tree grows vigorously, is upright and productive, bearing early. Its origin I have not learned, but procured the specimens from my valued friend, Jno. C. Teas, of Raysville, Indiana.

Fruit of good size, regular, flat; Surface rather rough, dull red, with indistinct stripes; Dots few, dark, sunken.

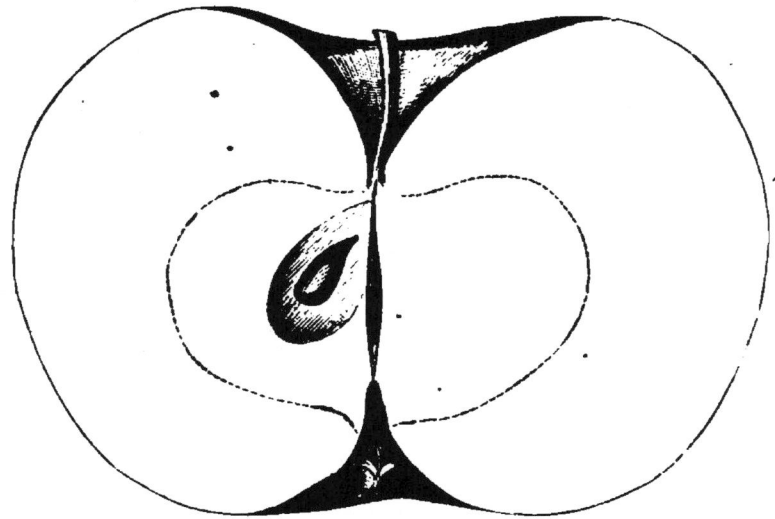

Fig. 62.—CONNETT SWEET.

Basin not deep, wide, regular; Eye rather large, closed. Cavity wide, regular, brown; Stem medium to long.

Core wide, closed; Seeds of medium size; Flesh compact, yellow, fine grained; Flavor very sweet; Quality very good; Season, December to March.

Granniwinkle.

This is supposed to be the famous cider apple of New Jersey, described by Coxe, except that the form is different; it has as good qualities for making a rich cider; specimens obtained from W. C. Hampton.

Fruit small, oblate, regular; Surface dull red, striped purple; Dots numerous, yellow.

Basin wide, regular; Eye large, open.

Cavity wide, regular, brown; Stem long, inclined.

Core medium, round, regular, closed, meeting the eye; Seeds numerous, angular, plump; Flesh yellowish-white, firm, tough; Flavor sweet; Use, cider; Season, winter.

Jersey Sweet.

AMERICAN.

In some parts of the country this is a favorite baking apple, but its great productiveness renders it small, and makes it rather a stock apple. Tree vigorous, round-headed; Shoots short-jointed and red; Foliage abundant.

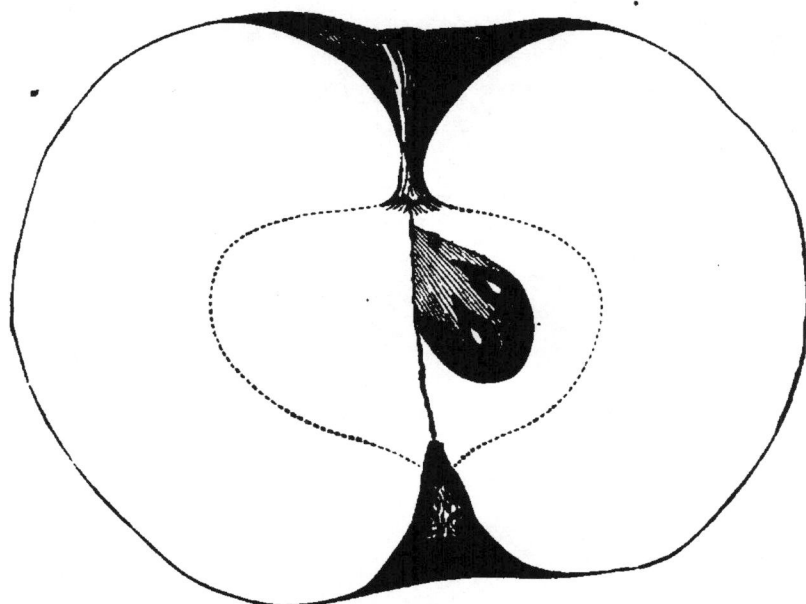

Fig. 63.—JERSEY SWEET.

Fruit medium, regular, globular-oblate, sometimes rather conical, (according to Elliott & Downing, roundish-ovate, but the drawing given by the latter is globular);

Surface smooth, yellow, nearly covered with red, mixed, striped and splashed carmine, more or less distinctly; Dots generally minute.

Basin medium to wide, regular; Eye small, generally closed.

Cavity wide, regular or wavy, rather deep, brown, and in Michigan often green; Stem medium to long, green.

Core wide, regular, partially open in some specimens, but generally closed; Seeds numerous, wide, pointed, plump; flesh pale yellow, tender, fine grained, juicy; Flavor very sweet, aromatic and rich; Use, the dessert, for those who like sweet apples, but especially valued for baking and for feeding stock. Season August to October.

Moore's Sweeting.

RED SWEET PIPPIN.—BLACK SWEET.

This valuable winter sweet apple is much cultivated throughout the West on account of its productiveness,

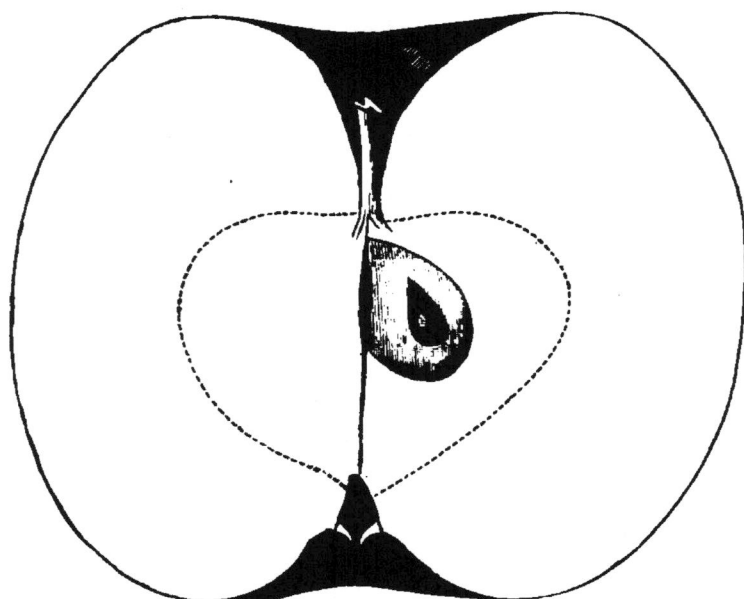

Fig. 64.—MOORE'S SWEETING.

and the amount of nutriment it furnishes to both man and

animals. Tree vigorous, healthy, spreading, round, with branches sufficiently open; Shoots dark olive; Foliage large, dark green.

Fruit medium to large, globular-oblate, regular; Surface smooth, greenish-yellow, covered with dull red in confused stripes and shaded with gray that gives the fruit a purple hue; Dots minute and few; Skin thick.

Basin wide, wavy or folded; Eye medium, closed.

Cavity wide or acute, deep, green or brown; Stem short, rather stout.

Core small, closed; Seeds numerous, plump, pale; Flesh yellow, dry, firm; Flavor very sweet; Quality inferior, for the dessert; Use, baking, market, stock, cider; Season from December to March and later, keeping very sound.

Putnam Sweet.

Originated near Marietta, Ohio.

Fruit large, flat, regular; Surface smooth, mixed, splashed and striped deep red; Dots numerous, large.

Basin wide, shallow, regular; Eye small, closed. .

Cavity wide, regular; Stem short.

Core roundish, flattened, open, clasping the eye; Seeds numerous, pointed, pale; Flesh tender; Flavor sweet; quality very good; Use, kitchen, stock; Season August, September.

Richmond.

Described by F. R. Elliott, author of *American Fruit Growers' Guide,* and named for our mutual friend, D. C. Richmond, near Sandusky, Ohio, who found it in an old seedling orchard with several other good varieties. The seeds were supposed to have been brought from the old French orchards of Canada. Tree large, vigorous, productive, and would appear to have been hardy.

Mr. Elliott says:

" Fruit large; Form roundish, occasional specimens have one side a little enlarged; Color light yellow ground, mostly or quite overspread with light and dark red stripes, many dots or specks of light russet; Stem varying, mostly short, slender; Cavity deep, open, regular, a little brownish at bottom; Calyx large, segments long; Basin deep, open, uniformly furrowed; Flesh white, tender, juicy, deli-

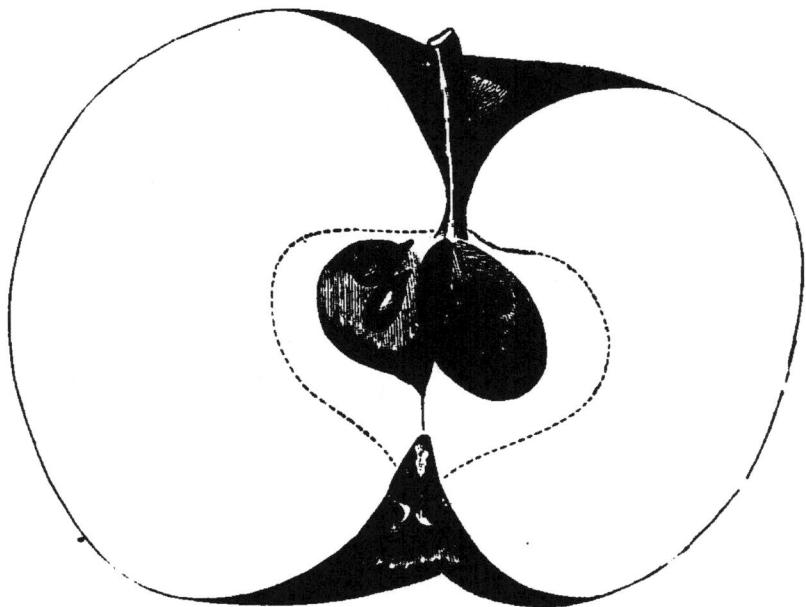

Fig. 65.—RICHMOND.

cate, sweet; Core medium; Seeds large, full; Season October to December."

Sweet Vandervere.

This is another western favorite with the admirers of sweet apples. Tree sufficiently vigorous, healthy, and productive; twigs slender, like those of the true Vanderveres.

Fruit of good size, from full medium to large, regular, oblate, and resembling the Pennsylvania Vandervere; surface very smooth, yellow, shaded with mixed red, and striped with dull or dark red; Dots yellow, scattered, indented.

Basin abrupt, wide, deep, regular; Eye small, closed.

Cavity sometimes wide and regular, or acute; Stem long, slender.

Core regular, heart-shaped, closed; Seeds medium to long, angular; Flesh firm, breaking, yellow; Flavor sweet,

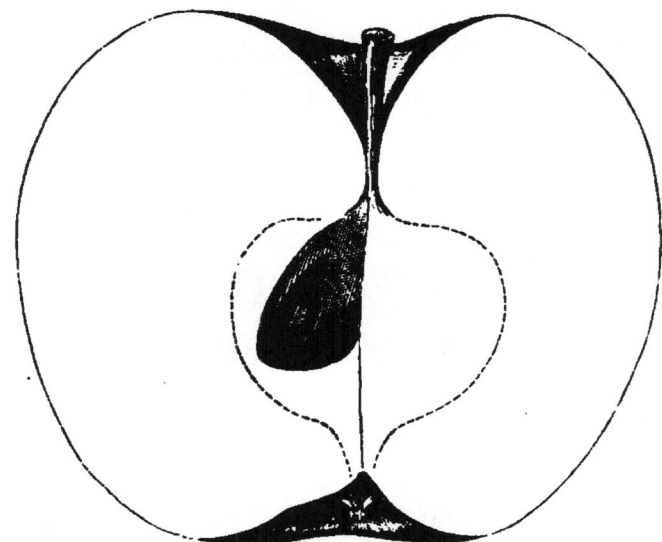

Fig. 66.—SWEET VANDERVERE.

pleasant; Quality not first rate, valued for baking and for stock; Season December and January.

CLASS I.—FLAT APPLES.

ORDER I.—REGULAR.

SECTION 1.—SWEET.

SUB-SECTION 3.—RUSSET.

NONE.

CLASS I.—FLAT APPLES.

ORDER I.—REGULAR.

SECTION 2.—SOUR.

SUB-SECTION 1.—SELF-COLORED.

Better Than Good.

JUICY BITE.

Like our standard authority, I am obliged to quote from the American Pomological Society's Transactions. Origin uncertain, (Elliott says from Pennsylvania); Tree thrifty, rather slender, very productive.

Fruit medium, oblate; Skin pale yellow, with a few brown dots.

Basin large and open; Calyx closed.

Cavity broad; Stem short.

Flesh yellowish, very tender, juicy; Flavor mild, pleasant, sub-acid; November to January.

Bohanon.

This apple was brought into notice by Lewis Sanders, that veteran agriculturist of Kentucky, who was equally

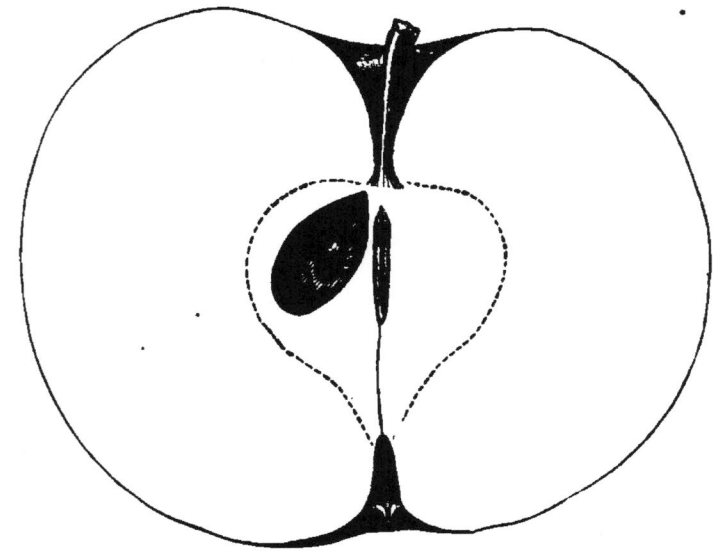

Fig. 67.—BOHANON.

remarkable as a planter of choice fruits, and breeder of fine cattle. Mr. Elliott thinks this variety may have had its origin in Virginia. Tree moderately vigorous and productive.

Fruit full medium, regular, oblate, rarely inclined to be angular, sometimes slightly conical; Surface very smooth, whitish, or waxen, occasionally blushed with pale carmine, making it very beautiful; Dots minute.

Basin abrupt, narrow, folded, wavy and irregular; Eye closed; Segments reflexed.

Cavity acute, brown; Stem rather long.

Core regular, small, pyriform, closed, clasping the eye; Seeds small, compressed; Flesh white, breaking, fine grained, juicy, sub-acid; Quality very good and preferred as a dessert fruit to the *Maiden's Blush*, which it much resembles without having the peculiar flavor of that variety.

Cornfield.

A southern variety received from J. S. Downer & Son.

Fruit medium, roundish-oblate or cylindrical, truncate, regular; Surface smooth, yellow, covered with mixed deep red, striped; Dots numerous, minute.

Basin deep, abrupt, regular, leather-cracked; Eye small, open.

Cavity wide, acute; Stem short.

Core round, regular, closed, hardly clasping; Axis short; Seeds numerous, plump; Flesh yellow, fine grained, tender, rather dry; Flavor sub-acid; Quality good; Use, table; Season, December.

Cracking.

This variety had its origin in the eastern part of Ohio. The tree is a strong grower and productive.

Fruit large, oblate, somewhat uneven and irregular, but handsome; Surface smooth, greenish-yellow until ripe, when it is often tinged with red; Dots numerous, minute, indented and green.

Basin wide, folded; Eye medium, closed.

Cavity acute, wavy, brown; Stem short, rather stout.

Core wide, open, clasping the eye; Seeds large, pointed, dark; Flesh yellow, breaking, juicy; Flavor sub-acid;

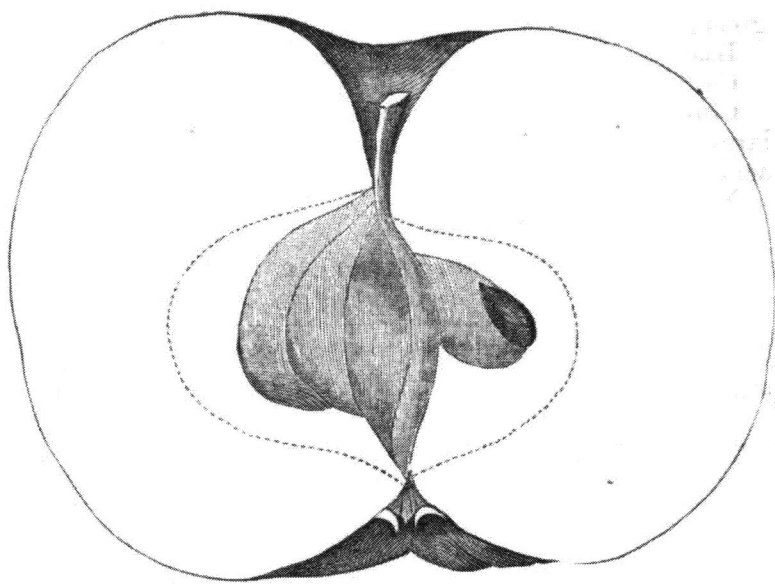

Fig. 68.—CRACKING.

quality nearly first rate; Use, kitchen and table; Season
September and October.

Cranberry Pippin.

This is a beautiful apple which originated near Hudson,
New York.   Tree vigorous, very productive.
Fruit large, flat, regular; Surface very smooth, bright,
clear yellow, with a shining scarlet cheek; Dots minute.
Basin wide, regular or wavy; Eye small, short, closed.
Cavity wide, wavy; Stem medium.
Core small, oval, just meeting the eye; Axis short; Seeds
numerous, long; Flesh white, breaking, juicy; Flavor mild,
sub-acid; Quality very good for cooking, not for dessert;
Season November to February in New York.

Dalton.

Specimens from Mr. Warren, of Massachusetts.   Origin
and history unknown.

Fruit medium, flat, uneven; Surface smooth, yellowish-green, becoming greasy; Dots scattered, green.

Basin medium, folded; Eye medium, closed.

Cavity deep, pointed; Stem medium.

Core medium, wide, closed, clasping the eye; Seeds large; Flesh greenish-white, tender, juicy; Flavor sub-acid; Quality good; Use kitchen, table; Season September.

Not particularly desirable.

Early Harvest.

This American apple has long been a prime favorite in the orchard, especially when planted for family use, since it is of excellent quality for table as well as in the kitchen. For the commercial orchard, however, it is falling into dis-

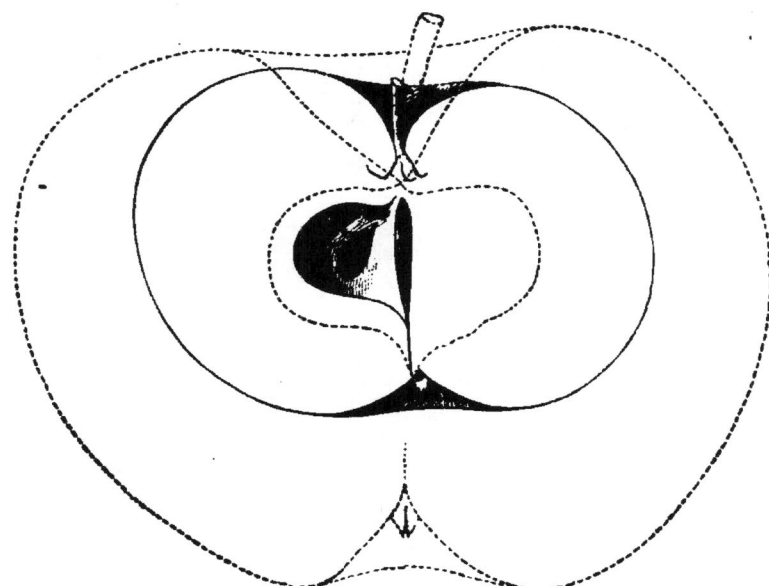

Fig. 69.—EARLY HARVEST.

favor with the market men, because of its uncertainty, and its proneness to be defective on some soils.

Tree spreading, healthy and vigorous; the limbs are very strongly attached to the trunk by a woody enlargement at their base, and the pale olive twigs are remarkable for their peculiar mode of production in twos and threes from a common origin.

Fruit medium, regular, oblate, sometimes almost round, as described by Downing, but this is rare in the West, where the oblate form prevails. Surface smooth, clear, waxy yellow, very rarely blushed; Dots numerous, minute, green.

Basin regular, narrow, abrupt; Eye small, closed.

Cavity wide, regular; Stem short.

Core round, closed, not meeting the eye; Seeds large, pointed; Flesh tender, breaking, juicy, acid to sub-acid, agreeable; Of first quality for table or kitchen during the month of July.

Faust.

This very nice apple, received from S. W. Westbrooke, of Greensboro, N. C., deserves the commendation of its southern admirers.

Fruit regular, globular-oblate, of medium size; Surface

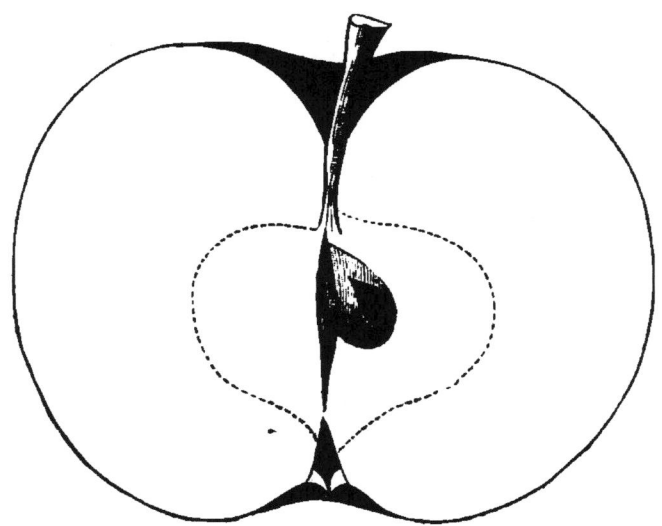

Fig. 70.—FAUST.

smooth, yellow, with a white bloom and sunken white dots.

Basin shallow, folded; Eye small, closed.

Cavity wide, green; Stem medium, to long.

Core wide, closed, scarcely meeting the eye; Seeds angular; Flesh yellow, fine grained; Flavor sub-acid, aromatic, and first quality for table or dessert use, in November or later.

Finley.

ABBOTT ?

This fine fruit originated in Kentucky and is cultivated to some extent in Southern Indiana, where it is considered entitled to the meed of excellence, and preferred to the Early Harvest on the one hand, and to the Maiden's Blush

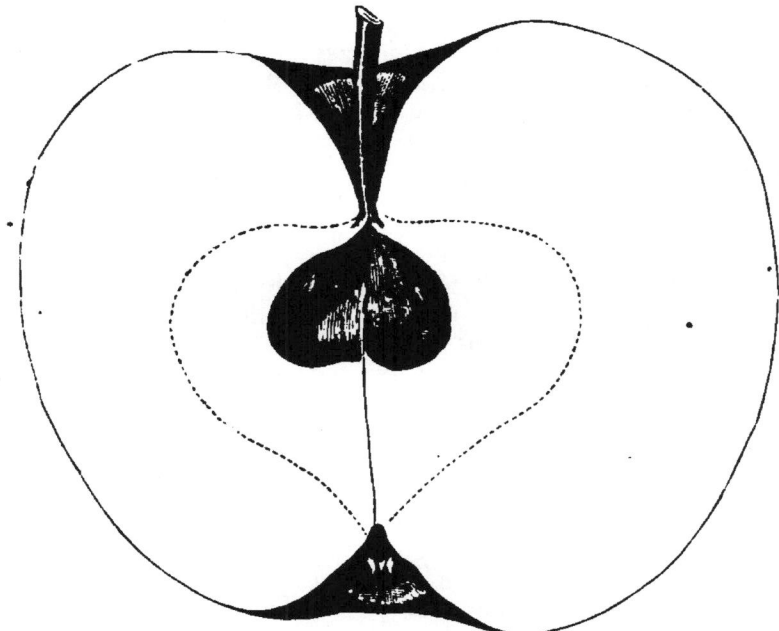

Fig. 71.—FINLEY.

on the other; and in its season, it competes with both, being useful in July for the kitchen, and ripening gradually until September.

Tree large, spreading, vigorous and productive.

Fruit large to very large, regular, globular-oblate, slightly conical; Surface smooth, greenish-yellow, becoming a clear lemon yellow at maturity; Dots minute, gray, scattering.

Basin rather wide, wavy; Eye small, closed; Segments reflexed.

Cavity acute, medium to deep, regular, brown; Stem long, yellow.

Core heart-shaped, regular, closed, clasping the eye; Seeds few, large, plump, and some imperfect; Flesh yellow, breaking, fine grained, juicy, acid, almost first quality; Valuable for kitchen and market; Season August and September.

Fink.

FINK'S SEEDLING.

This long keeper was brought before the notice of the Ohio Pomological Society many years ago by Mr. Clarke, of Somerset, Ohio. Mr. Elliott considered it the same as Tewksbury Winter Blush, and introduces Fink's Seedling as a synonym of that variety. Others think it a different fruit, among whom is that practical Pomologist, the Secretary of that association, M. B. Bateham, Esq., who has propagated and planted the trees extensively. It was described as Fink's Seedling in the Ohio Cultivator, May, 1847. At the meeting of 1854, the merits and claims of this variety were freely discussed, and the Society named it the *Fink*, after admitting that it was an original seedling, as stated by Mr. Fink, in whose seedling orchard it had originated.

Tree of strong upright growth, a profuse and annual bearer.

Fruit small, regular, roundish-oblate; Surface very smooth, polished, greenish-yellow, blushed with brownish-red; Flesh whitish, breaking, juicy, mild sub-acid; remarkable for its keeping qualities, remaining sound until the second season, and has been shown in May after having been kept over two winters.

Fulton.

Origin, Canton County, Illinois. Tree large, vigorous, productive, annual bearer.

Fruit large, globular-oblate, often oblique or unsymmetrical; Surface smooth, greenish-yellow, with a carmine blush; Dots minute, indented.

Basin abrupt, deep, folded; Eye medium to large, open.

Cavity deep, narrow or acute, green and brown; Stem rather long and slender.

Core small, round, clasping; Seeds numerous, small, short and plump; Flesh yellow, tender, fine grained, juicy; flavor sub-acid and aromatic; First quality for table; In

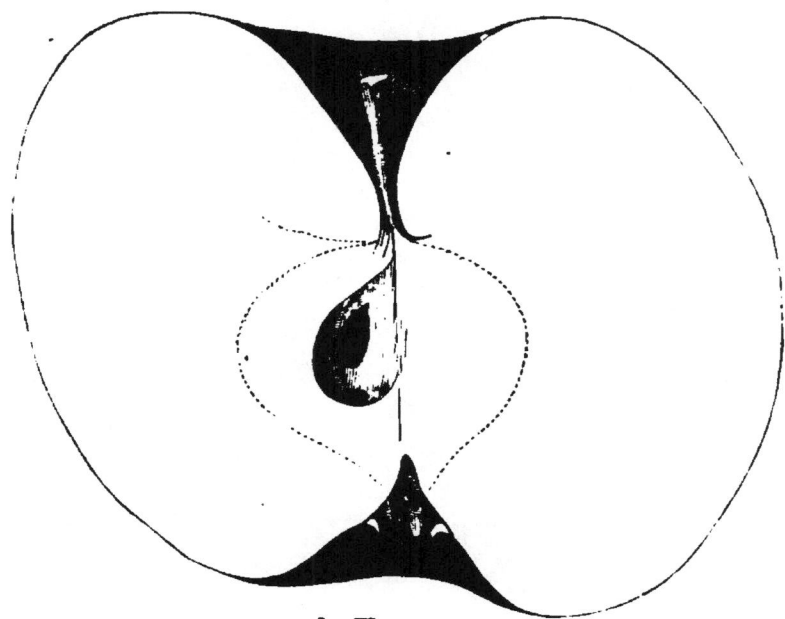

Fig. 72.—FULTON.

November and December. Our Illinois orchardists do not commend it so highly as when first introduced; not fully satisfactory where planted in Ohio on limestone clays.

Golden Seedling.

Said to have originated with Mr. Riehl, of St. Louis, cultivated and distributed by Geo. Husmann, of Hermann, Mo., in whose orchard I gathered it.

Fruit large, handsome, regular, and oblate; Surface smooth, greenish-yellow, and blushed; Dots scattered, minute.

Basin wide, regular; Eye medium, closed.

Cavity wide, wavy; Stem short.

Core medium, regular, meeting the eye, closed; Seeds

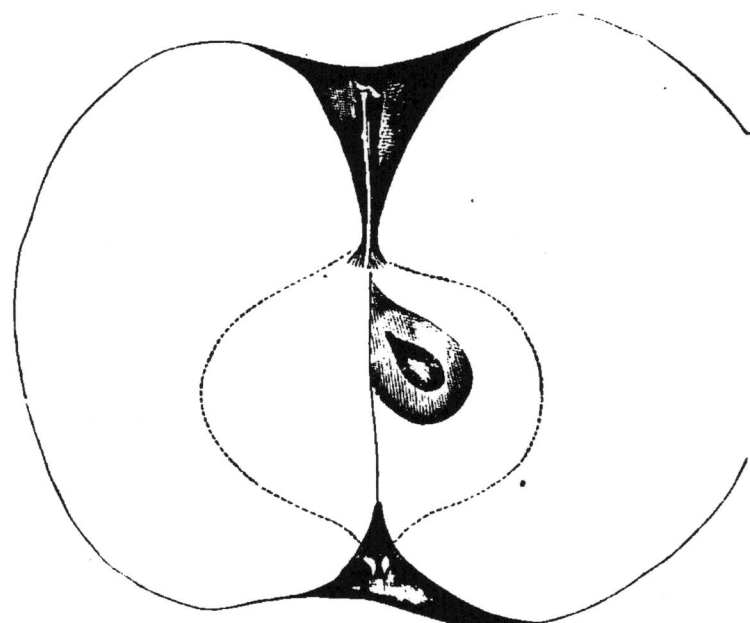

Fig. 73.—GOLDEN SEEDLING.

numerous, angular, pale; Flesh yellow, juicy, rich; "Very good."

Green Crank.

I have received this southern apple from Kentucky, Tenn., and also from Georgia, but have not yet fruited it. Tree moderately thrifty; Shoots brown; Foliage small.

Fruit medium to large, flattened somewhat, conical, regular; Surface green to yellow, sometimes bronzed; dots small, gray.

Basin medium, regular; Eye medium, closed.

Cavity wide, deep, acute, brown; Stem medium, green, thick.

Core wide, medium, closed, not clasping the eye; seeds numerous, plump, short, dark; Flesh yellow, firm, fine grained, juicy; Flavor sub-acid, aromatic, rich; Quality good to very good; Use table, kitchen; Season December to March.

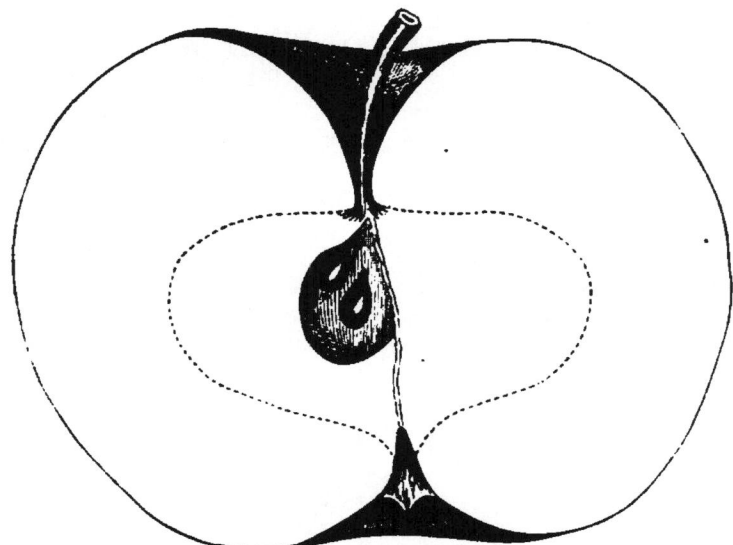

Fig. 74.—GREEN CRANK.

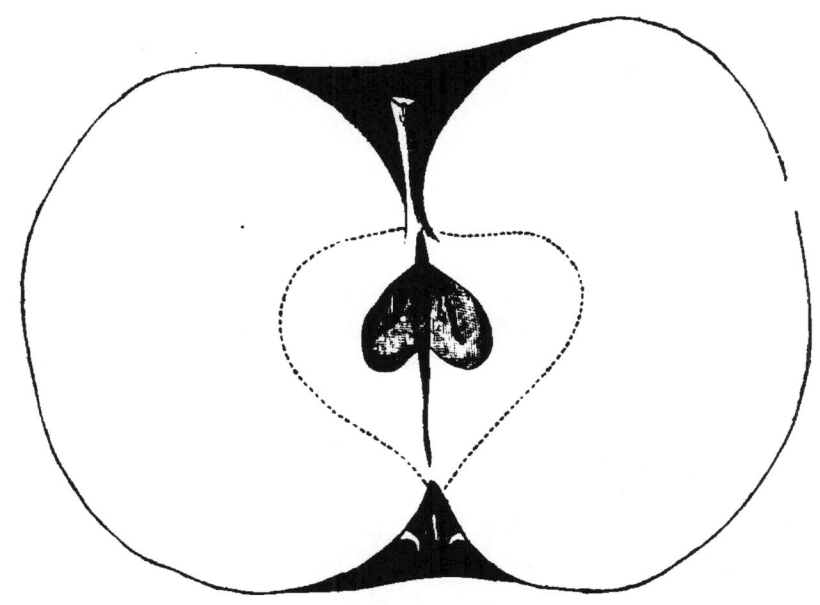

Fig. 75.—HAWLEY.

18

Hawley.

Originated in Columbia County, New York. Tree vigorous, with a round spreading head; Shoots stout, olive.

Fruit large, regular, oblate or slightly conic; Surface waxy yellow, rarely shaded or blushed, becomes oily or greasy when kept.

Basin rather wide, wavy; Cavity wide, sometimes folded; Stem short, medium and long.

Core regular, closed, scarcely clasping the eye; Seeds generally imperfect; Flesh yellowish-white, very tender, fine grained, juicy; Flavor very pleasant, mild sub-acid, rich; Season August to September; an amateur's fruit.

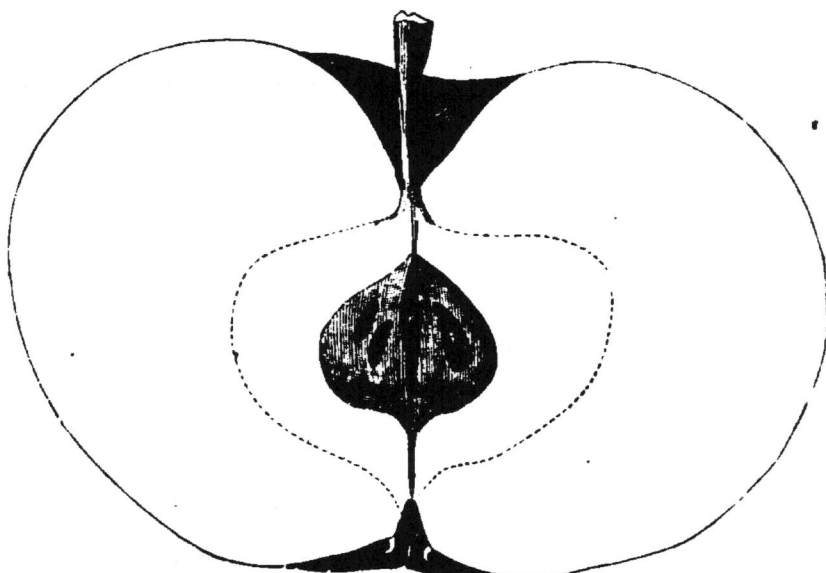

Fig. 76.—HAWTHORNDEN.

Hawthornden.

This famous Scotch fruit appears to do very well in this country, but it must yield the palm to its American cousin and representative, the Maiden's Blush, which possesses all its good qualities as a market and kitchen fruit, with attractive appearance.

Tree spreading, vigorous and productive: an early bearer.

Fruit large, regular, and very flat; Surface perfectly smooth, always fair, and of a beautiful white, very rarely and faintly blushed; Dots minute.

Basin shallow, narrow, regular; Eye small, closed.

Cavity wide, wavy, green; Stem medium.

Core wide, regular, somewhat open, meeting the eye; Seeds numerous, angular, imperfect, brown; Flesh greenish-white, breaking, fine grained, juicy; Flavor acid, aromatic; of second quality for table, but first rate for cooking; Uses, kitchen and market; Season October.

Junaliska.

This apple originated in the Cherokee country, where it is highly esteemed, and fruited in Ohio and Kentucky this year.

Fruit large, roundish or flattened, slightly conic, regular; Surface smooth, yellow, with some russet, chiefly about the apex; sometimes blushed; Dots minute, gray.

Basin rather small, regular; Eye small, long, closed.

Cavity deep, acute, brown; Stem quite short, knobby.

Core wide, heart-shaped, regular, closed; Axis short; seeds few, short, plump; Flesh yellow, breaking, granular; flavor sub-acid, spicy, rich; Quality good; Use, table and kitchen; Season November, and through the winter.

It may be destined to supply the place of the *Rhode Island Greening*, where that variety does not succeed.

Kane.

CAIN.

Origin, Delaware. Tree upright, sufficiently vigorous. Has been confounded with the Bohanon, but is distinct.

Fruit small, regular, oblate, somewhat conic; Beautiful for the dessert; Surface very smooth, waxen yellow, blushed with bright crimson; Flesh whitish, crisp, juicy, acid and pleasant; October and November.

Lady.

API PETIT, ETC.

This beautiful little French apple has been fully naturalized in our country, and has received the enthusiastic admiration of the American people. The fruit needs to be entirely perfect to meet with favor as an ornament to the table, for which use it is especially adapted; unfortunately it is often overgrown and irregularly developed. Wherever produced in proper size and color, it is one of the most profitable varieties, commanding fancy prices at the period of Christmas decorations. In the rich soils of the West it is apt to be too large, and has generally failed to meet the requisitions; but it succeeds well in Michigan, and the neighboring region of Indiana.

Tree of medium size, very close and upright, healthy and productive; Shoots very dark; the foliage small, crowded, curled, and very dark.

Fruit very small, quite flat, very regular; Surface very smooth, shining or polished, of a pale waxen yellow, nearly covered with bright carmine, which contrasts finely with the ground color, wherever the fruit has been shaded by a leaf; Dots minute.

Basin medium, rather abrupt; Eye small, closed.

Cavity acute, deep, regular; Stem short.

Core regular, wide, closed; Seeds numerous; Axis very short; Flesh white, breaking, tender and juicy when ripe; with a mild sub-acid flavor; Use ornament and dessert; Season December until March.

Maiden's Blush.

This beautiful and profitable fruit has received the unqualified approbation of thirteen out of the eighteen States that have reported to the American Pomological Society. It is a native of New Jersey, and is still held in high repute there as a market apple. The tree is hardy, vigorous, spreading and productive, beginning to bear quite early.

Fruit medium, to large, regular, flat and very handsome; Surface very smooth, polished, of a pale waxen yellow and blushed with bright carmine; Dots minute.

Basin shallow, regular or wavy; Eye small, closed.

Cavity wide, wavy; Stem medium to short.

Core regular, closed, meeting the eye; Seeds numerous, brown; Flesh white, breaking, fine grained, juicy; Flavor acid, aromatic, and to most palates not agreeable at the dessert, but very good when cooked, and requiring but a short time to be reduced to a delicious pulp of light color. This apple is also used for drying and makes a very light colored product, that is much admired by dealers. Season September and October, but may be used in the kitchen during August.

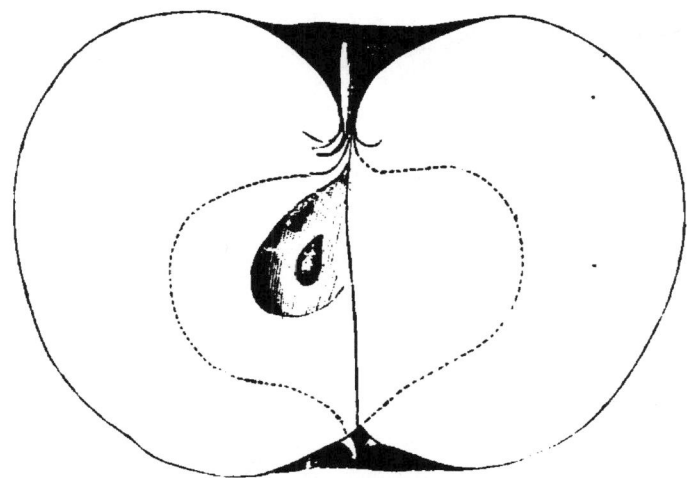

Fig. 77.—MAIDEN'S BLUSH.

Bachelor's Blush appears to be a variety of the above; found in Burlington County, New Jersey, and exhibited before the American Pomological Society at the Rochester meeting in 1864, by Wm. Parry, as a valuable and distinct variety. Having examined the trees as they grew together in the orchard, the resemblance to Maiden's Blush was very apparent. The fruit is larger, and for market purposes is considered more profitable. The two may be different, but are very much alike.

Pickard's Reserve.

Grown in Parke County, Indiana, from seed brought from North Carolina. This apple was first brought to my notice by Jno. C. Teas, of Raysville, Indiana. Considerably grown in that State. Tree hardy; the original is still standing in Rockville.

Fruit large, flat, somewhat unequal; Surface smooth, pale yellow; Dots scattered, minute.

Basin abrupt, regular, rather deep; Eye quite small, closed.

Cavity deep, wavy, brown; Stem short to medium.

Core irregular, closed, scarcely clasping the eye; Seeds

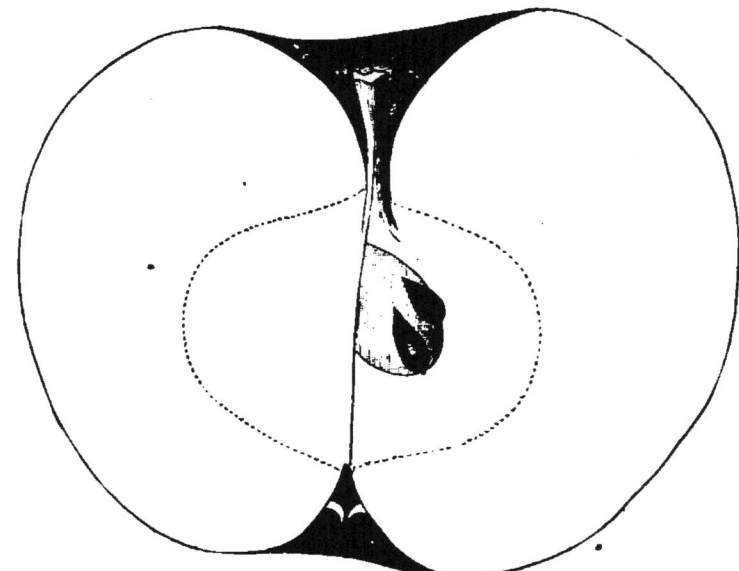

Fig. 78.—PICKARD'S RESERVE.

numerous, angular, dark brown; Flesh whitish-yellow, fine grained, tender, juicy, with a sub-acid, aromatic flavor, making this a fruit of first quality for table or kitchen use; Season December and January.

Rhode Island Greening.

From its name this apple would appear, like the Peck's Pleasant, to have come from the sea-girt State. It is a universal favorite, and is found to succeed well in a great many situations; but there are some portions of the West where it has failed to give satisfaction, being slow to come into bearing, becoming an autumn instead of a winter fruit, and falling badly from the trees before picking time. In sandstone soils, however, even in Southern Indiana and Illinois, it does better than on the limestone clays; the fruit attains an enormous size, but matures too early for a winter apple.

Tree very vigorous, crooked, spreading, productive; Shoots stout, dark, with dark foliage.

Fruit large to very large, varying in shape from globular or round to flat, which is the prevailing and characteristic form. Surface smooth in the North, somewhat rough and often quite russeted in the South, a dull green, becoming yellow at maturity; Dots grey, irregular, numerous.

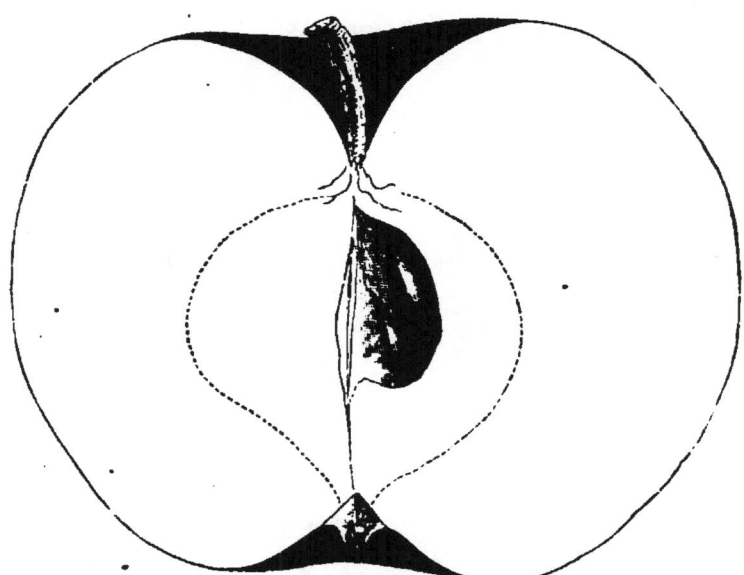

Fig. 79.—RHODE ISLAND GREENING.

Basin regular, small and russeted to a greater or less extent, sometimes extending half way down the sides of the fruit; Eye small to medium, closed.

Cavity wide, regular; Stem medium to long, curved, often reddish.

Core roundish-oval, regular, closed, clasping the eye; seeds numerous, angular, dark; Flesh very yellow, breaking, tender, juicy, with a rich, acid flavor, making it a superior cooking apple, and very fine for the dessert when fully ripe; Quality almost first rate; Season October to December—in the North, keeping until March.

Tewksbury Winter Blush.

This long-keeping variety was described by Coxe as having its origin in New Jersey. It has already been named in connection with the Fink, which resembles it very closely, and, like it, the chief excellence of this variety consists in its superior keeping qualities.

The tree is vigorous, upright, productive, and holds the apples well.

Fruit small, regular, flat; Surface smooth, yellow, blushed; Flesh yellow, breaking, juicy, well flavored, and retains its characters for a long time.

Virginia Greening.

This apple is supposed from its name to have originated in Virginia. It is cultivated chiefly in the Southern

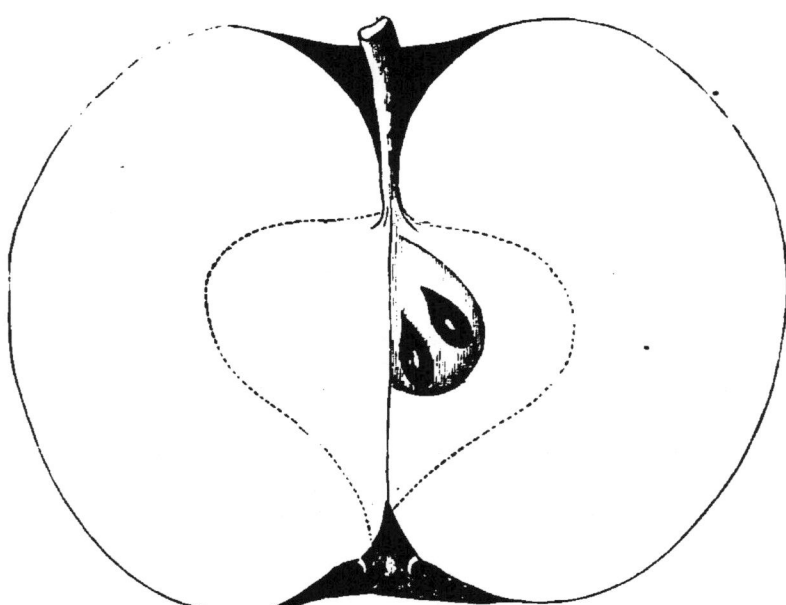

Fig. 80.—VIRGINIA GREENING.

States, and in those parts of the Northwest to which Southerners have migrated. Its chief merit is its long keeping. Tree large, spreading, productive.

Fruit large, regular, flat to roundish, generally the former; Surface smooth, dull green and often bronzy, never blushed; Dots scattered, large, white or gray, with whitish rings around them.

Basin regular, wide, shallow; Eye small, open.

Cavity wide, regular, green; Stem long to medium.

Core regular, turbinate, closed, meeting the eye; Seeds numerous, long; Flesh white, firm, breaking, sub-acid; Fit only for the kitchen; A long keeper; March and April; often subject to Bitter-rot.

White Fall Pippin.

FALL PIPPIN OF LOUISVILLE.

This handsome fruit is seen in quantities in the Louisville market every fall. Its cultivation does not appear to have been widely extended, nor has its origin been traced. It has been thought to resemble the Spanish Reinette, with which I have not had an opportunity to compare it.

Fruit very large, slightly uneven, roundish-flattened or globular-oblate; Surface smooth, pale yellow, not bronzed or blushed, but having a whitish striping toward the stem end; Dots scattered, minute, dark.

Basin abrupt, narrow, deep and folded; Eye small, long, closed.

Cavity wide, wavy; Stem very short.

Core wide, regular, somewhat open, clasping the eye; Seeds numerous, angular; Flesh yellowish-white, breaking, juicy; Flavor sub-acid, aromatic and rich; Useful for cooking, drying, and table; Season October.

White Juneating.

JUNEATING, *Coxe.*—YELLOW JUNE.—EARLY MAY?

Downing thinks this a very old variety, mentioned by Evelyn in 1660, and by Ray in 1688. It has long been known in the West and South as a very early apple, and valued on this account, though quite small. The tree resembles that of the Early Harvest in the color and arrangement of its twigs.

Fruit flat, regular; Surface smooth, pale yellow.

18*

Basin not deep, slightly folded; Eye small, closed.

Cavity wide, shallow; Stem long, slender.

Flesh breaking, whitish, juicy till over-ripe, when it is dry; Flavor sub-acid; Use table and market; Season June.

Winter Pippin.

WINTER PIPPIN OF GENEVA.

This very handsome fruit was received from T. T. Lyon, of Plymouth, Michigan, marked as having been received from Western New York. The same fruit was a very strong competitor for the Greeley prize before the Committee of the American Institute, and is believed to be the same as that described by Downing as the *Winter Pippin of Geneva*.

Tree thrifty, branches spreading; Said to be productive.

Fruit large, oblate, regular, or slightly unequal; Surface smooth, pale yellow, with a bright crimson cheek; Dots numerous, minute.

Basin wide, wavy, or plaited; Eye medium, closed.

Cavity regular, green, rather deep; Stem long.

Core medium, regular, closed, clasping the eye; Seeds numerous, plump; Flesh yellowish-white, fine grained, juicy, sub-acid; Season January until May. A limited acquaintance does not justify me in giving such high praises as those bestowed upon this fruit by Mr. Downing.

Yellow Foster.

This apple is a favorite with that worthy pioneer Pomologist of Southern Ohio, H. N. Gillett, of Lawrence County, to whom I am under obligations for this and many other varieties.

Fruit medium to large, regular, oblate; Surface smooth, greenish-yellow; Dots scattered, minute green.

Basin of medium depth and size, regular; Eye small, closed.

Cavity acute, regular; Stem of medium size and length.

Core medium, wide, closed, not meeting the eye; Seeds not numerous, medium; Flesh yellow, fine grained, tender, juicy; Flavor sub-acid and aromatic; Of first quality for table; During October.

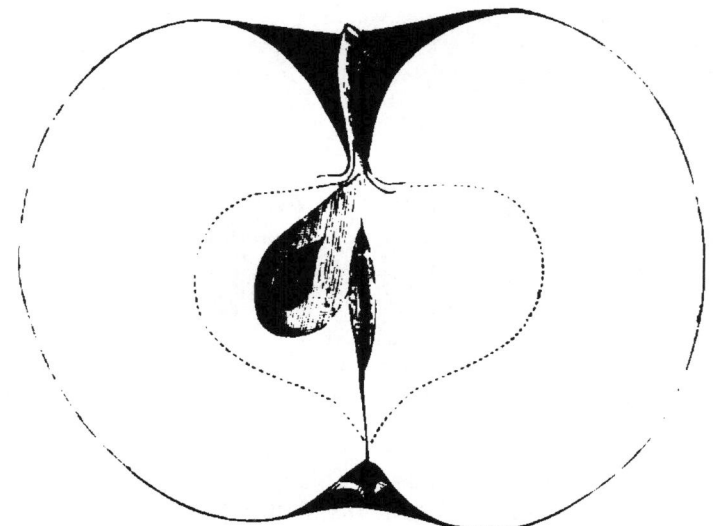

Fig. 81.—YELLOW FOSTER.

CLASS I.—FLAT APPLES.

ORDER I.—REGULAR.

SECTION 2.—SOUR.

SUB-SECTION 2.—STRIPED.

Abram.

FATHER ABRAHAM, of Illinois, not that of Coxe.

This little southern favorite is not extensively cultivated in the North, except where southern settlers have introduced it. It is found in Illinois, Indiana and Missouri. Origin believed to have been in Virginia, whence I have received specimens and trees. In Kentucky it is found to be a hardy drooping tree, holding the fruit well; annually productive, valued for cider, and keeping till July of next year.

Fruit medium, globular-oblate, uneven; Surface not smooth, yellowish green, mixed, red, with stripes and splashes; the whole presenting a gray appearance; Dots minute, scattered.

Basin shallow, wide, wavy; Eye small, closed.

Cavity acute, regular; Stem long, inclined.

Core medium, regular, closed; Seeds numerous, short, plump, pale; Flesh greenish-yellow, fine grained, juicy; flavor mild sub-acid, rich; almost first quality; keeping until May or later.

American Pippin.

GRINDSTONE.

This fruit is chiefly valued for keeping very late into the summer. Coxe commends it for its cider, rating it as nearly equal to the Grey-House; he says that fourteen bushels are required to make a barrel of cider. The apples hang well to the tree, and will bear a considerable amount of freezing. They are so firm as to suffer little from bruising, and are not disposed to rot when thus injured. A fruitman once said of their ability to withstand rough usage, that the apples might be whipped off the tree with a hoop-pole, shoveled into a cart, dumped upon the ground, and have some dirt thrown upon them, and that they would keep until next July; but, he added, they are then as good as dried apples; so lightly are they esteemed for table use.

The tree is thrifty, with a low, spreading head and depending branches; very productive; notwithstanding the fruit is dry and deficient in flavor, it is considered profitable, because so easily kept until May and June, when it commands the highest price, because of the rarity of green fruit at that season.

Fruit medium, regular, very flat; Surface rough, sometimes vein-russeted, dull green, covered with mixed red, and shaded with stripes of brick-dust color; Dots numerous, large, gray.

Basin very shallow, wide, regular or plaited; Eye quite small, open.

Cavity regular, brown, this color extending over the base of the fruit; Stem medium, often thick and knobby.

Core wide, irregular, closed; Seeds numerous, plump, brown; Flesh yellow, breaking, dry, very firm; Flavor mild sub-acid; Quality poor; Uses kitchen and market, which last means that it may be sold to those who do not appreciate the summer fruits of May and June.

Baldwin.

This celebrated apple of New England has been widely distributed over the country, but has not met with universal favor in the West and South; first, because it is apt to become a fall or early winter fruit, instead of a keeping apple; and secondly, because it is not well adapted to our palates; moreover, the tree has been considered tender, having suffered extensively during the cold winters; this is especially true in the nursery. Its productiveness and fair quality will, however, always make the Baldwin a favorite over a large portion of our country, and the New England settlers must have this variety.

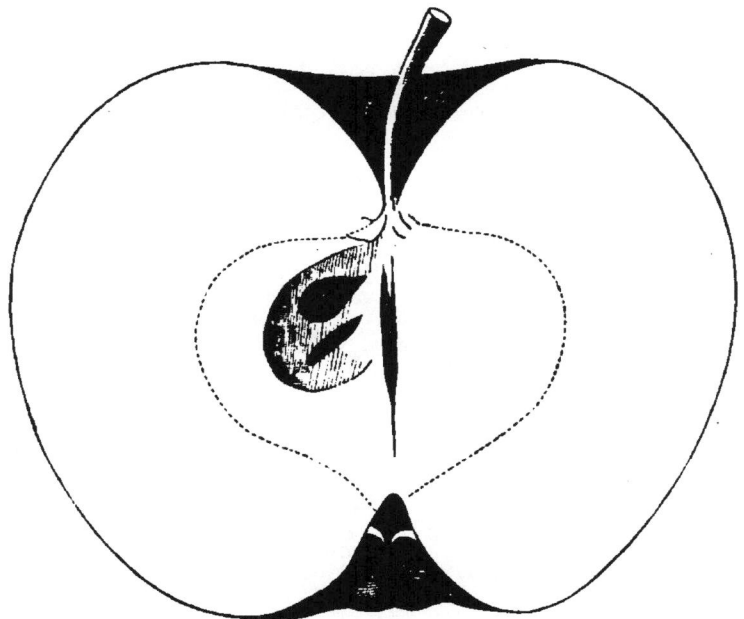

Fig. 82.—BALDWIN.

Tree robust, spreading, very productive; Foliage large, dark, on shoots that are stout and have a rich brown bark.

Fruit large, frequently round, and sometimes almost conical, but generally inclined to be flattened, so as to be classed by measurement as oblate; large specimens in southern latitudes are very apt to be unequal, and to have their axis inclined, or to be what is called lop-sided; surface smooth, rich yellow where shaded, but the exposed parts quite covered with deep red, which is mixed so as to conceal the ground color, and also to obscure the stripes of deeper red that prevail; this fruit is also frequently marked with veined russet, overlying the red color, or excluding it; Dots minute, and yellow, or gray where the red prevails.

Basin deep, often abrupt and narrow, generally waved, folded or plaited, and these marks are quite characteristic; Eye large and open, from the shortness of the calyx. On this account the variety is considered very subject to the attacks of the Codling-moth.

Cavity wide, regular or wavy, generally brown; Stem medium to long, often curved or inclined, sufficiently stout.

Core medium, regular, closed, meeting, sometimes clasping the eye; Seeds numerous, long, angular, imperfect; flesh yellow, breaking, frequently coarse-grained, juicy, sub-acid, rich; some northern specimens are fine-grained and almost first quality; those from the South are coarse, poor and scarcely second-rate for table use, but are good for cooking; Season October to January, occasionally keeping later.

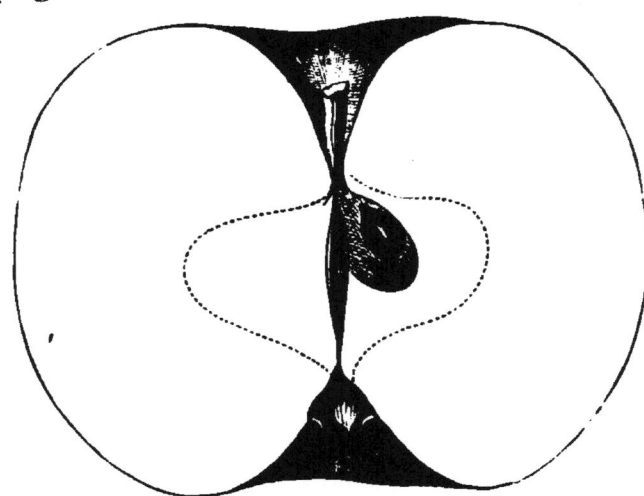

Fig. 83.—BETHLEMITE.

Bethlemite.

This apple has frequently been exhibited before the Ohio Pomological Society, by friends Lipsey, Morris and Benedict, of Morrow County, to which region its cultivation appears to have been confined. The origin of the fruit is obscure.

Tree thrifty, hardy, productive, upright.

Fruit medium, flat, or oblate-globular, regular; surface smooth, dull red or bright red, mixed, on yellow, with broken splashes of crimson; Dots distinct, large, gray and yellow.

Basin wide, deep, regular or folded, leather-cracked; Eye medium, closed.

Cavity rather wide, regular, brown; Stem medium to short.

Core regular, neat, closed, just meeting the eye; Axis short; Seeds numerous, short, very plump, pale; Flesh yellowish-white, breaking, juicy, sub-acid, aromatic; Quality good, for table and cooking; Season December.

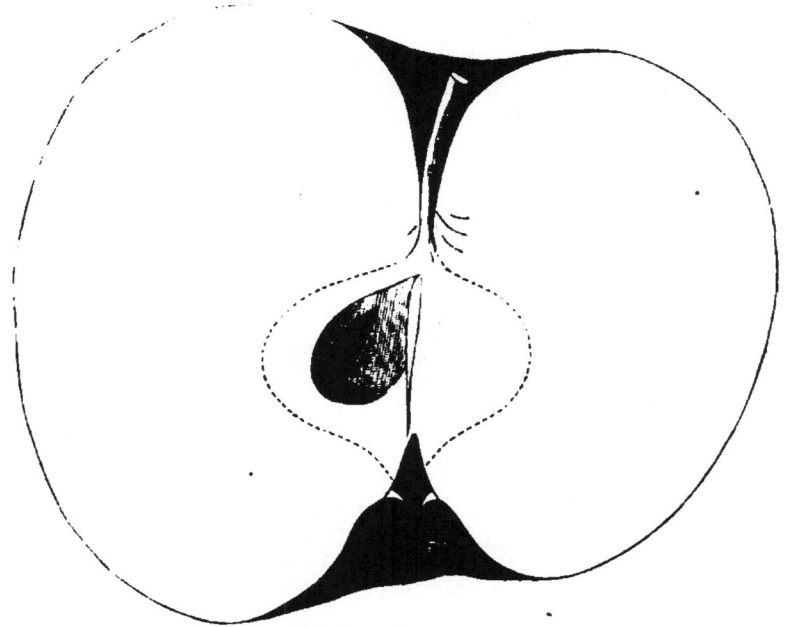

Fig. 84.—BLONDIN.

Blondin.

This fine fruit originated with the veteran Pomologist of Indiana, Reuben Ragan.

Fruit very large, oblate, unequal; Surface rough, greenish-yellow, splashed and striped with red; Dots numerous, large, gray.

Basin abrupt, folded; Eye small, closed.

Cavity acute, deep, brown; Stem short, rather slender inclined.

Core medium or small, regular, closed, clasping the eye; Seeds plump, pointed, brown; Flesh greenish-yellow, fine-grained, tender, juicy; Flavor sub-acid; almost first rate for table and market; Season October and November.

Blooming Orange.

Mr. Waring considers this the handsomest apple. In 1839 he brought a large number of sorts from the famous Herefordshire apple orchards of England, of which this is the only one he retains as fully adapted to the mountain region of Pennsylvania.

Tree a very strong, free, handsome grower, and an immense bearer, after six or eight years' growth.

Fruit very large, fair, beautiful, roundish-oblate, regular; surface dark, richly clouded with claret and mahogany, on yellow ground; Eye open; Flesh crisp, juicy, acid at first, but this merges into a rich, penetrating, very agreeable flavor.

It is of the Ribston Pippin, or Dutch Mignonne type of fruit.—[Mr. G. Waring's MS.]

Bonum.

MAGNUM BONUM.

This delicious southern fruit originated in Davidson County, North Carolina. The tree is vigorous, very productive and bears early. I received specimens from S. W. Westbrooke, Greensboro', North Carolina. Introduced to the American Pomological Society at the Philadelphia meeting, 1860, by Walter Steele, of Rockingham County, North Carolina, and highly recommended.

Fruit large, oblate, regular; Surface smooth, yellow, covered with mixed red, and striped; Dots distinct, large, yellow.

Basin medium, regular; Eye large, closed.

Cavity deep, regular, brown; Stem long, not thick, green.

Core oval, small, closed, scarcely meeting the eye; Axis

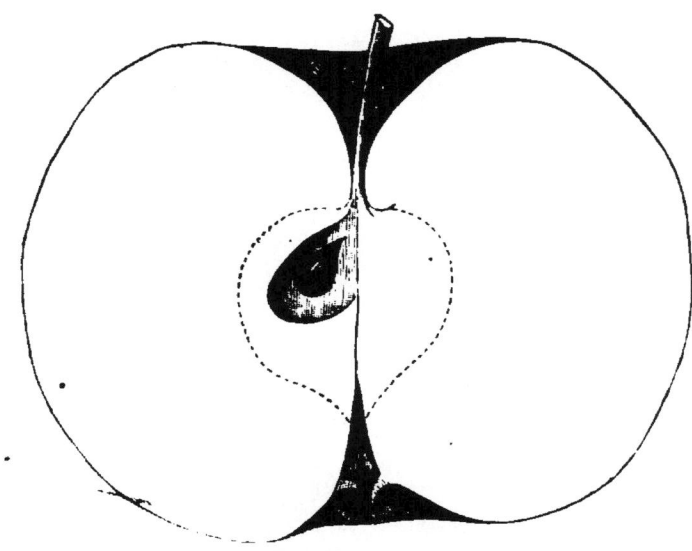

Fig. 85.—BONUM.

short; Seeds large, plump; Flesh yellow, firm, breaking, fine-grained, juicy; Flavor rich, sub-acid; first quality for the dessert; in September.

Brandywine.

This apple was found on the edge of the prairie, east of Quincy, Illinois, in the orchard of K. K. Jones, Esq., where it was supposed to have been brought from the State of Delaware.

Tree large, vigorous, spreading and productive.

Fruit medium, oblate, roundish, slightly conic, regular; surface smooth, greenish, covered with confused stripes of dull red; Dots scattered, white.

Basin shallow, abrupt, regular; Eye small, closed.

Cavity acute, regular, green; Stem very short.
Core small, round, closed, clasping; Seeds imperfect;

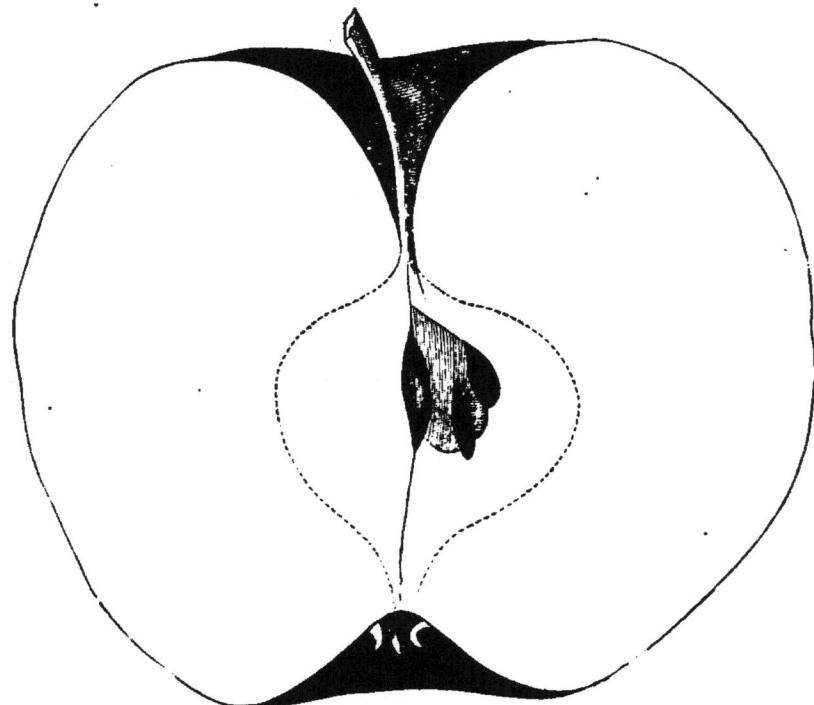

Fig. 86.—BRANDYWINE.

Flesh greenish-white, fine-grained, tender, juicy; Flavor sub-acid, aromatic; Quality only good; Use table, kitchen; Season January, February.

Buchanan's.

Origin near Cincinnati, Ohio, in the orchard of Robert Buchanan, Esq., a gentleman long devoted to pomology. It also closely resembles the Brandywine, as grown in Illinois, already described.

This variety is much like the Minkler, which originated in Illinois, and both may have come from seeds of the Gilpin, which they resemble.

Tree vigorous and productive.

Fruit medium, oblate, regular; Surface smooth, yellow, covered with mixed red and striped bright red; Dots scattered, minute.

Basin medium, folded or plaited; Eye large, closed.

Cavity wide, regular, green; Stem short or medium.

Core flattened, closed, clasping the eye; Seeds numerous, plump, dark; Flesh greenish-yellow, firm, breaking; Flavor sub-acid; Quality scarcely second rate, but useful for cooking, and keeps sound until May.

Carolina Baldwin.

This nice southern apple was received from S. W. Westbrooke, of Greensboro'. Of the tree I know nothing.

Fruit medium, oblate, regular; Surface yellow-green, with mixed red and stripes; Dots numerous, large, white.

Basin abrupt, regular; Eye large, closed.

Cavity wide, regular; Stem, medium to long.

Core small, regular, heart-shaped, closed; Seeds pointed; Flesh yellow, fine-grained, juicy; Flavor, sub-acid; good for table in November.

Cheese.

This fruit was received from Lewis Sanders, of Grass Hills, Gallatin County, Kentucky, by whom it was grown and esteemed.

Fruit medium to small, oblate, regular; Surface smooth, yellowish-green, striped purple red, splashed deep red; dots scattered, gray and purple.

Basin shallow, regular, or abrupt and deep, in different specimens; Eye small, closed.

Cavity wide, regular, brown; Stem long, slender.

Core regular, closed; Axis long; Seeds plump, pointed, dark; Flesh yellow, tender, fine-grained, juicy; Flavor sub-acid, agreeable; Quality good for the table in December and January.

Colvert.

Fruit large, roundish-oblate, slightly conic, regular, often unequal; Surface smooth, yellowish-green, mixed, striped, light red; Dots scattered, distinct, white.

Basin deep, abrupt, regular, folded; Eye medium.

Cavity rather deep, acute, brown; Stem medium.

Core round, flattened, slightly open, meeting the eye; Seeds numerous, long, pointed, imperfect; Flesh white, breaking, fine-grained, juicy; Flavor sub-acid; Quality scarcely good; Use, market chiefly; Season October, November.

Cooper.

This delicious apple was introduced into the West with the cions that were brought to the early Putnam nursery at the mouth of the Muskingum river in 1796. Though a general favorite from its beauty, its fine texture, and ex-

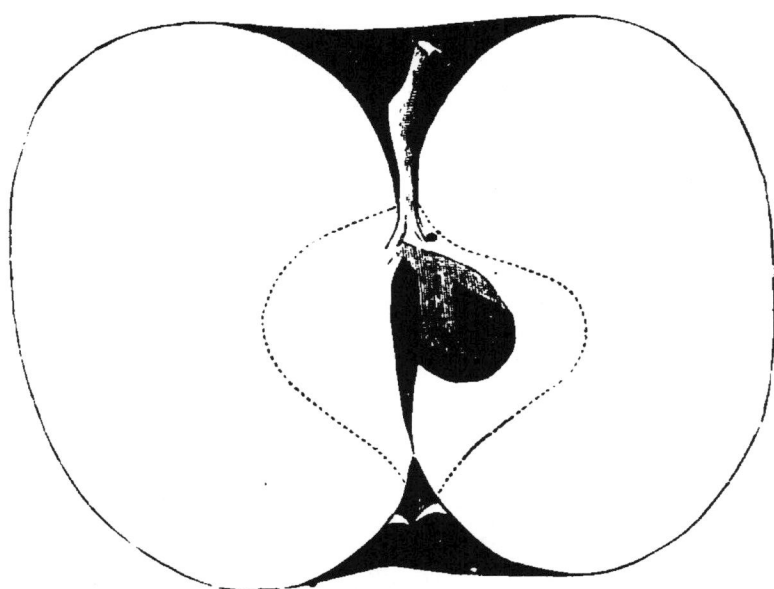

Fig. 87.—COOPER.

quisite flavor, this variety does not appear to have been so widely spread as others very inferior to it. Though occurring on the original Putnam list, and therefore an eastern variety, it does not appear to have been recognized by cultivators in the older States, and there are those in the West who claim that it is of French origin.

The tree has a stout, upright growth, which becomes spreading with age, when the limbs stand at a right angle with the trunk; they are frequently defaced with marks of diseased action that are called *canker*. The twigs are reddish and rather slender; the leaves are pale green, large, broad.

Fruit large, globular-oblate, regular, sometimes unequal, light; Surface smooth, pale waxen-yellow, with a little mixed scarlet and very distinctly marked carmine; Dots scattered, minute.

Basin regular, abrupt, deep; Eye small, closed.

Cavity wide, regular, green; Stem medium, green.

Core small, closed, just meeting the eye; Seeds numerous, plump, short, dark; Flesh pale yellow, fine-grained, tender, almost melting, juicy; very mild sub-acid, aromatic; of first quality for table, kitchen or market (too good for drying, but makes a superior article of *snits*); Season September and October.

Dr. Watson.

AUTUMN SEEK-NO-FURTHER OF INDIANA.

This delicious and beautiful dessert apple is much grown in Central and Eastern Indiana, particularly among the Friends. It was for a long time a puzzle to the pomologists. In the meanwhile it must have a name, and without waiting for the decision of the learned, the people in different sections, without consultation, called it the *Autumn Seek-no-further*. Finally the Horticultural Societies decided that it was an old sort named *Doctor Watson*, though upon what authority does not appear. The fruit has not been recognized by our Eastern friends, nor by the American Pomological Society, to which it was referred in 1860.

Tree large, spreading, very productive; Twigs slender, foliage small, pale green; in the nursery it is a poor grower.

Fruit medium to large, unless when too crowded, regular, oblate, sometimes unequal; Surface smooth, mixed pale and red on waxen-yellow, beautifully splashed with scarlet; Dots minute.

Basin abrupt, rather deep, wide, regular, sometimes cracked; Eye medium, open.

Cavity wide, regular or wavy, brown; Stem medium to short.

Core medium, regular, closed, just meeting the eye; Axis short; Seeds plump; Flesh yellow, fine-grained, very tender and juicy, almost melting, with a rich, aromatic,

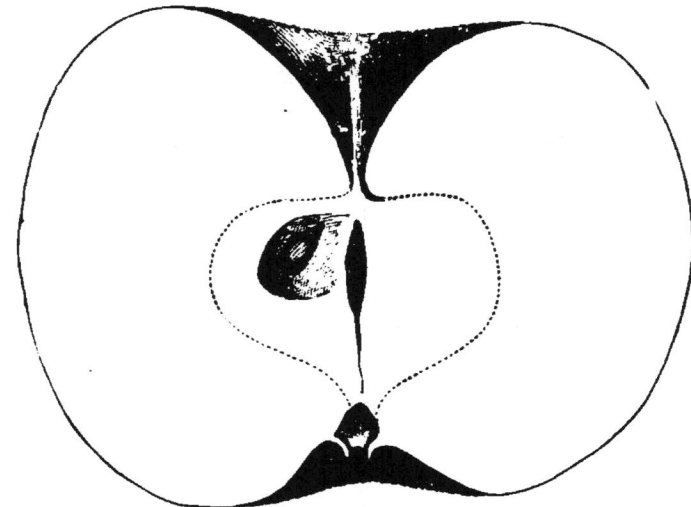

Fig 88.—DR. WATSON.

sub-acid flavor; Quality best, for table and kitchen, from September to November; also valuable for stock feeding.

Domine.

Supposed to be a native of this country; origin unknown. Tree very thrifty, making long, stout, brown shoots, which branch from the ends, and form spurs along their sides, so that the tree has a straggling, open head, and bears its fruit crowded along the smaller branches. It is hardy, upright, vigorous and productive. Foliage large and long, with a peculiar curl or folding upwards, so as to show the underside of the leaves.

Fruit large, flat, regular, sometimes unequal; Surface yellowish-green, nearly covered with mixed red, and striped indistinctly with carmine, often vein-russeted; Dots scattered, yellow and gray, large.

Basin rather shallow, folded or plaited; Eye medium to small, closed.

Cavity wide, wavy, brown; Stem medium to long, slender at its insertion into the fruit, and easily separated from it, but holding firmly to the tree; hence care is needed in picking the fruit.

Core regular, somewhat open, scarcely meeting the eye;

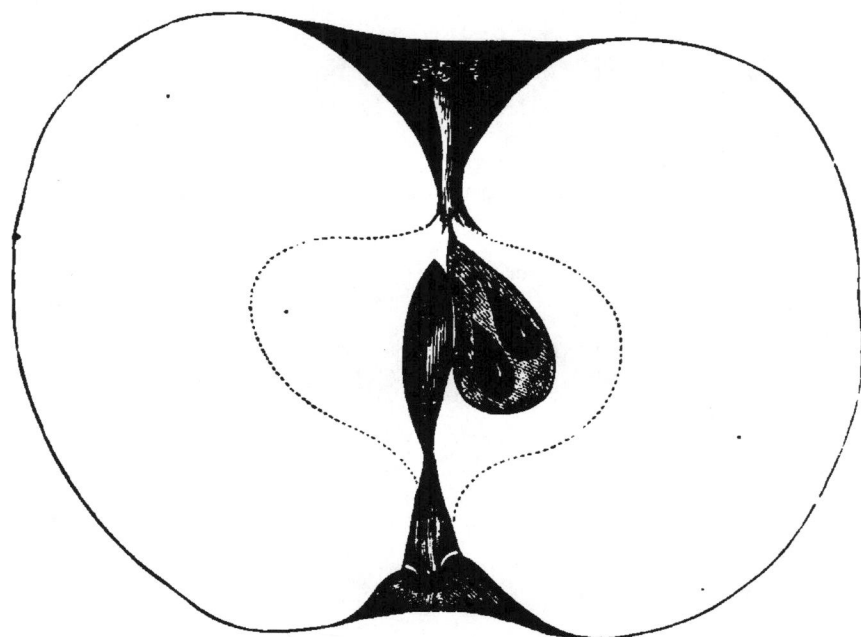

Fig. 89.—DOMINE.

Axis often short; Seeds numerous, pointed, plump; Flesh light yellow, breaking, tender, juicy; flavor slightly sub-acid, rich; good, for table, kitchen, or market; Season December and January, keeping until spring in the North.

,Duchess of Oldenburgh.

This very beautiful striped apple is from Russia, and has proved one of the hardiest apples in our trying climate. Reports from the Northwest are entirely satisfactory as to its hardiness.

Tree medium size, round-headed, sufficiently vigorous and perfectly hardy.

Fruit medium, regular, roundish-oblate; Surface smooth, waxen-yellow, partially covered with distinct and regular stripes and splashes of brilliant red and carmine; often having a light bloom, such as is found on most Russian apples.

Basin regular, pretty wide; Eye large and closed.

Cavity regular, acute; Stem medium to long, rather slender.

Flesh white, tender, juicy; Sour and suitable for cooking. Though attractive to the eye, it is unsuited for the dessert.

By Dr. Jno. A. Kennicott, the pioneer cultivator of Northern Illinois, this apple was considered the *ne plus ultra* for that and higher latitudes.

Equinetelee.

BACHELOR—BYERS—IOLA (Berckmans' M.S.) SOL. CARTER (Downing.)

This fine southern apple has its origin traced to Yancey County, in North Carolina. It has not yet been sufficiently

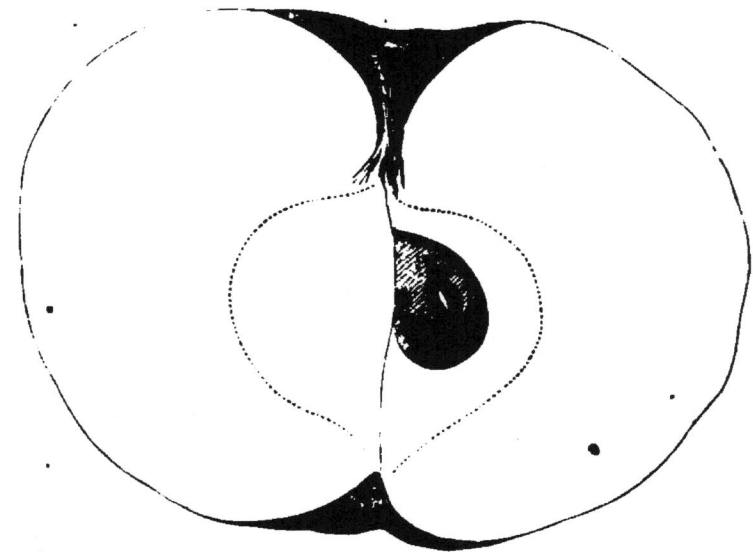

Fig. 90.—EQUINETELEE.

tested in the Northern States, but is considered one of the

best in the South, and is looked upon as having great promise in our northern orchards, where it is somewhat introduced. Berckmans says : "The finest of the late fall and winter apples."

The trees bear a strong resemblance to those of the *Buckingham*.

Fruit large, oblate, sometimes oblique ; Surface light yellow, mostly covered with bright crimson, obscurely striped ; Dots small, white.

Basin deep, narrow, irregular ; Eye medium, closed.

Cavity wide, deep ; Stem short.

Flesh pale yellow, very tender, juicy, melting ; Flavor very mild sub-acid, making it a very superior table fruit, from November to January in Georgia, according to Berkmans.

Evening Party.

This excellent dessert fruit originated in Berks County, Pennsylvania, and was brought into notice by the late la-

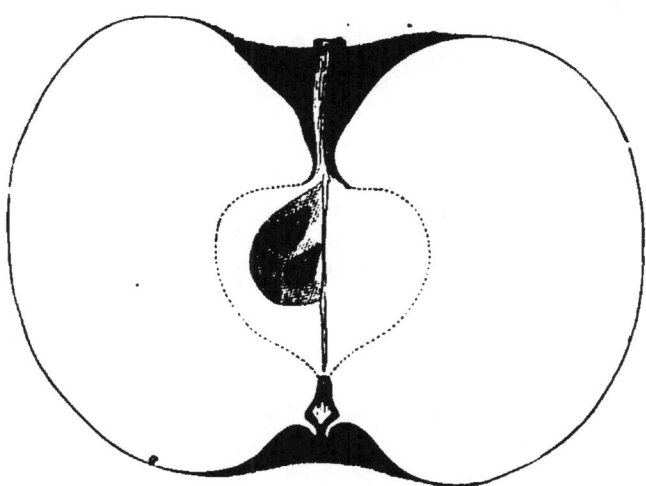

Fig. 91.—EVENING PARTY.

mented Dr. Brinkle, of Philadelphia, in his ad-interim reports, and also in Hoffy's Fruits. It has been tested with entire satisfaction by J. D. G. Nelson, President of the Indiana Horticultural Society, who always has admirers

19

of the fruit exhibited by him at the winter meetings. This apple takes the place at mid-winter which is occupied in summer by the Early Joe, and in autumn by the Jefferies, Dr. Watson and Cooper.

Fruit medium to small, regular, quite flat; Surface smooth, mixed red, and carmine stripes on waxen-yellow ground; Dots numerous, distinct, gray.

Basin abrupt, regular deep; Eye small, closed; Segments long.

Cavity wide, deep, regular, brown; Stem medium, green, slender.

Core small, regular, closed, touching the eye; Axis short; Seeds short, wide, dark; Flesh light yellow, very fine-grained, tender, juicy; Flavor sub-acid, aromatic; first quality, or very best, for the dessert, or the *evening party*, during December and January.

Fall Wine.

Origin unknown. A great favorite in the West as a table fruit; little grown in the Eastern States, whence it was brought. Downing supposes this is because the fruit is there defective. In virgin soil it is remarkably fair and handsome.

Tree of medium size, rather slender, but healthy, spreading, and annually productive.

Fruit medium, oblate, handsome; inclined to crack open if left on the tree till ripe; Surface very smooth, waxen-yellow, almost completely covered with bright, and often deep red, upon which it is indistinctly striped; Dots minute.

Basin abrupt, wide, regular or wavy; eye small, closed; Calyx reflexed.

Cavity wide, regular, uniformly green; Stem long, slender.

Core medium, regular, closed, meeting the eye; Seeds numerous, angular or plump; flesh yellow, breaking, tender, fine-grained, juicy; flavor mild sub-acid, and very aromatic; Quality best, for table and market, during September and October or later

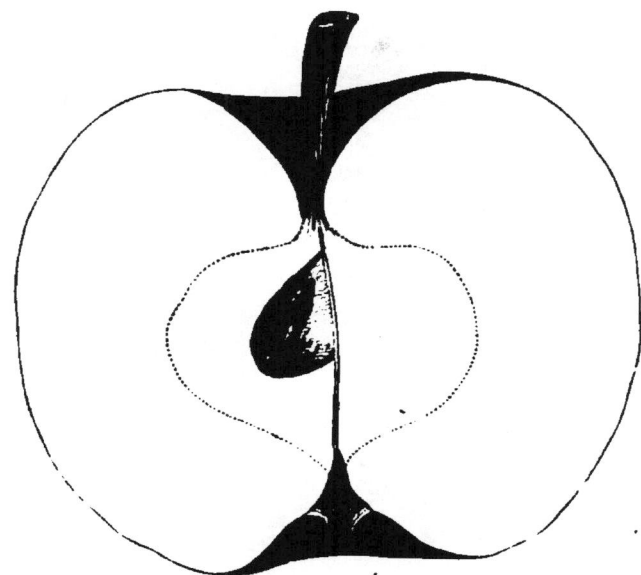

Fig. 92.—FALL WINE.

Garden.

GARDEN ROYAL.

This fine apple has been received from quite distant points, Chillicothe, Ohio, and Salem, Indiana. It is quite distinct in season from the *Beefsteak* or *Garden* of Downing, but in description corresponds very closely with the *Garden-Royal* of Elliott, which fruit I have not seen. Origin unknown.

Fruit pretty large, roundish, flat, regular; Surface smooth, yellowish-green, slightly shaded red, scattered stripes, carmine; Dots minute, black.

Basin wide, regular, small, closed.

Cavity deep, acute, regular, green; stem short to medium, sometimes knobby.

Core wide, closed or open, regular, clasping the eye; seeds small, pointed, brown; flesh pale yellow or whitish, tender, fine-grained, juicy; Flavor sub-acid, aromatic, saccharine, agreeable; Quality very good to best; Use dessert, kitchen, market; Season August to October; worthy of cultivation.

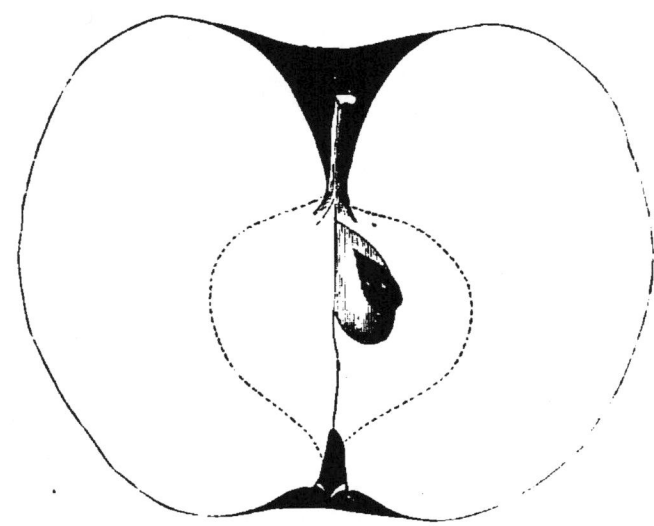

Fig. 93.—GARDEN.

Golay.

This fruit originated near Vevay, Indiana, and is supposed to be a seedling of the *Janet*, which it somewhat resembles.

Fruit medium, oblate, somewhat conic, truncated, regular; Surface smooth, yellow, mixed, striped, purplish-red; Dots minute, gray, scattered, indented.

Basin wide, regular; Eye small, closed.

Cavity wide, regular; Stem short.

Core very small, pyriform, closed, clasping; Seeds numerous, large, plump, brown; Flesh yellowish-white, breaking, tender, juicy; Flavor sub-acid, rich; Quality good to best; Use, table; Season, January to May.

Harvest Redstreak.

This old variety is valued only as an early cooking apple, for which it has been found very profitable, by those who attend market. Origin unknown. Introduced into the West by Silas Wharton, from the neighborhood of Philadelphia, where it was cultivated largely. Not recognized among the varieties described by Coxe.

Tree spreading, open, round-headed; Twigs stout; Leaves small, mealy.

Fruit medium, roundish-oblate, regular; Surface smooth, greenish-yellow, striped and splashed with red, more or less mingled; Dots minute, dark, and a light bloom.

Basin medium, folded; Eye medium, closed.

Cavity acute, regular, often brown; Stem medium, thick.

Core regular, closed; Seeds angular; Flesh whitish, breaking, coarse, juicy, becoming dry; Quality inferior, except for cooking; Season July.

High-Top.—[LEWIS JONES.]

This handsome apple is supposed to have originated in Wayne County, Indiana, and was brought into notice by Lewis Jones.

Fruit large, flat, roundish, regular; Surface smooth,

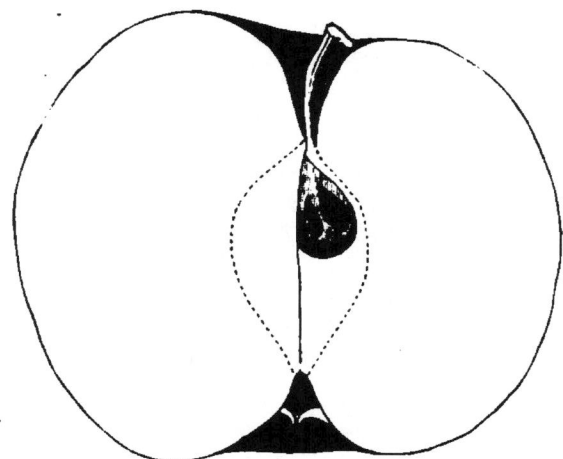

Fig. 94.—HIGH-TOP.

mixed dull red, striped carmine; Dots scattered, minute.

Basin wide, medium, folded; Eye medium, closed.

Cavity wavy, brown, acute; Stem short, green.

Core regular, closed, or wide and open, clasping; Seeds numerous, short, plump, pale; Flesh pale yellow, fine-grained, tender, juicy; Flavor sub-acid, aromatic; Quality good to very good; Use table, kitchen, market; Season, December, January; reminds one somewhat of Domine.

Hocking.

This variety has only been found in western orchards, and has not been mentioned by name in any fruit book with which I have met. At the second meeting of the Northwestern Fruit Growers' Convention, it was reported as having been brought from Fairfield County, Ohio; its resemblance to Townsend was also observed, but it was declared to be different in wood and buds. These apples may yet prove to be identical, but as the question is not settled, both will be described.

Tree thrifty, vigorous, productive—an early bearer.

Fruit medium to large, globular-oblate, regular; Surface smooth, yellow, covered with mixed red, and splashed carmine; Dots minute, yellow.

Basin medium, regular; Eye medium to large, closed.

Cavity medium, regular, green; Stem medium to long.

Core small, closed; Seeds large, brown; Flesh light yellow, breaking, juicy; Sub-acid; Quality good; Market and kitchen; September.

Hunt.

Another of Lewis Jones' apples, supposed to be a seedling of Eastern Indiana; productive.

Fruit medium, roundish-oblate, regular; Surface smooth, yellow, mixed, striped bright red; Dots numerous, yellow.

Basin rather wide, abrupt, folded; Eye small, closed.

Cavity wide, regular; Stem medium, slender.

Core small, roundish, flattened, closed, not meeting the eye; Seeds numerous, angular; Flesh yellow, breaking, fine-grained, juicy; flavor sub-acid, aromatic; Quality good to very good; Use table, market; Season December and January.

Indiana Favorite.

This fruit resembles the Pennsylvania Vandervere, from which it may have sprung. Origin believed to be Fayette County, Indiana. It is considerably cultivated in the eastern part of the State, where I procured specimens exhibited at the Richmond Horticultural Society.

Tree vigorous, spreading, productive.

Fruit medium, globular-oblate, regular; Surface very smooth, bright red, striped with darker red; Dots numerous, star-shaped, yellow.

Basin wide, regular, abrupt; Eye small, closed.

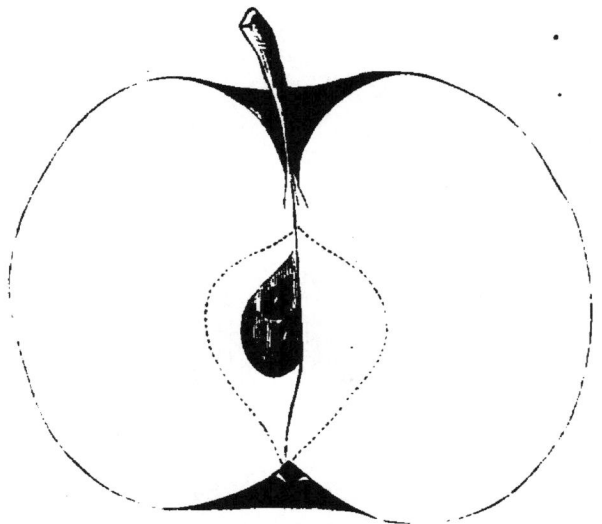

Fig. 95.—INDIANA FAVORITE.

Cavity acute, regular, green or brown; Stem medium to long, red.

Core regular, closed, clasping the eye; Seeds numerous, angular, imperfect; Flesh pale yellow, breaking, fine-grained, juicy; Mild sub-acid; Good to very good, for table and market, from January to March.

Jarminite.

This new fruit originated on the farm of Jarmin Ballard, in Highland County, Ohio, where it was grown from the seed of Gilpin.

The tree is very vigorous, and only too productive.

Fruit medium, regular, oblate, or roundish; Surface smooth, green, partially covered with mixed and striped dull red.

Basin regular, wide; Eye medium, closed.

Cavity regular, acute; Stem slender, medium to short.

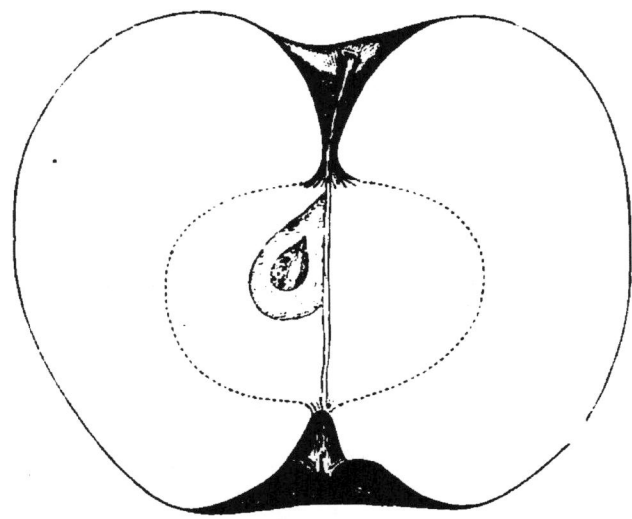

Fig. 96.—JABMINITE.

Core regular, closed, clasping; Seeds few, large, dark; flesh breaking, firm; Mild sub-acid, almost sweet; December until March.

Jefferies.

This delicious autumn apple originated in Chester County, Pennsylvania, and was first described by the ad-interim committee of the Pennsylvania Horticultural Society; also in the Farm Journal, for 1853, by David Townsend, of Westchester, Pa.

Tree healthy, sufficiently vigorous; shoots slender, foliage bright green; productive, early bearer.

Fruit full medium, oblate, regular; Surface smooth, yellow, mixed and splashed crimson; Dots large, scattered, yellow.

Basin wide, regular; Eye small, closed.

Cavity medium, regular, brown; Stem medium to long.

Core small, closed, regular, clasping; Seeds numerous, large, brown; Flesh yellow, breaking, fine-grained, juicy; flavor sub-acid, aromatic, delicious; Quality very good, for table and market, during August, September and October.

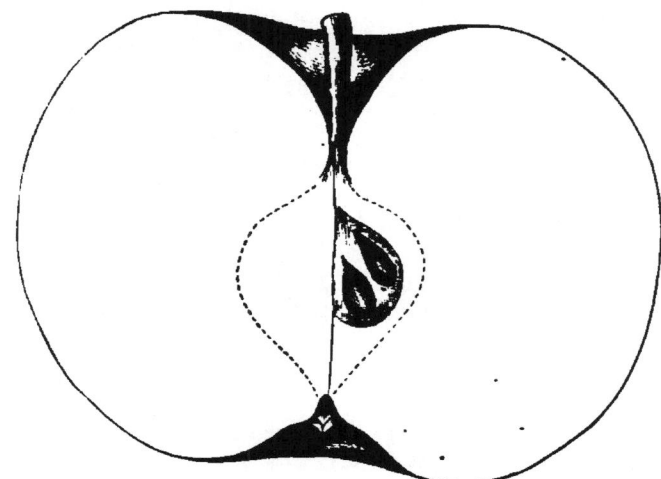

Fig. 97.— JEFFERIES.

Kentucky King.

Received from J. S. Downer & Son, Elkton, Kentucky. Further history not known.

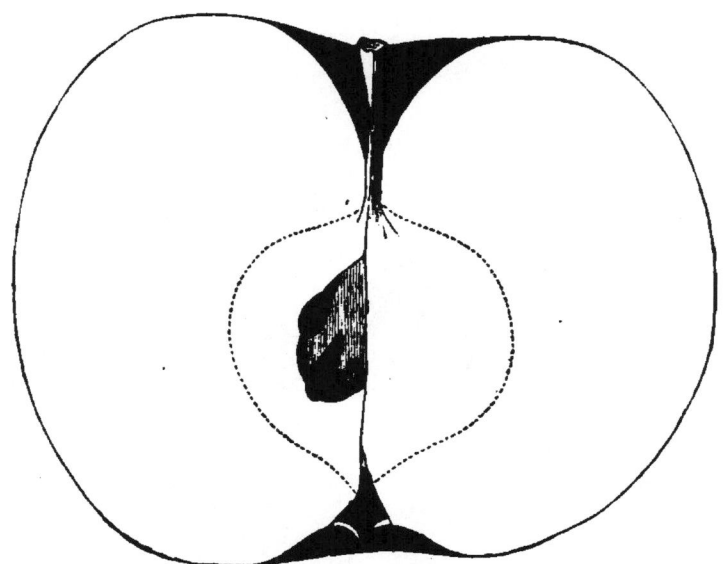

Fig. 98.—KENTUCKY KING.

19*

Fruit above medium, flat, regular; Surface smooth, yellow, with mixed and striped carmine; Dots scattered, minute.

Basin medium, regular; Eye medium, open.

Cavity medium, regular, brown and green; Stem medium to long.

Core medium, round, closed, clasping; Seeds numerous, angular, pointed, dark; Flesh yellow, breaking, fine-grained, juicy; Flavor sub-acid, aromatic; Quality good to very good; Use table, kitchen; Season December, February.

Klaproth.

Another Pennsylvania apple, introduced by my friend Dr. J. K. Eshleman. Tree vigorous, large, productive.

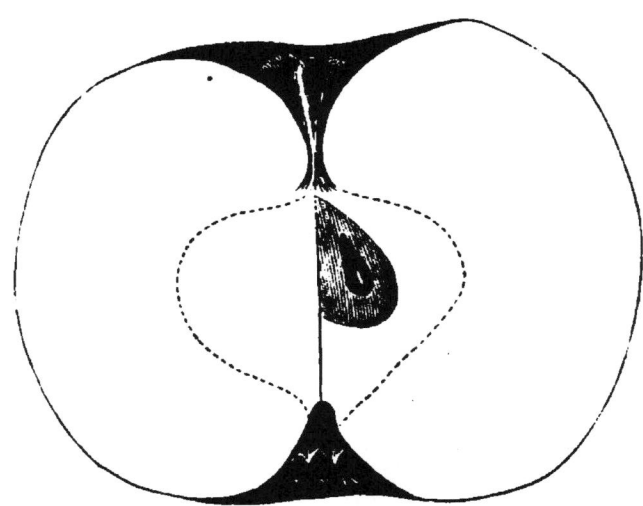

Fig. 99.—KLAPROTH.

Fruit medium, regular, oblate; Surface dull yellow, more or less covered with red stripes; Dots numerous, light.

Basin wide, regular; Eye closed, small; Calyx reflexed.

Cavity deep, regular, brown; Stem short to medium.

Flesh white, breaking, tender, very juicy; Flavor acid, to sub-acid when ripe; Good; August till October.

Lewis.—*Of Ragan.*

Originated in Putnam County, Indiana, as one of the many seedlings produced by my old friend Reuben Ragan.

Tree thrifty and productive.

Fruit medium, regular, oblate; Surface smooth, deep red on yellow; Dots, numerous, large, yellow.

Basin medium, regular, not deep; Eye small, closed

Cavity wide, regular, brown; Stem short.

Core wide, regular, closed, meeting the eye; seeds numerous, plump; Flesh yellow, tender, fine-grained, juicy; flavor sub-acid, aromatic; Quality nearly first-rate for table; Season, October.

Lacker.

This old Pennsylvania apple is cultivated to some extent in the Western States for its beauty. Specimens from Henry Myers, South Bend, Indiana, from his beautiful collections shown at the State Fairs.

Fruit full medium to large, very handsome, oblate, regular; Surface smooth, highly polished, bright red on pale yellow, striped dark red; Dots numerous, pale.

Basin wide, wavy; Eye small, closed; Segments short.

Cavity deep, narrow, wavy; Stem short to medium.

Core small, roundish or oval, closed, clasping; Seeds numerous, plump; Flesh whitish, breaking, fine-grained, juicy; Flavor mild sub-acid, aromatic, fine; Quality good; use table, market; Season January to March.

McDaniel.

This is a seedling of Green County, Ohio, to which was awarded a premium at the State Fair in 1855.

Fruit full medium, regular, oblate; surface very smooth, yellow, well covered with rich crimson, indistinct stripes; dots scattered, light gray.

Basin medium, regular; eye medium, closed.

Cavity narrow, regular; stem short.

Core medium, regular, closed; seeds plump, dark; flesh rich yellow, solid, juicy; flavor sub-acid, rich, piquant, like a Spitzenberg; October, November.

Minkler.

Produced by S. G. Minkler, of Kendall, Illinois.

This variety very closely resembles that described as *Buchanan*, though their origin is entirely distinct. The Minkler also bears a very close resemblance to an apple found at Quincy, Illinois, and known as the *Brandywine.*

Tree very thrifty, spreading, branches strong, forming a large angle with the stem.

Fruit medium to large, regular, globular-ovate; Surface

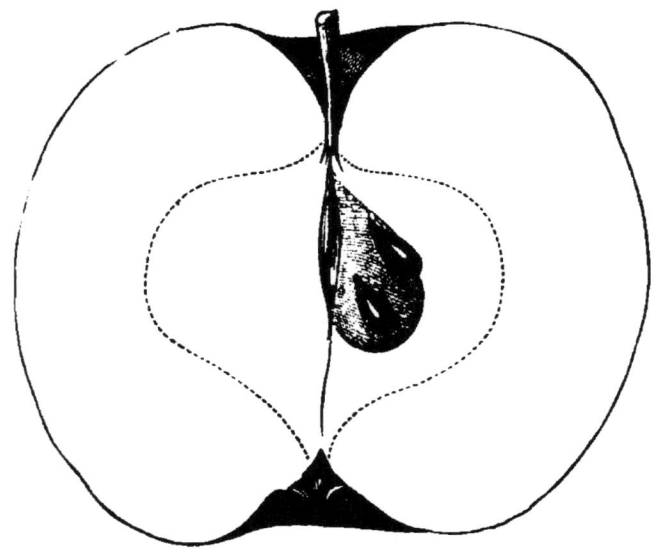

Fig. 100.—MINKLER.

smooth, greenish-yellow, covered with mixed red, and stripes of dark dull red; Dots scattered, minute, yellow.

Basin wide, shallow, regular; Eye small, closed.

Cavity acute, rather deep, brown; Stem medium.

Core large, closed, meeting the eye; Seeds numerous, long, pointed; Flesh yellow, or greenish-yellow, fine-grained, breaking, juicy; Sub-acid; Second quality; Use market and cooking; from March until May.

Newtown Spitzenberg.—[COXE.]

VANDERVERE, OF NEW YORK (Downing)—OX-EYE—JOE BERRY, ETC.

Origin, Newtown, Long Island.

Tree sufficiently vigorous, not of the largest size, spreading, compact, round head, foliage rather small, curled, showing the whitish underside. Productive.

Fruit medium to large, regular, globular-oblate, often inclined or lop-sided when overgrown in young orchards, apt to be scabby and defective on old trees, and falls badly; Surface smooth, deep red, mixed and striped, on rich yellow ground, often over-spread with whitish, giving the fruit a gray appearance; Dots numerous, minute, fawn color on dark specimens.

Basin medium, regular; Eye small, closed.

Cavity regular, medium, brown; Stem short.

Core regular, wide, somewhat open, meeting and sometimes clasping the eye; Seeds numerous, angular; Flesh rich, yellow, very fine-grained, very tender, juicy; Flavor rich sub-acid and saccharine, aromatic, eminently satisfying; Quality best, for table and kitchen, in December.

Nickajack.

SUMMEROUR—JACKSON RED—BIG HILL—CAROLINA, AND MANY OTHERS.*

This southern apple, which has extended more widely northward than most of its congeners, is believed to be a native of Macon County, Georgia.

Tree robust, spreading, large, very productive, young shoots stout and red.

The following description is that of a specimen sent by my friend, R. Peters, of Atlanta, Georgia, but it corresponds in all important particulars with those of fruits obtained from a dozen different sources in our own latitude:

Fruit large, globular-oblate, regular, not handsome; surface even but not smooth, mostly covered with mixed brick-dust red, striped indistinctly with dark red, some stripes very distinct; dots scattered, yellow.

Basin shallow, regular, even; eye small, closed.

---

* Vide Horticulturist for 1861 p. 40.

Cavity acute, regular, yellow and brown; Stem medium slender.

Core closed; Seeds numerous, large, plump; Flesh green-

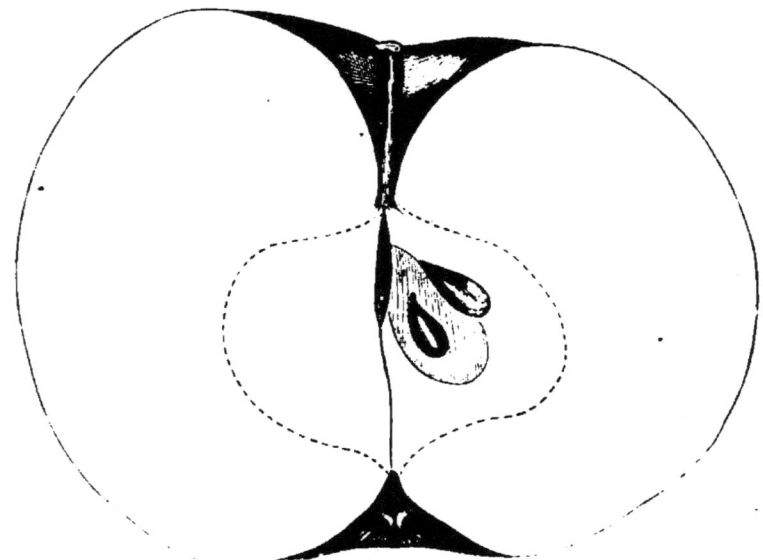

Fig. 101.—NICKAJACK.

ish-yellow, breaking, firm, coarse; Flavor sub-acid, not rich; Quality only good, a market fruit, keeping well; Season March until May.

Nyack.

NYACK PIPPIN.

Origin New York; specimen obtained from Mr. E. H. Warren, of Chelmsford, Massachusetts.

Fruit medium, flat, uneven; Surface smooth, greenish-yellow, mixed, striped, splashed bright red; Dots numerous, distinct, yellow, indented.

Basin shallow, folded; Eye small, closed; Axis short.

Cavity wide, deep, wavy, brown; Stem short, thick, knobby.

Core rather wide, closed, rather clasping; Seeds large; Flesh white, firm, juicy; Flavor acid, rich; Quality pretty good; Use table, market; Season December.

Ohio Nonpareil.

MYER'S NONPAREIL—WESTERN BEAUTY.

This fine fruit originated with Mr. Myers, near Massillon, Ohio.

It was described in the Western Horticultural Review for February, 1853.

Tree vigorous, healthy, spreading, limbs straight, stout

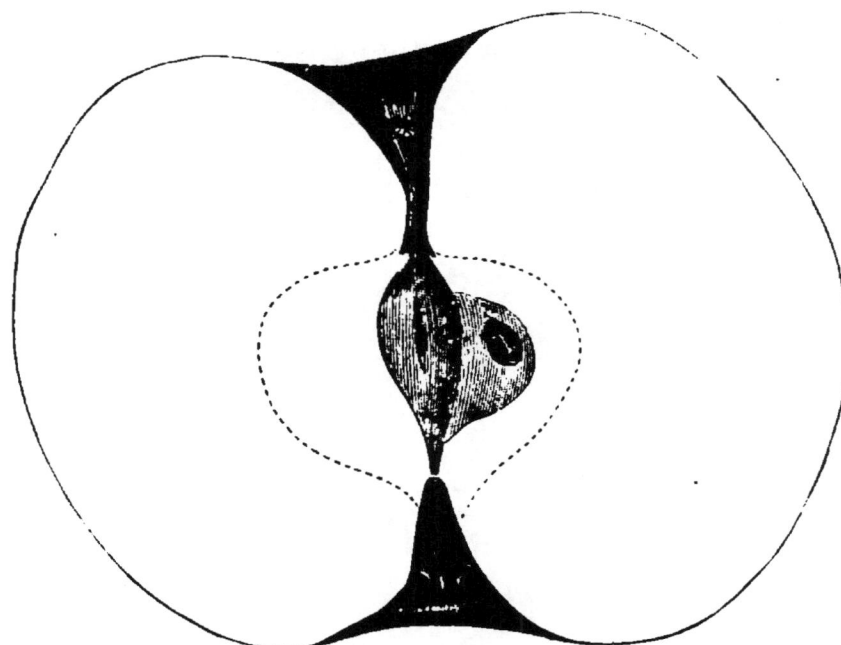

Fig. 102.—OHIO NONPAREIL.

and compact, not liable to break with the weight of fruit. The original tree had borne annual crops of even sized fruit for twenty years.

Fruit large to very large, regular, oblate, very handsome; Surface smooth, yellow, covered with bright red; Dots scattered, gray.

Basin medium, wide, regular; Eye large, closed.

Cavity deep, acute, regular; Stem short, small.

Core regular, somewhat open; Seeds numerous, medium; Flesh yellowish, tender, fine-grained, juicy; sub-

acid, rich ; First quality, for table, market, cooking or drying ; Season September to December. Compared with
some of the best dessert apples of the season, such as
Hawley, Fall Pippin, Fall Wine, Rambo, and others, this
variety was declared to be "better than the best."

Osceola.

Originated in Indiana, brought into notice by that earnest horticulturist, Henry Ward Beecher, who did much to
stimulate the culture of fine fruits when a resident of that
State.

Fruit medium, flattened, sometimes unequal, regular ;

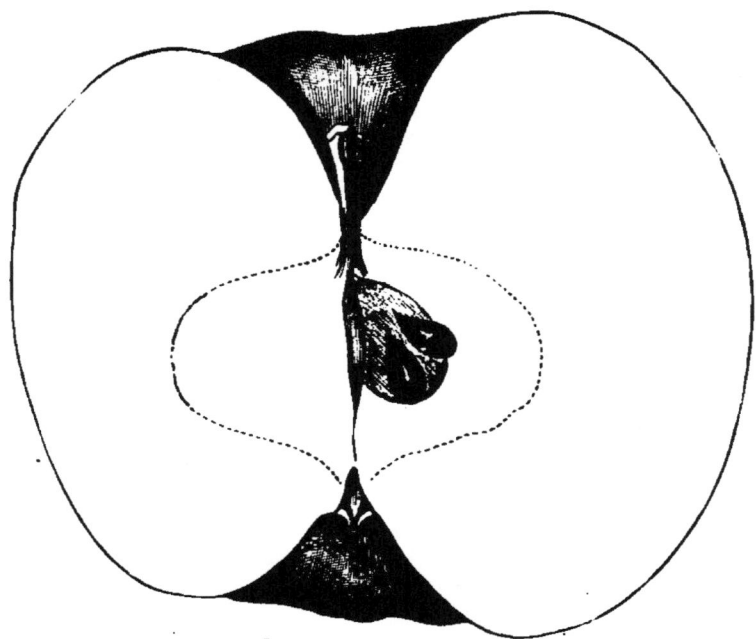

Fig. 103.—OSCEOLA.

Surface smooth, slightly colored red, and striped with the
same ; Dots scattered, irregular, more frequent and minute
about the apex, few and larger at base of the fruit.

Basin wide, regular ; Eye small, closed.

Cavity medium, acute ; Stem short.

Core small, round, closed, clasping ; Seeds numerous, plump, dark ; Flesh yellowish, firm, rich, juicy ; Flavor sub-acid, mild ; Quality good ; Use table and market ; Season January to March.

This variety does not seem to have won its way into public favor to the extent that was expected for it some years ago.

Pennock.

PENNOCK'S RED WINTER—ROMANITE—BIG ROMANITE.

This fruit, of Pennsylvania origin, is not introduced into this collection on account of its excellence, but because it is so universally cultivated in nearly all parts of the country.

Tree vigorous, large, spreading, very productive, bearing some fruit every year.

Fruit large to very large, form variable, but characteristically it is conic-oblate, often unequal, and lop-sided ; Surface greenish-yellow, covered with mixed and striped red ; Dots large, irregular and round, gray.

Basin wide, rather deep, uneven or wavy ; Eye large, open.

Cavity wide, deep, regular ; Stem short.

Core irregular, closed, meeting the eye ; Seeds numerous, angular, plump ; Flesh yellow, breaking, coarse-grained ; Flavor sub-acid, poor ; third quality ; for cooking and market only ; Season December ; very much disposed to bitter rot.

Pennsylvania Vandervere.

VANDERVERE (Coxe and Downing)—LITTLE VANDERVERE—GRAY VANDERVERE—STAALCUBS, ETC.

This old kitchen favorite, of Pennsylvania, has migrated westward until it has reached every State and county on its appropriate parallels of latitude, 39° to 42°.

Mr. Downing gives Delaware as its origin, on the authority of Coxe. In accordance with common acceptance in the regions where it is best known, I have adopted the above name, which was given to distinguish it from several other Vanderveres, and especially from the Newtown Spitzenberg, to which the name Vandervere had been applied in New York and westward on that parallel. Coxe describes the fruit in question under the name *Vandervere.*

Tree vigorous, healthy, large, spreading, very twiggy and drooping, with abundant fruit on the ends of the spray; Foliage bright yellowish-green, shining, pointed, the whole aspect of the tree peculiar and characteristic in summer or winter.

Fruit medium or less, oblate, or globular-oblate, regular; Surface smooth, but having raised hemispherical warts of a yellow russet color, yellow, mottled, and striped light red, often a gray appearance over the whole exterior; Dots large, yellow, indented.

Basin wide, regular, not deep; Eye small, closed.

Cavity wide, regular; Stem long, slender.

Core regular, closed, meeting and clasping the eye; seeds numerous, pointed, plump; Flesh yellow, breaking, granular, juicy; Flavor highly aromatic, acid; Quality for table third, for kitchen first, for cider Coxe says very good, yielding a heavy must; Season December and January.

The fruit is subject to bitter rot, and does not keep well, but may be used for cooking as soon as any other apple, making good sauce in July, when not half grown.

Pottinger.

BIG RED.

This large market fruit is found chiefly in regions settled by immigrants from the South, and it may prove to be the same as some other southern apple. Specimens first received from my friend J. B. Orange, in Southern Illinois, afterwards from several other points.

Tree vigorous, large, branches upright, shoots purple, warty, buds long, pointed.

Fruit large, regular, oblate; Surface not smooth, dull red, shaded and striped, covering the yellow ground; Dots small, prominent, with some roughness.

Basin regular, wide, not deep; Eye small, closed.

Cavity wide, regular, green and brown; Stem medium to short.

Core closed, or nearly so, meeting and partially clasping the eye; Axis short; Seeds numerous, plump, angular; Flesh yellow, breaking, granular, juicy; Flavor sub-acid, aromatic; Quality only good; Useful for kitchen and dry-

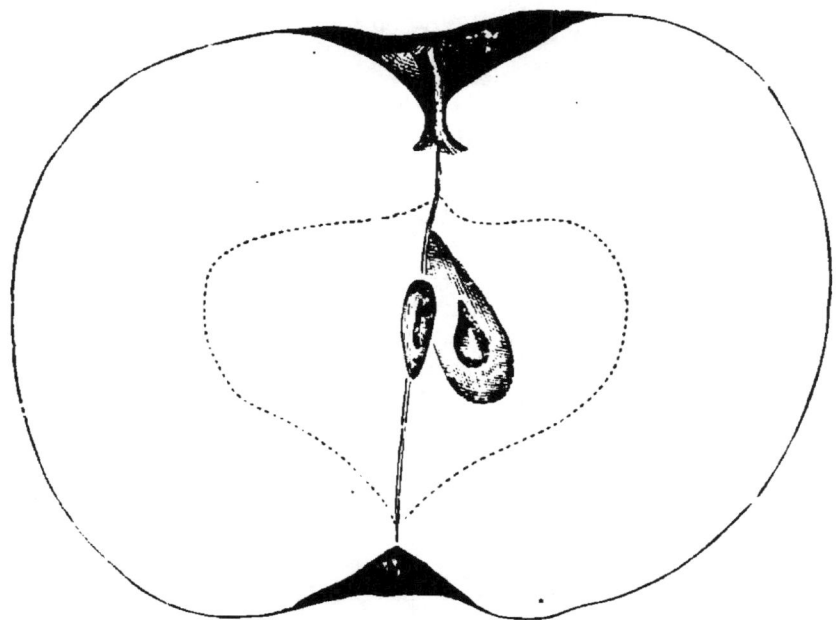

Fig. 104.—POTTINGER.

ing; Season December and January; keeps well.

Press Ewing.

This Kentucky apple was sent me by J. S. Downer, from whom trees were also procured which have already borne fruit.

Tree vigorous, healthy, and early productive.

Fruit resembles Smokehouse, medium, roundish-oblate, regular; Surface smooth, bright red, mixed, striped, and splashed, on greenish yellow; Dots numerous, brown and yellow.

Basin wide, wavy, regular, rather deep; Eye medium, open; calyx reflexed.

Cavity wide, wavy, brown; Stem long, slender.

Core medium, closed, meeting the eye; Axis short; Seeds numerous, angular, pointed; Flesh yellow, fine-grained, tender, melting, juicy; Flavor rich sub-acid; Quality

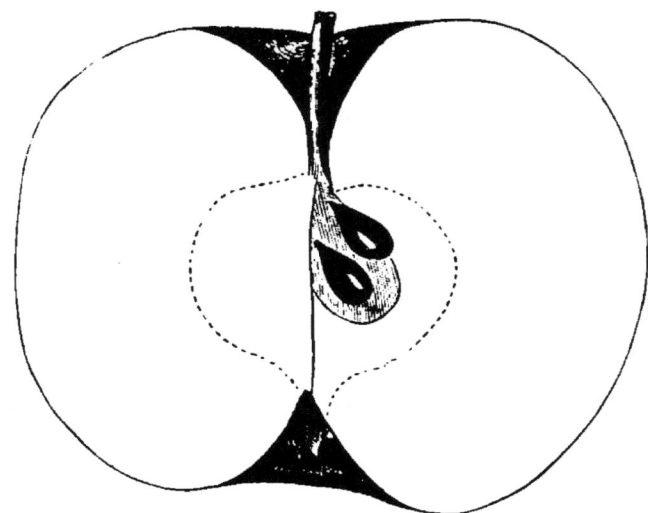

Fig. 105.—PRESS EWING.

nearly first rate; Use for table in December and January.

Powers.

This beautiful table apple was first brought to public notice by Geo. Powers, of Perrysburgh, Ohio. He exhibited specimens at the Toledo meeting of the Ohio Pomological Society in January, 1864, but the fruit was over ripe; at the State Fair at Dayton, Ohio, October 16th, it was shown in perfection of beauty and excellence, and was then examined by the Society, who commended it highly, and being satisfied that it was an original seedling, its local name, *Miller's Apple*, was then changed to *Powers*, in honor of the pomologist who had brought it into notice.

The tree appears to have been an accidental seedling, which sprang up in the town of Perrysburgh, where it grew almost without care until it fruited a few years ago, and attracted the attention of Mr. Powers.

The fruit is large and fair, round, somewhat flattened, and sometimes rather conic, generally regular, but large specimens are slightly angular; the surface is very smooth, a greenish waxen yellow, more or less shaded with mixed light red, upon which are laid numerous stripes and broken splashes of rich, dark carmine; Dots minute, scattered, gray.

Basin abrupt, regular, or folded; Eye small, closed.

Cavity deep, regular, sometimes brown; Stem medium or short.

Core medium or wide, regular, closed, meeting the eye; Seeds numerous, plump, sometimes imperfect; Flesh white,

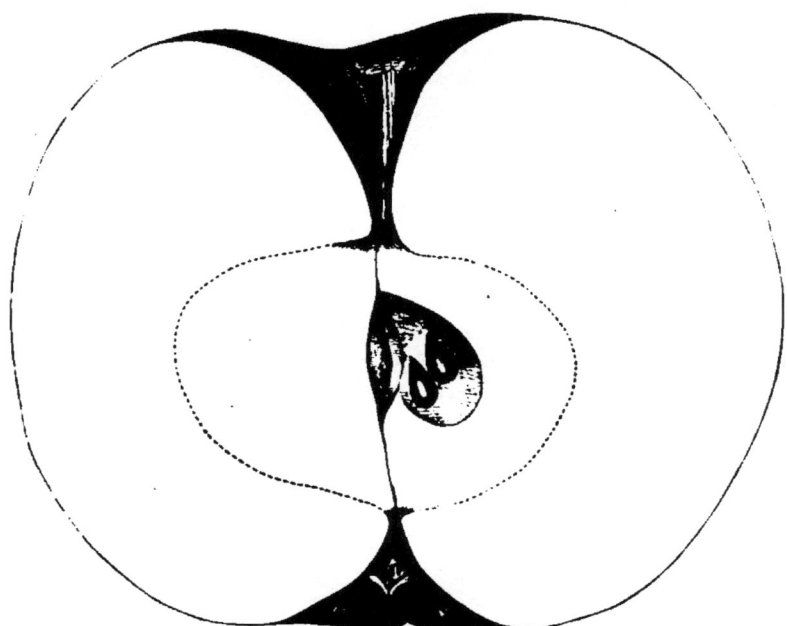

Fig. 106.—POWERS.

very tender, juicy; Flavor mild sub-acid, quite aromatic, very agreeable; Use especially for the table, as a highly ornamental dessert fruit, for which its extreme delicacy adapts it, while the same quality unfits it for general market purposes; Quality very good; in its season of ripening, in its beautifully white and tender flesh, and in its perfumed flavor, this fruit resembles the *Fameuse*, from which it may have been produced.

Prolific Beauty.

This showy fruit is one of the original Putnam list of Washington County, Ohio; it is somewhat singular that so few choice sorts are traceable to the seeds of these first good orchards of the West. Rome Beauty is almost the only one of great notoriety that is referable to this source.

Fruit large, sometimes quite large, oblate, somewhat conic, regular; Surface smooth, yellowish-green, partially covered with stripes of red; Dots minute, gray.

Basin medium, wide, regular; Eye small, closed.

Cavity wide, wavy, green; Stem medium.

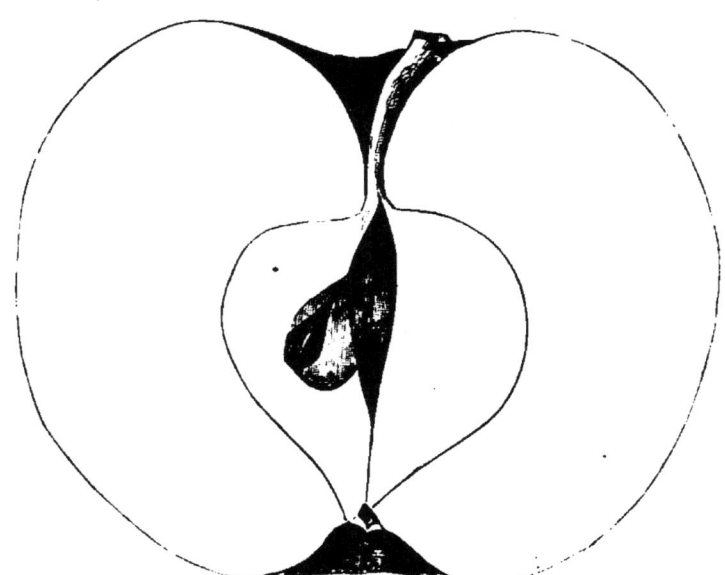

Fig. 107.—PROLIFIC BEAUTY.

Core large, regular, open, clasping; Seeds numerous, plump; Flesh whitish-yellow, tender, juicy; Flavor acid; quality scarcely good; Use kitchen, market; Season September to December.

Rambo.

ROMANITE OF NEW JERSEY—BREAD-AND-CHEESE, ETC.

This standard Eastern Pennsylvania variety is universally popular, and through the Western States it marks the progress of emigration from the Keystone State, though its admirers are not confined to that class of our population. It is a fall and early winter fruit, and some pomologists on the southern borders of its culture object to it that it will not keep long, and that it soon becomes dry and mealy when put away. When grown further north it is smaller, but more solid, and remains juicy until spring. It should be gathered early, even before it is well colored, and kept cool to make it retain its flavor and juiciness.

Tree upright, very thrifty, very productive; shoots dark, foliage large, light green, and thus the variety may

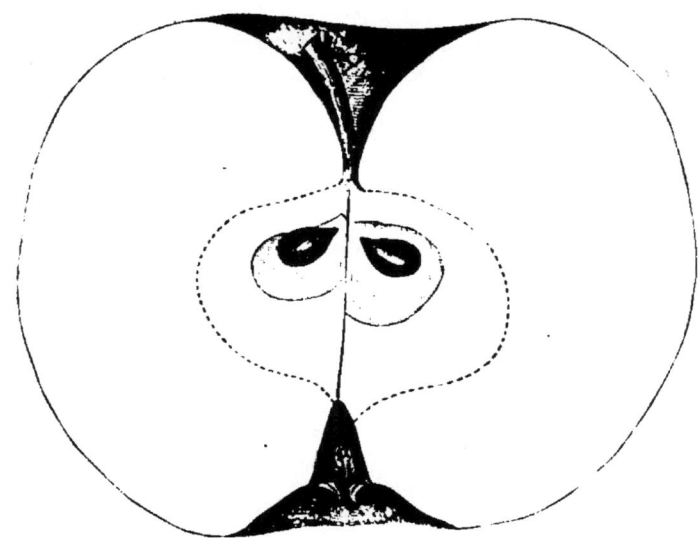

Fig. 108.—RAMBO.

easily be distinguished in the orchard. Not very hardy; whole nurseries and orchards were destroyed, in 1856, throughout the Northwest.

Fruit medium to small, when crowded upon the limbs as they generally are upon old trees, regular, oblate, or roundish-oblate, but sometimes unequal when overgrown; large specimens are flattened at the ends so as to appear truncate; Surface striped and splashed scarlet on greenish-yellow, in some the stripes coalesce so as to make the skin red, the ground color being covered; Dots numerous, small, prominent, rich bloom.

Basin wide, abrupt, regular or plaited, sometimes quite shallow; Eye small, closed.

Cavity wide, regular, always green; Stem medium.

Core regular, closed, meeting and clasping the eye; seeds numerous, large, angular; Flesh greenish-white, tender, breaking, granular, juicy; Flavor sub-acid, aromatic, vinous; Quality almost first rate for table, excellent for the kitchen; Season October to December, and if gathered early in the North, until spring.

Red Astrachan.

This Russian fruit has been perfectly adopted by our countrymen, and has proved itself a great favorite, parti-

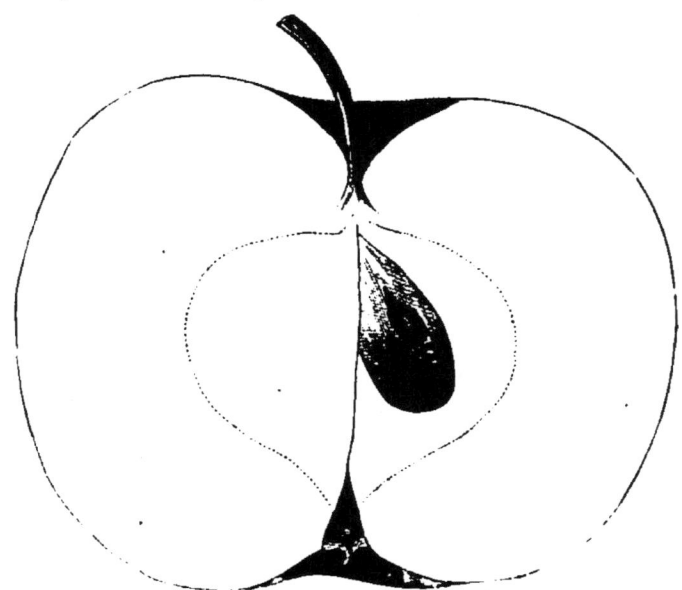

Fig. 109.—RED ASTRACHAN.

cularly in the North, by its hardiness and productiveness, beauty and good qualities.

Tree vigorous, upright, productive, hardy; Shoots reddish brown, foliage large, rich green.

Fruit medium to large, regular, oblate; Surface smooth, mottled, marbled and striped crimson on greenish-yellow; Dots minute, heavy bloom.

Basin medium, regular; Eye small, closed. .

Cavity shallow, regular; Stem long, yellow.

Core regular, closed; Seeds angular, small, dark; Flesh yellow, breaking, juicy; Flavor quite acid, not rich; Quality first rate for market and cooking, poor for table; Season July.

Richard's Graft.

RED SPITZENBERG—STRAWBERRY—WINE.

Supposed to have originated in Ulster County, New York. Tree vigorous, upright, very productive.

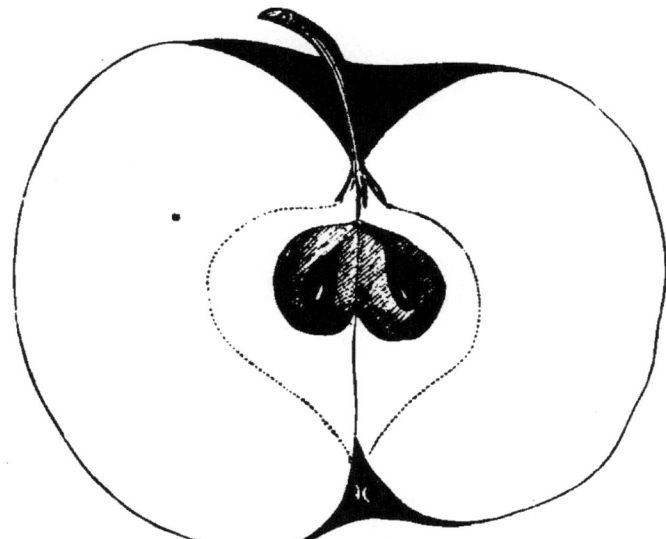

Fig. 110.—RICHARD'S GRAFT.

Fruit medium to large, regular, oblate; Surface smooth, greenish-yellow, mixed and splashed red; Dots numerous, white.

Basin medium, abrupt, folded; Eye small, closed.

Cavity wide, regular; Stem long, red.

Core small, closed, clasping the eye; Seeds numerous, plump; Flesh yellowish-white, fine-grained, tender, juicy;

20

Flavor rich, sub acid; Quality best; Use for the dessert; Season September and October.

Downing says: "One of the best dessert apples of its season."

Rome Beauty.

GILLETT'S SEEDLING.

This handsome market fruit was originated in Southern Ohio, by that sterling pioneer pomologist, II. N. Gillett, to whose contributions I acknowledge myself under many obligations.

Tree thrifty, hardy, round headed, very productive;

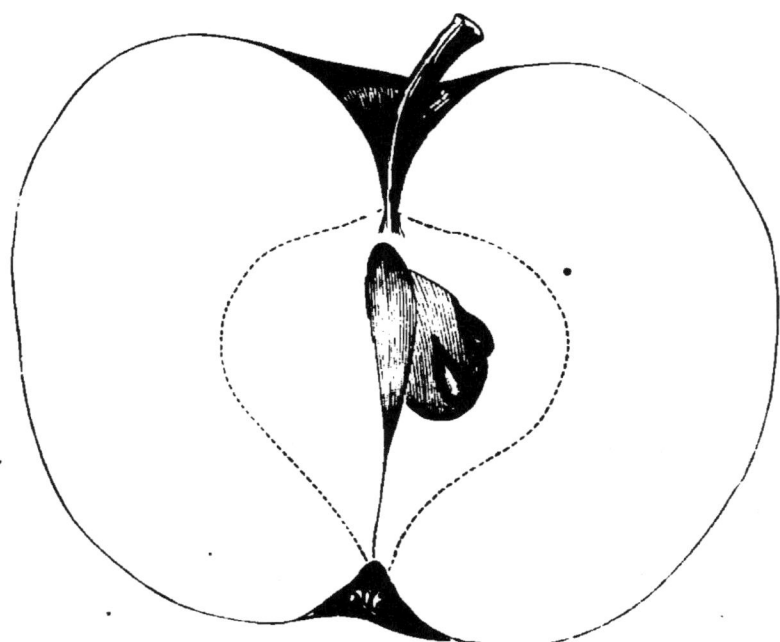

Fig. 111.—ROME BEAUTY.

shoots slender, red; Foliage healthy; Blossoms open late, and thus it often escapes a late frost; early productive.

Fruit large to very large, regular, handsome, fair, said to be scabby on old trees, regular oblate, roundish-oblate, and sometimes rather conical; Surface smooth, pale yellow, striped and mixed bright red; Dots minute, indented.

Basin wide, deep, regular; Eye quite small, closed.
Cavity wide, wavy, green; Stem long, slender.

Core wide, regular, closed, meeting the eye; Seeds numerous, long, pointed; Flesh yellow, breaking, coarsegrained; Flavor sub-acid, not rich; Quality scarcely good; valuable for market, on account of its productiveness, size and beauty, as well as for its certain bearing; Season December to February.

Shiawassee Beauty.

This Michigan apple may well be called *Beauty*. It was introduced at the meeting of the American Pomo-

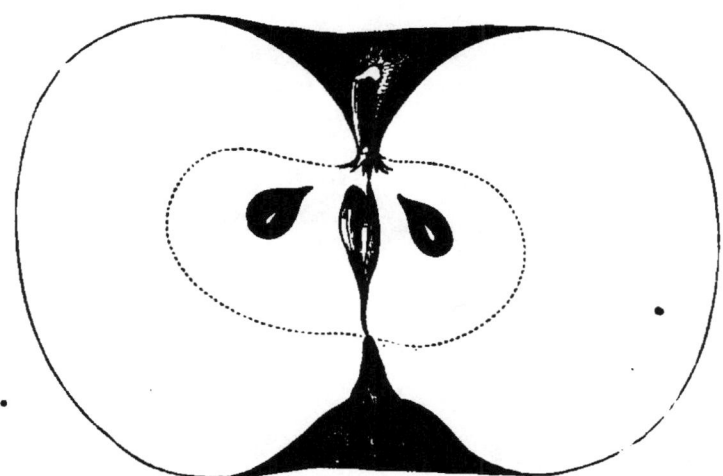

Fig. 112.—SHIAWASSEE BEAUTY.

logical Society in 1862, by T. T. Lyon, of Plymouth, Mich., who stated that it was a seedling of the Fameuse, the faults of which it does not inherit, though possessing all the good qualities of its parent, with a healthy and productive tree. (See Michigan Farmer, Dec. 11, 1859.)

Fruit medium, very handsome, very regular, quite flat; Surface very smooth, pale yellow, mixed and distinctly striped carmine; Dots scattered, minute.

Basin wide, folded; Eye medium, closed; Calyx reflexed.
Cavity wide, wavy; Stem short.

Core wide, regular, somewhat open, meeting the eye; seeds plump, short, dark; Flesh very white, fine-grained, tender, breaking; Flavor sub-acid, aromatic; Quality good to very good; Use dessert and market; Season October to January.

Summer Limbertwig.

Southern; obtained from S. Westbrooke, Greensboro', North Carolina.

Fruit medium, flat, regular; Surface pale yellow, mixed

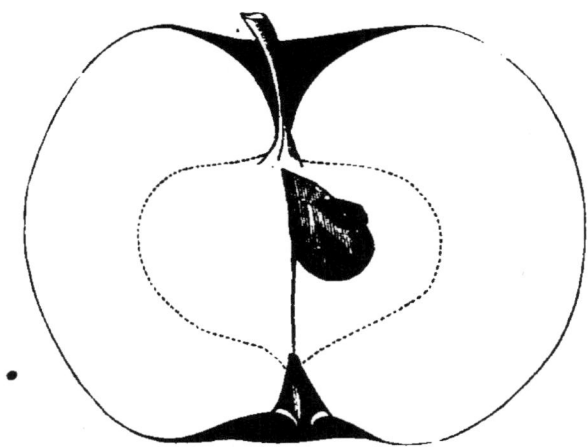

Fig. 113.—SUMMER LIMBERTWIG.

pink, striped dark red; Dots minute, gray, indented Basin shallow, wide, regular; Eye wide, open.

Cavity acute, regular, brown; Stem long, inclined.

Core wide, regular, closed, clasping; Axis short; Seeds numerous, plump, dark; Flesh white, tender, fine-grained, juicy; Flavor sub-acid, aromatic, agreeable; Quality very good, if not best; Use table; Season August, September.

Townsend.

Having been disappointed in my trees obtained for this variety, which proved to be Rawle's Janet, I prefer to quote from Mr. Downing. What I have fruited and described as the Hocking may prove to be the same.

" Origin Pennsylvania. Tree healthy, vigorous, very productive.

" Fruit medium, oblate, slightly conic. Skin pale yellow, striped and splashed with red, and covered with a thin bloom. Stalk rather long, slender, inserted into a medium cavity. Calyx closed, set in a basin of moderate depth. Flesh white, tender, very mild, agreeable, sub-acid flavor. Ripe middle of August to middle of September. Hocking of the West may prove to be the same."

Trader's Fancy.

This peculiar looking apple originated in Washington County, Pennsylvania. Tree vigorous, healthy, spreading, round-headed, very productive, bears regularly. As a long keeper, with dark skin, that does not show bruises, it became a favorite with shippers on the Ohio river, hence its name, the flat-boats that stop from port to port to dispose of their cargoes being called trading boats, and their masters traders.

Fruit medium, regular, oblate; Surface very smooth, greenish yellow, almost completely obscured with deep purple red, mixed and striped, and covered with a white bloom.

Basin wide, sometimes folded or plaited; Eye small, closed.

Cavity wide, regular; Stem medium, slender.

Core medium, closed; Seeds plump; Flesh whitish, tender, fine-grained; Flavor mild sub-acid; Quality only good; Use market and kitchen; Season January to May.

Twenty-Ounce Pippin.

Origin unknown, and the variety never should have been distributed; it is here named to put people on their guard against it when they desire to purchase the *Cayuga Red Streak*, also called the *Twenty-ounce apple.*

Fruit large, flat, regular; Surface greenish, more or less mottled and striped dull red.

Basin, wide, regular, or wavy; Eye small, open.

Cavity wide, regular, green; Stem short, thick.

Core large, closed; Seeds numerous, angular; Flesh yellow-white, breaking; Flavor acid, with a peculiar aroma, not agreeable; Quality poor; Use kitchen only; Season November to January. There are many better apples of its season.

Vance's Harvest.

A pretty little early apple grown in some parts of the West. Origin unknown.

Fruit small, flat, regular; Surface smooth, rich yellow, shaded and splashed bright red; Dots small, scattered, yellow.

Basin small, regular; Eye small, closed.

Cavity wide, regular, brown; Stem long.

Core wide, regular, meeting the eye; Seeds numerous, short, plump, dark; Flesh yellow, firm, breaking, not very juicy; Flavor acid to sub-acid; Quality pretty good; Use kitchen and market; Season August.

Vandervere Pippin.

LARGE VANDERVERE—WATSON'S VANDERVERE—VANDERVERE (Elliott)— YELLOW VANDERVERE—and several others in the books.

There appears to have been much confusion in the minds of authors who have written of this fruit, which, in some parts of the country is very well known and much cultivated. I have taken the name by which it is almost universally recognized by cultivators, though it is adopted only as a synonym by Mr. Elliott, who seems to have confounded this apple with the *Pennsylvania Vandervere* or *Staalcubs* described by Coxe.

Origin believed to have been Pennsylvania, but this is not well established.

Tree very vigorous, large, spreading, productive, bearing annually; Twigs and leaves much like the Pennsylvania Vandervere.

Fruit large to very large, regular, oblate; surface smooth, yellow, more or less covered with marbled red, and scarlet stripes; Dots large, yellow, indented, sometimes irregularly net-veined, making it less smooth.

Basin wide, regular; Eye small, closed.

Cavity wide, regular; Stem long, medium size.

Core regular, closed, meeting and clasping the eye; Seeds numerous, dark; Flesh yellow, firm, breaking, granular, juicy, heavy; Flavor rich, acid; Quality poor for table, excellent for cooking; Season December. Does not keep well, rather subject to bitter rot, but a great favorite with house-keepers, and a useful shade tree near the kitchen door.

Vaughan's Winter.

This Kentucky variety was sent to me by my friend J. S. Downer, of Fairview, Kentucky, with several other new southern apples of merit. Tree vigorous, hardy and productive, bearing fruit early.

Fruit medium, regular, round-oblate; Surface smooth,

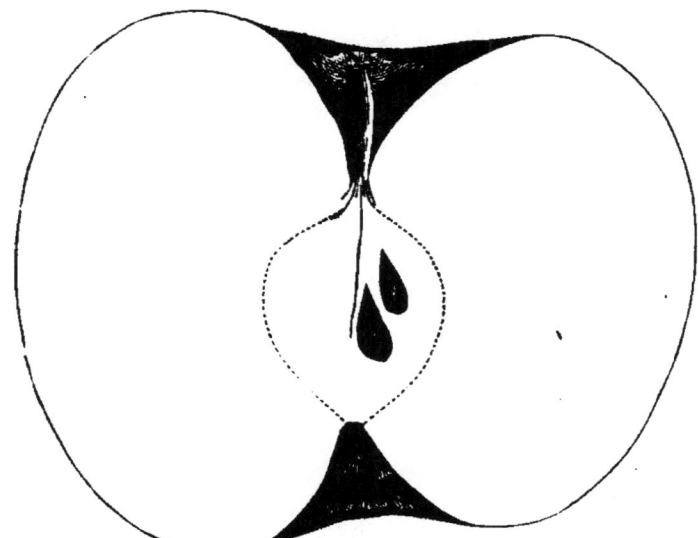

Fig. 115.—VAUGHAN'S WINTER.

greenish-yellow, mixed and splashed with bright red and splashes of carmine; Dots small, gray and yellow.

Basin regular, abrupt, medium, and leather-cracked; Eye large, open; Segments reflexed.

Cavity medium, yellow and brown; Stem short.

Core small, regular, closed, meeting the eye; Seeds few, large, brown; Flesh yellow, breaking, fine-grained, juicy; Flavor sub-acid, good; December.

Western Beauty.

MUSGROVE'S COOPER—BIG RAMBO—OHIO BEAUTY.

A valuable fall and early winter fruit, the origin of which is not known; it is considerably grown in Central Ohio, and has attracted attention under its synonyms as given. It was at one time thought to be the Cooper.

Mr. W. F. English, of Auglaize County, Ohio, carried grafts into that region from Pickaway County, and in a most disinterested manner exerted himself to distribute

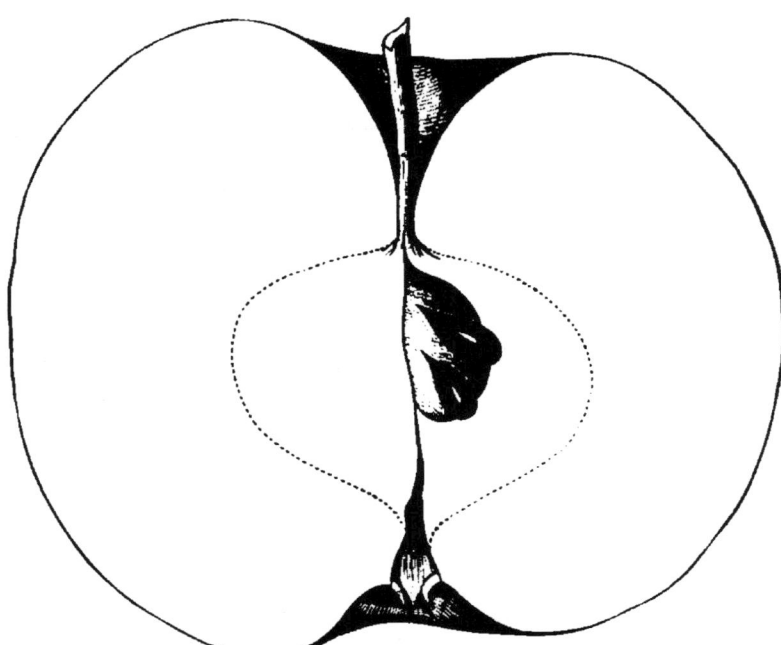

Fig. 116.—WESTERN BEAUTY.

the variety. In a communication to the *Western Horticultural Review*, for February, 1853, he says: "The tree is vigorous, leaves upon young shoots are often three to three and a half inches broad, and four or five, and even six inches long; shoots stout, being often as large as your little finger at the end of the summer's growth. The form of the tree is peculiar, and its appearance beautiful; once seen, it may be recognized anywhere by its habit."

Having fruited this variety in my own orchard, I can confirm the above, and add:

Tree vigorous, large, spreading, open head, productive, an early bearer.

Fruit large, sometimes very large, beautiful, regular, oblate, not disposed to rot, except when attacked by the birds, which are very fond of it; Surface smooth, pale yellow, partially covered with mixed red, striped and often distinctly splashed with bright red; Dots numerous, gray, prominent; Skin quite thin.

Basin wide, regular, sometimes cracked open; Eye large, closed.

Cavity wide, regular, green, and partly brown; Stem either short or long.

Core large, nearly closed, clasping the eye; Seeds numerous, medium, pointed; Flesh light yellow, almost white, brittle, tender, juicy, almost melting, never water-cored; Flavor sub-acid, vinous, delicious, satisfying; Quality best; either for table or cooking, for the latter purpose they may be taken when half grown in the beginning of July. In August they may be house-ripened and found good, but the proper season is September to Christmas; if properly cared for they may be preserved plump until March, but lose some of their refreshing flavor.

Wilson.

This very nice little apple was sent to me with this name from Western Virginia, by Julius Brace, who found it abundant on Paint Creek. I have not yet been able to identify it, but it may prove to be the same as some of our new southern varieties. An outline and description are here given with its local name, in the hope that if it should prove to be the same as the *Black Annette*, of the Clinch river region of Virginia, or some other variety, the identity may be the more readily traced.

Fruit small, regular, oblate, or globular-oblate; Surface smooth, nearly covered with very deep red, in which the stripes are almost obscured; Dots numerous, minute, white.

20*

Basin, deep, regular, plaited or folded; Eye small, closed.

Cavity regular, acute; Stem long, red.

Core regular, closed, meeting, not clasping the eye; Seeds small, plump; Flesh white, fine-grained, crisp, tender,

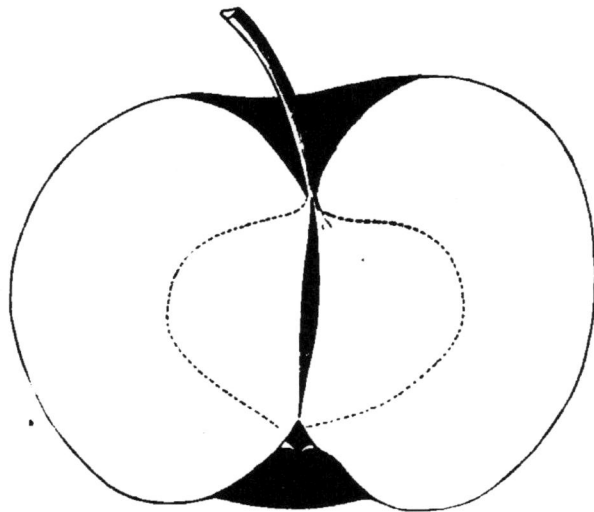

Fig. 117.—WILSON.

juicy; Flavor mild sub-acid, agreeable; Quality best; Use table; Season January.

This is different from Wilson's of Michigan, which is yellow.

Wine.—[*Coxe.*]

HAYS' WINTER—PENNSYLVANIA RED STREAK.

This handsome large apple is another index of the source of population in a western county. It is a favorite fruit with those who know it, either for market or the kitchen, for which its size and form render it peculiarly attractive.

Tree very large and handsome, spreading and very open head; leaves small, curled, and mealy, making the foliage appear rather meagre, and displaying the splendid fruit, which is evenly distributed.

Fruit large, globular-oblate, flattened or truncate, regular, occasionally unequal and lop-sided; Surface smooth, yellow, more or less covered with mixed and broken stripes of red, splashed with crimson; Dots scattered, large, gray.

Basin rather shallow, wide, abrupt; Eye small, closed, or open from breaking of the calyx.

Cavity acute, regular, brown; Stem short, thick.

Core medium, regular, closed; Seeds numerous, large, angular; Flesh yellow, firm, breaking, juicy; Flavor acid to sub-acid, rich; Quality good, for market and kitchen; Season, November and December.

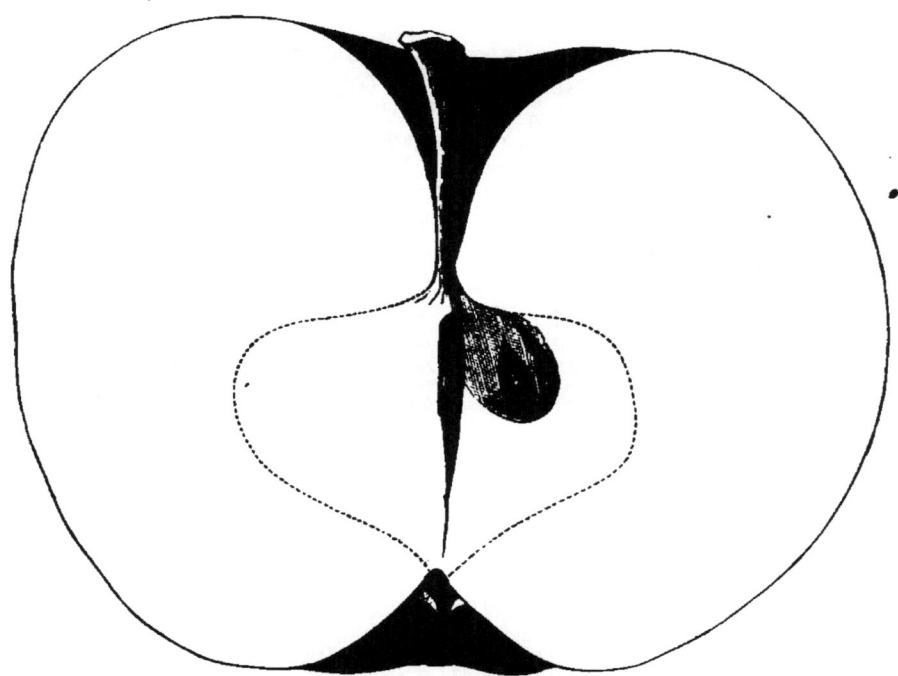

Fig. 117.—WINTER QUEEN.

Winter Queen.—[Coxe.]

FALL QUEEN—KENTUCKY QUEEN—ROBERTSON'S SUPERB (of Ga.)

This is a favorite, of southern origin, and has many synonims. An excellent apple for drying, for family use and for market. Tree thrifty, upright, productive, early bearer; limbs long and parallel while young; shoots dark, stout; foliage large, broad, rather pale.

Fruit large, often very large, globular-oblate, somewhat conic, regular; Surface smooth, often polished, yellow, almost wholly obscured with marbled dull red, and darker stripes that are often lost in the depth of tint; Dots generally small, indented; often a slight bloom covers the fruit, but it is easily removed, when the skin appears to be polished.

Basin deep, abrupt, narrow, often wavy or even ribbed; Eye medium, closed.

Cavity deep, wide, green, wavy or regular; Stem medium.

Core regular, closed, meeting, not clasping the eye axis is sometimes very short; Seeds large, plump; Flesh greenish-white, tender, almost melting, juicy; Flavor mild sub-acid, agreeable; Quality good to very good; Use dessert, kitchen and drying; Season October to January.

Yost.

Having been disappointed in receiving this apple, I give Dr. W. D. Brincklé's ad interim report:

Fruit rather large, roundish-oblate, beautifully striped, and delicately mottled with crimson on yellow ground; Stem short; Cavity wide, deep; Flesh yellow, tender, juicy; Flavor pleasant; Quality very good.

———————

CLASS I.—FLAT APPLES.

ORDER I—REGULAR.

SECTION 2.—SOUR.

SUB-SECTION 3.—RUSSET.

Perry Russet.

This variety is grown to some extent in the North-west. The specimen from which the description is made, was exhibited by Mr. Utters, at a meeting of the North-western Fruit Growers, in 1850.

Fruit medium to large, oblate, regular; Surface smooth, yellow, covered with fine russet; Dots minute, scattered. Basin medium, regular, wavy; Eye large, closed.

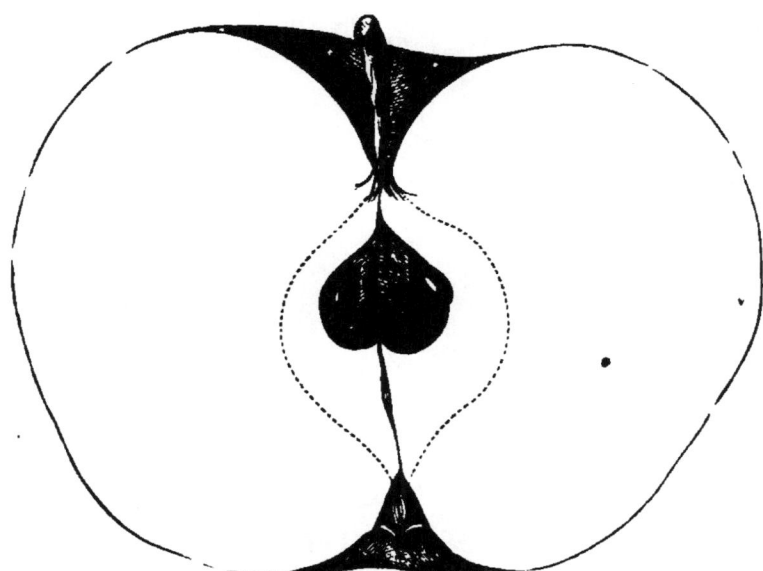

Fig. 118.—PERRY RUSSET.

Cavity medium, regular or wavy, brown; Stem medium size and length.

Core small, closed, meeting the eye; Seeds few, plump, brown; Flesh yellow, fine grained, juicy; Flavor acid, rich; Quality almost best, for table or kitchen; Season, December and January.

Pomme Grise.

Supposed to be of French or Canadian origin. Tree sufficiently vigorous, productive; shoots slender.

Fruit small, roundish-oblate, regular; Surface even but hardly smooth, yellow, overspread with fine russet, rarely blushed.

Basin wide, regular, sometimes abrupt; Eye very small, closed.

Cavity wide, regular; Stem short or medium.

Core full heart-shaped, regular, closed, scarcely meet-ing the eye; Seeds plump, angular; Flesh firm, yellow,

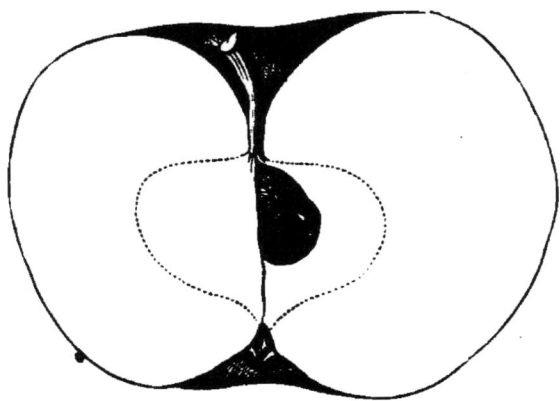

Fig. 119.—POMME GRISE.

breaking, fine grained, juicy; Flavor sub-acid, rich, aro-matic, delicious; Quality *best*, for dessert; Season, January to March; One of the very best of the Russets.

Willis Russet.

This apple was brought from Massachusetts, by my friend and neighbor B. F. Sanford, without any history of its origin. The quality of the fruit has induced me to give its description.

Fruit medium to small, roundish-oblate; Surface rough, yellow, shaded with light red, covered with russet.

Basin shallow, folded; Eye long, closed.

Cavity wide, wavy; Stem long.

Core large, wide, open, clasping; Seeds numerous, plump; Flesh yellow, breaking, fine grained, juicy; Flavor acid or sub-acid, aromatic; Quality almost first rate, for the table; Season, December and January.

CLASS I.—FLAT APPLES.

ORDER II.—REGULAR IN FORM.

SECTION 1.—SWEET.

SUB-SECTION 1.—SELF-COLORED.

Autumnal Sweet Swaar.

SWEET SWAAR.

The fruit is highly commended by J. J. Thomas, who thinks it "one of the finest autumnal sweet apples."

Tree vigorous, spreading, productive.

Fruit large, roundish-oblate, somewhat angular; Surface

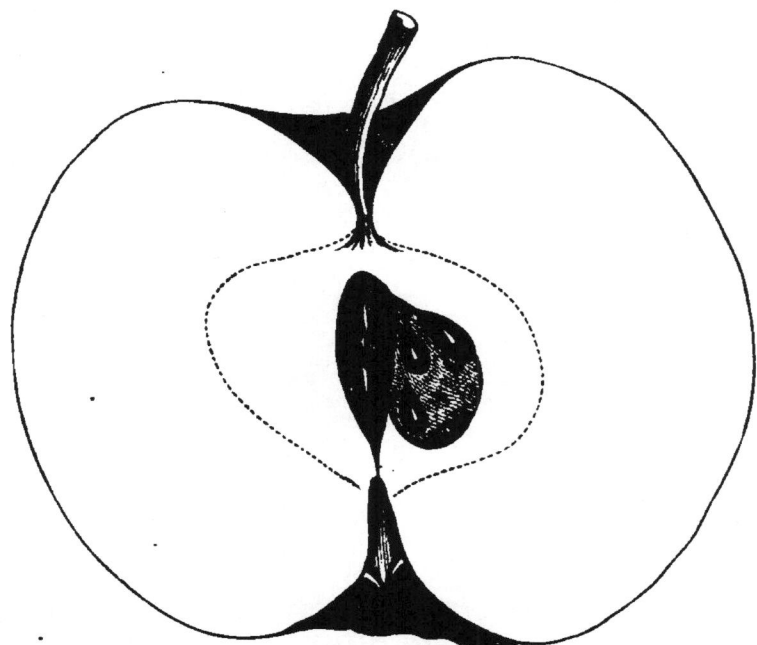

Fig. 120.—AUTUMNAL SWEET SWAAR.

smooth, waxen yellow, sometimes blushed; Dots rare, minute.

Basin wide, shallow, plaited or folded; Eye medium, long, closed.

Cavity acute, deep, wavy, green; Stem long, inclined, yellow and red.

Core regular, globular, somewhat open, clasping; Seeds numerous, plump, pale; Flesh white, fine grained, juicy; Flavor very sweet; Quality best, for baking and market; Season, September and October.

Challenge.

This is another of the apples introduced by Mr. Elliott, from the orchard of D. C. Richmond, near Sandusky, O.

Tree productive, hardy.

Fruit medium, globular-oblate; Surface smooth, pale

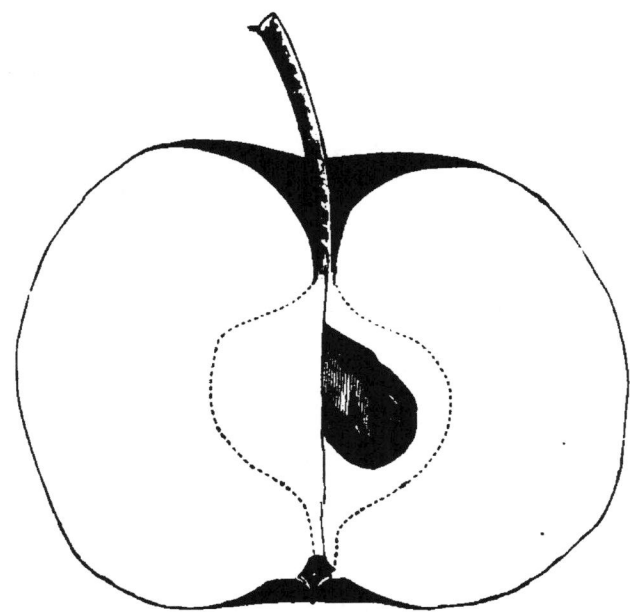

Fig. 121.—CHALLENGE.

yellow; Dots black, minute, scattered, and russet spots, becoming a rich vermillion where exposed.

Basin shallow, wide, plaited; Eye small, closed.

Cavity wide, regular, brown; Stem long, slender.

Core small, oval, regular, sometimes open, not meeting

the eye; Seeds large, dark; Flesh yellow, tender, fine grained, juicy; Flavor sweet; Quality almost first rate, for table; Season, October.

Delight.

This variety is grown in the southwestern part of Ohio; origin unknown.

Fruit medium to large, round-oblate, irregular; Surface smooth, yellow, bronzed; Dots minute.

Basin narrow, folded uneven; Eye medium, closed; Segments short.

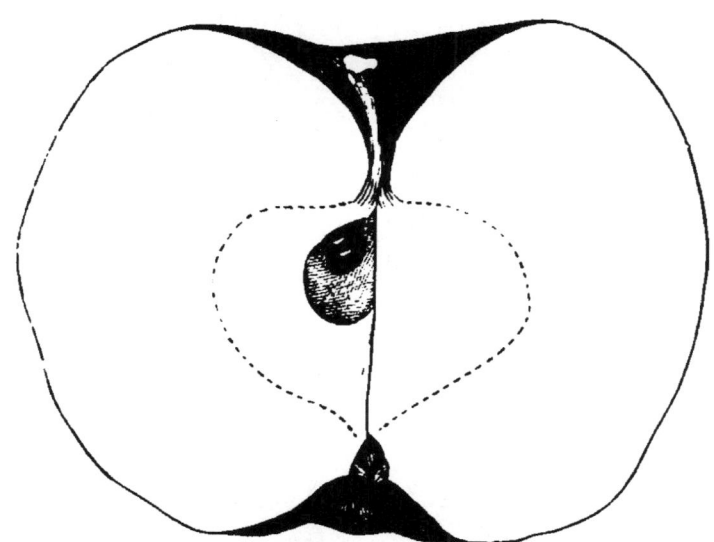

Fig. 122.—DELIGHT.

Cavity wide, regular, brown; Stem short, thick.

Core small, oval, closed, meeting the eye; Seeds numerous, plump, dark; Flesh yellow, tender, juicy; Flavor sweet; Quality pretty good; Use, market and baking; Season, January to June.

Maverack Sweet.

Origin South Carolina.

"Fruit large, roundish-oblate, angular; Skin yellow,

mostly shaded with crimson, sprinkled with gray or green-ish dots; Stalk short, inserted into a large cavity surround-ed by russet; Calyx open, set in a deep, irregular basin; Flesh rich, pleasant, vinous, almost saccharine." — [Downing.

Spice Sweeting.

The specimens described were from Mr. Warren, of Massachusetts. Others, found in Ohio and Illinois under this name, have a deep, abrupt basin, large or long eye, and yellow flesh; they must be different fruits.

An old variety; Tree vigorous, productive.

Fruit full medium to large, handsome, flat, irregular; Surface smooth, yellow, bronzy, crimson; Dots numerous, green.

Basin shallow, folded; Eye small, closed.

Cavity acute, wavy; Stem thick, knobby.

Core very wide, open, meeting the eye; Seeds pointed, long, dark; Flesh very white, tender, fine grained, juicy; Flavor sweet; Quality good; Use, kitchen, baking, stock; Season, September, October.

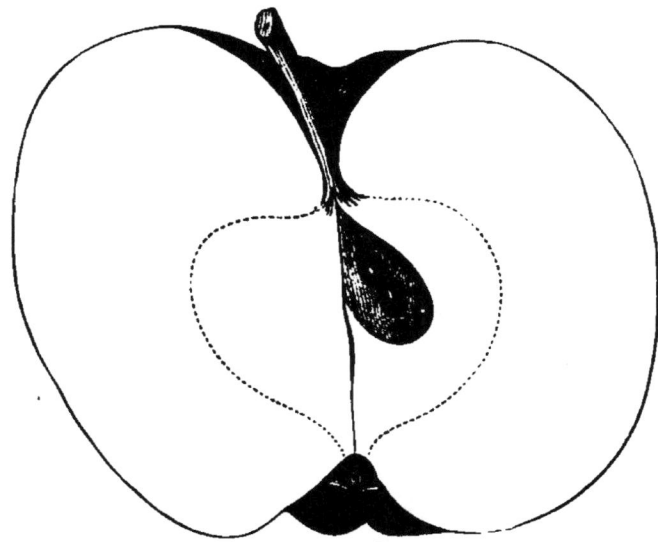

Fig. 123.—SWEET AND SOUR.

Sweet and Sour.

This variety is interesting as a curiosity, rather than valuable for its good qualities. It has been suggested that it might be a sport; no educated nurseryman will now believe the old story of its having been produced by the combination of the buds of two varieties, a sweet and a sour.

Fruit large, oblate, often unequal and lop-sided, ribbed, and deeply furrowed.

Surface yellow and green, the ribs being developed and ripening have flavor, but the furrows not being developed are flavorless and called sweet.

Sweet Sponge.

From H. N. Gillett; Origin unknown.

Fruit medium, oblate, irregular; Surface smooth, yellowish white; Dots minute.

Basin none or extremely shallow, folded; Eye long, closed.

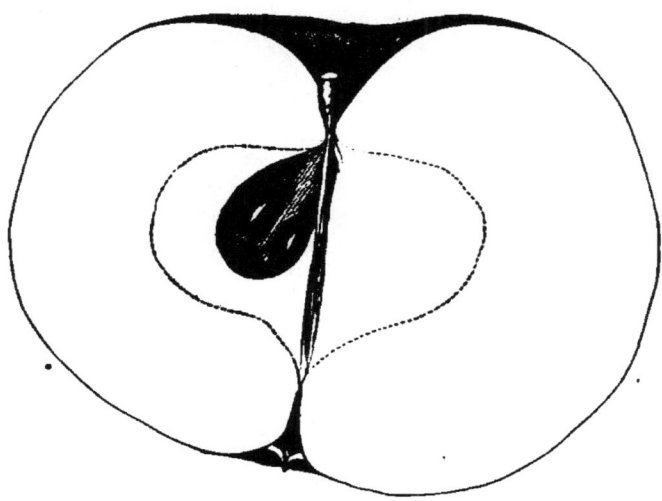

Fig. 124.—SWEET SPONGE.

Cavity wide, irregular; Stem short, thick.

Core wide, closed, scarce meeting the eye; Seeds numerous, plump, brown; Flesh white, tender; Flavor sweet; Season, July.

CLASS I.—FLAT APPLES.

ORDER II.—IRREGULAR.

SECTION 1.—SWEET.

SUB-SECTION 2.—STRIPED.

Angle Sweet.

Fruit medium, round-oblate, irregular; Surface smooth, yellow, covered with stripes and splashes of red, some darker; Dots white.

"Flesh yellow, tender, sweet, and good, fair and handsome; Season, first of September."—[Downing.

Peach Pond Sweet.

Origin Dutchess County, New York.

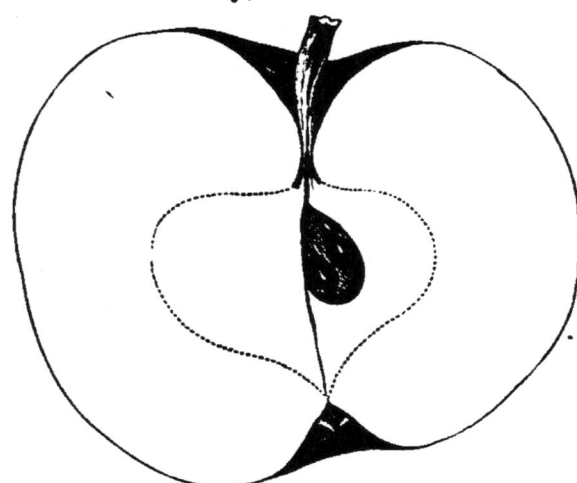

Fig. 125.—PEACH POND SWEET.

Fruit small to medium, round-oblate, pentangular, slightly conical; Surface smooth, pale yellow, lightly covered with mixed and striped red, and beautifully splashed crimson.

Basin narrow, regular or folded; Eye small, closed.

Cavity deep, acute, regular, brown; Stem medium to long, green, sometimes knobby.

Core regular, heart-shaped, closed, meeting the eye; Seeds small, short; Flesh yellow, tender, fine grained, juicy; Flavor very sweet; Quality almost first rate, very good; for table or baking; Season September.

Phillips' Sweet.

Origin believed to be Ohio; Downing says, Chotocton County, Ohio.

Tree vigorous, healthy, growth upright, very productive. Elliott thinks it may prove to be the same with Richmond.

Fruit roundish, flattened, slightly conical, obscurely angular or flattened on the sides; Surface smooth, yellow, more or less covered with red, striped crimson; Dots numerous.

Basin abrupt, regular, closed; Eye closed, segments of calyx long.

Cavity large; Stem medium length, rather slender.

Flesh yellow, tender, crisp, juicy; Flavor sweet, spicy, rich · Season, November to March.

Wing Sweet.

Tree very productive.

Fruit medium, oblate, angular; Surface very smooth, yellow, mostly covered with red, indistinctly striped darker red.

Basin wide, deep, regular or folded; Eye small, closed.

Cavity acute; Stem long.

Core small, regular, closed, scarcely touching the eye; Seeds ovate; Flesh yellow, tender, dry; Flavor sweet and rich; Quality good; baking; early winter.

CLASS I.—FLAT APPLES.

ORDER II.—IRREGULAR.

SECTION 2—ACID.

SUB-SECTION 1.—SELF-COLORED.

Blockley.

BLOCKLEY PIPPIN, O. POM. SOC.

Originated near Philadelphia, Pennsylvania. Tree moderately vigorous, upright, productive.

Fruit large, round-oblate, flattened at the ends, five-sided, angular; Surface smooth, greenish-yellow, blushed; Dots numerous, small, distinct, dark.

Basin wide, rather deep, wavy or folded; Eye small, closed, or partly open.

Cavity acute, narrow, uneven, brown; Stem quite short, rather thick.

Core medium, heart-shaped; Seeds numerous, angular and imperfect, dark; Flesh yellow, compact, almost melting, fine grained, juicy; Flavor rich sub-acid, sprightly; Quality almost best, for table; Season, November to January.

Bracken.

This variety has caused much discussion among the Western Pomologists, on account of its resemblance to the Early Harvest. The late Dr. Barker, one of the most intelligent fruit-growers of the country, said it was introduced as a seedling from Kentucky in 1812. Elliott does not mention it in his work, but in the discussions of the Society he is reported as having declared it the same as Early Harvest, with which it agrees in peculiar growth of twigs. H. N. Gillett, and others, familiar with the fruits of southern Ohio, consider it a distinct seedling of Kentucky. The specimen described was from that gentleman.

Fruit medium, oblate, somewhat conical, irregular and angular; Surface smooth, pale yellow; Dots scattered, dark.

Basin abrupt, medium, folded; Eye small, closed.

Cavity wide, deep, irregular, brown; Stem large, knobby.

Core irregular, closed, meeting the eye; Seeds angular,

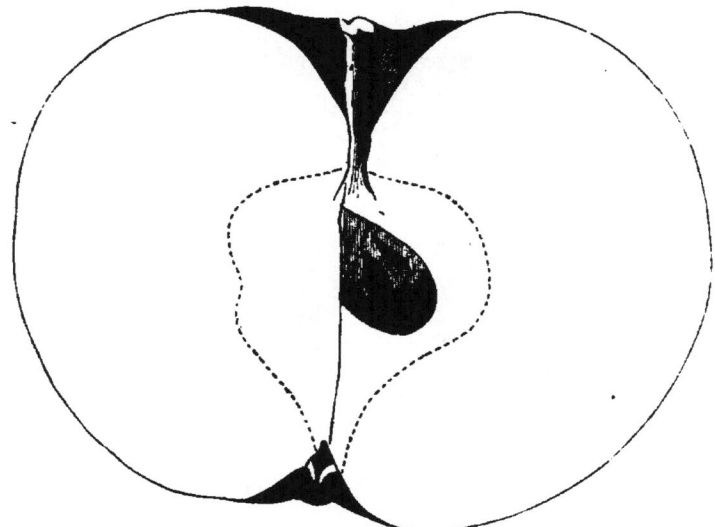

Fig. 126.—BRACKEN.

imperfect; Flesh white, very tender, fine grained; Flavor mild sub-acid; Quality good; Use, table and kitchen; Season, June, July; earlier than Early Harvest.

Canada Reinette.

This fine fruit does not appear to be well known to our orchardists, and some of our writers have given the White Pippin among its numerous synonims, and have suggested that they might be the same, which is not so; they are very distinct. I have omitted the synon'ms, as they can be of little interest to our planters; they are not used in this country. The origin of this variety is uncertain, probably European. Downing says that Merlet, a French writer, described the fruit in the 17th century.

Tree vigorous, robust, tall spreading, productive.

The following outline and description of a specimen presented by Irvin Jessup, of Laporte, Indiana, was kindly made for me by my lamented friend, Geo. M. Beeler, a short time before his death.

Fruit large, oblate, angular; Surface not smooth, yellow, blushed and spotted red; Dots numerous, small, gray.

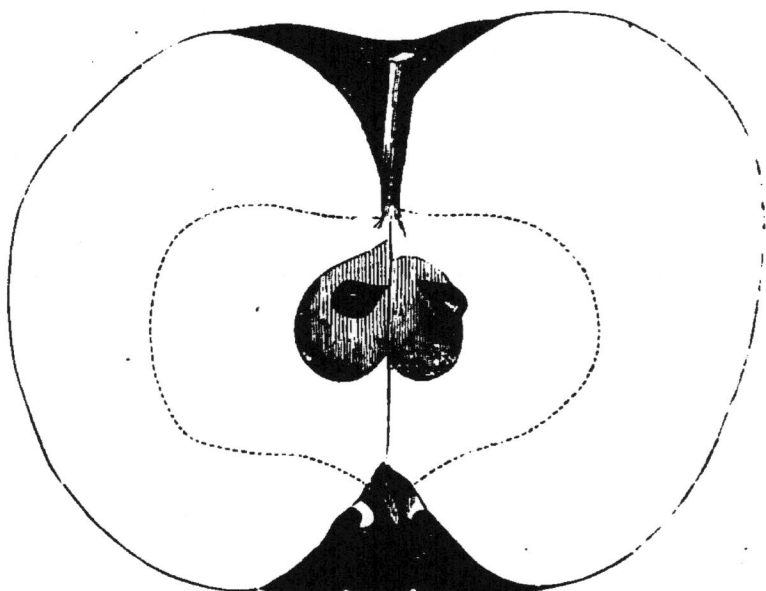

Fig. 127.—CANADA REINETTE.

Basin abrupt, deep, angular; Eye small, nearly closed. Cavity medium, acute; Stem medium, inclined.

Core wide, regular, closed, clasping; Seeds plump, angular, dark; Flesh breaking, fine grained, very juicy; Flavor acid to sub-acid, aromatic, rich; Quality very good; Use, table and cooking; Season, December to February, in northern Indiana.

Culp.

Origin Jefferson County, Ohio; exhibited at the meetings of the Ohio Pomological Society as early as 1855, by S. B. Marshall, of Massillon, whose friend, S. Wood, had cultivated it several years; my specimens and trees are from the Massillon nursery.

Tree vigorous, thrifty, symmetrical, spreading, very productive, not an early bearer.

Fruit fair, sound, large, somewhat angular, oblate, inclined to conic, hangs well on the tree; Surface smooth, green with bronze blush; Dots minute, with green bases.

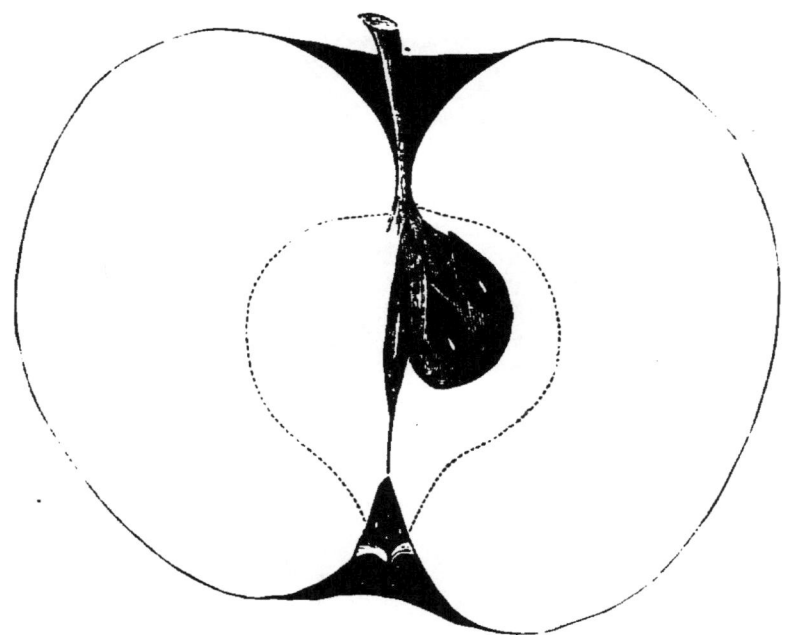

Fig. 128.—CULP.

Basin narrow, rather abrupt, regular; Eye rather large, closed.

Cavity rather deep, regular, brown; Stem long or short.

Core long heart-shaped, regular, nearly closed, clasping; seeds numerous, very large, dark brown; Flesh yellowish, compact, crisp, juicy; Flavor mild sub-acid, slightly perfumed; Quality good; excellent for cooking, "compared to Rhode Island Greening;" Season, December until April.

21

Fall Harvey.

Origin Essex County, Massachusetts. Specimen from Zanesville, Ohio.

Fruit large, oblate, irregular; Surface smooth, yellow or pale yellow; Dots minute, gray, distinct.

Basin wide, regular, leather-craked; Eye medium, closed.

Cavity wide, wavy, green; Stem long to medium.

Core wide or globular, regular, closed, not meeting the eye; Seeds medium, pointed and defective; Flesh yellow, breaking; Flavor rich, acid; Quality only good, but valuable for the kitchen; Season, October.

Garretson's Early.

Origin supposed to be New Jersey. Tree vigorous; an early and abundant bearer.

Fruit medium, globular-oblate, somewhat angular; Surface smooth, pale yellow; Dots whitish.

Basin small, abrupt, furrowed; Eye small, closed.

Cavity shallow; Stem short, inclined.

Flesh white, breaking, tender, juicy; Flavor pleasant sub-acid; Quality good; Use, table; Season, July and August.

Harris.

This variety was received from North Carolina, and fruited for the first time in the North during 1866. It was first described and figured, among other new apples, in the Horticultural Annual for 1867. In the South it is considered a summer and fall variety, being in season from August, and continuing for a long time. For specimens, I am indebted to Doctor E. Taylor, of Cleveland, Ohio.

Fruit medium to large, oblate, angular; Surface smooth, yellow, faintly blushed; Dots scattered, minute, with rosy spots.

Basin deep, abrupt, folded; Eye medium, rather open.

Cavity deep, wavy, clear yellow; Stem medium to long.

Core small, open, meeting the eye; Axis very short; Seeds numerous, angular; Flesh light yellow, breaking, fine-grained, juicy; Flavor acid to sub-acid, spicy, agree-.

able; Use table and kitchen; Season October; Quality
good to very good.

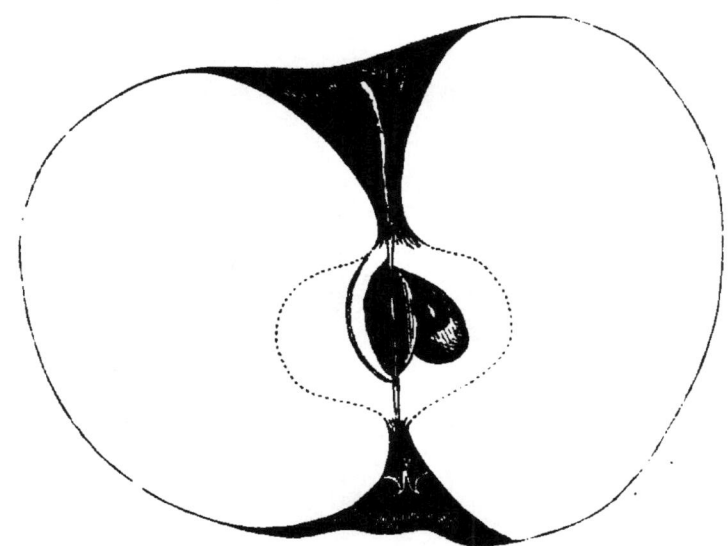

Fig. 120.—HARRIS.

Loudon Pippin.

LADY WASHINGTON?

Origin Loudon County, Virginia.   Exhibited before the
Ohio Pomological Society, by Joseph Sigler, of McConnellsville, Ohio.

Fruit large, oblate, conic, angular; Surface beautiful,
very smooth, waxy yellow, handsomely blushed, and
bright red spots; Dots scattering, gray.

Basin wide, regular or folded; Eye large, closed.

Cavity wide, not deep, regular, brown; Stem medium,
red.

Core heart-shaped, regular, closed, clasping the eye;
Seeds numerous, medium; Flesh yellowish, compact, tender, breaking; Flavor rich sub-acid, aromatic; Quality very
good; Dessert; Season, December to February.   A fine
fruit from Washington County, shown at the same time
as the *Lady Washington ;* was thought to be the same.

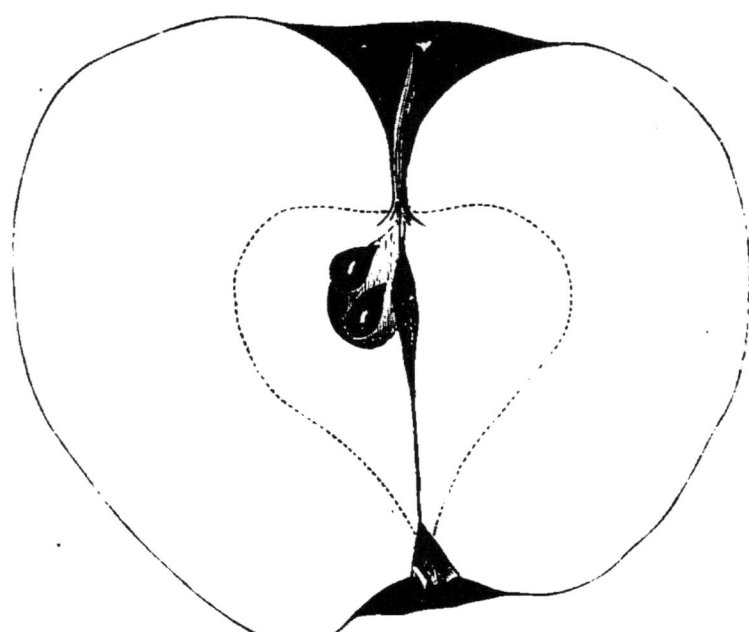

Fig. 130.—LOUDON PIPPIN.

Ohio Pippin.

ERNST'S APPLE.—BUCHANAN, ETC.—SHANNON.

We owe our acquaintance with this fine large fruit to the late Mr. A. H. Ernst, long President of the Ohio Pomological Society, who furnished trees to Mr. Robert Buchanan, an enthusiastic Pomologist of Cincinnati. Both these gentlemen were too modest to permit their names to be attached to a fruit which they did not originate, but which they have aided to distribute. Another focus of distribution was the orchard and nursery of R. W. Todd, at Madison, Indiana, and the fruit has been received under the name of Shannon, from Doctor J. A. Dibrell, of Van Buren, Arkansas. Origin Dayton, Ohio, from whence it was procured personally by Mr. Todd, many years ago, and the grafts set by him are the oldest trees known.

Tree healthy, vigorous, large, spreading; Shoots stout, dark; Leaves large.

Fruit large, often very large, oblate, somewhat conic, irregular; Surface smooth, greenish-yellow, sometimes blushed faintly near the base; Dots small gray.

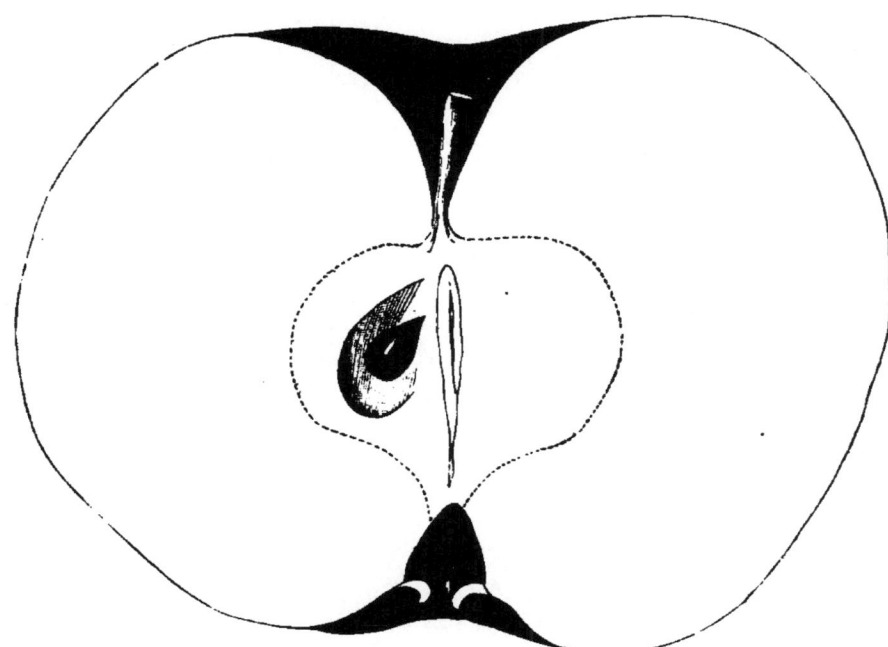

Fig. 131.—OHIO PIPPIN.

Basin wide, deep, folded; Eye large or very large, open; Segments short.

Cavity wide, wavy or regular, brown; Stem short, stout.

Core medium to large, regular, closed, meeting the eye; Seeds numerous, medium, plump, sometimes imperfect; Flesh yellowish, breaking, tender, juicy; Flavor acid to sub-acid; Quality good; Market and kitchen, too large for dessert, Season, December, January.

Western Spy.

Origin Jefferson County, Ohio. Tree healthy but medium growth, very productive; exhibited by Joel Wood.

Fruit large, roundish-oblate, uneven; Surface smooth, yellow, blushed; Dots numerous, minute, with white bases.

Basin abrupt, uneven; Eye large, closed.

Cavity medium, wavy; Stem short.

Core wide, closed, not meeting the eye; Seeds numerous, large, plump; Flesh yellow, breaking; Flavor acid; quality pretty good; Use, kitchen, table; Season, December, January.

CLASS I.—FLAT APPLES.

ORDER II.—IRREGULAR.

SECTION 2.—ACID.

SUB-SECTION 2.—STRIPED.

Berry.

Not having enjoyed an opportunity of examining this fruit, I quote from my friend Chas. Downing.

"Origin Virginia or North Carolina. Tree vigorous, upright, very productive, and a valuable market fruit.

"Fruit rather above medium, obliquely depressed; Skin striped and splashed with red, on greenish-yellow ground, with large dots, having a dark center; Stem short, in a generally broad, deep cavity; Calyx open; Basin shallow, and uneven; Flesh rather coarse, juicy, with a pleasant sub-acid flavor; November to March."

Buff.

For description of this fruit I take Downing's quotation from *White's Gardener*:

"Origin uncertain; Tree vigorous, erect; Fruit very large, irregular, roundish flattened and slightly irregular; Skin thick, yellow, striped, and shaded with red, very dark next the sun, marked with a few greenish russet spots; Stem three-fourths of an inch long, in a medium cavity; Calyx in a large, irregular basin; Flesh white, and when fully ripened, tender and excellent, sometimes indifferent; November to March.

Dana.

From Gabriel Sleath, near Cincinnati, Ohio.   The origin
of this pleasant dessert apple is not known.   Tree large,
productive.

Fruit small, flat, somewhat angular;   Surface smooth,
rich yellow partially covered mixed red, distinctly striped
carmine;   Dots pale fawn or yellow;   heavy white bloom.

Basin shallow, leather-cracked;   Eye small, long, closed.

Cavity medium, regular;   Stem quite long, slender.

Core wide, regular, open, clasping;   Seeds numerous,
short, plump, brown;   Flesh yellow, very fine grained, very
juicy;   Flavor sub-acid, sprightly, agreeable;   Quality good
to very good;   Use, dessert;   Season, August.

Gravenstein.

This fine European apple is said to have originated at
Gravenstein, Holstein.   It has long been in this country,
where it succeeds very well.

Tree vigorous, spreading, productive;   Shoots vigorous;
Leaves long, rolled, showing the white underside.

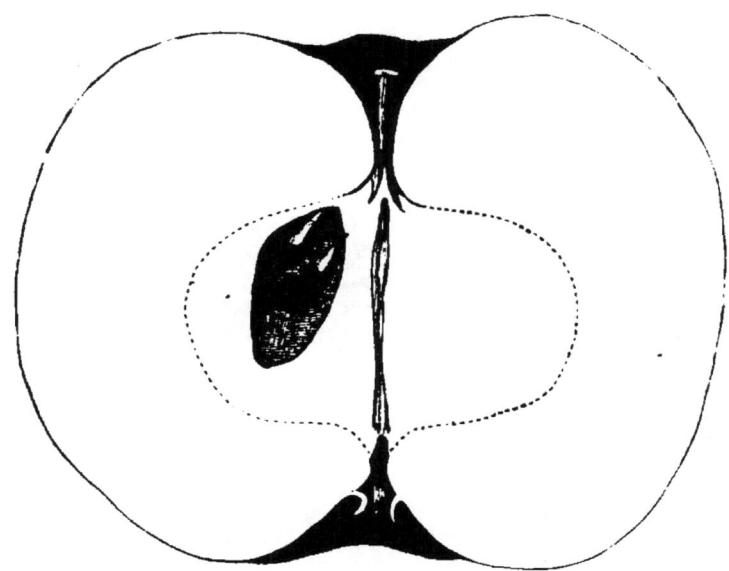

Fig. 132.—GRAVENSTEIN.

Fruit large, globular-oblate, angular; Surface smooth, yellow, partially covered with mixed and splashed scarlet; Dots rare.

Basin medium, regular; Eye small, closed.

Cavity deep, regular; Stem short.

Core regular, globular, or pointed toward the eye, closed, clasping; Seeds small, pointed; Flesh yellow, fine grained, breaking, juicy; Flavor sub-acid, aromatic; Quality best; table and kitchen; Season, August, September.

Kelser.

Origin Jefferson County, Ohio; not widely distributed. Tree thrifty, upright. The following description was made from fruit obtained of · my friend T. S. Humrick-house, of Coshocton.

Fruit full medium to large, oblate, uneven; Surface smooth, greenish-yellow, mixed and striped red; Dots scattered, minute.

Basin wide, deep, folded; Eye small, closed.

Cavity acute, deep; Stem quite short.

Core very small, regular, closed, clasping; Seeds numerous, short, plump; Flesh yellow, tender, fine grained, juicy; Quality good to best; for table and kitchen; Season, December to January.

Mangum.

A first rate southern fruit. Tree thrifty, and very productive.

Fruit medium, oblate, slightly conic, angular; skin yellowish, striped and mostly shaded with red, thickly sprinkled with whitish and bronze dots; Stem short and small, inserted in a broad cavity surrounded by russet; Calyx partially closed; Basin slightly corrugated; Flesh yellow, very tender, juicy, mild sub acid, excellent, highly prized in Georgia and the South; October and November. Carter of Alabama may prove the same."—[C. Downing.]

Melon.

Origin East Bloomfield, New York. Tree sufficiently vigorous, spreading, round-headed.

Fruit large, oblate, somewhat conical, angular; Surface smooth, waxen yellow, nearly covered with marbled and mixed scarlet, striped distinctly with darker shade; Dots minute.

Basin, wide, medium depth; Eye medium, open.

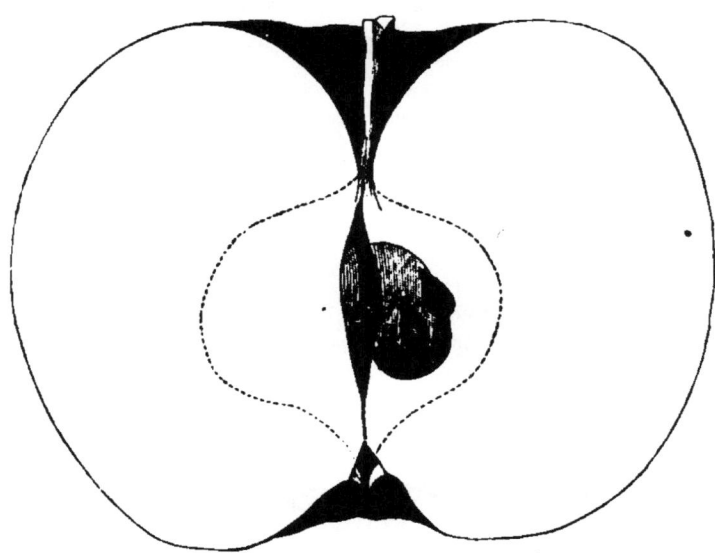

Fig. 133.—MELON.

Cavity deep, acute, wavy, green and brown; Stem medium.

Core regular, heart-shaped, wide, partially open, clasping; Seeds numerous, medium, angular; Flesh yellow, tender, fine grained, juicy; Flavor acid, sub-acid, aromatic, rich; Quality almost best; Use, table, market and kitchen; Season, November to January.

Muster.

This very nice apple was introduced to my attention by my very good friend Calvin Fletcher, Jr., of Indianapolis, in which neighborhood it grows. Its origin and history are unknown, nor do any satisfactory responses come to the oft-repeated question—What is this delicious apple?

Fruit large, oblate, angular; Surface yellow, mostly

21*

covered with mixed red and splashes of crimson; Dots scattering, large, yellow and gray.

Basin moderately deep, folded; Eye medium, open.

Cavity medium, regular, brown; Stem medium to short.

Core small, closed; Seeds plump, dark; Flesh yellow, fine-grained, tender, juicy; Flavor sub-acid, aromatic; Quality best for dessert; Season, August and September.

Pennsylvania Winesap.—[Local Name.]

Origin unknown; Grown in Wayne County, Indiana.

Fruit large, conical-oblate, truncated, angular.

Surface smooth, yellow, blushed, very little splashed; Dots scattered, minute.

Basin medium, folded, wavy; Eye medium, closed.

Cavity medium, wavy; Stem medium or short, stout, fleshy.

Core regular, closed; Seeds few, plump; Flesh yellowish-white, tender, fine-grained, juicy; Flavor sub-acid; Quality good; Use, table; Season, December, January.

Wagener.

This beautiful and useful apple originated at Penn Yan,

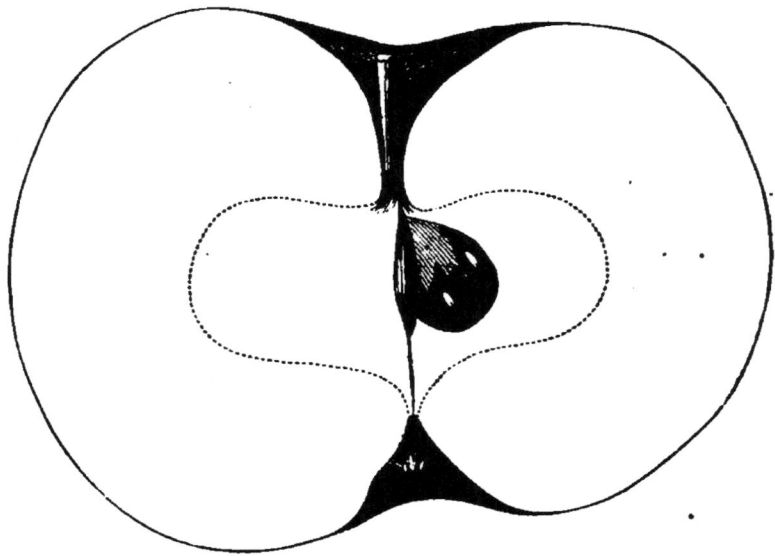

Fig. 134.—WAGENER.

Yates County, New York; was described and figured in the Transactions of the State Agricultural Society.

Tree thrifty, upright, productive, and very early bearer.

Fruit large, oblate or globular-oblate, pentangular; Surface very smooth, yellow, well covered with mixed bright red, stripes not distinct; Dots scattered, yellow.

Basin wide, abrupt, regular; Eye small, closed.

Cavity regular, brown; Stem medium, green.

Core regular, wide, heart-shaped, closed, meeting the eye; Seeds numerous, large, angular; Flesh yellowish-white, tender, fine-grained, juicy; Flavor mild sub-acid; Quality good; Uses, market, table and kitchen; Season, November and December.

CLASS I.—FLAT APPLES.

ORDER II.—IRREGULAR.

SECTION 2.—ACID.

SUB-SECTION 3.—RUSSET.

Cranberry Russet.

This apple was introduced to the notice of the Ohio Pomological Society by its Vice-President, J. Austin Scott, of Toledo, Ohio.

Fruit medium to large, oblate, flattened at the sides, irregular; Surface rough, russeted, blushed carmine, uneven; Dots numerous, large, gray, prominent.

Basin shallow, uneven; Eye small, partially open.

Cavity deep, acute, green; Stem long, slender, knobby.

Core wide, regular, closed; Seeds long, angular, brown; Flesh breaking, tender, not very juicy; Flavor quite acid; Quality second rate, but said to be superior for cooking; Season, November and December.

Roxbury Russet.

BOSTON RUSSET.—PUTNAM RUSSET.

This standard apple is perhaps as widely known and as much admired as any other in the catalogue. It was brought to the West by different routes—by the Ohio River and by the lakes—and has been universally distributed. Those brought to the mouth of the Muskingum River, and propagated by Mr. Putnam, had the name changed to that of the Marietta and the Putnam Russet; and at the same time the appearance of the fruit was so altered by increase in the russeting, that it was long thought to be a different variety, until the question was at length settled by interchange of grafts; and when these fruited the identity was proved.

It is claimed that more money has been realized from this than from any other variety, though, on the Ohio

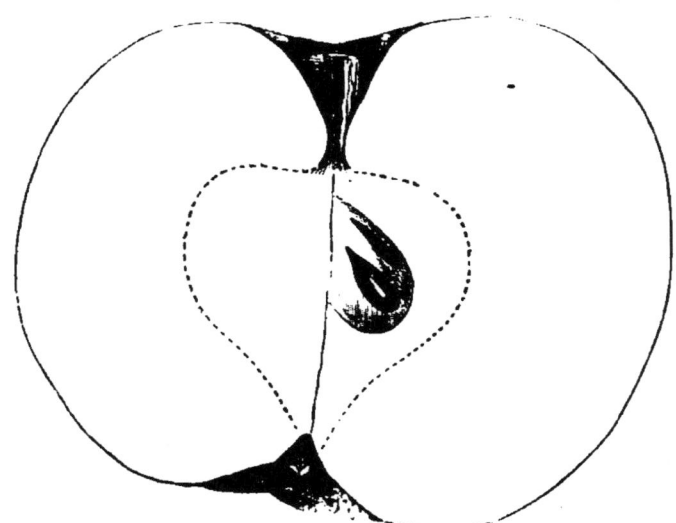

Fig. 135.—ROXBURY RUSSET.

River, the Rome Beauty is considered to be equally profitable. The popularity of this Russet is on the wane, however, as it is very subject to attacks of the Codling-moth, which makes it fall, and because it is apt to ripen too early in the season in southern locations and on limestone soils. Hence its value as a keeping apple is diminished.

Tree robust, vigorous, spreading; Shoots stout, straggling, dark; Foliage gray-green.

Fruit large, oblate, often lop-sided at the West, frequently angular, sometimes conic and truncated; Surface overspread with heavy brown russet in the South, but green, often bronzed, and with partial light russet at the north of latitude 41°; Dots minute, scattered.

Basin regular or wavy, green, often folded; Eye medium, closed.

Cavity regular, pointed; Stem medium, curved.

Core regular, closed, clasping; Seeds numerous, angular, imperfect; Flesh greenish-yellow, breaking, granular, often coarse, juicy; Flavor decidedly acid; Quality second rate; Use, market and cooking; Season, November to January; a better keeper in the North.

Whitney Russet.

Of uncertain or accidental origin in the extensive nurseries and orchards of my friend A. R. Whitney, of Franklin Grove, Lee County, Illinois, where my specimens and trees were procured.

Fruit medium or small, roundish-oblate, truncated, an-

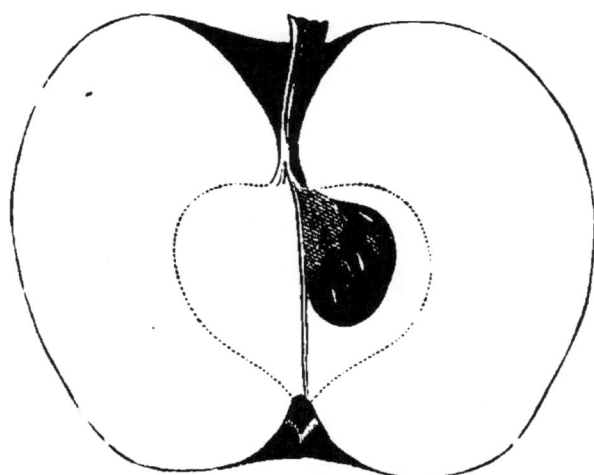

Figg. 136.—WHITNEY RUSSET.

gular; Surface smooth, yellow, rather thinly russeted; Dots minute, prominent.

Basin abrupt, regular, green; Eye medium, closed.

Cavity acute, deep, wavy; Stem medium to long, slender.

Core medium, regular, heart-shaped, rarely open, meeting the eye; Seeds very numerous, medium, plump; Flesh greenish-yellow, breaking, very fine-grained, juicy; Flavor sub-acid, aromatic, rich, spicy; Quality best; especially a dessert apple; Season, December to February.

CLASS II.—CONICAL APPLES.
ORDER I.—REGULAR.
SECTION 1.—SWÉET.
SUB-SECTION 1.—SELF-COLORED.

Large Bough.
LARGE YELLOW BOUGH, ETC.

A native fruit, much admired as an early sweet apple. Tree vigorous, compact head, rather productive.

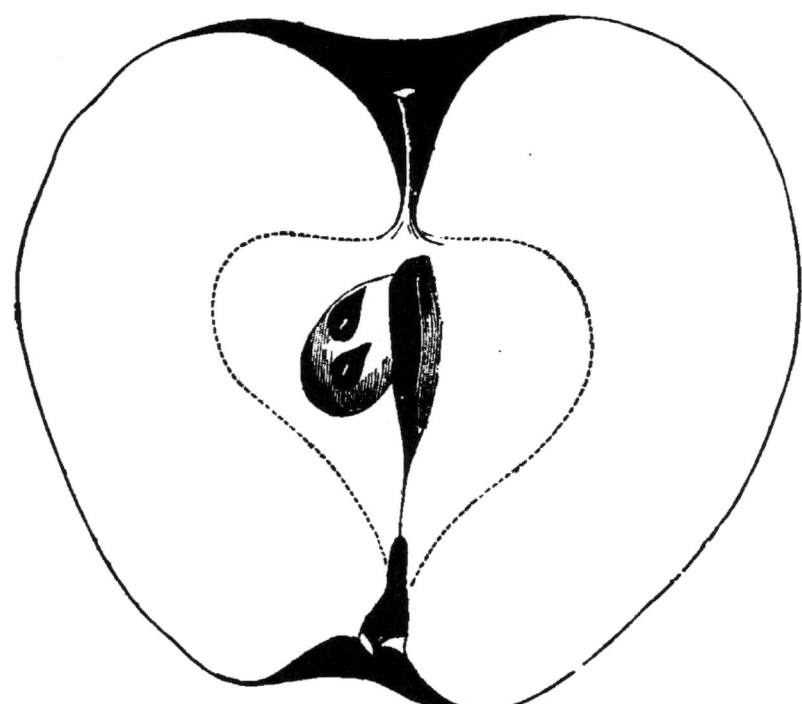

Fig. 137.—LARGE BOUGH.

Fruit round-conic, regular, very light; Surface smooth, white or pale yellow; Dots minute, dark, indented, few.

Basin rather shallow, regular; Eye small, closed.

Cavity acute, regular, deep, sometimes brown; Stem medium.

Core regular, nearly closed, clasping; Seeds medium, dark; Flesh white, very soft, light, juicy; Flavor very sweet when ripe, somewhat bitter when green; Quality only good—by some called best; Use, market, stock and dessert—tasteless when cooked; Season, July and August.

Fallawater.

TULPEHOCKEN, ETC.

A native of Pennsylvania, where it is a great favorite; extensively cultivated through the West.

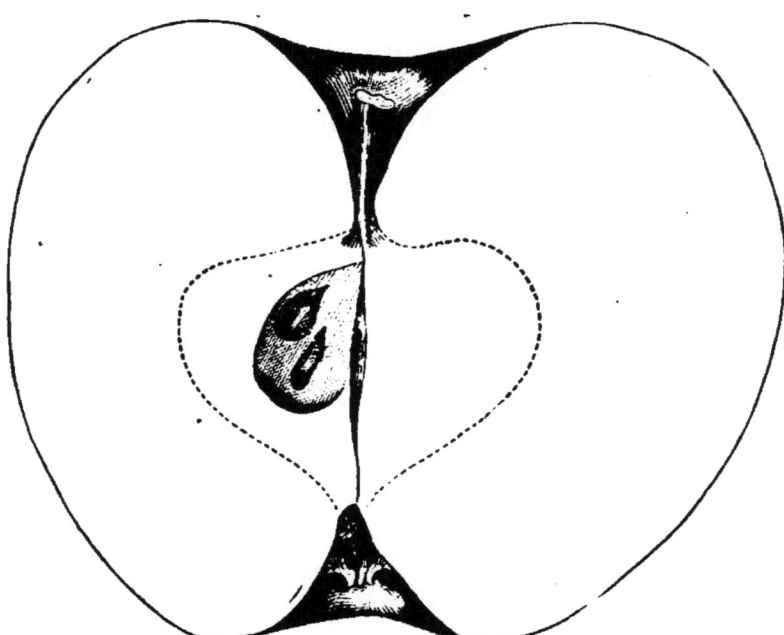

Fig. 138.—FALLAWATER.

This is essentially a market apple, having little to recommend it but its size, appearance and productiveness.

Tree very vigorous, spreading, productive, not long-lived; Shoots very stout, dark; Leaves large.

Fruit large, round or oblate-conic, regular; Surface sometimes smooth, greenish-yellow, often blushed crimson—large specimens covered with whitish veined marks; Dots numerous, gray, large, and having whitish bases.

Basin rather deep, regular; Eye large, open.

Cavity deep, regular, brown; Stem short, stout.

Core medium, closed, meeting the eye; Seeds numerous, angular; Flesh whitish, often greenish-white, light, tender, juicy; Flavor very mild sub-acid, or sweet, with little character; Quality scarcely good; Use, market and stock; Season, November, December, and may be kept longer if desired.

Michael Henry.

MICHAEL HENRY PIPPIN.—[*Coxe.*]

Origin Monmouth County, New Jersey. Extensively

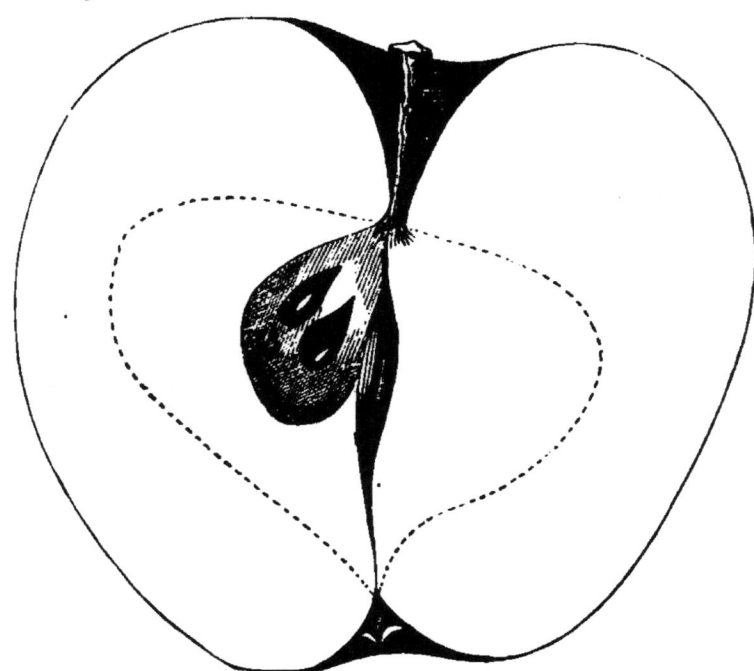

Fig. 139.—MICHAEL HENRY.

cultivated in the Western States, where it has many admirers.

Tree vigorous, not large, spreading, very productive, early bearer; Shoots dark, foliage medium and healthy.

Fruit fair, medium to large, conic, regular; Surface smooth, dull green, whitish stripes, pale yellow when ripe, rarely a faint blush; Dots scattered, prominent.

Basin abrupt, or shallow, regular; Eye medium, closed.

Cavity deep, acute, brown; Stem short to medium.

Core regular, heart-shaped, clasping, closed; Seeds numerous, plump, black; Flesh pale yellow, breaking, tender, light, juicy; Flavor sweet, slightly aromatic, little character; Quality good; Use, market, kitchen; Season, December and January; keeps well.

Premium of 1858.

Found in a seedling orchard near Springfield, Ohio, and awarded the premium in 1858.

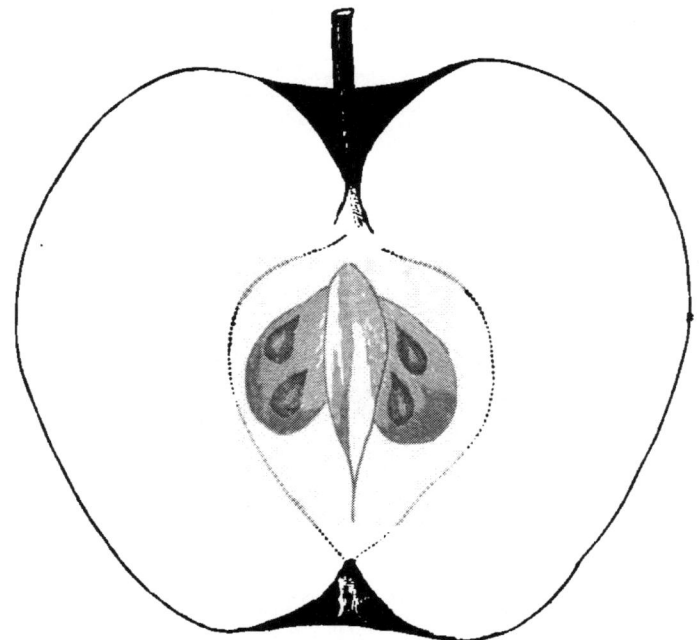

Fig. 140.—PREMIUM OF 1858.

Fruit medium, roundish-conic, regular; Surface smooth, pale yellow; Dots numerous, minute, white.

Basin shallow, regular, folded; Eye large, closed or open. Cavity wide, shallow, regular; Stem long, slender.

Core rather large, regular, open, meeting the eye; Seeds numerous, angular; Flesh yellow, fine grained, tender; Flavor very sweet, rich; Quality very good; Use, baking and stock; Season, October to December.

Shockley.

Origin Jackson County, Georgia. This long-keeper from the South promises to be an acquisition of value for market orchards, unless its small size may make an objection.

Tree vigorous, very productive.

Fruit medium to small, conic, truncated, regular; Surface very smooth, waxen yellow, marbled or blushed scarlet and crimson; Dots scattered, minute, gray.

Bas'n shallow, plaited; Eye small, closed.

Cavity acute, deep, regular; Stem slender, long.

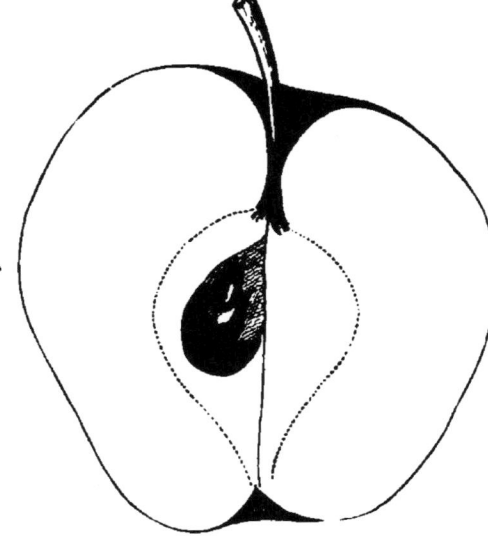

Fig. 141.—SHOCKLEY.

Core long heart-shaped, closed, meeting the eye; Seeds numerous, plump, dark; Flesh yellow, fine grained; Flavor mildly sub-acid, rich, saccharine, agreeable; Quality very good; Use, dessert; Season, March to June; a good keeper.

Sweet Pear.

The origin of this fruit is uncertain; the specimens were obtained in the orchard of H. P. Kimball, and his father-

in-law, Dr. George Haskell—zealous pomologists at Rockford, Illinois.

Fruit medium to large, round, somewhat conic, regular;
Surface smooth, yellowish-green, blushed; Dots numerous, minute, gray, indented; red spots.

Basin quite shallow, plaited; Eye small, but long, closed.

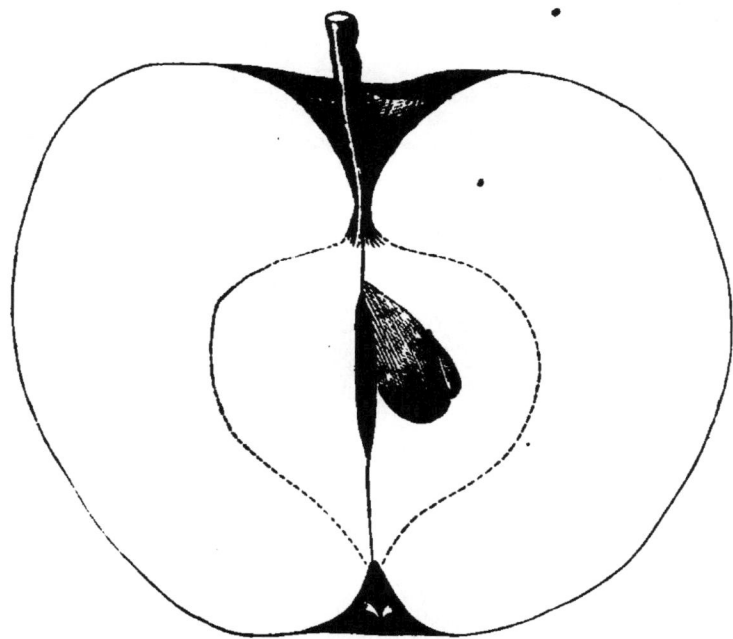

Fig. 142.—SWEET PEAR.

Cavity deep, acute, wavy, green; Stem long, rather
slender, green.

Core small, round, somewhat open, clasping the eye;
Seeds numerous, medium, pointed; Flesh greenish-white,
breaking, fine grained, juicy; Flavor sweet, aromatic;
Quality good to best; Use, table; Season, October.

Victuals and Drink.

GREEN SWEET OF INDIANA.—POMPEY.—FALL GREEN SWEET.

This old variety has met with great favor in its western
home, though not esteemed or much cultivated in the

Eastern States, unless about Newark, New Jersey, where it originated about 1750, according to Downing.

Tree spreading, large; Branches twiggy, slender, moderately productive.

• Fruit large, conical, regular, but uneven; Surface somewhat rough, dull green to dull yellow, often veined russet; Dots numerous, minute.

Basin medium, sometimes abrupt, regular or folded; Eye medium, closed.

Cavity wide, wavy, green; Stem short.

Core small, regular, oval, clasping, closed; Seeds numerous, angular, imperfect, dark; Flesh greenish-white or yellowish, very tender, fine-grained, light; Flavor very sweet, very rich; Quality best; Use, baking, table and stock; Season, September and October—in the North later, but is not a housing apple.

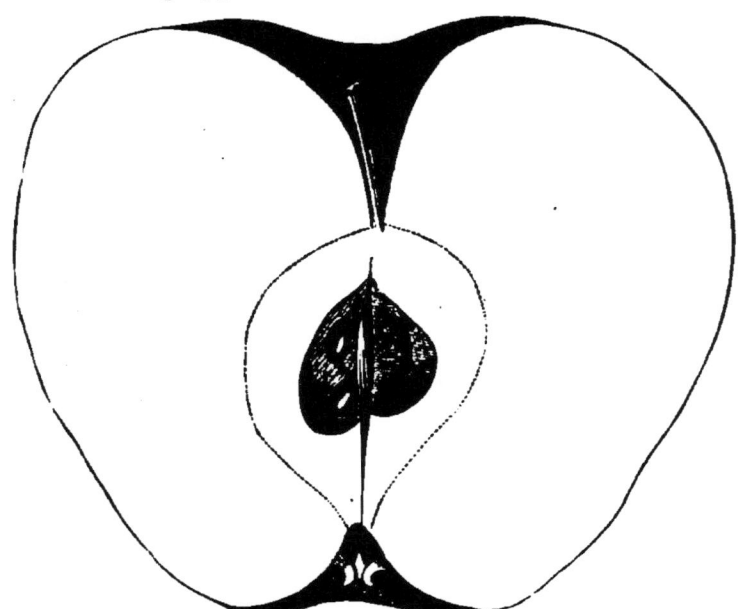

Fig. 143.—VICTUALS AND DRINK.

Virginia June.

Presented by W. P. Putnam, of Ohio, as brought from Adams County, Mississippi

Fruit medium to large, oblate-conical, regular; Surface greenish-yellow; Dots scattered, prominent.

Basin medium, regular, abrupt; Eye medium, open.

Cavity very wide, regular, brown; Stem very short.

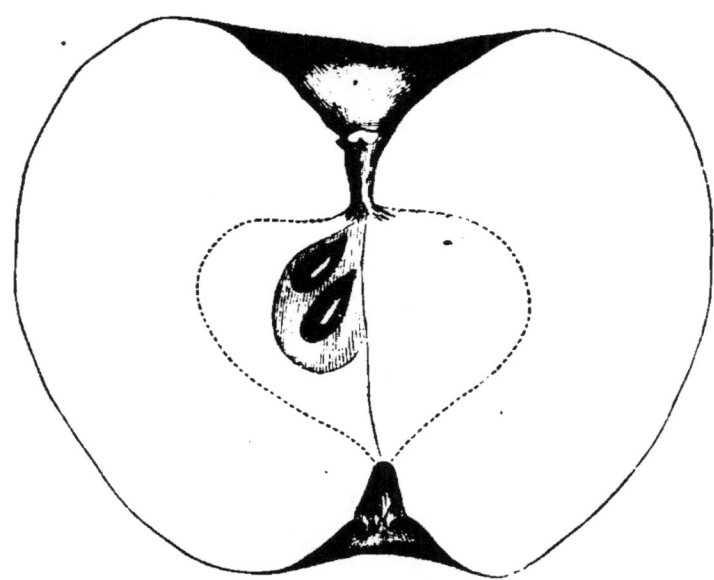

Fig. 144.—VIRGINIA JUNE

Core heart-shaped, regular, meeting the eye, closed; Seeds numerous, pointed; Flesh yellow; Flavor rich, sweet; Quality good; September to October, in Ohio.

This may prove to be some known variety, but it has not yet been recognized.

The *Virginia June*, grown in Kentucky and Indiana, is quite different, being round, striped and sub-acid. It is esteemed, where known, as a household apple, but becomes rather dry.

CLASS II.—CONICAL APPLES.

ORDER .I—REGULAR.
SECTION 1.—SWEET.
SUB-SECTION 2.—STRIPED.

Kentucky Sweet.

This is an apple of Kentucky or southern origin, found in many parts of the western country among the emigrants from Dixie Land, with whom it is a great favorite on account of abundant fruitage and rich sweetness.

Specimens, under name, were received from the intelligent southern pomologist, J. S. Downer, of Fairview, Kentucky, also from J. W. Dodge, of Pomona, Tennessee,

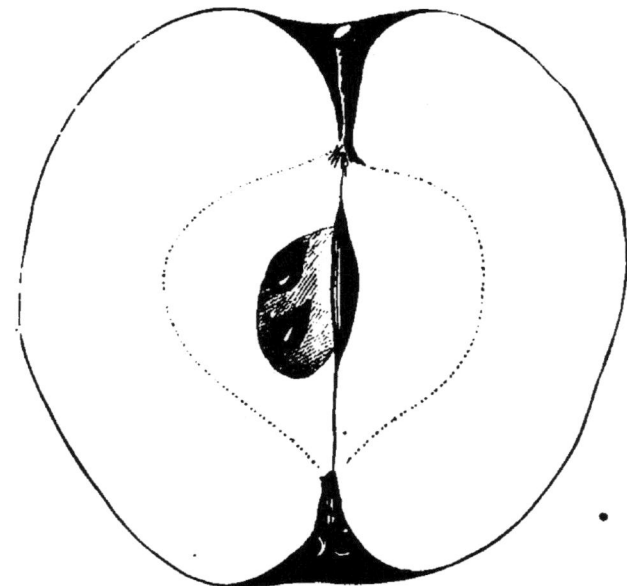

Fig. 145.—KENTUCKY SWEET.

from which the description and drawing are taken. It has also been seen frequently in Southern Illinois.

Fruit medium, conic, regular; Surface smooth, deep red, stripes obscured and scarcely visible, the yellow ground color rarely seen; Dots scattered, large, yellow.

Basin regular, narrow, not deep, leather-cracked; Eye medium, long, open; Segments short.

Cavity acute, not deep, brown ; Stem short to medium.
Core oval, regular, not meeting the eye, somewat open ;
Seeds numerous, large and imperfect, brown ; Flesh yellow,
tender, fine-grained, juicy ; Flavor very sweet, rich, slightly perfumed ; Quality very good to best ; Use, baking, market and stock ; Season November to January. Keeps well.

Milam.

BLAIR.—(Rarely.)

This is another little southern favorite, to be found by
almost every cabin in parts of the West. Whole orchards.
have been planted with sprouts from the mother trees,
among the people to whom the art of grafting was an un-

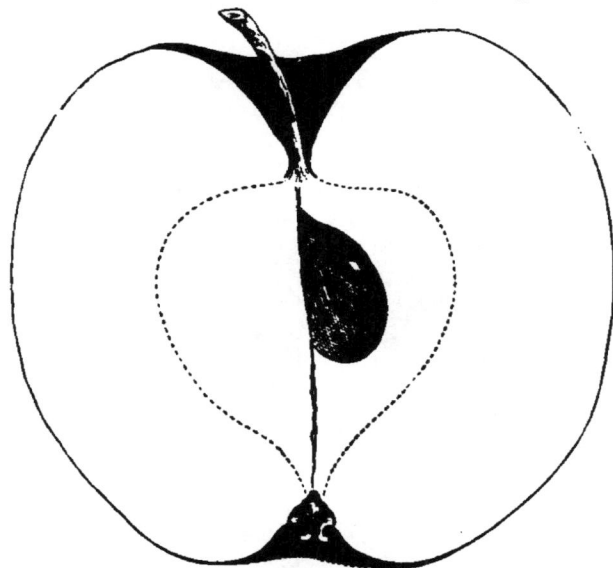

Fig. 146.—MILAM.

heard of mystery. Now distributed by nurserymen all
over the country.

Tree moderately vigorous, round-headed, twiggy; shoots
reddish ; foliage rather dark. Annually productive and
an early bearer.

Fruit small to medium, conical, regular; Surface smooth,
yellow, covered with marbled red, indistinct stripes ; Dots
small, gray, scattered, prominent.

Basin narrow, wavy, leather-cracked; Eye medium, closed.

Cavity regular, acute, brown; Stem long.

Core ovate, covering the eye, closed; Seeds numerous, some imperfect; Flesh white, tender, crisp, juicy; Flavor mild sub-acid or sweet, agreeable and refreshing, but without any decided character; Quality good; Use, dessert, in cooking it lacks flavor; Season, December, January.

CLASS II.—CONICAL APPLES.

ORDER I.—REGULAR.

SECTION 1.—SWEET.

SUB-SECTION 3.—RUSSET.

Pumpkin Sweet.

SWEET RUSSET, of Ohio.

Fruit was exhibited at the Ohio State Fair at Zanesville.

Fruit large, regular, roundish, conical; Surface dull green, covered with a rough coat of russet.

Basin medium, regular; Eye medium, closed.

Cavity deep, narrow, regular; Stem long, slender.

Core medium, regular; Seeds numerous, small, plump; Flesh spongy, light; Flavor sweet; Quality scarcely good; Use, baking, stock; Season, autumn.

This apple has never commended itself very highly to my notice in the limited opportunities I have had for its examination, but it is esteemed in some parts of the country for baking and for stock-feeding.

CLASS II.—CONICAL APPLES.

ORDER I.—REGULAR.

SECTION 2.—SOUR.

SUB-SECTION 1.—SELF-COLORED.

August Tart.

Origin unknown. Specimens procured from Marietta, Ohio.

Fruit medium to large, regular, conical, truncated; Surface smooth, yellow-green; Dots numerous, large, yellow.

Basin medium, wavy or folded; Eye medium or small, closed.

Cavity wide, regular, brown; Stem long, slender.

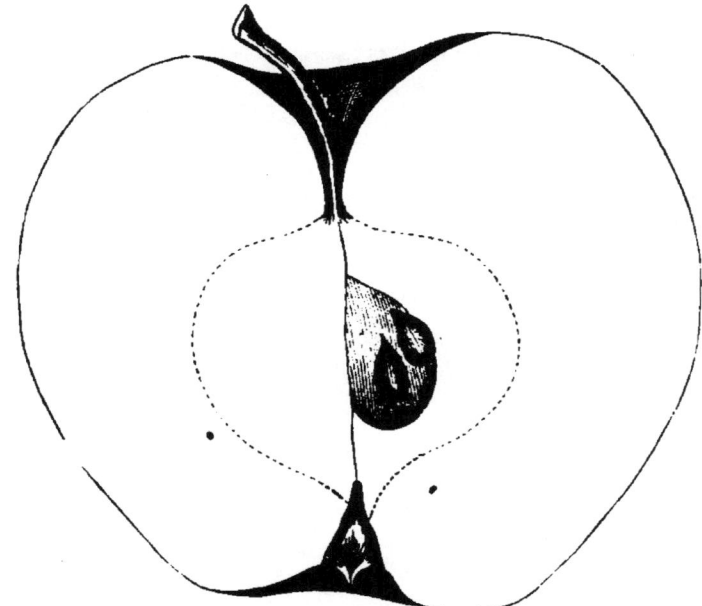

Fig. 147.—AUGUST TART.

Core medium, regular, closed, clasping; Seeds numerous, pointed; Flesh greenish-yellow, breaking; Flavor acid; Quality poor, except for cooking; Season August.

Democrat.

Origin unknown. Specimens obtained from George Powers, of Perrysburgh, Ohio.

Fruit medium, handsome, roundish-conic, regular; Surface yellow, blushed scarlet; Dots minute, indented.

Basin shallow, regular; Eye small, closed.

Cavity rather deep, very acute; Stem medium to short, slender.

22

Core heart-shaped, rather open, meeting the eye; Seeds large; Flesh yellow, breaking, juicy; Flavor sub-acid, aromatic, rich; Quality good to very good; Use dessert; Season October to December.

Holland Pippin.

There is a strange confusion existing in some of the books, by which this fruit has been associated with the Fall Pippin. The Holland, as grown in Western New York, and through the West, as derived from the former State, is entirely different; and as that is extensively known, its description is here given, that it may be compared with the other, which belongs to a different class.

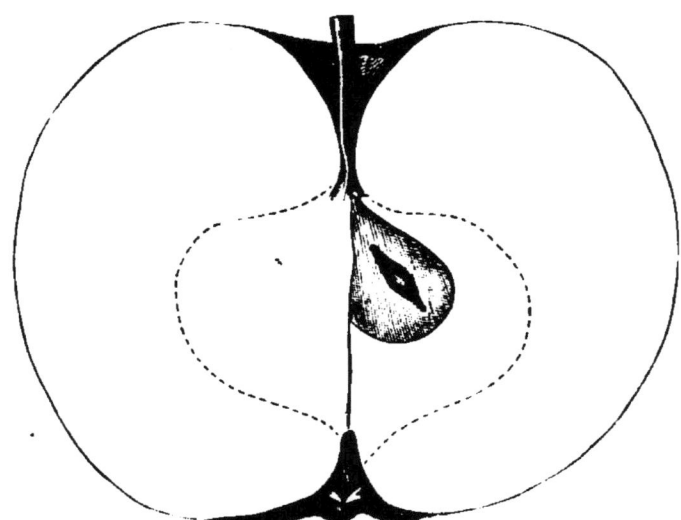

Fig. 148.—HOLLAND PIPPIN.

Fruit large, regular, conic, rather oblate; Surface dull yellowish-green, rarely bronzed; Dots minute.

Basin narrow, medium depth, regular; Eye medium, closed.

Cavity medium, acute, regular, brown; Stem medium to long.

Core medium, regular, closed, meeting the eye; Seeds numerous, sometimes imperfect; Flesh yellowish-white or greenish-white, breaking, coarse-grained, juicy; Flavor quite acid, not rich, not agreeable; Quality only fair; Use cooking only; Season, October to December at the North. Not seen in the southern counties of the States north of the Ohio River.

Middle.

A comparatively new fruit, from Herkimer County, New York, found in a division fence between two neighbors; hence its name. Considerably cultivated in the

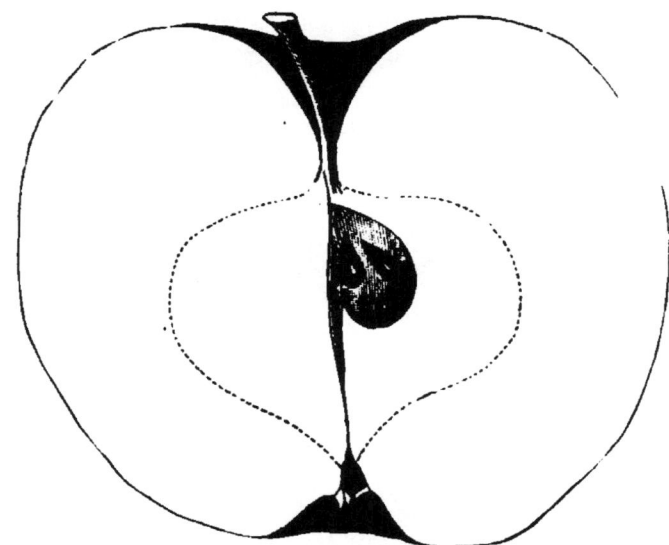

Fig. 149.—MIDDLE.

neighborhood, where it is highly esteemed. Introduced into Ohio by Mr. John Ludlow, of Springfield, in 1854, and propagated at the Oakland Nurseries near by.

Tree thrifty and productive.

Fruit medium to large, conical or oblate-conic, regular; Surface rather smooth, green to pale greenish-yellow; Dots small, irregular, rather abundant, gray, somewhat prominent.

Basin shallow, nearly regular, russeted, like Rhode Island Greening; Eye small, closed.

Cavity acute, sometimes lipped, wavy; Stem long, slender.

Core small, oval, regular, closed, just meeting the eye; Seeds small, very light colored; Flesh greenish-yellow, breaking, fine grained, tender, juicy; Flavor sub-acid, rich, aromatic; Quality nearly first rate; Use dessert; Season December and January, but is said to keep until May in New York.

White Winter Pearmain.

This favorite fruit was brought to Indiana by some of the early pomologists, in the days of saddle-bag transpor-

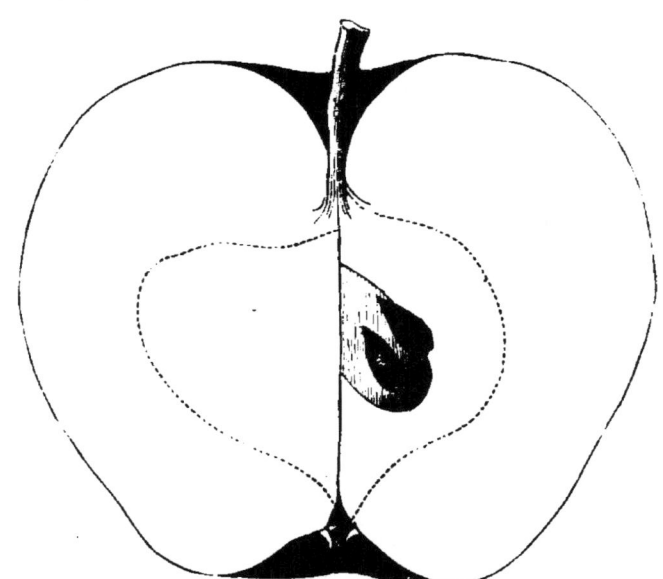

Fig. 150.—WHITE WINTER PEARMAIN.

tation. In a lot of grafts, two varieties, having lost their labels, were propagated and fruited without name. Being considered Pearmain-shaped, they were called respectively Red and White Winter Pearmains. The former proved to be the Esopus Spitzenberg; the latter has never yet been identified, though believed to be an old eastern variety. Mr. Downing suggests that it may be *Winter Harvey*, a description of which I have not seen. At one time this apple was confounded with the *Michael Henry* by many of us, and Mr. Elliott gives it as a synonym of that variety, but they are very distinct.

Tree spreading, vigorous, productive, the bark often marked by a kind of canker or crack. Foliage large, rather light green.

Fruit medium to large, handsome when fair, but often scabby on rich limestone soils and on old trees, conical, regular, sometimes obscurely angular; Surface smooth, yellow, often bronzy; Dots scattered, small, dark.

Basin abrupt, regular or shallow and folded; Eye medium, closed.

Cavity acute, wavy, brown; Stem medium to long, often knobby and clubbed.

Core regular, closed, slightly clasping the eye; Seeds few, pointed, pale or yellow; Flesh yellow, fine grained, tender, crisp, juicy; Flavor mild sub-acid, very rich; Quality best; Uses table, kitchen, market; Season December to March.

Woolfolks.

This is supposed to be a Kentucky seedling. It was received from my friend Ormsby Hite, of Louisville.

Fruit full, medium, truncated, regular; Surface very smooth, yellow-green; Dots scattered, gray, white bases.

Basin medium, wavy, plaited; Eye small, closed.

Cavity wide, acute, wavy, brown; Stem short, green.

Core small, heart-shaped, regular, closed, clasping; Seeds pointed, angular, dark; Flesh white, tender, breaking, juicy; Flavor sub-acid; Quality good; Use, table, kitchen; Season, December to March.

CLASS II.—CONICAL APPLES.

ORDER I.—REGULAR.

SECTION 2.—SOUR.

SUB-SECTION 2.—STRIPED.

Alexander.

This Russian apple, so much admired for its size and beauty, is not a favorite in the orchard, though some persons have found it profitable in the markets.

Tree medium size, spreading, moderately productive, early bearer.

Fruit large to very large, fair and handsome, conical, truncated, sometimes obscurely angular; Surface smooth, pale yellow, striped and splashed distinctly bright red, sometimes shaded mixed red; Dots minute.

Basin medium, regular; Eye small, long, closed.

Cavity rather deep, narrow, regular, brown; Stem medium to short, stout.

Core wide, regular, nearly closed, clasping; Axis short; Seeds large; Flesh whitish, breaking, not fine grained, juicy; Flavor acid, not rich; Quality scarcely good, except for cooking; Season, August and September. Fruit falls badly from the tree.

Cayuga Red Streak.

TWENTY OUNCE, ETC.

I have preferred to adopt the above name for this old Connecticut apple, to avoid the confusion arising from another and very indifferent fruit that is still considerably cultivated upon the same parallels with this, and known as the *Twenty Ounce Pippin*.

The Cayuga is a very great favorite as a market and family fruit in many parts of the country north of latitude 40°—being large, handsome and productive.

Tree thrifty, healthy, early productive, round-headed, twiggy; Shoots medium or slender, reddish brown, leaves large.

Fruit large to very large, regular, globular-conic; Surface generally smooth, yellow-green, nearly covered with mixed red, striped and splashed scarlet; Dots minute, scattered.

Basin regular, abrupt; Eye small, closed; Calyx long.

Cavity wide, folded, brown; Stem short.

Core wide, large, irregular, open, meeting or slightly clasping the eye; Seeds numerous, short, plump, pale; Flesh whitish, breaking, granular, juicy; Flavor sour, not

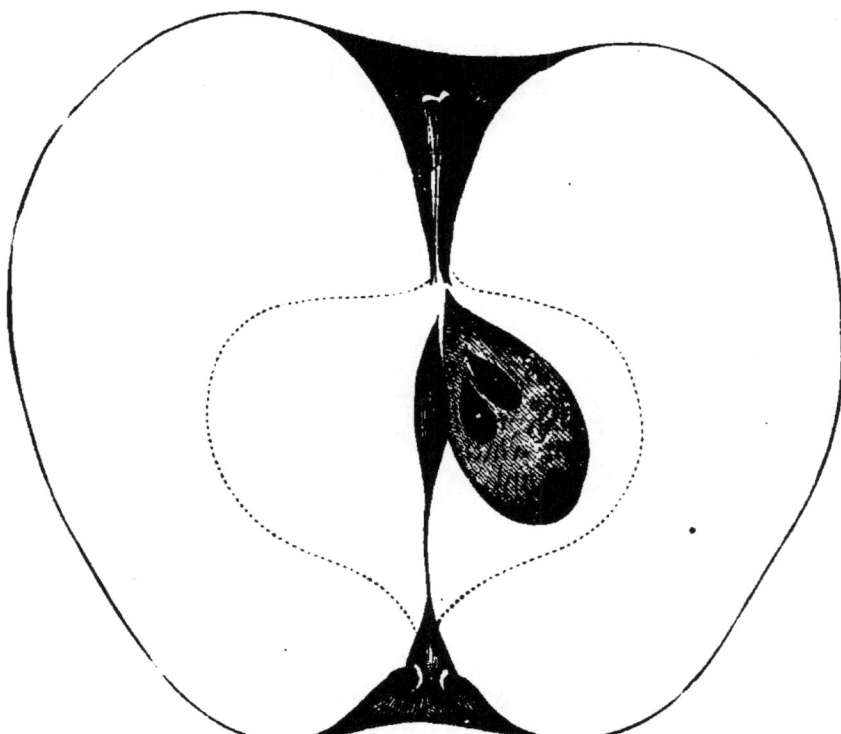

Fig. 151.—CAYUGA RED STREAK.

rich; Quality good, only for its special uses, market, cooking and drying; Season, October to December.

Clarke's Pearmain.

Origin North Carolina. Specimens from W. S. Westbrook. Tree grows slowly, but very productive.

Fruit medium, roundish-conic, truncated; Surface yellow, covered bright red and bronzed · Dots numerous, large, yellow.

Basin abrupt, folded; Eye small, closed; Segments short, reflexed.

Cavity deep, acute, sometimes lipped; Stem long, red.

Core small, pyriform, regular, closed, scarcely clasping; Seeds, some imperfect; Flesh greenish-yellow, fine grain-

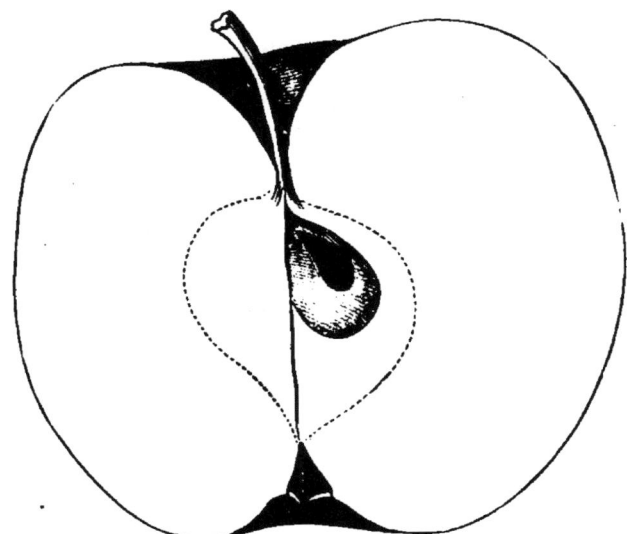

Fig. 152.—CLARKE'S PEARMAIN.

ed; Flavor sub-acid, rich; Quality good to very good; Use dessert and kitchen; Season December.

Clayton.

Believed to have originated in Central Indiana. Brought to my notice by Z. S. Ragan, of Clayton, Indiana; also exhibited by the Plainfield Horticultural Society at the meetings of the State Horticultural Society.

Fruit large, conical, flattened, regular; Surface smooth, greenish-yellow, covered with dull red, striped and splashed darker; Dots minute, scattered.

Basin narrow, abrupt, regular; Eye small, long, closed.

Cavity wide, acute, deep, wavy, green; Stem medium, stout.

Core wide, regular, open, clasping; Seeds numerous, plump, angular, short, dark; Flesh yellow, breaking, not

fine grained; Flavor sub-acid; Quality good; Use, kitchen
and market; Season, all winter until March.

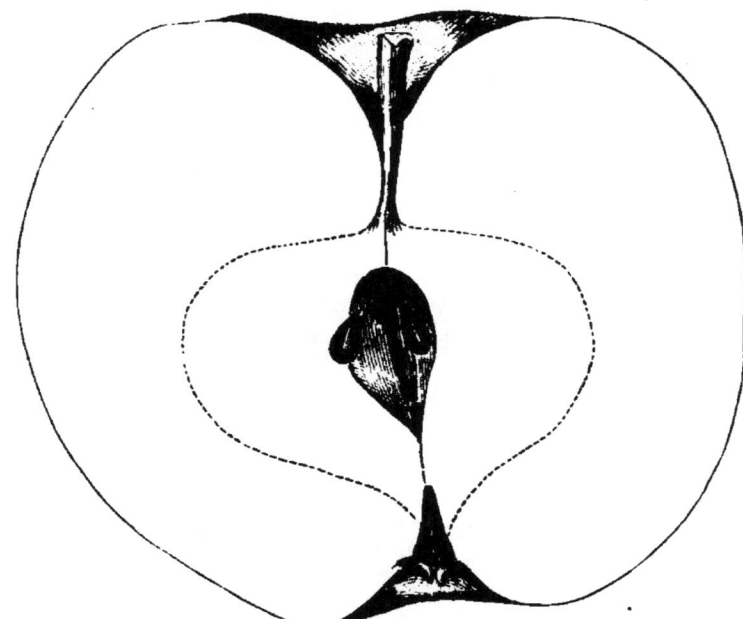

Fig. 153.—CLAYTON.

Cooper's Market.

COOPER'S REDLING.

"Fruit medium, oblong-conic; Skin yellowish, shaded
with red, and striped with crimson; Stem short, cavity
deep, narrow; Calyx closed, basin small; Flesh white,
tender, with a brisk sub-acid flavor; December to May."—
(Downing.)

Early Joe.

This delicious summer apple originated in Ontario County, New York; Tree moderately vigorous, bushy when
young, early bearer, very productive.

22*

Fruit small to medium, flat-conic, regular; Surface yellow or waxen, mixed red, splashed carmine; Dots minute, with yellow bases.

Basin abrupt, regular; Eye medium, long, closed; Segments reflexed.

Cavity wide, acute, wavy, green; Stem medium, thick.

Core wide, closed, clasping; Seeds plump, brown; Flesh light yellow, breaking, very fine grained, juicy; Flavor sub-acid, aromatic, spicy, rich, very satisfying; Quality best; Use, dessert only; Season, July.

Early Strawberry.

AMERICAN RED JUNEATING.

Origin New York; Tree thrifty, very upright, while young, spreading and large when older; Shoots dark col-

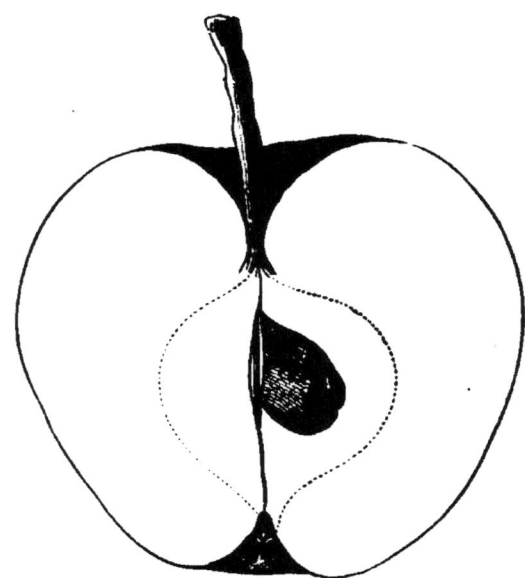

Fig. 154.—EARLY STRAWBERRY.

ored; Foliage abundant on long stems, bright green, almost shining, rather narrow, long, erect.

Fruit small to medium, round-conic, regular or rarely angular; Surface smooth, often shining, yellow, mostly covered with mixed red, striped crimson; Dots rare, very minute; Surface sticky or "greasy" when house-ripened.

Basin shallow, folded or plaited; Eye medium, long; Segments reflexed.

Cavity medium, regular; Stem long, rather slender, sometimes short, knobby.

Core regular, closed, not meeting the eye; Seeds numerous, broad, plump; Flesh whitish-yellow, breaking, fine grained, juicy; Flavor sub-acid, aromatic; Quality good to very good; Use, dessert, market; Season, July and August.

Family.

This new southern variety is not yet sufficiently known to enable me to give a full description. My trees have not borne.

Fruit medium, conic, striped red; Season, July and August.

Flushing Spitzenberg.

As some doubt has existed in the minds of many pomologists in respect to this variety, and as many have had this name applied to the *Baltimore* of Elliott, I quote that author's description:

"American. Tree vigorous, strong brown shoots; Fruit medium, roundish, slightly conical, greenish-yellow, mostly covered with warm yellowish-red; russet dots, with suffused fawn shade surrounding; Stem slender; Cavity narrow; Calyx small; Basin shallow; Core rather large; Flesh white, tinged yellow, juicy, crisp, mild, nearly sweet; 'very good.'" November to February.

Gabriel.

LADIES' BLUSH.—GARDEN OF INDIANA.

This is thought to be a southern apple, but the origin is unknown. It may yet prove to be a known variety in cultivation.

Tree moderately vigorous, productive.

Fruit medium, conic, regular; Surface smooth, greenish-yellow, mixed and striped pale red; Dots minute.

Basin medium, regular; Eye medium, closed.

Cavity regular, green; Stem medium, slender.

Core regular, closed; Seeds medium; Flesh tender, fine grained, juicy; Flavor sub-acid to sweet, aromatic; Quality almost best, for dessert; August and September, or later.

Limbertwig.

This well known southern apple is much cultivated in many parts of the West as a long keeping winter variety. It is a favorite with the southern immigrants, and found most abundant in regions occupied by them, but it has been carried pretty far to the north. The synonym *James River*, as given by Downing, is not met with among the

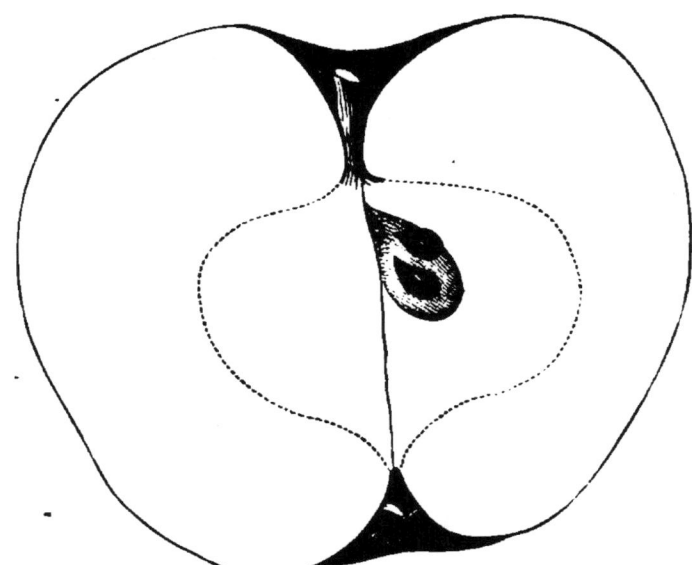

Fig. 155.—LIMBERTWIG.

people as applied to this apple, but the *Willow Twig* is often so named.

Tree thrifty, exceedingly productive; Shoots slender and drooping with the heavy crops.

Fruit medium to small, roundish conic, regular; Surface rather smooth, mixed dull purplish red, on green, stripes scarcely to be traced ; Dots numerous, large, irregular, brown.

Basin medium, regular; Eye small, open.

Cavity deep, acute, brown; Stem medium, curved.

Core rather large, regular, turbinate, closed, clasping; Seeds numerous, small, plump, long; Flesh greenish-yellow, firm; Flavor sub-acid, rich, aromatic; Quality very good; Use, table and kitchen; Season, March and April. Keeps very well, but wilts if exposed to the air—preserved very well in the ground.

Long Island Seek-no-Further.
WESTCHESTER SEEK-NO FURTHER.

This old variety still has its admirers in the Eastern States, but is not often seen in the West. I describe specimens from Wm. S. Carpenter, of Westchester County, New York.

The tree is vigorous and productive.

Fruit rather large, oblate, conic, regular; Surface greenish-yellow, splashed bright red; Dots numerous, scattered, russet.

Basin shallow, wavy; Eye medium, closed.

Cavity wide, regular, brown; Stem long.

Core regular, closed; Seeds pointed, angular, imperfect; Flesh greenish-white, breaking, juicy; Flavor sub-acid, aromatic; Quality good to very good; Use, table, cooking; Season, October, November.

Polly Bright.

Origin Virginia. Considerably cultivated in Eastern Ohio.

" Fruit elongated, conic; Skin light yellow, shaded carmine, obscurely striped; Stalk of medium length, in an acute cavity, russeted; Calyx in a small furrowed basin. Flesh tender, juicy, with a pleasant sub-acid flavor; September, October."—(Downing.)

Rawle's Janet.
JANETTING OR GENETON—NEVER FAIL—ROCK RIMMON, ETC., ETC.

This famous southern apple has been spread throughout the West, and even the Northwest where, however, it has

not proved hardy.   It also has the fault of over-bearing,
when the fruit is often small and insipid.   In suitable soils
it is very fine and deservedly a favorite with planters, some
of whom recommend fifty trees of this variety in an orchard of one hundred.   Origin Virginia.

Tree thrifty, not large, spreading; Twigs brownish, foliage medium, rather whitish.   Blossoms appear later than
other sorts, and thus they sometimes escape a spring frost.

Fruit medium, sometimes large when thinned, flattened,

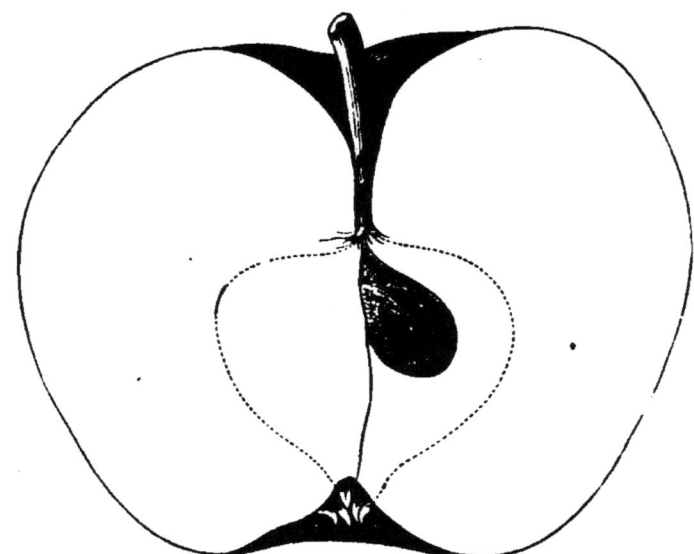

Fig. 156. — RAWLE'S JANET.

conic, regular; Surface smooth, mixed and striped crimson on yellow and green; Dots numerous, small.

Basin wide, regular; Eye small, closed; Segments reflexed.

Cavity acute, deep, regular, brown; Stem long, curved.

Core regular, heart-shaped, closed, clasping; Seeds numerous, plump; Flesh yellowish, crisp, breaking, fine
grained, juicy; Flavor sub-acid, vinous, refreshing; Quality good to very good; Use, dessert, kitchen, market and
cider; Season, February, March, and later.

Red Winter Pearmain.

RED GILLIFLOWER—RED LADY FINGER—BUNCOMBE? ETC.

This favorite southern apple is widely diffused through the South and West, and its good qualities have made it many admirers. Origin uncertain.

Tree sufficiently vigorous, upright, productive, annual bearer.

Fruit medium to large, conic, regular; Surface smooth, deep red, almost purplish on yellow, stripes nearly lost in the depth of coloring, whitish shading exteriorly, not a bloom; Dots numerous, minute.

Basin regular, plaited or folded; Eye long or large, open.

Cavity acute, regular, green; Stem medium length, thick, knobby.

Core medium, closed, clasping; Seeds numerous, large, plump; Flesh yellow, breaking, juicy; Flavor mild sub-acid, almost sweet, rich, satisfying; Quality good; Use, table and kitchen; Season, December and January.

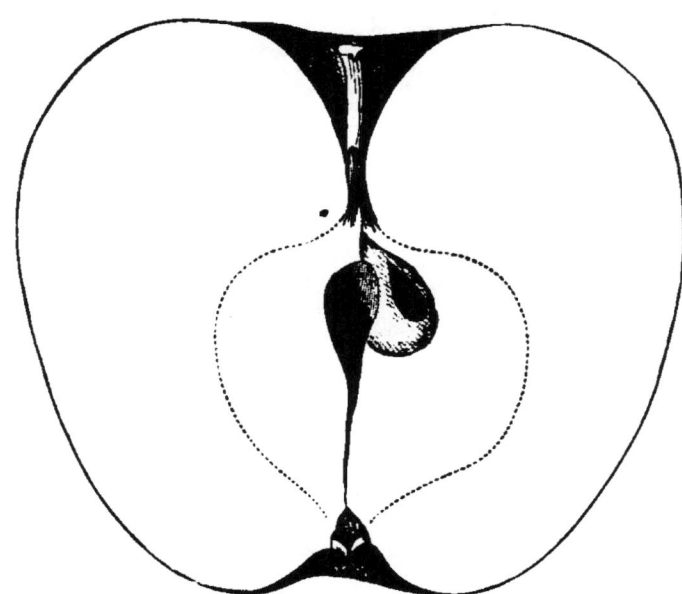

Fig. 157.—ROSY RED.

Rosy Red.

This is one of the valuable fruits which we owe to the indefatigable efforts of that earnest pomologist and thus philanthropist, Lewis Jones, of Cambridge, Indiana. Found in a seedling orchard.

Fruit medium, conical, truncated, regular; Surface smooth, bright red, generally diffused, indistinctly striped; Dots scattered, medium, yellow.

Basin medium, shallow, regular or folded; Eye medium, closed.

Cavity acute, narrow, deep, brown; Stem medium, slender, yellow.

Core wide, indistinct, partly open, scarcely meeting the eye; Seeds few, plump and imperfect; Flesh pale yellow, breaking, juicy; Flavor sub-acid; Quality good; Use, market and table; Season, December and January.

Westfield Seek-no-Further.

This favorite Connecticut apple has been widely disseminated throughout the country, and is universally ad-

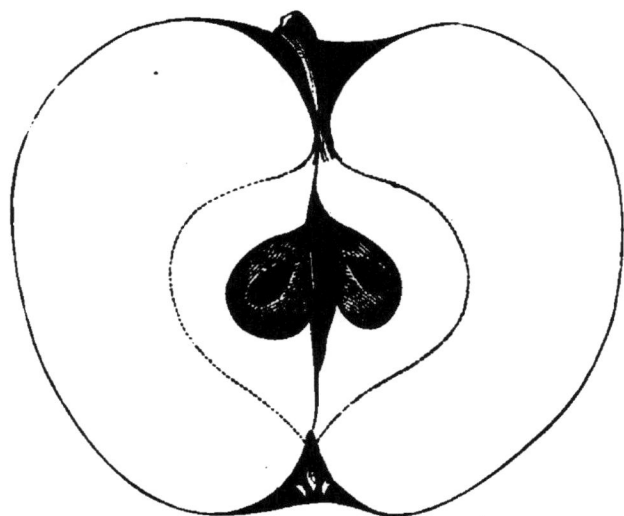

Fig. 158.—WESTFIELD SEEK-NO-FURTHER.

mired by those who come from the Northern States; on

lower parallels it is less known, and not so highly appreciated, nor is it so fine a fruit, being larger, but less compact, more spongy, less beautifully colored and sometimes almost a russet.

Tree vigorous, thrifty, spreading, productive.

Fruit medium, roundish-conic; Surface smooth dull red, mixed and striped on yellow, in the North clear bright red; Dots scattered, large, yellow; leather-cracked and russeted about the apex.

Basin shallow, regular, leather-cracked; Eye small, closed or open.

Cavity pointed, regular, brown; Stem long.

Core medium, regular, closed, meeting and clasping the eye; Seeds numerous, small, pointed; Flesh yellowish-white, tender, breaking; Flavor very mild sub-acid, aromatic, satisfying, not high flavored nor spicy; Quality only good in my estimation; Use, table and market; Season, December.

CLASS II.—CONICAL APPLES.

ORDER I.—REGULAR.

SECTION 2.—SOUR.

SUB-SECTION 3.—RUSSET.

American Golden Russet.
BULLOCK'S PIPPIN, ETC.

This delicious table apple is a universal favorite with all who can appreciate delicacy of flavor and fineness of flesh in an apple, and yet it is not a profitable variety for orchard planting, because the fruit is very apt to be imperfect. The best I have seen were from the South, and sandstone soils.

Tree vigorous, upright, round-headed, small; Foliage large, healthy.

Fruit small to medium, round-conic, regular when perfect; Surface smooth, yellow, covered with thin russet, sometimes faintly blushed; Dots minute.

Basin shallow, regular; Eye small, closed.

Cavity acute, regular; Stem long, slender.

Core medium, closed, meeting the eye; Seeds numerous, pointed; Flesh yellowish, very fine grained, tender,

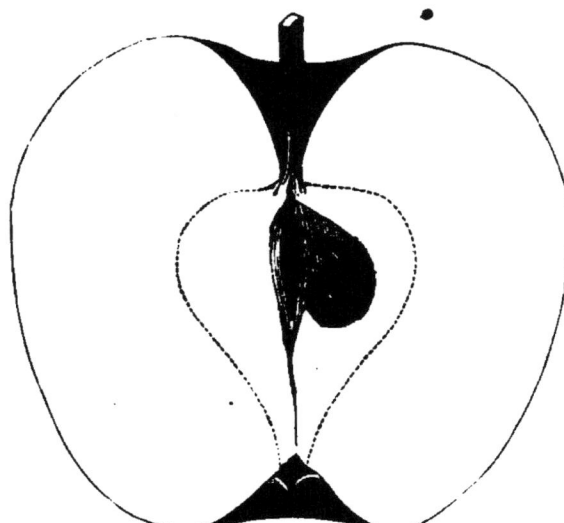

Fig. 159.—AMERICAN GOLDEN RUSSET.

when fully ripe almost melting, like a pear, juicy, becoming dry when over ripe; Flavor sub-acid, rich, aromatic; Quality very best; Use, dessert; Season, November and December.

Cheesborough.

This is one of the largest and one of the poorest of the Russet apples, and unworthy of cultivation; on that account put upon record to be avoided.

Fruit large and fair, conical, regular; Surface dull green, overspread with thin russet, or more southward.

Basin irregular, green; Eye large, closed.

Cavity pointed, regular; Stem short.

Core large, closed, clasping; Seeds long, pointed, angular; Flesh green, breaking, coarse, often dry; Flavor acid or sub-acid, not rich; Quality poor; Use, kitchen only; Season, November and December.

Egyptian Russet.

BAGBY RUSSET.

This capital dessert fruit was found in Southern Illinois
and introduced to his fellow pomologists of the State Society by Jno. M. Hunter, nurseryman, of Ashley.   Its ori-

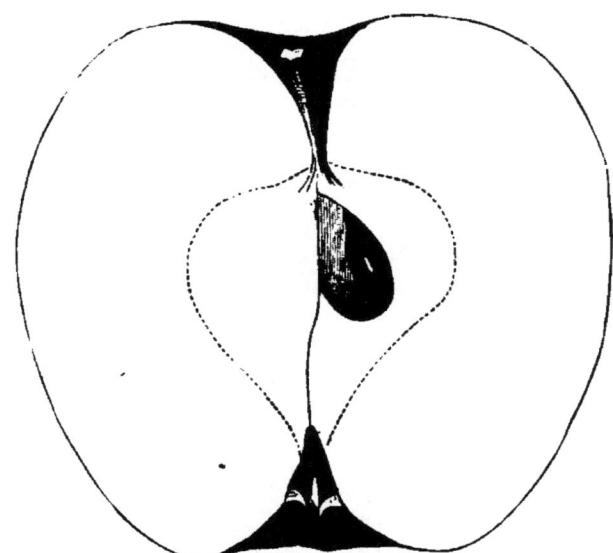

Fig. 160.—EGYPTIAN RUSSET.

gin is unknown, but supposed, like the pioneers of the region, to have come from Tennessee, or some other Southern State.

Tree symmetrical, moderately vigorous, productive;
Twigs slender.

Fruit medium, regular, conical, truncated; Surface
smooth, light yellow, covered with fine russet, obscurely
striped gray.

Basin wide, wavy, plaited, green; Eye medium to large,
open.

Cavity acute, wavy; Stem medium.

Core irregular, closed, scarcely meeting the eye; Seeds
large, plump; Flesh very tender, fine grained, juicy;

Flavor sub-acid, aromatic, rich, pear-like; Quality *very best ;* Use, dessert; Season, December and January, until March. Like other russets disposed to wilt if too much exposed to the air.

Poughkeepsie Russet.
ENGLISH RUSSET.

Origin New York; Tree tender, vigorous, upright, productive; Shoots brown, slender; Foliage healthy.

Fruit medium, conical or globular-conical, regular; Surface smooth, almost polished, dull yellowish-green, often bronzed near the base, more or less covered with fine russet.

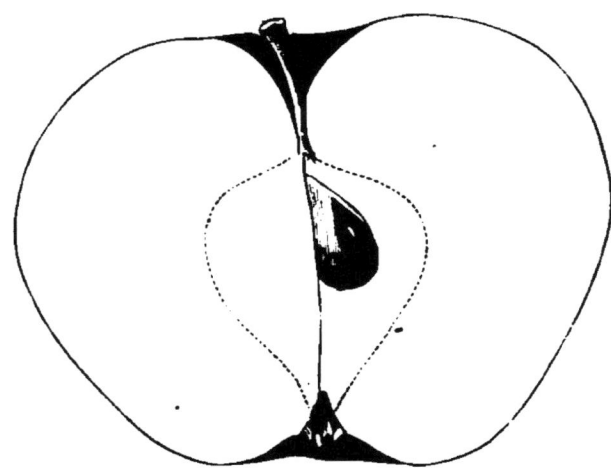

Fig. 161.—POUGHKEEPSIE RUSSET.

Basin shallow, regular; Eye large, closed.

Cavity pointed, wavy; Stem long.

Core closed, not meeting the eye; Seeds imperfect; Flesh greenish, firm, inclined to be tough; Flavor acid, poor; Quality third rate; Use, market and cooking only, and valued because it keeps soundly for a long time; Season, December until June.

Ross' Nonpareil.
SPICE RUSSET ? OF OHIO.

The delicious fruit about to be described is believed to be the celebrated Irish apple mentioned by Thompson,

Lindley, and others; if not, we have found another choice fruit, which deserves to be better known. It is frequently found at the exhibitions in Ohio and Indiana. Often shown as *Spice Russet*, flatter and irregular: *Vide conspectus*.

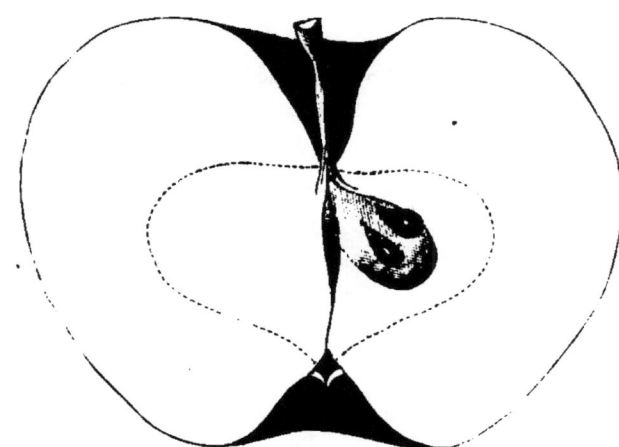

Fig. 162.—ROSS' NONPAREIL.

Fruit medium, regular, oblate-conical; Surface smooth, yellowish, thin russet, rarely blushed dull carmine; Dots minute, gray.

Basin wide, folded; Eye medium, closed.

Cavity deep, acute, wavy; Stem long, inclined.

Core regular, open, scarcely meeting the eye; Axis short; Seeds numerous, medium, plump; Flesh white, breaking, fine grained, tender; Flavor sub-acid, aromatic, rich; Quality almost best; for table; Season December.

Spafford Russet.

This apple is supposed to have originated near old Fort Miami, in Northern Ohio, and was introduced to the notice of the Ohio Pomological Society by its Vice-President, J. Austin Scott, of Toledo, who cultivates the variety on the banks of the Maumee, near the place of its supposed origin.

Fruit medium, flattened-conical, regular; Surface smooth, greenish-yellow, lightly russeted, rarely bronzed; Dots minute, green.

Basin medium, abrupt, narrow, regular; Eye small, closed.

Cavity wide, wavy, green; Stem medium.

Core small, open, regular, meeting the eye; Axis short

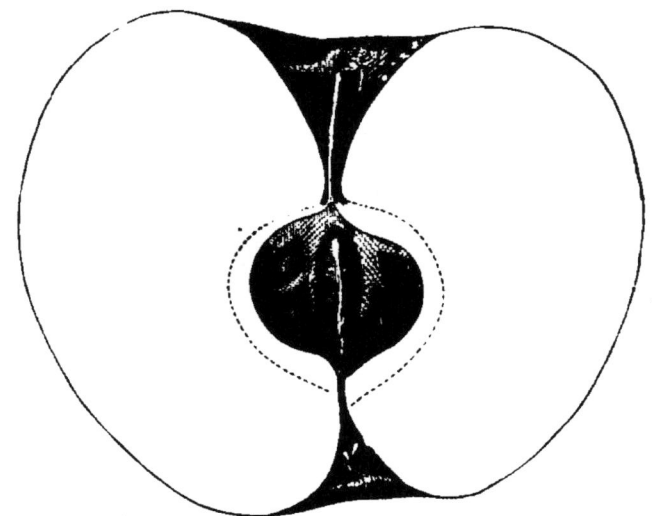

Fig. 163.—SPAFFORD RUSSET.

Seeds numerous, plump, angular; Flesh white, fine grained, juicy; Flavor sub-acid, rich, aromatic, agreeable; Quality good to very good; Use, table; Season, December until March.

CLASS II.—CONICAL APPLES.

ORDER II.—IRREGULAR OR ANGULAR.

SECTION 1.—SWEET.

SUB-SECTION 1.—SELF-COLORED.

Belden Sweet.

" Grown in Connecticut, very prolific; Fruit medium or below, conic, angular; Skin light yellow, with a warm cheek. Stem medium, in an acute deep cavity; Calyx closed, in a small basin; Flesh white, tender, juicy, saccharine, with a pleasant aromatic flavor; December to March."—(Downing.)

Lyman's Pumpkin Sweet.

POUND SWEET.

Origin, the orchard of S. Lyman, Manchester, Connecticut. A very handsome, large, sweet apple, valued for baking and for stock-feeding.

Tree vigorous, spreading, drooping, rather productive.

Fruit large to very large, roundish-conical, angular; Surface very smooth, pale yellow; Dots minute.

Basin deep, abrupt, regular; Eye medium, closed.

Cavity deep, acute, regular, brown; Stem medium or short.

Core large, closed; Seeds angular, dark; Flesh yellowish, breaking, juicy, often water-cored and heavy; Flavor very sweet; Quality good; Use, baking and stock-feeding; Season, October to December.

CLASS II.—CONICAL APPLES.

ORDER II.—IRREGULAR.

SECTION 1.—SWEET.

SUB-SECTION 2.—STRIPED.

NONE.

CLASS II.—CONICAL APPLES.

ORDER II.—IRREGULAR.

SECTION 1.—SWEET.

SUB-SECTION 3.—RUSSET.

Sweet Russett of Kentucky.

This fruit was received from J. S. Downer & Son, Elkton, Kentucky,

Fruit small, conical, truncated, angular; Surface rough, dark russet; Dots scattered, minute, white, prominent.

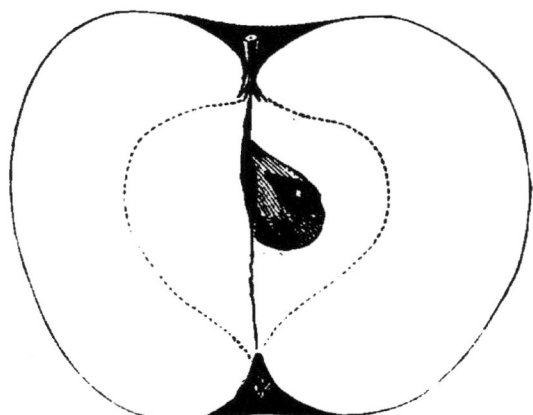

Fig. 164.—SWEET RUSSET OF KENTUCKY.

Basin shallow, regular; Eye small, closed.
Cavity very shallow, acute; Stem short, slender.
Core large, regular, nearly closed, meeting the eye; Seeds numerous, angular, pale; Flesh yellowish-white, fine-grained, not tender; Flavor sweet; Quality scarcely good; Season, December to February.

Sweet Russet.

Fruit medium, conical, uneven; Surface yellow, thin russet; Dots numerous, small, prominent.
Basin shallow, folded; Eye small, closed.
Cavity wide, wavy; Stem short.
Core oval, open, clasping the eye; Seeds plump; Flesh yellow, tender, fine grained, juicy; Flavor sweet; Quality good to very good; Use, baking; Season, August.
S. B. Parsons of Flushing, Long Island, considers it the best baking apple.

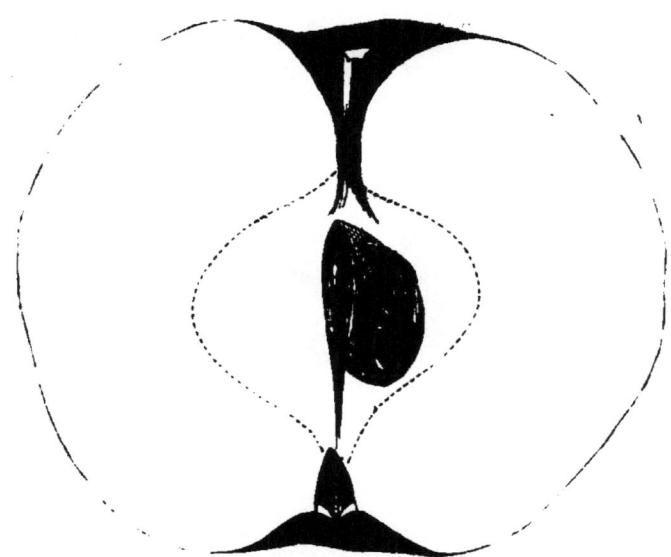

Fig. 165.—SWEET RUSSET.

CLASS II.—CONICAL APPLES.

ORDER II.—IRREGULAR.

SECTION 2.—SOUR.

SUB-SECTION 1.—SELF-COLORED OR BLUSHED.

Belmont.

GATE—MAMMA BEAN, ETC.

This beautiful apple is believed to be of Virginia origin, but was brought into public notice and notoriety in Belmont County, Ohio, whence its name. It is supposed to be the same as the *Waxen* of Coxe, which that author refers to Virginia.

Tree vigorous, spreading, productive, not hardy; Twigs light olive.

23

Fruit large, fair, oblate-conic, often angular; Surface very smooth, waxen-yellow, often faintly blushed orange, and spotted red; Dots minute, scattered.

Basin regular or wavy, not deep; Eye small, closed.

Cavity wide, wavy, brown; Stem long.

Core wide, regular, somewhat open, clasping; Axis short; Seeds numerous, large, flat; Flesh yellow, tender,

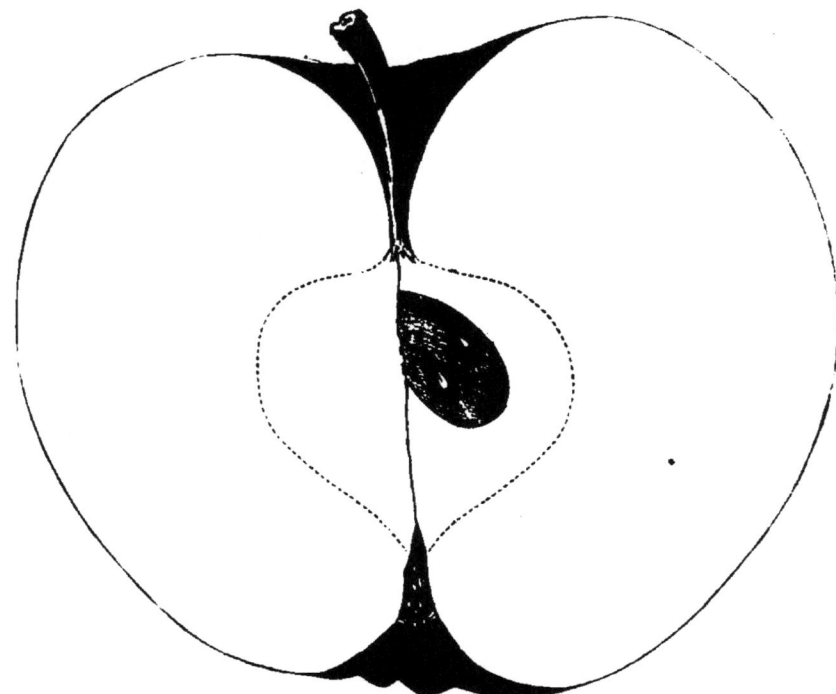

Fig. 166.—BELMONT.

fine-grained, juicy; Flavor mild sub-acid, refreshing, very agreeable; Quality nearly best; Use, table, kitchen, market; Season, October to December.

Celestia.

This fine amateur fruit, which appears destined to take the place of the Dyer, being more handsome, is a seedling from the *Stillwater Sweet*, and was produced by L. S. Mote, of Miami County, Ohio.

Fruit large, conical, truncated, angular; Surface some-what uneven, smooth, waxen-yellow; Dots scattered, distinct, gray, with green bases.

Basin narrow, folded; Eye small, long, closed.

Cavity wide, shallow, angular; Stem long or medium, sometimes knobby.

Core small, oval, open, clasping; Seeds numerous, long, angular; Flesh yellow, very fine grained, very tender,

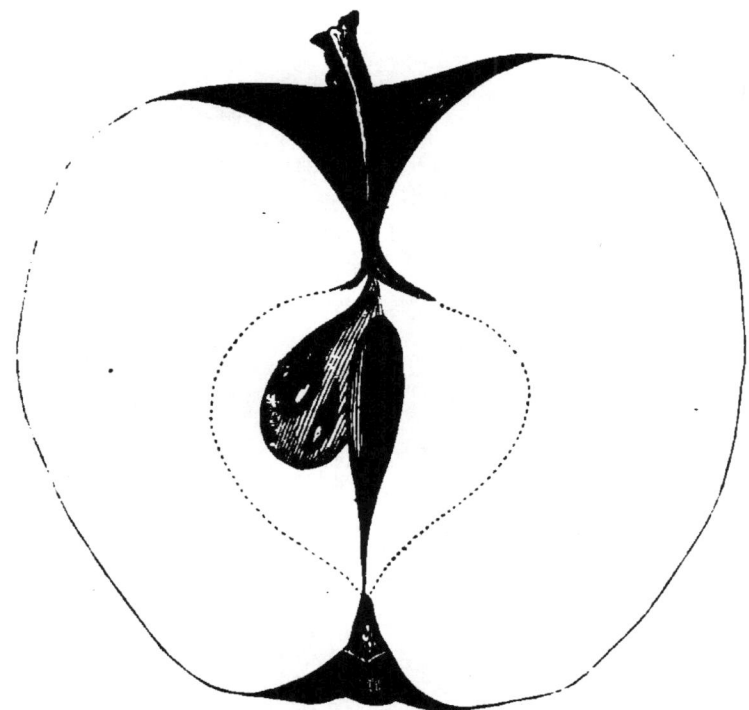

Fig. 167.—CELESTIA.

juicy; Flavor sub-acid, very sprightly, and spicy, aromatic; Quality very best; Use, table and kitchen; Season, September.

This is essentially an amateur's fruit, as its texture and

color disqualify it for market, while its delicious flavor renders it very attractive.

Detroit Black.

DETROIT RED?—GRAND SACHEM.

Supposed to be of Canadian origin, in the neighborhood of Detroit, Michigan. I have put these two names together, because the fruits presented as *Black* and as *Red Detroit* are so very much alike in all respects that it is not worth while to consider them distinct.

Fruit large to very large, conic, angular; Surface very smooth, shining, deep red shaded, almost black in some specimens, no striping; Dots, numerous, minute, indented, gray.

Basin deep, abrupt, folded; Eye small, open.

Cavity wide, wavy; stem very short.

Core wide, closed or open, clasping the eye; Seeds nu-

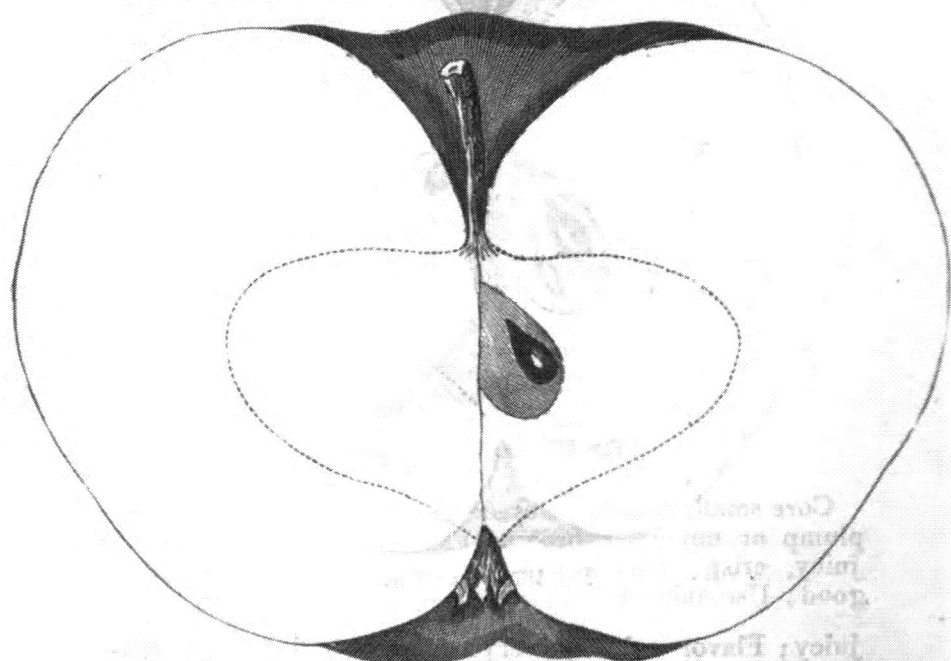

Fig. 163.—DETROIT BLACK.

merous, angular, brown; Flesh whitish, tender, breaking,

juicy; Flavor acid, poor; Quality second to third rate; Use, kitchen and drying; Season, September and October.

The Red variety may be distinct, as it keeps later.

Fall Geneting.

Elliott says this is an old Connecticut variety. Tree vigorous and productive.

Fruit large, flattened-conic, angular; Surface smooth, greenish-yellow, blushed; Dots rare, minute.

Basin shallow, plaited; Eye small, closed; Calyx reflexed.

Cavity deep, wide, regular, brown; Stem short.

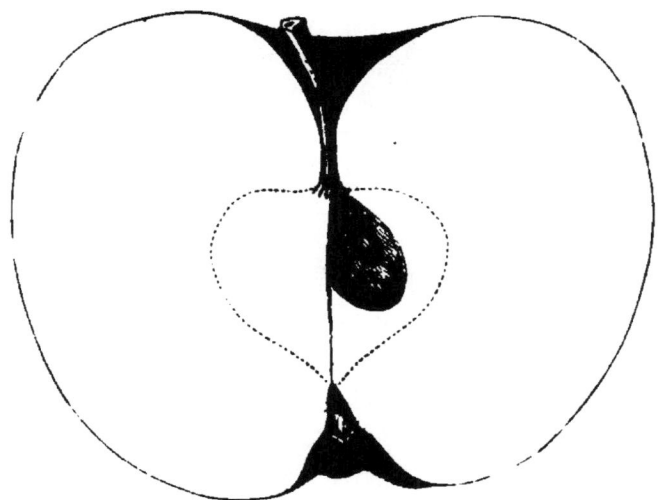

Fig. 169.—FALL GENETING.

Core small, regular, closed, clasping; Seeds numerous, plump or imperfect, brown; Flesh yellow, fine grained, juicy, crisp; Flavor sub-acid, not very rich; Quality good; Use, table, kitchen; Season, October.

Ferdinand.

I procured my trees from Virginia, where it originated. Tree vigorous, upright.

Fruit large, flattened-conic, irregular; Surface smooth, pale green or yellow.

Basin shallow; Eye medium, open.

Cavity medium; Stem stout.

Flesh yellow, tender; Flavor sub-acid; Quality good; Season, "November to March," according to Mr. Summer, South Carolina.

Harrison.

This famous Jersey cider apple, from Essex County in that State, has been carried westward over a great extent of territory, where it succeeds admirably well, and where

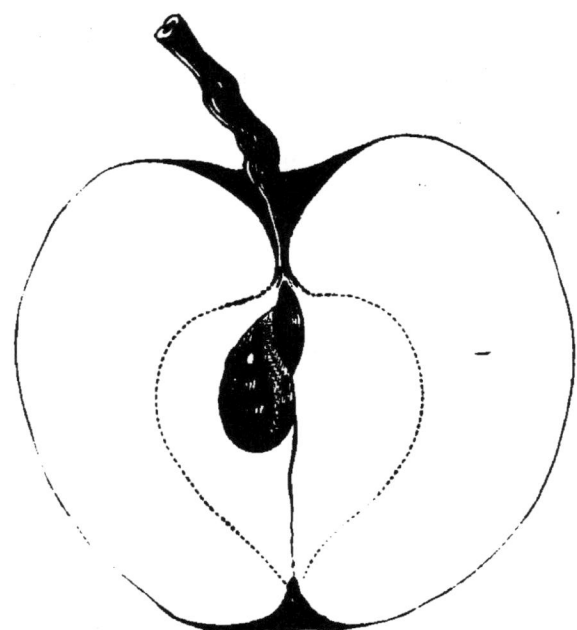

Fig. 170.—HARRISON.

the necessities of the people have brought to light its good properties for the kitchen as well as for the cider mill.

Tree vigorous, large, spreading, productive.

Fruit small, round-conical, somewhat angular and irregular; Surface not smooth, yellow, rarely blushed; frequent rose-colored spots, and marks radiating from the cavity over the base of the fruit; Dots small, distinct, gray.

Basin none, or very shallow, plaited; Eye small, closed; Segments long.

Cavity medium, regular, brown; Stem long, red, knobby.

Core regular, heart-shaped, closed, scarcely meeting the eye; Seeds numerous, small; Flesh yellow, compact, dry till ripe, then juicy; flavor acid to sub-acid, very rich, saccharine; Quality good; Use, especially for cider, also for cooking and for dessert in April. Keeps well.

Pound Royale.

This fine summer apple, received from H. N. Gillett, of Lawrence County, Ohio, has long been considered one of the very best summer apples along the Ohio River.

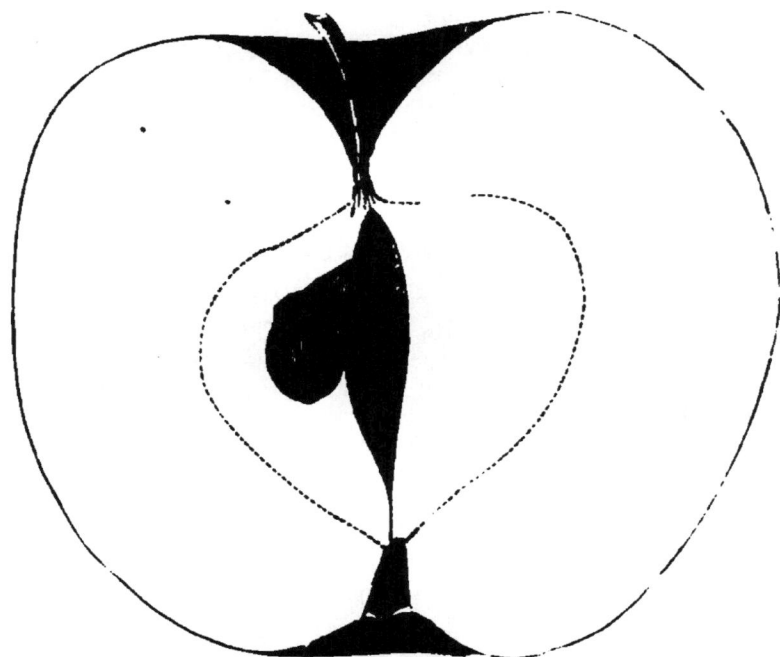

Fig. 171.—POUND ROYALE.

Tree a pretty good grower, an early and constant bearer, very productive; Shoots dark, foliage dark.

Fruit large, conical, slightly angular; Surface smooth, glossy, greenish; Dots small, green, indented.

Basin medium, folded; Eye medium, closed; Segments long, reflexed.

Cavity acute, wavy, brown; Stem medium, sometimes knobby.

Core small, closed or slightly open, meeting the eye; Seeds numerous, pointed, dark; Flesh white, very tender, juicy; Flavor very mild sub-acid, delicious; Quality very good to best; Use, table, kitchen; Season, August.

Different from *Pound Royal* of Downing, which is a winter-keeping fruit.

Ridge Pippin.

This fruit appears to be quite a favorite market apple in the neighborhood of Philadelphia, where it originated.

Fruit rather large, round-conic, very irregular, ribbed; Surface yellow, lightly shaded and blushed with red, and sprinkled with russet and crimson spots.

Basin abrupt, furrowed and folded; Eye small, closed.

Cavity wide, regular; Stem short.

Flesh yellow, crisp, juicy; Flavor mild sub-acid, rich.

Season, until March and April.

The Cook's Favorite.

This nice autumn apple comes to me from Oliver Albertson, a prominent and intelligent cultivator in Washington County, Indiana, marked "*Best.*" Origin unknown.

Fruit medium, flattish-conical, angular; Surface smooth, whitish-yellow; Dots minute.

Basin deep, folded, ribbed; Eye medium, closed.

Cavity wide, wavy, brown; Stem long, slender.

Core medium, roundish, closed, meeting the eye; Seeds numerous, dark; Flesh yellow, breaking, tender; Flavor sub-acid; Quality quite good; Use, kitchen especially—"cooks very well;" Season, September.

Trenton Early.

This fine autumn apple has been thought to be the *English Codling*. Of its origin and history we know little, except that it was one of Silas Wharton's varieties, and that it has been a great favorite wherever known. It was introduced to the notice of the Ohio Pomological Society, 1852, by R. W. Steele, Esq., of Dayton, Ohio, with the following notes: "A large, white apple, of excellent flavor, and is highly esteemed both for eating and cooking. It ripens in August. The tree is a vigorous grower and an abundant bearer. It was introduced here many years ago by Silas Wharton, of Warren County, to whom this portion of the Miami Valley is largely indebted for the introduction of many excellent varieties of apples and pears."

Fruit large, conical, angular; Surface smooth, very pale yellow or white; Dots rare, minute.

Basin narrow, folded; Eye medium or small, closed.

Cavity wide, regular, brown; Stem medium.

Core large, rather open; Seeds numerous, angular; Flesh white, very tender, juicy; Flavor sub-acid, pleasant; Quality very good; Use, dessert and kitchen; Season, August, September.

CLASS II.—CONICAL APPLES.

ORDER II.—ANGULAR.

SECTION 2.—SOUR.

SUB-SECTION 2.—STRIPED.

Buckingham.

BYER'S RED—FALL QUEEN (of some)—BLACKBURN (erroneously.)

This favorite southern apple, from Louisa County, Virginia, has worked its way northward into public favor at rapid rate, under the influence of railways and Pomological Societies. It was first presented to the American Society at the Philadelphia meeting, in 1860, when it was figured and reported on by the Committee on Native Fruits, to some of whom, as to thousands of others in the West, it was familiar as household words. This fruit was brought by settlers to Southern Illinois, and thence distributed, by taking up the sprouts that formed about the base of the stocks, and setting them out for an orchard. I have some of these growing, and they make nice plants.

23*

Tree vigorous, upright, compact while young, spreading with the weight of fruit, never large; the shoots rather slender, red, dark; Leaves medium, rather narrow, wider towards the end, dark, footstalks red. The stems of these trees are characterized by curious enlargements of an irregular, mammellar form, and reddish color, and appear to be like the knaurs of the olive tree.

When this apple was first brought to the notice of the Cincinnati Horticultural Society, twenty years ago, it was

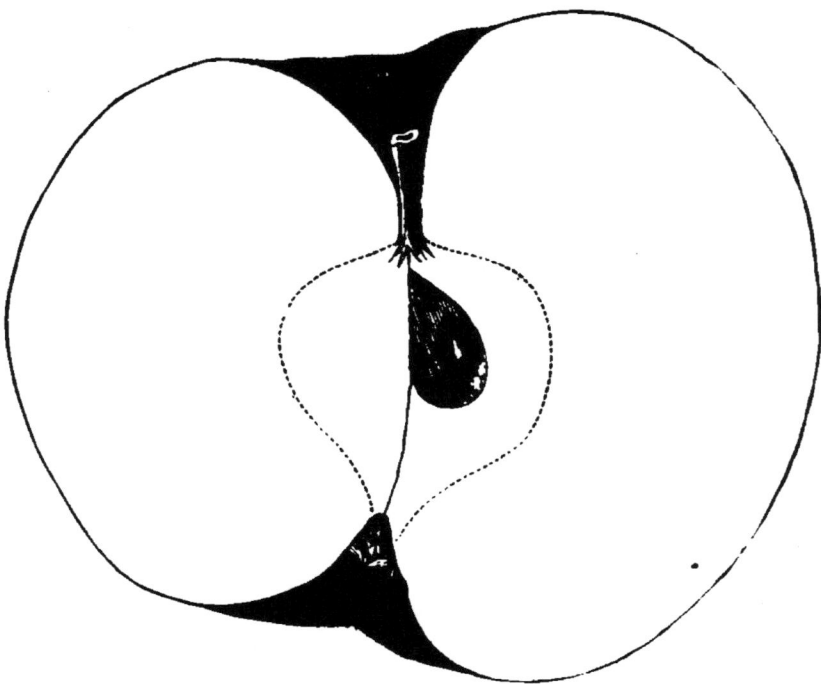

Fig. 172.—BUCKINGHAM.

thought to resemble the Winter Queen of Kentucky so closely that it was considered only a variety or sport, and called the *Striped Fall Queen*, but it has since been deemed a distinct sort.

Fruit large to very large, variable in form, but generally conical, or oblate-conic, truncated, angular; Surface smooth, greenish-yellow, mixed and striped pale purplish-red ; Dots scattered, prominent, yellow.

Basin deep, abrupt, wavy; Eye large, long, open.

Cavity wide, wavy, brown ; Stem short.

Core large, regular, closed ; Axis very short; Seeds numerous, long, pointed ; Flesh yellow, tender, fine-grained, juicy; Flavor mild sub-acid, rich, agreeable; Quality best, or nearly so; Use, table, kitchen, drying ; Season, October to December.

Esopus Spitzenberg.

Origin New York, on the Hudson. This fruit has changed its character in progressing westward and southward, becoming larger and more irregular, less brilliantly colored, less highly flavored, and less productive.

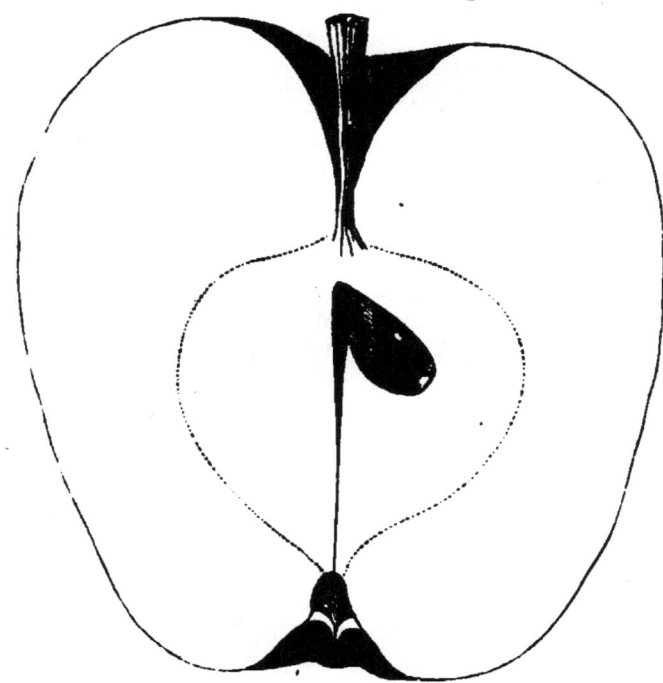

Fig. 173.—ESOPUS SPITZENBERG.

Tree vigorous, upright, thrifty, but in some regions subject to blight and unprofitable ; Shoots slender.

Fruit medium to large, conical, ribbed, irregular; Surface smooth, yellow, covered with bright red, marbled and mixed, striped more or less distinctly; Dots numerous, large, irregular, gray, always elongated near the base.

Basin deep, ribbed or folded, often-leather-cracked; Eye small, closed.

Cavity deep, acute, regular, or wavy; Stem long.

Core large, closed; Seeds long, pointed; Flesh rich, ye' low, breaking, juicy at the North, more fibrous than crisp at the South; Flavor quite acid till ripe, when it is rich, saccharine, highly aromatic, giving the idea of the Spitzenberg flavor; Quality best; Use, dessert and kitchen; Season, December to February.

Lansingburgh.

The origin of this long-keeper has not been traced. It has been common about Cincinnati, and along the Ohio River, for many years.

Tree upright, vigorous, brushy and thorny, looking like a wilding.

Fruit medium, conical, angular, oblique, often unequal; Surface smooth, green and yellow, bronzed and blushed, becoming very rich yellow and carmine—an indistinct gray-striping makes the ripe fruit appear to be striped yellow; Dots minute, indented, gray, with green bases.

Basin deep, plaited or folded; Eye small, closed.

Cavity acute, irregular, rough with brown; Stem short.

Core small, oval, closed; Seeds numerous, large; Flesh firm, compact; Flavor mild sub-acid, negative; Quality scarcely good; Use, market, ornamental, cooking; Season in the kitchen all winter—ornamental and eatable March to May, or later.

Late Strawberry.
AUTUMN STRAWBERRY.

The origin of this choice fruit appears to be unknown.

Tree upright, productive, thrifty, leaves serrate.

Fruit medium, roundish, conical, angular, furrowed; Surface smooth, waxen-yellow, mixed and striped scarlet; Dots minute, indented.

Basin folded, irregular; Eye medium, closed.

Cavity acute, wavy, irregular; Stem slender, long.

Core medium, regular, closed , Seeds large; Flesh yellow, very tender, fine-grained, very juicy; Flavor sub-acid, aromatic, refreshing, vinous; Quality best; Use, dessert especially; Season, August and September.

There is another similar fruit—the *Frank* or *Chenango Strawberry*, which is by some preferred to this.

Northern Spy.

Origin near Rochester, New York. Tree very vigorous, large, upright, spreading, when older; shoots reddish,

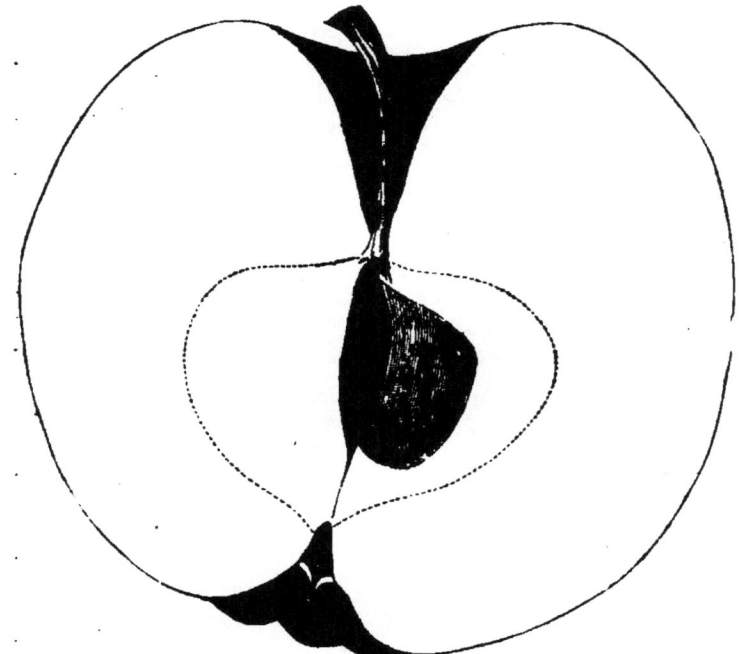

Fig. 174.—NORTHERN SPY.

leaves healthy, large, dark. Tree productive when old, but not an early bearer; needs trimming to admit light and air to the fruit.

Fruit large, flattened-conical, angular; Surface smooth, yellow, mixed, and splashed, scarlet, or crimson; Dots scattered, small.

19*

Basin abrupt, regular, or folded; Eye small, closed.

Cavity wide, regular or wavy, brown; Stem medium to short.

Core large, irregular, open; Seeds numerous, small, pointed, pale; Flesh yellowish-white, breaking, granular, juicy; Flavor acid, becoming sub-acid, aromatic, rich, with the spiciness of a Spitzenberg; Quality considered best, but rather coarse in texture; Use, table, kitchen and market; Season, December until May, and in the North longer.

Red Canada.

STEEL'S RED.

Origin New England. Tree thrifty, healthy, but slender, twiggy, productive.

Fruit medium, globular-conic, indistinctly angular; Surface smooth, yellow, covered with mixed and striped bright red; Dots numerous, gray, indented, elongated near the stem, as in Esopus.

Basin shallow, folded; Eye small, closed.

Cavity wide, acute, wavy; Stem long, inclined.

Core regular, closed, large; Seeds imperfect; Flesh yellowish-white, breaking, crisp, fine-grained, tender, juicy; Flavor sub-acid, aromatic, delicious; Quality best, for table; Season, December to February.

Red Stripe.

EARLY RED MARGARET (incorrectly)—ROCKHILL'S SUMMER QUEEN (Indiana).

This handsome and productive early apple has been extensively propagated in parts of Indiana, under the names above presented. It was introduced at Fort Wayne by Mr. Rockhill, who is reported to have "made more money from the trees of this variety than from twice as many of any other early apple." Recommended for general cultivation in that State.

Tree hardy in nursey and orchard, productive; Shoots very downy.

Fruit medium to small, long, conical, furrowed or ribbed; Surface polished, pale yellow, mixed and splashed crimson.

Basin very shallow, plaited; Eye very small, closed.
Cavity acute, regular, browned; Stem medium.

Core long, oval, embracing the eye; Flesh whitish, tender, fine-grained, juicy; Flavor acid; Quality good; Table or kitchen; Season, July and August.

Scalloped Gilliflower

This is supposed to be an old European variety. Its peculiarly irregular form makes it quite a remarkable fruit. It is sometimes called *Red Gilliflower ;* but that name is also very commonly applied to quite another fruit—the *Red Winter Pearmain*, described on a previous page, in Class II., Order I., Section 2., Sub-section 2.

Fruit large, round-conic, very irregular, furrowed and ribbed; Surface yellow, marbled and splashed scarlet.

Basin abrupt, deep, folded or ribbed; Eye medium, closed.

Cavity deep, acute, irregular, wavy; Stem medium.

Core regular, round, very open, meeting the eye; Seeds numerous, plump; Flesh yellow, breaking, tender; Flavor sub-acid, aromatic; Quality scarcely good; Use, table, kitchen; Season, November, December. Chiefly grown northward.

Seager.

This large, handsome fruit was exhibited at the American Pomological Society's meeting at Philadelphia, in 1860, by Chas. P. Davis, of Phillipsburgh, New Jersey. The Committee reported it "Good."

Fruit large, roundish-conic, irregular; Surface smooth, yellow, striped, splashed and mixed carmine; Dots scattered, yellow.

Basin abrupt, narrow, folded, plaited; Eye medium, large, closed.

Cavity wide, wavy, brown and yellow; Stem medium, knobby.

Core roundish, open, clasping; Seeds angular, imperfect; Flesh yellowish-white, breaking, fine-grained, juicy; Flavor sub-acid, aromatic; Quality good to very good; Use, table, kitchen; Season, September.

Stanard.

From Erie County, New York, this fruit has made its way westward, by the Lakes, having been distributed by Col. Hodge, of Buffalo, and brought to the notice of his western friends by Hon. M. L. Dunlap, of Champaign, Illinois, who esteems it very highly. I quote from his account of it:

"This proves one of our most profitable winter apples; the tree bears young and constantly, but fuller on alter-

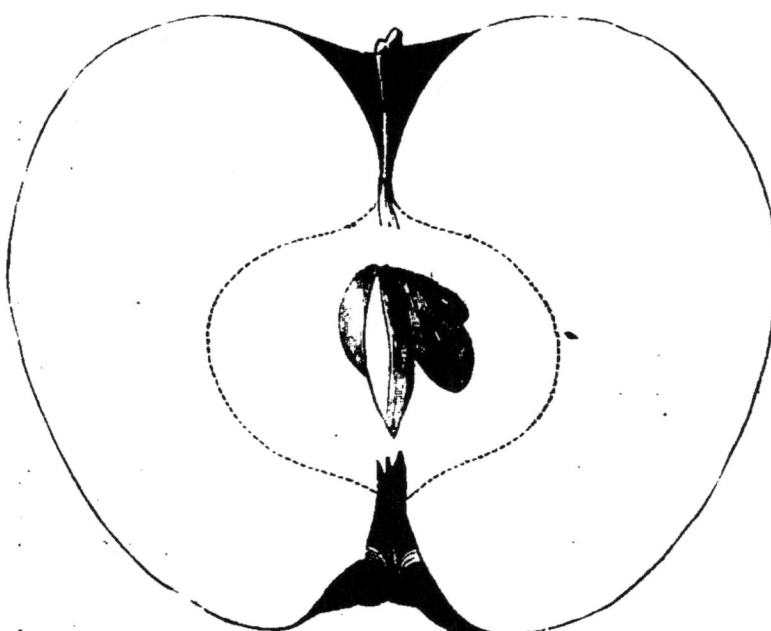

Fig. 175.—STANARD.

nate years; fruit large and showy, shoots large and downy; buds prominent, fruit buds large, and the earliest in the orchard to swell; but they do not open as soon as others. Tree spreading, trunk generally crooked." Very hardy.

Fruit large, roundish, conical, ribbed, angular; Surface smooth, yellowish-green, somewhat red, mixed and striped indistinctly; Dots numerous, minute, white.

Basin medium, folded and plaited; Eye large, closed; Segments long.

Cavity wide, acute, wavy, green; Stem medium to long.

Core small, globular, regular, closed or open; Seeds numerous, brown, angular; Flesh yellow, breaking, rather coarse, tender; Flavor acid to sub-acid, rich; Quality good; Use, market and table; Season, November to February.

Summer Queen.

American.   Tree vigorous, large, spreading, productive.

Fruit medium, round-conic, angular; Surface yellow,

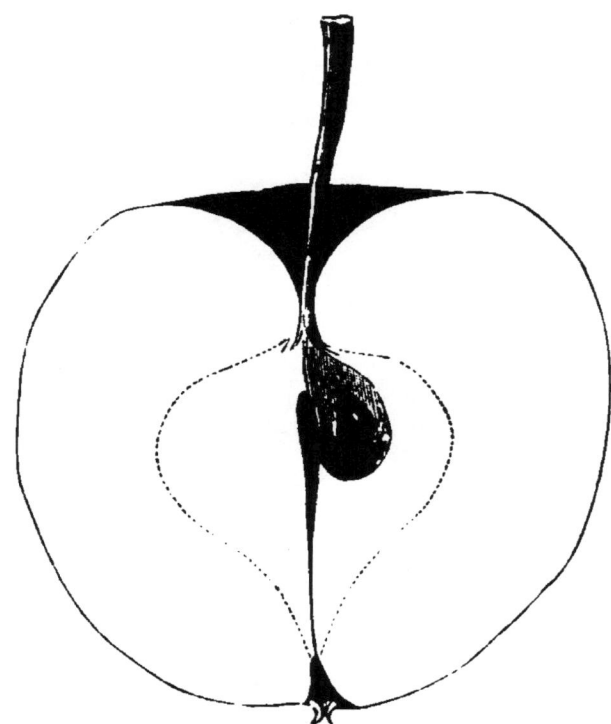

Fig. 176.—SUMMER QUEEN.

covered mixed red, striped, splashed scarlet; Dots minute, yellow.

Basin none or very shallow, folded or plaited; Eye medium, closed.

Cavity wide, regular, brown; Stem long, slender.

Core medium, regular, open; Seeds numerous, pointed, brown; Flesh firm, yellow, breaking; Flavor acid, very aromatic, spicy; Quality first rate; Use, kitchen; Season, July, August.

Winesap.—[*Coxe.*]

Tree vigorous, healthy, hardy, productive, early bearer; Branches open, straggling; Shoots strong, dark reddish-brown; Foliage curled, glaucous, sparse.

Fruit medium, conical, often obscurely angular, or slightly ribbed; Surface rather smooth, bright or dark red,

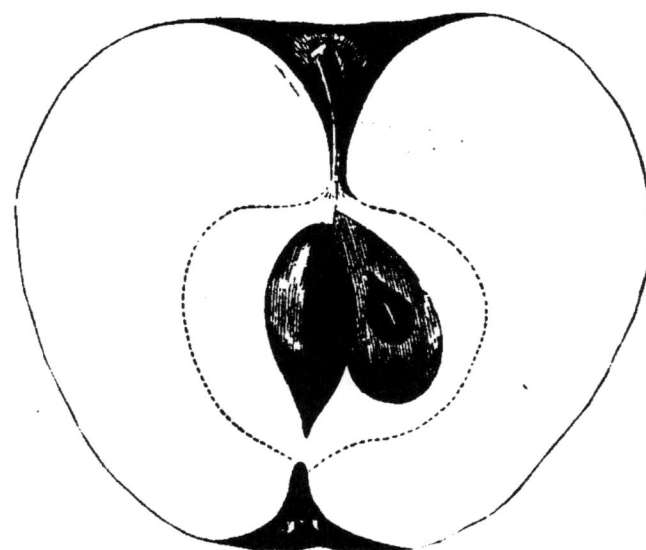

Fig. 177.—WINESAP.

mixed and obscurely striped on yellow, which is mostly covered, often veined russet; Dots few, minute, indented.

Basin narrow, shallow, plaited; Eye small, closed.

Cavity wide, reddish brown; Stem medium.

Core regular, somewhat open; Seeds large, rather light; Flesh firm, yellow; Flavor rich, acid to sub-acid; Use, market, kitchen, cider; Season, January to March.

CLASS II.—CONICAL APPLES.

ORDER II.—ANGULAR.

SECTION 2.—SOUR.

SUB-SECTION 3.—RUSSET.

Fort Miami.

This is another of the seedling russets of the Maumee, brought to the notice of the State Society by its Vice-President, J. Austin Scott, of Toledo. Mr. Elliott describes it from notes taken in 1846, when he received specimens from A. Spafford, Esq., Perrysburgh, Ohio.

Tree upright and spreading, healthy, thrifty; Shoots dark; not an early bearer, but productive when older.

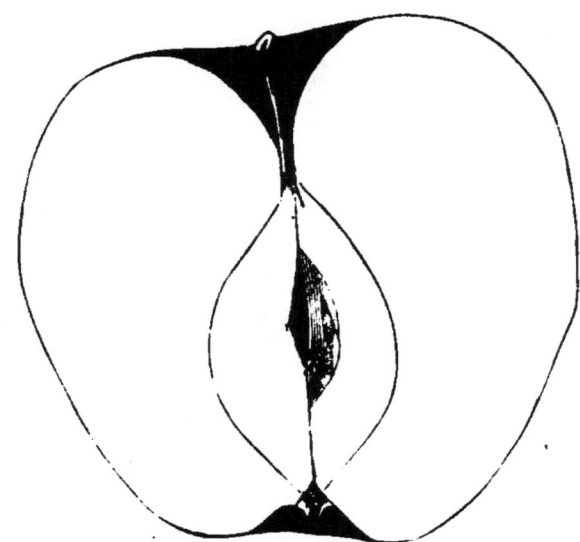

Fig. 178.—FORT MIAMI.

Fruit medium, roundish or oblong-conic, truncated, angular, often unequal; Surface rich yellow russet, often bronzed; Dots scattered, netted russeting.

Basin medium or shallow, folded; Eye small, closed.

Cavity acute, wavy, green; Stem medium.

Core oval, clasping the eye, regular, closed; Seeds often imperfect; Flesh greenish-yellow, firm; Flavor acid, rich; quality nearly best; Use, dessert; Season, February to April.

CLASS III.—ROUND APPLES.

ORDER I.—REGULAR.

SECTION 1.—SWEET.

SUB-SECTION 1.—SELF-COLORED.

Bluff Sweet.

This apple was found by G. M. Beeler on the banks of the White river, upon a farm devoted to pomology.

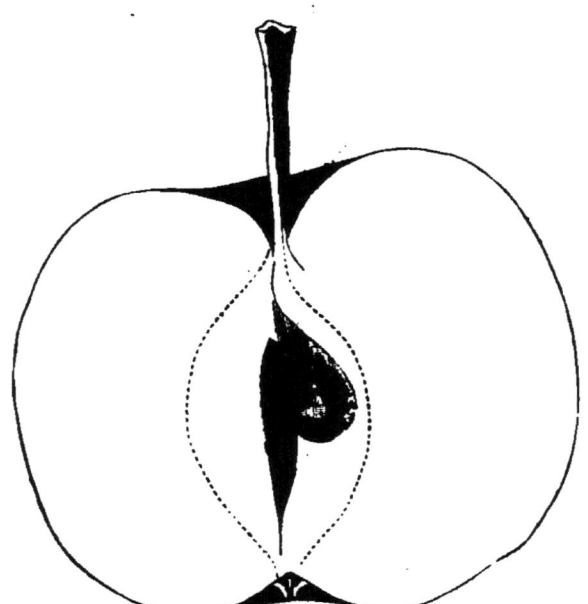

Fig. 179.—BLUFF SWEET.

Fruit medium to small, regular, round; Surface smooth, green; Dots minute.

Basin shallow; Eye small, closed.

Cavity shallow, regular; Stem long.

Core small, oval, pointed; Seeds plump, brown; Flesh greenish-white; Flavor sweet; Quality good; Use, market; Season, July.   Rather too small.

Broadwell.

This delicious winter sweet apple originated near Cincinnati, Ohio.   Tree thrifty, vigorous, spreading, productive.

Fruit large, varies from globular toward oblate, regular; Surface smooth, pale yellow or whitish, thinly blushed with carmine, often bronzed; Dots scattered, minute, dark.

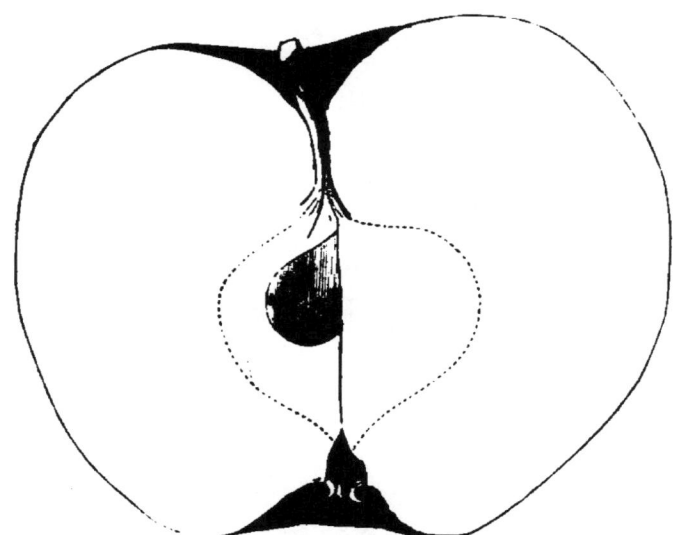

Fig. 180.—BROADWELL.

Basin abrupt, rarely folded or plaited; Eye small, closed. Cavity wide, regular brown; Stem short.

Core round, regular, closed, clasping the eye; Seeds short, plump; Flesh yellowish, fine-grained, very tender, juicy; Flavor very sweet, agreeable; Quality best winter sweet; Use, table, kitchen; Season, December.

Caleb.

"A Pennsylvania fruit.   Tree vigorous and productive; Fruit medium, roundish, flattened, skin yellow; Flesh rather fine, very sweet, excellent for cooking. Last of August and first of September".—[Downing.]

Danvers' Winter Sweet.

Origin Danvers, Massachusetts. Tree very thrifty, very productive.

Fruit large, globular, truncate, sometimes globular-oblate, regular; Surface smooth, uneven, greenish-yellow; Dots numerous, medium, prominent, with white and green bases.

Basin abrupt, deep, regular; Eye small, closed; Segments long.

Cavity wide, deep, brown; Stem long, slender, knobby.

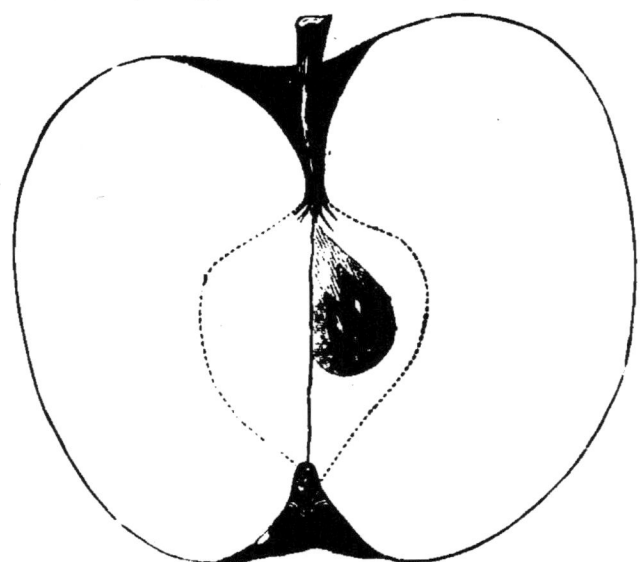

Fig. 181.—DANVERS' WINTER SWEET.

Core round, regular, closed; Seeds numerous, long, brown, pointed; Flesh yellow, breaking, fine-grained, juicy; Flavor very sweet; Quality good to very good; Use, baking; Season, December and January.

Fancher.

This new fruit was obtained from Mr. Thomson, at the State Fair at Zanesville, Ohio. Origin unkown. Not identified nor recognized.

Fruit large to very large, globular, regular; Surface smooth, yellow, blushed; Dots minute, scattered.

Basin shallow, regular; Eye small, closed.

Cavity acute, regular, green; Stem long, inclined.

Core wide, round, open, meeting the eye; Seeds numerous, plump, brown; Flesh white, fine-grained, breaking, juicy; Flavor very sweet; Quality good to very good; Use, baking; Season, September and October. ·

Golden Sweet.

ORANGE SWEETING.

From Connecticut.   Tree very robust, vigorous, spread-

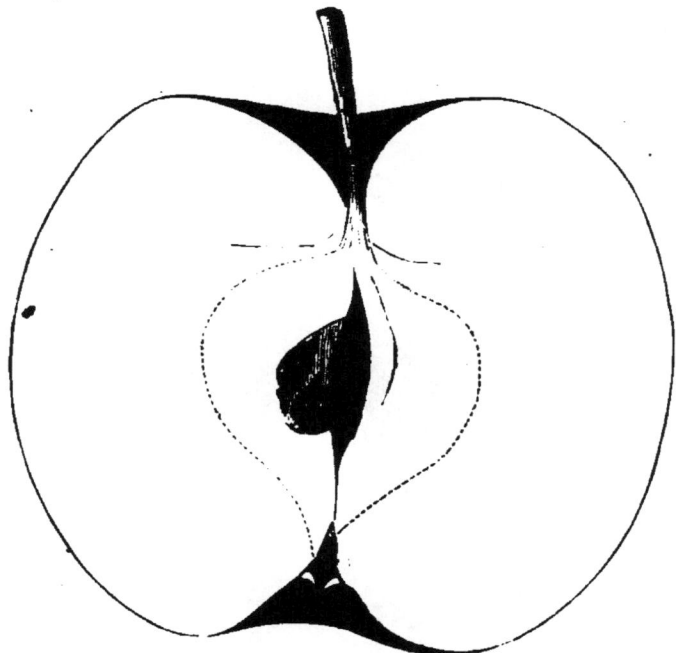

Fig. 182.—GOLDEN SWEET.

ing, round-head, early — productive; Shoots stout, dark, foliage large, dark.

Fruit large, globular, regular; Surface very smooth, waxen to rich yellow; Dots scattered, indented, green.

Basin shallow, wide regular; Eye medium, closed; Calyx reflexed.

Cavity wide, regular; Stem long, slender, yellow.

Core medium, regular, closed; Seeds numerous, small, pointed, light brown; Flesh yellow, breaking, fine-grained, juicy; Flavor very sweet, aromatic, like sassafrass; Quality good to very good; Use, baking and market; Season, August.

Higby Sweet.

LADY BLUSH.

Origin Trumbull County, Ohio; introduced by Dr. Kirtland.

Fruit large, round, truncated, regular; Surface smooth, greenish-yellow, blushed; Dots scattered, distinct, white and dark.

Basin abrupt, wavy, deep; Eye medium, closed.

Cavity deep, acute, regular, brown; Stem medium.

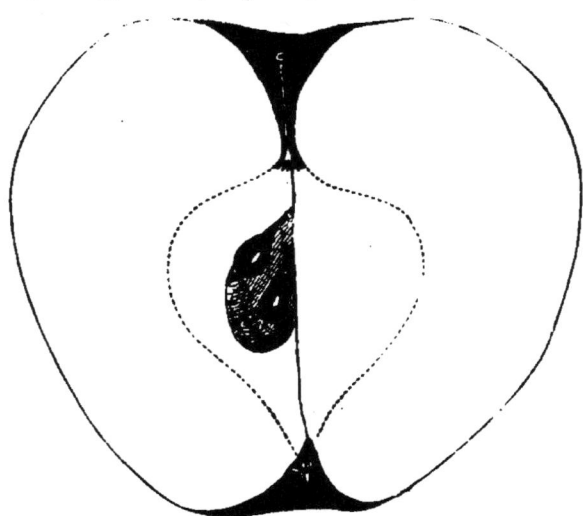

Fig. 183.—HIGBY SWEET.

Core small, regular, heart-shaped, closed, clasping the eye; Seeds plump; Flesh yellowish-white, tender, fine-grained, juicy; Flavor very sweet; Quality good; Use, baking; Season, October.

Hightop Sweet.

SWEET JUNE.

From Plymouth, Massachusetts.

Tree vigorous, very upright, exceedingly productive and profitable.

Fruit small to medium, round, regular; Surface smooth, greenish-yellow; Dots minute, black.

Basin medium, regular; Eye small, closed.

Cavity deep, narrow; Stem medium.

Core very small, oval, separate from the eye; Seeds numerous, angular, yellow; Flesh white, or greenish-white, fine-grained, tender, juicy; Flavor sweet; Quality good; Use, table and kitchen; Season, June and July.

Holston Sweet.

Origin unknown.   Not identified as any other variety; received from my brother, J. T. Warder, Springfield, Ohio

Fruit medium to large, round, regular; Surface smooth greenish-yellow, bronzy; Dots scattered.

Basin regular, small; Eye small, closed.

Cavity shallow, wide; Stem long to medium.

Core small, oval, regular, closed, clasping; Seeds short, plump, brown; Flesh whitish-yellow, very fine-grained, tender, juicy; Flavor very sweet, aromatic, rich; Quality best; Use, table, baking; Season, December to February.

One of the best sweet table apples—better than *Higby Sweet.*

May.

MAY (of Myers)—RHENISH MAY (of Illinois.)

This long-keeping apple has been widely disseminated throughout the West, and yet I do not find its history nor origin.   It has been exhibited at all our winter meetings, and finds favor on account of its productiveness and its long-keeping properties.   Tree healthy, vigorous and productive—believed to be hardy.   Its reputed foreign origin is discredited.

Fruit medium, round, inclined to conical, regular; Surface smooth, often shining, pale greenish-yellow, often faintly blushed, or bronzed.

24

Basin shallow, generally regular ; Eye small, closed.

Cavity deep, narrow, regular, brown ; Stem long, rather slender.

Core large, regular, heart-shaped, reaching the eye ; Seeds

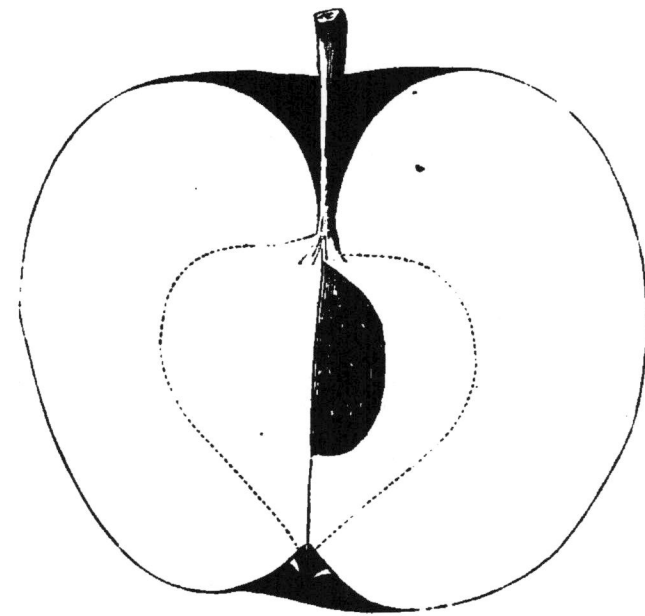

Fig. 184.—MAY.

numerous, pointed, plump, brown ; Flesh yellow, compact, fine, sufficiently juicy ; Quality fair ; Use market and kitchen ; Season spring and into summer.

Morton.

This undescribed fruit appears to have originated in Clermont County, Ohio. My specimens and trees came from my worthy friend, Wm. E. Mears, of Milford, Ohio.

Tree vigorous, healthy, round top, spreading, productive ; Shoots rather slender ; Leaves rich green, abundant.

Fruit large, round, regular ; Surface smooth, green, becoming yellow, with a dull bronzy blush ; Dots gray and brown.

Basin shallow, or deep and abrupt, regular or plaited; Eye medium, closed.

Cavity acute, regular, brown; Stem rather slender, often long.

Core very small, regular, closed, meeting the eye; Seeds

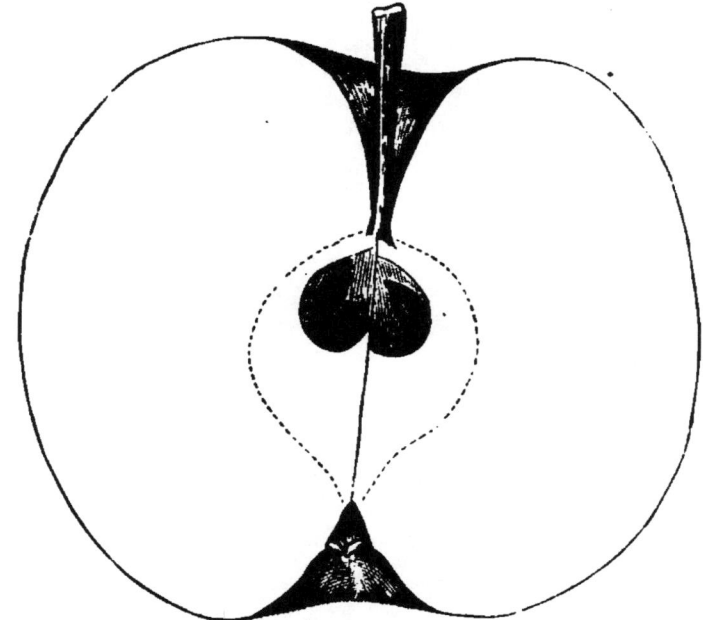

Fig. 185.—MORTON.

not numerous, flat, angular; Flesh white, tender, juicy; Flavor rather sweet, rich, agreeable; Season December to January.   Worthy of cultivation.

Paradise Summer Sweet.

Origin Eastern Pennsylvania.   Tree upright, vigorous, productive.

Fruit large, oblate-globular, regular; Surface greenish-yellow; Dots numerous, large, white.

Basin shallow, wide, folded; Eye small, closed.

Cavity deep, regular, acute, green; Stem long, inclined, yellow.

Core medium, regular, round, clasping; Seeds plump;

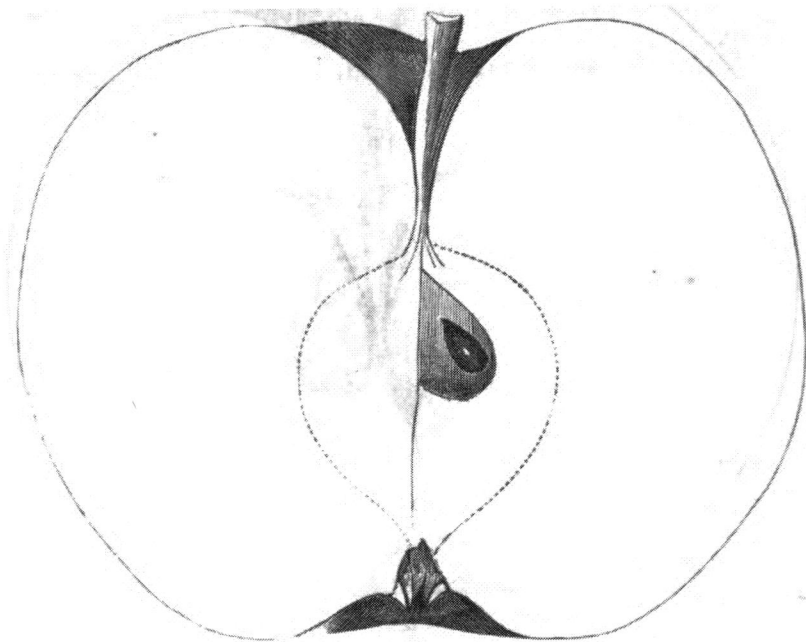

Fig. 186.—PARADISE SUMMER SWEET.

Flesh yellow, melting, juicy; Flavor rich, sweet; Quality best; Use table and kitchen; Season August, September.

Paradise Winter Sweet.

Origin believed to be similar to its predecessor—Lancaster County, Pennsylvania.

Fruit large, globular, often unequal; Surface smooth, yellowish-white; Dots scattered, minute.

Basin abrupt, regular; Eye small, closed.

Cavity deep, acute, brown; Stem long, slender.

Core large, wide, open, clasping; Seeds plump and dark; Flesh white, tender, breaking, juicy; Flavor very sweet; Quality good; Use, baking and stock; Season, December to March.

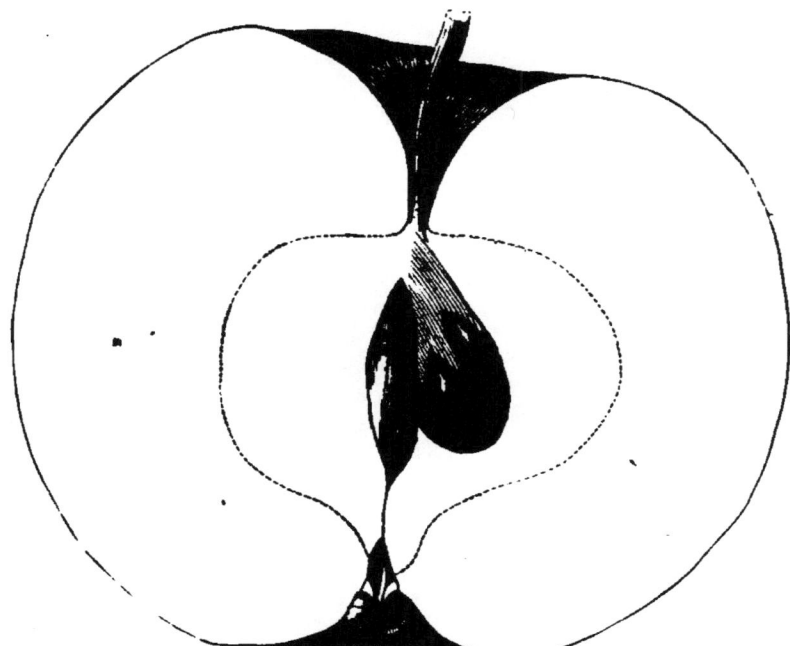

Fig. 187.—PARADISE WINTER SWEET.

Tallman's Sweet.

This favorite baking apple of New England has trav-
eled from Rhode Island wherever her hardy sons have
gone westward.

Tree hardy, very productive.

Fruit medium to large, nearly round, somewhat flattened, regular; Surface smooth, yellow; Dots minute, dark;
frequently a distinct line on one side from stem to eye.

Basin wide, regular, leather-crooked; Eye small,
closed.

Cavity rather wide, regular; Stem medium size, long.

Core heart-shaped, regular, closed, clasping; Seeds numerous, plump, pointed, dark; Flesh yellow, breaking,
firm; Flavor very sweet, rich; Quality good; Use, baking
and stock; Season, December and January.

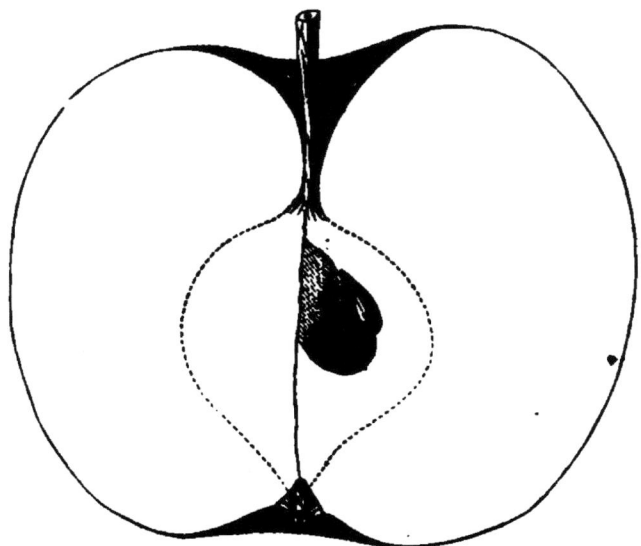

Fig. 188.—TALLMAN'S SWEET.

CLASS III.—ROUND APPLES.

ORDER I.—REGULAR.

SECTION 1.—SWEET.

SUB-SECTION 2.—STRIPED.

Bentley Sweet.

This long-keeping sweet apple was received in Eastern Ohio from some part of Virginia, where it is supposed to have originated.

Tree quite vigorous, upright while young, spreading, productive—an early bearer.

Fruit medium to large, globular, truncated, slightly flattened, regular; Surface smooth, yellow, or greenish, covered, mixed, blotched, striped and splashed dull red, becoming brighter when ripe; Dots minute.

Basin medium, abrupt, regular; Eye medium, open; Calyx reflexed.

Cavity deep, acute, regular; Stem slender, long.

Core round, flattened, regular, closed; Seeds numerous, plump, long; Flesh yellowish-white, firm, breaking, fine-grained; Flavor sweet; Quality good to very good; Season spring and all summer until September. Keeps sound.

Bowling Sweet.

From Spottsylvania County, Virginia. Tree vigorous, very productive.

Fruit medium roundish, dull red on yellow; Flesh rich, juicy, sweet; Entirely free from acid; October to January.—[H. R. Robey, in Downing.]

Cullasaga.

Origin Macon County, North Carolina. Good grower; a standard winter fruit for the South.

Fruit medium or large, roundish, inclining to oval, flattened at base and crown, skin yellowish, mostly shaded and striped with dark crimson, and sprinkled with whitish dots; Stem small and short, inserted in a deep cavity, surrounded by russet; Calyx open, set in a shallow, corrugated basin; Flesh yellow, tender, juicy, with a very mild, rich, almost saccharine flavor. January to April. —[Downing.]

Gilpin.

CARTHOUSE—LITTLE RED ROMANITE.

This valuable Virginia apple was cultivated and distributed by Coxe, and has found its way into the orchards and into favor all over the country, on account of its productiveness and early bearing.

Tree remarkably vigorous, strongly branched, spreading, open, round head, very productive; shoots stout, dark; foliage rather sparse, somewhat curled and glaucous.

Fruit medium, small on old trees, round, truncated at the ends, making it look cylindrical, mostly symmetrical, but large specimens often somewhat irregular; Surface very smooth, often polished, deep red all over, stripes indistinct; Dots minute, indented.

Basin wide, regular, or folded; Eye small, closed.

Cavity deep, acute, regular, brown; Stem very short.

Core medium, round, regular, closed; Seeds few, large, plump; Flesh greenish-yellow, firm, juicy; Flavor sweet, rich; Quality poor for dessert, though it is eatable in the

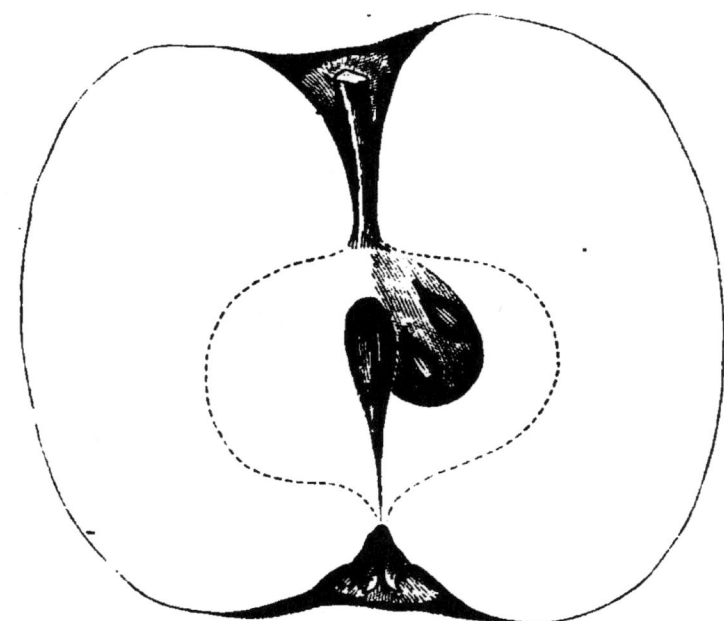

Fig. 189.—GILPIN.

spring—valuable for its cider from the richness of the must. Keeps sound until May—bruises do not rot as in other apples. Valuable also for stock.

Its early bearing makes it very desirable in a new country, and in the prairies it has received the soubriquet of "*Dollars and Cents.*"

Hall.

HALL'S SEEDLING—HALL'S RED.

From Franklin County, North Carolina, and now being spread throughout the Western States as a fruit of great promise.

Tree medium size, sufficiently thrifty, upright, hardy, very productive; Shoots long, rather slender, reddish, wood firm. Introduced into the West by the venerable R. Ragan, of Fillmore, Indiana. The specimens from which the following description was made were sent by J. S. Downer, of Elkton, Kentucky, from whom also my trees were obtained. Mr. J. P. Wilson, of Olney, Ill.,

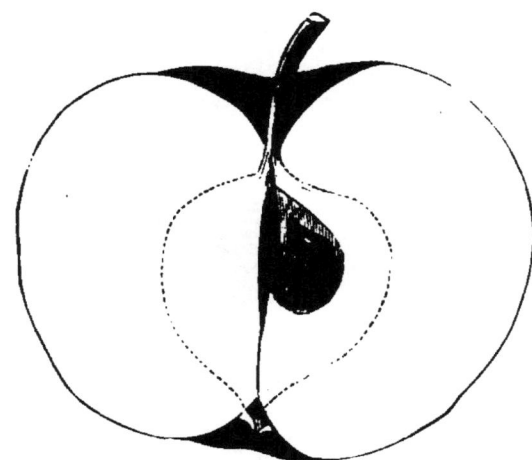

Fig. 190.—HALL.

says, it originated in Saline County, of that State, with Jonathan Hall, about forty years ago. [?]

Fruit small, round, slightly conical, regular; Surface smooth, yellow, covered with bright red, mixed and striped; Dots numerous, large, yellow.

Basin shallow, wavy or plaited, leather-cracked; Eye small, closed.

Cavity wide, regular, brown; Stem long, slender.

Core pyriform, regular, slightly open, clasping; Seeds large, plump; Flesh yellow, tender, fine-grained, juicy; Flavor sub-acid, rich, agreeable; Quality almost best; Use, table; Season, December to April.

Ladies' Sweeting.

This prime favorite of Chas. Downing originated near Newburgh, New York. Though having many admirers,

24*

it finds strong competitors in the *Broadwell, Paradise Winter,* and some others of the same season.

Tree thrifty, productive.

Fruit large, round, somewhat conic, occasionally angular; Surface smooth, light yellow, striped and splashed with bright red; Dots distinct, large, gray.

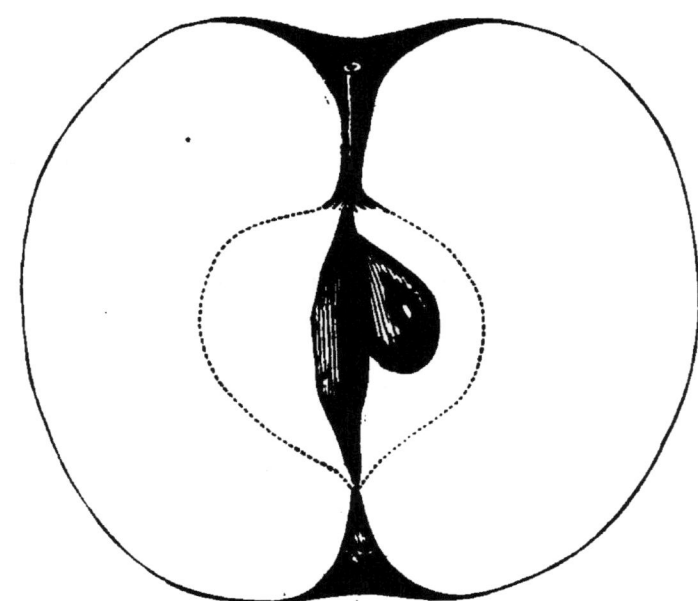

Fig. 191.—LADIES' SWEETING.

Basin medium, often abrupt, folded; Eye very small, closed.

Cavity medium or wide, regular, brown; Stem short, or long and slender.

Core medium, round, closed or open, clasping; Seeds numerous (16), angular; Flesh white, crisp, fine-grained, juicy; Flavor sweet, agreeable; Quality only good (to my taste); Use, table, baking and stock feeding; Season, December.

Scarlet Sweet.

This delicate fruit was received from *my good friend* Jas. Edgerton, of Barnesville, Ohio, who had exhibited it at the State Pomological Society at different times.

Fruit medium, round, somewhat flattened, regular; Surface smooth, yellow, striped and blushed scarlet; Dots minute.

Basin wide, abrupt, regular; Eye medium, open; segments short.

Cavity deep, acute, regular, brown; Stem medium, slender.

Core rather wide, regular, closed, clasping the eye; Seeds numerous, plump, angular; Flesh yellow, fine-grain-

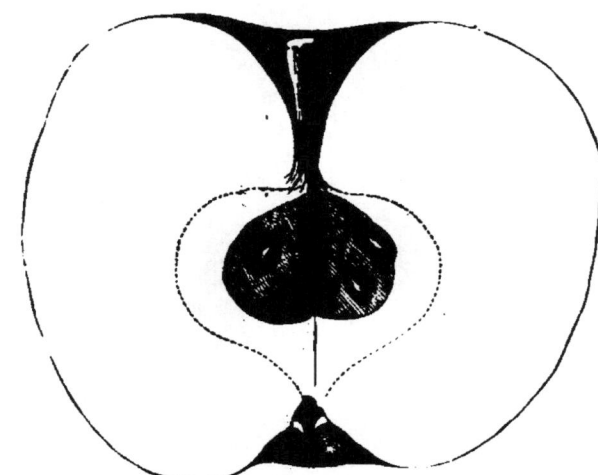

Fig. 192.—SCARLET SWEET.

ed, juicy; Flavor sweet; Quality good to very good; Uses, table, baking and market; Season, October to December.

This is different from the *Scarlet Sweeting* of Sigler, of Morgan County, Ohio—more like Hampton's Scarlet Sweet, of M.S. notes.

Sweet Janet.

This is another of the fine fruits originated by Reuben Ragan, of Indiana, from seed of *Rawle's Janet*. Tree large, healthy, vigorous, spreading; Shoots rather stout, brown; foliage rich green. Annually productive of fine, fair fruits, which are well distributed and hold well.

Fruit large, round, somewhat conical, regular; Surface smooth, covered with rich red or crimson, mixed and striped; Dots numerous, rather large, yellow, indented.

Basin regular or plaited; Eye medium, closed.

Cavity rather deep, very narrow, wavy; Stem quite short.

Core medium, turbinate, regular, slightly open, clasping; Seeds numerous, angular, pointed; Flesh yellow,

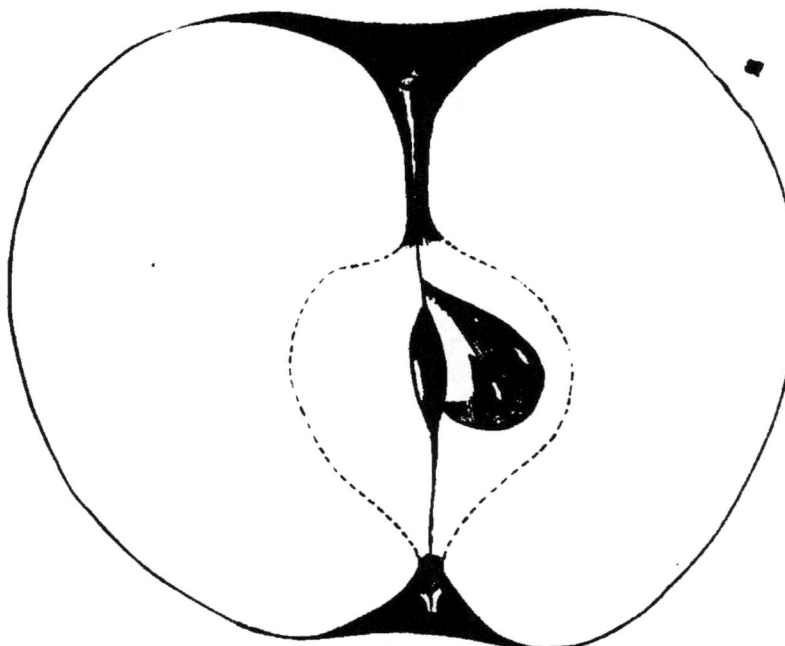

Fig. 193.—SWEET JANET.

breaking, juicy; Flavor very sweet; Quality good to very good; Use, baking, market; Season, December and January. Very profitable.

Sweet Romanite.

Origin unknown. Grown in Illinois; introduced at the State Society by the lamented Cyrus R. Overman, President—much esteemed by him.

Fruit medium, round, sometimes flattened or truncate, regular; Surface smooth, greenish-yellow, blushed, mixed bright red and dull red, stripes indistinct; Dots scattered, irregular, brown or fawn on the deeper colors.

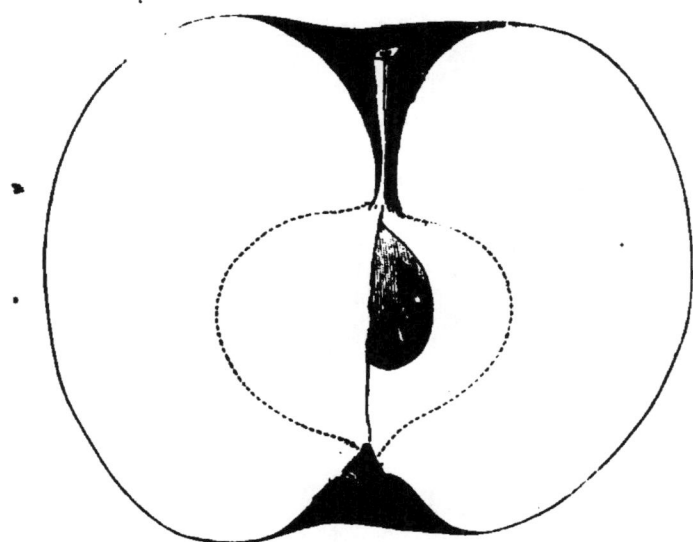

Fig. 194.—SWEET ROMANITE.

Basin medium, or deep and abrupt, folded, plaited; Eye small, closed.

Cavity deep, acute, wavy, brown; Stem medium to long, green.

Core roundish, closed, clasping; Seeds numerous, plump, angular; Flesh yellow, fine-grained, breaking, juicy; Flavor very sweet; Quality good to very good; Use, baking, cider, table and stock; Season, December to April.

CLASS III.—ROUND APPLES.

ORDER I.—REGULAR.

SECTION 1.—SWEET.

SUB-SECTION 3.—RUSSET.

Orange Sweeting or Russet.

An eastern variety—not much cultivated.

Fruit large, very round, regular; Surface greenish-yellow, bronzy-orange, russeted; Dots numerous, white, green bases.

Basin shallow, regular, or plaited; Eye small, closed.

Cavity acute, lipped, wavy; Stem short, green.

Core very large, turbinate, open, clasping; Seeds numerous, pointed, pale; Flesh green, rather tough, fine-grained, juicy; Flavor sweet; Quality good—for baking especially; Season, December.

Pumpkin Russet.

Fruit large, globular, regular; Surface covered with coarse russeting; Flesh spongy, light, very sweet; Used for baking and apple butter; Season, autumn. Not valuable, except for stock.

————•◦•————

CLASS III.—ROUND APPLES.

ORDER I.—REGULAR.

SECTION 2.—SOUR.

SUB-SECTION 1.—SELF-COLORED OR BLUSHED.

Ashmore.

The origin of this fine dessert fruit is not known. Though not commonly cultivated, it is considerably scattered, and has come to me from several points in the West with different local names.

Tree vigorous, upright, with long parallel branches that

become spreading. Shoots rather slender, foliage rich green.

Fruit rather large, handsome, round, frequently flattened, regular, rarely angular; Surface smooth, polished, very light waxen yellow, almost wholly covered with brilliant lively carmine, very rarely an indistinct stripe; Dots minute, gray, indented.

Basin medium, often wavy or even folded; Eye small, closed; Segments reflexed.

Cavity narrow, acute, regular or wavy; Stem medium to short.

Core indistinct, closed; Seeds plump; Flesh yellowish-white, crisp, tender, very fine-grained, juicy; Flavor sub-

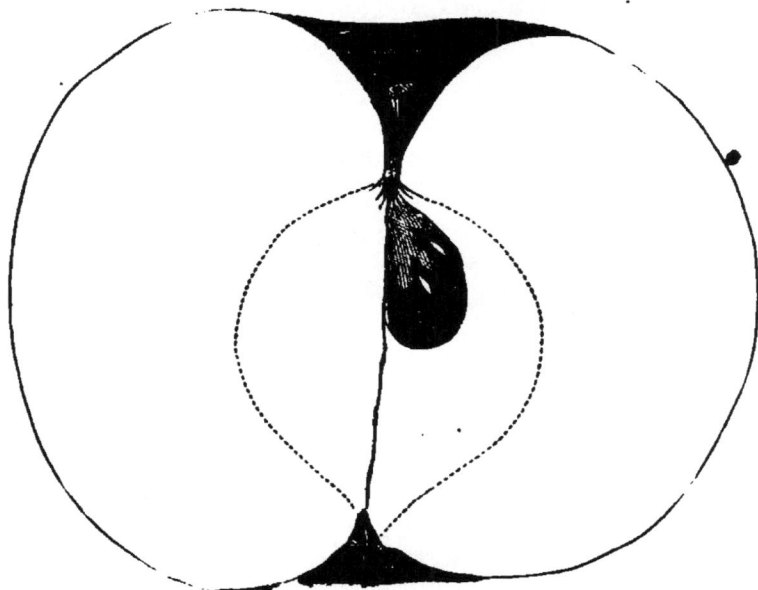

Fig. 195.—ASHMORE.

acid, very agreeable; Quality best, though not rich; Uses, table, kitchen and market; Season, September and October; May be kept into winter.

There is also a *Striped Ashmore*, resembling this in every respect, except in the distinct stripe. It is supposed to be a sport from the above. Both varieties have been propagated to some extent by suckers or sprouts.

Bledsoe.

From Carroll County, Kentucky; Sent to Ohio by Lewis Sanders. Tree moderately vigorous, spreading, productive.

Fruit large, round, somewhat conical, flattened at the base, regular; Surface greenish-yellow.

Basin sometimess folded; Eye medium, closed.

Cavity deep, brown; Stem short.

Flesh white, fine-grained, crisp, juicy; Flavor mild sub-acid, agreeable; Quality good—Kentucky Horticultural Society say "very good;" Season, September to April.

Bush.

Received from W. G. Waring, Tyrone, Pennsylvania. Supposed to be a seedling of Centre County. "Tree vigor-

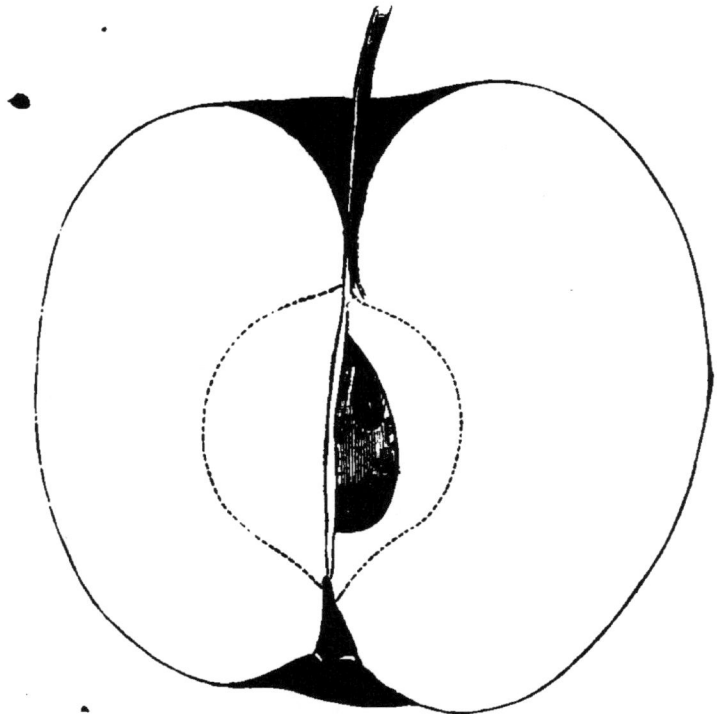

Fig. 196.—BUSH.

ous, hardy, thrifty, regularly productive."—[W. G. W.]

Fruit large, fair, round, regular; Surface smooth, waxy yellow, occasionally a faint blush; Dots minute, rare.

Basin wavy; Eye medium to small, closed.

Cavity deep, wavy, brownish; Stem long, slender, yellow.

Core medium, round, rather open, meeting the eye; Seeds few, plump, dark; Flesh whitish, tender, fine-grained, juicy; Flavor mild sub-acid, agreeable; Quality very good; Season August and September.

Mr. Waring considers it one of the best of the season, in which opinion I unite.

Cornish Aromatic.

This foreign variety was imported and tested at Louisville, Kentucky, by Mr. George Heinsohn, to whom I am indebted for specimens of other European varieties.

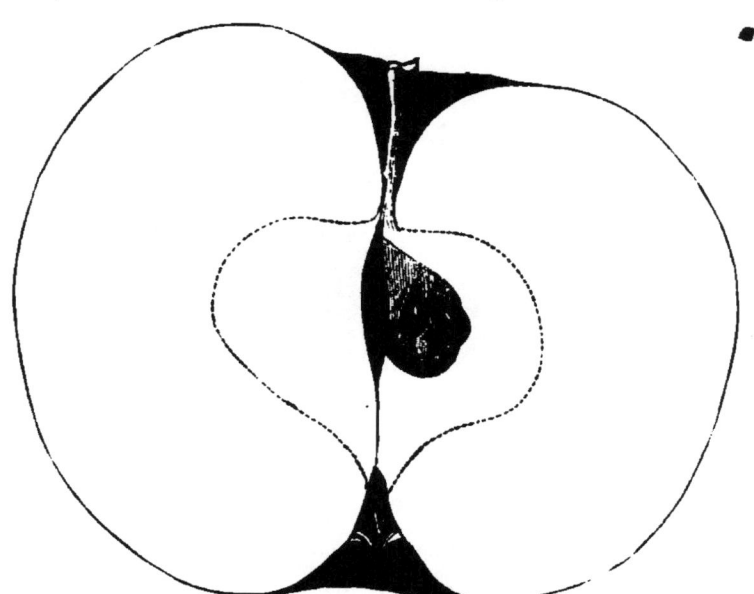

Fig. 197.—CORNISH AROMATIC.

Fruit medium to large, roundish, a little flattened, regular; Surface smooth, yellow, washed rich red; Dots and spots yellow russet.

Basin medium, abrupt, regular or furrowed; Eye medium, closed.

Cavity medium depth, narrow; Stem medium to long, slender.

Core medium, somewhat open, clasping; Seeds large, plump, angular; Flesh yellow, breaking, juicy; Flavor sub-acid, aromatic, spicy; Season November to February.

Duffield Pippin.

Specimens from my friend T. T. Lyon, of Michigan, who says it is a seedling that originated in Pennsylvania,

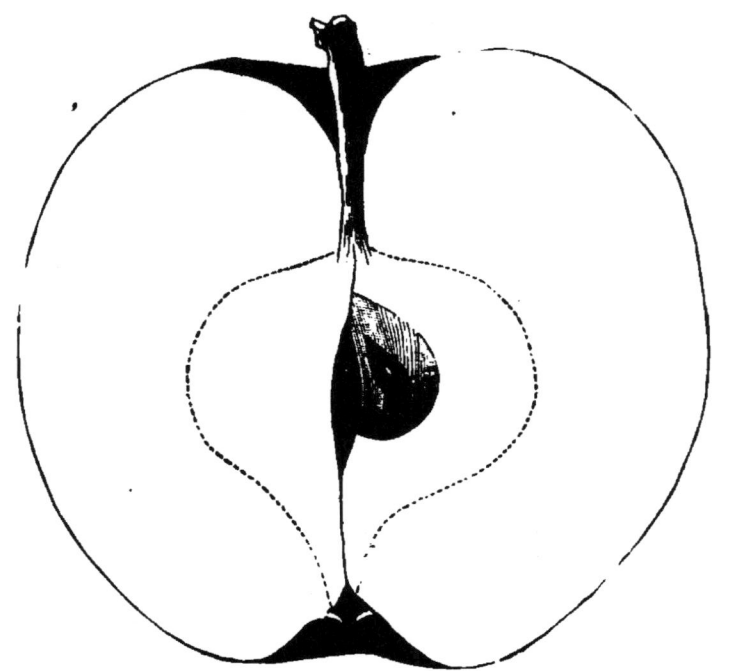

Fig. 198.—DUFFIELD PIPPIN.

at the beginning of the present century, with the ancestors of Geo. Duffield, D.D., for whom it was named, when it received a first premium at the Michigan State Fair, as a valuable winter variety.

Fruit large, handsome, round, sometimes conic, regular;

Surface smooth, yellowish-green, blushed; Dots scattered, minute, indented.

Basin abrupt, narrow, folded; Eye small, closed.

Cavity deep, narrow, acute; Stem medium to long.

Core closed, clasping; Seeds plump, brown; Flesh yellow, breaking, juicy; Flavor sub-acid; Quality good; Uses table, kitchen and market; Season January to April.

Fall Pippin.

It is unfortunate that since the days of Coxe there should have been a confounding of this noble and delicious

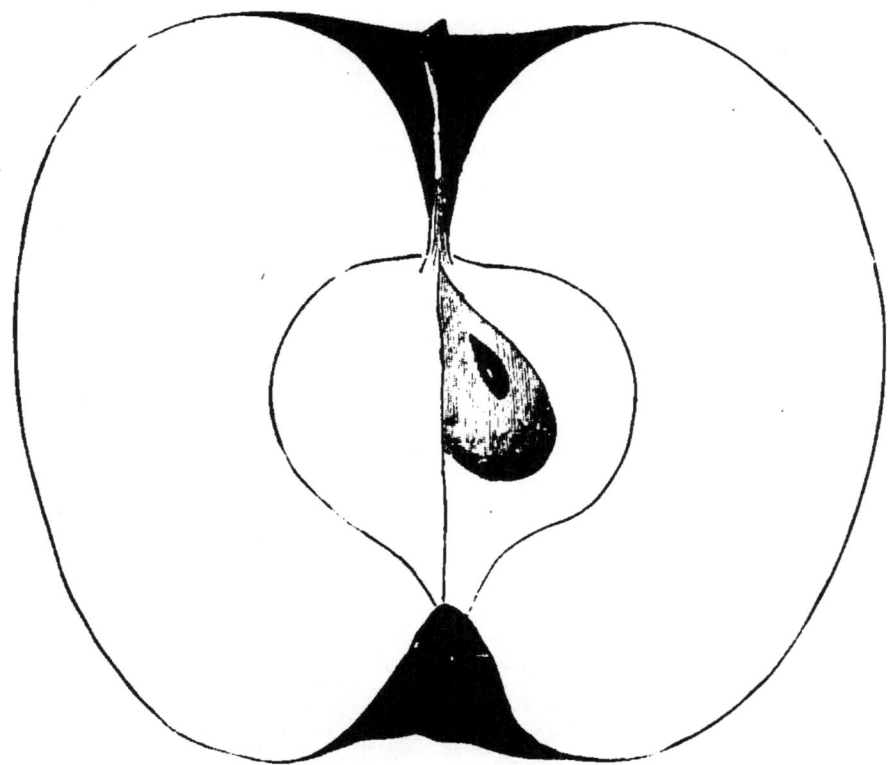

Fig. 199.—FALL PIPPIN.

American apple with the inferior foreign kitchen variety: the Holland Pippin.

Tree exceedingly vigorous, large, wide-branching, open head, not early bearer, moderately productive when old; Shoots stout, dark; Leaves large, broad.

Fruit large to very large, handsome, globular, truncated, making it cylindrical, regular; Surface smooth, rich yellow, rarely blushed South, frequently so North, with skin finer; Dots minute, gray.

Basin deep, abrupt, regular, marked with concentric rings which often crack open in large southern specimens; Eye large, open; Segments short.

Cavity wide, regular, or narrow, deep; Stem long.

Core large, regular, closed, meeting the eye; Seeds pointed, often imperfect; Flesh yellow, breaking, compact, very fine-grained; Flavor acid, becoming sub-acid, aromatic, delicious; Quality best for dessert, kitchen, market and drying; Season September to December.

Fall Swaar—[OF THE WEST.]

The origin of this apple is unknown. Like many others of our Western fruits, which have been received from vari-

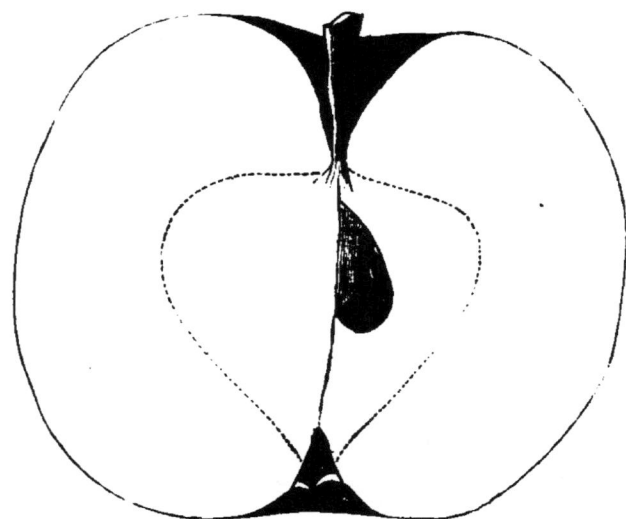

Fig. 200.—FALL SWAAR.

ous sources, and often from unreliable persons, and with wrong names, we have been obliged to re-christen this.

Fruit full medium to large, round, somewhat flattened, regular, handsome; Surface smooth, yellowish-green, with a bronzy blush; Dots numerous, large, gray.

Basin medium, regular; Eye small, closed.

Cavity medium, acute, regular, green; Stem medium to long, knobbed.

Core rather small, closed, clasping; Seeds numerous, large, plump; Flesh yellow, breaking, juicy; Flavor mild sub-acid, agreeable; Quality good; Uses table and kitchen; Season September.

Gloucester White.

This Virginia apple was highly prized by Coxe for its qualities as a cider fruit. Not having seen it, his description is quoted:

"This apple is of middling size, of a shape not very uniform, varying from oblong to flat; the color when ripe is a bright yellow, with clouds of black spots; the flesh is yellow, rich, breaking, and juicy; of a fine flavor as a table apple, and producing cider of an exquisite taste. The stalk is of the ordinary length, inserted in a cavity of medium depth; the crown is moderately deep. The time of ripening is about the first of October, after which the fruit soon falls and is fit for cider. It does not keep long, but while in season is a delicious table apple. The tree is very thrifty, hardy and vigorous, of a regular and beautiful form, and very productive. It is much cultivated in the lower counties of Virginia, from whence I procured it, as an apple of high reputation."

Horse.

Another southern favorite, much liked by its western cultivators, especially as a useful family apple.

Fruit large, round, somewhat conical, truncated, uneven; Surface yellow; Dots scattered, indented, large, gray and greenish.

Basin abrupt, fol'ed; Eye medium, closed.

Cavity deep, acute, wavy, brown; Stem medium to long.

Core large, somewhat open, clasping; Seeds numerous, medium, plump, brown; Flesh yellow, breaking, fine, juicy;

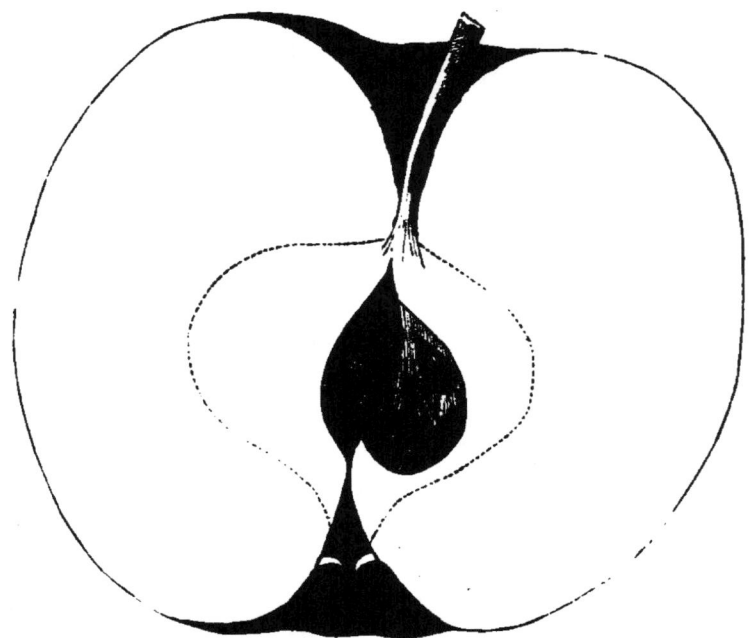

Fig. 201.—HORSE.

Flavor sub-acid; Quality good; Use, kitchen, market and drying; Season, August, September.

Hunge.

This southern apple was received from Mr. S. W. Westbrooke, Greensboro', North Carolina.

Fruit large, round, somewhat flattened, regular; Surface smooth, greenish-yellow, blushed; Dots scattered, white.

Basin regular, abrupt; Eye small, closed, very long; Calyx reflexed.

Cavity wide, wavy; Stem short, slender.

Core large, wide, irregular, open, clasping; Seeds numerous, angular, plump; Flesh white, fine-grained, tender, juicy; Flavor sub-acid, mild; Quality pretty good; Use, table, kitchen, drying; Season, September.

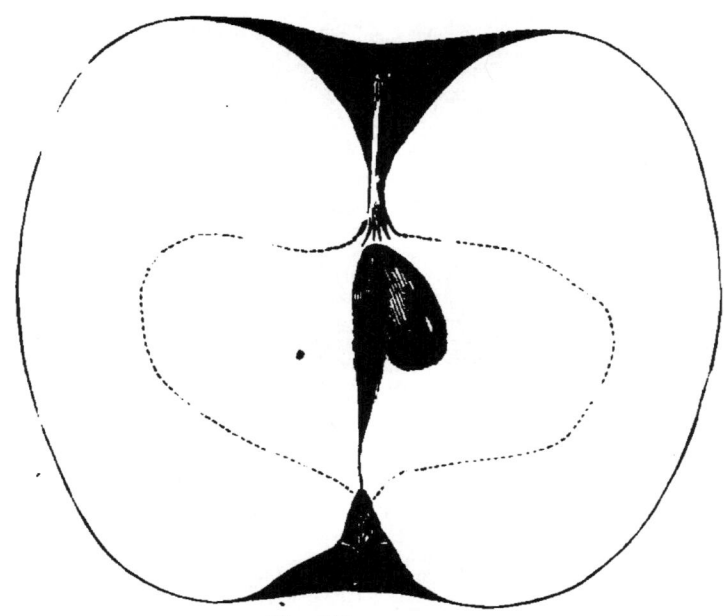

Fig. 202. —HUNGE.

Knickerbocker.

Specimens from W. S. Carpenter, New York.

Fruit above medium, roundish, conic, unequal; Surface smooth, greenish-yellow; Dots numerous, minute, distinct, whitish, indented.

Basin abrupt, wavy, folded; Eye medium, closed.

Cavity wide, wavy, brown; Stem long, slender, green.

Core very wide, closed, clasping the eye; Axis short; Seeds angular, pale; Flesh greenish-yellow, tender, fine-grained, juicy; Flavor sub-acid, rich, very agreeable; Quality best; Use, table, kitchen; Season, October.

Long Island Pippin.

Origin unknown.   Specimens received from T. T. Lyon, Plymouth, Michigan.

Fruit large, roundish, flattened, regular; Surface smooth yellowish-green; Dots minute, scattered.

Basin abrupt, deep, regular; Eye medium, closed.

Cavity medium, regular, green ; Stem medium to long.

Core large, oval, closed, clasping ; Seeds numerous, pointed, angular, pale ; Flesh greenish-yellow, breaking, fine-grained, juicy ; Flavor sub-acid ; Quality almost best ; Use, table ; Season, January.

Lowell.

TALLOW PIPPIN, QUEEN ANNE, &C.

Origin unknown.

Tree vigorous, healthy, round-headed ; Foliage yellowish green.

Fruit large, round, slightly conic, truncated, regular ; Surface smooth, waxy yellow, not blushed or bronzed, becoming greasy when kept indoors ; Dots numerous, green.

Basin deep, abrupt, regular ; Eye medium, closed.

Cavity medium, regular, green ; Stem long, slender.

Core medium, oval, closed, clasping ; Seeds numerous, angular, pointed, pale ; Flesh yellow, tender, fine-grained, juicy ; Flavor sub-acid, aromatic ; Quality very good ; Use, table, cooking, drying, market ; Season, August, September.

McAdow's June.—[Local Name.]

Specimens received from Chillicothe, Ohio. Thought at one time to be Tetofski, but the descriptions do not correspond.

Fruit medium to small, globular, slightly conical, regular ; Surface smooth, greenish, yellow, blushed ; Dots numerous, large, white.

Basin medium, wavy ; Eye small, closed.

Cavity rather wide, regular ; Stem long, stout.

Core small, round, closed, not meeting the eye ; Seeds numerous, brown; Flesh yellow, tender, fine-grained, juicy ; Flavor sub-acid ; Use, kitchen, table ; Quality good ; Season, June, July ; one of the earliest.

Pomologists have been in doubt whether this may not be the Tetofski. Comparison should be made of the tree characters.

Michigan Golden.

This beautiful apple was received from the accurate pomologist, T. T. Lyon, of Plymouth.

Fruit large, globular, slightly conic, truncated and some-what angular; Surface smooth, becoming greasy, greenish yellow; Dots minute, prominent.

Basin abrupt, folded; Eye small, closed.

Cavity wide, wavy; Stem long, inclined.

Core medium, closed, clasping; Seeds numerous, long,

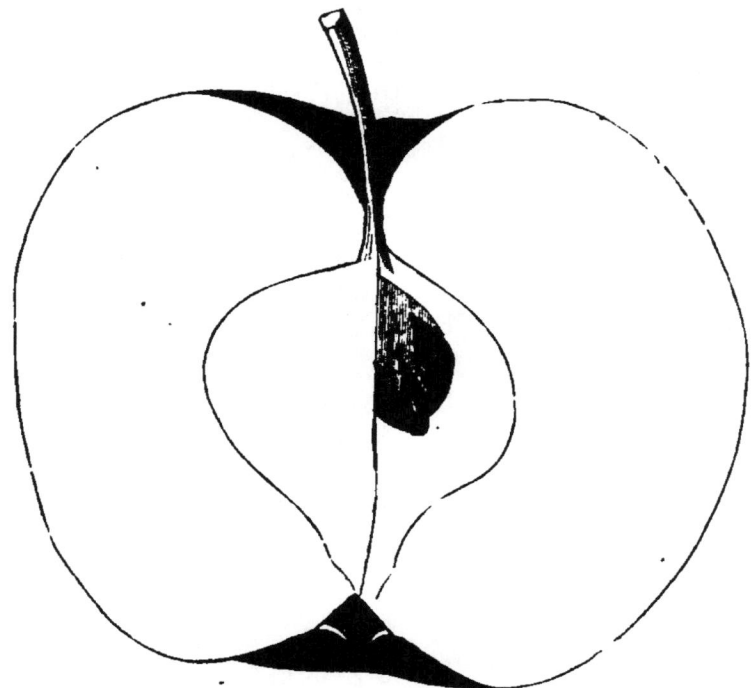

Fig. 203.—MICHIGAN GOLDEN.

pointed; Flesh yellow, breaking, juicy; Flavor sub-acid; Quality nearly best; Use, table, kitchen; Season, September to November.

Monmouth Pippin.

RED CHEEK.

Fruit rather large, handsome, roundish or flattened, regular; Surface smooth, greenish yellow, blushed and marbled; Dots minute, green.

25

Basin shallow, regular; Eye large, closed.
Cavity wide, regular or wavy, brown; Stem short, thick.
Core medium, closed, clasping; Seeds numerous, point-

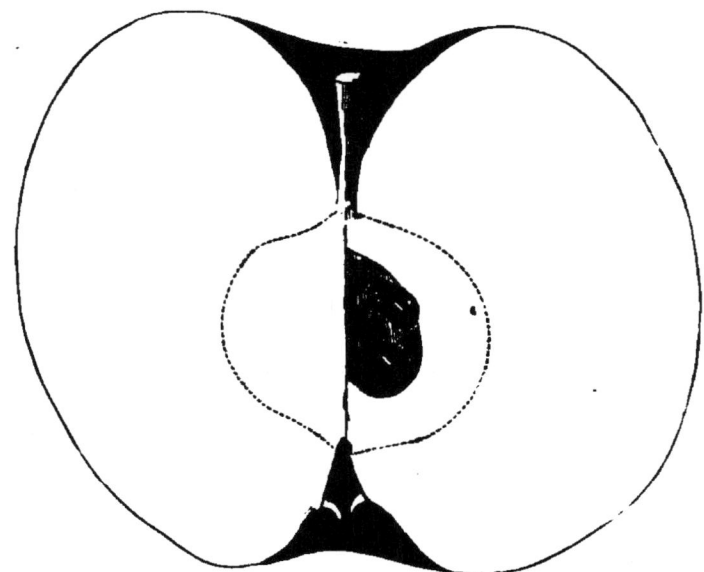

Fig. 204.—MONMOUTH PIPPIN.

ed, brown; Flesh white, breaking, fine-grained, juicy;
Flavor acid; Quality good for cooking only; Season, December to February.

Newtown Pippin.

GREEN NEWTOWN.

This is probably the original Newtown Pippin, but by
no means the more common, which is the *Yellow Newtown
Pippin*, to be described in another place.
Fruit medium to large, globular, flattened, sometimes
obscurely ribbed; Surface smooth, green, becoming yellowish green when fully ripe, sometimes bronzy, and always showing white irregular striæ near the base when
first gathered; Dots scattered, minute, dark.
Basin shallow, folded; Eye small, closed.
Cavity wide, wavy, brown; Stem long, slender.

Core round, regular, closed, meeting the eye; Seeds pointed, plump, dark; Flesh greenish white, crisp, tender, juicy; Flavor acid, aromatic, rich, very agreeable; Quality best; Use, dessert, cooking; Season, December to March.

Roman Stem.

Origin Burlington, New Jersey. Tree moderately vigorous, very productive.

Fruit medium, globular, regular; Surface smooth, yellow, often blushed; Dots minute, dark.

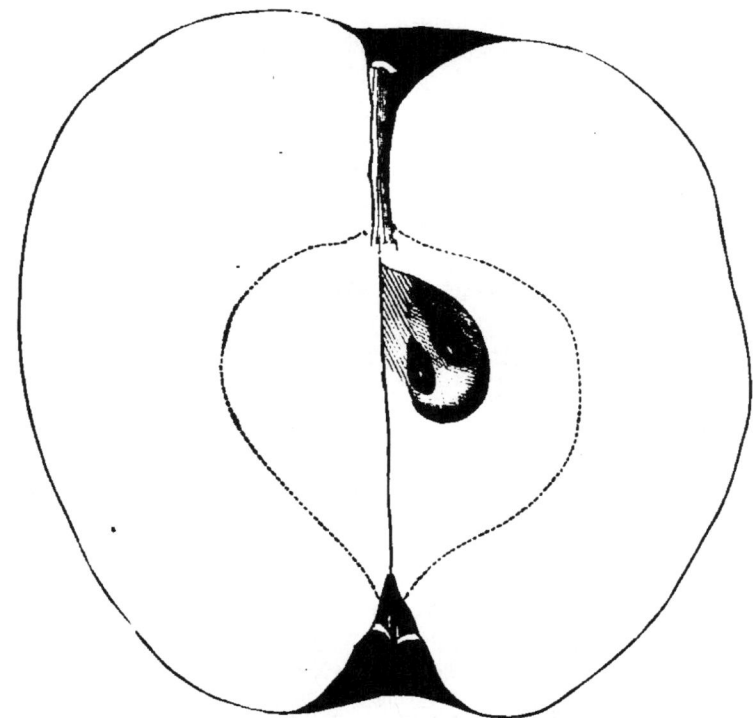

Fig. 205.—ROMAN STEM.

Basin shallow, regular, or wavy, russet; Eye small, closed.

Cavity acute, lipped; Stem long.

Core rather large, heart-shaped, regular, clasping; Seeds

numerous, plump; Flesh yellowish white, fine-grained, juicy; Flavor mild sub-acid, rich; Quality good to very good; Use, table; Season, December, January.

Royal Pearmain.

We have two different apples bearing this name, both very promising and desirable sorts. I shall, in this place, attempt to describe the one mentioned by Coxe, as my specimens are traced back to his nursery, though coming to the West by way of Georgia.

Fruit full medium to large, globular, rather flattened, regular; Surface not smooth, of a rich yellow, finely blushed, with carmine more or less diffused over the fruit, and overspread with a very thin russet; Dots medium, prominent, brown.

Basin medium, folded; Eye medium, closed.

Cavity acute, brown; Stem medium to long.

Flesh rich yellow, firm, juicy; Flavor acid, sprightly; Quality very good; Use, table; Season, October to February.

Virginia Quaker.

This very fine little apple was obtained from H. N. Gillett, Lawrence County, Ohio. Origin not known.

Fruit quite small, globular, flattened, slightly conic, regular; Surface smooth, greenish yellow; Dots scattered, minute, black.

Basin shallow, plaited; Eye small, closed.

Cavity wide; Stem medium.

Core ovate, closed; Seeds medium; Flesh yellowish white, firm, breaking; Flavor sub-acid; Quality good, Mr. Gillett says, best; Season, mid-summer.

Voss' Winter.

Southern. The specimens were obtained from Mr. Westbrooke, of North Carolina.

Fruit medium to large, globular, unequal; Surface smooth, white, with leather-cracking, and a heavy bloom; Dots minute, irregular, brown.

Basin abrupt, deep, wavy; Eye small, closed.

Cavity deep, wavy, brown; Stem long, curved.
Core small, regular, closed, clasping; Seeds irregular;

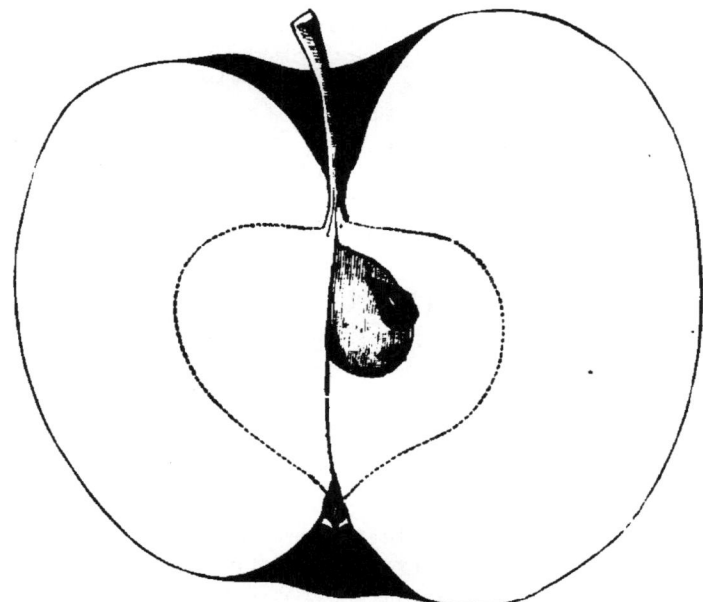

Fig. 206.—VOSS' WINTER.

Flesh whitish yellow, firm, juicy; Flavor sub-acid; Quality
good; Use, table and kitchen; Season, December.

White Pippin—[Of Kentucky.]

Fruit large, globular, somewhat oblate, regular; Surface smooth, green, becoming pale yellow, sometimes
faintly blushed; Dots numerous, white, rather large.
Basin small, abrupt, regular; Eye very small, long,
slender, closed.
Cavity acute, regular, green; Stem medium, regular,
knobby.
Core round, regular, closed, clasping; Seeds numerous,
long, pointed, angular, brown; Flesh white, breaking, fine-
grained, juicy; Flavor acid; Quality good; Use, market
and kitchen; Season, December, January.

Wilson—[Of Michigan.]

Fruit large, round, slightly conic, regular; Surface smooth, golden yellow; Dots scattered, dark.

Basin small, folded; Eye long, closed.

Cavity wide, very deep, wavy, green; Stem medium or short, crooked.

Core small, globular, open, clasping; Axis short; Seeds numerous, plump, short; Flesh very yellow, breaking, fine-grained, juicy; Flavor sub-acid, rich; Quality best; Use, the dessert; Season, January and February.

Yellow Ingestrie.

This old English variety has been propagated pretty extensively in the Northwest, and though too small for a profitable market fruit, it has been found desirable on account of its early and abundant productiveness.

Fruit small, globular, truncated, regular; Surface smooth, lemon yellow; Dots minute.

Basin wide, shallow, folded; Eye medium, open; Segments reflexed.

Cavity acute, brown; Stem long, slender.

Core medium, oval, regular, closed, clasping; Seeds few, large, pale; Flesh whitish yellow, breaking, juicy; Flavor sub-acid; Quality barely good; Use, cooking; Season, September, October.

CLASS III.—ROUND APPLES.

ORDER I.—REGULAR.

SECTION II.—SOUR.

SUB-SECTION II.—STRIPED.

American Summer Pearmain.

This delicious apple is supposed to be of American origin. It is essentially a fruit for the amateur; being of slender and slow growth in the nursery, it is not a favorite with the propagators, and though making a large and productive tree in the orchard, it is not profitable as a market variety.

Fruit medium, variable in form, being oblong, round, conic and even oblate, regular or unequal ; Surface smooth, greenish yellow, more or less covered with dull purplish red, marbled, and made up of very short splashes, with distinct stripes and splashes of brighter red ; Dots minute.

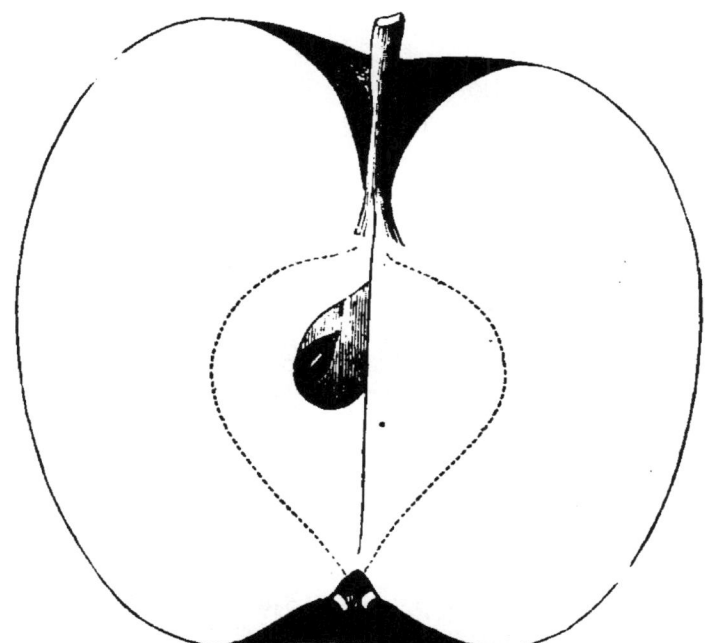

Fig. 207.—AMERICAN SUMMER PEARMAIN.

Basin medium, regular ; Eye rather large, nearly closed ; Segments recurved.

Cavity rather deep, acute, regular ; Stem medium to long.

Core small, roundish, closed ; Seeds small, pointed ; Flesh yellow, exceedingly tender, almost melting, crisp, fine-grained, juicy ; Flavor very mild sub-acid, aromatic, deliciously refreshing ; Quality best ; Use, the dessert ; Season, August and September..

Baccalinus.

Fruited by J. H. Crain, Pulaski County, Illinois, on trees nine years old, which produced ten bushels apiece, showing its productiveness.

This valuable Southern keeper bids fair to become a great favorite.

Tree thrifty, very productive; Fruit small, globular, truncated, regular, handsome; Surface smooth, mixed bright red, and splashed crimson on pale yellow; Dots few, minute.

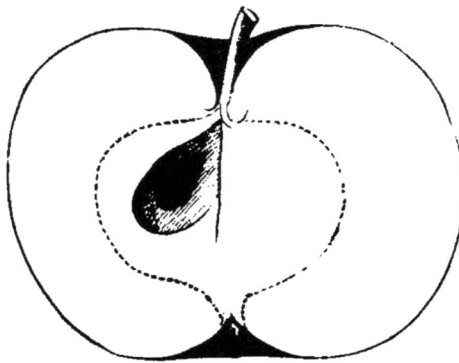

Fig. 208.—BACCALINUS.

Basin shallow, wide, regular; Eye small but long, closed; Calyx reflexed.

Cavity deep, regular, brown; Stem medium to long, slender.

Core medium, regular, closed, or slightly open, clasping; Seeds numerous, angular, dark; Flesh yellow, firm, fine-grained, juicy; Flavor sub-acid, agreeable; Use, dessert; Season, December till March or longer; Quality very good.

Beauty of Kent.

A large English apple, well adapted to the kitchen. Tree upright, vigorous, rather productive.

Fruit large to very large, roundish, flattened, somewhat conic, regular; Surface greenish yellow, more or less covered with bright red mixed, and splashed with a darker hue; Dots small.

Basin quite shallow, regular; Eye very small closed.

Cavity medium, acute, wavy, green; Stem medium to short.

Core regular, medium, ovate, slightly open, clasping the eye; Seeds angular, imperfect; Flesh whitish yellow, breaking, juicy; Flavor acid; Quality only good; Use, cooking and market, for which it is well adapted by its size and appearance; Season, September and October.

Ben Davis.

NEW YORK PIPPIN, &C.

This handsome Southern apple has attained a wonderful notoriety within a few years, and its culture has been greatly extended, not on account of its superlative excellence, but because of its many good qualities as an orchard tree or market fruit. It was long cultivated by Verry

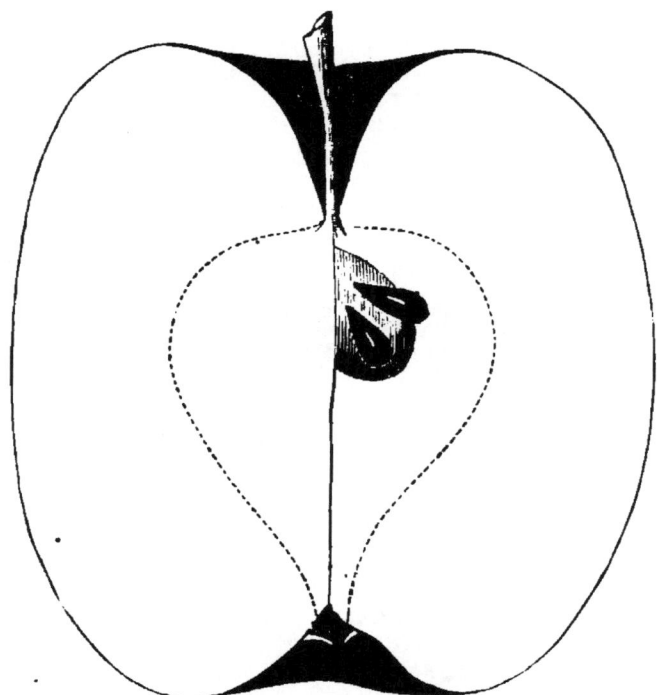

Fig. 209.—BEN DAVIS.

Aldrich, in Bureau County, Illinois, and exhibited as *New York Pippin*, which name gave an idea of its eastern origin, but in other localities its relations point clearly to its source in the South. To Mr. J. S. Downer we are indebted for a knowledge of its present name, and for confirmation of its identity under its several synonyms. This apple may be said to have succeeded as well in the

25*

northern parts of Indiana and Illinois as in their southern borders, where it has long been planted; though the northern orchards are still young, they are very promising. The fruit is modified somewhat by a cooler climate, and will keep later than that grown in the South.

Tree remarkably healthy and vigorous, an upright, rapid grower in the nursery, and has numerous short spur-branches along the stem. In the orchard the limbs are set very strongly, and the stems are marked by little mammillar projections or knobs, that are very characteristic. Tree large, spreading, productive, bears early; Shoots long, reddish brown, smooth; Foliage large, dark green.

Fruit large, variable in form, round, often apparently oblong, tapering to the eye, truncated, regular, sometimes inclined, generally very true, as though turned in a lathe; Surface smooth, often polished, yellow covered with mixed red, splashed bright red; Dots minute, scattered.

Basin generally shallow, in large developed specimens deep, abrupt, always regular; Eye large, open; Segments reflexed.

Cavity deep, acute, wavy, brown; Stem medium to long.

Core medium, regular, clasping the eye; Seeds large, plump; Flesh whitish, breaking, tender, juicy; Flavor sub-acid, not rich; Quality only good; Use, market, kitchen; Season, December, January and longer.

Blackburn.

Found in the markets at Louisville, Kentucky; not much seen elsewhere. Origin unknown, probably Southern.

Fruit large, round, somewhat flattened; Surface dull looking, dull green and gray, with broken stripes of dark dull red; Dots large, gray about the apex.

Basin narrow, regular; Eye medium, closed.

Cavity rather deep, acute, brown; Stem medium, curved, rather stout.

Core flattened, open, clasping; Flesh white, crisp, juicy; Flavor sub-acid, with a peculiar spicy, wild, rather astringent taste, that diminishes with the maturity of the fruit; Quality considered good; Use, family and market; Season September, November. *Blackburn* is sometimes used as a synonym of *Fall Queen*, a different fruit.

Capital.

A seedling of Z. S. Ragan, Clayton, Indiana.

Fruit small, globular, truncate at the ends, regular; Surface smooth, deep red on greenish yellow; Stripes and Dots indistinct.

Basin wide, deep; Eye medium, open, elongated.

Cavity wide, acute, regular; Stem medium.

Core round, open, clasping; Seeds numerous, pointed;

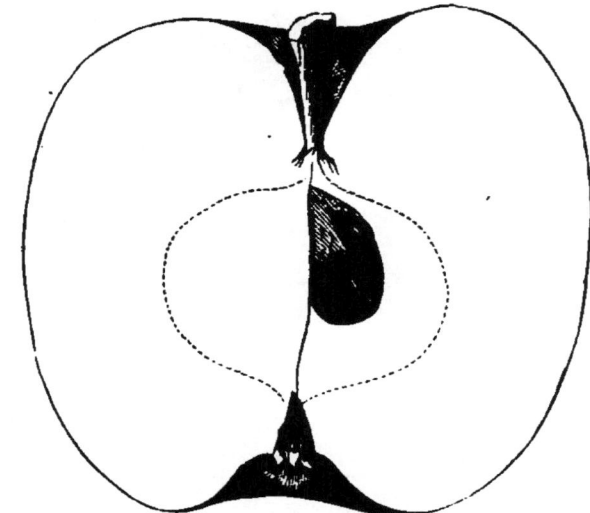

Fig. 210.—CAPITAL.

Flesh yellow, breaking, juicy; Flavor sub-acid, rich; Quality good; Use, the dessert; Season, December and January.

Carter.—[Of Massachusetts.]

Specimens from Luke Lincoln, of Leominster, Mass.

Fruit medium, round, flattened, slightly angular; Surface smooth, yellow, mixed and splashed scarlet; Dots rare, minute.

Basin shallow, folded; Eye small, closed.

Cavity deep, acute, wavy; Stem long.

Core rather large, regular, closed, clasping; Seeds plump

and imperfect, pointed; Flesh yellowish white, breaking,

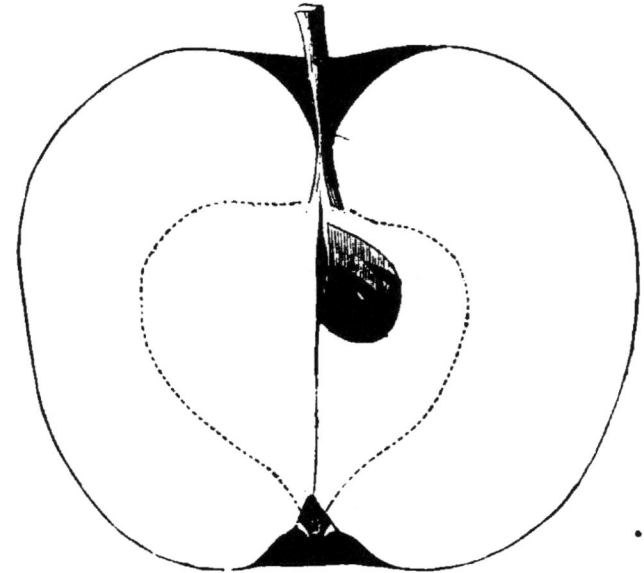

Fig. 211.—CARTER.

juicy; Flavor sub-acid, aromatic; Quality good; Use, table; Season, December, January.

Cary's Summer.

This is probably an old variety, but it has not been identified. Specimens from C. C. Cary, near Louisville, Kentucky.

Fruit large, round, flattened, regular; Surface smooth, rich yellow, mixed, splashed, carmine; Dots scattered, minute.

Basin wide, wavy; Eye small, closed.

Cavity deep, narrow, wavy brown; Stem short.

Core medium, roundish, regular, open; Seeds numerous, plump; Flesh yellow, tender, fine-grained, juicy; Flavor sub-acid; Quality very good; Use, table, kitchen, market; Season, June to September.

Cluster Pearmain.

Introduced by R. Ragan, of Indiana.

Fruit full medium, round, flattened, regular, inclined; Surface yellowish green, mixed and striped light red; Dots large, numerous, gray and yellow; white bloom.

Basin deep, abrupt, regular; Eye small, closed.

Cavity wide, regular, brown; Stem short.

Core medium, pyriform, nearly closed, clasping; Seeds numerous, angular, dark; Flesh yellowish white, break-

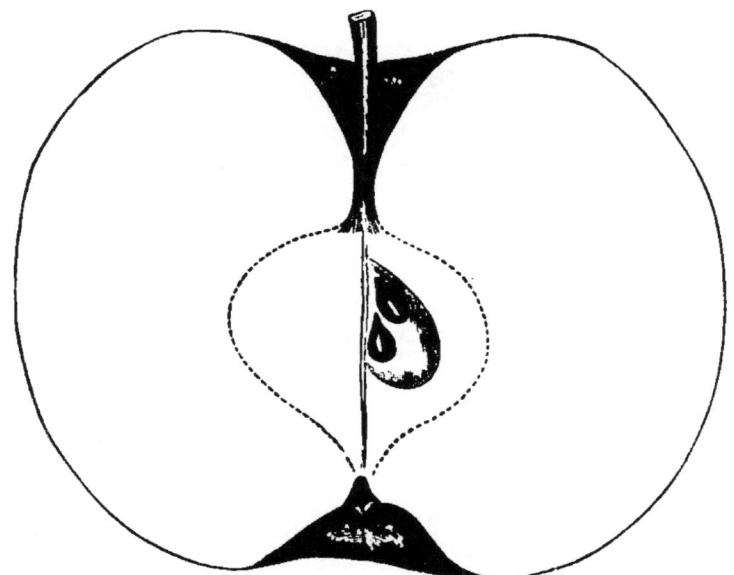

Fig. 212.—CLUSTER PEARMAIN.

ing, tender, granular; Flavor sub-acid, aromatic; Quality good to very good; Use, table; Season, September, October. A most acceptable substitute for Rambo, as an amateur's fruit.

Coggeswell.

Origin near Norwich, Connecticut. Tree vigorous, upright, productive on alternate years.

Fruit large, uniform, fair, beautiful, round, flattened, regular; Surface smooth, striped red on yellow.

Basin shallow, small; Eye small, closed.

Cavity wide, brown; Stem short.

Flesh yellow, tender, fine-grained, juicy; Flavor mild sub-acid, aromatic, rich; Quality best; Use, table; Season, December to March.

This fruit has been thought to resemble the Ohio *Nonpariel*, but I think it is different.

Cropsey's Favorite.

Originated with D. W. Cropsey, Plainfield, Will County, Illinois.

Fruit full medium, globular, looking oblong, regular; Surface smooth, yellow, mixed, splashed carmine; Dots few.

Basin medium, regular, russet; Eye medium, closed.

Cavity deep, acute, wavy, green; Stem short to medium.

Core roundish, heart-shaped, closed, meeting the eye; Seeds medium, angular; Flesh yellow, breaking, fine-grained, juicy; Flavor sub-acid, rich; Quality good to very good; Use, table, kitchen; Season, December.

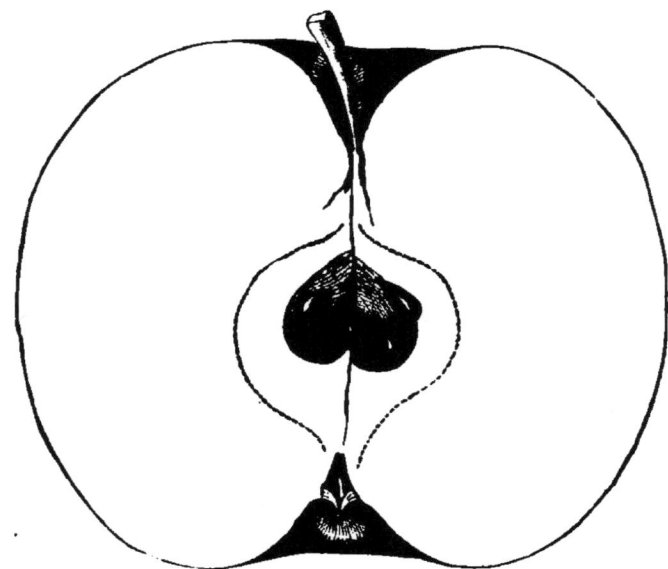

Fig. 218.—DAN PEARMAIN.

Daniel.

This delightful autumn dessert apple is grown in Henry County, Indiana.

Fruit medium to small, round, flattened, regular; Surface smooth, mixed scarlet on yellow, splashed carmine; Dots minute.

Basin shallow, regular; Eye medium, closed.

Core wide, regular, open; Seeds numerous, plump; Flesh yellow, very fine-grained, tender, juicy; Flavor sub-acid, aromatic, delicious; Quality best; Use, the dessert; Season, September.

Dan Pearmain.

This very beautiful seedling was procured by Reuben Ragan from near the battle-field of Tippecanoe, Indiana, where it was found in a seedling orchard.

Fruit medium to small, round, flattened, regular, fair and handsome; Surface yellow, covered with bright red, mixed, striped and splashed; Dots numerous, large, yellow, prominent.

Basin deep, regular or plaited; Eye small, closed.

Cavity deep, acute, regular, sometimes brown; Stem long, slender, red.

Core small, turbinate, closed; Seeds numerous, small, plump; Flesh yellow, breaking, tender; Flavor very mild sub-acid, rich; Quality almost best; Use, table, kitchen, market; on older trees too small for profit; Season, December to March.

Day.

ROYAL PIPPIN.

From Reuben Ragan. Fruit large, round, somewhat conic, regular; Surface smooth, yellow, striped, splashed, mottled, carmine; Dots numerous, gray, large.

Basin shallow, folded; Eye small, closed.

Cavity deep, acute, green; Stem medium, clubbed.

Core wide, pyriform, slightly open, clasping; Seeds numerous, pointed, angular, dark; Flesh yellowish white, firm, breaking, granular; Flavor sub-acid; Quality good; Use, kitchen; Season, January. Not destined to take a very high rank.

Doctor Fulcher.

A Southern apple of some merit. Originated in Todd County, Kentucky. Tree thrifty, an early and abundant bearer; Shoots slender; Foliage bright green. Received from J. S. Downer, of Elkton, Kentucky.

Fruit medium, globular, truncated, regular; Surface smooth, yellow, marbled, splashed carmine; Dots minute.

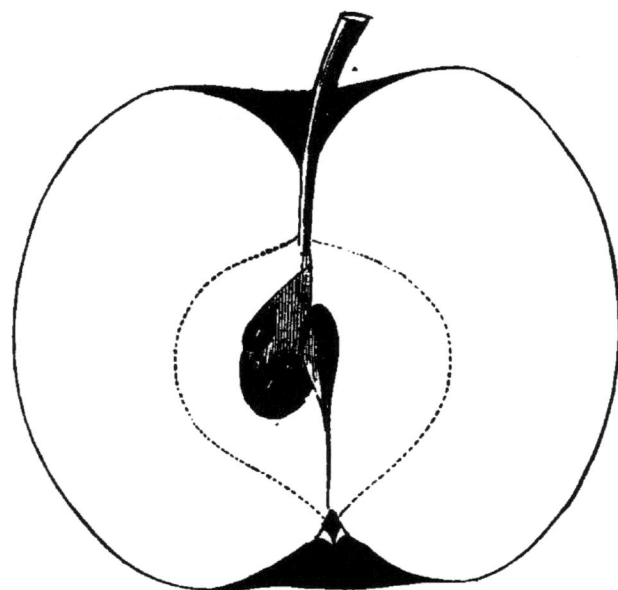

Fig. 214.—DOCTOR FULCHER.

Basin shallow, wavy, russeted, cracked; Eye small, closed.

Cavity sometimes wide, wavy, brown; Stem medium to long.

Core large, turbinate, regular open, meeting the eye; Seeds large, plump; Flesh yellow, fine-grained, tender, melting, juicy; Flavor sub-acid, rich; Quality good, Downer says "best;" Use, table; Season, December, January.

Dutch Mignonne.

REINETTE DOREE—And Several Others in Europe.

A fine large apple from Holland. Tree vigorous, upright, productive.

Fruit large or very large, roundish, flattened, sometimes conical, truncated; Surface rough, yellow, covered with red, splashed with bright red; Dots numerous, prominent, fawn-colored.

Basin wide, abrupt, regular; Eye short, wide, open; Segments short.

Cavity medium, acute, regular; Stem medium to long.

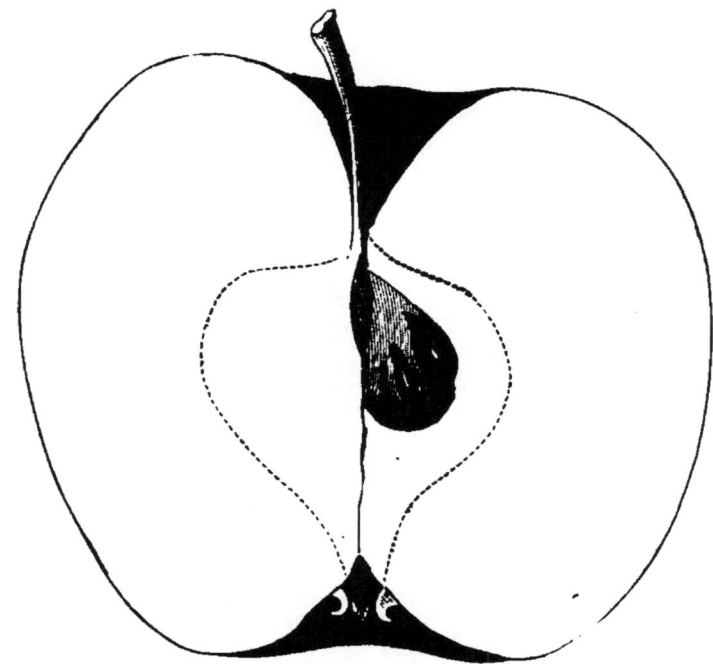

Fig. 215.—DUTCH MIGNONNE.

Core small, turbinate, regular, clasping; Seeds few, angular imperfect; Flesh yellowish white, breaking, coarse-grained, juicy; Flavor acid to sub-acid, rich; Quality good to very good; Use, kitchen, market, drying; Season, September, October.

Early Pennock.

SHAKER YELLOW—HOMONY, of the South ?

Origin unknown. Tree thrifty, upright, early bearer, productive, not long-lived.

Fruit large, variable in form, being sometimes oval, and conical, averaging roundish—conic, regular, handsome, sometimes inclined in the axis; Surface smooth, yellow, partially covered with mixed and striped scarlet, splashed carmine—often the yellow prevails; Dots numerous, dark.

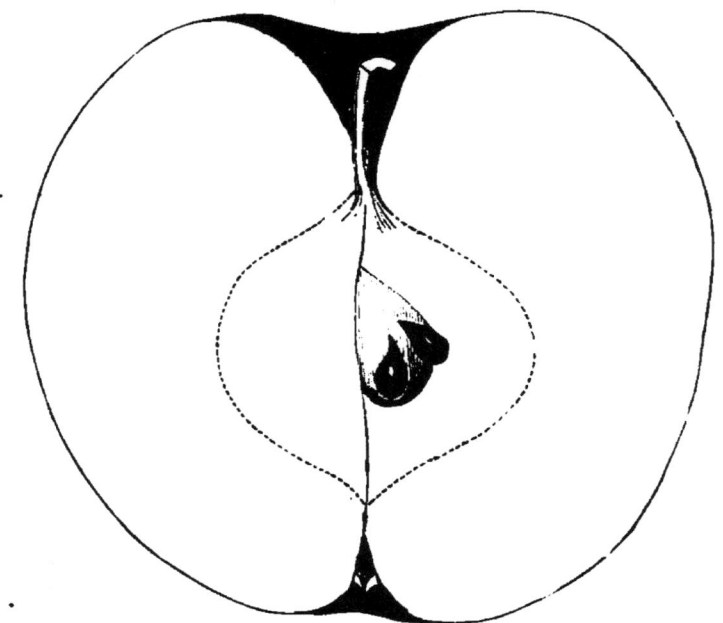

Fig. 216.—EARLY PENNOCK.

Basin shallow, plaited or regular; Eye small, closed. Cavity deep, regular, brown; Stem medium or short.

Core long, tapering to both ends, partially open in some, clasping the eye; Seeds large, numerous, plump, dark; Flesh yellow, breaking, rather coarse; Flavor acid; Quality poor; Use, market and kitchen; Season, July and August.

Fameuse.

SNOW—CHIMNEY—POMME DE NEIGE.

This is a favorite Northern fruit of great beauty. Origin uncertain—whether Canadian or French. It is greatly valued in the North and Northwest as an early winter apple. Tree vigorous, productive; Shoots red; Foliage dark, abundant.

Fruit medium, round, regular; Surface pale waxen yellow, almost wholly covered deep red, made up of stripes and splashes that are not always traceable in the depth of color—absent where a portion of the apple has been shaded by a leaf; Dots minute.

Basin medium, regular; Eye very small, closed.

Cavity wide, wavy, green; Stem short.

Core medium, heart-shaped, closed, meeting the eye; Seeds numerous, pointed, rich brown; Flesh snowy white, very tender, fine-grained, juicy; Flavor sub-acid, mild, delicately perfumed, not rich; Quality good; Use, dessert, kitchen, market; Season, October to December.

Farley Red.

A native of Kentucky, already somewhat extended northward. Tree healthy, moderately thrifty, very productive, making it small.

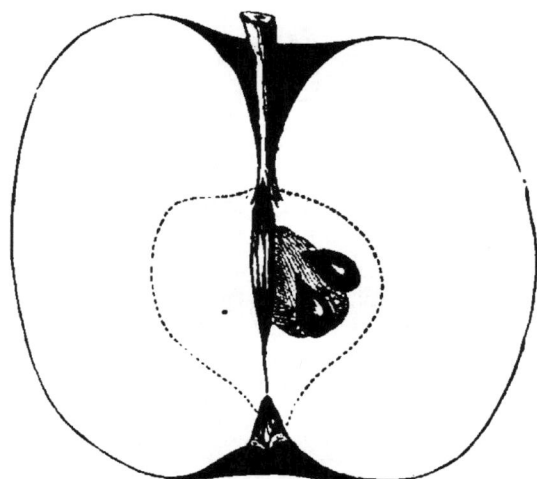

Fig. 217.—FARLEY RED.

Fruit small, round or oblong, flattened or truncated at the ends, barrel shaped; Surface dull red stripes on yellow; Dots minute, indented, purplish.

Basin shallow, folded or plaited; Eye small, closed.

Cavity deep, acute, wavy, brown; Stem medium.

Core regular, turbinate, open, clasping the point of the eye; Seeds numerous, plump, angular; Flesh yellowish white, firm, juicy; Flavor sub-acid; Quality only good; Use, Mr. R. Ragan finds it one of his best market fruits; Season, March and April, keeping sound and very salable.

Glendale.

Believed to have originated near Glendale, Hamilton County, Ohio, where I obtained it from A. A. Mullet.

Tree vigorous, thrifty, spreading, well formed head, productive.

Fruit large, roundish, somewhat conical; Surface smooth, bright yellow, striped and clouded with bright red; Dots small, russet.

Basin deep, abrupt; Eye small, closed.

Cavity medium, wavy, green; Stem long.

Core open; Seeds numerous, medium; Flesh yellowish, tender, juicy; Flavor very mild sub-acid, almost saccharine, rich; Quality good; Use, table; Season, September, October.

Hagloe.

This foreign variety has the general aspect of a Russian apple both in tree and fruit.

Excellent for cooking, highly esteemed by the market gardeners of New Jersey, where it is much grown.

Tree healthy, vigorous, round headed, productive; Shoots stout, blunt; Foliage large, light green.

Fruit medium to large, round, somewhat flattened; Surface pale yellow, distinctly striped and splashed bright red or carmine, covered with white bloom.

Basin small, regular; Eye small, closed.

Cavity wide, regular; Stem short, thick.

Flesh whitish, not fine-grained, breaking, juicy; Flavor acid; Quality good; Use, kitchen and market only; Season, August.

Hannah.

AUNT'S, not AUNT HANNAH of Massachusetts.

This large and rather handsome fruit is found in many parts of the country, but is not largely cultivated. Its occurrence among Southern emigrants would lead us to suspect that they might have brought it with them.

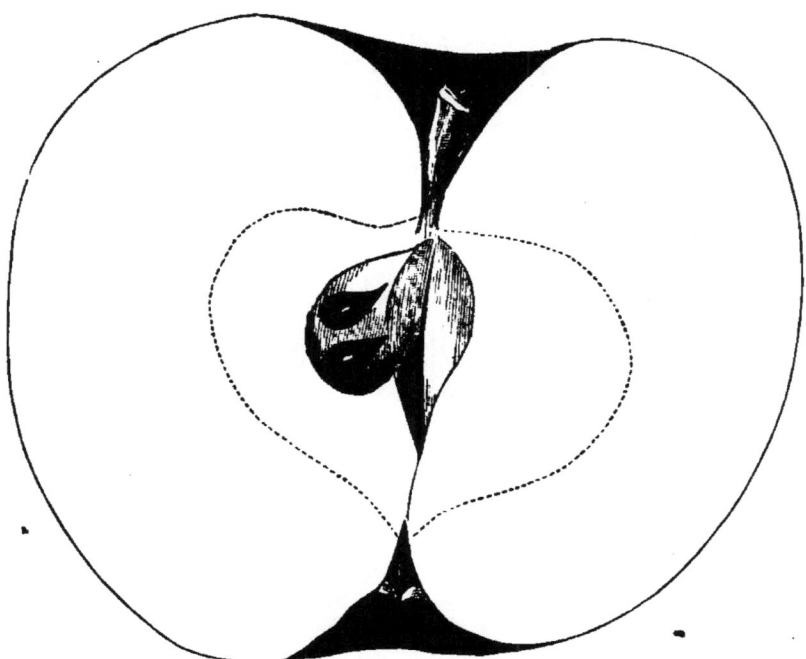

Fig. 218.—HANNAH.

Fruit large, showy, round, somewhat flattened, regular, sometimes unequal; Surface rather smooth, pale yellow, mixed, distinctly striped and splashed crimson and carmine; Dots scattered, large, gray.

Basin medium, abrupt, regular, often slightly russeted; Eye medium but long, closed.

Cavity wide, wavy, acute, deep, brown or green; Stem short or very short.

Core round, flattened or wide, regular, open; Axis very short; Seeds numerous, short, plump; Flesh light, yellowish white, breaking, tender, juicy; Flavor sub-acid, aromatic, peculiar, not agreeable to some palates; Quality only good; Use, kitchen, market, drying; Season, October to December.

Herefordshire Pearmain.

This is supposed to be an old English variety which has reached certain portions of the Western States from the East, though now rarely seen there, as its place has been taken by other *Pearmains* of American origin and more

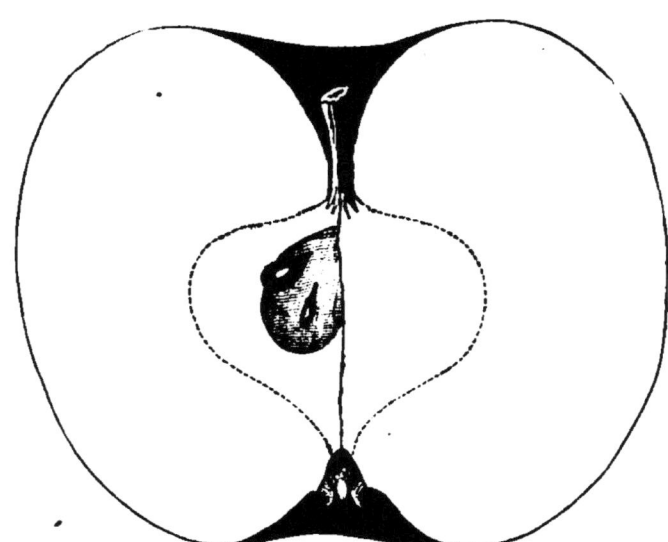

Fig. 219.—HEREFORDSHIRE PEARMAIN.

vigor, such as the *Long Island Pearmain*, described on another page. Tree slender and slow grower, medium size, very productive.

Fruit small to medium, roundish, slightly conic, truncated sharply; Surface smooth, deep red, splashes dark or maroon on rich yellow, which only shows where the fruit has been shaded by a leaf; Dots numerous, small, yellow.

Basin wide, regular, abrupt; Eye medium, open, reflexed.

Cavity medium, regular or wavy, green; Stem mostly short, stout, sometimes quite thick.

Core wide, turbinate, closed, regular, clasping the eye; Seeds numerous, small, pointed, dark, some imperfect; Flesh deep yellow, firm, breaking, very fine-grained, juicy; Flavor rich, sub-acid, aromatic, vinous, spicy, very agreeable; Quality best; Use, dessert; Season, December to February.

Especially adapted to amateur collections.

Hewes' Crab.

From Virginia. A famous cider apple, found in all extensive and good cider orchards. Tree of slender growth, but makes a large, spreading top, immensely productive alternate years, long lived; Twigs slender; Foliage sparse.

Fruit quite small, round, somewhat flattened, regular; Surface mixed, striped, purplish red on yellow; Dots numerous, large, pale or fawn.

Basin shallow; Eye small, closed.

Cavity deep, regular; Stem long, red.

Core round, regular, open, clasping; Seeds large, pointed; Flesh firm, yellowish and greenish, juicy; Flavor acid, rich; the must is very heavy; Quality best for cider; Season, November to January. Also useful for cooking, except on account of its small size; the rich and piquant acid makes it a particularly desirable ingredient in mince-pies.

In Kentucky there is a variety of this apple known as *Beeler's Crab*, with fruit of similar characters, but the tree is a better grower.

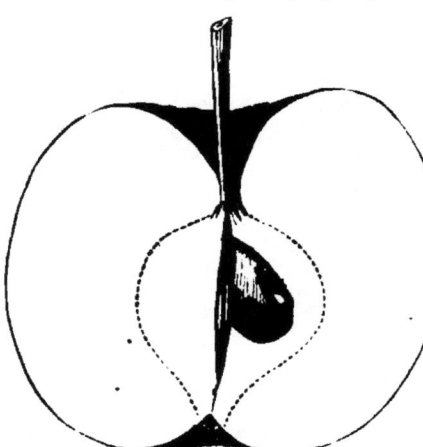

Fig. 220.—HEWES' CRAB.

Hubbardston.

HUBBARDSTON NONSUCH.

This fine apple originated in Hubbardston, Massachusetts. Tree vigorous, healthy, productive, early bearer, round-leaved, branching. At one time this and the Baldwin were confounded and mixed in some Western collections.

Fruit large, fair, handsome, round, somewhat ovate, tapering both ways from the middle, regular; Surface often

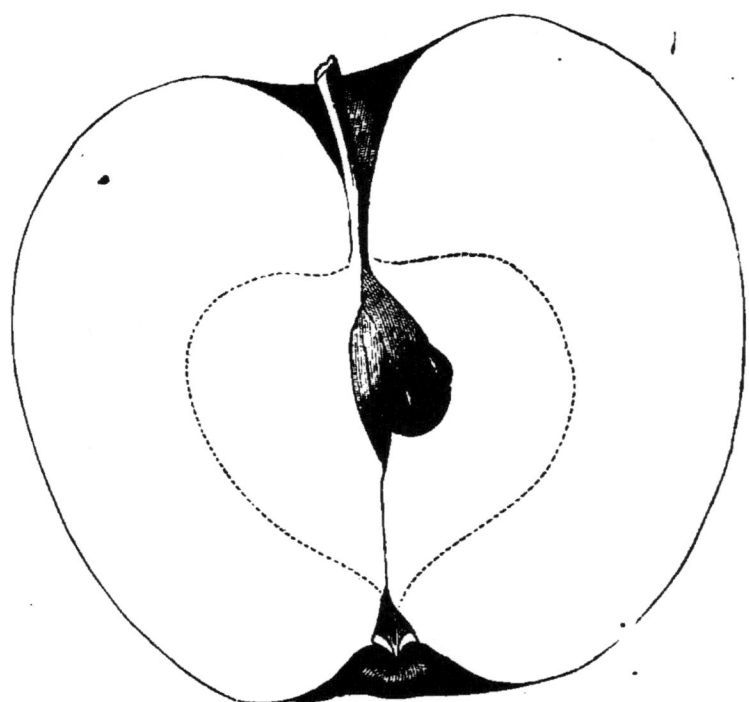

Fig. 221.—HUBBARDSTON.

uneven, yellow, covered with mixed red and broken stripes, presenting a rich brownish appearance; Dots scattered, gray, prominent.

Basin abrupt, wide, regular, leather-cracked, or russeted, or both; Eye medium or small, open.

Cavity wide, regular, brown ; Stem medium or short.

Core large, heart-shaped, regular, sometimes partially open, clasping the eye ; Seeds few, pointed ; Flesh yellow, breaking, fine grained, juicy ; Flavor acid, sub-acid, rich ; Quality very good ; Use, cooking early, table when perfectly ripe ; Season, November, December.

Krowser.

Origin Berks County, Pennsylvania, where I found it very popular as a productive winter apple for all purposes. Tree vigorous, healthy, large, spreading, and very productive.

Fruit medium to large, round, slightly conic, regular ; Surface rather smooth, pale yellow, nearly covered with red, and splashed carmine.

Basin small, folded ; Eye medium, closed.

Cavity medium ; Stem short to medium.

Flesh whitish, tender, juicy ; Flavor mild sub-acid, rich, agreeable ; Use, a good market fruit ; Season, December to March.

Large Striped Pearmain.

This choice Western apple is supposed to have originated in Kentucky—possibly further South. It is now to be found in Eastern Ohio, Southern Indiana and Illinois, and in Missouri. Much grown in Kentucky. In all places it seems to be doing well, and giving entire satisfaction, excepting that the bark bursts near the ground even in bearing trees, root-grafted.

Tree vigorous, thrifty, spreading, productive ; Shoots rather slender, dark ; Foliage dark green, abundant on young trees.

Fruit large, round, flattened, regular, fair, handsome, though not so beautifully colored as some others ; Surface smooth, mixed, splashed and striped, pale purplish red on yellow, which shows through the shading ; Dots minute, indented, gray, so that the fruit has a general gray appearance.

Basin medium, regular, sometimes cracked ; Eye small, closed.

Cavity wide, wavy, rather deep, brown ; Stem short, medium, or rather long.

26

Core roundish, medium, regular, open; Seeds numerous, large, angular, some imperfect; Flesh yellow, breaking, somewhat coarse-grained, juicy; Flavor sub-acid; Quality

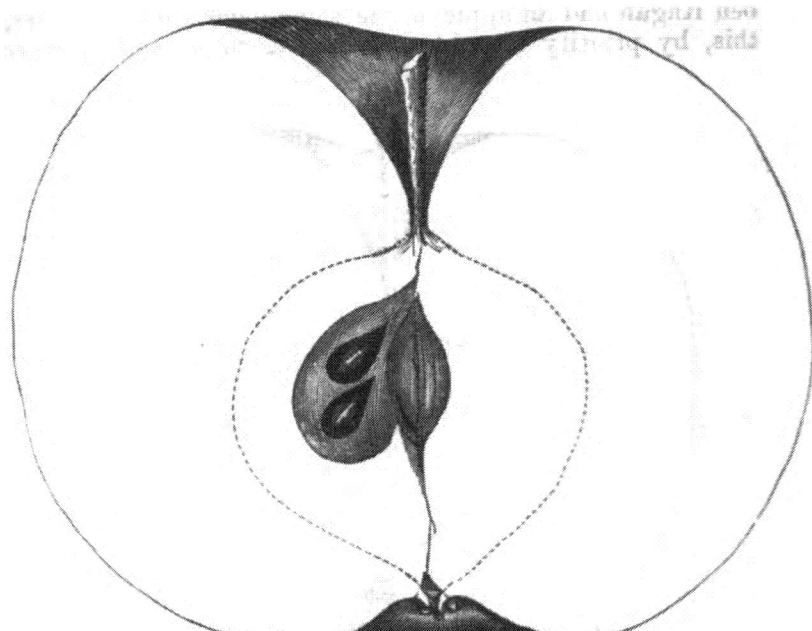

Fig. 222.—LARGE STRIPED PEARMAIN.

quite good; Use, market, kitchen, table; Season, December to February.

In the West it is more flattened than in Ohio, becoming in large specimens almost a flat or oblate apple. Highly recommended for commercial orchards, whether for shipping North or South—particularly the latter.

Lewis.

This delicious apple originated in Decatur County, Indiana, near Greensburgh, and was introduced to my notice by one of the early pomologists of the region, a nurseryman by the name of Lewis, from whom I obtained my trees after he had introduced me to the original, which I

found to be vigorous, healthy, upright, spreading and productive.

The fruit was described in the *Western Horticultural
Review* for 1852, before I was aware that my friend Reuben Ragan had an apple of the same name; nevertheless,
this, by priority of publication, will stand, unless there

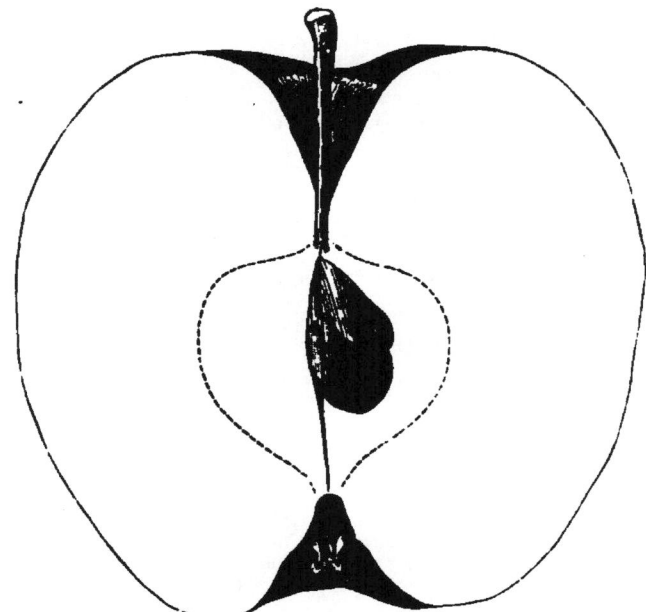

Fig. 223.—LEWIS.

should prove to be another Lewis that can claim seniority
of publication.   I distinguish the other apple by calling it
Lewis of Ragan; it is in another class.—[See Downing, p.
164.]

Fruit medium to large, round, somewhat ovate, regular;
Surface smooth, yellow, striped and marbled scarlet; Dots
scattered, gray and yellow.

Basin deep, abrupt, regular; Eye medium, closed.

Cavity acute, deep, regular; Stem long, slender.

Core regular, oval, heart-shaped, closed, meeting the
eye; Seeds numerous, plump, brown; Flesh yellow, very
tender, crisp, juicy; Flavor acid to sub-acid, rich, deli-

cious; Quality best; Use, table and kitchen; Season, August. Marked in my notes "One of the very best of the new apples."

Liberty.

This valuable market variety originated near Columbus, Ohio, where it was brought into notice by M. B. Bateham, the excellent Secretary of the Ohio Pomological Society, and founder of the Columbus Nurseries.

Tree vigorous, healthy, large, spreading and productive; believed to be entirely hardy.

Fruit full medium to large, globular, inclining to oblong in appearance, turbinated or flattened at the ends, regu-

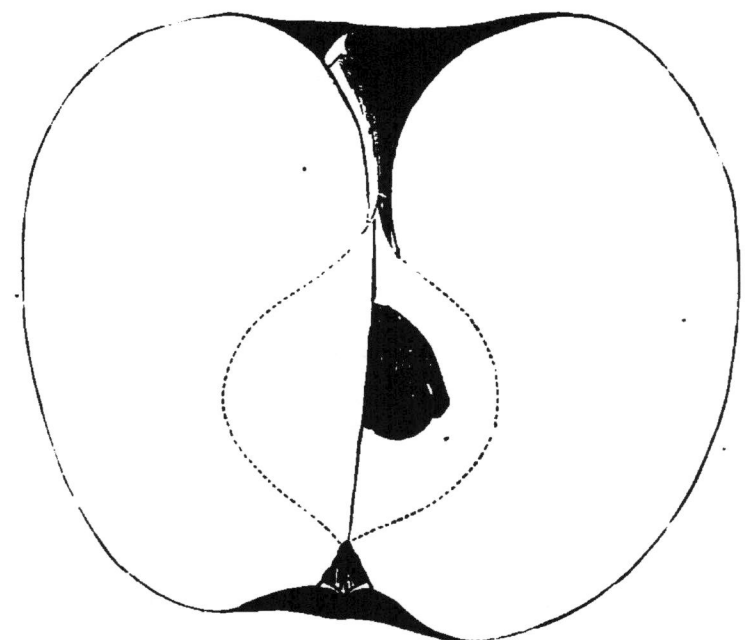

Fig. 234.—LIBERTY.

lar; Surface not smooth, yellow, covered with dull red and scarlet, mixed and splashed, stripes indistinct; Dots minute, gray, prominent.

Basin medium, quite shallow, regular, indistinctly leather-cracked; Eye small, closed.

Cavity medium, acute, wavy; Stem medium, inclined.

Core small, oval, closed, meeting the eye; Seeds numerous, pointed; Flesh yellow, breaking, rather coarse, juicy; Flavor acid to sub-acid; Quality good; Use, market and kitchen or table; Season, January to March, or later.

Lyscom.

Origin Massachusetts. This pleasant dessert apple is not generally known.

Fruit large, roundish, flattened, regular; Surface smooth, yellowish, striped and splashed with red.

Basin large, plaited; Eye large.

Cavity deep, regular; Stem short.

Flesh whitish, fine-grained, tender, juicy; Flavor mild sub-acid, agreeable; Quality good; Use, table and kitchen; Season, September to November.

Margil.

A famous old English dessert apple, rarely seen in this country, but much better adapted for the closing of a feast than many which are more pretentious in style and im-

Fig. 225.—MARGIL.

posing in size. Certainly much more economical to him who provides even at a higher price per bushel than those which are too large to be eaten, and are only cut to be left on the table and wasted. Tree of slender growth, but very productive.

Fruit quite small, round, somewhat conic, abruptly truncated, regular; Surface smooth, red, mixed and striped; Dots yellow, prominent.

Basin wide, shallow, regular; Eye small, open; Calyx reflexed.

Cavity wide, not deep, regular, brown; Stem long.

Core turbinate, regular, closed, meeting the eye; Seeds numerous, pointed, long; Flesh yellow, crisp, fine-grained, juicy; Flavor sub-acid, rich, aromatic, very agreeable; Quality best; Season, November to January.

Meach.

From Vermont; Fruit large, roundish, conic; Skin greenish-yellow, striped and mottled with light red, and sprinkled with brown dots; Stalk long, rather slender, set in a pretty large cavity; Calyx closed in a corrugated basin; Flesh yellowish, rather fine, juicy, rich, mild, sub-acid, aromatic; October and November.—[Downing.]

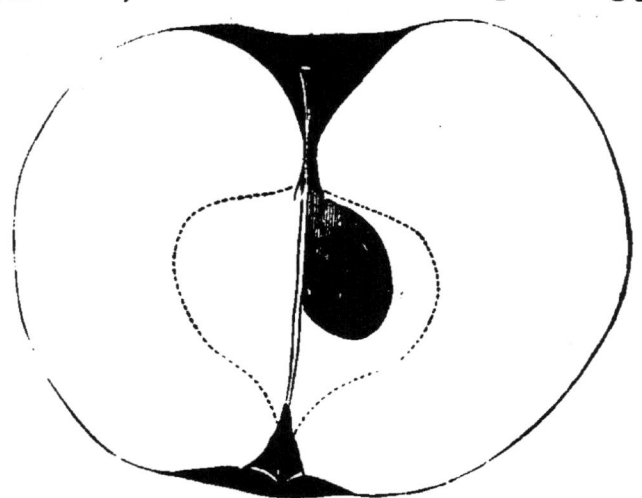

Fig. 226.—M'KINLEY.

McKinley.

Highly esteemed by Reuben Ragan, of Indiana, who finds it profitable.

Fruit medium, roundish, flattened, slightly conic, regular; Surface smooth, dull red on greenish-yellow, stripes indistinct; Dots scattered, large, gray.

Basin regular, shallow; Eye large, closed.

Cavity deep, acute, regular, brown; Stem slender, medium to short.

Core medium, ovate, regular, closed, meeting the eye; Seeds numerous, plump, brown; Flesh breaking, very fine-grained, very juicy; Flavor sub-acid, good; Quality good to very good; Use, table; Season, December and January.

Mexico.

Origin Canterbury, Connecticut. Tree hardy, productive. Not much known in the West.

Fruit—obtained from E. Newburg, Brooklyn, Connecticut—medium, round, regular; Surface bright crimson-red, striped darker; Dots numerous, yellow-green.

Basin shallow, regular; Eye medium, closed.

Cavity acute, regular; Stem long or medium, slender.

Core large, open, meeting the eye; Seeds numerous, angular, pointed; Flesh white, tender, fine-grained, juicy; Flavor sub-acid; Quality best; Use, table; Season, August and September.

Monk's Favorite.

This large, showy apple originated in Delaware County, Indiana, and was introduced to the public by Dr. J. C. Helme, of the State Horticultural Society.

It was described in the *Western Horticultural Review*, some years ago, as a promising fruit, and was favorably noticed at the time of its introduction, but has not yet been sufficiently known for general recommendation.

Tree vigorous, upright, spreading, productive.

Fruit large, globular, flattened, regular; Surface smooth, yellow, pretty well covered with stripes and splashes of bright red; Dots medium, ragged, gray, scattering.

Basin medium, regular; Eye medium, open.

Cavity wide, wavy; Stem medium to long, stout.

Core wide, heart-shaped, open, clasping; Seeds pointed; Flesh whitish, breaking, juicy; Flavor sub-acid; Quality good; Use, kitchen, table, and promising for market; Season, November to January.

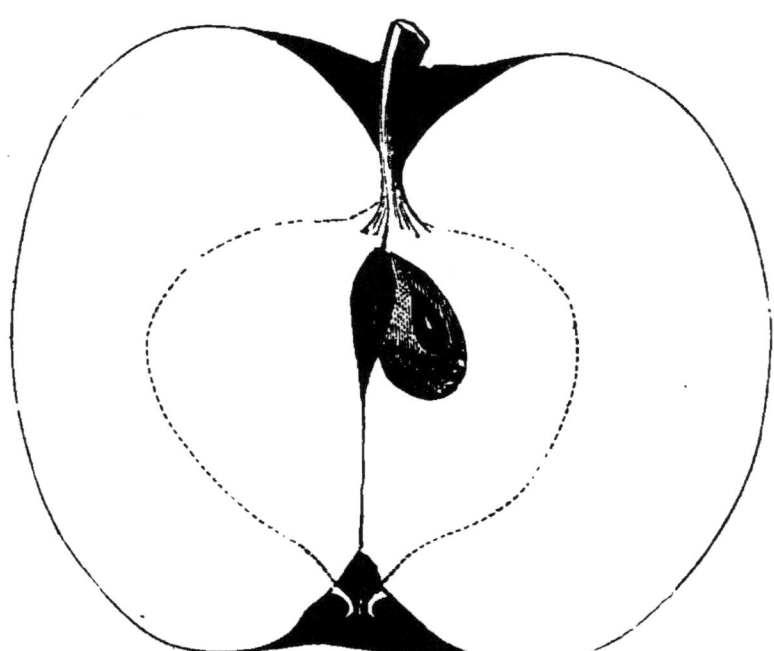

Fig. 227.—MONK'S FAVORITE.

Neversink.

Not having had an opportunity of examining this fruit, I quote the *ad interim* report of the Pennsylvania Horticultural Society:

"Origin Berks County, Pennsylvania.

"Fruit large, roundish, exterior of an exceedingly beautiful waxen orange-yellow color, with a few russet dots, and a delicately striped and richly mottled carmine cheek; Stem very short and rather stout, cavity narrow, acuminate, shallow; Calyx large, basin deep, rather wide, furrowed; Flesh yellowish, somewhat tough, owing to the fact of its being shriveled; Flavor approaches to that of a pineapple; Quality very good; December to April."

Newark King.

An old apple, supposed to have come from New Jersey; found in the oldest orchards of grafted fruits in Southwestern Ohio, seldom elsewhere in the West that I have seen.

Tree thrifty, upright, spreading, productive; Foliage dark.

Fruit full medium to large, roundish, flattened or truncated conic, mostly regular, sometimes ribbed; Surface not very smooth, rich yellow, nearly covered with dull

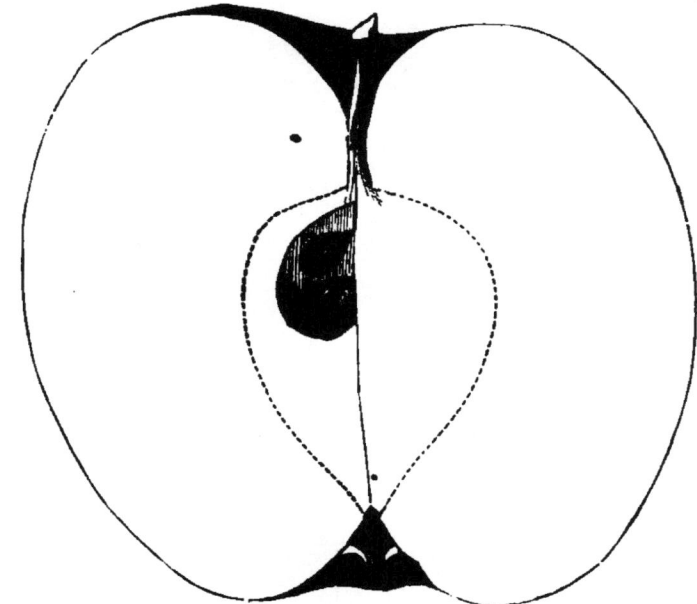

Fig. 228.—NEWARK KING.

red mixed, and darker stripes, giving the fruit almost a mahogany color; Dots numerous, gray, elongated at the extremities, and coalescing into russet about the blossom end.

Basin deep, abrupt, folded or plaited, covered with fine russet; Eye small, closed.

Cavity acute, often lipped; Stem rather long, slender.

Core small, oval, closed, not clasping but meeting the eye; Seeds numerous, angular; Flesh rich yellow, breaking, fine grained, juicy; Flavor acid, rich, sprightly, high-flavored; Quality very good; Use, kitchen, table and cider; Season, December, January, or longer.

Patton.

CARTER of Alabama—MANGUM—ALABAMA PEARMAIN of Peters.

This is a great favorite in the South, and deservedly so, on account of its good qualities. Specimens from Dr. Jas. S. Blair, Limestone County, North Alabama, afford me data for the following description. I have preferred the name *Patton* because of the other *Carters:*

Fruit large, roundish, somewhat flattened; Surface smooth, mixed, marbled and splashed carmine on yellow; Dots scattered, distinct, yellow.

Basin deep, abrupt, folded; Eye medium, open.

Cavity deep, acute; Stem long to medium, inclined, red.

Core small, regular, closed, half clasping; Seeds plump and imperfect; Flesh yellow, firm, breaking, juicy; Flavor acid, agreeable; Quality good; Season, November to January.

Pomme Water.

An apple by this name is found in Northern Illinois; little is known of its origin or history.

Fruit full medium, globular truncate, slightly conic, regular; Surface mixed, splashed scarlet on yellow; Dots minute, numerous, brown.

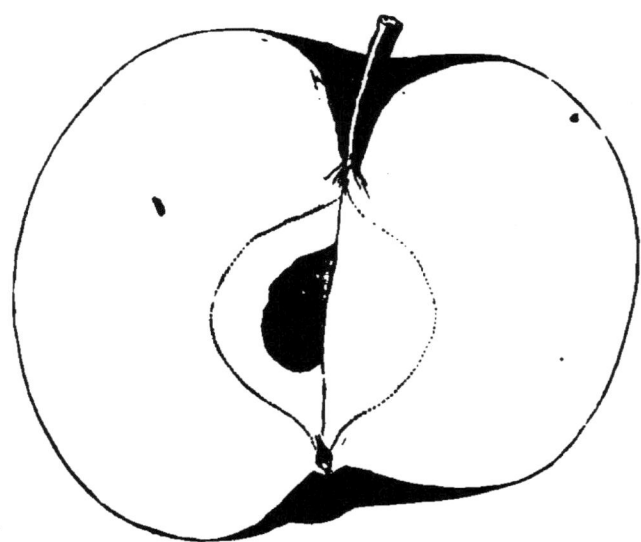

Fig. 229.—POMME WATER.

Basin wavy, medium; Eye large, closed.

Cavity medium, regular; Stem short, thick, green.

Core medium, round, closed, scarcely meeting the eye; Seeds numerous, angular, imperfect; Flesh yellow, breaking, fine grained, juicy; Flavor sub-acid; Quality good to very good; Use, table; Season, September and October.

Specimens obtained from Henry Kimball, of Rockford, Winnebago County, Illinois.

Ragan's Red.

Origin Putnam County, Indiana, by R. Ragan. Tree vigorous, productive.

Fruit large, round, slightly conic, regular; Surface

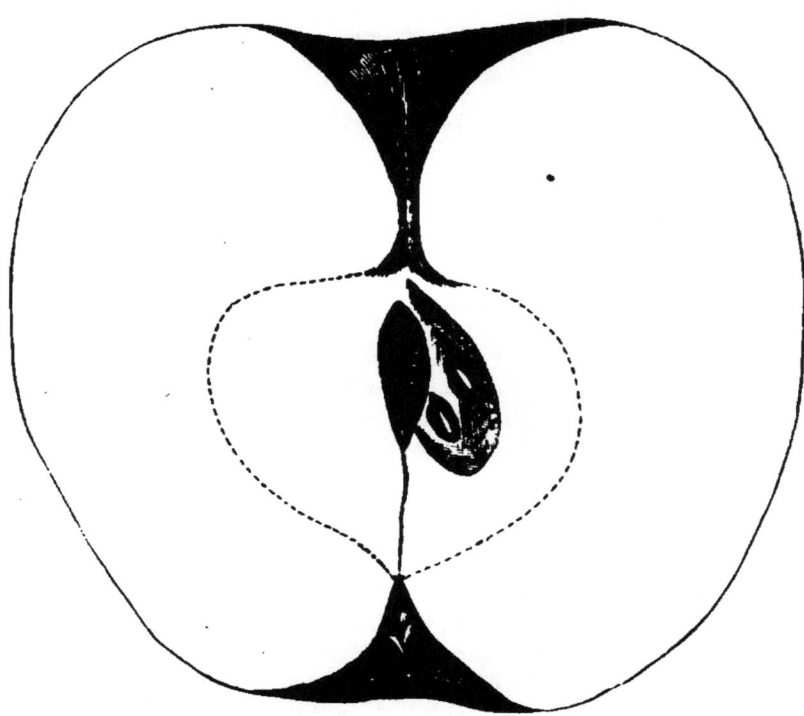

Fig. 230.—RAGAN'S RED.

smooth, bright red, splashed darker; Dots numerous, small.

26*

Basin abrupt, deep, regular; Eye small, closed.

Cavity deep, acute, regular; Stem long.

Core small, pyriform, regular, nearly closed; Seeds numerous, plump; Flesh yellow, breaking, fine grained; Flavor sub-acid, aromatic; Quality good; Use, table and market; Season, October and November.

Ribston Pippin.

This famous English apple does not seem to have many admirers among our orchardists, but on some accounts it merits a place in the amateur's collection.

Tree productive, early bearer.

Fruit medium to large, round, truncated, regular; Surface rough, splashed and mixed dull red on yellow; Dots numerous, minute, prominent, russet.

Basin abrupt, plaited or regular, russeted; Eye small, closed.

Cavity acute, wide, regular, brown; Stem long, slender.

Core regular, closed; Seeds numerous, angular, imperfect; Flesh yellow, crisp, firm, juicy; Flavor acid, rich, aromatic; Use, kitchen—scarcely for table; Season, October and later, but apt to wilt.

Sigler's Red.

This very handsome apple, from near McConnellsville, Morgan County, Ohio, was shown before the Ohio Pomological Society, at different times, by Jos. Sigler, for whom it was named, because it was not identified as any known variety.

Fruit medium, globular, slightly flattened, regular; Surface smooth, mixed and splashed bright red; Dots minute, rare.

Basin shallow, regular; Eye small, closed.

Cavity acute, wavy; Stem short to medium, knobby.

Core wide, indistinct, closed, meeting the eye; Seeds pointed, plump; Flesh yellow, fine-grained, juicy; Flavor sub-acid, aromatic, rich; Quality almost best; Use, table; Season, September.

A beautiful dessert fruit. Elliott gives it as synonym to *Autumn Pearmain.*

Small Black.

BLACK APPLE of Coxe and Downing—AMERICAN BLACK.

This useful little apple is found in many collections where the *Jersey Black* is cultivated, but it seems to be quite distinct.   Origin unknown.

Fruit medium to small, globular, sometimes nearly ob-

Fig. 231.—SMALL BLACK.

late, regular; Surface smooth, deep red, sometimes purplish, striping indistinct; Dots numerous, indented, minute, pink or purple.

Basin shallow, abrupt, regular or folded; Eye small to medium, closed; Segments reflexed.

Cavity acute, sometimes lipped, brown; Stem long, inclined, red or green.

Core regular, round, slightly open, clasping the eye; Seeds numerous, plump and angular; Flesh yellowish, often pink, tender, fine grained; Flavor sub-acid, agreeable; Quality good; Use, dessert; Season, November to January.

Smith's.

SMITH'S CIDER.

Origin Bucks County, Pennsylvania, where it still continues a favorite variety. Its cultivation has extended widely to the westward, giving great satisfaction as a market fruit, for culinary purposes, but cannot be recommended for table.

Tree vigorous, hardy, productive, an early bearer; Limbs straggling, shoots rather slender, light olive; Foliage large, light green.

Fruit medium to large, round, varying from flattened to elongated, mostly regular, sometimes lop-sided; Surface

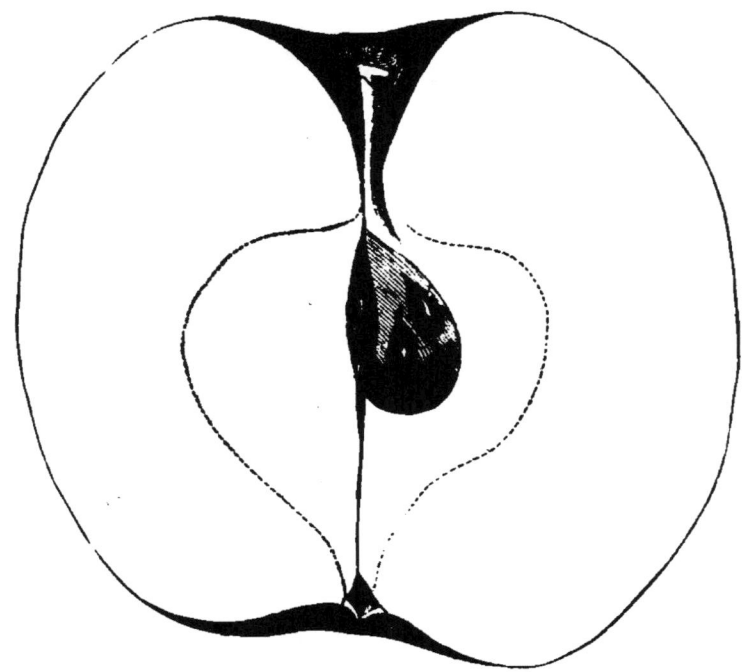

Fig. 232.—SMITH'S.

smooth, pale yellow, covered with mixed light red, splashed indistinctly with bright carmine, beautiful; Dots distinct, rather large, light gray.

Basin shallow, wide, or more often plaited; Eye small, closed.

Cavity acute, regular, brown; Stem medium to long, variable.

Core wide, pyriform, open, clasping; Seeds numerous, plump, pointed; Flesh white, breaking, juicy; Flavor acid, sub-acid, aromatic, not rich, peculiar, not agreeable; Quality good for cooking only, making very fine apple sauce—makes much cider, but thin and watery; Season, December, January and later.

This is essentially a market fruit, and is one of the most profitable apples planted in Southwestern Ohio and adjacent counties of Indiana.

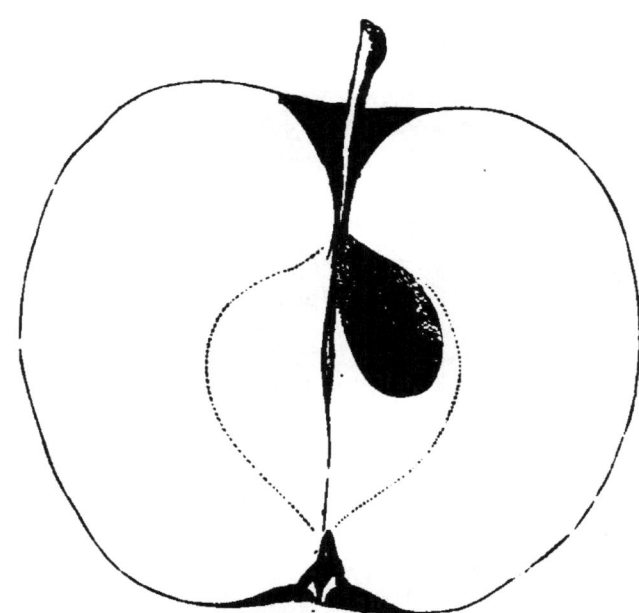

Fig. 233.—SOPS OF WINE.

Sops of Wine.

European. Tree vigorous, spreading, productive.

Fruit small to medium, round, slightly conic, regular; Surface smooth, mixed red, shaded dark red throughout; Dots small, scattered, yellow.

Basin shallow, plaited; Eye small, closed.

Cavity medium, wavy, somewhat browned; Stem long, red.

Core distinctly marked with a red line, wide, oval, closed, meeting the eye; Seeds numerous, pointed, brown; Flesh yellow, fine grained, tender, juicy; Flavor acid to sub-acid, agreeable; Quality good to very good; Use, dessert: Season, August and September.

Summer Janet.

Specimens received from Mr. Johnson, Louisville. Ky.

Fruit medium, round, truncated, regular; Surface smooth, pale yellow, mixed red, striped darker red; Dots scattered, gray.

Basin deep, abrupt, regular; Eye small, open.

Cavity shallow, regular, yellow; Stem medium to long, green.

Core pyriform, indistinct, closed, clasping; Seeds pointed, imperfect; Flesh yellow, tender, fine grained; Flavor sub-acid, aromatic; Quality good; Use, market; Season, September.

Summer Rose.

Origin New Jersey. Tree vigorous, healthy, spreading, productive, early bearer; Shoots stout; Foliage large, glaucous.

Fruit small, roundish, flattened, regular; Surface smooth polished, very pale yellow, striped and splashed distinctly bright red and carmine; Dots minute.

Basin abrupt, wide, regular; Eye small, closed.

Cavity acute, regular; Stem medium.

Core large, regular, closed, meeting the eye; Seeds numerous, short, plump; Flesh white, crisp, fine grained, juicy; Flavor sub-acid, agreeable, not rich; Quality, one of the best early apples; Use, family, table and kitchen; Season, June to August—ripening gradually.

Sutton Beauty.

An old Massachusetts apple, occasionally found in the West, where it attains increased size and beauty. My specimens were from W. Hampton, with many other sorts of interest grown by him in Northwestern Ohio.

Fruit large, handsome, globular, regular; Surface smooth, yellow, mottled and splashed carmine; Dots scattered, brown, vein-reflexed.

Basin wide, regular, russety; Eye large, open; Segments reflexed.

Cavity wide, acute, wavy, brown; Stem long, inclined.

Core medium to large, closed, clasping; Seeds numerous, pointed, angular, dark; Flesh whitish, tender, break-

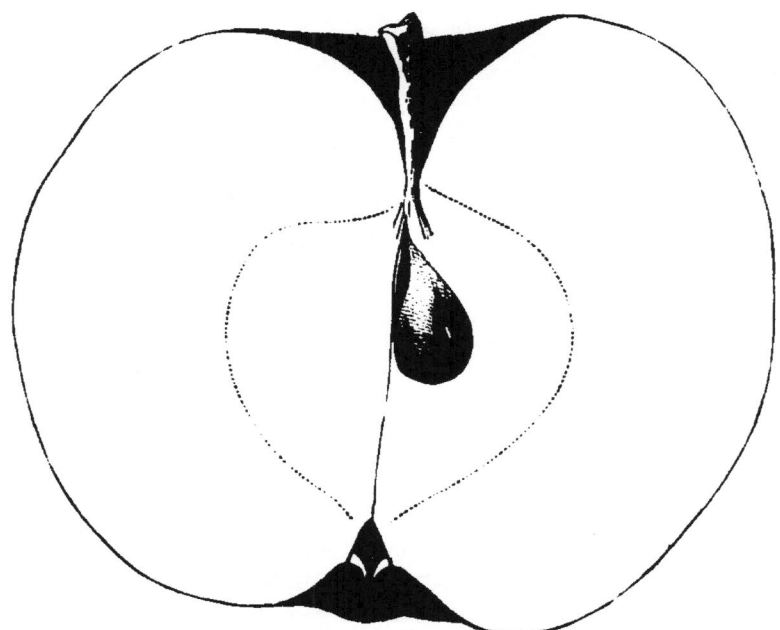

Fig. 234.—SUTTON BEAUTY.

ing, juicy; Flavor acid, sub-acid, agreeable; Quality good; Use, table, kitchen and market; Season, December to March.

Thought by Mr. Hampton to be a seedling brought from Southern Ohio.

Sylvester.

Introduced by Dr. Ware Sylvester, of Lyons, New York.

Fruit small to medium, round, regular; Surface smooth, white, blushed and striped bright carmine; Dots scattered, minute.

Basin very shallow, plaited; Eye small, closed.

Cavity deep, acute, wavy; Stem medium.

Core indistinct, slightly open; Seeds numerous, plump,

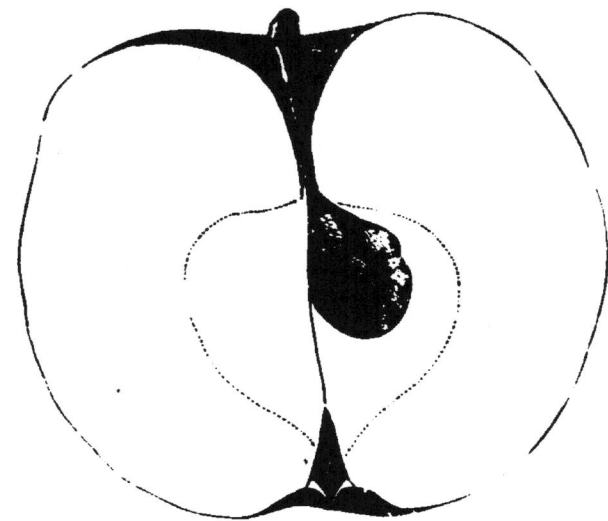

Fig. 235.—SYLVESTER.

angular, long; Flesh white, tender, fine grained, juicy; Flavor sub-acid; Quality very good; Use, table and cooking; Season, September.

Williams' Favorite.

WILLIAMS' EARLY.

Origin Roxbury, Massachusetts.

Fruit small to medium, round, regular; Surface smooth, dark purplish red, indistinctly striped; Dots none.

Basin abrupt, folded; Eye medium, closed.

Cavity wide, shallow; Stem long, slender.

Core large, round, closed; Seeds pointed, brown; Flesh whitish-yellow, streaked red, breaking, not juicy; Flavor sub-acid, peculiar; Quality scarcely good; Season, July and August.

Willow.

WILLOW TWIG—JAMES RIVER, ETC.

This Virginia fruit has obtained a wide spread notoriety as a valuable market apple throughout the West.

Tree very vigorous, healthy, productive, branching, twiggy, thorny while young; Shoots slender, olive brown.

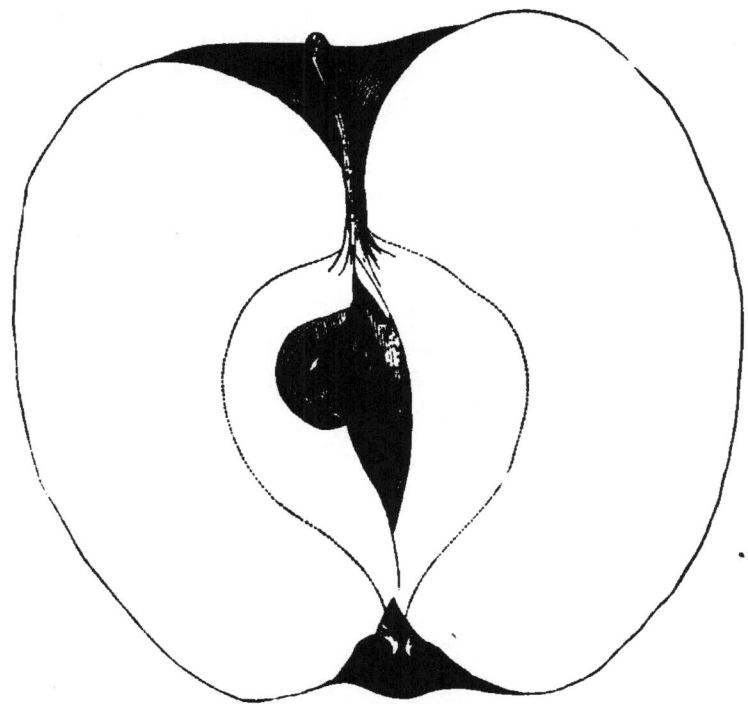

Fig. 236.—WILLOW.

Fruit globular, truncated, looking oblong from its cylindrical sides; Surface smooth, dull greenish-yellow, marbled and striped dull red; Dots minute, gray.

Basin wide, abrupt, plaited; Eye medium, closed.

Cavity wide or acute, regular; Stem long, slender, inclined.

Core medium, round, regular, closed, meeting, not clasping the eye; Seeds numerous, plump, brown; Flesh greenish-yellow, breaking, juicy; Flavor acid; Quality only good, but valuable for market and culinary uses; Season, December to April. Excellent for shipping South.

Wilson's Volunteer.

Origin believed to be a seedling or "Volunteer" on the banks of the Ohio River. Received from George Sibbald.

Fruit large, globular, truncated or flattened, regular; Surface yellow, mostly covered with mixed red, striped darker; Dots large, gray and yellow.

Basin deep, regular, leather-cracked; Eye medium, closed.

Cavity deep, acute, regular; Stem long, slender.

Core small, round, regular, closed, clasping; Seeds numerous, pointed; Flesh greenish-yellow, tender, juicy; Flavor sub-acid; Quality only good; Use, kitchen; Season, December to February.

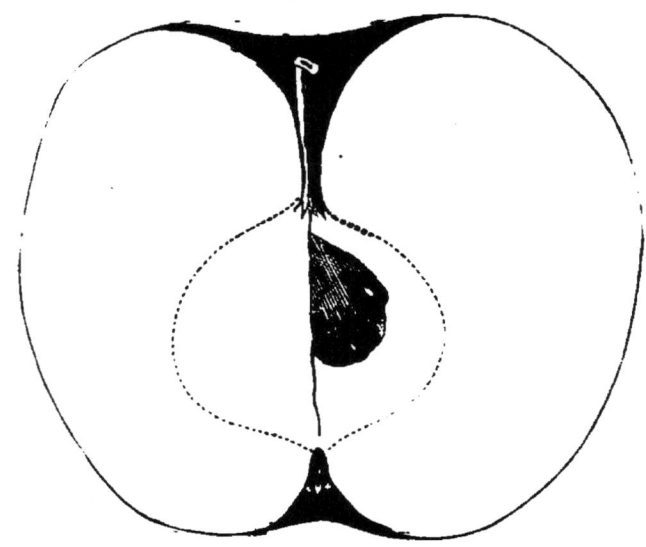

Fig. 237.—WRIGHT'S JANET.

Wright's Janet.

This fine keeping apple, received from N. J. Colman and other zealous pomologists of St. Louis, Missouri, is supposed to have originated in that region with Mr. W. G. Wright.

Fruit medium to large, round, sometimes flat, regular; Surface smooth, waxen yellow, mixed, striped and splashed carmine; Dots minute, prominent, scattering.

Basin medium, regular; Eye small, acute, closed.

Cavity deep, wavy, brown; Stem long, short, or very short.

Core medium, regular, somewhat open, clasping; Seeds numerous, small, plump; Flesh deep yellow, breaking, very fine grained, juicy; Flavor sub-acid, rich, very agreeable; Quality good to very good; Use, table, kitchen and market; Season, January to June and keeps until August.

Yadkin.

Southern. Received from S. W. Westbrooke, of Greensboro', North Carolina.

Fruit large, round, regular; Surface red, striped dark red; Dots large, scattered, distinct, gray.

Basin abrupt, deep, regular; Eye small, open.

Cavity acute, regular, brown; Stem medium, brown.

Core small, closed, meeting the eye; Seeds small, pointed, brown; Flesh white, breaking, dry; Flavor sub-acid; Quality only good; Season, August—and on that account scarcely worth carrying to the North.

CLASS III.—ROUND APPLES.

ORDER I.—REGULAR.

SECTION 2.—SOUR.

SUB-SECTION 3.—RUSSET.

Beeler's Russet.

Origin not known. Found in an old orchard on the banks of White River, in Marion County, Indiana, by my lamented young friend, Geo. M. Beeler.

Fruit medium to small, round, truncated or cylindrical, inclined; Surface russeted; Dots minute, prominent.

Basin abrupt, uneven, green; Eye medium, closed.
Cavity regular; Stem long.

Core large, wide, heart-shaped, closed, clasping; Seeds numerous, angular; Flesh yellow, crisp, fine-grained, ten-

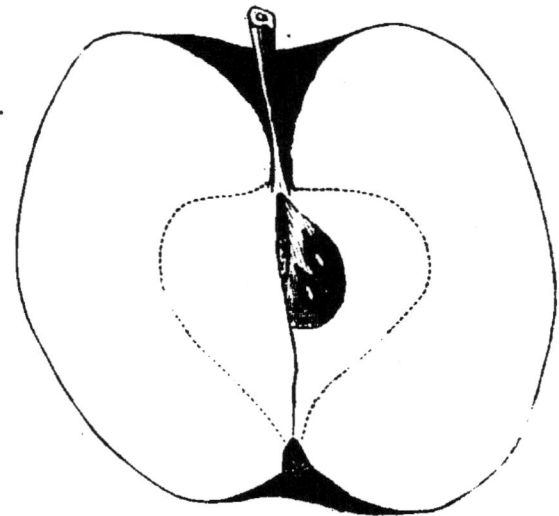

Fig. 288 —BEELER'S RUSSET.

der, juicy; Flavor sub-acid to acid, aromatic, spicy, very agreeable; Quality best; Use, table, kitchen; Season, November, December.

A choice dessert apple.

Columbian Russet.

The origin of this fine, long-keeping russet is not known. Specimens were received from H. N. Gillett, Lawrence County, Ohio. If the tree be healthy and productive, this variety will be a valuable addition to our orchards.

Fruit medium to small, round, truncated, lop-sided; Surface smooth, russeted; Dots minute, scattered, prominent.

Basin medium, regular; Eye large, open.
Cavity acute, regular; Stem, long, slender.
Core medium, closed, pyriform, meeting the eye; Seeds numerous, slender, angular, dark; Flesh very yellow,

breaking, fine-grained, juicy; Flavor acid to sub-acid, rich, aromatic; Quality best; Use, table; Season, February to April.

Very like the *Golden Pearmain*, from J. S. Downer, which see; they may prove to be the same variety.

Court of Wyck.

This spicy English apple, which has so many synonyms as evidences of its popularity, has not been a favorite in this country, but occasionally succeeds well; it has little to recommend it in its looks.

Fruit very small, round, truncated abruptly, much flattened, regular; Surface yellow, covered russet.

Basin wide, very shallow; Eye small, open; Segments reflexed.

Cavity rather wide; Stem long, slender.

Core small, ovate, closed, meeting the eye; Seeds numerous, large, brown; Flesh rich yellow, firm, juicy; Flavor acid, aromatic, rich, spicy, sharp; Quality good in its way; Use, "dessert;" Season, December, January.

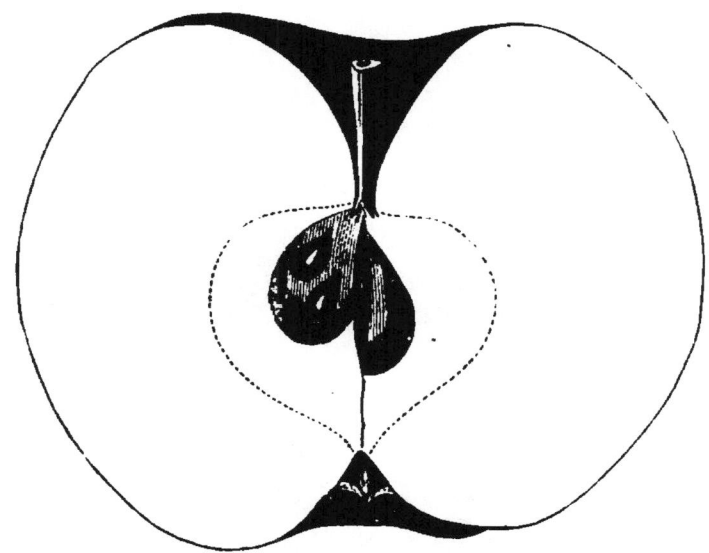

Fig. 239.—CROWNEST.

Crownest.

Originated at Kelley's Island, Ohio, in the orchard of Chas. Carpenter.

Tree vigorous, thrifty, brushy, productive.

Fruit full medium, round, truncated or flattened, often unequal and inclined; Surface greenish yellow, thinly covered with russet.

Basin regular, wide; Eye large, open.

Cavity irregular, lipped; Stem short, curved, fleshy.

Core round, regular, closed, meeting the eye; Seeds long, pointed, angular; Flesh green, tender, breaking; Flavor sub-acid; Quality only good for culinary uses; Season, November to January.

English Golden.

RUSSET GOLDEN, of Barry.

Among the russets there has been much confusion, which it is very difficult to clear up. The apple about to

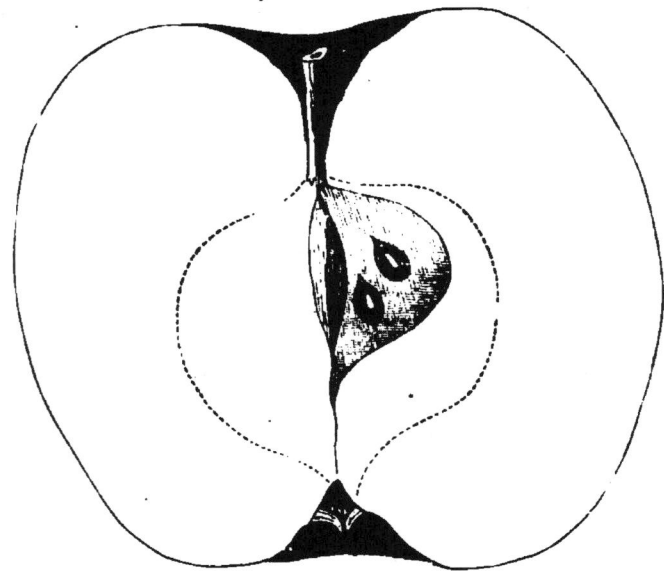

Fig. 240.—ENGLISH GOLDEN.

be described came to the West from the nurseries about Rochester; a very superior variety to many others that resemble it, and may be distinguished by the palate, or by the character of the twigs.

Tree thrifty, vigorous, spreading, productive, a rather early bearer; Shoots slender, olive, speckled.

Fruit medium, round, large ones are oblate, often cylindrical, sometimes inclined, regular; Surface greenish yellow, covered with thick russet; Dots minute, white, scattered.

Basin regular, deep, leather-cracked; Eye small, closed. Cavity wide, regular, rough; Stem short.

Core wide, regular, closed, clasping; Seeds small, flat; Flesh greenish yellow, breaking, granular, juicy; Flavor sub-acid, rich; Quality good to best; Use, table, kitchen; Season, January, February.

A choice dessert fruit. Succeeds well in parts of Kentucky.

English Russet.

Origin unknown. Procured from Mr. C. C. Cary, near Louisville, Kentucky.

Fruit large, globular, flattened, somewhat one-sided; Surface uneven, green; Dots minute, russety and russet streaks.

Basin medium, uneven; Eye small, closed. Cavity acute, wavy, russeted; Stem medium, green.

Core medium, heart-shaped, closed, clasping; Seeds numerous, plump and angular, some imperfect; Flesh yellow, firm, breaking, juicy; Flavor acid; Quality good; Use, kitchen; Season, December, January.

Golden Pearmain—[Of Kentucky.]

This is another very promising Southern variety, received from J. S. Downer, of Kentucky; Origin unknown; he procured it from Tennessee.

Tree vigorous, but tardy and shy in bearing; Shoots stout, dark; Foliage medium.

Fruit small to medium, globular, rather conical, truncated, lop-sided; Surface yellow, blushed and russeted.

Basin abrupt, wide, regular; Eye large, open. Cavity acute, regular; Stem short to medium, slender.

Core somewhat open, meeting the eye; Seeds plump and imperfect; Flesh yellow, breaking, fine-grained;

27

Flavor acid, aromatic, sprightly; Quality very good, almost best; Use, dessert; Season, December, February. —See *Columbian Russet*.

Green Russet.—[N. C.]

Specimens from Reuben Ragan.

Fruit quite large, globular, slightly oblate, regular; Surface yellow, blushed dull red; Dots green, indented, russet veined.

Basin medium, regular; Eye medium, open.

Cavity deep, acute, regular, brown; Stem medium, thick.

Core regular, wide, closed, clasping; Axis short; Seeds numerous, plump, dark; Flesh yellowish white, breaking, granular; Flavor sub-acid; Quality only good, for culinary use; Season, December, January.

Hampton's Russet.

Fruit small, globular-truncate, to flat; Surface yellow russet, bronzed, broken russet stripes; Dots 'scattered, large, yellow.

Basin wide, regular; Eye large, open, green.

Cavity medium, regular, brown; Stem long, inclined.

Core medium, round, closed, meeting the eye; Seeds numerous, pointed, brown; Flesh yellow, tender, breaking, fine-grained; Flavor sub-acid, rich; Quality good; Use, table; Season, December.

Knox Russet.

A very nice little apple, found in the orchard of J. Knox, Pittsburgh, Pennsylvania; trees obtained from near Greensburgh, Pennsylvania. Tree spreading, very productive; Shoots slender.

Fruit small to medium, globular, somewhat conic, regular; Surface smooth, yellow green, blushed, covered with light russet.

Basin shallow, regular; Eye medium, open; Segments reflexed.

Cavity deep, acute, regular; Stem long, red.

Core round, regular, slightly open, clasping the eye;

Seeds numerous, short, plump; Flesh yellow, very fine-

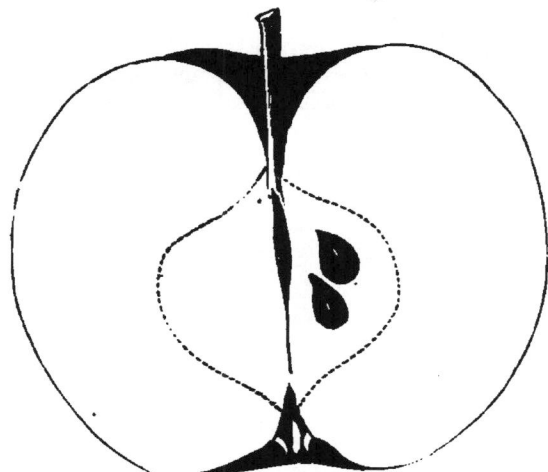

Fig. 241.—KNOX RUSSET.

grained; Flavor mild sub-acid, aromatic; Quality good to very good; Use, dessert; Season, December, January.

Pryor's Red.

This southern apple, probably from Virginia, has been carried through all the Western States, where it is a great favorite, though there are some objectors, on account of its having shown signs of failure in certain situations. The fruit is singularly affected by change of soil and climate; thus, on the Ohio River, it is seen quite flat and regular, with a dull green russeted skin, becoming yellow and ruddy; in one part of the State of Indiana, on lime-stone, it is gibbous, round, often very large, and covered with a rich cinnamon russet, while on the coal measures, west of the center of the State, it is smaller, regular, and distinctly striped deep red on red, with very little russet. Specimens from Rochester, New York, have been shown with scarcely a trace of russet, and having the stripes as distinct and almost as beautiful as those of a *Duchess of Oldenburgh*, so that no southern or western man would have recognized it for his home favorite. The distinctive *leather-cracking* about the eye was present, however, in all.

Tree thrifty, growth upright, twiggy, attaining large size, productive when old; Shoots slender, reddish olive, speckled; Foliage scattering, folded, grayish green; Subject to leaf-blight.

Fruit large, globular-oblate, often unequal; Surface greenish, or dull red, striped, russeted; Dots numerous, large, gray.

Basin shallow, regular or plaited, leather-cracked; Eye small, closed.

Cavity shallow, acute, often lipped; Stem medium.

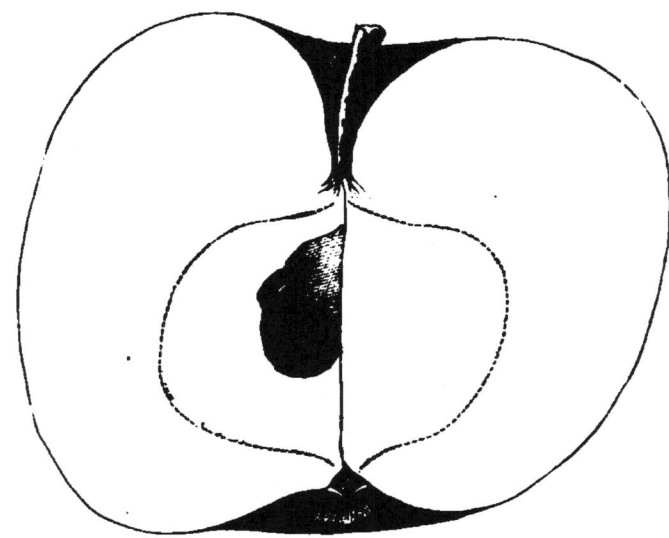

Fig. 242.—PRYOR'S RED.

Core round, regular, closed, meeting the eye; Seeds numerous, angular, pointed; Flesh yellow, tender, melting, fine-grained, juicy; Flavor sub-acid, rich; Quality best; Use, table, kitchen; Season, December, February.

Red Russet.

Origin Hampton Falls, New Hampshire.

Tree very vigorous and productive; resembling Baldwin in almost every particular.

"Fruit large, roundish, conic; Skin yellow, shaded with dull red and deep carmine in the sun, and thickly covered with gray dots, and an appearance of rough russet on most of the surface; Stalk rather short and thick, inserted in a medium cavity, surrounded with thin russet; Calyx nearly closed; Segments long, recurved, in a narrow, uneven basin; Flesh yellow, solid, crisp, tender, with an excellent, rich, sub-acid flavor, somewhat resembling *Baldwin*; Season, January to April."—Downing.

This fruit is rarely seen in the West. It has been thought by some to have originated as a sport from the Baldwin.

Rolen's Keeper.

Received from H. N. Gillett, Lawrence County, Ohio. Origin not given.

Fruit medium, round, regular; Surface rough, splashed red on russet; Dots scattered, small, white.

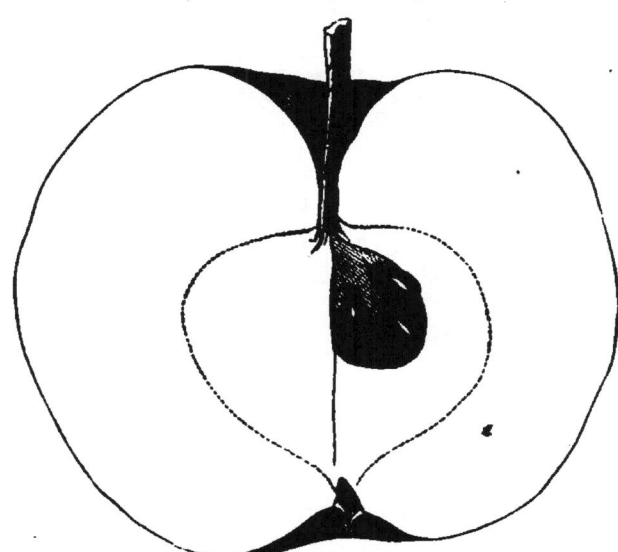

Fig. 243.—ROLEN'S KEEPER.

Basin shallow, regular, leather-cracked; Eye small, closed.

Cavity deep, acute, regular; Stem long, slender.

Core roundish-ovate, regular, closed, clasping; Seeds very numerous, short, plump; Flesh greenish yellow, fine-grained; Flavor acid, rich; Quality good to very good; Use, table; Season, March, April.

Very promising as a keeper.

Rustycoat Milam.

Fruit medium, globular, conic, regular; Surface russet-ed; Dots minute, prominent.

Basin narrow, abrupt, shallow; Eye small, closed.

Cavity acute, regular; Stem medium to long.

Core medium, regular, closed, clasping; Seeds numer-

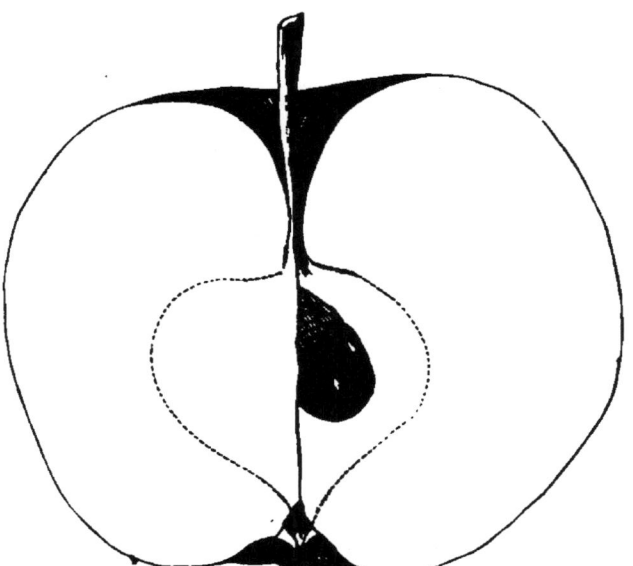

Fig. 244.—RUSTYCOAT MILAM.

ous, pointed, plump; Flesh greenish yellow, breaking, fine-grained, tender; Flavor sub-acid, aromatic; Quality good; Use, table; Season, December to February.

CLASS III.—ROUND APPLES.

ORDER II.—IRREGULAR.

SECTION 1.—SWEET.

SUB-SECTION 1.—SELF-COLORED OR BLUSHED.

Mote's Sweet.

This seedling from the *Stillwater Sweet*, grown by L. S. Mote, of Miami County, Ohio, is quite an improvement upon its parent, which has obtained a high reputation as

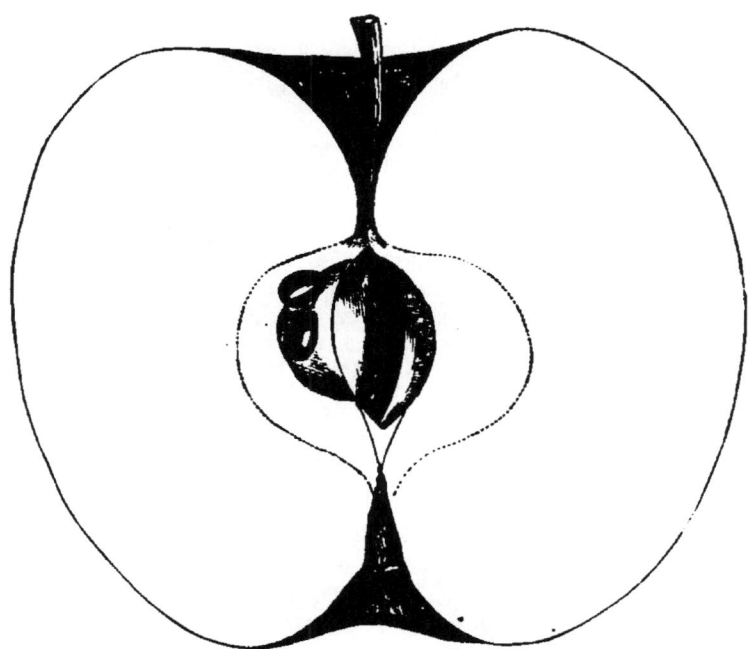

Fig. 245.—MOTE'S SWEET.

a choice autumnal sweet apple. Tree round, spreading, vigorous; Shoots pale; Foliage large, wide, finely serrated, and rather pale.

Fruit large, globular, somewhat flattened, or conic-truncated, rather angular; Surface very smooth, greenish yellow to whitish, with a rare faint blush; Dots scattered, gray, often rosy, whitish bases.

Basin medium, abrupt, wavy; Eye medium, long, closed.
Cavity deep, wide, wavy; Stem long, yellow, curved.
Core medium, open, clasping; Seeds numerous, angular, pale; Flesh yellow, very fine-grained, almost melting, juicy; Flavor very sweet, pleasant; Use, table and kitchen; Quality best; Season, September. One of the most delicious sweet apples.

Northern Sweet.

Origin unknown; supposed to be Vermont. Tree sufficiently healthy and productive. Not generally nor extensively cultivated.
Fruit large, globular, somewhat flattened, angular or regular; Surface smooth, very pale yellow, rarely blushed; Dots minute, with white bases.
Basin deep, abrupt, regular; Eye long, closed.
Cavity rather wide, regular, green; Stem medium.
Core very small, closed, almost clasping; Seeds numerous, short; Flesh whitish, breaking, juicy; Flavor very sweet; Quality pretty good; Use, baking; Season, September, in Northern Indiana and Illinois. Downing says "rich and excellent; September and October."

Swaar.

Origin on the banks of the Hudson, in New York State. Tree vigorous, spreading, productive; Shoots stout, dark colored; Foliage large, curled.
Fruit large, form variable, being sometimes flat, where unusually developed, generally roundish, somewhat flattened, more or less angular or flattened on the sides, but not ribbed; Surface not smooth, often rough, greenish yellow, bronzed, becoming a dead golden yellow when ripe; Dots large, numerous.
Basin medium, wide, regular; Eye small, not long, closed.
Cavity wide, regular or wavy, green; Stem long, curved, pretty stout.
Core medium, regular, heart-shaped, closed, clasping; Seeds numerous, angular, pale; Flesh very heavy, yellow, fine-grained; Flavor very mild sub-acid, or sweet, very rich; Quality best; Use, table and kitchen; Season, March.

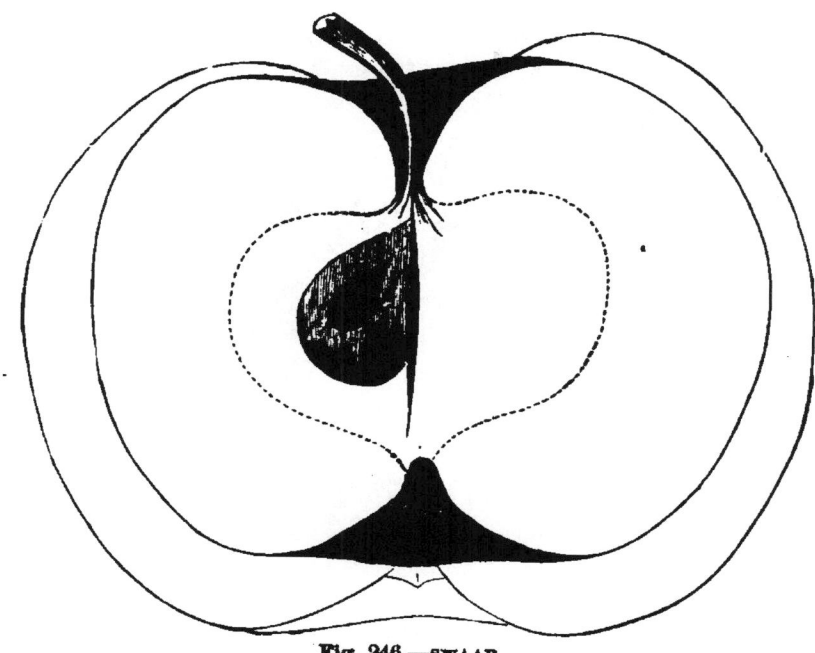

Fig. 246.—SWAAR.

CLASS III.—ROUND APPLES.

ORDER II.—IRREGULAR.

SECTION 1.—SWEET.

SUB-SECTION 2.—STRIPED.

Bailey Sweet.

From Wyoming County, New York. Tree vigorous, productive.

Fruit large, round, sometimes flattened, sometimes angular or ribbed; Surface smooth, mottled, mixed and striped deep red; Dots numerous, large, gray.

Basin narrow, abrupt, regular or folded; Eye small, closed.

27*

Cavity regular, acute green; Stem long.

Core rather large, turbinate, open, clasping; Seeds numerous, angular, dark; Flesh yellow, tender, fine-

Fig. 247.—BAILEY SWEET.

grained, juicy; Flavor very sweet, rich; Quality good to very good; Use, kitchen, table; Season, October.

A very valuable variety also for stock.

Brittle Sweet.

" Origin unknown; good grower, and very productive.

" Fruit above medium, roundish, approaching conic, sometimes elongated, angular; Skin greenish yellow, shaded and splashed with crimson, sprinkled with gray dots; Stem short, inserted in a broad, shallow cavity; Calyx closed, set in a small corrugated basin; Flesh yellowish, crisp, tender, juicy, sweet, and excellent; Season, September, October."—Downing.

Hull Blossom.

This is an Eastern or European variety, which I have not seen in the West. Specimens from Massachusetts.

Fruit small, roundish-truncate, or flattened, uneven; Surface smooth, yellow, mixed and striped, carmine; Dots large, yellow.

Basin shallow, folded; Eye small, closed.

Cavity deep, wavy; Stem short.

Core small, closed, roundish, meeting the eye; Seeds large, pale; Flesh yellow, fine-grained; Flavor sweet; Quality good to very good; Use, table, kitchen; Season, November.

Sweet Pearmain.

"This variety, according to Downing and Thomas, is the *English Sweeting;* but, according to Manning, the English Sweeting is the *Ramsdell's Sweeting* of Downing. This fruit is extensively grown in Central Ohio, and further West, suiting well the rich soils; keeping finely all winter; highly valued for baking or eating."

"Fruit medium size or often above; Form roundish, slightly angular; Color dull red, rough russet dots, and blueish bloom; Stem long, slender; Cavity deep, wide, open; Calyx woolly; Basin medium; Flesh yellowish, tender, moderately juicy, sweet; Core medium, with outer or concentric lines; Seeds ovate, pyriform, dark brown; Season, December to March."—Elliott.

I am not familiar with the above, but find a very strong resemblance in the characters to those of my *Red Winter Pearmain*, Class II, I, 2, 2, from which, however, Elliott's outline would exclude it.

Willis Sweet.

This apple is supposed to have originated on Long Island, where it is highly valued for baking.

Tree vigorous, productive; Fruit medium, round, somewhat angular, striped red, very sweet and rich; Use, baking and stock.

CLASS III.—ROUND APPLES.

ORDER II.—IRREGULAR.

SECTION 1.—SWEET.

SUB-SECTION 3.—RUSSET.

NONE.

———

CLASS III.—ROUND APPLES.

ORDER II.—IRREGULAR.

SECTION 2.—SOUR.

SUB-SECTION 1.—SELF-COLORED.

American Golden Pippin.

GOLDEN PIPPIN, of Downing.—NEW YORK GREENING, &C.

Having mislaid my notes of this apple, I am obliged to quote Mr. Downing's description of this fine fruit, which

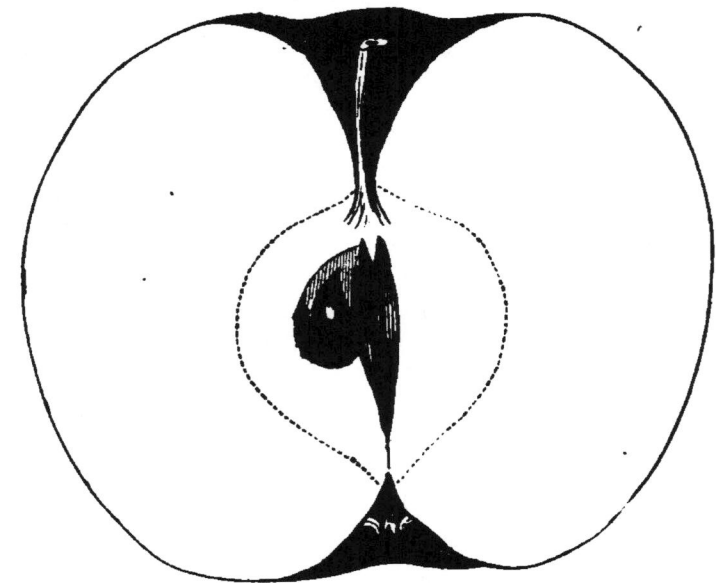

Fig. 248.—AMERICAN GOLDEN PIPPIN.

is believed to be American; cultivated in parts of New York, and found to be profitable.

"Growth strong, similar to that of Rhode Island Greening, but less drooping, making a round, spreading head ;
does not bear young, but very productive when a little
advanced, and a popular fruit where known."

"Form variable, oblate, globular or conic, angular or
ribbed ; Stem stout, short, inserted in a deep cavity ;
Calyx closed, set in an irregular basin ; Skin fine golden
yellow, thinly sprinkled with dots, sometimes slightly
netted with thin russet ; Flesh yellowish, tender, juicy,
nearly melting, with a rich, refreshing, almost vinous,
aromatic flavor ; Core rather large ; November to February."

Brooke's Pippin.

"Origin, Essex County, Virginia. The original tree is
very large, bears regular and large crops of fruit, which
is always fair, of the largest size, keeps well till May ;
Flesh fine, yellow, juicy and rich, and of the finest flavor ;
young trees grow very thriftily."—[H. R. Robey, Fredericksburgh, Va.]

Fruit large, roundish, inclining to conical, obscurely
ribbed, greenish yellow, faintly blushed.

Basin small, shallow, wavy, sometimes furrowed ; Eye
medium, closed.

Cavity deep, wavy, brown ; Stem short, thick.

Flesh yellow, crisp, juicy, fine-grained ; Flavor acid,
spicy, rich ; Quality very good ; Season, November to
March.

As grown in Indiana, both tree and fruit resemble the
Newtown Pippin in appearance, and may prove identical
after further trial.

Champlain.—[*Downing.*]

PAPER—PAPER-SKIN.

This very delicate fruit was exhibited before the Ohio
Pomological Society by A. L. Benedict, of Morrow County, as the *Paper* apple. He obtained the cions from the
celebrated apple region, Grand Isle, Vermont, where it is
sometimes called Champlain, and where it had been introduced from Rhode Island, without a name, by his friend
Macomber. My friend Benedict informs me that " the
growth of the tree is strong and stocky, and that the fruit

never scabs nor rots on the tree. It is increasing in es-
teem as it becomes better known, and is preferred to the
Red Astrachan, ripening with it. When sent to J. J.
Thomas, he thought it synonymous with the *Primate*, but
Jos. Newcomber, having both varieties growing side by
side, assured me they were quite unlike, and that the *Paper* was much the better apple of the two."

Tree medium size, vigorous, stocky.

Fruit full medium, globular, rather conical, angular;
Surface smooth, yellowish green, slightly blushed; Dots
minute, indented.

Basin small, abrupt, folded; Eye small, long, closed.

Cavity acute, wavy, green; Stem long, slender.

Core medium, round, slightly open, clasping; Seeds
numerous, angular, dark; Flesh white, tender, fine-grained,
juicy; Flavor sub-acid, aromatic, delicate; Quality best;
Use, the dessert especially; Season, August, September.

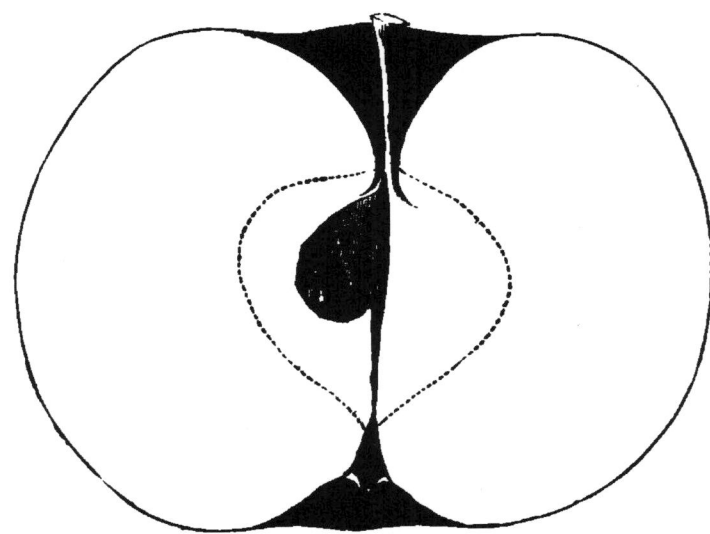

Fig. 249.—DRAP D'OR.

Drap d'Or.

VRAI DRAP D'OR.—[Dahamel.]

This is an old French variety, respecting which there is
some uncertainty among cultivators.

Fruit large, globular, but variable, being conical-truncate to oblate; Surface smooth, pale waxen yellow, rarely blushed.

Basin wide, plaited; Eye small, closed.

Cavity wide, wavy, brown; Stem long, inclined, yellow or red, angular.

Core large, regular, closed, clasping; Seeds numerous, angular, long; Flesh pale yellow, breaking, fine-grained, juicy; Flavor sub-acid, aromatic; Quality good to best; Use, market, kitchen, table; Season, August, September.

For the table its place is supplanted by the *Primate*, *Dyer* and others.

Dyer, or Pomme Royale.

POMMEWATER, in Illinois.

Believed to be a French apple, but named Dyer by the Massachusetts Horticultural Society, in the belief that it was a seedling of Rhode Island.

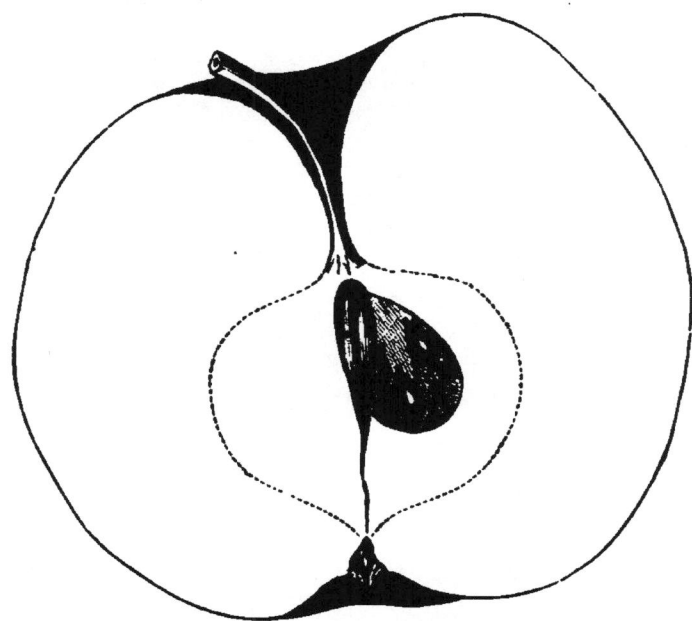

Fig. 250.—DYER, OR POMME ROYALE.

Tree of moderate vigor, spreading, not very productive.

Fruit medium to large, globular, uneven, somewhat angular; Surface not smooth, pale yellow, vein-russeted; Dots numerous, minute, dark.

Basin medium, shallow, folded or plaited; Eye small, closed.

Cavity deep, acute, lipped, brown; Stem long, slender.

Core regular, round, open or closed, clasping; Seeds numerous, plump, short; Flesh yellowish, very tender, very fine-grained, very juicy; Flavor sub-acid, aromatic, rich, delicate; Quality best; Use, the dessert; Season, September, October.

Not attractive in appearance, but very fine for the amateur.

Ewalt.

Origin Pennsylvania. Introduced by Dr. Brinckle in his *ad-interim* reports to the Pennsylvania Horticultural Society. Mr. Waring considers it a valuable winter apple. Tree vigorous, handsome grower in the nursery; Shoots erect, dark colored; an early, regular bearer.

Fruit large, very handsome, roundish, rather angular; Surface smooth, yellow, with clear bright red in the sun, not striped; Dots numerous about the base, greenish.

Basin medium, narrow, plaited; Eye medium, closed.

Cavity medium, acute; Stem short.

Flesh tender, fine-grained; Flavor acid, becoming mild, aromatic, sprightly; Quality very good; Season, February to April.

Golden Ball.

A favorite Maine apple. Tree vigorous, productive, hardy.

Frut large, round, ribbed; Surface smooth, greenish yellow; Dots few, distinct, white bases.

Basin deep, abrupt, folded; Eye large, closed.

Cavity narrow; Stem medium.

Core indistinct, open, clasping; Seeds defective; Flesh yellowish, tender, juicy; Flavor sub-acid, rich; Quality good; Use, table, kitchen, market; Season, December to March in the North.

Morgan White.

Origin unknown. Sent from Morgan County, Illinois, by Professor J. B. Turner, of Jacksonville.

Fruit large, globular, somewhat flattened, irregular, ribbed, uneven; Surface smooth, greenish, marked with gray striæ, rarely a faint blush; Dots white, large.

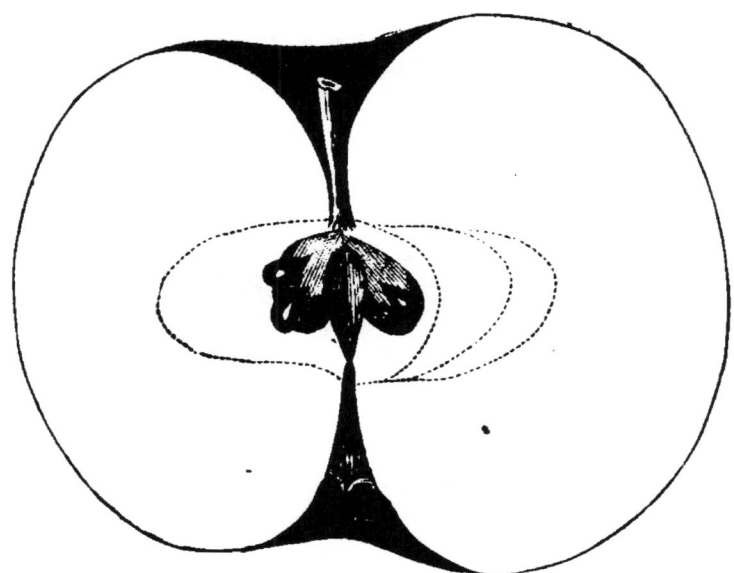

Fig. 251.—MORGAN WHITE.

Basin abrupt, ribbed; Eye small but long, closed.

Cavity deep, acute, wavy; Stem short to medium.

Core small, very wide, open, clasping; Axis short; Seeds numerous, plump, short; Flesh greenish white, breaking, tender, fine-grained, juicy; Flavor acid to sub-acid, agreeable; Quality good; Use, kitchen and table; Season, September to January.

Peck's Pleasant.

This fine fruit is credited to Rhode Island. The tree is healthy, spreading, moderately vigorous, but productive, and a regular bearer. This apple is said to resemble the Newtown Pippin, but I have never been able to trace any resemblance, except that both are green; at any rate there is no danger of the merest tyro in pomology confounding the two varieties. There is, however, a remarkable diversity in the fruit arising from the different soils and climates in which it is cultivated, North and South, and while, like many other varieties, its size is greatly developed, its texture and flavor are depreciated in the migrations southward.

Fruit large, flattened, globular, somewhat angular, or flattened, sometimes having a shallow sulcus or furrow on

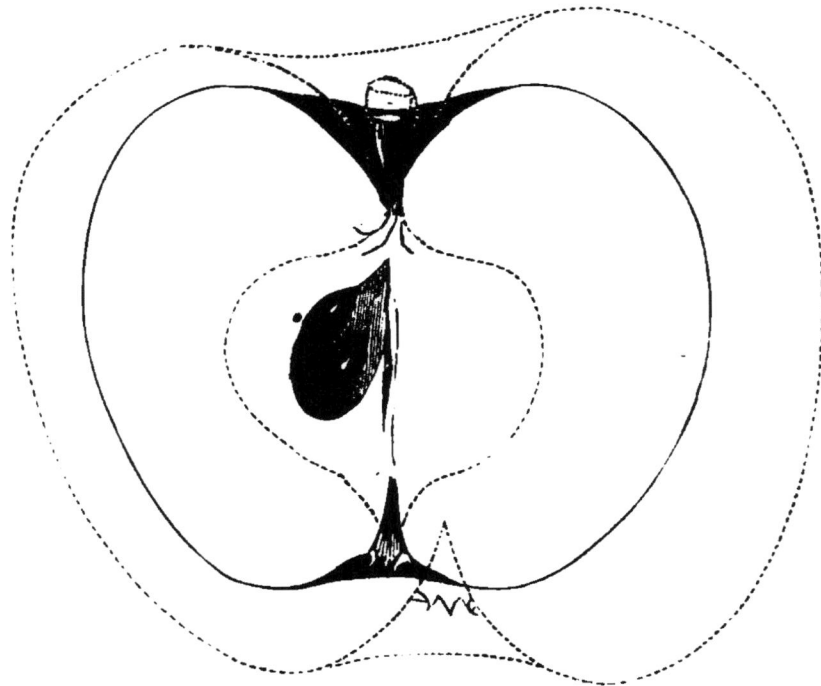

Fig. 252.—PECK'S PLEASANT

one side; Surface smooth, yellow or orange, being sometimes faintly blushed; Dots gray, with white bases.

Basin rather shallow and folded; Eye small and open, calycinal segments being short.

Cavity wide, but often lipped, brown; Stem short, very thick, clubbed or knobby.

Core large, closed, clasping the eye; Seeds numerous, angular; Flesh yellow, tender, breaking, fine-grained; Flavor sub-acid and somewhat aromatic; of first quality in the North; Use, table, kitchen or market; Season, December to January, or later.

Primate.

This delicious table apple has strong claims upon our admiration, on account of its good qualities as a dessert fruit, for the extreme delicacy of its skin and flesh render it unfit for market; it is therefore not profitable for the commercial orchard.

Tree thrifty, stocky, vigorous, strongly branched, pro-

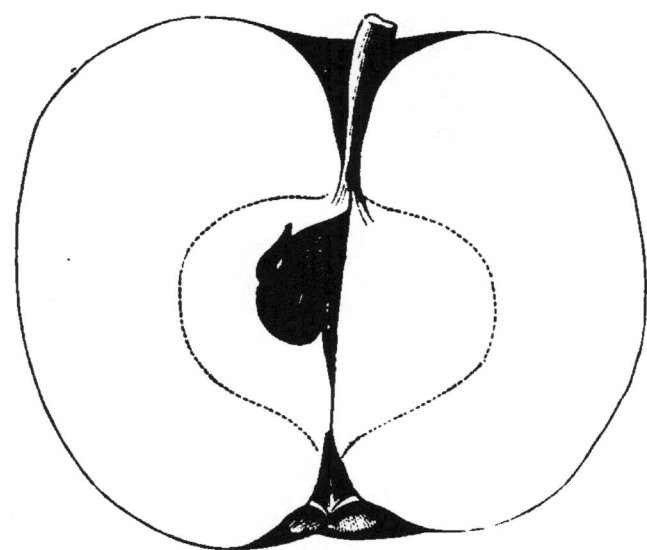

Fig. 253.—PRIMATE.

ductive; Shoots stout, short, light olive; Buds prominent, foliage pale green.

Fruit full medium, globular, angular, irregular; Surface smooth, greenish-yellow, becoming almost white, sometimes faintly blushed; Dots minute.

Basin abrupt, folded; Eye small but long, closed; Segments reflexed.

Cavity acute, wavy, green; Stem medium to long, thick.

Core medium, round, closed, clasping; Seeds numerous, angular, long, dark; Flesh greenish-white, very tender, fine-grained; Flavor mild sub-acid, very agreeable; Quality best; Use, the dessert; Season, July and August.

Progress.

Not having had the good fortune to study this apple, I quote the description given by Downing:

"A native of Middletown, Connecticut. Tree a moderate grower and forms a handsome head, bears early and very productive.

"Size above medium, rather globular, inclining to conic, sometimes oblate, somewhat angular; Stem short, inserted into a round cavity, surrounded by russet; Calyx large, partially closed, set in a shallow, open basin; Skin smooth, yellow, with a sunny cheek, sometimes a few scattered, gray dots; Flesh solid, tender, crisp, juicy, with a very refreshing, vinous flavor. Ripe October until April."

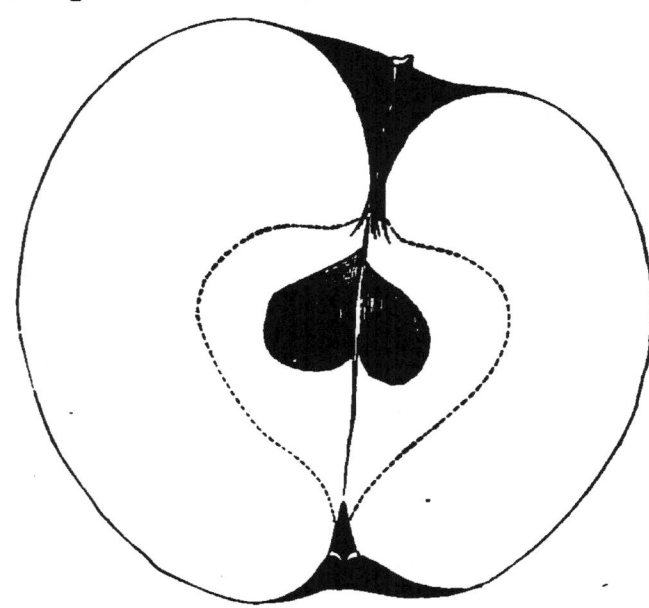

Fig. 254.—QUINCE.

Quince.

COLE'S QUINCE.

This does not appear to be exactly the same as that described by Coxe, and later by Downing. This fruit is not very extensively cultivated. The specimens described are from that precise pomologist T. T. Lyon, of Michigan.

Fruit full medium, globular, angular, ribbed; Surface smooth, greenish-yellow, pale.

Basin narrow, folded, plaited; Eye small, closed.

Cavity acute, wavy; Stem medium, yellow.

Core oval, closed, meeting the eye; Seeds numerous, angular, plump, brown; Flesh yellowish-white, tender, fine-grained, juicy; Flavor sub-acid, aromatic; Quality good for cooking; Season, November to January.

September.

This apple is highly esteemed by Mr. W. G. Waring, of Center County, Pennsylvania, where it originated.

Tree hardy and vigorous, a good and regular bearer.

"Fruit large, globular, somewhat depressed, slightly conic, angular; Skin yellow, slightly shaded and thinly sprinkled with brown dots; Stalk short, inserted in a deep, abrupt cavity, surrounded by thin russet; Calyx partially closed, set in an open basin; Flesh yellowish, tender, juicy, with a very agreeable sub-acid flavor; October."— [Downing.]

Sheepnose—*of Mears.*

This substantial little apple was presented by Wm. E. Mears, a zealous horticulturist of Clermont County, Ohio, where it is considerably cultivated. Origin unknown.

Fruit medium, round, slightly conic, irregular; Surface smooth, greenish yellow, white striæ about the base, like *White Winter Pearmain*, which it resembles in some other respects; Dots minute.

Basin shallow, wavy; Eye long, closed.

Cavity acute, narrow, bronzed; Stem medium, knobbed.

Core roundish oval, irregular, open, clasping; Seeds numerous, plump, dark; Flesh yellowish-white, breaking, tender, juicy; Flavor sub-acid; Quality good; Use, table and kitchen; Season, December to February.

Summer Pippin.

A favorite apple about New York—not known extensively. Tree vigorous, forming a beautiful head, a regular
and good bearer.

Fruit medium to large, variable in form, sometimes ob-
long-oval, or inclining to conic, angular and irregular; Skin
pale waxen yellow, shaded with a delicate crimson blush,

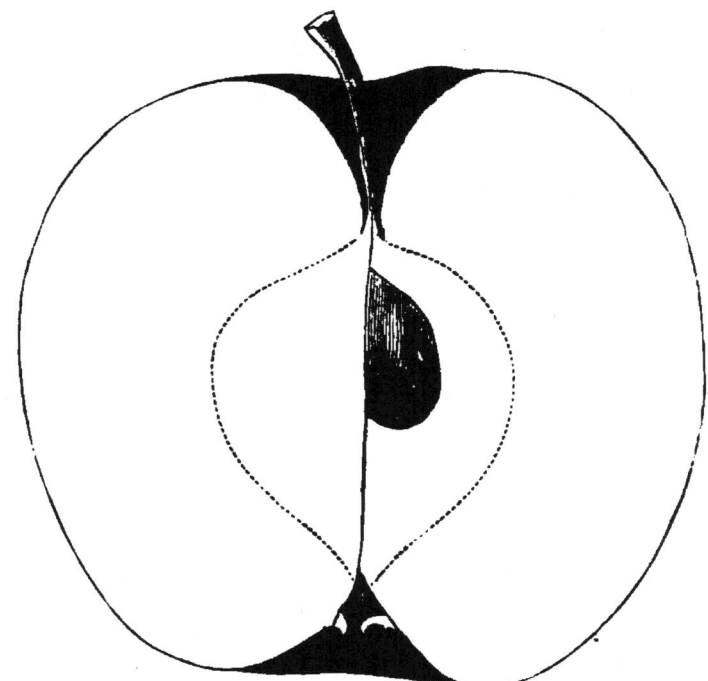

Fig. 255.—SUMMER PIPPIN.

and sprinkled with green and grayish dots; Stalk varies
in length and thickness, inserted in a deep, abrupt cavity;
Calyx closed, set in a deep, abrupt, corrugated basin;
Flesh white, tender, moderately juicy, with a pleasant, refreshing sub-acid flavor ; Valuable for culinary uses; Ripens in August and continues a month or more.—[Downing.]

Transport.

Another of Reuben Ragan's Indiana seedlings. Tree poor in the nursery—good in the orchard. Very productive.

Fruit large, globular, flattened, angular; Surface smooth, pale yellow, blushed carmine; Dots scattered,

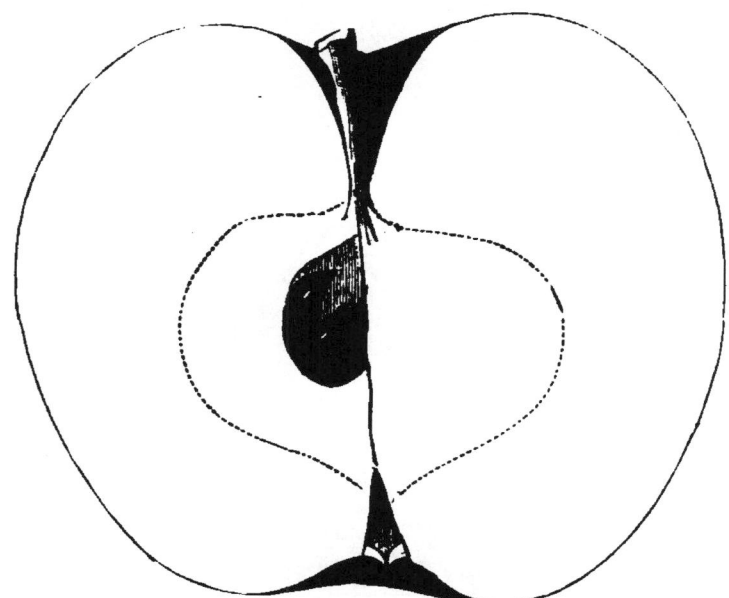

Fig. 256.—TRANSPORT.

green, with white bases, becoming purple where exposed; Bloom white.

Basin medium, plaited; Eye small, closed.

Cavity deep, acute, brown; Stem medium to long.

Core irregular, closed, clasping; Axis short; Seeds dark, pointed, imperfect; Flesh, yellowish-white, tender, melting, fine-grained, juicy; Flavor mild sub-acid, rich; Quality good to very good; Use, table, kitchen, market; Season, December to February. Not very profitable.

White Pippin.

The origin of this valuable fruit is entirely unknown, and its history can only be traced to the nursery of Silas

Wharton, who may have brought it with him from the East. For a time some of our leading pomologists thought it was the *Canada Reinette*, but this idea has long since been relinquished, and all agree that it is *sui generis*, though it may have had a different name. In some of its external characters it more nearly resembles

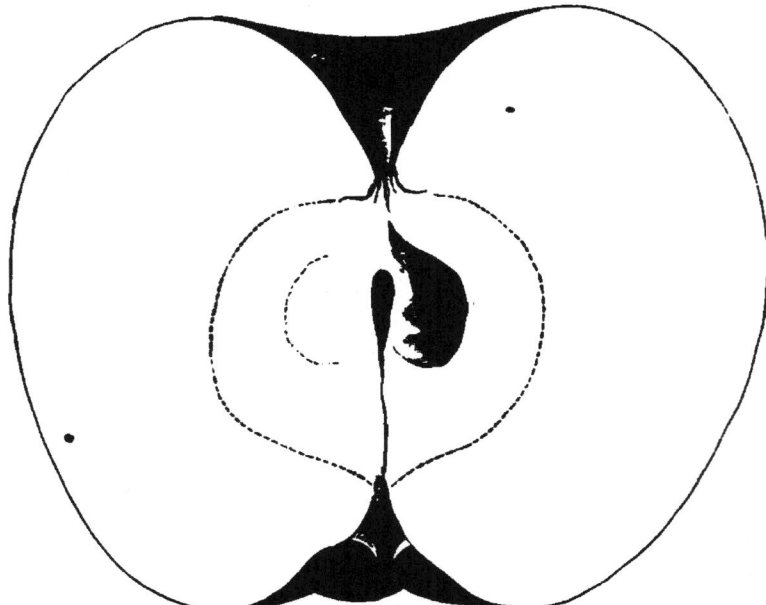

Fig. 257.—WHITE PIPPIN.

the *Yellow Newtown Pippin* than any other fruit; but, while it lacks the high, spicy flavor of that apple, it is found to be much more profitable in the orchard.

The tree is remarkably thrifty, vigorous and productive, upright, with very dark shoots, covered with down, bearing large leaves that are quite downy beneath, and deep green above.

Fruit large, variable in form, angular, sometimes lopsided, generally fair, free from scab; Surface smooth, green or greenish-white to very pale yellow when ripe; the skin toward the base is often marked on the unripe apple with indistinct wavy stripes of white, the interspaces are sometimes colored by exposure, and assume a pink or purplish hue, making the fruit appear to be striped; Dots very minute, and surrounded by green bases that are most distinct before the fruit is perfectly ripe; these and the white stripes are very characteristic.

Basin deep, abrupt, regular, wavy or folded; Eye small, closed.

Cavity wide, deep, wavy, brown and green: Stem short, sometimes thick.

Core small, pyriform, closed, clasping; Seeds numerous, angular, pale brown, pointed; Flesh white or yellowish-white, breaking, granular, juicy; Flavor acid to sub-acid, not spicy; Quality good; Use, kitchen rather than table, cooks very well; Season, December and January; not a very good keeper; may be preserved until March.

Yellow Newtown.

The origin of this variety of the Newtown Pippin, which has obtained such a world-wide notoriety as the "Ameri-

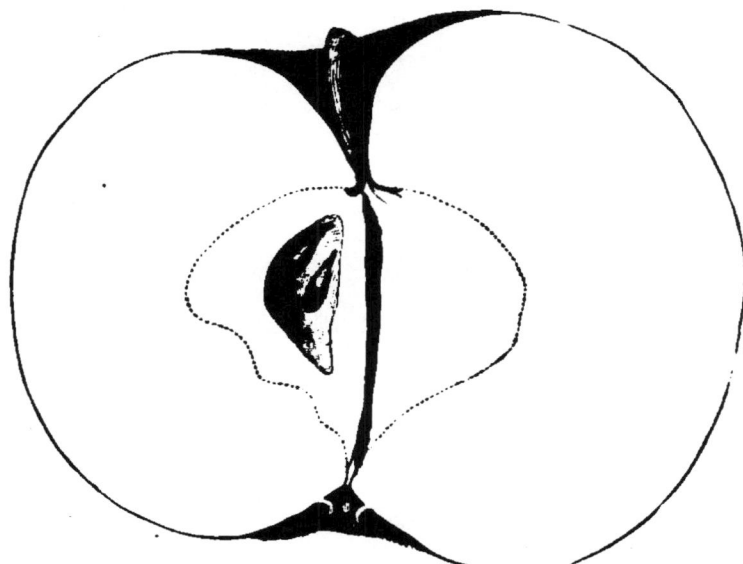

Fig. 258.—YELLOW NEWTOWN.

can Apple," is very uncertain. The distinction between this and the *Green Newtown*, as described under Class III, I, 2, 1, was well known to Coxe.

28

Tree resembling that of the Green variety, slow grower in the nursery, having rough bark when old, not an early bearer, but large, spreading, and productive, and in suitable soils profitable. From some cause, however, the orchards of both these apples are much less satisfactory in their results than formerly in many parts of the country. Still it is often seen in great perfection, and I am compiling this description from outlines and notes of a large number that were very fine.

Fruit large, round, more or less modified by being cylindrical, truncated, lop-sided, ribbed, and irregular, sometimes even conic; Surface smooth, yellowish-green, sometimes bronzy, becoming yellow when ripe, like the *White Pippin*, it is marked with gray striæ near the base while green; Dots minute, scattered, whitish bases.

Basin large, folded, ribbed or plaited; Eye medium, rather open.

Cavity deep, acute, brown; Stem medium or short, rarely long.

Core medium, oval, regular, closed, meeting or clasping the eye; Seeds pointed, brown, sometimes imperfect; Flesh yellow, firm, breaking, juicy, not crisp like the Green variety; Flavor acid, aromatic, rich, very agreeable; Quality best; Use, table, kitchen, market and cider; Season, March.

CLASS III.—ROUND APPLES.

ORDER II.—IRREGULAR.

SECTION 2.—SOUR.

SUB-SECTION 2.—STRIPED.

Benoni.

This handsome and delicious early apple is a native of Dedham, Massachusetts. Its good qualities have caused its culture to be widely extended, and it appears to give very general satisfaction; though not so early as some other kinds, for the dessert especially, it is indispensable to the amateur.

Tree small, upright, close, productive, early bearer; Shoots slender, brown, leaves thin, long.

Fruit small to medium, round, truncated, somewhat angular, irregular; Surface smooth, yellow, covered mixed red, striped scarlet and carmine; Dots minute.

Basin wide, abrupt; Eye large, open or closed.

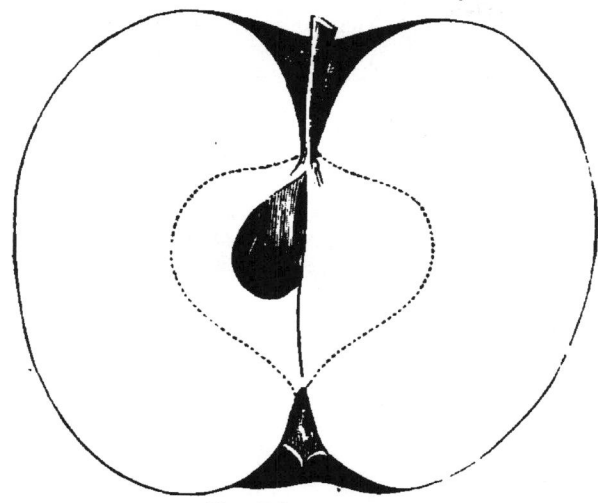

Fig. 259.—BENONI.

Cavity acute, wavy, brown; Stem medium, green, often stout.

Core small, closed, meeting the eye; Seeds angular, dark; Flesh yellow, fine-grained, juicy; Flavor rich, sub-acid, spicy; Quality best; Use, dessert, kitchen and market; Season, July and August.   Delicious and profitable.

Brennaman.

This fine apple, from Lancaster County, Pennsylvania, was reported on by the *ad interim* Committee of the Pennsylvania Horticultural Society, and was brought to my notice by Dr. J. K. Eshleman, of Downingtown, in whose beautiful orchard I had an opportunity of studying the variety.

Tree large, spreading, vigorous, productive, said to be hardy.

Fruit medium to large, round, somewhat angular; Surface smooth, yellow, nearly covered with stripes of bright rich red.

Basin deep, wavy; Eye closed.

Cavity large, brown; Stem short to medium.

Flesh whitish, breaking, fine-grained, juicy; Flavor sub-acid, agreeable; Quality good, especially for culinary use and market; Season, August and September.

Chronicle.

This is a famous long keeper of Indiana origin. The honors of its discovery are divided between the Sigersons and R. Ragan.

Tree vigorous, healthy, productive, said to be hardy.

Fruit full medium to large, globular, truncated, cylindrical, irregular, flattened at the sides or angular; Axis

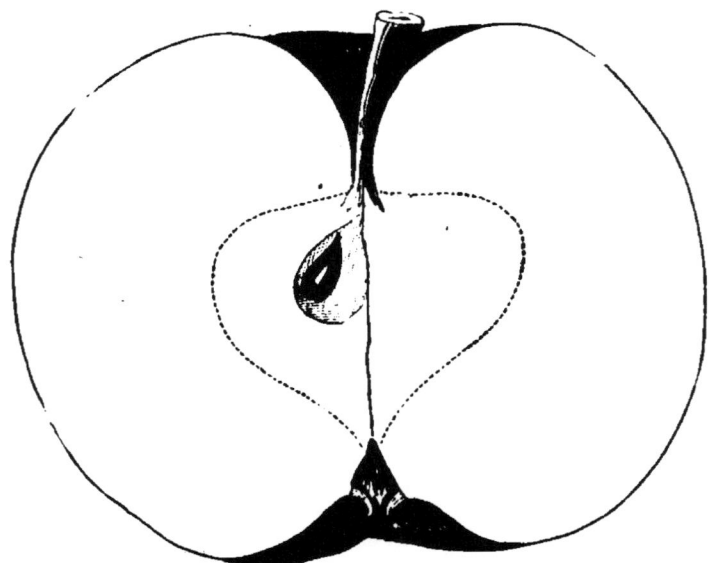

Fig. 260.—CHRONICLE.

inclined in some; Surface yellowish-green to yellow, mixed and striped dull red; Dots large, scattered, yellow, indented.

Basin, wide, deep, regular or wavy; Eye small to medium, closed.

Cavity wide, wavy or acute, sometimes lipped, brown; Stem medium to long, sometimes thick.

Core small, closed, meeting; Seeds numerous, pointed, plump; Flesh greenish to yellow, firm; Flavor sub-acid, not spicy; Quality scarcely good, except for culinary Use and for market; Season, March to May. Keeps sound even when bruised.

Foundling.

" From Massachusetts. Tree moderately vigorous, spreading, productive."—[Downing.]

Fruit medium to large, round, flattened at the ends, angular or uneven; Surface yellowish-green, mixed red, splashed deep red; Dots minute, indented.

Basin wide, abrupt, folded; Eye small, closed.

Cavity deep, acute, wavy, green; Stem short or medium.

Core large, wide, open, clasping; Seeds numerous, small, pointed; Flesh white, tender, fine-grained, juicy; Flavor sub-acid, aromatic; Quality good; Use, table; Season, September.

Specimens obtained from Mr. Warren.

Jersey Black.
BLACK APPLE of Coxe?

This admirable but unpretending fruit has extended its way quietly through the country, along the parallels 40° to 42°, without ever having had any extra puffing, such as has given notoriety to some of its competitors for places in the orchard. Nobody speaks about this apple, nor writes about it, and yet it is everywhere to be found. This cannot be the *Black Apple* of Coxe and Downing, being quite different in some of its strong characters. Origin unknown, supposed to have been introduced into the West by Silas Wharton, of Warren County, Ohio, as it is found with the White Pippin and other favorite sorts of his introduction, and is in his published list.

Tree sufficiently vigorous, but does not grow large, spreading, often drooping when old, branches open, always fruitful, either well distributed in a light crop, or crowded in a full one.

Fruit full medium, round, angular and irregular, sometimes ribbed; Surface smooth, completely covered with deep red, striped darker, giving a purple, almost black hue to the fruit, often covered with a thin bloom; one variety is always lighter, stripes more distinct, and the flesh more stained; Dots numerous, minute, indented, purple.

Basin mostly shallow, folded and plaited; Eye small to medium, closed.

Cavity deep, acute, brown, often wavy or folded; Stem short, medium or long, usually stout, sometimes knobbed.

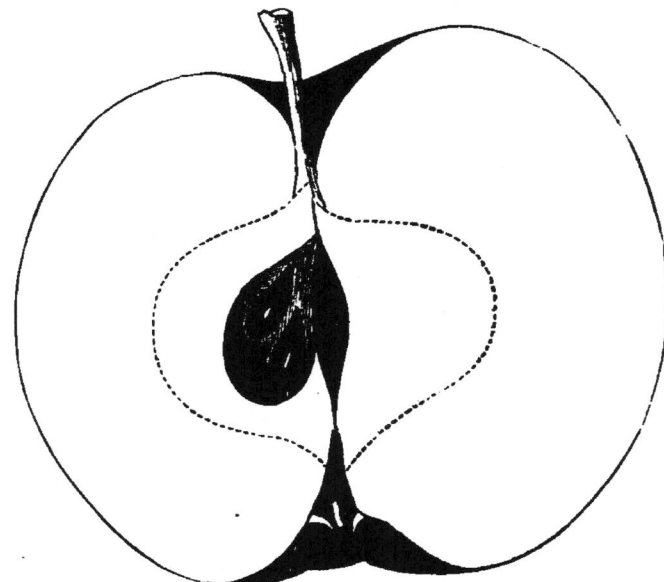

Fig. 261.—JERSEY BLACK.

Core medium, regular, generally closed, clasping the eye; Seeds numerous, short, plump, pointed, dark; Flesh yellow, crisp, fine-grained, juicy, often stained pink or reddish; Flavor rich, mild sub-acid, aromatic, not spicy, satisfying; Quality good; Use, table, kitchen, cider and for stock; Season, December, January; keeps sound. A good market apple.

King.

KING OF TOMPKINS COUNTY.

This splendid apple, which has attracted so much attention of recent years, had its origin, as is supposed, in Tompkins County, New York, where it has been much cultivated.

Tree vigorous, healthy, large and spreading, an abundant annual bearer.

Fruit large, handsome, globular, irregular, somewhat

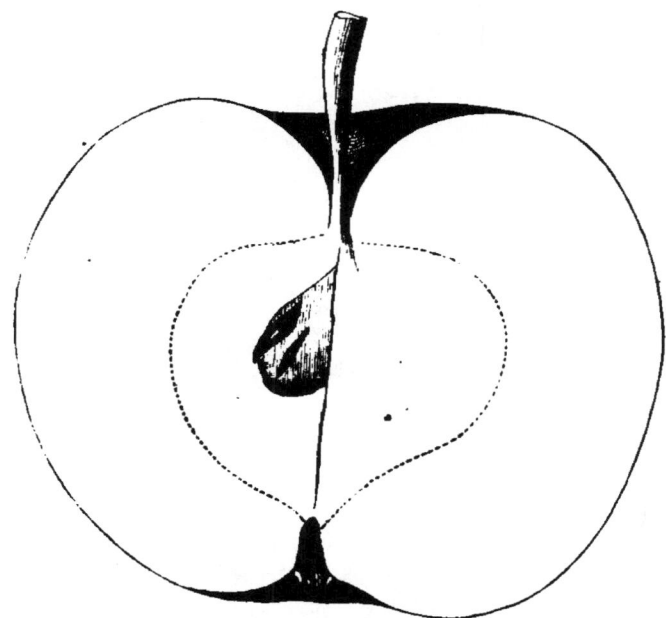

Fig. 262.—KING.

conic, angular; Surface smooth, yellow, covered deep red, marbled and striped; Dots numerous, gray, large.

Basin shallow, folded; Eye large, short, closed.

Cavity wide, shallow, wavy; Stem short or long, thick or slender, red.

Core very large, turbinate, regular, closed; Seeds imperfect, angular; Flesh yellowish-white, tender, breaking; Flavor sub-acid, aromatic; Quality best; Use, table, kitchen and market; Season, December and longer.

Missouri Keeper.

Specimens from Norman J. Colman, Esq., Editor of the Rural World, St. Louis, Missouri. Origin unknown.

Fruit medium to small, round, irregular; Surface smooth, shaded, mixed, striped red; Dots numerous, large, white, distinct.

Basin abrupt, regular; Eye small, closed.

Cavity narrow, regular; Stem medium to short, knobby, thick.

Core regular, closed; Seeds numerous, long, plump, angular; Flesh yellow, breaking, tender, fine-grained, juicy; Flavor sub-acid; Quality good to very good; Use, table, market and kitchen; Season, January to July.

Specimens cut and described on the 25th of June were in perfect condition.

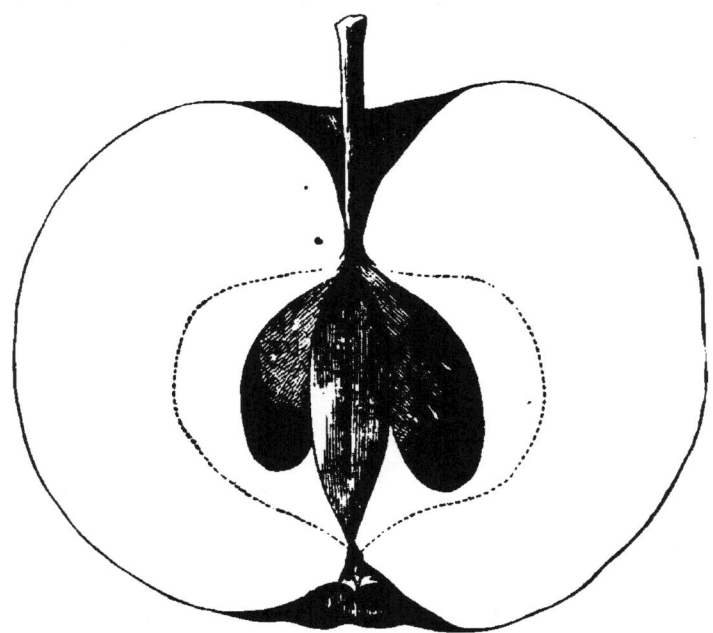

Fig. 263.—NONPAREIL.

Nonpareil.

The history and origin of this nice autumn fruit have not been ascertained, and it may prove to be an old variety with a changed name—considerably grown in Northern Illinois. Specimens from Dr. Geo. Haskell, of Rockford, are here described.

Fruit medium to large, round, somewhat conic, angular, ribbed; Surface smooth, waxy-yellow, splashed crimson; Dots minute.

Basin shallow, folded and plaited; Eye small, closed.

Cavity deep, acute, wavy, sometimes lipped; Stem long to medium, thick, green.

Core wide, regular, open, meeting the eye; Seeds numerous, angular, brown; Flesh white, tender, fine-grained, juicy; Flavor acid, aromatic; Quality quite good; Use, table; Season, September and October.

Stewart's Nonpareil—Local Name.

This early apple is quite a favorite in Clarke County, Ohio, and may prove to be the Tetofski, or some other known variety, when it comes to be more thoroughly examined. Fruits received from my brother, J. T. Warder.

Fruit medium, roundish, conical, irregular, angular; Surface smooth, yellowish-green, splashed carmine; Dots minute, scattered, indented.

Basin small, abrupt, folded; Eye very small, closed.

Cavity deep, acute, narrow; Stem long, slender.

Core large, oval, open, clasping the eye; Seeds numerous, brown; Flesh white, tender, fine-grained, juicy; Flavor sub-acid; Quality good to best; Use, table and kitchen; Season, July and August, in latitude 40°.

Tetofski.

This little foreigner was brought from Russia, and seems as well adapted to our climate and tastes as are its companions from the same region.

Tree vigorous, hardy, productive, upright, leaves broad, pale or light green.

Fruit small to medium, round, flattened, somewhat conic, angular; Surface smooth, yellow, striped, splashed carmine, white bloom.

Basin shallow, folded; Eye large, closed.

Cavity wide, wavy, or deep, acute; Stem short, yellow.

28*

Core large, closed, clasping; Seeds numerous, plump, brown; Flesh yellowish-white, breaking, fine grained, juicy; Flavor acid; Quality good; Use, market, kitchen; Season, June, July—before *Early Harvest.*

CLASS III.—ROUND APPLES.

ORDER II.—IRREGULAR.

SECTION 2.—SOUR.

SUB-SECTION 3.—RUSSET.

Golden Harvey.

BRANDY APPLE.

This highly flavored English apple is often referred to, but is rarely seen in American collections; but as it may be interesting to some, I quote Downing's brief description:

"Fruit small, irregularly round; Skin rather rough, dull russet over a yellow ground, with a russety red cheek; Flesh yellow, of fine texture, with a rich sub-acid flavor. The fruit is apt to shrivel."

Tree of slender growth.

CLASS IV.—OBLONG APPLES.

ORDER I.—REGULAR.

SECTION 1.—SWEET

SUB-SECTION 1.—SELF-COLORED.

Downing's Paragon.

Originated at Canton, Illinois. Tree upright, bears annually, productive.

Fruit large, round, but appearing oblong, regular; Surface smooth, yellow to golden, slightly bronzed or blushed when fully ripe; this and the dots can scarcely be seen while the fruit is immature.

Basin deep, abrupt, plaited ; Eye medium, closed.
Cavity deep, acute, irregular ; Stem long.
Core very small, oval, closed, meeting the eye ; Seeds

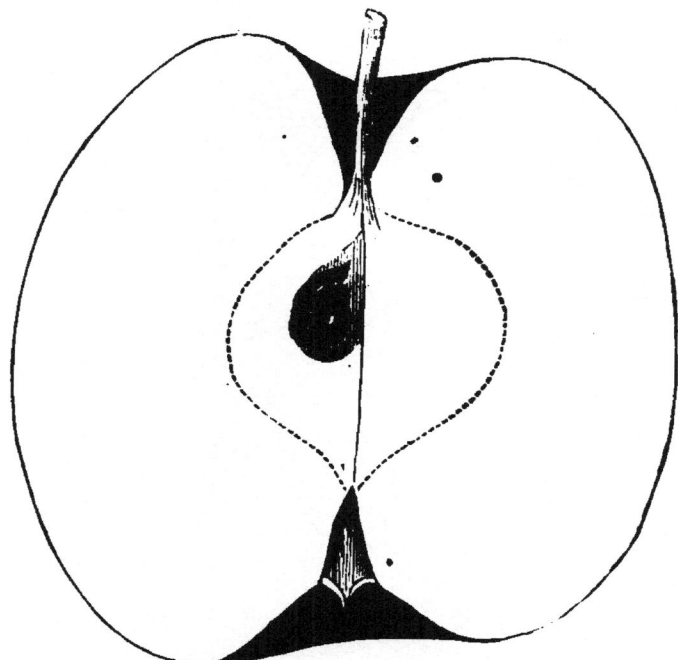

Fig. 264.—DOWNING'S PARAGON.

numerous, plump ; Flesh very tender ; Flavor sweet, rich,
aromatic ; Quality good ; Use, table ; September to December.

Honey.

Native of Pennsylvania. Tree very erect and an excellent bearer. Fruit rather small, oblong or oblong-conical,
greenish ; Flesh tender, juicy. If this apple ripened in
October (apple butter season) it would be more valuable.
—[W. G. Waring's MS.]

Pennsylvania Sweeting.

Found in Southern Illinois. Origin and history unknown.

Fruit large, oblong, regular; Surface dull greenish-yellow; Dots numerous, dark, distinct.

Basin deep, abrupt, regular; Eye large, closed.

Cavity deep, acute, irregular; Stem medium.

Core irregular, large, open, clasping; Seeds numerous,

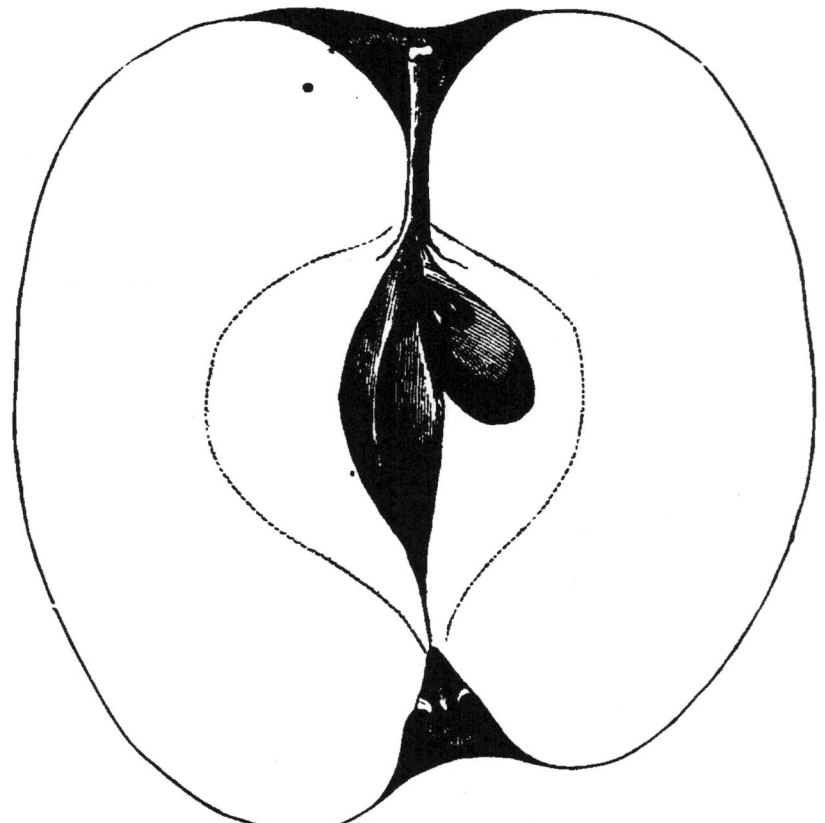

Fig. 265.—PENNSYLVANIA SWEETING.

small; Flesh tender, melting, fine-grained; Flavor very sweet; Quality good; Use, baking and stock; Season, early winter.

Wells' Sweeting.

Origin and history unknown.

Fruit medium, round or oblong, regular; Surface smooth, white, some blush; Dots scattered, prominent.

Basin wide, regular, leather-cracked; Eye large, closed.

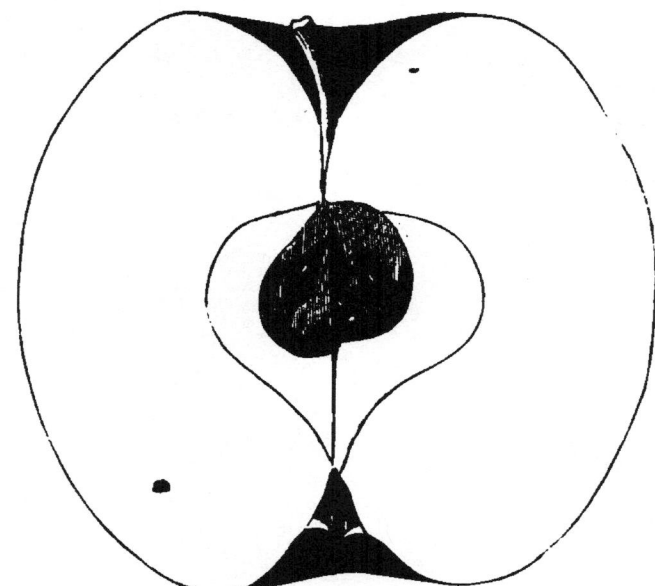

Fig. 266.—WELLS' SWEETING.

Cavity medium, regular, green; Stem medium.

Core pyriform, closed; Seeds numerous, angular, plump; Flesh white, firm, juicy; Flavor sweet; Use, baking and stock; Season, October and December.

CLASS IV.—OBLONG APPLES.

ORDER I.—REGULAR

SECTION 1.—SWEET.

SUB-SECTION 2.—STRIPED.

Black Gilliflower.

An old variety, which cannot be very highly praised, for it is but an indifferent fruit, and yet, on account of its productiveness and keeping properties, it is considered profitable for orchard planting.

Fruit rather large, oblong-ovate, regular; Surface near-

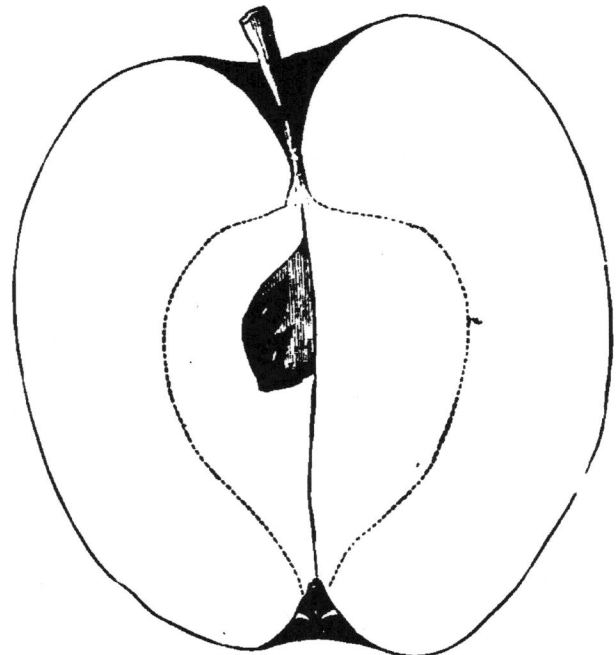

Fig. 267.—BLACK GILLIFLOWER.

ly covered with stripes of very deep red that make it look nearly black.   •

Basin very shallow, often plaited; Eye small, closed.

Cavity deep, acute, brown; Stem long, slender.

Core very large, oval, regular, meeting the eye; Seeds numerous, plump or imperfect; Flesh whitish, dry; Flavor only sweet; Use, essentially market, may be valuable for stock; Season, November to March.

Mother.

'   Origin Bolton, Massachusetts.   Tree rather slender, but productive.

Fruit medium to full medium, oblong, regular; Surface

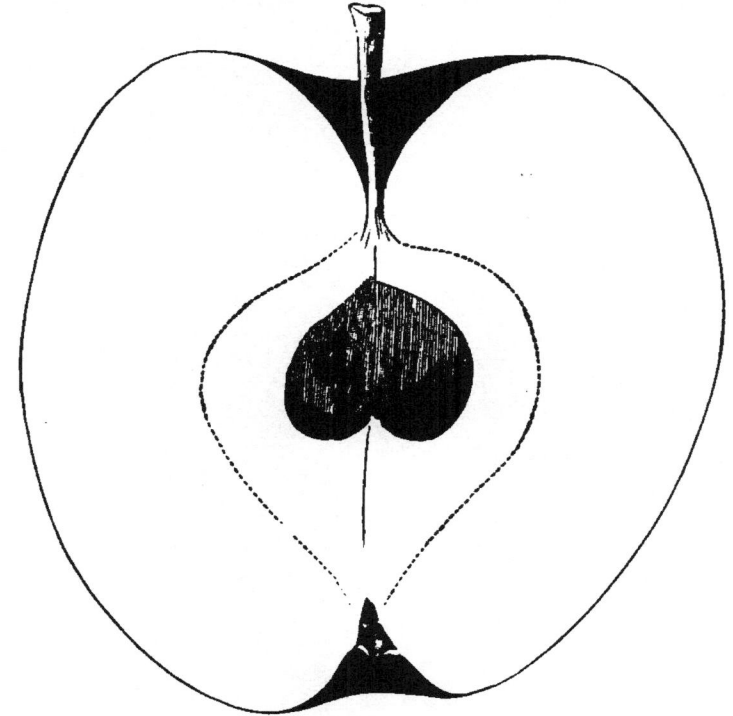

Fig. 268.—MOTHER.

smooth, shaded red on yellow, with close, fine stripes of red; Dots minute.

Basin medium, regular or plaited; Eye long, small, closed.

Cavity acute, regular or wavy; Stem long, slender.

Core medium, turbinate, regular, closed, clasping; Seeds numerous; Flesh yellow, crisp, very fine-grained, juicy;

Flavor sweet, very rich, vinous, aromatic; Quality best; Use, dessert; Season, October to January.

Ramsdell's Red.

Origin Connecticut. Tree vigorous, upright, many branches, productive, early bearer; Shoots slender, reddish; Foliage rather light green.

Fruit medium to large, oblong, regular, truncated; Sur-

Fig. 269.—RAMSDELL'S RED.

face smooth, yellow, hidden by bright red, mixed and striped; Dots numerous, yellow, distinct.

Basin rather deep, abrupt, wavy; Eye small to medium, closed.

Cavity deep, acute, wavy; Stem medium to long, often red.

Core large, oval, closed, clasping the eye; Seeds large; Flesh yellow, breaking, juicy; Flavor very sweet, rich; Quality very good; Use, baking and stock; Season, September to December.

———◦◦———

CLASS IV.—OBLONG APPLES.

ORDER I.—REGULAR.

SECTION 1.—SWEET.

SUB-SECTION 3.—RUSSET.

Mansfield Russet.

" Brought into notice by Dr. Joseph Mansfield, of Groton, Massachsetts. Tree vigorous and very productive. Fruit small, oblong, inclining to conic; Skin cinnamon russet; Stem long, inserted in a deep, furrowed cavity; Calyx partially closed, set in an open basin; Flesh not very juicy, rich, aromatic, saccharine, vinous; Keeps until April and May."—[Downing.]

———◦◦———

CLASS IV.—OBLONG APPLES.

ORDER I.—REGULAR.

SECTION 2.—SOUR.

SUB-SECTION 1.—SELF-COLORED.

Bailey's Golden.

" Origin Kennebec County, Maine. Tree productive; Fruit large, oblong, flattened at base and crown; Skin yellowish, slightly russeted, with a warm cheek; Stem short, surrounded by russet, in a broad, deep cavity; Calyx large and open, basin shallow; Flesh white, with a pleasant sub-acid flavor; January to March."—[Downing.]

Carolina Red June.

Origin southern, though long extensively grown in the North, and everywhere in the West a favorite early fruit.

Tree hardy, vigorous, healthy, upright, early bearer, productive; Shoots slender, dark; Foliage dark.

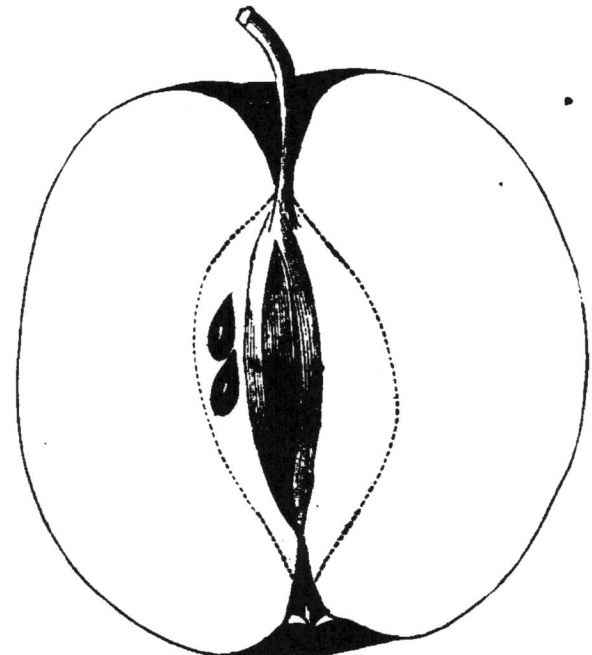

Fig. 270.—CAROLINA RED JUNE.

Fruit small to medium, form variable, but generally oblong-ovate, regular; Surface smooth, deep red on white, nearly universal; Dots minute.

Basin shallow, folded, plaited; Eye small, closed; Segments reflexed.

Cavity narrow, acute; Stem medium or short.

Core oval, open, meeting the eye; Seeds numerous, small, plump; Flesh white, very tender, fine-grained, juicy; Flavor sub-acid, not rich; Quality good; Use, table and market; Season, June and July—one of the earliest.

There is a striped variety, the *Striped June*, from Virginia, similar in every respect except the external markings. It is, of course, quite different from the *Virginia June.*—(Q. vide p. 500.)

Crawford Keeper.

This fruit was received from H. N. Gillett, Lawrence County, Ohio.

Fruit large, cylindrical, oblong, lop-sided; Surface smooth, purplish red; Dots numerous, fawn colored.

Basin wide, shallow, wavy; Eye small, closed.

Cavity acute, regular, rough, brown; Stem medium.

Core regular, open; Seeds numerous, brown; Flesh yellow, breaking, tender, fine-grained, juicy; Flavor sub-acid, rich; Quality good to very good; Use, table; Season, February to April. Very desirable.

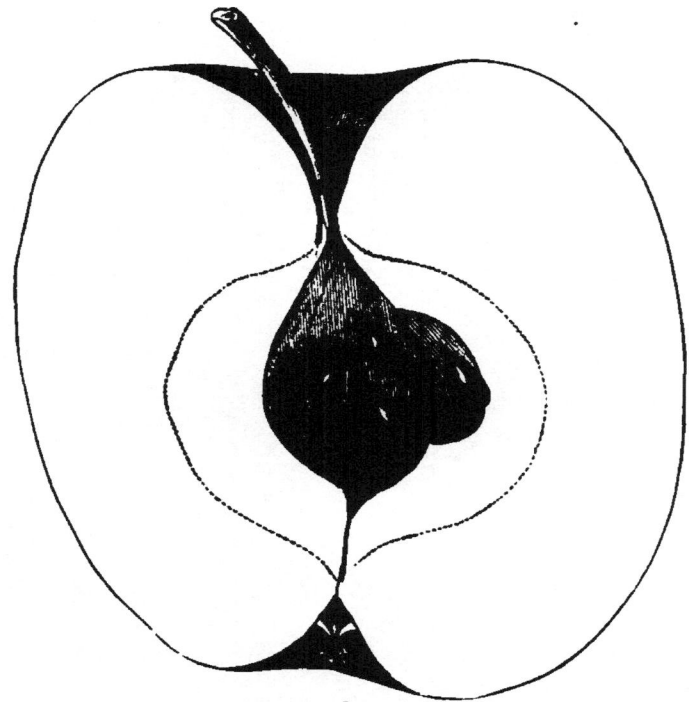

Fig. 271.—CUMBERLAND SPICE.

Cumberland Spice.

Origin New Jersey; not very extensively cultivated, for, though sometimes excellent, it is not found to be a profitable sort.

Fruit rather oblong, contracted toward the eye, or ovate, regular; sometimes the Axis is inclined; Surface pale yellow; Dots large, brown, scattered.

Basin shallow, regular or folded; Eye large, partially closed.

Cavity deep, acute; Stem generally long.

Core large, round, very open, not touching the eye; Seeds numerous, large, pointed; Flesh yellow, tender, breaking, juicy; Flavor acid to sub-acid, rich, aromatic; Quality good to best, but uncertain; Use, table, kitchen, not profitable; Season, October to December.

Curtis Greening.

This fruit was found in Illinois; origin uncertain.

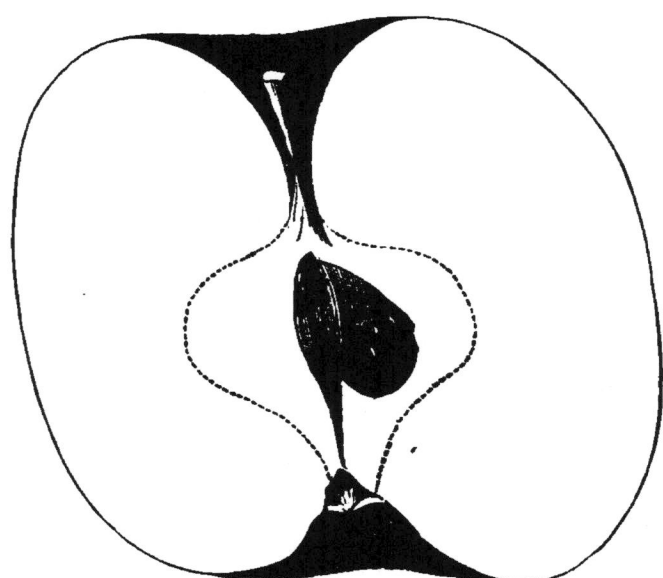

Fig. 272.—CURTIS GREENING.

Fruit medium to large, cylindrical, oblong, truncated;

Axis inclined; Surface yellow, bronzy; Dots numerous, dark, indented.

Basin abrupt, wide, regular; Eye large, open.

Cavity deep, acute, regular; Stem short.

Core small, fig-shaped, closed, clasping; Seeds numerous, small, plump; Flesh yellow, breaking; Flavor sub-acid, rich; Quality good; Use, table and kitchen; Season, January and February.

Dawson's Cluster.

From Clark County, Ohio.

Fruit full medium, oblong-truncate or ovate, regular;

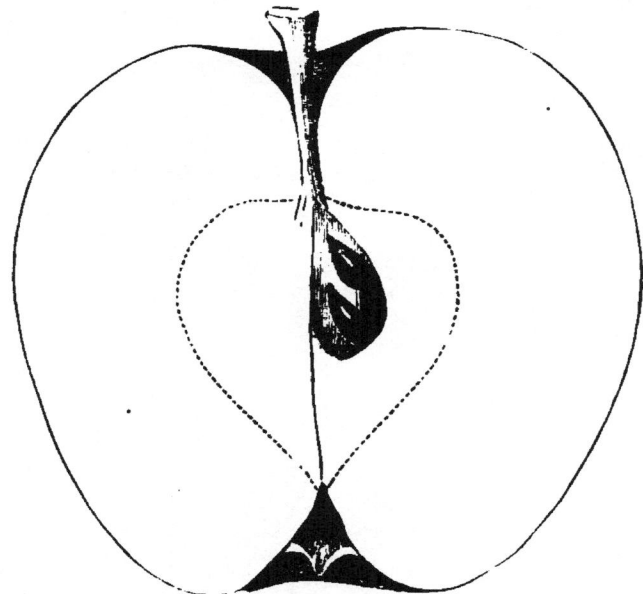

Fig. 273.—DAWSON'S CLUSTER.

Surface smooth, pale yellow, blushed lightly with brown; Dots scattered, gray.

Basin abrupt, regular; Eye large, closed.

Cavity very acute, wavy; Stem long, with a knob.

Core medium, heart-shaped, regular, closed, clasping; Seeds numerous, plump, large; Flesh yellowish-white, fine-grained, tender, juicy; Flavor sub-acid; Quality good; Use, kitchen, but chiefly recommended for cider; Season, November. An enormous bearer.

Franklin Golden.*

HUGHES' AMERICAN GOLDEN PIPPIN.

Tree thrifty, upright, moderately productive; Fruit oblong, cylindrical; Surface smooth, yellow; Dots distinct, gray, not numerous.

Basin wide, shallow, finely plaited; Eye long, closed.

Cavity medium, greenish; Stem long.

Core small, pyriform, regular, closed, clasping; Seeds plump, pointed; Flesh yellow, tender, fine-grained, juicy; Flavor acid, rich; Quality very good; Use, table; Season, mid-winter.

A choice dessert fruit.

Grimes' Golden.

Another apple of similar and equally high character. Origin, Brooke County, Virginia. Introduced to the State Pomological Society by our zealous fellow member

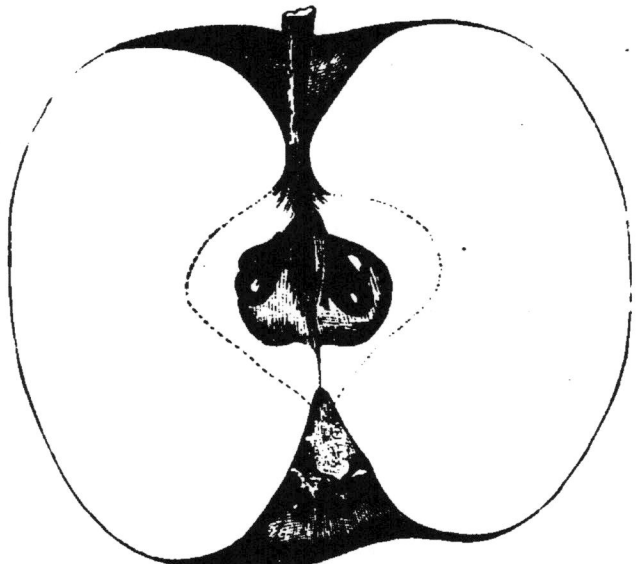

Fig. 274.—GRIMES' GOLDEN.

* Fall Butter. on page 677, belongs here.

S. B. Marshall, Massillon, Ohio, who obtained it from N. Wood, of Belmont County.

Tree vigorous, healthy, spreading, productive, bears early; Shoots stout, dark; Foliage abundant, dark green.

Fruit full medium, cylindrical, regular; Surface yellow, vein-russeted; Dots numerous, minute.

Basin abrupt, folded; Eye large, closed.

Cavity wide, regular, green; Stem long, curved.

Core small, pyriform, closed, meeting the eye; Seeds numerous, plump, brown; Flesh yellow, firm, breaking, very fine-grained, juicy; Flavor sub-acid, aromatic, spicy, rich, refreshing; Quality very best; Use, dessert, too good for aught else; those who have tried it say that it is excellent for cooking; Season, January to March.

Kirkbridge White.

This fruit has been pretty extensively cultivated in some parts of the Western States, and sometimes mistaken

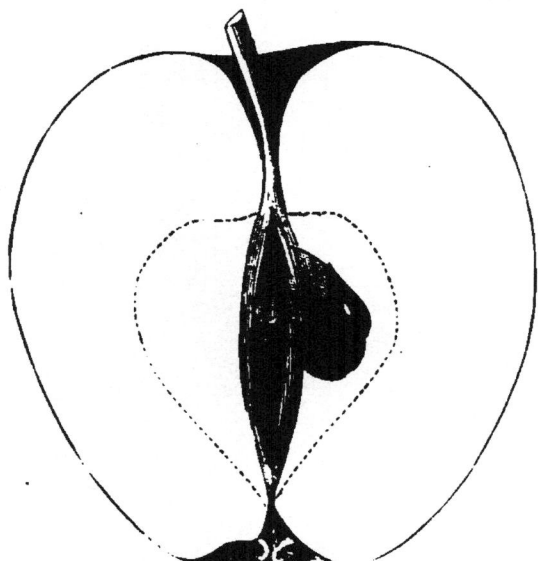

Fig. 275.—KIRKBRIDGE WHITE.

for the *Yellow June*. Tree of moderate growth, bears early, productive.

Fruit small, oblong-conic, regular; Surface smooth, pale yellow or white; Dots minute, gray, scattered.

Basin small, shallow or abrupt, narrow, regular; Eye small, closed; Segments reflexed.

Cavity deep, acute, regular, brown; Stem long, slender, green.

Core medium, pyriform, regular, open, meeting the eye; Seeds numerous, plump, pointed, brown; Flesh white, fine-grained, tender, juicy; Flavor sub-acid; Quality very good; Use, table, market; Season, July, August, after Early Harvest.

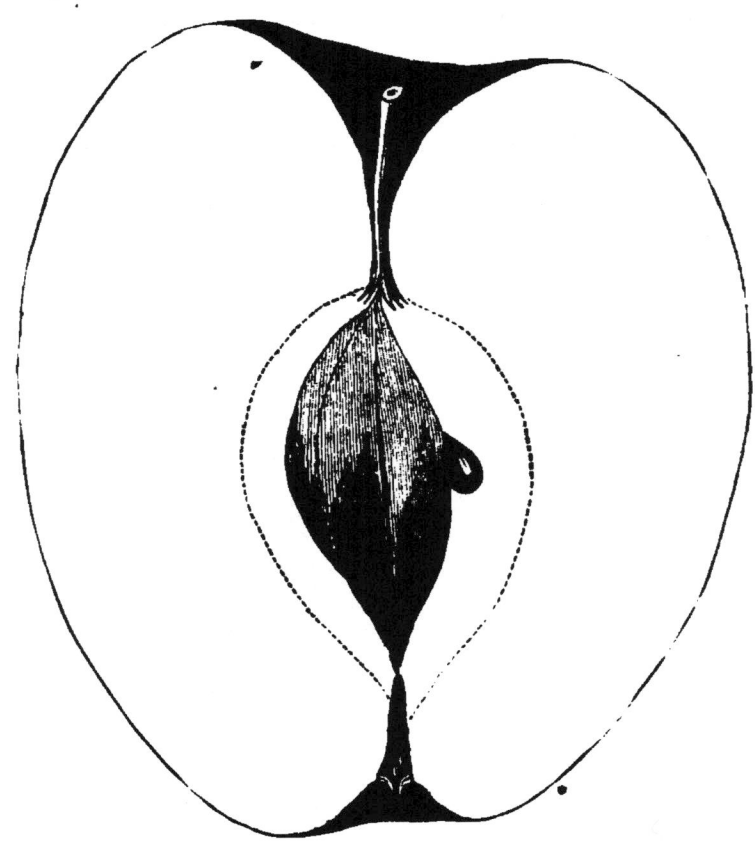

Fig. 276.—ORTLEY.

Ortley.

WHITE BELLFLOWER, And Many Others.

This excellent New Jersey apple has been cultivated very satisfactorily over a great extent of our country, and is still seen in some Western collections, exhibiting all its peculiar beauty, but in many places where it was a great favorite but a few years since, it has become so defective from scab and bitter-rot that it is rapidly disappearing from the nurseries and orchards.

Tree vigorous, healthy, upright, becoming large and spreading, very productive; Shoots stout, dark, bearing limbs brittle, and often broken by the fruit.

Fruit large, oblong, conic, truncated, regular; Surface smooth, pale yellow, rarely blushed light carmine, and red spots; Dots minute, indented, white bases seen only in the unripe fruit.

Basin medium, regular, plaited; Eye small, very long, closed.

Cavity deep, acute, regular, brown; Stem long, slender.

Core medium, oval, regular, open, meeting the very long eye; Seeds numerous, short, plump, pointed, dark, easily loosened, when they rattle in the large open capsules; Flesh yellowish, tender, breaking, juicy; Flavor acid to sub-acid, sprightly, refreshing; Quality best; Use, table, kitchen; Season, November to January.

The threatened failure of this fine fruit is much to be regretted. Its tissue is so fine as to suit even the invalid or convalescent, who could not safely partake of a more solid apple.

Porter.

Native of Sherburne, Massachusetts. Tree vigorous, healthy, productive.

Fruit rather large, oblong, somewhat conic, often truncated; Surface smooth, yellow, often faintly blushed; Dots few, sunken.

Basin abrupt, folded; Eye large, closed.

Cavity acute, wavy, brown; Stem medium.

Core medium, oval, regular, closed, meeting the eye; Seeds numerous, plump; Flesh yellowish white, breaking, tender, juicy; Flavor acid to sub-acid; Quality good to very good; Use, kitchen, table, market; Season, August to October.

29

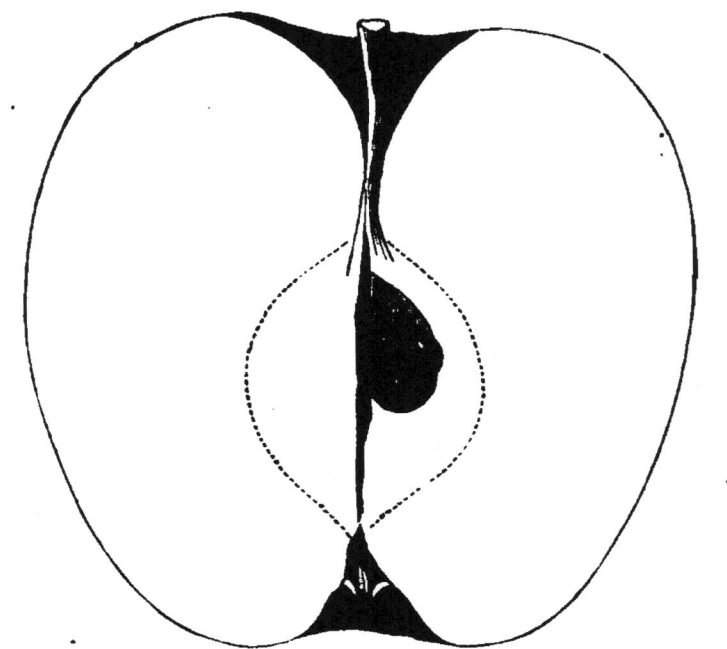

Fig. 277.—PORTER.

Spark's.

SPARK'S LATE.

Fruited by Jas. H. Crain, of Undulation, Pulaski County, Illinois, on trees received from J. W. Felt & Co., Crystal Springs, Mississippi.

Special origin unknown, but believed to be southern. Tree vigorous, upright and productive; Shoots stout.

Fruit full medium to large, oblong, conic, regular, handsome; Surface greenish-yellow; Dots numerous, rather large, gray and rough.

Basin shallow, small, regular; Eye very small, closed.

Cavity deep, acute, regular, green; Stem medium to long.

Core medium, oval, closed, meeting the eye; Seeds numerous, plump; Flesh yellow, breaking, fine-grained, juicy; Flavor sub-acid, rich, very aromatic; Use, dessert especially; Season, December and January; Quality best.

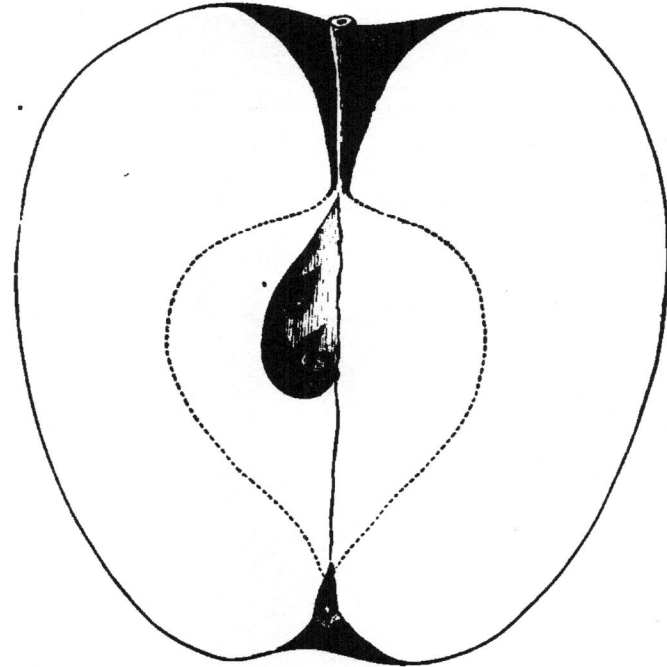

Fig. 278.—SPARK'S.

CLASS IV.—OBLONG APPLES.

ORDER I.—REGULAR.

SECTION 2.—SOUR.

SUB-SECTION 2.—STRIPED.

Boalsburg.

"A seedling of Center County, Pennsylvania. Large, oblong, inclining to conical, delicately mottled, and striped with red on yellow ground; Stem short, thick, inserted in a deep, acuminate, russeted cavity; Basin deep, moderately wide; Flesh yellow, juicy, sprightly, refreshing; Very good; February."—[*Ad interim* Reports.]

Mr. Waring, of Tyrone, Pennsylvania, writes me that the Boalsburg has not proved to be productive, and that he has discontinued its propagation.

Cannon Pearmain.

A southern apple; probably from North Carolina. Grown to some extent in parts of the West, where it proves a substitute for the Ben Davis, keeping longer.

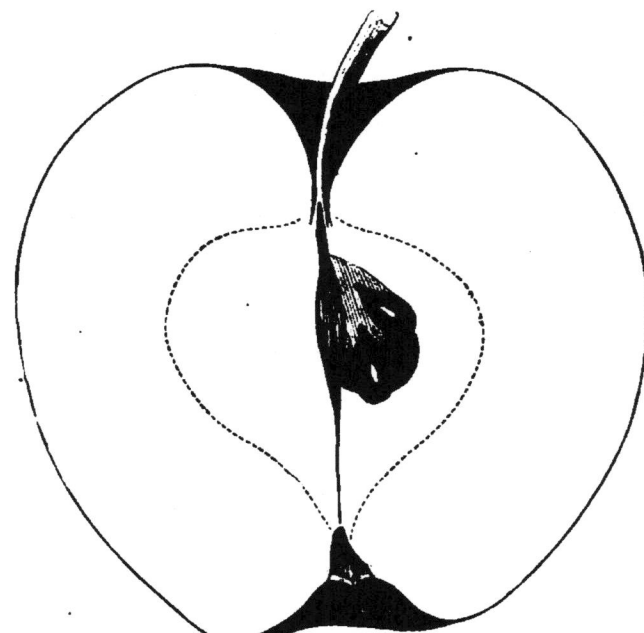

Fig. 279.—CANNON PEARMAIN.

Tree vigorous, healthy, productive when old; Fruit medium, round, oblong or ovate, regular; Surface smooth, yellow, shaded red, faintly striped; Dots large, yellow, gray.

Basin deep, abrupt, regular, rarely wavy; Eye small, closed.

Cavity acute, often lipped; Stem long, slender, red.

Core medium, regular, oval, closed, clasping; Seeds numerous, long, pointed; Flesh yellow, firm, breaking;

Flavor mild sub-acid; Quality only good; Use, market, kitchen, table; Season, January to April.

Cooper's Market.

"Tree vigorous, upright, with long, slender branches; productive and a late keeper.

"Fruit medium, oblong, conic; Skin yellowish, shaded with red, striped crimson; Stem short; Cavity deep, narrow; Calyx closed; Basin small; Flesh white, tender, with a brisk, sub-acid flavor; December to May."—[Downing.]

Full Butter.—[L. Jones.] *

There are many apples with this name, but my good friend Lewis Jones thinks this is the only genuine kind, and deserving the name from its adaptation to the making of apple butter. Found in a seedling orchard of Eastern Indiana, and a distinct sort.

Fruit large, handsome, globular; Surface smooth, greenish-yellow; Dots minute, prominent.

Basin regular, abrupt, brown; Eye medium, closed.

Cavity deep, narrow, green; Stem short.

Core medium, round, open, clasping; Seeds numerous, short, plump, dark; Flesh yellowish-white, breaking, fine-grained, juicy; Flavor sweet; Quality best for table, baking and apple butter; Season, December and January.

Hague.

Introduced by Lewis Jones, Wayne County, Indiana. Believed to be a seedling.

Fruit large, roundish, oblong, cylindrical, truncate; Surface smooth, greenish yellow, shaded more or less with red, striped and splashed deep red; Dots numerous or scattered, large, distinct, yellow.

Basin medium, regular; Eye medium, closed.

Cavity deep, acute, regular, brown; Stem short to medium, curved.

Core large, heart-shaped, regular, closed or open, clasping; Seeds numerous, short, pointed, plump; Flesh yellow, tender, fine-grained, juicy; Flavor sub-acid, aromatic, rich; Quality very good to best; Use, table, market; Season, December to February. Worthy of attention.

* See page 670.

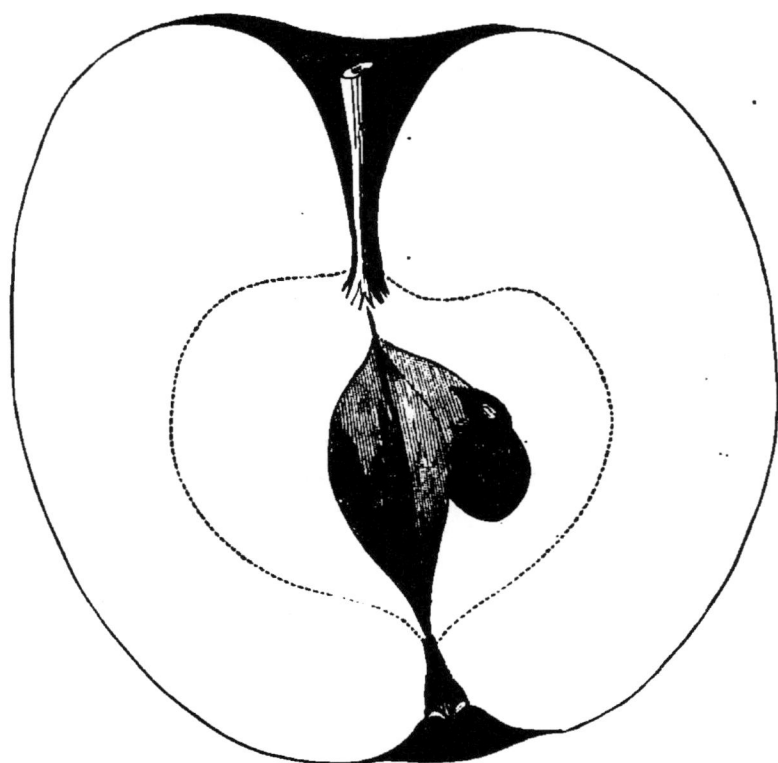

Fig. 280.—HAGUE.

Herman.

" From Cumberland County, Pennsylvania. Tree vigorous, spreading, quite prolific.

Fruit medium, oblong, conic; fine red, striped on green, Flesh greenish white, tender, juicy, sub-acid, and high flavor; November to April."—[Saml. Miller, in Downing.]

Indiana Beauty.

This beautiful Indiana seedling always attracts attention by its external appearance, but it is not destined to become a general favorite.

Fruit large, cylindrical, oblong, unequal; Axis inclined; Surface very smooth yellow, partially covered mixed scarlet, splashed carmine; Dots numerous, small.

Basin deep, abrupt, folded ; Eye medium to large, closed.
Cavity acute, wavy ; Stem medium.
Core small, oval, closed, clasping the eye ; Seeds nu-

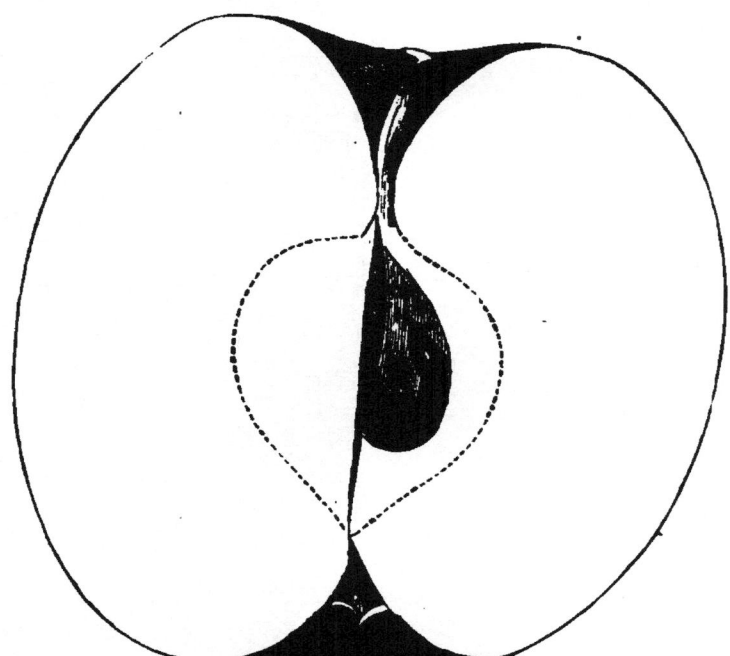

Fig. 281.;—INDIANA BEAUTY.

merous, long, pointed, imperfect; Flesh yellowish, breaking,
juicy ; Flavor sub-acid, aromatic ; Quality only good ;
Use, market, kitchen ; Season, September, November.

Jonathan.

Origin, Kingston, New York. Described by Judge
Buell. A very superior dessert fruit ; good for all purposes, and seems to do well everywhere. Its excellence has
caused it to be called, particularly, a gentleman's apple,
though quite acceptable to the farmers' boys.

Tree of rather slender growth ; hence top-grafted in
the orchard and stock-grafted in the nursery to produce

early results; Spreading, rather drooping, productive; Shoots slender, light brown, buds small; Foliage rather sparse, grayish.

Fruit medium, round or oblong, conic, truncated, regular; Surface very smooth, waxy yellow, wholly covered

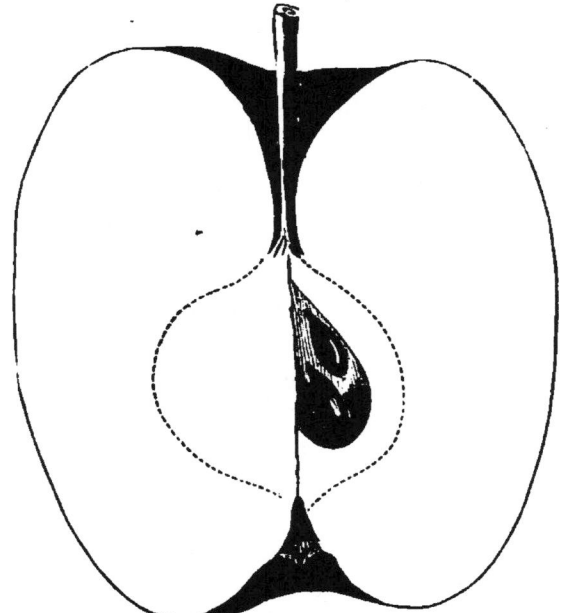

Fig. 282.—JONATHAN.

brilliant dark red, mixed and striped; Dots minute, russet-veined.

Basin deep, regular, russet-veined; Eye small, closed, green.

Cavity acute, deep, regular, reddish brown; Stem long, slender.

Core medium, roundish–oval, regular, closed, scarcely clasping the eye; Seeds numerous, large, angular; Flesh whitish yellow, tender, breaking, very juicy; Flavor sub-acid, aromatic, equal to Spitzenberg; Quality best; Use, dessert, cooking, &c.; December, January.

Should be in every orchard.

Kaighn's Spitzenberg.—[*Coxe.*]

From Gloucester County, New Jersey. Tree spreading, very productive; Shoots slender.

Fruit large, handsome, oblong, slightly conic, truncated, regular; Surface smooth, yellow, striped crimson; Dots minute.

Basin deep, abrupt, folded or regular; Eye medium, closed; Segments reflexed.

Cavity deep, acute, regular, brown; Stem long, slender, red.

Core large, pyriform, regular, clasping, generally open; Seeds numerous, plump, angular, loose; Flesh yellow,

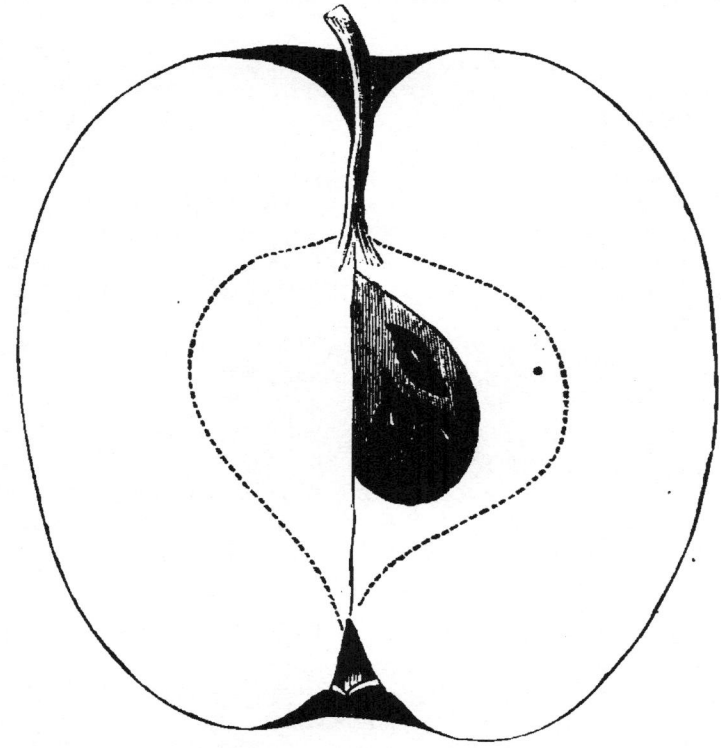

Fig. 283.—KAIGHN'S SPITZENBERG.

breaking, juicy; Flavor acid to sub-acid, rather rich; Quality good for culinary use; Market and drying; Season, November, December.

29*

Knowles' Early.

A favorite early apple about Philadelphia. Origin supposed to be Bucks County, Pennsylvania.

Tree medium, thrifty, very productive, early bearer.

Fruit small, conical, oblong, striped dull red on yellow.

Basin shallow, plaited; Eye small, closed.

Cavity acute, regular; Stem medium to long.

Flesh yellowish, very tender, juicy; Flavor mild subacid, aromatic, agreeable; Quality good; Use, table, kitchen; Season, July and August.

Long Island Pearmain.—[Cox.]

AUTUMN PEARMAIN, Thompson, according to Downing.—WINTER PEARMAIN, Western markets.

An old variety found in all the early orchards of Ohio and Indiana, that were within the influence of Silas Wharton's nursery. A good, profitable variety that has been overlooked in the rage for novelties.

Tree large, spreading, very productive; Fruit full medium, round, elongated, tapering slightly from the base, always truncated at the apex, regular; Surface smooth, yellowish green, covered with dull red, and striped maroon; Dots numerous, minute, gray; russet-veined towards the base.

Basin regular, wide, rather deep, slightly leathercracked; Eye medium, open; Segments long.

Cavity rather wide; Stem long.

Core medium, heart-shaped, regular, closed, not clasping; Seeds numerous, large, plump, brown; Flesh yellow, breaking, firm, not very juicy; Flavor sub-acid, aromatic, rich, agreeable; Quality good; Use, family and market; Season, November till March.

Marston's Red Winter.

As I have never seen this fruit, I again quote from Downing:

"I received this beautiful apple from Nathan Norton, of Greenland, New Hampshire, who said the original tree was more than a hundred years old, and still standing.

"Tree hardy, of moderate growth, great bearer, and keeps as well as Baldwin, and by many preferred to that variety, and is a popular fruit in the neighborhood.

"Fruit above medium size, oblong, oval, inclining to ovate; Stem three-quarters of an inch long, rather slender, in a narrow, deep, compressed, slightly russeted cavity, sometimes with a lip; Calyx partially closed; Segments long, · in a deep, corrugated basin; Color whitish yellow, shaded and striped with bright green and crimson, thickly sprinkled with minute dots; Flesh whitish yellow, very juicy, tender, sprightly, sub-acid flavor; December to March.

Mifflin King.

Origin Mifflin County, Pennsylvania. Fruit small, color of *Rambo*, perhaps a trifle more red, oblong; Flesh remarkably tender, juicy and pleasant; First rate.— [American Pomological Society's Report.]

CLASS IV.—OBLONG APPLES.

ORDER I.—REGULAR.

SECTION 2.—SOUR.

SUB-SECTION 3.—RUSSET.

NONE.

CLASS IV.—OBLONG APPLES.

ORDER II.—IRREGULAR.

SECTION 1.—SWEET.

SUB-SECTION 1.—SELF-COLORED.

Sweet Bellflower.

This apple is supposed to have originated in the neighborhood of Dayton, Ohio, and is cultivated chiefly in the adjacent regions, and when found elsewhere is traceable to this source.

Fruit large, roundish oblong, angular; Surface uneven, greenish yellow, becoming creamy yellow, very rarely blushed or bronzed; Dots minute, indented, surrounded by green in the unripe fruit.

Basin medium, folded; Eye small, closed; Segments long, reflexed.

Cavity acute, wavy, green; Stem long, slender.

Core regular, roundish, open, meeting the eye; Seeds

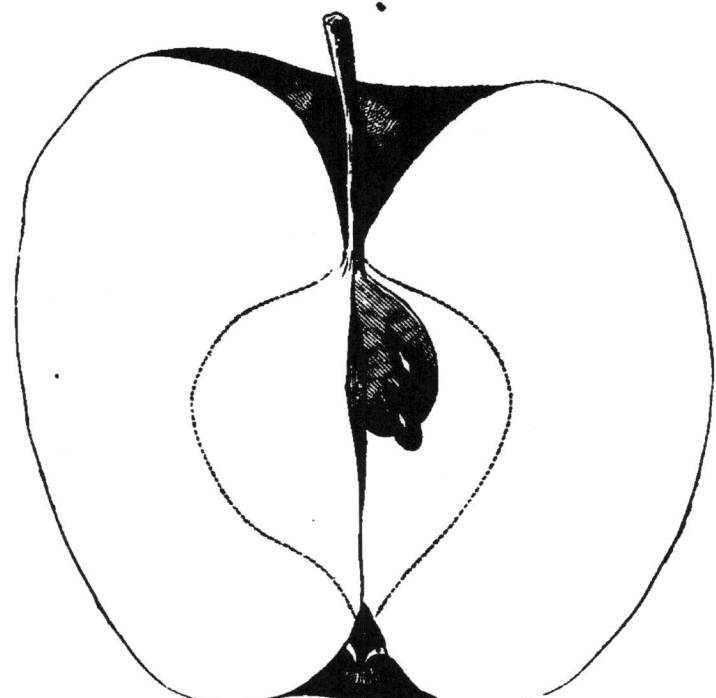

Fig. 284.—SWEET BELLFLOWER.

numerous, plump, angular, imperfect; Flesh white, fine-grained, breaking, juicy; Flavor very sweet; Quality good to very good; Use, baking, table; Season, December.

Not equal to Broadwell.

CLASS IV.—OBLONG APPLES.

ORDER II.—IRREGULAR.

SECTION 1.—SWEET.

SUB-SECTION 2.—STRIPED.

Harnish.

"From Lancaster County, Pennsylvania. Fruit medium, oblong, oval, slightly angular; Skin mostly shaded with dark red, and sprinkled with grayish dots; Flesh compact, tender, not juicy, almost sweet, pleasant; September to October."—[Downing.]

Illinois Pumpkin Sweet.

This apple was found in Illinois. From the orchard of Mr. Montagu, who esteemed it very highly.

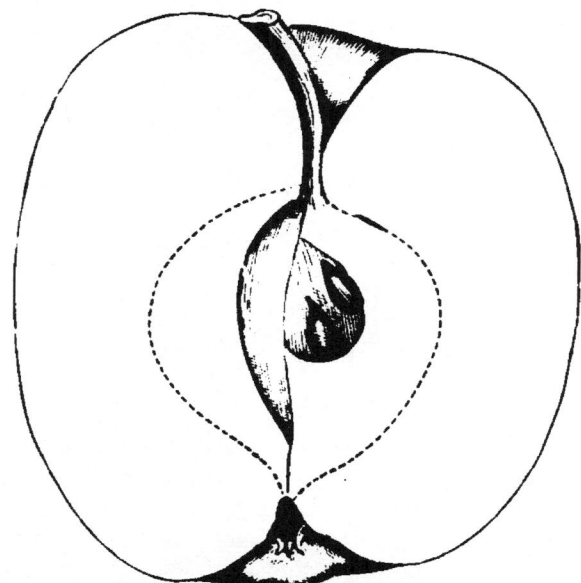

Fig. 285.—ILLINOIS PUMPKIN SWEET.

Fruit medium, oblong, ovate, angular; Surface mixed, splashed and striped with dull red; Dots scattered, distinct, yellow.

Basin abrupt, folded ; Eye medium, closed.

Cavity acute, folded ; Stem medium, inclined.

Core medium, pyriform, regular, closed, clasping ; Seeds numerous, angular, plump ; Flesh yellow, rather tough in winter, but "becomes melting in June"; Flavor very sweet; Quality good, Montagu says best; Use, kitchen, table; Season, January till June.

CLASS IV.—OBLONG APPLES.

ORDER II.—IRREGULAR.

SECTION 1.—SWEET.

SUB-SECTION 3.—RUSSET.

NONE.

CLASS IV.—OBLONG APPLES.

ORDER II.—IRREGULAR.

SECTION 2.—SOUR.

SUB-SECTION 1.—SELF-COLORED.

Genesee Chief.

Fruit large to very large, roundish oblong, ribbed or angular ; Surface smooth, pale yellow, sometimes bronzed ; Dots scattered, minute.

Basin shallow, medium ; Eye small, but very long, closed.

Cavity narrow, pointed, green ; Stem medium, knobby.

Core very large, round, clasping, very open ; Seeds numerous, defective, angular, brown ; Flesh white, tender, breaking, juicy ; Flavor acid, thin ; Quality second rate— good only for cooking ; Season, August.

Fig. 286.—GENESEE CHIEF.

Henwood.

A seedling of Indiana. Brought into notice by Lewis Jones, of Wayne County, who has frequently exhibited the fruit, and distributed grafts of this excellent apple, which may compensate for the failure of its reputed parent, the *Ortley.*

Fruit large, oblong, conic or ovate, often angular or ribbed; Surface smooth, pale yellow, rarely blushed; Dots scattered, dark.

Basin shallow, often abrupt, folded or plaited; Eye small, closed.

Cavity deep, acute, wavy; Stem long, slender.

Core rather small, round, regular, open, meeting the eye; Seeds numerous, long, angular; Flesh yellow, ten-

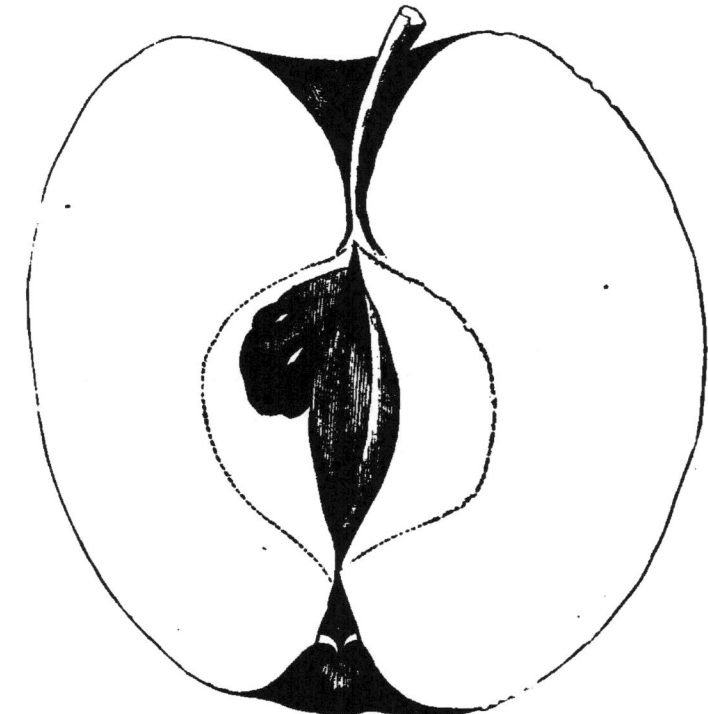

Fig. 287.—HENWOOD.

der, fine-grained, juicy; Flavor acid to sub-acid, rich; Quality very good to best; Season, December to February.

Keswick Codling.

An old English variety, which has greatly pleased the people of our country, who find it a valuable market and family fruit, particularly desirable in the North and Northwest.

Tree vigorous, hardy, productive, an early bearer; Shoots branching in a peculiar manner, dark.

Fruit medium, oblong, conical, truncated, ribbed; Surface smooth, pale yellow; Dots scattered, minute.

Basin medium, folded; Eye medium to large, closed.

Cavity acute, regular, browned; Stem long, yellow.

Core large, open, clasping; Seeds numerous, angular; Flesh greenish yellow, fine-grained, tender, juicy; Flavor

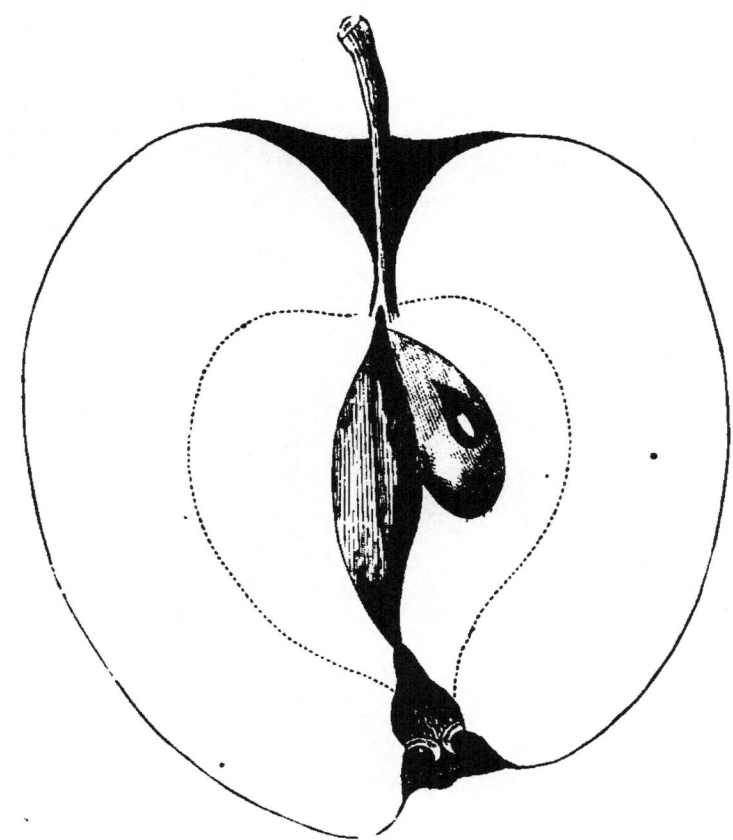

Fig. 288.—KESWICK CODLING.

acid; Quality good to very good for its use—cooking; Season, August to October.

The fruit may be cooked in June.

Newark Pippin.

Origin, New Jersey. Tree not large, orushy, limbs crooked, twiggy, drooping, not very productive or satisfactory.

Fruit above medium, oblong, cylindrical, truncated very abruptly, slightly angular; Surface smooth, rich yellow when ripe; Dots minute.

Basin wide, regular; Eye large, open.

Cavity wide, regular; Stem long, slender.

Core large, oval or pyriform, regular, closed, clasping; Seeds numerous, angular, plump; Flesh deep yellow, breaking, fine-grained, juicy; Flavor sub-acid, aromatic,

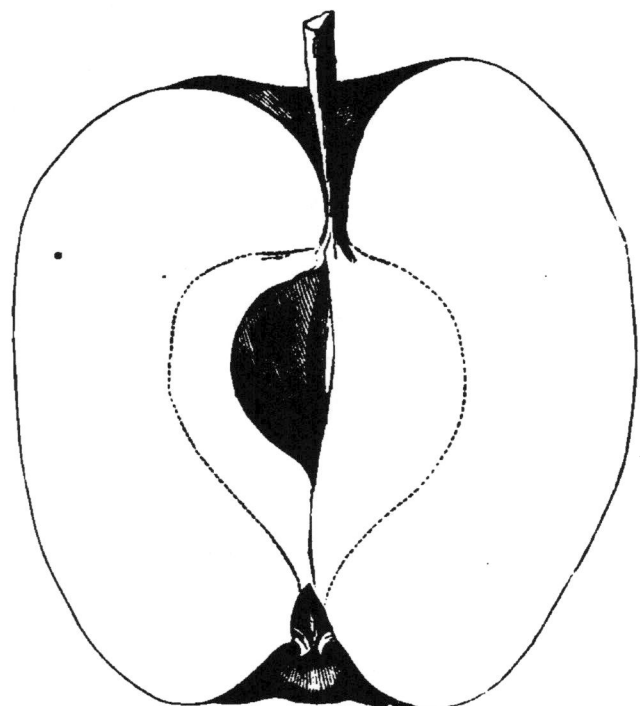

Fig. 289.—NEWARK PIPPIN.

rich, sprightly; Quality best; Use, dessert, cooking; Season, December to February.

A delicious fruit for amateurs, but its place is supplanted by *Grimes' Golden,* which is a much better tree, with fruit of similar good qualities, and better.

Rock Pippin.

RIDGE PIPPIN, LEMON, &C.

This admirable long-keeper has claims upon the attention of the commercial orchardist, on account of its

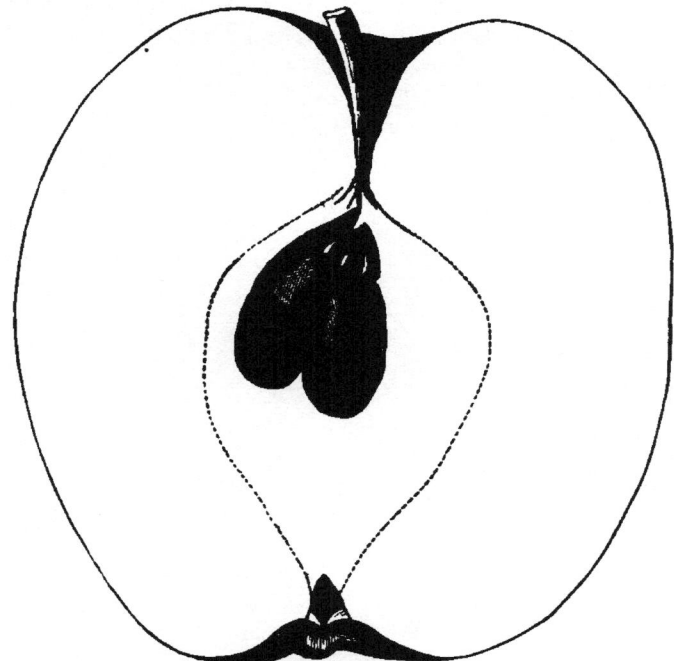

Fig. 290.—ROCK PIPPIN.

soundness and beauty in the spring.   Tree very thrifty, large, productive; Branches open, spreading; Shoots stout, dark; Foliage large, scattered.

Fruit full medium, oblong, ovate, angular, often ribbed, truncate at the apex, sometimes unequal; Surface very smooth, very rich yellow, blushed bright carmine when ripe; Dots few, small, dark.

Basin shallow, plaited or folded; Eye small, short, closed. Cavity acute, often lipped; Stem medium.

Core medium, pyriform, open, somewhat clasping; Seeds numerous, long, brown; Flesh yellow, breaking, rather dry; Flavor acid to sub-acid, rich; Quality only good; Use, market and kitchen; Season, December to May; of most value to sell at the latter period.

Cooks well all winter.

Yellow Bellflower.

This noble and valuable constituent of our orchards came from Burlington County, New Jersey, where it was first

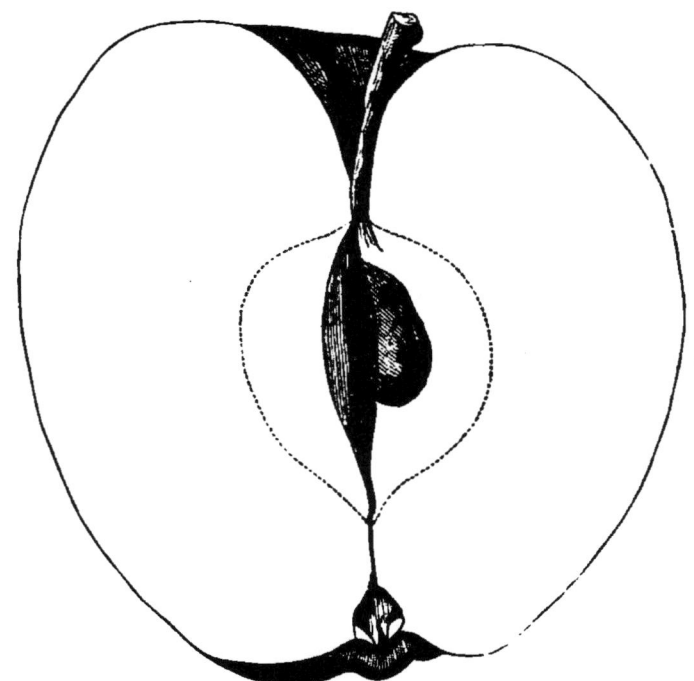

Fig. 291.—YELLOW BELLFLOWER.

described by Coxe. This apple has succeeded in almost all parts of the country, North and South, and has proved remarkably hardy. The quality of the fruit varies with the soil, being best and most highly flavored and colored on exposed ridges of rather thin soil, while those on rich low bottoms or prairies are slow in bearing, and then produce very large fruit. The crops, however, are not always satisfactory in such situations, though the trees become very large; the blossoms are often destroyed by spring frosts.

Tree vigorous, thrifty, hardy, large, spreading, drooping; Twigs slender, brown; Foliage abundant, long, wavy; Blossoms very large, on long stems, exposed to the weather and not protected by the leaves.

Fruit large to very large, oblong, ovate, angular, ribbed; Surface smooth, rich yellow, sometimes blushed; Dots scattered, gray.

Basin shallow or moderately deep, plaited or folded; Eye small, closed.

Cavity deep, acute or wide, wavy; Stem long, curved.

Core large, oval, open, clasping; Seeds dark, large, angular, imperfect; Flesh yellow, breaking, fine-grained, juicy; Flavor acid to sub-acid, aromatic, very rich and satisfying; Quality best; Use, table, kitchen, market; Season, December.

One of the finest culinary apples in the catalogue.

York Imperial.

From the neighborhood of York, Pennsylvania. Exhibited before the State Society at the meeting in Lebanon, 1855. Tree said to be healthy and productive.

Fruit large, rather oblong, somewhat angular; Surface smooth, mixed bright red on greenish yellow.

Basin wide, plaited; Eye medium, closed.

Cavity deep, wide; Stem short.

Flesh yellowish, tender, juicy; Flavor sub-acid, aromatic; Quality quite good; Use, market, kitchen; Season, January, February.

CLASS IV.—OBLONG APPLES.

ORDER II.—IRREGULAR.

SECTION 2.—SOUR.

SUB-SECTION 2.—STRIPED.

Clyde Beauty.

"Origin, Wayne County, New York. Tree vigorous, upright, very productive.

"Fruit large, roundish, conic, angular; Skin greenish,

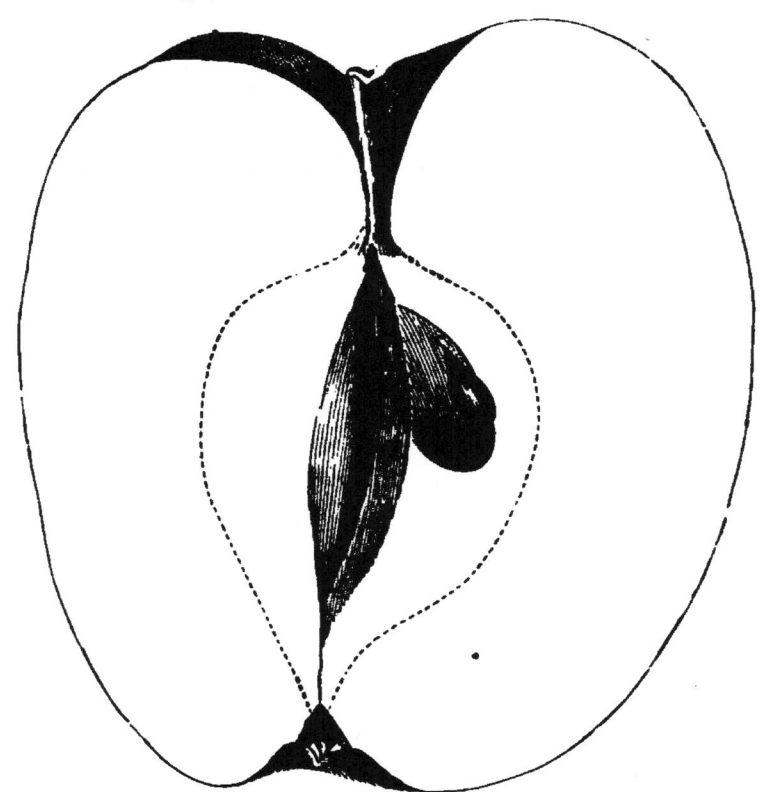

Fig. 292.—CLYDE BEAUTY.

oily, sprinkled and mottled with dull red, and bright red in the sun· Stem short, slender, inserted in an acute cavity; Calyx closed, set in a small corrugated basin; Flesh white, tender, juicy, with a brisk sub-acid flavor; October to January."—[Downing.]

Frank or Chenango.
CHENANGO STRAWBERRY.

This beautiful apple has been called also the *Late Strawberry*. So, to avoid confusion, perhaps, it were better to adopt its local name *Frank*. It is a native of New York.

Fruit medium to large oblong, tapering, irregular; Surface smooth, beautifully striped on waxen yellow.

Basin folded and plaited, abrupt; Eye medium, closed. Cavity acuminate; Stem medium.

Flesh tender, juicy; Flavor sub-acid, aromatic; Quality very good; Use, dessert; Season, autumn.

Minister.

This New England apple was introduced by Mr. Manning; when he brought it before the American Pomological Society, it met with so much favor from the members of that body that it was adopted and recommended. In the Western States it has failed to give satisfaction and is generally discarded, but further North it may do as well as in New England. In Ohio it becomes an autumn apple, and is only used for cooking, when we have plenty of others that are preferred.

Tree healthy, vigorous, early bearer, and constantly productive.

Fruit full medium to large, oblong, tapering to the eye, ribbed, irregular; Surface smooth, yellow, covered bright red mixed, splashed carmine, often handsome; Dots minute.

Basin very narrow, folded, plaited; Eye small, closed. Cavity deep, acute, sometimes brown; Stem long, slender.

Flesh yellowish, breaking, juicy; Flavor acid; Quality only good; Use, kitchen; Season, September and later; not a winter fruit in latitude forty.

Striped Gilliflower.

Fruit quite large, oblong, conical, truncated, ribbed; Surface smooth, yellowish white, mixed red, splashed carmine; Dots rare, gray.

Basin abrupt, folded; Eye large, closed.

Cavity wide, wavy, brown; Stem short, curved.

Core large, round, very open, meeting the eye; Seeds

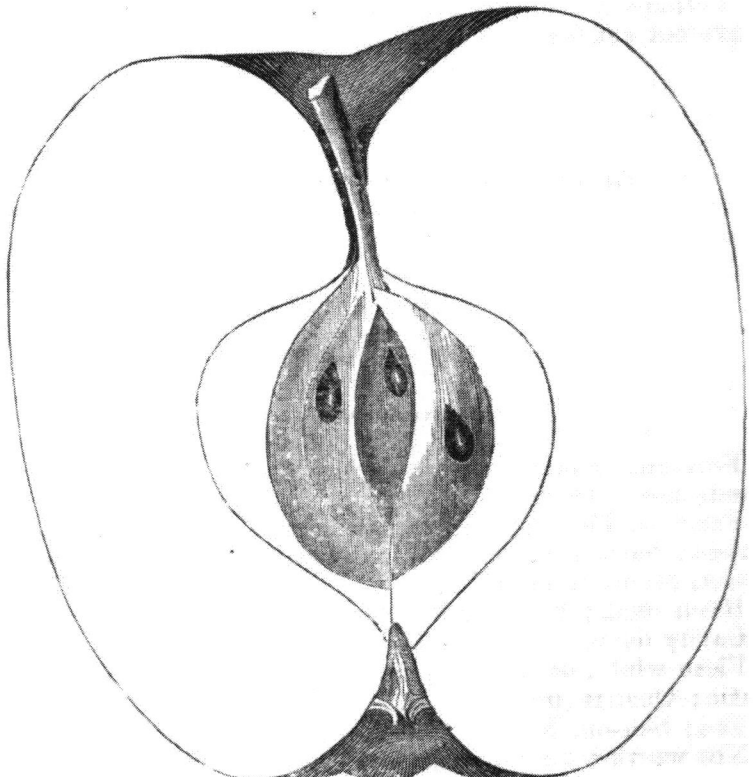

Fig. 293.—STRIPED GILLIFLOWER.

small, plump, black; Flesh yellowish white, breaking; Flavor sub-acid; Quality scarcely good; Use, market only; Season, September.

Less ribbed than the *Scalloped Gilliflower*.

Toccoa.

"From Toccoa Falls, Habersham County, Georgia.

"Fruit rather large, conical, irregular or oblong; Skin whitish yellow, considerably shaded with carmine, and sprinkled with a few brown dots; Stem short, inserted in a deep cavity; Calyx partially closed, set in a rather large basin; Flesh whitish, juicy, tender, pleasant, mild sub-acid; November to February."—[Downing.]

Perhaps not an early bearer; my trees, set six years, have not yet fruited.

CLASS IV.—OBLONG APPLES.

ORDER II.—IRREGULAR.

SECTION 2.—SOUR.

SUB-SECTION 3.—RUSSET.

Bourrassa.

Foreign. Said to do well in the North; have seen it handsome at Detroit.

Fruit medium, oblong, ovate, somewhat angular and ribbed; Surface yellow, covered lightly with a rich red russet, giving it an orange hue.

Basin small; Eye small, closed; Segments very long.

Cavity deep, acute, wavy; Stem long.

Flesh white, or stained, tender; Flavor acid, spicy, aromatic; Quality pretty good, but apt to be tough and wilted; Season, November to December.

Not worth trying in the South.

CHAPTER XVII.

FRUIT LISTS.

— ◦◦ —

Every orchard planter who examines the extended variety of fruits presented to him in the books, and by the nurserymen, must feel greatly embarrassed when he comes to select the varieties for his own orchards. Almost every one of the long lists is recommended for some good quality, and the number of *best*, which he is apt to conclude means indispensable for him, is wonderfully large. Some persons are bewildered by the array presented in the catalogue, and fall back upon their own slender stock of information, selecting only one well known variety; but most persons commit a far greater fault by attempting to grasp all the varieties that are offered and commended, which is very well for some one person in every region to do. It is a labor of love for the benefit of his fellow townsmen; but it is far better for him who is about to plant an orchard, either large or small, to determine which varieties are best adapted for his purposes. For the small planter, who is providing for the wants of his family, a number of varieties that will ripen in succession will be best, and the sorts should be selected with regard to their qualities for household uses. The planter of extensive commercial orchards, on the contrary, will need but a limited number of varieties, which should be selected with a view to the wants of the markets he intends to supply, as well as to the productiveness of the fruit, and its ability to bear transportation. While it is desirable to have but a few well selected varieties in such an orchard, it must be recollected that even when there is a general failure of the crop, there are always some sorts that bear fruit, and this is an argument against making the list too small.

All attempts to make out lists of fruits for general cultivation over the great extent of our country have been abortive. State and regional lists are made by the Pomological and other societies, which are useful in rendering approximate information; but, at last, every planter should observe the fruits that succeed in his own neighborhood, and upon soil similar to his own, and select his varieties for planting accordingly.

In making up our judgment of the excellence of a fruit, there are many elements that enter into the question of what constitutes a good apple, and so much depends upon the tastes of the individuals who have the question to decide, that at last every one is left to make up his own mind as to what will be best for his particular case.

The American Pomological Society, many years ago,

attempted to make out lists that would be applicable to the whole country, but it was very soon discovered that their recommendations were by no means of universal application, and that what was valuable in one section was worthless in another. The State and local societies took up the work, and the result of their labors has been of great value to persons similarly situated. In some States, regions, with peculiar soils and different underlying rocks, were found to be more or less fitted for the production of different varieties, and partial or local lists have been made out upon this principle. The greater value of the data thus obtained commended itself to the National Society, which has since collated these lists so far as possible in a tabular form, which shows the relative appreciation in which many varieties are held in the several regions that have reported; to these the reader is referred.* At present I propose to present a few lists which have been given by eminent pomologists, in different parts of the country, as the result of their extended observations, and applicable in their several districts.

Henry Little and others recommend for Maine:

Baldwin,
Blue Pearmain,
Bough,
Danvers,
Duchess of Oldenburgh,
Fameuse,
Golden Ball,
Golden Sweet,
Gravenstein,
Hubbardston,
Jewett's Fine Red,
Minister,
Mother,
Northern Spy,
Porter,
Red Astrachan,
Rhode Island Greening,
Ribstone Pippin,
Roxbury Russet,
Sops of Wine,
Tallman Sweet,
Vandervere (Newtown Spitzenberg),
Vermont,
Williams' Favorite,
Winthrop.

* See Reports of *American Pomological Society*.

The following list was furnished by C. Goodrich for Vermont:

Baldwin,
Bough,
Duchess of Oldenburgh,
Early Harvest,
Esopus Spitzenberg,
Gravenstein,
Newtown Pippin,
Northern Spy,
Porter,
Red Astrachan,
Rhode Island Greening,
Roxbury Russet.

Recommended by Thomas Hancock for New Jersey:

American Golden Russet,
Bough,
Early Harvest,
Fall Pippin,
Hagloe,
Juneating,
Maiden's Blush,
Monmouth Pippin,
Newtown Pippin,
Rhode Island Greening,
Summer Rose,
Striped Harvest,
Tewksbury Blush,
White Seek-no-further.

Wm. Parry, of Burlington County, New Jersey, an excellent judge of market qualities, recommends, after thorough trial, the following for profit:

Bachelor's Blush,
Bough,
Hagloe,
Maiden's Blush,

Jno. Diehl gave this list as desirable for Delaware:

American Summer Pearmain,
Baldwin,
Bough,
Caleb,
Danvers' Winter,
Early Harvest,
Early Red Margaret,
Early Red Streak,
English Russet,
Fallawater,
Fall Pippin,
Gilpin,
Greening,
Herefordshire Pearmain,
Lady,
Maiden's Blush,
Newtown Pippin,
Rambo,
Roman Stem,
Smokehouse,
Summer Golden Pippin,
Summer Queen,
White Juneating,
Winesap,
Yellow Bellflower.

Mr. Robey, of Fredericksburgh, recommends for that part of Virginia:

Abram,
Baltimore Pippin,
Bowling Sweet,
Brooke's Pippin,
Carter,
Garden,
Gloucester White,
Green Newtown Pippin,
Hollady,
Ladies' Favorite,
Leather Coat,
Limbertwig,
Milam,
Ogleby,
Pryor's Red,
Rawle's Janet,
Red Cathead,
Roberson's White,

Russet (?),
Spice (Va.),
Strawn's Seedling,
Summer Cheese,
Summer Golden Pippin,

Vandervere,
Waugh's Crab,
Winesap,
Winter Cheese,
Winter Queen.

Daniel K. Underwood, Michigan, gives the following extended catalogue:

SUMMER.

Early Harvest,
Early Joe,
Early Strawberry,
Golden Sweet,
Maiden's Blush,
Red Astrachan,
Sweet Bough,
Sine-qua-non,
Summer Queen,
Summer Rose.

AUTUMN.

Alexander,
Daniel,
Duchess of Oldenburgh,
Dyer,
Fall Pippin,
Fameuse,
Gravenstein,
Hawley,
Jersey Sweet,
Keswick Codling,
Late Strawberry,
Porter,
Rambo,
Cayuga Red Streak,
Fall Wine.

WINTER.

Baldwin,
Belmont,
Black Detroit,
Blue Pearmain,
Bourrassa,
Cornish Gilliflower,
Domine,
English Russet,
Esopus,
Green Newtown,
Golden Russet,
Herefordshire,
Hubbardston,
Jonathan,
Ladies' Sweeting,
Lady,
Northern Spy,
Peck's Pleasant,
Red Canada,
Rawle's Janet,
Roxbury,
Swaar,
Stone,
Twenty Ounce Pippin,
Rhode Island Greening,
Vandervere (Newtown Spitzenberg),
Westfield,
Yellow Bellflower.

J. D. G. Nelson, President of the Indiana State Society, an extensive orchardist at Fort Wayne, presented the following list as the result of long experience in Northern Indiana:

SUMMER.

Red Astrachan, less profitable.
Early Harvest, less profitable.
Duchess of Oldenburgh, more profitable.
Keswick Codling, more profitable.
Sweet Bough.
High-top Sweet, for profit.

FALL.

Maiden's Blush,
Porter,
Rambo,
Trenton Early,
Dyer,
Lowell,
Hawley,

FALL.

Golden Sweet.

WINTER APPLES FOR EXTENSIVE CULTIVATION FOR MARKET.

DARK.—Ben Davis, 500 trees.
Smith's Cider, 300 trees.
Jersey Black, 200 trees.

LIGHT.—Belmont, need careful handling
Wagener, " . "
Yellow Bellflower. "

SWEET.—Bentley Sweet, keeps well.
London Sweet, " "
Talman Sweet, " "

AMATEUR LIST.

American Summer Pearmain,
American Golden Russet,
Evening Party,
King of Tompkins County,
Swaar,
Newtown Pippin.

Dr. Cornett, of Versailles, Indiana, advised to plant

American Summer Pearmain,
Bohanon,
Carolina Red June,
Cooper,
Early Harvest,
Fall Pippin,
Fall Wine,

Golden Russet (American ?),
Newtown Pippin,
Pryor's Red,
Rambo,
Rawle's Janet,
Winesap,
Yellow Bellflower.

Messrs. Lawyer, of South Pass, Union County, Illinois, recommends of 1,000 trees for profit:

250 Ben Davis,
100 Early Harvest,
50 Nickajack,
50 Pryor's Red,
150 Rawle's Janet,

150 Red Astrachan,
50 Rome Beauty,
50 Smith's Cider,
50 White Pippin,
100 Winesap.

Parker Earle, President of the Illinois State Horticultural Society, an intelligent fruit cultivator in the Southern portion of that State (called Egypt), recommends the following list as being well adapted for profit:

Ben Davis,
Buckingham,
Carolina Red June,
Early Harvest,
Golden Sweet,
Jonathan,
Keswick Codling,
Newtown Pippin,

Rambo,
Rawle's Janet,
Red Astrachan,
White Pippin,
White Winter Pearmain,
Winesap,
Yellow Bellflower.

Wm. C. Hampton, Hardin County, Ohio, recommends for a select list of winter apples:

Broadwell,
Hubbardston,
Michael Henry,
Ortley,

Rome Beauty,
Seedling Jersey Sweet,
Yellow Bellflower,
Yellow Newtown Pippin.

H. B. Spencer, of Rockport, Cuyahoga County, Ohio, recommends the following :

Baldwin,	Peck's Pleasant,
Baltimore,	Red Canada,
Belmont,	Roxbury Russet.
Esopus Spitzenberg,	

Mr. G. W. Dean, of Welshfield, Geauga County, Ohio, gives the following list of ten :

Baldwin,	Peck's Pleasant,
Baltimore,	Rambo,
Canada Red,	Rhode Island Greening,
Hubbardston,	Swaar,
Ladies' Sweeting,	Westfield Seek-no-further.

Recommended by M. B. Bateham, Secretary Ohio Pomological Society, for the Central and Southern portion of the State :

SUMMER.

American Summer Pearmain,
Bough,
Early Harvest,
Early Pennock.
Early Strawberry,
Golden Sweeting,
High-top Sweet,
Keswick Codling,
Red Astrachan,
Summer Queen,
Tetofski.

AUTUMN.

Cooper,
Fall Pippin,
Gravenstein,
Jersey Sweet,
Lowell,
Malden's Blush,
Ohio Nonpariel,
Orange Sweet,
Rambo,
Smokehouse.

WINTER.

Bullock's Pippin,
Domine,
Fallawater,
London Sweet,
Milam,
Mount Pleasant Sweet,
Newtown Spitzenberg,
Pryor's Red,
Rawle's Janet,
Rome Beauty,
Smith's Cider,
Tallman,
Western Spy,
White Pippin,
Willow,
Winesap,
Yellow Bellflower.

Select lists from H. N. Gillett for Southern Ohio, Western Virginia and Kentucky :

SUMMER VARIETIES.

Benoni,
Early Harvest,
Early Chandler,
Primate,
Pound Royal,
Red Astrachan,
Summer Rose,
Summer Queen,
Summer Seek-no-further,
Sine-qua-non.

FALL VARIETIES.

Corse's Favorite,
Cooper,
Favorite,
Fall Pippin,
Fall Wine,
Fallawater,
Gravenstein,
Maiden's Blush,
King of Pippins,
Porter.

WINTER VARIETIES.

Ben Davis,
Black Coal,
Broadwell,

Buckingham [Autumn],
Bullock's Pippin,
Carolina Red [Nickajack ?],
Defiance,
Harrison,
Hewes' Crab,
Lady,
Pryor's Red,
Rawle's Janet,
Red Cedar,
Rolen's Keeper,
Rome Beauty,
Roxbury Russet,
Smith's Cider,
Winesap,
Yellow Bellflower.

By Henry Hefflebower, an extensive orchardist at Mont-clovia, Lucas County, Ohio:

American Golden Russet,
Baldwin,
Bellflower,
Belmont,
Bongh,
Early Harvest,
Fallawater,
Fall Pippin,
King of Tompkins,
Maiden's Blush,
Newtown Pippin,
Newtown Spitzenberg,
None Such,

Porter.
Primate,
Rambo,
Rawle's Janet,
Red Astrachan,
Seek-no-further,
Smokehouse,
Summer Queen,
Summer Rose,
Swaar.
Sweet Bellflower,
Tallow Pippin,
Twenty Ounce.

HARDY AND TENDER.

After the sad experiences in many portions of the Northwest, where in some severe winters whole orchards of trees and extensive nurseries were ruined by the cold, it has become a most important question for planters to ask whether the varieties recommended are *hardy.* The testimony of some of our best observers has been collected, and will be of value, though it may be observed that there is some discrepancy as to certain sorts.

The following list of hardy and tender varieties was prepared by Reuben Ragan, Putnam County, Indiana, and has since been carefully revised. Soil a rich argillaceous loam on lime stone:

TENDER.

Baldwin,
Bullock's Pippin,
Early Harvest,
Esopus,
Fall Pippin,
Gravenstein,
Michael Henry,
*Newtown Spitzenberg,
Ortley,
Pryor's Red,
Rambo,
Rawle's Janet,
Rhode Island Greening.
*Roxbury Russet,
*Summer Queen.

HARDY.

American Summer Pearmain.
Carolina June (Red),
Carolina June (Striped),
Chronicle,
Danvers' Winter Sweet,
Early Strawberry,

Fall Queen.
Fall Wine,
Farley Red,
Hannah,
Hoops,
Horse,
Lewis (of Ragan),
McAffee,
Newtown Pippin,
Northern Spy,
Pennock,
Pottinger,
President,
Priestley,
Ragan's Red,
Red Astrachan,
Red Streak,
Rome Beauty,
Sine-qua-non,
Transport,
Vandervere Pippin,
Winesap,
Yellow Bellflower,
Yellow Juneating.

A. L. Benedict, of Monroe County, has taken great pains in making out lists of those that were entirely destroyed, partially injured, and slightly affected by the terribly severe winter of 1855–6 :

ENTIRELY DESTROYED.

Baldwin Sweet,
Blue Pearmain,
Cheeseboro Russet,
Egg Top,
English Russett,
Esopus Spitzenberg,
Fall Pippin,
French Pippin,
Lowre Queen,
Newtown Spitzenberg,
Red Juneating,
Rhode Island Greening,
Robinson,
Romanite,
Spice Sweeting,
Wing Sweet,
Yellow Vandervere.

PARTIALLY INJURED.

American Golden Russet,
Belmont,

Black,
Bough,
Butter,
Colvert,
Detroit Black,
Early Harvest,
Fall Wine,
Golden Sweet,
Gray Vandervere,
Hoops,
Kaighn's Spitzenberg,
London Winter Sweet,
Newtown Pippin,
Ortley,
Peck's Pleasant,
Pennock,
Pine,
Rambo,
Raritan Sweet,
Roxbury Russet,
Scallop Gilliflower,
Streaked Vandervere,

* These suffered in the nursery especially.

PARTIALLY INJURED.

Swaar,
Sweet Gilliflower,
Tift's Sweet,
Tulpehocken,
White Pippin,
Winesap,
Yellow Bellflower.

HARDY OR BUT SLIGHTLY INJURED.

Bethlemite,
Black Gilliflower,
Blockley,
Gloria Mundi,
Grindstone,
Harrison (Newark King),
Jersey King,
Maiden's Blush,
May,
Molasses,
Pennsylvania Red Streak,
Pound Pippin,
Pumpkin Sweet,
Red Winter Sweet,
Roman Stem,
Saint Lawrence,
Saner's Early Sweet,
Summer Queen,
Summer Rose,
Sweet Vandervere,
Tallman Sweet.
Westfield Seek-no-further,
White Rambo,
Whitmore's Sweeting,
Yellow Newtown Pippin.

M. L. Comstock, of Iowa, gives the following list of apples that are found to be tender in that region:

Baldwin,
Esopus Spitzenberg,
Fall Pippin,
Fameuse,
Gravenstein,
Golden Russet,
Hubbardston,
Jonathan,
Ladies' Sweet,
Newtown Spitzenberg,
Peck's Pleasant,
Pomme Grise,
Rawle's Janet,
Red Canada,
Rhode Island Greening,
White Winter Pearmain.

F. W. Landon, Janesville, Wisconsin, thinking the hardy list would be too long, gives the following as tender:

Autumn Strawberry,
Baldwin,
Cloth of Gold,
Early Strawberry,
Esopus Spitzenberg,
Lady,
Newtown Spitzenberg,
Northern Spy,
Norton's Melon,
Westfield Seek-no-further.

J. C. Brayton, Azatlan, Wisconsin, gives the following list of hardy and valuable fruits for the rich lands in the western part of the State:

SUMMER.

American Summer Pearmain,
Benoni,
Early Harvest,
Early Pennock,
Early Red,
Fall Stripe,
High-top Sweet.

AUTUMN.

Bailey Sweet,
Fall Orange,
Fall Winesap,
Fameuse,
Late Strawberry,
Red Streak,
Rosean,
Saint Lawrence,
Sweet Pear,
Trenton Early,
Utter's Large,

AUTUMN.	White Winter Pearmain,
White Gilliflower.	Winesap.
WINTER.	Yellow Bellflower.
Broadwell,	
Domine,	HARDY, IF TOP-GRAFTED.
Flushing Spitzenberg,	
Golden Russet,	Autumn Swaar,
Hoops ?	Belmont,
Limbertwig,	English Russet,
Northern Spy,	Fulton,
Perry Russet,	Golden Sweet,
Rawle's Janet,	Herefordshire Pearmain,
Red Spitzenberg,	Jonathan,
Tallman's Sweet,	Lowell,
Wagener,	Maiden's Blush,
Westfield Seek-no-further,	Red June,
	Sops of Wine.

SWEET APPLES FOR BAKING AND FOR STOCK FEEDING.

With many persons the consumption of sweet apples becomes an important item of household economy; for the feeding and fattening of stock sweet apples have deservedly attracted the attention of intelligent farmers, and they may yet be much more extensively planted in many places where the land is not well adapted to the production of grain and other staple crops for the support of man and the animals under his care.

With a view to aid the planter the following lists have been collated:

Sweet apples to be planted for stock feeding. Recommended by T. S. Humrickhouse, of Coshocton, Ohio, in Ohio Cultivator, vol. VI, page 283:

SUMMER.	Ramsdell's,
*Duling Sweet,	Spice Sweet,
Golden Sweet,	*Superb Sweet.
*Jersey Sweet,	WINTER.
Pumpkin Sweet,	
Red and Green Sweet,	Baldwin Sweet,
Summer Sweet,	Broadwell,
*Summer Sweet Paradise,	Butter Sweet,
*Sweet Bough.	*Danvers' Winter,
AUTUMN.	Honey Sweeting,
*Haskell Sweet,	*Ladies' Sweeting,
*Kinsey's Sweet,	Late Pound Sweet,
Lyman's Pumpkin,	May,
	McKay's Favorite,

*Phillips' Sweeting,
*Tallman's Sweeting,
Wells' Sweeting,
Winter Sweeting.

ALSO, LESS KNOWN,

Acid Sweet,
Akeson's Sweet,
Beauty of the West,
Cash Sweet,

Charlotte Sweet,
Climb Sweet,
Ling Sweet,
London Sweet,
Merritt's Sweet,
Mt. Pleasant Sweet,
Morgan's Favorite,
Red Sweet Pippin,
Stone Sweet.

Planted by A. L. Benedict, Morrow County, Ohio, in a lot to be devoted to hogs. The numbers of each might be varied:

2 Bough,
3 Golden Sweet,*
6 Jersey Sweet,*
16 May of Myers,
10 Moore's Sweeting,
82 Pumpkin Sweet,

8 Raritan Sweet,
17 Spice Sweet,
1 Tift's Sweet,
19 Tallman Sweet,
30 Whitmore Sweet,
14 Wing Sweet.

L. Hampton's list† for a succession through the year:

Bentley Sweet,
Bough,
Broadwell,
Fall Sweet,
Federal Sweet,
Golden Sweet,
Hightop Sweet,
Honey Greening,

Kentucky Sweet,
Paradise Winter,
Scarlet Sweet,
Simpson's,
Smith's Sweet,
Sweet Favorite,
Winter Sweet.

For Illinois, by W. Cutter, in *Prairie Farmer:*

Broadwell,
Golden Sweet,
Paradise Winter,

Ramsdell Sweet,
Sweet June,
Sweet Nonesuch.

Sweet apples arranged in succession for stock. Those marked *T.* are also fine for the dessert; those marked *B.* are superior for baking:

Hightop, *B.*
Bough, *T.*
Golden Sweeting, *B.*
Victuals and Drink, *B. T.*
Jersey Sweet.
Lyman's Pumpkin, *B.*
Bailey Sweet, *B. T.*
Ramsdell's, *B.*
Mote's Sweet, *B. T.*

Stillwater Sweeting, *B.*
Higby Sweet, *B.*
Dr. Watson, *T.*
Molasses,
Fall Queen, *B. T.*
Buckingham,
Baltimore,
Fallawater,
Michael Henry,

---

* My friends write that they would have preferred more of these sorts, and that they planted such trees as were at hand at that time.

† Ohio Cultivator, vol. VI, page 269.

Broadwell, *T. B.*
Sweet Bellflower,
Sweet Janet, *B.*
London Sweet, *B.*
Winter Sweet Paradise, *T. B.*
Jersey Black,
Ladies' Sweeting, *T. B.*
Tallman's, *B.*

Holton's,
Moore's Sweeting,
Gilpin,
Campfield,
Sweet Vandervere,
Red Winter Pearmain,
Swaar,
Black Gilliflower,

In giving selections of Cider Apples I will begin with the veteran *Coxe's list:*

American Pippin,
Campfield,
Cooper's Russeting,
Gloucester White,
Golden Reinette,
Hagloe Crab,
Harrison,

Hewes' Crab,
House, or Gray-House,
Red Streak,
Roane's White Crab,
Ruckman's Pearmain,
Styre,
Winesap.

A select list of Cider Apples that may be found in many collections, all good bearers :

Campfield.
Gilpin.
Harrison,
Hewes' Crab,
Newtown Pippin,

Priestley,
Rawle's Janet,
Waugh's Crab
Winesap.

CATALOGUE AND INDEX OF APPLES.

EXPLANATION.

The first column presents the name of the apple, next its size, then its origin; or, if in brackets, the place where the variety is cultivated and was found. The Roman numerals indicate the *Class* and *Order* to which it is referred, and the Arabics, the *Section* and *Sub-section*, according to the classification adopted in this work. After this comes the season of maturity, Summer, Autumn, Winter, Spring, and the estimate of quality, from very best, best, very good, good; good? meaning almost good; poor? meaning rather so, and last plainly poor, when considered decidedly inferior. The names of varieties described in this volume are given in **full faced** type, with reference to the pages, while synonyms are printed in *Italics*. Abbreviations will explain themselves.

Name.	Size.	Orig.	Class.	Season.	Quality.	P.
Abbott Sweet	large	N. H.	II. I. 1. 2.	Winter	good	
Abram	small	Va. ?	I. I. 2. 2. } III. I. 2. 2. }	Spring	good	419
Adams	large	Penn.	I. I. 2. 2.	L. Wint.	good	
Agnes	small	Penn.	I. II. 2. 2.	Autumn	good	
Ailes	large	Penn.	I. I. 2. 2.	L. Wint.	good	
Akeson's Winter Sweet		South		Winter		
Alabama Winter		Ala.		Winter		
Albemarle	large	Va.	III. II. 2. 1.	Winter	good	
Alexander	large	Russ.	II. I. 2. 2.	Summ'r	good	510
Alexander	large	?	III. II. 2. 2.	Autumn	good	
Allen's Pippin	med.	Ga.	II. I. 2. 2.	Autumn	good	
Allen's Sweeting	med.	Mass.	III. I. 1. 1.	Winter	good	
All Summer			I. I. 2. 1.	Summ'r		
All Summer Sweeting			III. I. 1. 1.	Summ'r		
Allum	med.	N. C.	I. II. 2. 2.	Spring	good	
Alsace			II. I. 2. 1.			
Amber Crab	small	Eur.	II. I. 2. 1.	Autumn	good	
American Beauty	large	Mass.	III. I. 2. 2.	Winter	good	
American Black	small	?	I. I. 2. 1.	Wint'r?	good	
American Black	med.	?	I. I. 2. 2.	Winter	good	
Am. Golden Pippin	med.	Am.	III. II. 2. 1.	Winter	v. good	636
Am. Golden Russet	med.	Am.	II. I. 2. 3.	E. Wint.	best	521
American Marygold		Am.	I. I. 2. 1.	Autumn		
American Pippin	small	Am.	I. I. 2. 2.	Spring	poor	420
Am. Sum. Pearmain	med.	N. J.	II. I. 2. 2. } III. I. 2. 2. }	Summ'r	best	582
Angle Sweet	med.	?	I. II. 1. 2.	Winter	good	476
Anglo-American	med.	Can.	II. II. 1. 2. } III. II. 1. 2. }	Autumn	v. good	
Annette	small	Va.	I. I. 2. 2.	Winter	v. good	
Apple Butter	small	?	I. I. 1. 2.	Autumn	good	
Aromatic	med.	South	III. I. 2. 2.			
Aromatic	large	Car.	I. I. 2. 2.	Summ'r	good	
Ashland	large	?	II. II. 2. 2	Winter	good	
Ashmore	med.	Am.	III. I. 2. 1.	Autumn	good	566
Ashmore Striped	med.	Am.	III. I. 2. 2.	Autumn	good	
August		Ohio		Summ'r	good	
Augustine	large	Am.	II. II. 1. 1.	Summ'r	poor	

711

Name.	Size.	Orig.	Class.	Season.	Quality.	P.
August Stripe	med.	?	II. I. 2. 2.	Summ'r	good ?	
August Tart	med.	?	II. I. 2. 1.	Summ'r	good	504
August Vandervere	large	(Ind.)	II. I. 2. 2.	Summ'r	poor	
Aunt Anna	med.	Ohio	I. I. 2. 2.	Autumn	good ?	
Aunt Hannah	large	Mass.	III. I. 2. 1.	Winter	good ?	
Aunt's Apple	large	?	I. I. 2. 2.	E.Wint.	good ?	
Autumnal Bough	med.	Am.	III. I. 1. 1.	Autumn	good	
Autumnal Paradise			I. I. 1. 1.	Autumn	good	
Autumn Seek-no-further. Synonym of Dr. Watson.						
Autumn Swaar, see Fall Swaar of the West						
Autumnal Sweet	large	?	I. I. 1. 1.	Autumn	good	
Autumnal Sw. Swaar	large	?	I. II. 1. 1.	Autumn	good	471
Autumn Pearmain	med.	?	IV. I. 2. 2.	Winter	good	
Autumn Sweet			I. I. 1. 1.	Autumn	good	
Averill	large	Conn.	II. II. 2. 2.	Spring	good	
Baccallnus	small	South	{ III. I. 2. 2. / I. I. 2. 1. }	L.Wint.	good	588
Bachelor is Equineteley.						
Bachelor's Blush	large	N. J.	I. I. 2. 1.	Summ'r	good	
Badger's Bellflower	large	Ohio?	IV. I. 2. 2.	Winter	good	
Baer	small	Penn.	III. I. 2. 2.	Spring	"v. gd."	
Banby Russet, Synonym of Egyptian Russet.						
Bailey's Golden	large	Maine	IV. I. 2. 1.	L.Wint.	good	665
Bailey's Spice	med.	N. Y.	II. I. 2. 1.	Autumn	good	
Bailey's Sweet	large	N. Y.	{ III. II. 1. 2. / II. I. 1. 2. }	Winter	good	688
Bake Apple	small	(N.Y.)	III. I. 2. 2.	Autumn	good ?	
Baker		Penn?	III. I. 2. 1.			
Baker's Sweet	med.	Conn.	III. I. 1. 1.	E.Wint.	good	
Baldwin	large	Mass.	{ I. I. 2. 2. / III. II. 2. 2. }	Winter	good	421
Baldwin, N. C.	large	N. C.	I. I. 2. 2.	Winter	good	
Baldwin Sweet	large		III. I. 2.	Winter	good	
Baltimore, Synonym of Mammoth Pippin.						
Baltimore, (Elliott)	med.	?	{ I. I. 1. 2. / III. I. 1. 2. }	Winter	good	391
Baltzley			I. I. 1. 1.			
Barbour	med.	Penn.	I. I 2. 2.		good	
Barrett	med.	Conn.	II. I. 2. 2.	Winter	good	
Bars	large	R. I.	III. I. 2. 2.	Summ'r	good	
Bartlett, Synonym of Priestley.						
Barton		Penn.				
Basom Sweet			III. I. 1. 1.			
Bassett Sweet	small	Ohio.	II. I. 1. 1.	Autumn	good	
Bastard Geneton, Synonym of Wright's Janet.						
Battlefield	med.	South	I. I. 1. 1.			
Beard's Seedling	med.	Ohio	III. II. 2. 2.	Winter	good	
Beaufin Norfolk	med.	Engl.	I. I. 2. 2.	Winter	poor	
Beauty of Kent	large	Engl.	III. I. 2. 2.	Autumn	only gd.	584
Beauty of the West	large	Am.	III. I. 1. 2.	E.Wint.	poor	
Bedfordshire Foundling	large	Engl.	IV. II. 2. 1.	Winter	good ?	
Beefsteak	med.	Mass.	I. I. 2. 2.	Winter	poor	
Beeler's Russet	med.	(Ind.)	III. I. 2. 3.	Winter	best	621
Belle et Bonne	large	Conn.	IV. I. 2. 1.	E.Wint.	good ?	
Belden Sweet	small	Conn?	II. II. 1. 1.	Winter	good	526
Bellflower Pippin	large	Ind.	III. I. 2. 1.	Autumn	good	
Belmont	large	Va.	{ II. II. 2. 1. / III. II. 2. 1. }	E.Wint.	best	529
Ben or *Eustis*	large	Mass.	IV. I. 2. 2.	E.Wint.	good ?	
Ben Davis	large	Ky.	{ III. I. 2. 2. / IV. I. 2. 2. }	Winter	good	595
Ben Harris		South	I. I. 2. 2.	Winter		
Benoni	small	Mass.	{ III. II. 2. 2. / IV. I. 2. 2. }	Summ'r	best	650

Name.	Size.	Orig.	Class.	Season.	Quality.	P.
Bentley Sweet..........	large	Va. ?	III. I. 1. 2. IV. II. 1. 2.	Spring	good	558
Berkely Red..............		South	I. II. 2. 2.			
Berry............	large	Va. ?	I. II. 2. 2.	E.Wint.	good	486
Bethlemite............	med.	Ohio	I. I. 2. 2. III. I. 2. 2.	Winter	v. good	423
Betsey's Fancy...........	med.	?	I. I. 2. 2.	Winter	good	
Better than Good......	med.	Penn.	I. I. 2. 1.	E.Wint.	good	400
Bevan's Favorite...........	med.	N. J.	I. I. 2. 2.	Summ'r	good	
Beverley Red...........						
Big Hill, Synonym of Pryor's Red.						
Big Rambo, Synonym of Western Beauty.						
Big Red Sweet............		South	III. I. 1. 2.			
Bigger's Late Red...........		South				
Birmingham................	med.	Penn?	I. I. 2. 1.	Autumn	good	
Black, Synonym of Jersey Black.						
Black's Annette............	med.	(Ky.)	II. II. 2. 1.	Summ'r	v. good	
Blackburn............	large	Ky. ?	III. I. 2. 2. I. I. 2. 2.	Autumn	good ?	586
Black Canada............	med.	Can. ?	II. I. 2. 1.	E.Wint.	good ?	
Black Coal............	large	?	III. I. 2. 2.	Winter	good ?	
Black Detroit............	large	Can. ?	II. II. 2. 1.	Autumn	poor	
Black Eyes, Synonym of Cheese.						
Black Gilliflower......	large	?	IV. I. 1. 2.	Spring	poor	662
Black Jack............	small	Ohio	I. I. 1. 2.	Winter	poor	
Black Lady Apple...........	small	Eur.	I. I. 2. 1.	Winter	poor	
Black of Michigan...........	med.	Can. ?	I. I. 2. 1.	Winter	poor	
Blackshear............		South	I. I. 2. 1.			
Black's Late Sweet...........		South		Winter		
Black Tom............	med.	Md.	I. I. 2. 1.	Autumn	poor	
Blakeley............	large	Vt.	I. I. 2. 1.	Winter	good	
Bledsoe............	med.	Ky.	III. I. 2. 1. I. I. 2. 1.	Winter	good ?	568
Blenheim Orange....	large	Eng.	III. I. 1. 2.	Autumn	good	
Blockley..............	large	Penn.	I. II. 2. 1. III. II. 2. 1.	Winter	v. good	478
Blockley Pippin, Synonym of Blockley.						
Blondin..............	large	Ind.	I. I. 2. 2. III. I. 2. 2.	E.Wint.	good	424
Blooming Orange......	large	Eng.	I. I. 2. 2. III. I. 2. 1.	Autumn	v. good	424
Bloomington........ ?.....	med.	Ills.	IV. I. 1. 2.	Winter	good	
Blue Bloom............	med.	?	III. I. 2. 2.	Autumn	good ?	
Blue Pearmain............	large	?	III. I. 2. 2.	Autumn	good ?	
Bluff Sweet............	med.	Ind.	III. I. 1. 1.	Winter	good	548
Boalsburgh............	large	Penn.	IV. I. 2. 2.	Autumn	good	675
Boas or Kelter............		Penn.	I. I. 2. 1.			
Bohanon............	med.	Va. ?	I. I. 2. 1.	Autumn	v. good	400
Bonum............	med.	N. C.	I. I. 2. 2.	Autumn	v. good	424
Boravitski............	med.	Russ.	III. II. 2. 2.	Summ'r	poor	
Borsdorffer............	small	Germ.	I. II. 2. 1.	Winter	good	
Boston Russet, Synonym of Roxbury.						
Bough	large	Am.	III. I. 1. 1. II. I. 1. 1.	Summ'r	v. good	494
Bourrassa............	large	Eur. ?	IV. II. 2. 3.	Winter	poor	697
Bowback Sweet............		Ohio				
Bowker............		?	I. II. 2. 1.	Autumn	good	
Bowling Sweet......	med.	Va.	III. I. 1. 2.	Winter	good	559
Brabant Bellflower...........	large	Holl.	III. II. 2. 2.	E.Wint.	good ?	
Brace's Seek-no-further, Synonym of White Seek-no-further.						
Bracken..............	small	Ky.	I. II. 2. 1.	Summ'r	v. good	478
Bradford's Best.............						
Brandywine.....	med.	Del.	I. I. 2. 2. III. I. 2. 2.	Winter	good ?	425
Brennaman............	large	Penn.	III. II. 2. 2.	Autumn	v. good	651

Name.	Size.	Orig.	Class.	Season.	Quality.	P.
Brigg's Auburn	med.	Me.	I. I. 2. 1.	Autumn	v. good	
Brittle Sweet	med.	?	III. II. 1. 2.	Autumn	v. good	634
Broadwell	large	Ohio	III. I. 1. 1.	Winter	best	549
Brooke's Pippin	large	Va.	III. II. 2. 1.	Winter	v. good	637
Brown's Superior	large	Ohio?	III. II. 2. 2.	Winter	good	
Bruce	large	?	II. I. 1. 2.	Summ'r	good ?	
Buchanan's	med.	Ohio	I. I. 2. 2.	Spring	good ?	426
Buckingham	large	Ga.	II. II. 2. 2.	Autumn	v. good	537
Buck Meadow	large	Conn.	III. I. 2. 2.	Winter	good	
Buck's County	large	Penn.	I. II. 2. 1.		good	
Buff	v. lar.	N. C.	I. II. 2. 2.	E. Wint.	good ?	486
Buffington's Early	small	Penn.	I. II. 2. 1.	Summ'r		
Bush	large	Penn.	III. I. 2. 1.	Autumn	v. good	508
Bush's Beauty	med.	Ohio?	II. II. 2. 2.	Autumn	poor	
Bullock's Pippin, Synonym of American Golden Russet.						
Butter	small	Ohio	I. I. 1. 2.	Autumn	good	392
Butter	large	Ind.	III. I. 1. 2.	Winter	good	
Butter	med.	Penn.	III. I. 1. 1.	Autumn	good	
Butter	large	?	IV. I. 2. 1.	Autumn	good ?	
Butter Sweet						
Button			I. I. 1. 2.			
Button Core	med.	Mass.	III. I. 2. 1.	Winter	good ?	
Byer's, Synonym of Equinetelee.						
Cabashea	large	?	I. II. 2. 2.	Winter	poor	
Cabin	med.	?	I. I. 2. 1.	Winter	poor	
Cache	med.	(Ills.)	II. II. 2. 1.	L. Wint.	good	
Cake	med.	Conn.	I. I. 2. 2.	Winter	good ?	
Caleb	med.	Penn.	III. I. 1. 1.	Summ'r	good	549
Calville White Winter	med.	Fr.	III. II. 2. 1.	Winter	poor	
Camack Sweet	med.	N. C.	I. I. 1. 1.	Spring	good ?	581
Campfield	med.	N. J.	I. I. 1. 1.	Spring	poor	382
Canada Black	large	Can. ?	III. I. 2. 1.	E. Wint.	poor	
Canada Red	large	"	II. I. 2. 2.	Winter	best	
Canada Reinette	large	Eur. ?	I. II. 2. 1.	Winter	v. good	479
Cane Creek Sweeting		South	IV. I. 1. 1.			
Cann	large	?	II. I. 1. 1.	Winter	good ?	
Canon	med.	South	I. I. 1. 1.	Autumn		
Canon Pearmain	med.	Va.	IV. I. 2. 2.	Spring	good	676
Capital	med.	Ind.	III. I. 2. 1.	Winter	good	587
Capron's Pleasant	med.	?	I. I. 2. 1.	Autumn	good	
Carbage	large	?	II. I. 1. 1.		poor	
Carey's Pippin	large	Ohio	III. I. 1. 1.	Winter	v. good	
Carmell Sweet		N. Y.	I. I. 1. 1.			
Carnahan's Favorite	large	Ohio	III. I. 2. 1.	E. Wint.	poor	
Carnation	med.	South	I. I. 2. 2.	Autumn	" best "	
Carolina Baldwin	large	South	I. I. 2. 2.	Winter	good	427
Carolina Greening		South	I. I. 2. 1.			
Carolina Horse	large	South	III. I. 2. 1.	Autumn	good	
Carolina Pippin	large	South	III. I. 2. 2.			
Carolina Red June	small	N. C.	IV. I. 2. 1. / II. II. 2. 1.	Summ'r	good	666
Carolina Russet	med.	N. C.	III. I. 2. 3. / I. I. 2. 3.	L. Wint.	v. good	
Carolina Striped June	small	N. C.?	IV. I. 2. 2. / II. II. 2. 2.	Summ'r	good	
Caroline	med.	N. J.	I. II. 2. 1.	Winter	good	
Caroline Watson			III. I. 2. 2.		good	
Carpenter's No. 1	med.	Ohio	III. I. 2. 1.	Winter	good	
Carter	med.	Mass.	III. I. 2. 2. / III. II. 2. 2.	Winter	good	587
Carter, Synonym of Patton.						
Carter		N. C.		Winter		
Carter's Blue		South	I. I. 2. 2.			
Carver						
Cary's Summer	large	?	III. I. 2. 2.	Summ'r	good	588

Name.	Size.	Orig.	Class.	Season.	Quality.	P.
Cash Sweet..................	med.	?	II. I. 1. 1.	Autumn	poor	
Cataling....................			II. I. 2. 2.	....	....	
Cathead Sweet.............	large	?	II. I. 1. 1.	Autumn	poor	
Catline....................	small	Md.	I. I. 2. 2.	E. Wint.	good	
Cat's-head................	large		III. I. 2. 1.	Autumn	good ?	
Cattel....................	small	Ohio	....	Autumn	good	
Cattell, Synonym of Ohio Nonpareil.						
Cayuga Redstreak.....	large	Conn.	II. I. 2. 2.	Autumn	good	510
Caywood..................	med.	N. Y.	I. I. 2. 1.	Spring	good ?	
Celestia..............	large	Ohio	II. II. 2. 1.	Autumn	best	530
Centers..................		N. C.	....	....	....	
Challenge.............	med.	Ohio	I. II. 1. 1.	Autumn	v. good	472
Champlain.............	large	(Vt.)	III. I. 2. 1.	Autumn	good	637
Chandler.................	large	Conn.	III. II. 2. 2.	Winter	v. good	
Charlotte Sweet..........			....	....	....	
Chattahoochie Greening......		Ga.	I. II. 2. 1.			
Cheese...............	med.	Va.	I. I. 2. 2. / I. II. 2. 2.	E. Wint.	good ?	427
Cheese...................	large	(Ind.)	I. I. 2. 1.	Winter	good	
Cheeseboro...........	large	?	II. I. 2. 3.	E. Wint.	poor	522
Cheltenham..............			III. II. 2. 2.	....	....	
Cherokee Red............		South	....	....	....	
Cherry Crab.............	small	?	III. I. 2. 1.	Autumn	good	
Chestatee...............		South	II. II. 2. 1.	....	....	
Chester..................	med.	Penn.	I. I. 2. 1.	E. Wint.	"good"	
Chester Red..............		Sou. ?	....	....	....	
Chillicothe..............	large	Ohio	I. I. 2. 1.	Winter	good	
Chillicothe Redstreak......	large	Ohio	II. I. 2. 2.	Winter	good	
Christiana...............	med.	Del.	III. I. 2. 2.	Autumn	"v. gd."	
Chronicle.............	med.	Ind.	III. II. 2. 2.	Spring	good ?	652
Churchhill Greening........	large	?	I. II. 2. 1.	Winter	good	
Clark's..................			IV. II. 2. 1.	....	....	
Clark's Greening.........		Va.	I. I. 2. 1			
Clark's Pearmain.....	med.	N. C.	II. I. 2. 2.	Winter	good	511
Claybank................	med.	Ohio	I. I. 2. 1.	Autumn	v. good	
Clayton..............	large	Ind.	II. I. 2. 2.	Winter	good	511
Climb Sweet.............			....	....	....	
Close Set, (Lindsley)..........	med.	(O.)	III. II. 2. 2.	Autumn	good	
Cloth of Gold............	large	Eur.	II. II. 2. 1.	Autumn	good	
Cloud....................		South	I. I. 2. 2.	....	....	
Cluster..................	small	?	I. I. 1. 2.	Winter	good	
Cluster Pearmain......	med.	Ind.	III. I. 2. 2. / I. I. 2. 2.	Autumn	v. good	589
Clyde Beauty........	large	N. Y.	IV. II. 2. 2.	Autumn	good	694
Codling Keswick, Synonym of Keswick.						
Coe......................			....	....	....	
Coggswell............	large	Mass?	III. I. 2. 2.	Autumn	v. good	589
Cole.....................	large	Engl.	III. II. 2. 2.	Summ'r	poor	
Cole's Quince.............	med.	Mass?	III. II. 2. 1. / IV. II. 2. 1.	Autumn	good	
Columbia................			....	....	....	
Columbian Russet.....	small	Sou.?	III. I. 2. 3.	Winter	v. good	622
Columbus Red............	med.		III. I. 2. 2.	L. Wint.	good	
Colvert..............	large	N. Y.?	I. I. 2. 2.	Autumn	good ?	427
Companion...............		South	I. I. 2. 1.	....	....	
Conant's Red.........	med.	?	I. I. 1. 2.	Winter	good	393
Congress................			....	....	....	
Connett Sweet........	med.	Ind. ?	I. I. 1. 2.	Winter	good	394
Conrad's Eating..........		?	I. I. 2. 2.	....	....	
Conway..................	med.	?	I. II. 2. 1.	Winter	good	
Cook's Favorite..........	med.	Ind.	II. II. 2. 1.	Summ'r	good	
Cook's Greening..........	large		III. I. 2. 1.	Winter	good ?	
Cook's Red...............			II. II. 2. 1.	....	....	
Cooper...............	large	?	I. I. 2. 2.	Autumn	best	428
Cooper's Early White........	small	?	I. I. 2. 1.	Summ'r	good	

Name.	Size.	Orig.	Class.	Season.	Quality.	P.
Cooper's Market.......	med.	?	{ II. I. 2. 2. / IV. I. 2. 2. }	Winter	good	518
Cooper's Redling, Synonym of Cooper's Market.						
Cooper's Russeting...........	small	N. Y.	IV. I. 2. 3.	Winter	good	
Cope's Red Sweet...........	small	Ohio	IV. I. 1. 2.	Winter	good	
Cope's Sweet...............	small	Ohio	III. I. 1. 2.	Winter	good ?	
Cornell's Fancy.............	med.	Penn.	IV. I. 2. 2.	Autumn	good	
Cornfield..................		South	I. I. 2. 1.	Winter	....	
Cornfield...............	med.	Ohio	IV. I. 2. 2.	Winter	good ?	401
Cornish Aromatic......	med.	Engl.	III. I. 2. 1.	Winter	v. good	569
Cornish Gilliflower....	med.	Engl.	II. II. 2. 2.	Winter	good	
Corse's Favorite.............			I. I. 2. 1.			
Cos	large	N. Y.	III. II. 2. 2.	Winter	good	
Court of Wyck........	small	Engl.	{ III. I. 2. 3. / III. I. 2. 1. }	Winter	good ?	623
Court Pendu Plat.............	med.	Eur.	I. I. 2. 1.	Winter	"gd."	
Crackling............	large	Ohio	{ I. I. 2. 1. / III. II. 2. 1. }	Autumn	good	401
Cranberry Pippin......	large	N. Y.	{ I. I. 2. 1. / I. II. 2. 1. }	Winter	good ?	409
Cranberry Russet......	med.	Ohio	I. II. 2. 3.	Winter	good ?	491
Crawford's Keeper.....	med.	Sou. ?	IV. I. 2. 1.	Winter	"gd."	667
Creighton	small	Ohio	I. I. 2. 2.	Summ'r	good	
Crib.....................	small	Ohio	III. I. 2. 2.	Winter	poor ?	
Crooked Limb, Synonym of Watson's Dumpling.						
Cropsey's Favorite.....	med.	Ills.	{ III. I. 2. 2. / IV. I. 2. 2. }	Winter	good	590
Crow's Egg................	med.	Ind.	IV. II. 1. 2.	Winter	poor ?	
Crow's Egg................		South				
Crownest..............	large	Ohio	III. I. 2. 3.	Winter	good	694
Cullasaga....	med.	S. C.	III. I. 1. 2.	Winter	good	559
Cullawhee.................		South	III. II. 2. 2.			
Culloden.................		South	II. I. 2. 2.			
Culp..................	large	Ohio	III. II. 2. 1.	E.Wint.	good ?	480
Cumberland Spice......	large	N. J.	IV. I. 2. 1.	Winter	good	668
Curtis Greening........	med.	Ills.	IV. I. 2. 1.	Winter	good	666
Curtis Pippin.............	med.	Ills.	IV. I. 2. 2.	Winter	good	
Curtis Sweet...............	large	?	IV. II. 1. 2.	Autumn	good	
Dahlonega.................		Ga.	IV. I. 2. 2.			
Dalton................		Ga.	I. I. 2. 1.	Summ'r	good	402
Dana.................	small	?	I. II. 2. 2.	Summ'r	good	487
Daniel................	med.	?	III. I. 2. 2.	Autumn	v. good	591
Dan. Pearma'n........	med.	Ind.	III. I. 2. 2.	Winter	good	591
Danvers Wint. Sweet	large	Mass.	III. I. 1. 1.	Winter	good ?	550
Darby Pippin..............	large	Penn.	IV. I. 2. 2.	Winter	....	
Darlington.................		Penn?	III. I. 2. 3.			
Davis....................	small	Mich.	IV. I. 2. 2.	Winter	good	
Davis' Ortley.............	large	Ind.	IV. I. 2. 1.	Winter	good	
Davis		Miss.				
Dawson's Cluster.......	med.	Ohio	IV. I. 2. 1.	Winter	good	669
Day..................	large	Ind.	III. I. 2. 2.	Winter	good ?	591
Deacon's Pryor......	large	Ky.	III. II. 2. 3.	Winter	good	
Deal's Red...	med.	(Ind)	I. I. 2. 2.	Winter	good ?	
Dean's Sweeting.............	med.	(Ind.)	III. I. 2. 2.	Winter	good	
Defiance..................	large	Ga.	{ II. II. 2. 2. / II. II. 1. 2. }	Summ'r	good	
Degruchy.................		South	....	.... ..		
Delasure		South	III. I. 2. 1.			
Delight................	med.	Ohio	I. II. 1. 1.	Winter	good	473
Democrat..............	med.	(O.)	II. I. 2. 1.	E.Wint.	good	505
Demurry..................		South				
Derry Nonsuch..............	large	N. H.	IV. II. 2. 2.	L.Wint.	good	
Detroit Black..........	large	Can. ?	II. II. 2. 1.	Autumn	good ?	633
Detroit Red................	large	Can. ?	II. II. 2. 1.	Autumn	good ?	
Devonshire Quarrenden......	small	Engl.	I. I. 2. 2.	Autumn	good ?	

Name.	Size.	Orig.	Class.	Season.	Quality.	P.
Dewees	med.	Ind.	II. II. 2. 2.	E.Wint.	good ?	
Dewitt. Synonym of Doctor Dewitt.						
Dick's Seedling		?	III. I. 2. 2.			
Dillaways		Ohio				
Dillingham	med.	Ohio	III. I. 1. 1.	Spring	good	383
Disharoon	med.	Ga.	II. I. 1. 2. / III. I. 2. 1.	E.Wint.	good	
Doctor Dewitt	large	Penn.	I. I. 2. 2.	E.Wint.	good	
Doct. Fulcher	med.	Ky.	III. I. 2. 2.	Winter	good	592
Doct. Watson	med.	Penn?	I. I. 2. 2.	E.Wint.	v. good	429
Dodge's Crimson, Synonym of Ashmore ?						
Dodge's Early	med.	?	III. I. 2. 2.	Summ'r	good	
Dol's Red	med.	Ohio	III. I. 2. 2.	Winter	good	
Domine	large	N. Y.	I. I. 2. 2.	Winter	v. good	430
Downing's Paragon	large	Ills.	IV. I. 1. 1.	Winter	good	658
Downton Pippin	small	Engl.	III. I. 2. 1.	Autumn	good	
Drap d'Or	large	Eur.	III. II. 2. 1. / II. II. 2. 1.	Autumn	v. good	638
Drumore						
Duchess of Oldenburg	large	Eur.	I. I. 2. 2. / III. I. 2. 2.	Summ'r	good	431
Duckett	large	South	I. I. 2. 1.	Autumn	good	
Duffield Pippin	large	Penn.	III. I. 2. 1.	Winter	v. good	570
Duling Sweet						
Dumelow	large	Engl.	III. I. 2. 1.	Winter	good	
Dumpling, Synonym of Watson's Dumpling.						
Dunlevy		(O.)				
Durable Keeper	large	(Ind.)	III. I. 2. 2.	Spring	poor ?	
Durham Winter Pearmain			III. I. 1. 1.			
Dutch Codling	large	Eur.	III. II. 2. 1.	Autumn	good ?	
Dutch Miguonne	large	Eur.	III. I. 2. 2.	Autumn	good ?	593
Dyer	large	Fr.	III. II. 2. 1.	Autumn	best	639
Early Chandler	small	?	I. I. 2. 1.	Summ'r	good	
Early Cider	med.	?	II. I. 2. 2.	Summ'r	good...	
Early George, Synonym of George.						
Early Harvest	large	N. Y.	I. I. 2. 1.	Summ'r	best	408
Early Joe	med.	N. Y.	II. I. 2. 2. / I. I. 2. 2.	Summ'r	best	513
Early Longstem	small	?	IV. II. 2. 1.	Summ'r	good ?	
Early Nonsuch	small	?	III. I. 2. 2.	Summ'r	good	
Early Pennock	large	Am.	III. I. 2. 2. / II. I. 2. 2.	Summ'r	good ?	594
Early Greening	med.	Penn.	I. I. 2. 2.	Summ'r		
Early Red Margaret	med.	Engl.	III. II. 2. 2. / II. II. 2. 2.	Summ'r	good	
Early Redstreak, Synonym of Harvest Redstreak.						
Early Red Stripe, Synonym of Red Stripe.						
Early Ripe		Penn?		Summ'r		
Early Strawberry	med.	N. Y.	II. I. 2. 2.	Summ'r	v. good	514
Early York			III. II. 2. 2.	Summ'r		
Easter Pippin	med.	Engl.	I. I. 2. 1.	Spring	good ?	
Eaton	med.	N. Y.	IV. II. 2. 2.	Winter	good	
Egg Top	med.	?	IV. II. 2. 2.	E.Wint.	poor ?	
Egypt Red Summer	med.	(Ills.)	III. I. 2. 2.	Summ'r	good ?	
Egypt Red Winter	med.	(Ills.)	I. I. 2. 2.	Winter	good ?	
Egyptian Russet	med.	(Ills.)	II. I. 2. 3.	Winter	v. good	523
Elarkee		South	II. I. 2. 1.			
Eldorado		South	III. I. 2. 1.			
Elgin Pippin	large	Miss.	II. I. 2. 2.	Winter	v. good	
Hicke's Winter	med.	Penn.	I. I. 1. 2.	Winter	good ?	
Ellis	small	Conn.	III. I. 2. 2.	Spring	good ?	
Ellwill's Late		South		Winter		
Emersine Sweet	med.	Ohio?	I. I. 1. 1.	Winter	good ?	
Emperor, see Alexander.						

Name.	Size.	Orig.	Class.	Season.	Quality.	P.
Emperor................	large	(Ill.)	I. II. 2. 2.	Winter	good	
Emperor. (Dickson's)........	.....	Scotl.	I. II. 2. 2.			
Ene's Winter Sweet...	med.	Ky.	I. I. 1. 1.	Winter	good	364
Enfield.................			III. I. 2. 2.			
Enfield Pearmain...........	small	?	III. I. 1. 2.	Winter	good	
English Codling............	large	Engl.	III. I. 2. 1.	Autumn	good	
English Golden Pippin......	.....	Engl.	III I. 2. 1	Winter	good	
Engl. Golden Russet..	med.	Engl?	III. I. 2. 3.	Winter	v. good	624
English Pearmain..........	large	?	I. I. 2. 2.	Autumn	good	
English Redstreak.........	large	(Ind.)	I. I. 2. 2.	Winter	v. good	
English Redstreak........	large	Engl.	III. I. 2. 2.	Winter	good ?	
English Red Sweeting......	.....	Engl.	IV. I. 1. 2.			
English Russet........	med.	Engl?	III. I. 2. 3.	Winter	poor	625
English Sweeting..........	.....	Engl.	II. I. 1. 2.			
Epse Sweeting, Synonym of Danvers.						
Epsy....................	small	Vt.	II. I. 1. 1.	Winter	good	
Equinetelee............	.....	Ga. ?	{ I. I. 2. 2. / I. II. 2. 2. }	E. Wint.	....	432
Ernst's Pippin, Synonym of Ohio Pippin.						
Esopus Spitzenberg...	med.	N. Y.	II. II. 2. 2.	Winter	best	639
Esten...................	large	R. I.	IV. II. 2. 1.	Autumn	good	
Eustis, Synonym of Ben.						
Evening Party..........	med.	Penn.	{ I. II. 2. 2. / I. I. 2. 2. }	Winter	best	433
Ewalt................	large	Penn.	III. II. 2. 1.	Winter	good ?	640
Excel...................	large	Conn.	I. II. 2. 2.	Winter	good	
Exquisite.....	small	Ills.	{ I. I. 1. 2. / I. I. 2. 2. }	Autumn	v. good	
Fairbanks.............	med.	Me.	{ I. I. 2. 2. / II. I. 2. 2. }	Autumn	good	
Fair Maid............	.....	Penn.	I. I. 2. 1.	....	....	
Fair Winter.............	.....	.....	III. I. 2. 2.			
Falder.............	.....	Penn.	IV. I. 2. 2.	Winter	....	
Fallawater............	large	Penn.	II. I. 1. 1.	Winter	poor ?	495
Fall Butter............	large	Ind.	IV. I. 2. 2.	Autumn	good	677
Fall Chandler........	.....	.....	II. II. 2. 1.	Autumn	....	
Fall Geneting..........	large	Conn.	II. II. 2. 1.	Autumn	good	533
Fall Greening.............	.....	?	I. II. 2. 1.	Autumn	....	
Fall Harvey............	large	Mass.	I. II. 2. 1.	Autumn	good	482
Fall Orange............	large	Mass.	III. II. 2. 1.	Autumn	good	
Fall Pearmain..........	large	Conn.	II. I. 2. 1.	Autumn	good	
Fall Pippin......	large	Am.	III. I. 2. 1.	Autumn	best	571
Fall Pippin..............	large	(Ky.)	{ IV. II. 2. 1. / III. II. 2. 1. }	Autumn	good	
Fall Queen............	large	South	{ II. I. 2. 2. / IV. I. 2. 1. }	Autumn	v. good	
Fall Seek-no-further........	large	(Con.)	I. I. 2. 2.	Autumn	good	
Fall Swaar of West...	large	?	{ III. I. 2. 1 / III. II. 2. 1 }	Autumn	good	572
Fall Vandervere...........	large	(O.)	{ I. I. 2. 2. / III. I. 2. 2. }	Autumn	good	
Fall Wine............	med.	Am.	I. I. 2. 2.	Autumn	best	434
Fall Winesap............	med.	.....	III. I. 2. 2.	Autumn	good ?	
Fameuse.........	med.	Can.-	III. I. 2. 2.	Autumn	v. good	595
Family................	.....	South	II. I. 2. 2.	....	....	515
Fancher...........	large	South	III. I. 1. 1.	Autumn	good	550
Farley Red........	small	Ky.	{ III. I. 2. 2. / IV. II. 2. 2. }	Winter	good	595
Farrer's Summer............	.....	.....	III. II. 2. 1.	Summ'r	....	
Father Abraham............	med.	Va.	{ I. I. 2. 2. / III. I. 2. 2. }	Spring	good	
Faust.....	small	N. C.	{ I. I. 2. 1. / III. I. 2. 1. }	Spring	v. good	404
Favorite....................	small	Ky.	III. I. 2. 2.	E. Wint.	good	
Fay's Russet................	small	Vt.	II. I. 2. 3.	Spring	good	

Name.	Size.	Orig.	Class.	Season.	Quality.	P.
Fay's Sweet.............			I. I. 1. 1.			
Federal.............	large	Ohio?	III. I. 2. 2.	Winter	good?	
Felt's Strawberry.............	large	N. Y.	II. I. 2. 2.	Summ'r	"v.gd."	
Fenley.............	large	Ky.	I. I. 2. 1.	Summ'r	good	405
Fenouillet Rouge.............	med.	Fr. ?	III. I. 2. 1.	Autumn	....	
Fenton Sweet, Synonym of Trumbull Sweet.						
Ferdinand.............	large	Va.	II. II. 2. 1.	Winter	good?	538
Fink.............	small	Ohio	I. I. 2. 1.	Spring	good?	406
Fisk's.............	med.	N. H.	I. I. 1. 2.	Autumn	good	
Flamingo.............		South	III. I. 1. 2.			
Flat Sweet.............	large	Am.	I. II. 1. 1.	Winter	good	
Fleiner.............	large	Eur.	IV. I. 2. 1.	Summ'r	poor	
Flora.............	large	South	I. I. 2. 2.	Summ'r	....	
Flower of Kent.............	large	Engl.	III. II. 2. 2.	Winter	good?	
Flushing Spitzenberg	med.	L. Isd	II. I. 2. 2.	Winter	good	515
Focht.............	large	Penn.	I. II. 2. 1.	E. Wint.	good	
Ford.............	large	N. Y.	III. I. 2. 1.	E. Wint.	good	
Forest Sweet.............	med.	Ohio	I. I. 1. 1.	Winter	good?	
Fort Meigs.............	med.	Ohio	I. I. 2. 2	Winter	good	
Fort Miami.............	med.	Ohio	II. II. 2. 3 / IV. I. 2. 3.	Winter	v. good	547
Foster.............	med.	Ohio	I. I. 2. 1.	Autumn	good	
Foundling.............	large	Mass.	III. II. 2. 2. / I. II. 2. 2.	Autumn	good	658
Fourth of July, supposed Synonym of Tetofski.						
Foxite.............	large	(Ind.)	III. I. 2. 1.	Autumn	good?	
Frank or Chenango...	large	N. Y.	IV. II. 2. 2.	Autumn	good	695
Franklin.............			I. I. 1. 2. / IV. I. 2. 1.			
Franklin Golden.......	large	Am.	II. I. 2. 1.	Winter	good	670
Freeze and Thaw.............		Penn?	II. I. 2. 2.	Winter	....	
French.............		(Pa.)	III. I. 2. 1.			
French Pippin.............	large	(Pa. ?)	IV. II. 2. 1.	Winter	good	
French Pippin.............	large	N. J.	I. I. 2. 1.	E. Wint.	good	
French Pippin.............	large	(O.)	I. II. 2. 1.	E. Wint.	v. good	
French Royal.............	med.	?	IV. I. 2. 1.	Winter	poor	
French's Sweet.............	large	Mass.	III. I. 1. 1.	Autumn	good	
Fronclin.............	med.	Penn.	III. I. 2. 2.	....	good	
Fuller.............		Sou. ?	I. II. 2. 1.			
Fulton.............	large	Ills.	I. I. 2. 1.	Winter	good	406
Fulton Strawberry.............	med.	Ills.	III. I. 2. 2.	E. Wint.	good	
Gabriel.............	med.	?	III. I. 2. 2.	Autumn	v. good	515
Gabriel.............		South	II. I. 2. 2.			
Gallup's Russet.............	large	(O.)	II. I. 2. 3.	Winter	poor	
Galusha.............	med.	(Ills.)	III. I. 2. 1.	Winter	good?	
Garden.............	large	(O.)	I. I. 2. 2.	Autumn	v. good	435
Garden Royal.............	small	Mass.	III. I. 2. 2.	Autumn	good	
Garretson's Early.....	small	N. J.	I. II. 2. 1. / III. II. 2. 1.	Summ'r	good	482
Gatch.............	med.	Ohio.	II. I. 2. 2.	Winter	good?	
Genesee Chief.........	large	N. Y.	IV. II. 2. 1.	Summ'r	poor	686
George.............	med.	Ohio	I. I. 2. 1.	Summ'r	good	
Germanite, Synonym of Jarminite.						
Gewiss Good.............	med.	Penn.	I. I. 2. 1. / III. I. 2. 1.	Winter	good	
Giles.............	med.	Conn.	II. I. 2. 2.	Autumn	"v.gd."	
Gillett's Profusion.............		Ohio	....	....	....	
Gillett's Sweet Bellflower.....		Ohio	....	....	....	
Gillett's Winesap....		Ohio	....	....	....	
Gilpin.............	med.	Va.	III. I. 1. 2.	Spring	good?	559
Gilpin Seedling.............	med.	Ills.	III. I. 2. 2.	Spring	good?	
Giltner's.............	med.	?	I. I. 2. 2.	Autumn	good	
Gladney Red.............		South	II. II. 2. 1.	....	....	
Glendale.............	large	Ohio?	III. I. 2. 2.	Autumn	good	596
Gloria Mundi, Synonym of Mammoth Pippin.						

Name.	Size.	Orig.	Class.	Season.	Quality.	P.
Gloucester White	med.	Va.	III. I. 2. 1.	Autumn	good	573
Goff	large	Ohio	III. II. 2. 2.	Autumn	good	
Golay	med.	Ind.	I. I. 2. 2. / II. I. 2. 2.	Winter	good	435
Golden Ball	large	Conn.	III. II. 2. 1. / III. I. 2. 1.	Winter	good	640
Golden Drop, Synonym of Court of Wyck.						
Golden Drop		South		Winter		
Golden Harvey	small	Engl.	III. II. 2. 3.	Winter	good ?	658
Golden Pearmain	small	?	III. I. 2. 3.	Winter	good	
Golden Pearmain	small	(Ky.)	III. I. 2. 1. or 3.	Winter	v. good	635
Golden Pippin	small	Eng. ?	III. I. 2. 1.	Winter	good ?	
Golden Pippin—American		Am.	I. II. 2. 1. / III. II. 2. 1.	Winter	good	
Golden Reinette	small	Eur.	I. I. 2. 2. / III. I. 2. 2.	Winter	good ?	
Golden Rose		Sou. ?		Winter		
Golden Russet	med.	?	III. I. 2. 3.	Winter	good ?	
Golden Russet of Mass.	med.	Mass.	III. I. 2. 3.	Winter	good	
Golden Seedling	large.	Mo.	I. I. 2. 1.	Winter	good	407
Golden Sweet	large	Conn.	III. I. 1. 1.	Summ'r	good	551
Golden Winter Sweet		(N.Y.)	I. I. 1. 1.	Winter		
Good Russet	med.	(O.)	III. I. 2. 3.	Winter	poor ?	
Gordon's Seedling	med.	N. C.	II. I. 2. 2.	Winter	good	
Governor	large	Vt.	III. I. 2. 1.	E.Wint.	good	
Gov. Morrow	med.	Ohio	I. I. 2. 2.	Winter	good	
Grandfather	large	N. E.	I. II. 2. 2. / III. II. 2. 2.	Autumn	good ?	
Grand Sachem. Synonym of Black Detroit.						
Granite Beauty	large	Mass.	IV. II. 2. 2.	Winter	good	
Granniwinkle	med.	N. J.	I. I. 1. 2.	E.Wint.	good	394
Gravenstein	large	Germ.	I. II. 2. 2.	Summ'r	v. good	437
Great Keeper			I. I. 2. 3.	Spring		
Green Cheese	med.	Tenn.	I. I. 2. 1.	Winter	good ?	
Green's Choice	med.	Penn.	III. I. 2. 2.	Summ'r	good	
Green Crank	large	South	I. I. 2. 1. / III. I. 2. 1.	Winter	good	408
Green Domine	med.	Pen. ?	I. I. 1. 2.	Winter	good ?	
Green Everlasting, Synonym of American Pippin.						
Green Flat		?	I. I. 2. 1.			
Green Flour		Penn.	II. I. 2. 1.			
Green Gilliflower			II. I. 1. 1.			
Green Horse		South				
Green Mountain Pippin	med.	Ga.	I. I. 2. 1. / III. I. 2. 1.	Winter	good	
Green Newtown Pippin	large	L. Is.	III. I. 2. 1.	Winter	v. good	
Green Pearmain		Sou. ?	I. I. 2. 1.	Winter	good	
Green Pippin	large	(Ind.)	III. I. 2. 1.	Winter	good	
Green Russet	large	N. C.	III. I. 2. 3.	Winter		636
Green Seek-no-further	large	L. Is.	II. I. 2. 1.	Autumn	good	
Green Skin	med.	N. C.	I. I. 2. 1.	E.Wint.	good	
Green Sweet	med.	Mass?	I. I. 1. 1.	Spring	good	555
Green Winter	large	(O.)	II. I. 1. 1.	Winter	v. good	
Gregson, Synonym of Catlin.						
Greyhouse	med.	?	III. I. 2. 2.	Winter	poor ?	
Griest's Favorite		Penn.	III. I. 2. 2.			
Griffith. Synonym of Clay Bank.						
Grimes' Golden	med.	Va.	IV. I. 2. 1.	Winter	best	670
Grosh		Penn.	I. I. 2. 2.			
Grosser Erdbeere	med.	Eur.	III. I. 2. 2.	Summ'r	good ?	
Gullett						
Gully		N. C.				
Gully, Synonym of Mangum.						
Gully	small	Penn.			good	
Hagloe	large	N. J.	III. I. 2. 2.	Summ'r	good	586

Name.	Size.	Orig.	Class.	Season.	Quality.	P.
Hagloe Crab	small	Engl.	IV. II. 2. 1.	Wint. ?	good ?	
Hague	large	Ind.	IV. I. 2. 2. / III. I. 2. 2.	Winter	good	677
Hain	large	Penn. N. C.?	III. I. 1. 2.	Winter	good	
Halleck's Favorite	med.	(O.)	I. I. 2. 1.	Autumn	good ?	
Halliday		Va.	I. I. 1. 1.	Winter		
Hall	small	N. C.	III. I. 1. 2.	Winter	best ?	560
Hamilton		South	III. II. 2. 2.			
Hamilton's	large	(Ind.)	II. I. 2. 1.	Winter	good	
Hampton's Honey	med.	Ohio	I. I. 1. 1.	Winter	good	
Hampton's Red Winter Sweet	med.	Ohio	I. II. 1. 2.	Winter	good ?	
Hampton's Russet	small	Ohio	III. I. 2. 3. / I. I. 2. 3.	Winter	good ?	626
Hannah	large	?	III. I. 2. 2. / II. II. 2. 2.	Winter	good	597
Harnish	med.	Penn.	IV. II. 1. 2.	Autumn	good ?	685
Harper Sweet	med.	Ills.	I. I. 1. 2.	Autumn	good	
Harris	large	N. C.?	I. II. 2. 1.	E. Wint.	good	482
Harrison	med.	N. J.	II. II. 2. 1.	Winter	good	534
Hartford Sweet	med.	Conn.	I. I. 1. 2. / III. I. 1. 2.	Winter	good	
Harvest Redstreak	large	Penn.	I. I. 2. 2.	Summ'r	good ?	436
Haskell Sweet	large	Mass.	I. I. 1. 1.	Summ'r	good	385
Hawley	large	N. Y.	I. I. 2. 1. / II. II. 2. 1.	Summ'r	best	410
Hawthornden	large	Scotl.	I. I. 2. 1.	Autumn	good	410
Hayboys	large	(O.)	I. I. 1. 1.	Summ'r	good	385
Hays, Synonym of Wine.						
Hector	large	Penn.	IV. I. 2. 2.	Winter	"v.gd."	
Heister		Penn.				
Helen's Favorite	med.	Ohio	III. I. 2. 2.	Winter	"v.gd."	
Hemphill	med. ?	N. C.	III. I. 2. 1.	Winter	good	
Henley		Sou. ?	II. I. 1. 1.			
Henrick Sweet	med.		I. I. 1. 2.	Winter	good ?	
Henry	large	Vt.	II. II. 2. 1.	E. Wint.	good	
Henwood	large	Ind.	IV. I. 2. 1.	Winter	v. good	687
Hepler	med.	Penn.	I. I. 2. 1.	Winter	good ?	
Herefordshire Pearm.	med.	Engl.	I. I. 2. 2.	Winter	best ?	598
Herman	med.	Penn.	IV. I. 2. 2. / II. I. 2. 2.	Winter	good	678
Hersey Keeper			III. I. 2. 2.			
Hess	med.	Penn.	III. I. 2. 2.	Winter	"v.gd."	
Hewes' Crab	small	Va.	III. I. 2. 2.	Winter	best	599
Hick's		Penn.				
Higby Sweet	med.	Ohio	III. I. 1. 1. / II. I. 1. 1.	Autumn	good	552
Highlander	med.	Vt.	I. I. 2. 2.	Autumn	good	
Hightop, (Jones)	large	Ind.	I. I. 2. 2.	Winter	good	437
Hightop Sweet	small	Con. ?	III. I. 1. 1.	Summ'r	good	553
Hiker's	med.	Ky.	I. I. 2. 2. / III. I. 2. 2.	Spring	good	
Hill's Favorite	med.	Mass.	III. II. 2. 2.	Summ'r	good	
Hilton	large	N. Y.	III. I. 2. 1.	Autumn	good	
Hinesley	large	(Ind.)	I. I. 1. 2.	Winter	poor	
Hoary Morning	large	Engl.	I. I. 2. 2.	E. Wint.	good ?	
Hockett Sweet		South	III. I. 2. 2.			
Hocking	large	?	I. I. 2. 2.	Summ'r	good ?	438
Hodge's Limbertwig	med.	West?	II. I. 2. 2.	Winter	good	
Hog Island Sweet	med.	N. Y.	I. I. 1. 1.	Autumn	good	
Hog Snout	med.	N. C.	III. I. 2. 2.	Winter	good ?	
Holland Pippin	large	Eur. ?	II. I. 2. 1. / III. I. 2. 1.	Autumn	good ?	506
Holland's Red Winter		(O.)		Winter		
Holland's Sweet	med.		II. I. 1. 2.			

31

Name.	Size.	Orig.	Class.	Season.	Quality.	P.
Hollow Crown	med.	?	I. I. 2. 2.	E.Wint.	good	
Holly		South	III. I. 1. 2.			
Holman, ? Synonym of Nickajack.						
Holston Sweet	med.	?	III. I. 1. 1.	Winter	good	553
Hommacher	large	Penn.	III. I. 2. 1.	Winter	good	
Homony	large	South	II. I. 2. 2. / IV. II. 2. 2.	Summ'r	good	
Hovey		?	I. I. 1. 2.			
Honey		Penn.	IV. I. 1. 1.			659
Honey Greening	large	West.	IV. II. 1. 1.	Winter	good	
Honey Pippin			II. I. 1. 2.			
Honey Sweet	large	(O.)	III. I. 1. 1.	Winter	good	
Honiker		Penn.				
Hooker	med.	Conn.	II. I. 2. 2.	Winter	good ?	
Hoopbole	small	(O.)	III. I. 2. 2. / I. I. 2. 2.	Winter	good	
Hoops	med.	Penn.	I. I. 1. 2.	Spring	poor	
Hoosier	med.	Ind.	IV. I. 2. 2.	Winter	good	
Hoosier Red	med.	Ind.	III. I. 2. 1.	Winter	good ?	
Hoover	large	S. C.	II. I. 2. 1. / III. I. 2. 1.	Winter	good ?	
Hopkin's Red Cheek, Synonym of Monmouth Pippin.						
Hopper		South	II. I. 2. 2.			
Horn	med.	Ga.	I. II. 2. 2. / I. I. 2. 1.	Winter	good ?	
Hornet	large	Penn.		Autumn	good	
Horse	large	N. C.	III. I. 2. 1. / IV. II. 2. 1.	Autumn	good	573
Horton Sweet		(O.)				
Housnm Red	large	Penn.	IV. I. 2. 2. / IV. II. 2. 2.	E.Wint.	"v. gd."	
Howe's Russet		Mass.	I. II. 2. 3.			
Hoyle's Nonpareil		Sou. ?	I. II. 2. 2.			
Hubbardston	large	Mass.	III. I. 2. 2. / IV. I. 2. 2.	E.Wint.	v. good	600
Hubbardton	large	N. H.?	III. II. 2. 2.	Winter	good	
Hughes	large	Penn.	III. I. 2. 1.	Spring	good	
Hughes' Am. Golden Pippin	large	Am.	III. I. 2. 1.	Winter	v. good	
Hull Blossom	small	N. E.	III. II. 1. 2.	E.Wint	good	635
Hunge	large	N. C.	III. I. 2. 1.	Autumn	good ?	574
Hunt	med.	Ind.	I. I. 2. 2.	Winter	good	438
Hunter	med.	Penn.	III. I. 2. 2.	Autumn	good	
Hunter's Sweet		(O.)				
Huntsman Russet			II. I. 2. 3.			
Hunt's Russet	small	Mass.	II. I. 2. 3.	Winter	good	
Hurlbutt	med.	Conn.	I. I. 2. 2. / I. II. 2. 2.	E.Wint.	good	
Hutching's Seedling, Synonym of Sugar Loaf Pippin.						
Hyatt's Wonderful		Sou. ?	I. I. 2. 1.			
Ice Cream	med.	Ky.	I. I. 2. 1.	Autumn	good ?	
Illinois Greening	med.	Ills.	III. I. 2. 1.	Winter	good ?	
Illinois Pippin	med.	Ills.	III. I. 2. 1.	Winter	good ?	
Ills. Pumpkin Sweet	med.	Ills.	IV. II. 1. 2.	L.Wint.	good	685
Imperial Russet, Synonym of Spice Russet.						
Indiana Beauty	large	Ird.	IV. I. 2. 2.	E.Wint.	poor	678
Indiana Favorite	med.	Ind.	I. I. 2. 2.	Winter	good	438
Indian Prince	med.	Am.	III. I. 2. 1.	Autumn	good ?	
Indian Winter		South	II. I. 2. 1.			
Innes		?	I. I. 2. 2.			
Iola, Synonym of Equinetelee.						
Irish Peach	med.	Eur.	III. II. 2. 2.	Summ'r	good ?	
Iron		South	III. I. 2. 1.			
Iron Mountain	med.	Mo.	III. I. 2. 1.	Winter	good	
Iron Pippin	med.	Ky.	III. I. 2. 2.	Winter	poor	
Isom		?	I. I. 2. 1.			

Name.	Size.	Orig.	Class.	Season.	Quality.	P.
Jabez	med.	Conn.	III. I. 1. 1.	Winter	good	
Jackman's Sweet		Penn.	III. I. 1. 1.	E.Wint.		
Jackson		Ga.	I. I. 2. 1.			
Jackson	med.	Penn.	II. I. 2. 1. / III. I. 2. 2.	Winter	"v. gd."	
Jacksonian			III. II. 2. 2.			
Jarmivite	med.	Ohio	I. I. 2. 2. / II. I. 2. 2.	Winter	good	489
Jefferies	med.	Penn.	I. I. 2. 2.	Summ'r	best	440
Jefferson		Ky.	III. I. 2. 2.			
Jefferson County	med.	N. Y.	III. I. 2. 2.	Winter	good	
Jenkins	small	Penn.	III. I. 1. 1.	L.Wint.	"v. gd."	
Jersey Black	med.	N. J.?	III. II. 2. 2.	Winter	good	653
Jersey Greening	large	N. J.	III. I. 2. 1.	Winter	good?	
Jersey King	med.	(O.)	II. I. 2. 2.	Winter	good?	
Jersey Pippin	med.	Eur.	III. I. 2. 2.	Winter	good	
Jersey Sweet	med.	N. J.	I. I. 1. 2. / II. I. 1. 2.	Summ'r	v. good	395
Jewett's Best	large	Vt.	I. II. 2. 2.	Winter	good	
Jewett's Fine Red	med.	N. H.	I. II. 2. 2.	Winter	good	
John Carter	large	(Con.)	III. II. 2. 2.	Autumn	good?	
John Snepp's, Synonym of Snepps.						
John's Sweet	med.	N. H.	IV. I. 1. 2.	L.Wint.	good?	
Johnson	large	Conn.	III. I. 1. 2.	Summ'r	good	
Johnson's Sweet	med.	Ohio	IV. I. 1. 1.	Winter	good	
Jonathan	med.	N. Y.	IV. I. 2. 2.	Winter	best	679
Julien	med.	N. C.	II. I. 2. 2. / III. I. 2. 2.	Summ'r	good	
July	med.	(O.)	II. I. 2. 2.	Spring	poor	
Junaliska	large	N. C.	I. I. 2. 3. / I. I. 2. 1.			411
June	med.	Va.	II. I. 1. 1.	Summ'r		
Kaighn's Spitzenberg	large	N. J.	IV. I. 2. 2.	Winter	good	681
Kane	med.	Del.	I. I. 2. 1.	Autumn	v. good	411
Keepwell	small	(O.)	III. I. 1. 2.	Spring	poor?	
Keim	med.	Penn.	IV. I. 2. 1.	Winter	v. good	
Keiser	med.	Ohio	I. II. 2. 2. / III. I. 2. 2.	Winter	good?	488
Kelsey	med.	Penn.	I. I. 2. 1.	L.Wint.	v. good	
Kelter, or Boas		Penn.	I. I. 2. 1.			
Kennedy	large	Ga.	III. I. 2. 2.	Autumn	good?	
Kenrick's Autumn	large		III. I. 2. 2.	Autumn	good	
Kentish Fillbasket	large	Engl.	III. II. 2. 1.	Autumn	poor	
Kentucky	large	Ky.	IV. I. 2. 2.	Autumn	good	
Kentucky Cream	med.	Ky.	III. I. 2. 1.	Winter	good?	
Kentucky King		Ky.	II. I. 2. 2.	Winter		441
Kentucky Streak		(Ark)		Winter		
Kentucky Sweet	med.	Ky.?	II. I. 1. 2.	Winter	good	503
Kerry Pippin	med.	Irel'd	IV. I. 1. 1.	Autumn	good?	
Keswick Codling	large	Engl.	IV. II. 2. 1.	Autumn	good	688
Ketchum's Favorite	med.	Vt.	II. II. 2. 1.	Winter	good	
Kilham Hill	large	Mass.	III. II. 2. 2.	Autumn	poor	
King	large	(Ind.)	I. II. 2. 2.	Autumn	poor	
King—Newark	large	N. J.	IV. I. 2. 2.	Winter	v. good	
King of Pippins	med.	Engl.	I. I. 2. 2.	Autumn	poor	
King of Tompkins	large	N. Y.	III. II. 2. 2.	Winter	v. good	655
King Solomon		South				
Kingsley	med.	N. Y.	III. I. 2. 2.	Winter	good	
King's Winter						
King Tom	med.	Mo.	II. I. 2. 1.	Winter	poor	
Kinsey's Sweet						
Kirkbridge White	small	?	IV. I. 2. 1.	Summ'r	good	671
Kirke's Lord Nelson	large	Engl.	III. I. 2. 2.	Autumn	good?	
Kitchen	med.	(O.)	I. I. 2. 1.	Winter	poor	
Kitchmor's Favorite	med.	Ohio	II. II. 2. 1.	Winter	good?	

Name.	Size.	Orig.	Class.	Season.	Quality.	P.
Kittagesgee.................... .	....	South	I. I. 2. 1.			
Klaproth..................	med.	Penn.	I. I. 2. 2.	Summ'r	good	442
Knickerbocker.........	med.	N. Y.	III. II. 2. 1. / I. II. 2. 1.	Autumn	v. good	575
Knight's Red June..........	med.	Ky.	....	Summ'r	good	575
Knowles' Early........	small	Penn.	IV. I. 2. 2. / III. I. 2. 2.	Summ'r	good	682
Knox's Russet..........	small	Penn.	III I. 2. 3.	Winter	good	626
Kolb's Winter.................	......	Sou. ?	....	Winter	....	
Kratz............................		Penn.				
rowser.................	med.	Penn.	III. I. 2. 2. / II. I. 2. 2.	Winter	good	601
Lacker....................	med.	Penn.	I. I. 2. 2.	Winter	good	443
Ladies' Ear Drop........	med.	N. Y.	IV. II. 2. 1.	Winter	good ?	
Lady...................	small	Fr.	I. I. 2. 1.	Winter	good	411
Lady Blush....................	....	South	II. II. 2. 1.			
Lady Finger Pippin, Synonym of Red Winter Pippin.						
Lady Healy's Nonsuch........	med.	Engl.	I. I. 2. 1.	Autumn	good ?	
Lady Washington............	large	?	III. I. 2. 1.	Winter	good	
Ladies' Favorite. Synonym of Fall Queen.						
Ladies' Sweeting........	large	N. Y.	III. I. 1. 2	Winter	v. good	561
Lake.......................	small	Ohio	I. I. 2. 1.	Autumn	good ?	
Lake...................	med.	Ohio	II. I. 2. 2. / IV. I. 2. 2.	Autumn	good	
Lancaster.....................	......	?	III. I. 1. 1.	....		
Lancaster...................	......	(Va.)	IV. I. 2. 1.			
Lancaster Greening.........	med.	Penn.	I. I. 2. 1.	L.Wint.	good ?	
Lancaster Sweet........	med.	Ind.	I. I. 1. 1.	Autumn	good	386
Landon.....................	med.	Vt.	III. I. 2. 2.	L.Wint.	good	
Landrum...................	med.	Ga.	II. I. 1. 1.	Autumn	good ?	
Lane's Redstreak............	large	Ills.	II. I. 2. 2.	Autumn	good ?	
Lane's Sweet..............	med.	Mass.	I. I. 1. 1.	Winter	poor	
Langendorffer...............	......	Eur.	III. I. 2. 1.			
Lansingburgh..........	med.	N.Y.?	II. II. 2. 2.	Spring	poor	510
Lav. Striped Pearmain	large	Ky.	III. I. 2. 2.	Winter	good	601
Large Bough..........	large	Am.	II. I. 1. 1.	Summ'r	good	494
Late Chandler...............	med.	?	II. II. 2. 2. / III. II. 2. 2.	Winter	poor	
Late Golden Sweet............	med.	?	III. I. 1. 1.	Autumn	v. good	
Late Pound Sweet............	......					
Late Strawberry........	med.	N. Y.	II. II. 2. 2.	Autumn	best	510
Laurence....................	large	Ohio?	....	Winter	poor ?	
Lawrens' Greening............	......	South				
Ledge Sweet.................	large	N. H.	I. I. 1. 1. / III. I. 1. 1.	Spring	good ?	
Leland Spice...............	large	Mass.	III. I. 2. 2.	Autumn	good	
Leming Sweet................	large	Ohio	I. I. 1. 1.	Summ'r	good	
Lemon, Synonym of Rock Pippin.						
Lemon Pippin................	med.	Engl.	II. I. 2. 1.	Winter	poor	
Lester Sweet................	large	Mass.	I. I. 1. 1.	Winter	v. good	
Lever	......		II. I. 2. 2.			
Levett's	......	Ky.				
Lewis....................	med.	Ind.	III. I. 2. 2.	Summ'r	best	602
Lewis, (Ragan's)..........	med.	Ind.	I. I. 2. 2. / III. II. 2. 1.	Winter	v. good	443
Lewis Jones' Seedling.......	large	Ind.	I. I. 2. 2.	Winter	poor	
Lexington.....................	......		IV. II. 2. 2.			
Liberty...................	large	Ohio	III. I. 2. 2.	Spring	good	604
Limber Limb................	large	(O.)	III. I. 2. 1.	Winter	good	
Limbertwig.............	med.	South	II. I. 2. 2.	Spring	good	516
Limbertwig--Summer........	med.	South	I. I. 2. 2.	Summ'r	v. good	
Ling Sweet.................						
Linsley's Favorite............	....	Ohio	I. I. 2. 1.	....		
Linsley's Sweet............	....	Ohio	I. I. 1. 2.	Spring	....	
Lippencott's Early, Synonym of Summer Rose.						

Name.	Size.	Orig.	Class.	Season.	Quality.	P.
Lipsey's Russet	med.	Ohio	IV. I. 2. 3.	Winter	v. good	
Little Pearmain	small	Ohio	III. I. 2. 3.	Winter	v. good	
Locy	med.	?	III. I. 2. 2.	Winter	good ?	
Logan Berry	large	N. C.	I. I. 1. 1.	Autumn	good	
London Sweet	large	Ohio	I. I. 1. 1.	Winter	good	387
Long Island Pearmain	med.	L. Isl.	IV. I. 2. 2.	Winter	good	682
Long Island Pippin	large	N. Y.	III. I. 2. 1.	Winter	good	575
Long Island Russet	med.	L. Isl.	IV. I. 2. 3.	Winter	good	
L. I. Seek-no-further	large	L. Isl.	II. I. 2. 2.	Autumn	v. good	517
Long Limb	large	Ohio	III. I. 2. 2.	Winter	poor	
Long Stem	med.	Ky.	I. I. 2. 2.	Winter		
Long Stem, (L. Jones)	med.	Ind.	I. I. 2. 2.	Autumn	good	
Longstem	med.	Mass.	III. I. 2. 1.	Autumn	good	
Longstem	small	Penn.	III. I. 2. 2.	Winter	v. good	
Longville's Kernel	small	Engl.	IV. I. 2. 2.	Autumn	poor	
Lopside	med.	Ohio	I. I. 2. 2.	Winter	good	
Lorick's Cluster		Va.				
Loring's Sweet	med.	Mass.	I. I. 1. 2.	Winter	good	
Loudon	large	Va.	I. II. 2. 1.	Winter	v. good	483
London Pippin, Synonym of Loudon.						
Loure Queen	large	Ohio ?	I. I. 2. 2.	Winter	good	
Lovett's Sweet	med.	Mass.	II. I. 1. 1.	Winter	good ?	
Lowell	large	Am.	III. II. 2. 1. / III. II. 2. 1.	Autumn	v. good	576
Lucombe's Seedling	large	Engl.	III. II. 2. 2.	Autumn	good ?	
Lyman's P'pkin Swt.	v. lar.	Conn.	II. II. 1. 1. / III. II. 1. 1.	E. Wint.	good	527
Lynn	med.	(Ky.)	I. I. 2. 2.	Winter	good	
Lyscom	large	Mass.	III. I. 2. 2.	Autumn	good	605
Macomber	med.	Me.	I. II. 2. 2.	Winter	good ?	
Madison Red		?	I. I. 2. 2.			
Magnolia	med.	Mass.	I. I. 2. 2.	Autumn	good ?	
Magnum Bonum, Synonym of Bonum.						
Maiden's Blush	large	N. J.	I. I. 2. 1.	Autumn	v. good	412
Maiden's Favorite	med.	N. Y.	IV. II. 2. 1.	Winter	good	
Major	large	Penn.	I. I. 2. 2.			
Malamuskeet	large	South	I. II. 2. 2.	Winter	good ?	
Male Carle	large	Eur.	I. I. 2. 1.	E. Wint.	good ?	
Mammoth June		South		Summ'r		
Mammoth Pippin	v. lar	Am.	III. II. 2. 1.	E. Wint.	poor	
Mangum	med.	Ala.	I. II. 2. 2.	Winter	v. good	488
Munomet	med.	Mass.	III. I. 1. 1.	Autumn	good	
Mansfield Russet	small	Mass.	IV. I. 1. 3.	L. Wint.	good ?	665
Margil	small	Engl	III. I. 2. 2.	Winter	good	605
Maria Bush	large	Penn.	III. I. 2. 2.	Autumn	good	
Market		Va.	III. I. 2. 2.			
Marks	med.	Penn.	III. I. 2. 2.	L. Wint.	v. good	
Marshall's Sweet Favorite		(O.)	II. I. 1. 2.	Winter		
Marston's Red Winter	large	N. H.	IV. I. 2. 2.	Winter	good	682
Mary Chester		South	I. I. 2. 2.			
Mary Moyer		South	I. I. 2. 2.			
Mary Womack	med.	Ky.	I. I. 1. 2.	Autumn	good ?	
Massey's Winter		South		Winter		
Matthew Stripe, Synonym of Lyscom.						
Maverick Sweet	large	S. C.	I. II. 1. 1. / III. I. 1. 1.	Winter	good	473
May, (of Myers)	med.	Va.	III. I. 1. 1. / IV. I. 1. 1.	Spring	good	558
Mayberry Seedling		Va. ?				
Maynard's No. 1		Ky.				
May Queen	small	(O.)	I. I. 2. 1.	Summ'r	good	
McAdow's June	small	(O.)	III. I. 2. 1. / II. I. 2. 2.	Summ'r	good	576
McAffee	large	South	III. I. 2. 2.	Winter	good ?	
McBride's Waxen			II. II. 1. 1.			

Name.	Size.	Orig.	Class.	Season.	Quality.	P.
McCloud's Family............	.....	South	.. ..	......	......	....
McCormack's................	large	Ohio	II. II. 2. 1.	Winter	good	
McDaniel	med.	Ohio	I. I. 2. 2.	Autumn	v. good	443
McDowell's Red............	.....	Va. ?	......	......	......	
McDowell's Sweet..........	.....	South	III. II. 1. 2.	......	......	
McHenry................	med.	Ohio	I. II. 2. 2.	Autumn	good	
McHenry's White..........	med.	Ohio	I. I. 2. 1.	E. Wint.	good?	
McKay's Sweeting............	.....	.....	......	......	......	
McKinley..............	large	Ind.	III. I. 2. 2.	Winter	v. good	606
McLean.......	.....	.....	III. I. 2. 2.	......	......	
McLelan	med.	Penn.	{ I. I. 1. 2. / III. I. 1. 2. }	Winter	good	
Meach......	large	Vt.	III. I. 2. 2.	Autumn / Winter	good?	606
Mead's Keeper............	.....	.....	......	......	......	
Mear's Seedling......	small	Ohio	I. II. 2. 1.	Winter	good	
Meister........	small	Penn.	III. I. 2. 2.	Autumn	v. good	
Melon	large	N. Y.	{ I. II. 2. 2. / II. II. 2. 2. }	Autumn	v. good	488
Melt in Mouth.	med.	Penn.	L. I. 2. 2.	Autumn	good	
Melville Sweet............	med.	Mass.	III. I. 1. 2.	Winter	good?	
Menagere	v. lar.	Eur.	I. I. 2. 1.	Winter	good?	
Merritt's Sweet............	med.	?	III. I. 2. 2.	Summ'r	good	
Methodist............	med.	Conn.	IV. I. 2. 2.	Autumn	good?	
Mexico	med.	Conn.	III. I. 2. 2.	Autumn	v. good	607
Michael Henry Pippin	med.	N. J.	III. I. 1. 1.	Winter	good	496
Michenor's Red Sweet........	med.	Ohio?	III. I. 1. 2.	Winter	good?	
Michigan Golden......	large	Mich?	{ III. I. 2. 1. / III. II. 2. 1. }	Winter	good	576
Michigan Winter Pippin......	large	Mich?	I. I. 2. 1.	Winter	good	
Middle................	med.	N. Y.	II. I. 2. 1.	Winter	v. good	507
Mifflin King............	small	Penn.	IV. I. 2. 2.	Winter	v. good	683
Milam	small	South	II. I. 1. 2.	Winter	good	503
Miller..............	large	Penn.	III. I. 2. 2.	Autumn	good	
Miller's Apple......	large	N. Y.	IV. I. 2. 2.	Autumn	good	
Miller's, Synonym of Powers.						
Milliken's Sweet..............	large	Ohio?	III. II. 1. 1.	Winter	good	
Milwood Green............	.....	.....	......	......	......	
Minister............	large	Mass.	IV. II. 2. 2.	Autumn	good?	695
Minkler............	med.	Ills.	I. I. 2. 2.	Winter	good?	444
Minkler's Molasses......	med.	Ills.	I. I. 1. 1.	Winter	good?	
Missouri Keeper........	small	Mo.	III. II. 2. 2.	Spring	good	656
Molasses................	small	(O.)	II. I. 1. 1.	Winter	good?	
Molasses	med.	N. C.	I. II. 1. 2.	L. Wint.	good	
Monarch..............	med.	(W.)	{ L. I. 2. 2. / II. II. 2. 2. }	Summ'r	good	
Monk's Favorite........	large	Ind.	III. I. 2. 2.	Autumn	good	607
Monmouth Pippin.....	large	N. J.	III. I. 2. 1.	Winter	v. good	577
Monroe............	.....	(O.)	......	......	......	
Monstrous Pippin, Synonym of Mammoth Pippin.						
Moore's Greening............	large	Conn.	III. I. 2. 1.	Winter	good	
Moore's Seedling............	large	Ohio	III. I. 2. 2.	Winter	v. good	
Moore's Sweeting	large	?	{ I. I. 1. 2. / III. I. 1. 2. }	Spring	good	396
Morgan White........	med.	Ills.?	III. II. 2. 1.	Winter	good	641
Morgan's Favorite............	.....	.....	......	......	......	
Morris..................	large	(Ills.)	IV. I. 2. 3.	Winter	good	
Morrison Red................	med.	Mass.	II. II. 2. 2.	Winter	good?	
Morton..............	large	Ohio	III. I. 1. 1.	Winter	good	554
Moseley Sweet......	.....	.....	I. I. 1. 2.	......	......	
Moses Wood................	med.	Me.	III. I. 2. 2.	Autumn	good	
Mote Sweet..........	large	Ohio	{ III. II. 1. 1. / II. II. 1. 1. }	Autumn	v. good	631
Mother	med.	Mass.	IV. I. 1. 2.	Autumn	v. good	663
Mountain Belle..............	.....	South	III. I. 2. 2.	......	......	
Mountaineer, Synonym of Mount Pleasant Sweet, or Weaver Sweet.						
Mountain Pippin, Synonym of Fallawater.						

Name.	Size.	Orig.	Class.	Season.	Quality.	P.
Mountain Sprout............	large	N. C.	II. II. 2. 1.	Autumn	good	
Mountain Sweet........	large	Penn.	I. I. 1. 1.	Winter	good	388
Mount Pleasant Sweet........	large	Ohio	I. II. 1. 1.	Autumn	good	
Mount Swaager.............	med.	Mass?	III. I. 2. 1.	Winter	poor	
Mouse....................	large	N. Y.	IV. I. 2. 1.		good ?	
Mrs. De Caradeuc......... ...		South	I. I. 2. 2.			
Mudd's Market............			II. I 2. 1.			
Mudd's No. 1................	large	Ills.	III. I. 2. 1.	Autumn	good	
Munson Sweet........	med.	Mass.	I. I. 1. 1. / IV. I. 1. 1.	E. Wint.	good ?	388
Murphy Red...............	large	Mass.	III. I. 2. 2. / II. I. 2. 2.	Autumn	good ?	
Musgrave's Cooper. Synonym of Western Beauty.						
Muskingum Keeper..........	med.	Ohio	I. I. 2. 2.	Spring	good?	
Muster.................	med.	Ind.	I. II. 2. 2.	Autumn	v. good	489
Myer's Nonpareil. Synonym of Ohio Nonpareil.						
Nantahalee.................	large	Ala.	II. II. 2. 1.	Summ'r	good	
Neat Russet................	small	(W.)	II. I. 2. 3.	Winter	good	
Ned......................		Penn.	....			
Ne Plus Ultra.............	v. lar.	Ga.	I. II. 2. 1.	Autumn	good	
Nequassa.................	large	N. C.	I. I. 1. 2.	Winter	good ?	
Neverfail (of Tenn.)........			II. I. 2. 2.			
Neverfail. Synonym of Rawle's Janet.						
Neversink.............	large	Penn.	III. I. 2. 2.	Winter	v. good	608
Newark King..........	large	N. J.	III. I. 2. 2.	Winter	v. good	608
Newark Pippin........	large	N. J.	IV. II. 2. 1.	Winter	v. good	690
Newcomer.................		(Va.)	I. I. 2. 1.			
New England Red..........	large	(Ky.)	III. I. 2. 2.	Autumn	good ?	
Newtown Pippin Gr.	large	L. Isl.	III. I. 2. 1.	Winter	best	578
Newtown Pippin Yell.	large	L. Isl.	III. II. 2. 1. / I. II. 2. 1.	Winter	best	649
Newtown Spitzenberg	large	L. Isl.	I. I. 2. 2.	Winter	best	445
Nickajack.............	large	N. C.	I. I. 2. 2. / III. I. 2. 2.	Winter	poor ?	445
Nix's Green Winter.........		Ga.	I. I. 2. 1.	Winter		
Noble.....................		(O.)	II. I. 2. 2.			
Nonpareil...........	small	(W.)	III. II. 2. 2. / II. II. 2. 2.	Autumn	good	656
Nonpareil—Old...........	small	Engl.	III. I. 2. 3.	Winter	good ?	
Nonpareil—Scarlet.........	med.	?	III. I. 2. 2.	Winter	good	
Nonsuch..................	med.	Engl.	I. I. 2. 2.	Winter	good ?	
Norfolk Beaufin..........	large	Engl.	I. I. 2. 2.	Winter	poor	
Northern Spy..........	large	N. Y.	II. II. 2. 2.	Spring	v. good	541
Northern Sweet........	f. med.	N. Y.	III. II. 1. 1.	Autumn	v. good	632
Norton's Melon, Synonym of Melon.						
Nutmeg..................	small	(Ind.)	II. I. 1. 2. / III. I. 1. 2.	Autumn	v. good	
Nyack Pippin..........	large	N. Y.	I. I. 2. 2.	Winter	good	446
Oats Harvest..............	small	Ohio	III. I. 2. 1.	Summ'r	good	
Oconee Greening...........	v. lar.	South	III. I. 2. 1. / I. I. 2. 1.		best	
Ogleby		Va.	III. I. 2. 1.			
Ohio Beauty, Synonym of Western Beauty.						
Ohio Nonpareil........	large	Ohio	I. I. 2. 2.	Autumn	v. good	447
Ohio Pippin..........	large	Ohio	I. II. 2. 1.	Winter	good	484
Ohio Redstreak...........	v. lar.	Ohio	I. I. 2. 2.	L. Wint.	good	
Ohio Winter..............	med.	(Ills.)	III. I. 2. 2.	L. Wint.	good	
Ohlinger..................		Penn.	III. I. 2. 1.			
Old Dapple..............	med.	?	II. I. 2. 2.	E. Wint.	poor	
Old English Codling..........	large	Engl.	IV. II. 2. 1.	Autumn	good ?	
Old Field................	med.	Conn.	I. I. 2. 1.	L. Wint.	good	
Old House................	med.	Penn.	I. I. 2. 1.	Winter	v. good	
Oneida Chief.............		N. Y.	....			
Orange, Synonym of Lowell.						

Name.	Size.	Orig.	Class.	Season.	Quality.	P.
Orange..........................	large	N. J.	I. I. 2. 1.	Autumn	good	
Orange..........................		Penn.	I. II. 2. 1.	......	......	
Orange..........................	large	Conn.	III. I. 2. 1.	E. Wint.	good	
Orange Sweet, Synonym of Golden Sweet.						
Orange Sweeting........	large	(Mas.)	III. I. 1. 3.	Winter	good ?	566
Orndorff.....................	med.	Ohio	III. II. 2. 2.	Autumn	v. good	
Orne's Early.................	large	Eur.	III. II. 2. 1.	Autumn	good	
Ortley......................	large	N. J.	IV. I. 2. 1.	Winter	v. good	673
Osborn's Rambo............	med.	Ind.	III. I. 2. 2.	Autumn	v. good	
Osburn Sweet...............		?	III. I. 1. 1.	......	......	
Osceola...................	med.	Ind.	I. I. 2. 1. / III. I. 2. 2.	Winter	v. good	448
Oslin........................	small	Scotl.	I. 1. 2. 1.	Summ'r	good	
Overman's Sweeting........	med	Ills.	II. I. 1. 2.	Winter	good	
Paper, Synonym of Champlain.						
Paradise Summer......	large	Penn.	III. I. 1. 1.	Summ'r	good	555
Paradise Winter.......	large	Penn.	III. I. 1. 1.	Winter	good	556
Parrot Reinette.............	large	Eur.	III. II. 2. 2.	Winter	good ?	
Patterson Sweet, Synonym of Bailey's Sweet.						
Patton....................	med.	Ala.	III. I. 2. 2.	Winter	v. good	610
Pawpaw......................	large	Mich.	III. I. 2. 2.	Winter	good ?	
Peach Pond Sweet.....	med.	N. Y.	I. II. 1. 2. / III. II. 1. 2.	Autumn	v. good	475
Pearmain Russet............	small	?	III. I. 2. 8.	Winter	v. good	
Pearson's Plate.............	small	Engl.	I. I. 1. 1.	Winter?	v. good?	
Peck's Pleasant.......	large	R. I.	III. II. 2. 1.	Winter	v. good	641
Pennington..................	med.	Engl.	I. II. 2. 1.	Winter	good ?	
Pennock..............	large	Penn.	I. I. 2. 2. / III. II. 2. 2.	Winter	poor	449
Pennsylvania Redstreak, Synonym of Wine.						
Pennsylvania Sweetg.	large	Pen. ?	IV. I. 1. 1.	Winter	poor	659
Penn. Vandervere.....	med.	Pen. ?	I. I. 2. 2.	Winter	good	449
Penn. Winesap........	med.	Penn.	I. II. 2. 2.	Winter	good	490
People's Choice.............	med.	Penn.	I. I. 2. 2. / III. I. 2. 2.	Winter	good	
Perkins	small	South	III. II. 2. 1.	Winter	good ?	
Perry Russet..........	med.	(Ills.)	I. I. 2. 3.	Winter	good	468
Peter........................	med.	(Mas.)	IV. I. 2. 1.	Summ'r	poor	
Petit Apl Noir,.............	small	Eur.	III. I. 2. 2.	Winter	good ?	
Pfeiffer.....................	small	Penn.	III. II. 2. 2.	Summ'r	?	
Phillippi....................	large	Penn.	I. I. 2. 1.	Winter	v. good	
Phillip's Sweet........	large	Ohio	II. II. 1. 2.	Winter	good ?	477
Pickard's Reserve.....	large	Ind.	I. I. 2. 1. / III. I. 2. 1.	Winter	v. good	413
Pickman.....................	med.	Mass.	I. I. 2. 1.	Winter	good ?	
Pie..........................	large	(O.)	IV. I. 2. 2.	Autumn	poor	
Pigeon Hill.................		Eur.	III. I. 2. 2.	......	......	
Pigeon Rouge...............	small	Eur.	II. I. 2. 2.	Autumn	good ?	
Pine Apple..................	small	(O.)	II. I. 2. 3.	Winter	good	
Pine Apple Russet..........	med.	Eur. ?	II. II. 2. 3.	Autumn	good ?	
Pine Strawberry............		South				
Pink Sweeting..............	small		III. I. 1. 2.	Autumn	good	
Pittsburgh Pippin..........	large	Penn.	I. I. 2. 1. / I. II. 2. 1.	Winter	good	
Polly Bright...........	large	Va.	II. I. 2. 2.	Autumn	good	517
Pomme Grise	small	Fr.?	I. I. 2. 3.	Winter	best	469
Pomme Royale........	large	Fr'ch	III. II. 2. 1. / II. II. 2. 1.	Autumn	v. good	639
Pomme Water........	med.	?	III. I. 2. 2.	Autumn	good	610
Poplar Bluff................			III. I. 2. 2.			
Poppy Quamp...............	large	(O.)	III. I. 1. 1.	Autumn	poor	
Porter...................	large	Mass.	IV. I. 2. 1.	Autumn	v. good	673
Porter Spitzenberg.........	large	Conn?	III. II. 2. 2.	Winter	good	
Pottinger...............	large	South	I. I. 2. 2.	E. Wint.	good ?	450
Poughkeepsie Russet	med.	N. Y.	II. I. 2. 3.	Winter	poor	594

Name.	Size.	Orig.	Class.	Season.	Quality.	P.
Pound Royal	large	(W.)	II. II. 2. 1.	E. Aut.	v. good	535
Pound Royal	large	?	III. I. 2. 1.	Winter	good	
Pound Sweet	large	Mich?	III. I. 1. 1.	Winter	good	
Pound Sweet	large	(Ind.)	III. I. 2. 2.	Winter	v. good	
Powers	large	Ohio	I. I. 2. 2.	Autumn	v. good	452
Pownai Spitzenberg	med.		I. I. 2. 2.	Winter	good	
Premium	med.	Ohio	II. I. 1. 1.	Autumn	good	497
Premium		Ala.				
President	large	(Ind.)	III. I. 2. 2.	Winter	poor	
President	large	Mass.	III. I. 2. 1.	Autumn	good ?	
President	large	Mich.	IV. I. 2. 1.	Winter	good	
Press	large	Penn.	I. I. 2. 2.	L.Wint.	good ?	
Press Ewing	med.	Ky.	I. I. 2. 2.	Winter	v. good	451
Price						
Priestly	med.	Penn.	IV. II. 2. 2.	Spring	poor	
Priest's Sweet	med.	Mass.	III. I. 2. 2.	Spring	good ?	
Primate	med.	N. Y.	III. II. 2. 1. / II. II. 2. 1.	Summ'r	best	643
Prince's Fall Pippin	large	?	III. II. 2. 1.	Autumn	good	
Prince	large	Enr.	IV. II. 2. 2.	Autumn	good ?	
Princely		Penn.	I. I. 2. 2.			
Prinz		Penn.	II. II. 2. 2. / IV. II. 2. 2.			
Progress	large	Con. ?	III. II. 2. 1.	Winter	good	644
Prolific Beauty	large	Ohio	I. I. 2. 2. / III. I. 2. 2.	Winter	poor	454
Prolific Sweet	med.	Conn.	II. I. 1. 1.	Winter	good ?	
Prother's Winter		South	II. II. 2. 1.			
Pryor's Red	large	Va.	III. I. 2. 3. / III. II. 2. 3.	Winter	v. good	627
Pumpkin Russet	large	N. E.	III. I. 1. 3.	Autumn	good ?	566
Pumpkin Sweet	large	?	II. I. 1. 3. / I. I. 1. 3.	Autumn	good ?	504
Purple Siberian Crab	small	Eur.	I. I. 2. 1.	Autumn	good	
Putnam Keeper	large	Ohio	I. I. 2. 2.	Spring	poor	
Putnam Russet, Synonym of Roxbury Russet.						
Putnam Sweet	large	Ohio	I. I. 1. 2.	Winter	good ?	397
Quaker		Penn.	I. I. 2. 2.			
Quaker Harvest	small	(O.)	I. 1. 2. 1.	Summ'r	good	
Quaker Pippin	med.	Am.	IV. I. 1. 1.	Autumn	poor ?	
Quaker—Virginia		Va.	III. I. 2. 1.			
Quarrenden—Red, Synonym of Devonshire Quarrenden.						
Quince	med.	?	III. II. 2. 1. / I. II. 2. 1.	Autumn	good	645
Quince—Coles	med.		III. I. 2. 1.	Autumn	v. good	
Rabum		South	IV. II. 2. 2.			
Ragan's Red	large	Ind.	III. I. 2. 2	Autumn	v. good	611
Ragan's Seedling		Ind.	I. II. 2. 2.			
Ralph			I. I. 2. 1.			
Rambo	med.	Penn.	I. I. 2. 2.	E.Wint.	v. good	454
Rambour Franc	med.	Eur.	I. II. 2. 2.	Summ'r	good ?	
Ramsdell Red	large	Con. ?	IV. I. 1. 2.	Autumn	good	604
Randall's Best	med.	Ohio?	III. I. 1. 2.	Winter	good	
Raritan Sweet	large	N. J.	I. II. 1. 1.	Winter	good	
Rasche	large	Mo.	I. I. 2. 2.	Winter	good	
Rawle's Janet	med.	Va.	II. I. 2. 2.	L.Wint.	v. good	517
Rebecca	large	Del.	I. I. 2. 1.	Summ'r	good	
Red and Green Sweet	large	?	II. II. 1. 2. / IV. I. 1. 2.	Summ'r	good ?	
Red Astrachan	large	Russ.	I. I. 2. 2.	Summ'r	good	456
Red Bellflower	large	Fr. ?	II. II. 2. 2.	Winter	poor	
Red Canada	med.	Mass.	II. II. 2. 2.	Winter	best	542
Red Cathead	large	Va.	III. II. 2. 1.	Autumn	good ?	
Red Cedar	med.	Ohio?	III. I. 2. 2.	Spring	good	
Red Cheek Pippin, Synonym of Monmonth Pippin.						

Name.	Size.	Orig.	Class.	Season.	Quality.	P.
Red Detroit..............	large	Can. ?	II. II. 2. 2.	Autumn	poor	
Red Gilliflower...............	large	South	II. I. 2. 2. / IV. II. 2. 2.	Winter	good ?	
Red Ingestrie........	small	Engl.	IV. I. 2. 2.	Summ'r	good ?	
Red June.............	small	Car.	IV. I. 2. 1.	Summ'r	good	
Red Juneating, Synonym of Early Red Margaret.						
Red Ladyfinger, Synonym of Red Winter Pearmain.						
Red Ox.......................	.....	Penn.				
Red Pound Sweet............	v. lar.	?	II. I. 1. 2.	Autumn	good ?	
Red Quarrenden, Synonym of Devonshire Quarrenden.						
Red Rance....................	small	?	IV. II. 2. 2.	Winter	good	
Red Republican...............	large	Penn.	I. I. 2. 2.	E. Wint.	poor	
Red Robinson.................			III. I. 2. 2.			
Red Russet........	large	N. H.	III. I. 2. 3.	Winter	good ?	628
Red Seedling.................	large	Ohio	I. I. 2. 2.	Autumn	poor	
Red Streak...................			III. I. 2. 2.	Winter	....	
Red Streak—English.........	large	Eur. ?	III. I. 2. 2.	Winter	good ?	
Red Stripe.................	med.	(Ind.)	II. II. 2. 2. / IV. II. 2. 2.	Summ'r	good	543
Red Sweet....................	med.	Ohio	I. II. 1. 2.	Winter	good ?	
Red Sweet....................	med.	Ohio	III. I. 1. 2.	E. Wint.	v. good	
Red Sweet Spice.............	small	(O.)	I. I. 1. 2.	Autumn	good	
Red Warrior........	......	South	....			
Red Winesap.................	med.	Penn.		Winter	good	
Red Wint. Pearmain	med.	South	II. I. 2. 2. / IV. I. 2. 2.	Winter	good	519
Reine des Reinettes......	med.	Eur.	II. I. 2. 2.	Winter	good	
Reinette du Canada, Synonym of Canada Reinette.						
Reinette Triomphante.......	large	Germ.	IV. I. 2. 1.	E. Wint.	good ?	
Reinette Van Mons...........	small	Eur.	I. II. 2. 3.	Winter	poor ?	
Republican Pippin............	large	Penn.	I. II. 2. 2.	Autumn	good	
Rhode Isl. Greening..	large	R. Isl.	I. I. 2. 1.	E. Wint.	v. good	414
Ribston Pippin......	med.	Engl.	III. I. 2. 2.	E. Wint.	good ?	612
Richard's Graft........	large	N. Y. ?	I. I. 2. 2.	Autumn	good	457
Richardson..................	large	Mass.	III. I. 2. 1.	Summ'r	good	
Richardson Winter...........		Mass.	I. I. 2. 1.	Winter	good ?	
Richmond..................	large	Ohio	I. I. 1. 2.	Autumn	v. good	397
Richmond's No. 1..........	med.	Ohio	III. I. 1. 2.	Winter	good	
Richmond's No. 4.		Ohio	III. II. 2. 2.	Autumn	good	
Richmond's No. 5.	......	Ohio	III. I. 2. 1.	Winter	good	
Richmond's No. 6............	......	Ohio	III. I. 2. 2.	Autumn	good	
Richmond's Red............	large	Ohio	III. I. 2. 1.	Autumn	good	
Rich Pippin, Synonym of Rock Pippin.						
Ridge Pippin...	large	Penn.	II. II. 2. 1. / IV. II. 2. 1.	Winter	good	536
Riest.....................	large	Penn.	III. II. 2. 1.	Summ'r	v. good	
River	med.	Mass.	IV. II. 2. 2.	Summ'r	good ?	
Roadstown Pippin..........	large	N. J.	I. I. 2. 2.	Spring	good	
Robertson's Red............	med.	Ky.	IV. I. 2. 2.	Winter	poor	
Robertson's White..	med.	Va.	IV. I. 2. 1.	E. Wint.	good ?	
Robey's.....................	large	Va.	III. I. 2. 2.	E. Wint.	v. good	
Robinson Stripe.............	med.	(O.)	II. I. 2. 2.	Autumn	poor	
Rock Apple..................	large	N. H.	I. I. 2. 2.	Winter	good	
Rock Pippin...........	large	?	IV. II. 2. 1.	Spring	poor	601
Rock Sweet..................	med.	Mass.	I. I. 1. 2.	Autumn	good ?	
Rockhill Summer, Synonym of Red Stripe.						
Rockport Sweet.....	med.	Mass.	I. I. 1. 1.	L. Wint.	good	
Rolen's Keeper	med.	Ohio ?	III. I. 2. 3.	Spring	good	629
Rollin......................	med.	N. C.	I. I. 2. 2.	E. Wint.	v. good	
Romanite, Synonym of Gilpin and of Pennock.						
Roman Stem..............	med.	N. J.	III. I. 2. 1.	Winter	good	579
Rome Beauty...........	large	Ohio	I. I. 2. 2. / III. I. 2. 2.	Winter	good ?	458
Ross' Green.................	......	(Va.)	I. I. 2. 1.	....	....	
Ross' Nonpareil........	small	Irld ?	II. I. 2. 3.	Winter	v. good	624

Name.	Size.	Orig.	Class.	Season.	Quality.	P.
Rosy Red	med.	Ind.	II. I. 2. 2.	Winter	good	520
Roxbury Russet	large	Mass.	I. II. 2. 3. / II. I. 2. 3.	Winter	good ?	491
Royal Pearmain	large		I. I. 2. 1.	Winter	good	580
Royal Pearmain	large	(O.)	III. II. 2. 1.	Winter	v. good	
Royal Pippin, Synonym of Day.						
Royal Pippin	large	Va.	III. I. 1. 1.	Spring	good	
Royal Red	med.	Ills.	II. I. 2. 2.	Autumn	good ?	
Ruckman's Pearmain	med.	?		Winter	poor	
Ruckman's	med.	N. C.	III. I. 2. 2.	L.Wint.	good	
Rum Apple	med.	Vt.	I. I. 2. 2.	Winter	good ?	
Russet Pearmain	med.	?	III. I. 2. 3.	Winter	good ?	
Rusticoat Milam	small	?	III. I. 2. 3.	Winter	good ?	630
Rymer	large	Eur.	I. II. 2. 2.	Winter	poor ?	
Sailly Autumn	med.	N. Y.	I. I. 2. 1.	Autumn	good	
Saint Lawrence	large	Can. ?	I. II. 2. 2.	Autumn	good ?	
St. Louis Ortley	large	Mo.	IV. I. 2. 1.	Winter	good	
Salem Seedling			II. I. 2. 2.			
Sam Young	small	Ire'd	I. I. 2. 3.	Winter	good ?	
Santa		South	IV. II. 2. 1.			
Santauchee		South	II. II. 2. 1.			
Sassafrass Sweet		Va. ?		Summ'r		
Sawyer Sweet						
Scalloped Gilliflower	med.	Eur.	II. II. 2. 2.	E.Wint.	poor	543
Scarlet Nonpareil	small	(O.)	I. I. 2. 2. / II. I. 2. 2.	Summ'r	poor ?	
Scarlet Pearmain	med.	Engl.	II. I. 2. 2.	Summ'r	good	
Scarlet Sweet	med.	Ohio	III. I. 1. 2.	E.Wint.	good	562
Seager	med.	Mass.	II. II. 2. 2.	Autumn	good	543
Seaver	med.	Ohio	III. I. 2. 2.	Autumn	good	
Secrist's	large	Ind.	I. I. 1. 1.	Winter	v. good	
Seedling Janet	med.	Ind.	II. II. 2. 2.	Winter	poor	
Seedling Gilpin	med.	Ills. ?	III. I. 2. 2.	L.Wint.	poor	
Seedling Neverfail	med.	Ind.	I. I. 2. 1.	Winter	good	
Seedling Paul			I. I. 2. 2.			
Seek-no-further—Autumn, Synonym of Dr. Watson.						
Seek-no-further—Summer	large	?	III. II. 1. 2	Summ'r	good	
Seek-no-further—Westchester	large	?	II. I. 2. 2.	Autumn	good	
Seek-no-further—Westfield	med.	Conn.	II. I. 2. 2.	Winter	good	
Seek-no-further—White	large	L. Isl.	III. II. 2. 1.	Autumn	good	
Seek-no-further—White	large	?	I. I. 2. 1.	Autumn	v. good	
Selby Bellflower	large	?	III. II. 2. 1.	Winter	good	
Selma	med.	Ohio	I. I. 2. 1.	E.Wint.	"v. gd."	
Selma	large	Ala.	IV. II. 2. 2.	Winter	"v. gd."	
Seneca Favorite		N.Y.?				
September	large	Penn.	III. II. 2. 1. / IV. II. 2. 1.	Autumn	good	645
Shaker, Synonym of Early Pennock.						
Shaker Redstreak	large	?	II. I. 2. 2.	Autumn	good	
Shannon, Synonym of Ohio Pippin.						
Sharke's Greening			II. I. 2. 1.			
Sheepnose, (Sigerson)		Mo.	II. I. 2. 1.	Winter		
Sheepnose, (Mears)	med.	Ohio?	III. II. 2. 1. / IV. II. 2. 1.	Winter	good	645
Sheepnose, (Ohio)	small	Ohio?	II. I. 2. 1.	Winter	good	
Sheppard Sweet	med.	Conn.	IV. II. 1. 2.	Autumn	good	
Shiawassee Beauty	med.	Mich.	I. I. 2. 2.	Autumn	v. good	459
Shipley's Green	med.	(Va.)	III. I. 2. 1.	Winter	poor ?	
Shockley	med.	Ga.	II. I. 1. 1.	Spring	good	498
Shop		Penn.	III. I. 2. 2.			
Shreeve, Synonym of Hannah.						
Siberian Crabs:						
Cherry	small		III. I. 2. 1.	Autumn	good	
Double Flowering	small		III. II. 2. 1.	"	poor	
Lady Crab	small		I. I. 1. 1.	"	good	

Name.	Size.	Orig.	Class.	Season.	Quality.	P.
Siberian Crabs:						
Large Yellow	small		III. I. 2. 1.	Autumn	good	
Montreal Beauty	small		III. I. 2. 1.	"	"	
Powers'	small		I. I. 2. 1.	"	"	
Yellow	small		III. II. 2. 1.	"	"	
Sigerson's Ortley	large	Mo.	IV. I. 2. 1.	Winter	good ?	
Sigler's Pound	v. lar.	Ohio	I. II. 2. 1.	E. Wint.	good ?	
Sigler's Red	med.	Ohio	III. I. 2. 2.	Autumn	good	612
Sillix		Penn.	IV. I. 1. 1. III. I. 2. 1.			
Sine qua non	large	L. Isl.	III. I. 2. 1.	Summ'r	v. good	
Sknnk	large	N. J.	I. II. 2. 1.	Autumn	poor	
Sleathe's Ivory	small	Ohio	I. I. 2. 1.	Winter	good ?	
Slingerland Pippin	large	N. Y.	I. II. 2. 2.	Winter	good	
Slug Sweeting	med.	R. I.	II. II. 1. 1.	Autumn	good	
Small Black	small	?	III. I. 2. 2.	Winter	good ?	613
Smalley	med.	Conn.	I. I. 2. 2.	Autumn	good	
Small's Pippin	small	?	IV. I. 2. 2.	Winter	poor	
Smith's	large	Penn.	III. I. 2. 2. IV. I. 2. 2.	Winter	good ?	614
Smokehouse	large	Penn.	I. I. 2. 2.	Autumn	good ?	
Smokytwig		Ky.				
Snepp's	large	Ind.	I. I. 1. 1.	Winter	v. good	389
Somerton Sweet		(O.)	I.	L. Aut.		
Sops-of-Wine	med.	Eur.	III. I. 2. 2.	Summ'r	good	615
Sour Rambo		(O.)				
Southern Golden Pippin		South	III. I. 2. 1.			
Southern Greening	med.	Ga.	I. I. 2. 1.	Winter	good	
South Mountain		Penn.		Winter		
Spafford Russet	med.	Ohio	II. I. 2. 3.	Winter	good	535
Spark's	large	South	IV. I. 2. 1.	E. Wint.	v. good	674
Speckled Oley		Penn.	III. I. 2. 2.			
Spice	med.	(O.)	III. II. 2. 1.	Winter	good	
Spice		Va.				
Spice Pippin	large	(O.)	III. II. 2. 1.	Winter	good	
Spice Russet	med.	(O.)	I. II. 2. 3.	Winter	v. good	
Spice Sweet	med.	?	I. I. 1. 1.	Autumn	good ?	
Spice Sweeting		(Ind.)	III. I. 1. 1.			
Spice Sweeting	med.	East.	I. II. 1. 2. III. II. 1. 2.	Autumn	good ?	474
Spiceland Sweet	med.	Ind.	II. I. 1. 2.	Winter	good	
Spitzenberg--Flushing	med.	L. Isl.	II. I. 1. 2.	Winter	good	
Spitzenberg--Red	med.	(Ills.)	II. II. 2. 2.	Winter	poor	
Sponge	large	?	III. I. 2. 2.	Autumn	poor	
Spotted Pippin	large	(Ills.)	III. I. 2. 1.	Winter	v. good	
Sprague	small	?	IV. I. 2. 1.	Autumn	good ?	
Spring Pippin			III. I. 2. 1.	Spring		
Springer's Seedling	small	Ohio	II. I. 2. 2.	Spring	poor	
Stack	med.	Ind.	II. I. 2. 2.	Winter	good	
Stannard	large	N. Y.	II. II. 2. 2.	Winter	good	544
Stanley's		South	IV. I. 2. 1. II. I. 2. 1.			
Stansill		South	III. II. 2. 1.			
Stark	large	Ohio	III. I. 2. 2.	Winter	good	
Steele's Red	med.	Mass?	II. II. 2. 2.	Winter	good	
Steele's Sweet	med.	Conn.	III. II. 1. 1.	Winter	good ?	
Stehley	large	Penn.	I. II. 2. 2.	L. Wint.	good	
Stevenson's Winter	med.	Miss.	I. I. 2. 1.	L. Wint.		
Stewart			II. II. 2. 2.			
Stewart's Nonpareil	small	(O.)	III. II. 2. 2.	Summ'r	good	657
Stillman's Early	small	N. Y.	III. II. 2. 1.	Summ'r	good	
Stillwater Sweet	large	Ohio	II. II. 1. 1.	Autumn	good	
Stockade Sweet			II. I. 1. 2.	Spring		
Stock Sweet		(O.)				
Stone		Mich.		Winter		

Name.	Size.	Orig.	Class.	Season.	Quality.	P.
Stone's Sweet	......	Ohio		......	....	
Stonewall		Ala.	IV. II. 2. 2.			
Straat	med.	N. Y.	IV. I. 2. 1.	Autumn	good ?	
Strandt	med.	Penn.	III. I. 2. 2. / II. I. 2. 2.	Autumn	v. good	
Strawn's Seedling	......	South	III. I. 2. 2.			
Stribling	......	South	II. I. 2. 2.			
Striped Ashmore	large	(O.)	III. I. 2. 2.	Autumn	v. good	
Striped Bellflower	large	Ohio ?	IV. II. 2. 2.	Autumn	good	
Striped Gilliflower	large	Eur.	IV. II. 2. 2.	Autumn	poor ?	696
Striped June	small	Va.	IV. I. 2. 2.	Summ'r	good	
Striped Sweet	med.	(O.)	III. I. 1. 2.	Autumn	poor	
Strode's Birmingham	small	Penn.	IV. I. 2. 1.	Autumn	poor	
Strother	....	Va.				
Sturmer Pippin	small	Engl.	I. I. 2. 1.	Spring	good ?	
Styre	med.	Engl.	III. I. 2. 1.	E.Wint.	good	
Sudbury Sweeting	large	(Mas.)	III. II. 1. 2.	Winter	good	
Suffolk Beauty	f. med	L. Isl.	I. I. 2. 1.	Autumn	good	
Sugar	small	?	II. I. 1. 1.	Winter	poor ?	
Sugar and Water	med.	(O.)	*II. I. 1. 2.	Summ'r	poor	
Sugarloaf	....	Penn.	IV. II. 2. 1.	Summ'r	good	
Sugarloaf Pippin	med.	Engl.	IV. II. 2. 1.	Summ'r	good ?	
Sugar Sweet	large	Mass.	II. II. 1. 1.	Winter	poor ?	
Summer Bellflower	med.	N. Y.	II. I. 2. 1. / II. II. 2. 1.	Summ'r	good	
Summer Bellflower	large	Penn.	IV. I. 2. 1. / II. II. 2. 1.	Summ'r	v. good	
Summer Cheese	med.	(Va.)	I. I. 2. 2.	Summ'r	good ?	
Summer Golden Pippin	small	Engl.	IV. I. 2. 1.	Summ'r	good ?	
Summer Green	med.	Penn.	II. I. 2. 2.	Summ'r	v. good	
Summer Hagloe, Synonym of Hagloe.						
Summer Janet	med.	Ind.	III. I. 2. 2.	Summ'r	good ?	616
Summer Limbertwig	med.	Va.	I. I. 2. 2.	Summ'r	good	460
Summer Pippin	med.	N. Y	III. I. 2. 1. / III. II. 2. 1.	Summ'r	good	646
Summer Queen	med.	N. Y.?	II. II. 2. 2.	Summ'r	v. good	545
Summer Rambo	....	Son. ?	I. I. 2. 2.			
Summer Red	....	South		Summ'r	....	
Summer Rose	small	N. J.	III. I. 2. 2.	E. Sum.	v. good	616
Summer Russet	small	?	III. I. 2. 3.	Summ'r	....	
Summer Seek-no-further	large	(O.)	III. II. 1. 2.	Summ'r	good	
Summer Sweet	large	Ga.	I. I. 1. 1.	Summ'r	good ?	
Sum'r Sweet Paradise	large	Penn.	III. I. 1. 1.	Summ'r	good	555
Summum Bonum, Synonym of Bonum.						
Sunday Sweet	large	(Ills.)	I. I. 1. 1.	Winter	good	
Superb	f. med	N. C.	I. I. 2. 1.	E.Wint.	v. good	
Superb Sweet	large	Mass.	I. I. 1. 1. / III. I. 1. 1.	Autumn	good	390
Surprise	small	Eur.	III. I. 2. 1.	Winter	poor	
Susan Spice	......	Penn.				
Sutton	large	Con.?	III. I. 2. 2.	Winter	good	
Sutton Beauty	large	Mass.	III. I. 2. 2. / III. II. 2. 2.	Winter	good	616
Sutton's Seedling	....	South	III. I. 2. 2.			
Swaar	large	N. Y.	III. II. 1. 1. / I. I. 1. 1.	Winter	v. good	632
Sweet and Sour	large	?	I. II. 1. 1.	E.Wint.	poor	475
Sweet Bellflower	large	Ohio	IV. II. 1. 1.	Winter	good	683
Sweet Bough, Synonym of Bough.						
Sweet Fall Pippin	large	N. Y.	I. I. 1. 1.	Autumn	good	
Sweet Gate	med.	(O.)	I. I. 1. 1.	Autumn	good ?	
Sweet Gilliflower	med.	?	III. I. 1. 2.	Autumn	good	
Sweet Gilliflower	med.	Mich.	II. I. 1. 2.	Winter	poor	
Sweet Janet	large	Ind.	III. I. 1. 2. / II. I. 1. 2.	Winter	good	563
Sweet June, Synonym of Hightop Sweet.						

Name.	Size.	Orig.	Class.	Season.	Quality.	P.
Sweet--Kentucky............	med.	Ky.	II. I. 1. 2.	Winter	good	
Sweetmeats................	small	Ind.	II. II. 1. 3.	Winter	good	
Sweet Pear..............	med.	Ohio	II. I. 1. 1.	Winter	good	498
Sweet Pearmain........	med.	(O.)	III. II. 1. 2. / III. I. 1. 2.	Winter	good ?	635
Sweet Rambo.............	med.	Penn.	I. I. 1. 2.	E.Wint.	good ?	
Sweet Romanite.......	med.	West	III. I. 1. 2.	Winter	good	564
Sweet Russet..........	small	Ky.	II. II 1. 3. / II. 1. 1. 3.	Winter	v. good	527
Sweet Russet..........	med.	?	II. II. 1. 3. / III. II. 1. 3.	Winter	good	526
Sweet Sponge..........	med.	(O.)	I. II. 1. 1. / II. II. 1. 1.	Summ'r	good	475
Sweet Vandervere.....	med.	(W.)	I. I. 1. 2. / III. II. 1. 2.	Winter	good	398
Sweet Wine..............	small	Ohio	III. I. 1. 2.	Autumn	good	
Sweet Winesap..........	med.	Pen. ?	I. I. 1. 2. / II. I. 1. 2.	E.Wint.	good	
Sweet Winter Pennock......	large	(O.)	III. I. 1. 2.	Winter	poor ?	
Sylvester..............	med.	N. Y.	III. I. 2. 2.	Autumn	good	617
Symmes' Harvest........		Va.	III. I. 2. 2.	Summ'r	....	
Tallman's Sweet.......	med.	R. I.	III. I. 1. 1.	Winter	good	557
Tart Bough...............	large	Ohio?	I. I. 2. 1.	Summ'r	good	
Taunton................		South	III. II. 2. 2.		....	
Taylor Red....	med.	Ohio?	I. II. 2. 2.	Winter	good ?	
Tender Skin.............	small	S.Car.	III. I. 2. 2.	Winter	v. good	
Tennessee Red..........	med.	Tenn.	II. I. 1. 2.	Autumn	good	
Tennessee Wilding.......	med.	Tenn.	IV. II. 2. 2.	Winter	good ?	
Terrall's Late...........	large	South	IV. I. 2. 2.	Winter	good	
Tetofski..............	small	Eur.	III. II. 2. 2. / II. I. 2. 2.	Summ'r	good	657
Tewksbury W. Blush	small	N. J.	I. I. 2. 1. / III. I. 2. 1.	Spring	good	416
The Cook's Favorite..	med.	(Ind.)	II. II. 2. 1.	Autumn	good	536
Thos. Gatch............	med.	Ohio	II. I. 2. 2.	Summ'r	poor	
Thomas' Late...........		South	I. I. 2. 2.	Winter	....	
Thurmond, Synonym of Julien.						
Tift's Sweeting..	med.	Mass.	I. I. 1. 1. / III. I. 1. 1.	Autumn	good	
Tinmouth.............	large	Vt.	I. I. 1. 1.	Winter	poor ?	
Titus Pippin.............	large	Ohio?	IV. I. 2. 1.	E.Wint.	good ?	
Toccoa................	large	Ga.	IV. II. 2. 1. / II. II. 2. 2.	Summ'r	good	637
Topal..................		(Va.)	I. I. 2. 2.	....	....	
Townsend...........	med.	Penn.	I. I. 2. 2.	Summ'r	good	460
Trader's Fancy.......	med.	Penn.	I. I. 2. 2.	Winter	good	461
Tranham................		South		....	.....	
Transparent..............			I. I. 1. 1.	....	.....	
Transport............	med.	Ind.	III. II. 2. 1. / II. II. 2. 1.	Winter	good	647
Trenton Early....	large	?	II. II. 2. 1.	Autumn	best	586
Trenton Pippin..........		Ohio		....	....	
Trippes' Horse..........		South	II. II. 2. 1. / III. II. 2. 2.		.	
Trippes' Railroad........		South	III. II. 2. 2.			
Trumbull Sweet.......	med.	Ohio	I. I. 1. 1.	Autumn	good	390
Tucker.................			III. I. 1. 1.	Winter	....	
Tudor Sweeting.........		Penn.	III. I. 1. 1.		....	
Tuft's Baldwin..........	large	Mass?	I. II. 2. 2.	Autumn	good ?	
Tulpehocken, Synonym of Fallawater.						
Turkey Greening............	large	Conn.	I. I. 2. 1.	Winter	poor	
Turner's Green............	med.	......	II. I. 2. 1.	Winter	poor	
Turn-off-lane.............	med.	N. J.	I. I. 2. 2.	L.Wint.	good	
Tuscaloosa............		Ala.	I. I. 2. 2		......	
Twenty oz. Pippin....	large	(W.)	I. I. 2. 2.	Winter	poor	461

Name.	Size.	Orig.	Class.	Season.	Quality.	P.
Twitchell Sweet	med.	N. H.	II. II. 1. 2.	E. Wint.	good	
Union	med.	Ohio	I. I. 2. 2.	Summ'r	poor	
Uri Manly	med.	(Ills.)	III. I. 2. 1.	Winter	v. good	
Van Buren	large	Ga. ?	III. I. 2. 1.	Winter	good ?	
Vance's Harvest	small	Ills.?	I. I. 2. 2.	Summ'r	v. good	462
Vandervere, Synonym of Newtown Spitzenberg.						
Vandervere—August	large	(Ind.)	I. I. 2. 2.	Summ'r	poor	
Vandervere—Fall	med.	(O.)	III. I. 2. 2.	Autumn	good	
Vandervere—Pennsylvania	med.	Del.	I. I. 2. 2.	Winter	good	
Vandervere Pippin	large	Penn.	I. I. 2. 2.	Winter	good	462
Vandyne	large	?	III. I. 2. 1.	Autumn	good	
Vaughn's Winter	med.	Ky.	{ I. I. 2. 2. } { I. II. 2. 2. }	Winter	good	463
Veineal Russet	small	(Ills.)	III. I. 2. 3.	Autumn	poor	
Vestal, Synonym of Maiden's Blush.						
Victuals and Drink	large	N. J.	II. I. 1. 1.	Autumn	good	499
Vincent Sweet	med.	(O.)	III. I. 1. 1.	Autumn	poor	
Virginia Greening	large	Va.	I. I. 2. 1.	L. Wint.	poor	416
Virginia June	med.	Va.?	II. I. 1. 1.	Autumn	good	500
Virginia June	med.	(Ind.)	III. I. 2. 2.	Summ'r	....	
Virginia May	small	Va.	III. I. 2. 1.	E. Sum.	good	
Virginia Quaker	small	Va.	III. I. 2. 1.	Summ'r	good ?	580
Voss' Winter	large	(Va.)	III. I. 2. 1.	Winter	good	580
Waddell Hall	.....	South	IV. I. 2. 2.		....	
Wagoner	large	N. Y.	I. II. 2. 2.	Winter	good	490
Walker's Greening		South	I. I. 2 1.	Winter	....	
Walker's Pippin		South	III. I. 2. 1.	Winter	....	
Walker's Yellow	large	Ga.	II. I. 2. 1.	Winter	good	
Wall, Synonym of Berry.						
Wallace's Green Pippin		Ky.		Winter	....	
Walpole	med.	Mass.	III. I. 2. 2.	Summ'r	good	
Walworth		N. J.	III. I. 2. 1.		....	
Ward	v. lar.	Ohio	IV. I. 2. 2.	E. Wint.	good	
Washington Royal	large	Mass.	I. I. 2. 2.	Spring	good	
Water			II. II. 2. 1.		....	
Wateree		South	I. I. 2. 2.		....	
Watson's Dumpling	large	Engl.	III. II. 2. 2.	Winter	good	
Waugh's Crab	small	Va.	III. I. 2. 2.	Winter	good	
Waxen, Synonym of Belmont.						
Weaver Sweet	large	(O.)	I. II. 1. 1.	Winter	good	
Webb's Winter		South	II. I. 2. 2.	Winter	....	
Wellford's Yellow	small	Va.	{ I. I. 2. 2. } { III. I. 2. 2. }	Spring	good	
Wells	med.	Md.	III. I. 2. 2.	Winter	good	
Wells, Synonym of Domine.						
Wells' Sweeting	small	N. Y.	{ III. I. 1. 1. } { I. I. 1. 1. }	E. Wint.	good	661
Westbrooke		Va.		Winter	....	
Westchester Seek-no-further	large	N. Y.	II. I. 2. 2.	Autumn	good	
Western Beauty	large	Ohio	I. I. 2. 2.	E. Wint.	v. good	464
Western Spy	large	Ohio	{ I. II. 2. 1. } { I. 2. 1. }	Winter	poor	485
Westfield Seek-no-fur.	med.	Conn.	II. I. 2. 2.	Winter	good	520
Weston	med.	Mass.	III. II. 2. 2.	Autumn	good	
Wetherill's White	large	N. J.	III. I. 1. 1.	Autumn	good ?	
Wharton	large	Ohio ?	III. I. 2. 2.	E. Wint.	good	
Wharton's Favorite	large	?	I. I. 2. 2.	E. Wint.	good ?	
Wheeler's Sweeting			IV. II. 1. 1.		....	
Whig		South	II. I. 2. 1.		....	
White Alexander	med.	?	I. I. 2. 1.	Summ'r	good ?	
White Apple	small	Ky.	IV. I. 1. 1.	Winter	....	
White Astrachan	med.	Russ.	III. I. 2. 1.	Summ'r	poor	
White Baldwin	large	(O.)	II. I. 2. 1.	Autumn	poor	
White Beauty			III. I. 2. 1.		....	
White Doctor	large	Penn.	{ I. I. 2. 1. } { III. I. 2. 1. }	Autumn	good ?	

Name.	Size.	Orig.	Class.	Season.	Quality.	P.
White Fall Pippin	large	(Ky.)	I. I. 2. 1.	Autumn	good?	417
White Juneating	small	Engl.	I. I. 2. 1. / I. I. 2. 1. / III. I. 2. 1.	Summ'r	good	417
White Paradise	small	Ky.	IV. I. 2. 1.	E. Wint.	poor	
White Pippin	large	?	III. II. 2. 1. / III. I. 2. 1.	Winter	v. good	415 647
White Pippin	large	(Ky.)	III. I. 2. 1. / I. I. 2. 1.	Winter	good?	581
White Rambo	med.	Ohio?	I. I. 2. 1.	E. Wint.	good?	
White's Long Keeper	large	Ind.	III. I. 2. 2.	Spring	good?	
White Seek-no-further	large	L. I.	III II. 2. 1.	Autumn	good	
White Spitzenberg	med.	Penn.	IV. I. 2. 1. / III. I. 2. 1.	Winter	good	
White Sweet	med.	Me.	I. I. 1. 1.	Autumn	good	
White Sweeting		N. J.	III. I. 1. 1.			
Whitewater Sweet	med.	Ohio	III. I. 2. 1.	Autumn	good	
White Winter	small	Penn.	III. I. 2. 1.	L. Wint.	good?	
Wh. Wint. Pearmain	med.	Am.	II. I. 2. 1.	Winter	v. good	508
Whitmore	med.	N. Y.	III. I. 1. 1.	Autumn	good	
Whitney Russet	small	Ills. ?	I. II. 2. 3.	Winter	v. good	493
Wiley's	large	?	II. II. 2. 2.	Winter	poor	
Willey's	large	Ind.	III. II. 1. 2.	Summ'r	good?	
William Penn	large	Penn?	I. I. 2. 2.	Winter	"v. gd."	
William Penn	large	Vt.	III. II. 2. 1.	Winter	v. good	
Williams' Favorite	med.	Mass.	III. I. 2. 2.	Summ'r	good	618
Willis Russet	small	Mass.	I. I. 2. 3. / I. II. 2. 3.	Winter	good	470
Willis Sweet	large	L. I.	III. II. 1. 2.	Autumn	good	635
Willow Leaf	large	(O.)	I. I. 2. 2.	Winter	good?	
Willow	large	Va.	III. I. 2. 2.	L. Wint.	good	619
Willson	small	W. Va.	I. I. 2. 2.	Winter	v. good	465
Wilson	large	Mich.	III. I. 2. 1.	Winter	good	582
Wilson Pippin	med.	(Ind.)	I. I. 2. 1.	Winter	good	
Wilson's Volunteer	large	Ohio	III. I. 2. 2. / I. II. 2. 2.	E. Wint.	good?	620
Winchell Seedling	large	(O.)	I. I. 2. 2.	Autumn	v. good	
Wine, or Hays	large	Del.	I. I. 2. 2. / III. I. 2. 2.	E. Wint.	good	466
Wine—Fall	med.	?	I. I. 2. 2.	Autumn	best	
Winesap	med.	N. J.	II. II. 2. 2. / II. I. 2. 2.	Winter	good	546
Winfield			III. I. 2. 1.			
Wing Sweet	med.	N. Y.	I. II. 1. 2. / III. I. 1. 2.	Autumn	good?	477
Winn's Russet	large	Me.	III. I. 2. 3.	Spring	good	
Winslow	large	Va.	III. I. 2. 2.	Winter	good?	
Winter Bough	large	N. Y.	II. I. 1. 1.	Winter	good	
Winter Brook		South	I. I. 2. 1.	Winter		
Winter Cheese	large	Va.	I. I. 2. 2.	Winter	good	
Winter Green	large	(O.)	II. I. 1. 1.	E. Wint.	v. good	
Winter Grixon, Synonym of Catline.						
Winter Harvey			II. II. 2. 1.	Winter		
Winter Janet	med.	?	III. I. 2. 2.	Winter	good?	
Winter Maiden Blush			II. II. 2. 1.	Winter		
Winter Nonsuch	large	(Ills.)	I. I. 2. 2.	Winter	good	
Winter Pearmain	med.	(Ills.)	II. I. 2. 2.	Winter	poor	
Winter Pippin	large	N. Y.	I. II. 2. 1.	Winter	good	
Winter Pippin	large	Ind.	III. II. 2. 1.	Winter	good	
Winter Pippin of Mich.	large	?	I. I. 2. 1.	Winter	good	418
Winter Pippin	v. lar.	Vt.	III. II. 2. 1.	Winter	good	
Winter Queen	large	Va.	I. I. 2. 2.	Autumn	good	467
Winter Rambo	med.		III. I. 2. 2.	Winter	v. good	
Winter Red	med.	(S. Ill)	III. II. 2. 2.	Winter	poor	
Winter Strawberry			IV. I. 2. 2.	Winter		
Winter Sweet—Dauvers'	large	Mass.	III. I. 1. 1.	Winter	good	

Name.	Size.	Orig.	Class.	Season.	Quality.	P.
Winter Sweet—Golden		(N. Y.)	I. 1. 1. 1.	Winter		
Winter Sweet—(Milwads)				Winter		
Winter Sweet Paradise	large	Penn.	III. I. 1. 1.	Winter	good	
Winter Sweeting						
Winthrop Greening	large	Me.		Autumn	good	
Winthrop Pearmain	large	Me.		Winter	good	
Wonder		South				
Woodburn Spi'zenberg		(Va.)	IV. I. 2. 2.	Winter		
Woodland	med.	N. C.	III. I. 2. 2.	Winter	good ?	
Woodside Cider	med.	Ohio	II. I. 2. 2.	Winter	good ?	
Wood's Greening	med.	N. J.	I. I. 2. 1.	Winter	good ?	
Wood's Sweet	large	Vt.	I. II. 1. 2.	Autumn	good	
Woolfolks	med.	Ky.	II. I. 2. 1.	Winter	good ?	500
World's Wonder		South				
Wormsly Pippin	med.	Engl.	III. I. 2. 1.	Autumn	poor	
Wreston's Prolific		Ky.				
Wright's Apple	med.	Vt.	I. I. 2. 1.	Autumn	good	
Wright's Janet	med.	Mo.	} III. I. 2. 2. { / I. I. 2. 2. \	Winter	good	620
Yacht	large	Penn.	III. I. 2. 2.	Winter	good	
Yadkin	large	South	III. I. 2. 2.	Autumn	poor	621
Yahaula		South	I. I. 2. 1.			
Yankee Russet		(O.)				
Yates		South	I. I. 2. 1.			
Yellow Bellflower	large	N. J.	IV. II. 2. 1.	E. Wint.	best	692
Yellow Crank, Synonym of Green Crank.						
Yellow English Crab		Engl.	III. I. 2. 1.			
Yellow Foster	med.	(O.)	I. I. 2. 1.	Autumn	good	418
Yellow Horse	large	South	I. I. 2. 1.	Autumn	good	
Yellow Ingestrie	small	Engl.	III. I. 2. 1.	Summ'r	good ?	582
Yellow June	small	?	{ I. I. 2. 1. / I. II. 2. 1. }	Summ'r	good	
Yellow Meadow	large	South	I. I. 2. 1.	E. Wint.	good	
Yellow Newtown	large	L. I.	III. II. 2. 1.	Winter	best	649
Yellow Pearmain	med.	South	II. I. 2. 1.	Wint'r	good	
Yellow Siberian Crab	small	Eur.	III. I. 2. 1.	Autumn	good	
Yellow Vandervere	med.	(O.)	III. II. 2. 1.	Winter	good	
Yocomb's	large	South	I. I. 2. 2.	Summ'r	good ?	
Yopp's Favorite	large	Ga.	} I. I. 2. 1. / II. I. 2. 1.		v. good	
York Imperial	large	Penn.	} IV. II. 2. 1. { III. I. 2. 2.	Winter	good	693
York Russet, Synonym of Pumpkin Russet.						
Yost	med.	Penn.	I. I. 2. 2.	Winter	good	468
Zieber	small	Am.	III. I. 2. 1.		poor	
Ziesler's Sweet		Penn.	I. I. 1. 1.			
Zaar Greening		Ohio				

GENERAL INDEX.

For Index to the Varieties of Apples see page 711. The names, given below in small caps, refer to headings of chapters.

738